Directions in Sociolinguistics

DIRECTIONS IN SOCIOLINGUISTICS

The Ethnography of Communication

Edited by

John J. Gumperz
University of California, Berkeley

Dell Hymes
University of Pennsylvania

HOLT, RINEHART AND WINSTON, INC.

New York   Chicago   San Francisco   Atlanta   Dallas
Montreal   Toronto   London   Sydney

Preface

The present work integrates in a single volume some major directions of research on the social basis of verbal communication, a subject which has become of considerable interest to social scientists working at both theoretical and applied levels. In recent years most linguists, in their concern with formal methods of description, have concentrated on the internal relations of linguistic signs, ruling out consideration of extra linguistic factors. Today, semantics is once more a legitimate subject, and syntax is seen to raise questions of the status of sentences as acts of speech and parts of discourse. Basic theoretical problems of the nature of grammar and its relation to speakers' verbal competence are therefore once more becoming relevant. Similarly, questions of the functions of language are again receiving serious attention.

The importance of language in social problems, especially education and national development, also is drawing linguistics into wider concerns. The last decade has seen an increasing number of conferences, interdisciplinary symposia, and monographs attempting to stimulate serious behaviorally oriented research on stylistics and expressive speech, intrasocietal diversity of language, attitudes to language, language politics and policy, and other similar peripheral subjects (Sebeok 1960; Bright 1966; Lieberson 1966b; Capell 1966; Haugen 1966; MacNamara 1967; Fishman *et al.* 1968).

Although sustained empirical work is only beginning, the response so far seems highly promising. Social scientists are showing interest in linguistic data as a means of studying behavior independently of overtly expressed attitudes, while linguists are beginning to see that many important questions of language change, education, and policy cannot be solved without information on the social factors affecting speech. Almost overnight sociolinguistics has emerged as a distinct field, one of a series of border disciplines which promises to provide novel insights into the bases of human conduct.

The ready currency of the term *sociolinguistics,* however, does not reflect fundamental agreement on common problems, sources of data, or methods of analysis. On the contrary, the recent publications reveal almost as many methods of operation as there are workers in the field. Many scholars—probably a majority of those who identify themselves as sociolinguists—are interested in language data as they contribute to the solution of problems already posed by the academic dialogue in their own disciplines. Some simply measure attitudes to language or speakers' self-reports on their usage. Others analyze usage through counts of individual words, or syntactic constructions and the like, using such counts as indexes in somewhat the same way in which income, education, and attitudes are used by other social scientists. Others again, seeking to make better use of the full potential of linguistic description, tend to draw direct parallels between features of the linguistic structure of a particular dialect or speech style and independently measured social characteristics of its users. A fourth group, oriented toward policy issues, has begun to utilize descriptive and historical linguistics in the creation of new orthographies and scientific terminologies, and in other aspects of language development and planning.

The gradual accumulation over the years of ethnographic information and insight into verbal practices of human groups, however, has also raised some entirely new questions about the very place of speaking in human interaction. No one claims, that grammar, as the term is normally understood, covers everything that is rule governed in speech. Linguists and social scientists of many persuasions have long called attention to the importance of prestige, politeness, expressive, ritual, and religious values, and similar aspects of language. It has been argued that such nonreferential functions may be determinant in language behavior and language change. Language usage—i.e., what is said on a particular occasion, how it is phrased, and how it is coordinated with nonverbal signs—cannot simply be a matter of free individual choice. It must itself be affected by subconsciously internalized constraints similar to grammatical constraints. But although issues of language function have stimulated considerable discussion, they have, so far, not been integrated into any general theory of language and society and, as a result, are rarely taken account of in the research designs which underlie field procedures.

The special issue of the *American Anthropologist* published in 1964 under the title "The Ethnography of Communication" (Gumperz and Hymes 1964) was an attempt to stimulate empirically oriented work on such problems. In the years since the publication of that collection, considerable progress has been made both in theory and in field techniques. The articles in the present volume, many of which are contributed by the same authors, attempt to capture these advances, while at the same time bringing in relevant lines of work not previously included.

The theoretical goal of the type of sociolinguistic investigation represented here is best illustrated by the notion of communicative competence: What a speaker needs to know to communicate effectively in culturally significant settings. Like Chomsky's term on which it is patterned, communicative competence refers to the ability to perform. An attempt is made to distinguish between what the speaker knows—what his inherent capacities are—and how he behaves in particular instances. However, whereas students of linguistic competence seek to explain those aspects of grammar believed to be common to all humans independent of social determinants, students of communicative competence deal with speakers as members of communities, as incumbents of social roles, and seek to explain their use of language to achieve self-identification and to conduct their activities. While for linguistic theory in the former sense the ability to formalize sentences as grammatically acceptable is the central notion, for sociolinguistics as represented in the book, the central notion is the appropriateness of verbal messages in context or their acceptability in the broader sense.

The contributors and their contributions represent an unusually broad range of fields. Different readers will recognize concepts and techniques drawn from linguistics, ethnography, sociology, dialectology, psychology, componential analysis, ethnoscience, paralinguistics and kinesics, folklore, ethnomethodology, stylistics, and possibly other sources as well. While most chapters are empirically oriented, none are merely descriptive. Many new and general concepts, suitable for the analysis of verbal interaction processes everywhere, are proposed. Yet there is by no means complete agreement on theory. Sociolinguistics is still many steps removed from the formal rigor of an integrated grammatical theory. It seems clear, however, that progress is not a matter merely of refining analytical apparatus. Since many of the relevant questions have only recently begun to be asked, we lack the empirical information on which generalizations must be built. Our aim here is to present evidence documenting the existence of a level of rule-governed verbal behavior which goes beyond the linguists' grammar to relate social and linguistic constraints on speech, to illustrate the type of data that must be collected for its analysis and the elicitation methods by which it can be gathered.

We hope that this book will stimulate students and professionals in the linguistic and social sciences as well as educators concerned with language arts. Because of the newness of the subject, it was impossible to modify the content of the articles without seriously impairing their utility.

Additional explanatory material has, however, been provided in the Introduction, the Plan of the Book, and in notes preceding each chapter. The Introduction relates the interactional approach to language to past and present theory and fieldwork practice. The Plan of the Book outlines the scope of the volume and the rationale for its organization. Each chapter is introduced by an explanatory note pointing out its significance for our concerns and giving additional background readings. A general bibliography lists all references cited. A list of background readings brings together some basic background material relevant to modern sociolinguistics. Also included in the appendix is the "Outline Guide for the Ethnographic Study of Speech Use," by Joel Sherzer and Regna Darnell. We hope that the reader will enjoy direct contact with work that seeks to build something and will gain new perspectives from which to approach existing research on language and social interaction and its application to education and policy making.

J.J.G.

D.H.

Contents

Introduction

JOHN J. GUMPERZ

The interactional approach to language behavior, which is the unifying theme of this volume, exemplifies both new theoretical insights and changes in research orientation. Since such changes are best understood in historical perspective, we will begin this introduction by outlining the background of modern sociolinguistics: early speech community studies, descriptive linguistics, generative grammar, and correlational sociolinguistics. We will then proceed to treat some of the most important research paradigms and analytical concepts emerging from the work of the last decade, and conclude with a discussion of implications for future fieldwork.

Early Speech Community Studies

The systematic investigation of the speech of human groups dates to the beginning of the nineteenth century and is part of the general interest in organized knowledge concerning the variety of human customs and beliefs which arose in the Enlightenment. For example, in the 16th century, Montaigne collected oral literature from Brazilian Indians brought to France. A unique manual of ethnography including language appeared in the seventeenth century in France, and word lists were gathered extensively in the eighteenth century. But cultural description focused on speech behavior was almost nonexistent. Most scholarly work of the era was dominated either by a concern with evolution in which the institutions of Western industrial society were seen as the end product of a series of evolutionary stages of which the languages and customs of primitives represented the beginning and/or with legitimizing the cultural origins of nations [e.g., the Italians (Vico) and the Germans (Grimm)].

Linguists of all persuasions, like other scholars, were concerned with documenting historical processes, but the source material for their studies differed. There were many linguists who, in the manner of the early classical philologists, worked primarily with manuscript remains of extinct languages or with literary texts, inscriptions, or documents exemplifying earlier stages of modern literary languages. Work with single or at most a few manuscripts of earlier epics, tales, chronicles, or Bible translations, each relatable to a particular modern vernacular, led them to visualize speech distribution as describable in terms of a limited number of discrete languages and dialects. Their goal was to document the development of these modern varieties from earlier prehistoric protolanguages in somewhat the same way that biological scientists studied the evolution of animal organisms.

A second group of scholars preferred to concentrate on more recent, historically documented linguistic changes. Arguing that peasant communities and tribal societies furnished living proof of evolutionary processes, many of them turned away from written documents to the direct study of the oral practices of such communities. The first-hand empirical investigation of speech received particular impetus from the neo-grammarian doctrines of sound change. The Neo-grammarian thesis that language change is regular and that sound changes which relate contemporary vernaculars to earlier forms of speech are describable by means of laws which, like the laws of natural science, allow no exceptions, was the first statement of historical linguistic processes sufficiently explicit to suggest practical field tests. It could be argued that if local peasant dialects of a literary language represent divergent historical development of earlier stages of that language, and if sound correspondences are regular, then dialects should be separated by sharp boundaries reflecting the historical linguists' statement of these correspondences.

Motivated by these and similar questions, dialectologists launched into a series of field surveys in which peasant speech was studied either through mail questionnaires or directly through fieldwork by investigators, who often covered many miles on foot in order to collect dialect samples through direct methods. Other scholars, more skeptical of the Neo-grammarian hypothesis, sought to disprove the latter theory by studying the linguistic consequences of large-scale immigration or conquest or by investigating "language mixture" as revealed in pidgins and trade languages found in regions of interethnic contact.

Writings on these issues in the years 1875–1940 are often quite speculative and poorly documented when compared with studies based on textual materials dating from the same period. Nevertheless, they served to demonstrate that language is basically a social institution and to document the importance of social factors in language change, thus disproving earlier ideas of biological or geographical determinism. Although it is evident that new expressions are always created by individuals, the acceptance of such innovations by others, their spread, and their ultimate effect on the linguistic system is in large part socially determined. Conquest, population migration, or other less dramatic forms of social change can lead to the disappearance of old languages and the spread of others. Similarly, new languages, pidgins, and creoles may be created as a result of forced population resettlement and intensive intergroup contact. Classification by language, therefore, need not be correlated with groupings of mankind on other bases.

Perhaps the most detailed and, for the modern social scientist, the most interesting evidence of the working of social factors in the spread of linguistic innovations comes from the dialect surveys conducted during the first decades of this century. The Swabian dialectologist Fischer (Bach 1960), e.g., found that the rural dialect boundaries of the area of southwestern Germany closely reflected the political borders of the seventeenth and eighteenth centuries. So close was the connection that subregional borders drawn on the basis of dialect isogloss bundles were almost as accurate as frontiers reconstructed on the basis of historical records alone. A comparative study of dialect boundaries in Germany, France, and Italy by Jaberg (1936) suggests that dialect diversity in these countries is a direct function of the degree of centralization of political power in a particular area. France, dominated for the last few centuries by a single center of political and economic power, shows few sharp dialect boundaries; transitions are gradual. Except in outlying areas, preexisting differences seem to have been largely obliterated. In Italy, with a few highly centralized city-states, dialect distribution follows the frontiers of these states and boundaries are sharp. Germany, where political fragmentation and small states were the rule, shows many small dialect areas, separated by relatively large transition zones, reflecting the lack of political stability and the many territorial changes of recent history.

Our understanding of the mechanisms by which social factors affect language change has been clarified by Leonard Bloomfield's (1933) discussion of speech communities, which argues that linguistic diversity in human societies is directly related to density of communication or to the amount of verbal interaction among speakers. Bloomfield writes:

Imagine a large chart with a dot for every speaker in the community and imagine that every time any speakers uttered a sentence an arrow were drawn into the chart printing from his dot to the dot representing each one of his hearers. At the end of a given period of time, say 70 years, that chart would show us the density of communication in the community. . . . Subgroups are separated by lines of weakness in this net of oral communication.

Whereas previous scholars had attempted to find direct correlations between language and various environmental factors, Bloomfield here postulates an intervening level of human communication which mediates between linguistic and nonlinguistic phenomena. Political, economic, or even geographical factors are no longer seen as directly reflected in speech. They affect language only to the extent that they can be shown to channel verbal communication among speakers, causing certain individuals to have more verbal contact with some than with others and thereby influencing the rate at which innovations diffuse. Recent sociolinguistic research leads us to question the relation between diffusion and mere density of communication as too simplistic, but the basic point about the effect of interaction on language structure is nevertheless valid and has become a central issue in modern sociolinguistic research.

Unfortunately, Bloomfield's suggestive remarks did not directly lead to empirical investigations, perhaps because at the time they implied an impossibly massive task. While there was widespread agreement about the importance of extralinguistic factors in language change, efforts to reconcile the linguistic findings of dialect surveys with the results of comparative reconstruction based on manuscript sources aroused considerable controversy. Although the issues are usually phrased in theoretical terms, failure to resolve them is at least partly attributable to the imperfections of field elicitation techniques and analytical tools. While scholars working with literary texts were limited to relatively few written manuscripts for each period, dialectologists sampled large numbers of speakers and were faced with the additional problem of reliability in transcription. For a time, accuracy in the recording of interspeaker differences became a major issue. One of the nineteenth-century pioneers of European dialectology, Gilliéron, fearing that scholars might permit their notions of language history to influence their field recordings (Pop 1950), sought out and trained as a fieldworker E. Edmond, a "naïve" speaker of the language whose main qualification was a good ear for sound and who, not being a philologist, was presumably unencumbered by preconceived notions about what he heard. Edmond received training only in phonetics, and traveled in person from locality to locality interviewing local residents and setting down on paper just what he heard without attempting to interpret it. Gilliéron's approach set the pattern for dialect elicitation procedures through the first third of the present century. Fieldwork was viewed as a process of behavioral observation aimed at the production of faithful records of natural speech. Interpretation and analysis were kept separate from this elicitation stage, being deferred until the data were in.

Geographical surveys, conducted on these principles, produced a wealth of new and startling information on intracommunity variation in pronounciation and word usage. Yet the larger the amount of data, the greater the number of problems in evaluating the significance of what was found. In spite of the basic insights gained into processes of change, the very question of dialect borders and their relation to sound laws, the problem which initially had provided the impetus for these surveys, defied solution. Since in many instances there was no basis for deciding which of the many isoglosses that marked the transition from one region to another was the actual boundary, some scholars maintained that each word had its own history. Others attempted to group isoglosses into bundles of greater and lesser importance so as to distinguish major from minor boundaries, but there were no generally agreed upon criteria for such bundling (Bloomfield 1933; Bach 1960). It seemed impossible to reconcile the many interpersonal, interregional and social variations discovered in the course of direct field surveys with the prevailing view of languages and dialects as quasi-organic, internally uniform wholes. Clearly, objectivity and accuracy in the recording of speech was not enough, no matter how detailed and unbiased the data. What was needed was a theoretical basis for judging the relative importance of the many potential indexes of linguistic diversity

Descriptive Linguistics

Ferdinand de Saussure's (1916) distinction between speech (*parole*) and language (*langue*) can be seen as an attempt to resolve the dialectologists' dilemma. "Speech" refers to the actual sounds produced by speakers, while "language" represents shared pattern, which is distinct from what is actually said in somewhat the same way that Durkheim's social facts are separate from behavior. Language structure is defined in terms of the regularities derived from utterance sequences by a process of analysis in which utterances are segmented into minimal segments and these segments then classified by comparison with other similar elements. The goal is to arrive at the minimum number of symbols necessary to account for observed articulatory characteristics and thus to eliminate redundant features. The distinctive units derived in this way form a system which is defined by the relationship of contrast among units and which does not depend on the phonetic value of any one of them.

With the notion of structure established, the emphasis in fieldwork shifts from a search for greater accuracy to classification and contrastive analysis. While detailed phonetic records continue to be important, they are only the first step in linguistic research. Once recorded, the overtly distinct or *etic* units must be converted into structurally distinct or *emic* units (Pike 1964). The dialectologists' failure to agree on dialect and language boundaries could thus be attributed to a tendency to emphasize surface differences at the expense of structural relationship. Variations recorded in fieldwork are of equal significance only if they alter the structural relationships among elements. While speech may change from place to place and person to person, grammatical systems tend to be more stable and less subject to change. With increased analytical refinement, the notion of languages and dialects as discrete wholes seemed saved, or at least salvageable. Henceforth it was argued that comparative statements, generalizations about verbal behavior and linguistic change must be based on emic analyses, not on raw field data. Homogeneity of languages and dialects was to be sought at the level of structural abstraction.

Edward Sapir's article on the psychological reality of phonemes dramatically demonstrated the importance of the notion of linguistic structure for our understanding of human cognition. Using evidence from his own efforts to train naïve natives to transcribe the sounds of their language, Sapir shows that his subjects' phonetic accuracy is significantly affected by the phonological system of their own native language. He explained what at first hand seemed to be errors in transcription by demonstrating that these errors occur where structural and phonetic reality conflict, and that the former takes precedence over the latter. Gilliéron's quest for unbiased native transcribers is thus demonstrably futile. All human beings, informants and linguists alike, tend to prejudge or edit the sounds they hear. Linguistic structure is more than a mere scholarly construct. Structure constrains and potentially predicts the speaker's perception of verbal stimuli.

Furthermore, since linguistic constraints operate largely below the level of consciousness, speakers themselves cannot be expected to provide adequate explanations for their own verbal behavior. Information on language structure must be discovered indirectly by trained investigators. Emphasis on phonetic accuracy gave way to a search for techniques which would enable the linguist to overcome his own perceptual limitations so as to discover the system of a second language.

The demand for better and more systematic analytical tools was especially strong among the growing numbers of American anthropologists and linguists who, following the pioneering work of Gatchett, Boas, and others, had set out to record and preserve the many languages spoken by American Indians. Information on these languages at first derived in large part from word lists or text translations collected by missionaries or government officials. As scholarly interest in tribal cultures deepened and linguistic skills increased, anthropologists began to record indigenous tales and myths as part of their regular ethnographic descriptions. A native speaker, usually someone well versed in tribal traditions, would dictate texts which the investigator would then record phonetically as best he could. Even the most careful investigators, however, frequently failed to note important aspects of these tales and tended to misinterpret the speaker's utterances. It became evident that the systematic analysis of linguistic form and of phonological and grammatical structures had to take precedence over evaluation of content. Anthropological linguistic analysis at the level of sound had to precede that at the higher levels of syntax, semantics, and culture.

Among the most valuable accomplishments of this period is the development of techniques which go beyond the mere recording of data to enlist the native speaker's assistance in improving the validity of the linguist's perception of sound. In order to determine if what was recorded as different was actually different, or whether what was transcribed as similar was actually similar, the method of variation within a frame was employed. This method consists of contrasting like items varying only in one feature. Thus, if an investigator wanted to test his transcription of the English 'i' in 'bid,' he would search for other items in the speaker's vocabulary, such as 'bed' and 'bead,' which shared the initial 'b' and the final 'd' and differed only in the vowel. In this way, by keeping the elicitation frame constant, he could concentrate all of his attention on one feature. The method served both to discover new distinctions and as a way of ear training or drill, helping the linguist to overcome the limitations imposed by his own phonological system. Linguistic analysis became an integral part of the fieldwork process. Moreover, since all speakers of a language are equally affected by the subconscious perceptual constraints of the system, structural linguists came to prefer intensive work with a single informant to the dialectologist's language surveys.

As anyone who has tried it can attest, the linguist-informant elicitation procedure just described is not at all simple. Most naïve speakers are unaware of the formal features to which the linguist wishes them to attend and think of language only in terms of meaning. The process thus involves learning for both the linguist and the informant. Not any native can serve as an informant. Linguists working in this tradition tend to search out "good" speakers of the language, people with both the time and leisure to work over a long period of time who had sufficient intelligence and verbal ability to learn the required task (Samarin 1967). Statistically, their sample is thus always biased.

The interview setting, furthermore, is often formal and contrived and almost always quite different from the settings within which people usually interact. Some of the best-known work of the Sapir era was, in fact, based on the speech of native speakers who had long been isolated from other native speakers of the language. Sapir's informant on Nootka was a student in a Pennyslvania college. Benjamin A. Whorf derived his basic data on Hopi from an Indian resident of New York City (Hoijer 1954). Even those linguists who worked in or near actual communities often found it necessary to do most of their elicitation in their own quarters, away from the distracting noise of the native community.

In spite of these limitations, however, the success of the new elicitation procedures and the analytical techniques built upon them is well known. As compared to earlier grammarians, descriptive linguists achieved a unique degree of explicitness and replicability. Armed with the new methodological tools, any two investigators making independent study of similar data could expect, with fair certainty, to arrive at similar or at least comparable results.

The new techniques of structural analysis earned for linguistics the reputation of the most scientific of the social-science disciplines. But these techniques proved to be quite limited in their application. Single isolated utterances, rather than entire texts, became the chief units of study, with meaning—and to some extent even syntax—frequently deferred for later attention. Minor dialect variations, loan words, and other diffusionary phenomena were also frequently dismissed as either marginal or not relevant for formalization.

The result was that much potentially important information on speech behavior was lost in the process of converting etic into emic categories. The notion of grammars as internally consistent systems, which must be explained in their own terms without reference to outside information, furthermore led to a reaction against earlier, premature, cross-language generalizations. It became fashionable to emphasize the infinite variability of phonemic and grammatical structures (Joos 1962).

Generative Grammar

Fortunately, many of these limitations in scope proved to be short-lived. During the 1950s, when some of the basic problems of phonology and word morphology seemed settled, interest turned once more to syntax and semantics. Concern with meaning in the makeup of sentences led to some fundamental changes in notions of grammatical structure, changes which were in some ways every bit as basic as those associated with the shift to descriptive linguistics. The key factor in these theoretical developments was Chomsky's demonstration that mere taxonomic analysis and classification of phonological and morphological units fails to explain some very basic grammatical relationships. Sentence pairs like the by now well known "he is eager to please" and "He is easy to please" are, Chomsky argues, overtly similar, yet native speakers of English have no difficulty in recognizing that in the first item "he" refers to the subject of "please," i.e., the one who does the pleasing, while in the second item "he" refers to the object, i.e., the one who is being pleased. In order to account for such underlying grammatical differences it is necessary to recognize two distinct levels of syntactic structuring, a level of "deep structure" dealing, among other things, with grammatical relationships (subject-object-verb, modifier-noun, etc.) and a level of surface structure representing the overt arrangement of phonological forms in actual sentences.

The relationship of sound to meaning thus proves to be much more complex than the earlier descriptivists had imagined. Segmentation and analysis of utterance elements does not automatically lead to an understanding of the basic mechanism of language. The goal of linguistic description therefore shifts from taxonomy of texts to grammar as a theory of the speaker's "linguistic competence," i.e., a set of abstract rules which account for his ability to generate and understand sentences.

This change in research paradigm has some important consequences for linguistic elicitation procedures. While much of the basic data for grammatical analysis continues to be collected in linguist-informant interview sessions of the type just described, the investigator, in order to prove the speaker's ability, takes an increasingly active role in the elicitation process. Rather than simply collecting speech forms and classifying them, he seeks ways of challenging his informant by asking him to perform grammatical operations on sentences, i.e., changing sentences from active to passive, positive to negative, singular to plural. He may himself test his own understanding of grammatical rules by creating new sentences and ask the informant to judge their grammaticality. The linguist thus ceases to be an impartial observer and increasingly takes on the role of an active experimenter.

Whereas descriptive linguists had seen their work as being closely related to the ethnographers' descriptions of foreign cultures, the generative grammarians' interest in grammar as a model of speakers' knowledge or ability takes them into the realm of the human. Chomsky explicitly characterizes linguistics as a branch of cognitive psychology. Generative grammar has a profound effect on psychological theory. The notion of linguistic competence clears the way for radically new approaches to cognition (Miller, Galanter, and Pribham 1960) and has made significant contributions to our understanding of human learning (Smith and Miller 1966).

It must be emphasized, however, that generative grammar studies speakers as individuals, not as members of specific groups. Speakers' abilities are dealt with at a very abstract level, with emphasis on those abilities that are shared by all humans. Recent linguistic research has in fact provided increasing evidence for the universality of basic grammatical processes, and much attention has been devoted to the formalization of universal grammatical rules (Chomsky and Halle 1968; Bach and Harms 1968). However, generative grammarians see the theory of grammars as having little relevance as an explanation for the social basis of verbal behavior (Hymes 1969).

Typology of Language Situations

Apart from grammatical theory, the last two decades have also seen an expansion in the depth and range of empirical research on the verbal habits of human groups. The Prague School linguists' writings on diffusion and stylistics (Garvin 1969; Sebeok 1960), Weinreich (1953) and Haugen's (1953) work on language contact as well as the British linguists' studies of dialect and register (Halliday, McIntosh, and Strevens 1964) had served to dispel the earlier structural preconceptions that formal analysis is applicable only to internally homogeneous systems.

Interest in problems of diversity grew as descriptive linguists working as ethnographers, second language teaching specialists, or government officers began to come in close contact with the complex societies of Asia and Africa. In these societies it was by no means unusual to find several distinct and sometimes unrelated languages spoken in what for reasons of communication density and on political and administrative grounds would have to be regarded as a single community. Bilingualism, bidialectalism or diglossia, as Ferguson (1964a) has called it, seemed to be the rule rather than the exception. Since speakers may alternate among such distinct local speech varieties in much the same way and for the same communicative ends as monolinguals select among styles of the same language, there is good justification for treating these communities as single multilingual or multidialectal speech communities.

During the last two decades descriptive linguistic analysis has with increasing frequency been applied to such diverse groups and the resulting descriptions compared with independently collected cultural and social information. As a result, the scope of linguistic fieldwork has also been broadened. The growing political importance of hitherto almost unknown languages, the unsuspected intricacies of language distribution in the so-called developing nations, called attention to the lack of first-hand information on verbal communication practices. Linguists began to go beyond structural analysis of grammatical systems to concentrate directly on the language usage of human groups and to record how the varieties in questions were used in particular nations, geographical regions, market networks, etc. To this end it became necessary to account for the fact that the grammatical characteristics of a language variety are not always directly related to its communicative functions and that the same language may have quite different functions in different social groups.

A major sociolinguistic goal is to devise schemes for the comparative study of language distribution which allow for the comparison of social systems in terms of what languages are spoken, by how many people in what contexts, and in terms of what the local attitudes to these languages are. In one of the first attempts to deal with this issue Stewart (1962) classifies languages along two dimensions: inherent characteristics and communicative function. The first dimension distinguishes among such categories as (1) standard languages, with highly condified literary norms; (2) vernaculars, or spoken idioms having no literary style;(3) classical languages, preserved only in texts; (4) creoles resulting from recent pidginization processes, etc. The second category distinguishes between (1) private or in-group media; (2) languages of wider communication used as scientific idioms; (3) trade languages, etc. Building on Stewart's classification, Ferguson (1966) has worked out a system of national language profiles capable of providing statistically codable information on language situations in nation states, comparable to the comparative sociologists cross-cultural studies of social variables.

During the last few years several large-scale countrywide surveys have been undertaken in Africa by teams of linguists, psychologists, and other social scientists. In these surveys structural and historical analysis of local languages and dialects is supplemented by sociological survey information on language usage and attitudes to local languages and tests of mutual intelligibility and multilingual competence (Ferguson 1971; Prator 1970). Other interdisciplinary studies have focused on politics and language planning, the processes by which formerly low prestige vernaculars are transformed into standard languages. Haugen's (1966) detailed history of this process in Norway shows how minor differences in grammar and pronunciation, which do not affect mutual intelligibility, have nevertheless caused major political problems over the last century. J. Das Gupta (1970), a political scientist, demonstrates that questions of language reform are intimately connected with pressure group politics and the competing aspirations of rival political power groups in modern India.

Recent Social Dialect Studies

A second major source of new sociolinguistic data derives from the adaptation of dialect survey techniques to the study of language usage in modern urban settings. The linguistic survey of Scotland, which leans in part on J. R. Firth's notions of context of situation (1964), was the first to take account of the fact that wherever education is widespread local languages always coexist with the standard languages of the schools and of public affairs. Such standard language features were found to have quite different distribution patterns than local dialect features thus dem-

onstrating the fact that speech variation is primarily a function of networks of social relationships (Barnes 1954) and is only indirectly dependent on geography.

In the United States, Labov's now classic study of English in New
York City (1966) while building on the work of the Linguistic Atlas of
the United States (Kurath 1941) makes a radical break with the cumbersome and often unreliable traditional dialect questionnaire interviews.
Rather than seeking out long-term local residents who are regarded as
"good dialect speakers" and surveying all significant aspects of their
speech as his predecessors had done, Labov begins by isolating a limited
number of locally current phonological and grammatical features, those
which are most frequent in everyday usage, most subject to interpersonal
and stylistic variation and which carry the greatest amount of social information. He charts the distribution of these class-stratified features in a
sample of speakers sufficiently large to be representative of the area as a
whole, using elicitation techniques designed to record talk in a variety of
formal and informal contexts. When mapped along the dimensions of
stylistic variation and social identity of speakers, the distribution of
dialect variables proved to be a highly accurate index of both social class
and ethnic identity, as reliable as the best of the conventional sociological
survey measures.

Labov's New York study has provided the impetus for a new tradition
of social dialectology in urban United States, much of it focused on the
speech of low-income minority groups: Blacks, Puerto Ricans, Chicanos,
etc. One aim is to provide linguistic information for curriculum reform in
urban primary schools. Typically these studies employ tape-recorded
questionnaire data with statistically representative population samples
and seek to relate the distribution of linguistic variables to the sociologist's measures of such factors as class, educational achievement, sex,
status, etc. (Wolfram 1969, Shuy, Wolfram, and Riley 1969).

The recent surveys of bilingualism and bidialectalism have brought
about some important insights on attitudes to language and language stereotypes. It has been shown that speakers regularly use dialect variables
as a basis for judging their interlocutors' social background, prestige and
personality characteristics. Such conscious judgments are often independent of the speakers own subconscious use of similar variables in his own
natural speech, so that a speaker may downgrade others for using speech
features which he himself also employs. Wallace Lambert (1967) in his
well-known "speech guise" experiments has built on this phenomenon to
develop some highly interesting measures of ethnic stereotypes.

Historical problems arising from the findings of urban dialectologists
have also led to a revival of the long dormant research on pidgin and
creole languages. Many of the so-called nonstandard features of Afro-

American dialects have their source in Carribean Creoles, which in turn seem to derive from West African pidgins. Attempts to explain some of the historical processes involved here are leading to renewed questioning of some of the basic assumptions regarding the interplay of linguistic and social factors in borrowing, diffusion, and related types of linguistic change (Hymes 1971).

The above approaches to language and society, termed correlational here because they seek to compare results from what are seen as two distinct types of enquiry, have served to establish the study of speech behavior as an important subdiscipline of language study requiring field elicitation procedures and analytical tools which go considerably beyond those of linguistics. While the recent work in theoretical linguistics with its emphasis on formalization and its insistence on maintaining a strict distinction between linguistic and nonlinguistic data has played a determining role in shaping our understanding of grammatical rules, of the relation of linguistic to cognitive processes, and in advancing our knowledge of language history, speech community studies on the other hand are equally essential for the study of ongoing processes of linguistic change for the development of linguistic indices to the study of social phenomena and for most areas of applied linguistics.

In the realm of theory, speech community studies have shown that the question of structural uniformity of languages is largely a matter of the linguist's basic assumptions: the extent to which his analysis is abstracted from everyday behavior and above all of the field elicitation procedures he employs. When studied in sufficient detail, with field methods designed to elicit speech in significant contexts, all speech communities are linguistically diverse and it can be shown that this diversity serves important communicative functions in signaling interspeaker attitudes and in providing information about speakers' social identities. Speech communities vary in the degree and in the nature of the linguistic relationship among intracommunity variables and it is this relationship which is most responsive to social change and most revealing of social information.

Studies of the incidence of linguistic variables have thus opened up many new avenues of research and have achieved some important breakthroughs in the study of language usage and linguistic change, yet important as they are, such correlational studies of linguistic and social variables also leave unanswered a number of basic questions concerning the nature of the relationship of linguistic to social facts.

Why is it for example that in some societies, such as those of South and Southeast Asia, major distinctions of language maintain themselves in spite of centuries of intensive contact, while elsewhere as in Europe, North and South Americas groups tend to give up their native tongues after only a few generations? While it is true that in most cases bilingualism leads to convergence or decrease in language distance among the varieties concerned, a number of cases have been reported where the opposite seems to occur. Certain features of upper-class dialects in India, for example, can be explained only on the assumption that they are neologisms created in response to contact with other groups (Ramamijan 1967). Similarly in the United States the increasing participation of Blacks in public life seems to be leading to the creation of new local prestige dialects which emphasize distinctness from standard English. How do we explain the fact that language conflict between competing intergroup aspirations and interethnic stereotypes are symbolized by what to the linguist are almost trivial linguistic differences? There seems to be almost no correlation between the linguistic distinctness of relevant variables and the social information they carry. The urban dialectologists' attitude studies moreover show that variable selection like the choice of grammatical features is largely subconscious and is independent of overt attitudes (see also Blom and Gumperz, Chapter 14). If this is the case and if variable selection does communicate social information, then how and in what way is this information communicated? What does the speaker have to know to speak appropriately? Clearly these questions cannot be answered by mere descriptions of linguistic variables. No more than the structural linguists' taxonomic approach to phonemes and morphemes could account for the relations of meaning to sound. What is needed is a more basic enquiry into the nature of communication processes, an enquiry which extends the notion of linguistic competence to enquire into the nature of communicative competence and the sociolinguistic rules which enable us to use and produce appropriate speech.

The remainder of this introduction will deal with some of the basic concepts and elicitation techniques relevant to this type of enquiry as they are described in this volume and from related writings (for a discussion of sociolinguistic rules see Ervin-Tripp, Chapter 7).

Some Basic Sociolinguistic Concepts

Before starting discussion of individual concepts it is necessary to comment on the assumptions about social structure that these concepts imply. Correlation sociolinguistics sees the relationship of linguistic to social categories as a match between closely connected but nevertheless independent systems. Language is regarded as a set of rules enabling speakers to translate information from the outside world into sound. Social categories are part of this outside world along with physical environments, cultural artifacts, myths, etc. The model is one of social structures seen as fixed jural rules. When these rules are followed behavior is said to be normal, failure to follow rules constitutes deviant behavior (Schegloff, Chapter 12). Like physical objects such jural rules are regarded as measurable by measures which are independent of communicative processes.

An approach to social theory which is somewhat more in line with sociolinguistic findings is the interactionist approach exibited in the writings of Goffman (1965), Garfinkel (1967), and Cicourel (1966). Noting that most individuals in everyday situations have considerable freedom in choosing which of several role relationships to enact, interactionists deny the parallel between social and physical measurement. They point out that information on social categories is obtainable only though language and that sociological measurement therefore always involves both the informant's and the investigator's perception of the categories that are being measured. This perception is seen as subject to the same culturally determined cognitive processes that ethnographic semanticists (Frake, Chapter 3) have discovered to be operative in human naming behavior. Just as the meaning of words is always affected by context, social categories must be interpreted in terms of situational constraints.

Concepts such as status and role are thus not permanent qualities of speakers, instead they become abstract communicative symbols, somewhat like phonemes and morphemes. Like the latter they can be isolated in the analyst's abstract description but they are always perceived in particular contexts. The division between social and linguistic categories is thus obliterated. Communication is not governed by fixed social rules; it is a two-step process in which the speaker first takes in stimuli from the outside environment, evaluating and selecting from among them in the light of his own cultural background, personal history, and what he knows about his interlocutors. He then decides on the norms that apply to the situation at hand. These norms determine the speakers selection from among the communicative options available for encoding his intent.

In analyzing the factors entering into the selection of communicative signs, it is important to distinguish between the perceptual clues and background information that serve as the input to the selection process and the actual stages that the analyst must postulate as part of his explanatory theory. The former are like the acoustic signals through which speech is identified as speech, whereas the latter are equivalent to the linguist's abstract grammatical categories. We assume that a speaker begins with a certain communicative intent, conscious or subconsious. He may want to ask for something specific: a favor, some information, or he may want to persuade the other or simply talk to be sociable. One of his first steps is to determine what if any limitations the environment imposes on his choice of interactional statetgies. Each culture classifies its surroundings into discrete categories of environment (Blom and Gumperz, Chapter 14), e.g., home, church, public square, classroom, etc. (see also Fishman, Chapter 15). The speaker must scan his surroundings to decide which classification applies. Simultaneously the speaker utilizes his knowledge of his audiences and their possible social identities (Goodenough 1965a) to determine what role to enact. Social rules, therefore, are much like linguistic rules, they determine the actor's choice among culturally available modes of action or strategies in accordance with the constraints provided by communicative intent, setting, and identity relationships.

Speech Communities

To the extent that speakers share knowledge of the communicative constraints and options governing a significant number of social situations, they can be said to be members of the same *speech community* (Gumperz 1964; Hymes, Chapter 1). Since such shared knowledge depends on intensity of contact and on communication networks, speech community boundaries tend to coincide with wider social units, such as countries, tribes, religious or ethnic groupings. But this relationship is by no means a one to one relationship. The adequacy of existing methods for delineating communities or other types of social groupings has been a subject of considerable controversy in recent years (Moerman 1968a; Barth 1969). It is not always possible to assume that a functioning community exists merely from information about ethnic identity, territorial boundaries, or genetic relationship about language varieties. The existence of shared values and of regular communication patterns requires empirical investigation.

As was mentioned above, members of the same speech community need not all speak the same language nor use the same linguistic forms on similar occasions. All that is required is that there be at least one language in common and that rules governing basic communicative strategies be shared so that speakers can decode the social meanings carried by alternative modes of communication. Ervin-Tripp (Chapter 7) and Albert (Chapter 2) discuss relevant communication problems.

While it is true that all speech communities are linguistically and socially diverse there is some relationship between the size and ecological characteristics of the communicating group and the nature of this diversity. In small face to face groups, where speakers have detailed knowledge of each others background and personal affairs, the signalling of social information is less important than in large diverse industrial societies (Das Gupta and Gumperz 1969).

Speech Events

The basic unit for the analysis of verbal interaction in speech communities is the *speech event* (discussed in detail in Hymes, Chapter

1). The speech event is to the analysis of verbal interaction what the sentence is to grammar. When compared with the sentence it represents an extension in size of the basic analytical unit from single utterances to stretches of utterances, as well as a shift in focus from emphasis on text to emphasize on interaction. Speech event analysis focuses on the exchange between speakers, i.e., how a speaker by his choice of topic and his choice of linguistic variables adapts to other participants or to his environment and how others in turn react to him. It is this emphasis on exchanges as stressed in this volume by Dundes (Chapter 4), Mitchell Kernan (Chapter 5), Sacks (Chapter 11), and Schegloff (Chapter 12) that distinguishes the interactional approach to sociolinguistics from the correlational study of language and society, and from recent linguistic analyses of larger utterance units (Halliday 1971; Hasan 1972) from the structural analysis of myth (Barthes 1966) and the philosophers' discussion of speech acts (Searle 1969). Speech event analysis derives its empirical validity from the fact that, as Hymes (Chapter 1⁄) and Albert (Chapter ⁄1) have pointed out, members of all societies recognize certain communicative routines which they view as distinct wholes, separate from other types of discourse, characterized by special rules of speech and nonverbal behavior and often distinguishable by clearly recognizable opening and closing sequences (Frake 1964a; Sacks, Chapter 11). Like the verbal duels described by Dundes (Chapter 4) and the signifying, marking, and other routines discussed by Mitchell-Kernan (Chapter 5) these units often carry special names. Although speech events are popularly thought of as units of content or activities, their social significance derives from the relationship they establish between certain types of content and certain types of verbal routines. Following the usual linguistic practice such restrictions can be analyzed along two dimensions: (1) the syntagmatic, involving the temporal ordering of subunits, including allocation of rights to speaking, and (2) the paradigmatic, referring to the selection among alternates within a contextual frame.

Just as sentences consist of ordered sequences of clauses, phrases, and words, conversations subdivide into episodes (Watson and Potter 1962) or discourse stages as Frake (1964a) has called them in his highly revealing and suggestive analysis of speech events in a Philippine tribal group. In some societies, such as the Burundi described by Albert in Chapter 2, verbal encounters begin with highly ritualized introductions, where wording is relatively predetermined and they end with similarly ritualized codas. In order to communicate effectively under these conditions a speaker must know how to insert his message between such ritualized sequences. A dramatic example of the communicative importance of order in conversation is provided by Schegloff (Chapter 12) in his analysis of opening gambits in telephone conversations. Schegloff shows how expectations about sequencing affect the interpretation of the social significance of messages and can in turn be manipulated for communicative ends.

Paradigmatic constraints govern selection among the constituent factors in speech events described by Hymes (Chapter 1) as well as selection among the linguistic variables which will be discussed below. Of particular interest for our understanding of social interaction processes is Sacks' (Chapter 11) utilization of constraints on topic selection as a basis for the semantic analysis of speakers' social categorization practices. Sacks works out empirical procedures for determining the social categories which speakers use to regulate everday conversation and demonstrates that social categories, at the interactional level at least, are in essence semantic categories.

Although speech event analysis has in large part focused on bounded, readily isolable sequences, where the form of what is said and done is relatively narrowly constrained, it is clear that not all interaction is analyzable into such discrete and ritualized units. In everyday informal interaction choice of linguistic form tends to be much less constrained and events often merge into one another without perceptible boundaries. But even in such informal situations the notion of speech events is important in determining the analysis of social meaning. Whenever particular linguistic forms or other formal features of speaking are associated with particular activities or with particular identity relationships, the formal features in question come to symbolize the cultural values attached to these environments. Such association between linguistic form and extralinguistic context can be used for communicative ends when, as in the cases of metaphorical code switching discussed by Blom and Gumperz (Chapter 13) or in some of the instances of signifying discussed by Mitchell-Kernan (Chapter 5), contextually marked modes of speaking are used in other than their normal context. In these cases, values associated with the original context are mapped onto the new message. The association between linguistic forms and social meanings is part of a community's rules of speaking and is used to interpret social meanings even by those speakers who themselves do not ordinarily engage in the event in question. Thus speech events are cognitive phenomena that play an essential part in managing and interpreting everyday communications.

Sociolinguistic Variables

How are social meanings encoded linguistically? Despite the narrowing in the scope of linguistic analysis, the problem has never been completely neglected. Sapir (1964) and his students (Haas 1964;

Newman 1964) are responsible for some highly interesting studies of grammatical differences in the speech of men and women and expressive speech forms in non-Western societies. Differences between high and low status styles in formal and informal speech have been described in considerable detail, e.g., in Java (Geertz 1960), Korea and elsewhere (Howell 1969). All these studies take as their point of departure structural data of the type collected in the course of ordinary linguistic analysis. A more general notion is the notion of sociolinguistic variable.

Linguists concerned with language usage had frequently observed considerable variation in the pronunciation of phones in some words. Some had explained this phenomena by postulating two alternating phonemic systems (Pike and Fries 1949). Others, noting the frequency with which such variations occurred in linguistically diverse communities, preferred to analyze them as shifts between allophones of phonemes within the same system (Ferguson 1964a; Gumperz and Naim 1960). Labov, using elicitation techniques capable of generating stylistically differentiated speech samples from large numbers of speakers, found similar phenomena among monolingual residents in New York City. In particular he noted that variations in the pronunciation of certain words were so extensive as to cut across the articulatory range of what structural dialectologists using traditional field techniques had analyzed as distinct phonemes. The vowel in 'bad,' e.g., could be homophonous with the [I·] in 'beer,' the [ɛ·] in 'bear,' or the [æ·] in 'bat.' Three distinct phonemes thus seemed to collapse into a single articulatory range. Since there is no phonetic basis for isolating distinct articulation peaks within this range, Labov argues that any attempt to deal with such shifts by postulating alternation between distinct systems is without empirical foundation. They must be treated as variables within a single system. He goes on to suggest that the descreteness of phonemic systems is an artifact of the linguist's field practice of abstracting rules from the speech of one or at most a few informants and of deemphasizing variation. Intensive study of speech behavior should, in any one speech community, reveal both phonemes and variables. While phonemes are characterized by pronunciations clustering around definable articulation peaks, variables are defined by a starting point and a scale of values varying in a certain direction. The values along such scales are conditioned by social factors in a manner analogous to that in which phonological environments condition the phonetic realizations of allophones.

Although the term *variable,* as used by Labov, applies primarily to pronunciation phenomena, similar types of socially determined variation have also been found in morphology and syntax and in the lexicon. Fischer's (1958) study of the alternation between 'ing' and 'in' in such English participles as 'going' and Geertz's (1960) analysis of high, middle, and low speech levels in Javanese are cases in point. Particular attention has been devoted to pronouns and terms of address such as the second person singular *tu* and *vous* in French (Brown and Gilman 1960) or their equivalents in Russian (Friedrich, Chapter 9), Korean, and Japanese (Martin 1958; Howell 1967), which serve both as symbols of social structure and indexes of social change.

Not all grammatical or lexical alternates in a language can automatically be regarded as sociolinguistic variables, however. Since the same language may be spoken in a number of socially distinct societies, it must be demonstrated that selection among alternates carries social significance for some groups of speakers. Furthermore, since social meaning is always embedded in reference, it is useful to speak of sociolinguistic variables only when alternates are referentially equivalent, i.e., when they signify the same thing in some socially realistic speech event. Items with the same or similar dictionary meanings may not be substitutable in actual conversation and, per contra, some variables are semantically equivalent only in specific contexts. An example will illustrate the problem. Few would ordinarily claim that the words 'wife' and 'lady' are homonyms in English. Yet they are used as such in the following extract from an invitation to an army social quoted in a recent issue of the San Francisco *Examiner:* "Officers with their ladies, enlisted men with their wives." Referential equivalence here underlines social differences.

The concept of the variable as discussed here is a general one, referring to the selection of elements or strings of elements at any component or level of linguistic structure (i.e., phonology, syntax, or lexicon). It is important to note that as long as the condition of referential equivalence in some speech event is met, the values or alternates of such a variable need not be confined to items normally considered part of the same language or dialect. As it was just pointed out, in some societies the shift between linguistically distinct codes may carry social meanings equivalent to the selection of stylistic alternates in others. In his analysis of kinship terminology in this volume Tyler (Chapter 8) finds it necessary to deal with Koya and Telugu forms as part of the same system. He sets up rules which select among these alternates in terms of group membership of speakers and addressee.

Linguistic Repertoires

The totality of linguistic resources (i.e., including both invariant forms and variables) available to members of particular communities refers to the linguistic repertoire of that community (Gumperz 1964b). This concept is advanced to account for the fact that the linguist's grammatical analysis seldom matches verbal behavior of actual populations. A grammar of English, for example, deals with the linguistic competence of speakers in a number of societies in England, in the United States, or even in India, Africa, and elsewhere. Speakers in these societies differ not so much in the way they speak English but in the fact that in their everyday interaction they alternate between English and various other local dialects or even languages. The concept of the repertoire enables us to capture these distinctions and thus uniquely describe the speech behavior of a population in terms of their selection within particular clusters of linguistic variants or sets of grammatical systems.

The mere listing of variables is however not enough. It becomes necessary to show how these component varieties are kept distinct in communication. In the process of analysis, the boundaries between subsystems must be determined. There is evidence that variables tend to be selected in *co-occurrent clusters*. In other words, the speaker's choice of a particular value of a variable is always constrained by previous selections of variables. Thus, if a speaker varies between [i·], [ɛ·], and [æ·] in 'bad' and, in addition, has alternates 'ain't,' 'is not,' 'going,' and 'goin',' he is most likely to say, "This ain't gonna be [bi·d]," in some situations and, "This is not going to be [bæd]," in others. It would be unusual for him to say, "This is not going to be [bi·d]." It is important to note that sociolinguistic selection constraints which generate such co-occurrences cut across the normal components of grammar (see Ervin-Tripp, Chapter 7; Blom and Gumperz, Chapter 14). Their study, therefore, extends the application of linguistic analysis to data not ordinarily considered a part of grammar.

The existence of sociolinguistic rules, selecting co-occurrent clusters of variables, lends some empirical validity to notions such as code, variety, dialect, or language. Whenever features in several components of linguistic structure alternate simultaneously, we can speak of switching among entire speech varieties rather than choice among individual features. Note that when a language variety (whether dialect, style, language, or whatever) is defined in this way (i.e., when the speech event is used as a starting point, the unit in question emerges from the analysis), we need no longer, as in the traditional field methods just discussed, start by asking informants to speak in a particular style or dialect with the concurrent risk that their attitudes will interfere with their response.

The Genesis and Maintenance of Speech Differences

How do different subgroups, co-resident within a larger social unit, develop different ways of speaking? Bernstein's notion of code explained in Chapter 17 represents one of the first attempts to deal with this problem in cross-cultural terms. According to Bernstein, the key to the acquisition and maintenance of different patterns is the socialization process. While basic grammatical competence is innate, the network of social relationships in which the individual interacts and the communicative tasks that these relationships entail ultimately shape the way in which he uses language. Such patterns of language usage are referred to as "linguistic codes" (see prefatory to Chapter 17). Once learned, a linguistic code constrains the individual's perception of his and his interlocutor's social role, just as lexical structures constrain the individuals perception of features in the physical environment. Intrasocietal differences in social relationships and especially in family role systems give rise to different linguistic codes and thus to differences in role perception. Following Bott (1957) a scalar distinction is made between closed or positional family role systems and open systems. Closed systems emphasize communal values stressing status distinctions and propriety in speech and lead to "restricted codes," a way of language usage which is highly formulaic. Open or person-oriented role systems, on the other hand, emphasize individual creativity, and ability to "take the role of the other" and lead to elaborated codes which are more suited to the transmission of new information and more acceptable to novel situations.

Bernstein's earlier largely exploratory work has led to some highly interesting studies in the area of socialization and has pioneered the use of linguistic indices to the study of socialization and social control (Cook 1972). Several linguistic analyses of interviews with mothers and children have revealed some important social differences in the use of sentence connectives, noun modifiers, deictic pronouns, etc. (Turner and Mohan 1971; Hassan 1972). In the present state of our knowledge there is, however, no evidence to assume that the distinction between restricted and elaborated codes corresponds to class-related differences in verbal skills. On the contrary, Labov (1969) using elicitation techniques which relied heavily on natural conversation and on his knowledge of culture specific speech events such as "sounding" found that the very children who in school or in interviews with strangers tend to speak only in short, seemingly truncated utterances of the type usually characterized as instances of restricted codes, show themselves to be highly creative and effective communicators when interviewed in settings which they perceive as culturally realistic or when their natural interaction with peers is recorded.

An alternative explanation of the issues raised by the distinction between elaborated and restricted codes, one which relates the problem to more basic communication processes is suggested by Garfinkel's (Chapter 10) concept of indexicality (see Cicourel 1968 for a discussion of this concept in relation to socialization). Indexicality refers to the fact that the interpretation of communicative acts always without exception depends upon the speakers background knowledge. For this reason the spoken message is always an imperfect realization of what was in the minds of the speakers and hearers. Background assumptioned may be signaled as part of the message through choice of words, speech style or stress and intonation; or they may be implicit in the actors' view of the speech event. Seen from this point of view, elaboration and restriction are simply two different modes of signaling or calling upon background knowledge. Elaborated messages are messages where the maximum communication load is carried by words; restricted messages, on the other hand, rely on other nonlexical communicative devices (e.g., code switching, stress, intonation, etc.). The greater the reliance on words, the more accessible the message is to others who do not share similar speakers' knowledge or personal background. In many written and spoken formal (elaborated) communications an interpretation at the level of dictionary meanings of words is adequate. Elaborated codes in this sense are thus more suited for cross-cultural communication and are typically taught in school systems. The fact that so much of literature and art relies on nondiscursive devices suggests that elaborated codes are not always the most effective means of communication.

Some Implications for Fieldwork

Although the preceding discussion of sociolinguistic concepts does not give a complete theory, it does however carry some clear implications for what is or is not adequate fieldwork. Throughout this discussion evidence has been presented for the close interdependence between linguistic data and elicitation procedures. Since language choice is largely subconscious, and since the signalling of social information is crucially dependent on context, the study of social meaning requires fieldwork techniques capable of challenging the verbal skills employed by speakers in everyday interaction. It is evident that the linguist informant method described earlier is not in itself adequate for this task. Single person informant interviews are essential starting points for the discovery of basic grammatical information; yet, once this information is known, such methods seem hardly suitable for eliciting natural conversations. The very artificiality of settings where speech samples must be produced on demand, apart from the customary circles of friends and family, is hardly likely to generate the subtleties in selection of speech forms, shifts in formality, intimacy, etc. by which members categorize each other in every day interaction. Even a highly skilled writer has difficulty in reproducing natural conversations. Certainly an ordinary informant cannot be expected to do it. At best the linguistic informant interview yields samples of a single speech style, generally relatively formal speech. The setting in such interviews tends to reduce to a minimum the very type of linguistic devices by which social meaning is conveyed in normal interaction.

The common linguist's practice of asking speakers to speak in a particular language or dialect, furthermore, implies the assumption that the delimitation of such entities presents no elicitation problems, and that both linguists and informants agree on what forms should be omitted from consideration and what forms included. This practice begs the question. Variants are not always assigned to particular languages on the basis of their grammatical characteristics alone. Religion, ethnicity, socioeconomic position of speaker and similar social criteria may play a more important role than a grammatical similarity or difference (Ferguson and Gumperz 1959). Since in such a diverse community the linguist's request to a speaker to produce particular forms of languages may be interpreted by speakers as a request to behave in a certain way (i.e., to be formal or informal), or to emphasize otherwise some aspect of his social personality, the social implications of linguistic forms thus elicited may seriously affect the validity of the linguist's analysis, for in effect, the question has filtered out significant aspects of the potential corpus of data.

The definition of sociolinguistic variables in terms of referentially equivalent units in some natural speech event defines a basic task of sociolinguistic fieldwork: to generate socially conditioned variations in speakers natural performances. The basic elicitation method can be regarded as an extension of the linguist's practice of studying the same linguistic forms in different linguistic environments. What is constant here is the basic message and what is varied is the social relationship. The search for natural speech or "good" language is therefore abandoned in favor of efforts to sample significantly different speech events. Such sampling of speech in a representative range of events clearly requires some knowledge of the rules of speaking discussed by Hymes (Chapter 1). Mere behavioristic observation of daily activities is not enough. Albert (Chapter 2) basing herself on her own analysis of Barundi speech lists in detail some of the difficulties the observer may encounter and suggests field procedures for learning rules of speaking. Yet it would be premature to demand that all sociolinguistic analyses start with a complete taxonomy of speech events in particular societies. This is a major task in itself, equivalent to furnishing a description of a whole culture. A more practical goal would be to begin with a significant and representative range of different contexts. But even for this task it is necessary to find some consistent criteria of defining or singling out particular contexts.

Frake (Chapter 3) adapts the ethnoscientist's analysis of native terminological systems to the definition of speech events (e.g., litigants) among the Yakan. Albert (Chapter 2) points out that ritual events—ceremonies, formal greetings, and speech making—are more sharply defined, and thus more easily separable from other events, than everyday happenings. Labov achieves contrast in setting by contrasting formal interview sessions in which speakers are asked to perform such tasks as reading word lists or reciting paradigms with more natural conversations. In these conversations he generates further variations by alternately involving his respondents in neutral, emotionally charged, or humous subjects. Blom and Gumperz utilize the anthropologist's ethnographic data to organize local discussion groups with different social characteristics in order to compare their treatments of similar conversational topics. Bernstein's more recent studies adopt the social psychologist's role-play technique to test the speaker's ability to respond to a variety of communicative tasks.

The need to generate natural speech frequently makes it necessary for the investigator to concentrate on group interviews rather than working with single individuals. The role of the interviewer in such groups is simply to act as an observer who may introduce a topic, but who then allows group processes to determine further treatment of the topic. Although it would seem difficult to induce people to speak normally while a tape recorder is operating, it has been found that when speakers are interviewed in groups, the social obligations among members frequently lead them to disregard the recording instrument and to behave as if they were unobserved.

Obviously, the investigator's skill in managing interaction is an important factor in sociolinguistic elicitation. If the investigator wishes to vary social stimuli, he must be able to predict which stimulus will produce what reaction. The most successful investigators are those who can utilize their own background knowledge of the culture in elicitation. It is not enough, as some behaviorally oriented students of natural speech suggest, simply to observe performances. The investigator must find ways of testing the speakers' ability to vary their performances. Hence his success depends on his knowledge of sociolinguistic rules.

Plan of the Book

This book has three major divisions. Each part addresses itself to a question at the forefront of sociolinguistic research. Part 1 is concerned with how ways of speaking are shaped by both cultural values and social institutions. Part 2 is concerned with how the rules of conversation and address can be discovered and adequately stated. Part 3 is concerned with how varieties of language arise and come to be appropriate to specific social and cultural contexts—why they persist, why they change, and why they disappear.

The three divisions of the book are not independent, nor can they be. Aspects of the structure and meaning of speech have a unity such that focus on one aspect involves consideration of each of the others. To ask about the meaning of a pattern of speech (1) involves being able to recognize an instance of it, that is, to describe its structure. The structure of speech in a given segment of interaction (2) is not fully intelligible apart from the context of values and institutions in which it is embedded. Each of these aspects is intimately bound up with the genesis, maintenance, and change of language varieties or codes (3). A topical index has been provided to help trace the connections among parts of the book.

If the three divisions of the book form an integrated whole, the different questions along which major divisions of the book are organized reflect somewhat different sources of interest in the emerging field of sociolinguistics. The first major division indicates the place of speech patterns in the nexus of the cultural or social institution in which it occurs. The second major division of the book focuses on discovery and descriptive methods used in current sociolinguistic analysis. The third major division focuses on variance in linguistic codes in terms of their genesis, maintenance, and change. It is, in effect, a synthesis of the first two major divisions.

In Part 1, Hymes suggests a general frame of reference for ethnographic description and comparison. In addition, the volume includes, as an appendix, a short field guide by Darnell and Sherzer, listing some basic questions relevant for comparative study. Hymes shows the relationship of the ethnographic approach to other work in the first section and in the sections which follow. Albert provides a sensitive perspective on the significance of speech in one particular society. Her work serves as a useful datum point for a number of the articles which follow. In a similar vein, Frake analyzes an institution which, he observes, "is manifested almost exclusively by one kind of behavior, talk." He carefully analyzes native categories for kinds of talk, and for settings in which they occur. He concludes with an instructive contrast between these features in two cultures. Dundes and his collaborators provide a vivid analysis of a particular speech genre, a verbal form of social strategy. This strategy, verbal dueling, is important throughout much of the world. Mitchell-Kernan discusses several common Afro-American speech acts. By means of skillfully selected examples from everyday interaction, she shows how rhetorical devices reflecting these events are used to enrich conversation and to convey subtle nuances of meaning. Roberts and Forman are also concerned with explaining the presence or absence of a genre in a particular society, and with what motivates differential involvement in it. The particular value of this study, apart from the fact that it describes a particular case, is its use of a comparative cross-cultural method combined with analysis of individual variation in our society, in terms of a model of the role of verbal genres, such as riddling, in socialization. Thus, Part 1 is designed to provide the reader with a sense of speech as part of larger cultural patterns of behavior, using data drawn from a broad geographical sphere—Africa, Turkey, the Philippines, and the United States.

While Part 1 may strike many linguists as ethnographic, Part 2 may strike many social scientists as primarily of concern to linguists. In this section, as in the first, however, the analysis is rooted in social science: Ervin-Tripp is a social psychologist, Tyler and Friedrich are anthropologists, Garfinkel, Sacks, and Schegloff are sociologists. Birdwhistell is an anthropologist with training in social psychiatry and, like many of the other contributors, with training in linguistics as well.

Studies of the sort in Part 2 are, and must be, concerned, like those in Part 1, with the kinds of settings of speech events, with what underlies and brings participants into them, as well as with the difficulties that are involved in providing accounts of the events themselves. What may make the studies in Part 2 seem instances of "linguistic" rather than "social science" subjects of inquiry is that they point the way toward a formal, that is, explicit, account of some specific segment of behavior. In a variety of ways such studies reflect the fact that speech manifests kinds of knowledge and abilities (kinds of competence), largely outside the range of immediate individual awareness, that can be characterized just as can the competence that underlies language proper. Such analysis may be said to extend the notion of "rule-governed creativity" (cf. Chomsky 1966, 1968) to speech—from the structure of sentences to the structure of their use.

The charter for this generalization can in fact be found in the work of a linguist who was an anthropologist, Sapir, and an anthropologist who was something of a linguist, Malinowski, both of whom came to be concerned with "living speech" (Sapir 1949a:592–593; Malinowski 1964:63). Sapir recognized the continuity of linguistic form with the patterning of all cultural behavior (1949c). Malinowski viewed language as a mode of action, not merely as a countersign of thought (1935). In this synthesis of language, thought, and behavior, the goals of leading schools of linguistic theory and ethnography converge (Goodenough 1964).

In Part 2 Ervin-Tripp provides the first general survey of kinds of rules and forms of statement in sociolinguistic study of interaction. Her paper is an invaluable introduction to the subject, and embodies original research as well. Tyler takes a subject central to social life and social anthropology, kinship; and whereas anthropological formal analysis of kinship has tended to neglect context just as much as linguistic analysis of sentences, Tyler shows the necessity and possibility of taking context formally into account. Friedrich uses interaction as described in Russian novels to show the subtlety and power of a grammatical choice when, although in itself a detail, it is deeply embedded in social life.

Garfinkel sketches a central concern of the movement of which he is the pioneer and which is gaining increasing recognition in modern sociology: to recognize the data of verbal interaction as neither trivial nor "degenerate" but rather as an artful accomplishment, one with profound import for understanding man's nature. Developing this theme, Sacks seeks to make us see everyday, taken-for-granted behavior as presupposing complex rules of interpretation, as being something to wonder at and wish to explain. He suggests that children early sense and make skillful use of some of these rules. Schegloff, taking data that might have been treated only statistically or by content analysis, attends strictly to its formal structure. Finding an exception to a generalization that accounts for 99 percent of the cases, he does not dismiss it, but discovers a deeper generalization. Schegloff's rules govern nonverbal as well as verbal behavior. Birdwhistell shows that nonverbal signals can countermand or replace speech; from that standpoint, he demonstrates in precise detail that the study of speech in interaction is part of the study of communicative conduct as a whole.

Between Parts 1 and 2, we noted, there is an apparent difference of scale; the significance of the genres dealt with in 1 is immediately apparent, and in dealing with them one can learn something without technical analysis of actual speech. One lesson of the kind of work represented in Part 2, however, is that it is in the nature of communicative interaction for matters of great significance to be presupposed or expressed in slight cues. Language—physically a matter of little marks and displacements of air—is itself an example. The more that patterns and meanings of behavior come to be shared, the more likely is it that bits of behavior, seemingly trivial or unnoticed, are for the persons involved not trivial but economical. Our present understanding of the complexity, rapidity, and power of the human brain makes it no surprise that much of communicative behavior must be understood on the analogy of an improvised motet or fugue.

Part 3 takes up a subject initially linguistic, but recast in the larger context that the preceding sections provide. The multiplicity of forms of speech has interested mankind from earliest times. For much of human history the most salient form of change has been that which has produced the several thousand different languages now found in the world; some of the great achievements of historical linguistics have been in discovering common ancestors and past contacts among languages now separate, and in establishing the methods by which this could be done. Folk explanations of diversity have been replaced with work based on the simple yet fundamental fact that language changes, inevitably and continually, and that, to the extent that communities become separate, subsequent changes in each, being independent of those in the other, eventually will produce distinct forms of speech. Recent work in theoretical linguistics has added depth of understanding of the form of change, and of ways in which it may depend upon common, even universal, properties of linguistic structures. Beyond recognition of the fact of change, however, lies the question of its cause and mechanism. Explanation has been sought in the speech organs, habits of articulation, the brain, the patterning of language itself—operative perhaps in terms of a cumulative drift, a functional gap, or the discontinuity between generations. The facts of "language history"—the conquest, extinction, or migration of populations, contact with other languages and new environments—causing new needs and providing new models, have, of course, been taken into account; but seldom has explanation been sought in the matrix of social relationships in which a language is used. Such relationships have been seen as a factor contributing to the diffusion of changes but not usually as a source of change. Change, like structure, has usually been considered something to be explained within linguistics itself.

Change, moreover, has been conceived essentially as change with respect to some one form or variety of a language, so far as explicit theory has been concerned, seldom as change in the functional role of a language. Seldom has persistence been seen as the other side of the coin, and equally in need of explanation. Rarely have modern linguists conceived the locus of persistence and change as the *repertoire* of a community—as lying in the relations among, and constituency of, a *set* of forms of speech. The existence of a set of alternative forms of speech is characteristic of every community, however, and by far the dominant process of change, today and for the future, is not diversification of whole languages (genetic diversification will rarely, if ever, occur again), but differentiation of the resources of languages into new functional varieties, together with the integration of different languages into new functional unities—for example, the development of new standardized varieties from former trade argots or pidgins, on the one hand, and specialization and revitalization of the role of surviving vernaculars, on the other, in new nations.

In this book we can broach only the issues most closely tied to social interaction. An essential step is to get at the social meaning of alternative forms of speech. Blom and Gumperz investigate the relation between a standard and a local dialect, and show the meaning of each to depend upon participation in different types of social relationships. Their approach provides a quite general way of studying any choice of form of speech, whether whole language, dialect, or style. Notice that it shows (as does Labov's work) that usage may be as much out of awareness as grammatical structure; self-report by informants would not suffice. Fishman seeks to relate fine-grained study of interaction to study of larger social systems through the concept of *domains* of language choice. He provides information on a situation in which an immigrant group alternately uses two wholly distinct languages, and where, situation and participants and even topic sometimes remaining constant, the expressive import of the choice is made manifest.

Both Barth and Bernstein deal with cases of shift from one form of speech to another, Barth between distinct ethnic groups, Bernstein within a single society. Barth succinctly analyzes a case in which neither gross "prestige" nor demonstrated dominance—the usual catchall explanations—can account for change of language and of linguistic boundaries. Explanation must be sought in the choices available within two contrasting types of social system and in the relationships of power and authority internal to the ethnic groups in question.

Bernstein argues that contrasting types of social interaction—particularly, of social control within the family—may introduce a boundary within a single society, by giving rise to distinct "linguistic codes" that express and perpetuate distinct orientations toward social reality. Where Blom and Gumperz dealt with maintenance of forms of speech, and Barth with shift from one to another, Bernstein deals with their genesis. Where social scientists, Durkheim and others, have sometimes seen correlations between type of society and type of language, Bernstein seeks to explain the mechanism by which such a link could come about, relating division of labor, class structure, family role systems, social control, and speech in a general theory. Nowhere is it more explicit that the unit of ordinary linguistic work, the named language, "English" or the like, is inadequate as a basis for understanding the meaning of language in social life. When, as in the case of Bernstein's work, the phonology, lexicon, and grammar are essentially the same from the standpoint of ordinary linguistic analysis, the need for new units and modes of description is evident.

Bernstein here develops his concepts of *elaborated* and *restricted codes*. Notice that they are more complex than the simple dichotomy they are usually taken to be. The same person may command more than one, and there may be varieties within each type, differing as to primary orientation toward persons or objects. Bernstein's suggestions as to the implications of these concepts for education are controversial (he himself has been critical of their application to the American situation), but the body of work on which they are based remains the most substantial of any so far.

Fischer shows that a difference between two related languages in a phonological detail (and also perhaps in other features) fits with a general contrast in outlook, social structure, and the role of speech between the two societies. Thus he shows the outcome, aided by geographical separation, of what may have begun as differential use of common linguistic means. In addition, he suggests that the feature with regard to which the languages differ has a universal expressive value, thus implying the possibility of inferring from phonology something of the orientation of the social worlds languages occupy. Like Bernstein and Labov, Fischer sees a social origin for linguistic change; again like both, his conception of such origin requires a description of language use as well as language structure.

Where Fischer deals with a stylistic feature, Labov demonstrates that the central phonological systems of languages change in ways that cannot be explained apart from social motivation. Linguists have tended to see social factors as secondary, contributing to the diffusion of changes whose source must be sought elsewhere. Labov shows social factors to be primary, and argues that the fact of inevitable, continual change in language is due to a further fact, namely, that at any given time some features of language are variables with social meaning, and differentially selected for use accordingly. Thus, whereas some sociolinguistic research requires linguists to add to the scope of their interests, commonly, it might be felt, to choose to "go beyond language," Labov shows that to explain a matter already regarded as part of linguistics—sound change—one *must* go outside language, to the social matrix of speech with which, in one way or another, all the contributions to this book are concerned.

part one

ETHNOGRAPHIC
DESCRIPTION
AND
EXPLANATION

1

Models of the Interaction
of Language and Social Life[1]

DELL HYMES

Dell Hymes is Professor of Anthropology at the University of Pennsylvania. He received his B.A. in anthropology and literature from Reed College, and his Ph.D. in linguistics from Indiana University. He has taught at Harvard and the University of California at Berkeley, and has lectured at Cambridge University. He has done fieldwork among American Indians of the northwest coast. His research interests include ethnography of speaking, verbal art, the history of linguistics and anthropology, and historical linguistics. This chapter has evolved from a paper published in 1967 (Macnamara 1967).

To claim that sociolinguistics is a distinct field is to imply that there are both problems and types of linguistic data that have not been adequately considered before. Language, after all, is all around us, and its description is among the oldest of man's scientific enterprises. What does it mean to do a description of a sociolinguistic system, and how does this differ from doing a grammar of a language or dialect, mapping dialect boundaries, determining historical relationships, studying rules of rhetoric

[1] Revised from Hymes 1967, particularly elaborating the treatment of taxonomy and recasting the presentation of components of speaking. Many of the examples come from an examination of ethnographic data undertaken with support of the culture of Schools program of the Office of Education in 1966–1967. I am greatly indebted to Regna Darnell, Helen Hogan, Elinor Keenan, Susan Philips, Sheila Seitel, Joel Sherzer, K. M. Tiwary, and my wife, Virginia, for their participation in that work. My own thinking on the general problem has benefited from a small grant from the National Institute of Mental Health in spring 1968. I thank Meyer Fortes, Edmund Leach and J. L. M. Trim for discussion of some of these problems, and many kindnesses, while a visiting fellow at Clare Hall, Cambridge, in 1968–1969.

and literary style, or analyzing the speech varieties characteristic of the various ethnic groups or social classes
coresident in a particular region? Which of the many
aspects of verbal behavior do we observe, and what concepts do we utilize in classifying what we observe to
insure comparability of data? This chapter addresses
itself to these issues. It is general in scope in that it suggests criteria for gathering information on rules of speaking rather than focusing on a particular social group. It is
thus in a sense complementary to the chapters by Ervin-
Tripp (Chapter 7), Bernstein (Chapter 17), and Garfinkel
(Chapter 10), which deal with similarly general problems
of theory and analysis.

Rules of speaking are the ways in which speakers associate particular modes of speaking, topics or message
forms, with particular settings and activities. The concern is, first of all, with the attitudes and knowledge of the
members of the community, as manifest in contrasts in
native terminologies and conduct. Except for occasional
references in ethnographies or grammatical descriptions
of certain linguistically distinct special parlances (such as
Vedic recitation styles, African praise singing, thieves
argots, and the like) there is almost no systematic information on such matters. What ethnographic information
we have suggests considerable cross-cultural variation in
rules of speaking (see Albert, Chapter 2; Frake, Chapter
3; Philips 1970). Yet the range of this variation and its
relation to social structure and linguistic form is as yet
unknown. What is needed at this stage are new types of
discovery procedures and concepts designed to facilitate
the empirical collection of data.

Since one human groups's theories of speaking can
best be isolated by contrast with those of another, the
comparative approach to fieldwork is probably the most
useful at this stage. Note, however, that the basic unit of
analysis is a community or group rather than a language
or dialect. Recent work with Afro-American speech
groups in the urban United States highlights the importance of this distinction. Linguistically, urban Afro-
American dialects (at least those of the urban northern
United States) do not differ greatly from standard English. Yet Afro-American speakers differ radically from
their white neighbors by the cultural emphasis they place

on speech acts such as "signifying," "sounding," "toasts," etc. Such speech acts, until quite recently, were almost unknown in the community at large, and the average white educator's ignorance of relevant rules of speaking has been responsible for perpetuating some rather tragic misconceptions about lower-class black children's low linguistic competence. Labov and his colleagues (1968) have shown that if, rather than studying black teen-agers' responses to psycholinguistic tests (which, after all, are quite unfamiliar and at times seem threatening to ghetto children), one studies performance in these typically black speech acts, children who in formal interviews seem almost nonverbal in fact, prove to be highly skilled in the use of English.

Emphasis on human groups rather than grammar per se does not mean a neglect of careful linguistic analysis. Both linguists and sociolinguists deal with linguistic form, but they do so from different perspectives. As Hymes puts it, "A linguistic sign is a relation between linguistic form and a linguistic value. A sociolinguistic feature is a relation between a form and a sociolinguistic value." Whereas linguists deal with dictionary meanings (denotation, or meaning abstracted from context), socio-linguists deal with what Sacks calls situated meaning (meaning mediated and sometimes transformed by rules of speaking) which reflects speakers attitudes to each other, and to their topics. [Sacks (see Chapter 11) provides one analysis of the process by which such meanings are communicated.] Sociolinguistic value is discussed either directly or indirectly in several chapters (Friedrich, Chapter 9; Fischer, Chapter 18; Labov, Chapter 19).

Note also Hymes' distinction between the marked or ordinary value of sociolinguistic features and the un-marked value of sociolinguistic features. This is analyzed formally in Geoghegan's study of address rules among the Samal of the southern Philippines (1970).

Although the term *ethnography of speaking* has only begun to gain currency, a number of studies recently completed, or still in progress, give evidence of growing scholarly interest. The field elicitation problems raised in the present paper are dealt with explicitly in Darnell and Sherzer's outline guide for the ethnographic study of speech use (Appendix), which lists some of the basic questions to be covered by ethnographers interested in speech behavior. "A Field Manual for the Cross-Cultural Study of the Acquisition of Communicative Competence" (Slobin et al. 1967) also deals with relevant questions. Tanner (1967), Hogan (1967), Sankoff (1968), and Seitel (1969) provide additional related readings.

Diversity of speech has been singled out as the hallmark of sociolinguistics. Of this two things should be said. Underlying the diversity of speech within communities and in the conduct of individuals are systematic relations, relations that, just as social and grammatical structure, can be the object of qualitative inquiry. A long-standing failure to recognize and act on this fact puts many now in the position of wishing to apply a basic science that does not yet exist.

Diversity of speech presents itself as a problem in many sectors of life—education, national development, transcultural communication. When those concerned with such problems seek scientific cooperation, they must often be disappointed. There is as yet no body of systematic knowledge and theory. There is not even agreement on a mode of description of language in interaction with social life, one which, being explicit and of standard form, could facilitate development of knowledge and theory through studies that are full and comparable. There is not even agreement on the desirability or necessity of such a mode of description.

Bilingual or bidialectal phenomena have been the main focus of the interest that has been shown. Yet bilingualism is not in itself an adequate basis for a model or theory of the interaction of language and social life. From the standpoint of such a model or theory, bilingualism is neither a unitary phenomenon nor autonomous. The fact that two languages are present in a community or are part of a person's communicative competence is compatible with a variety of underlying functional (social) relationships. Conversely, distinct languages need not be present for the underlying relationships to find expression.

Bilingualism par excellence (e.g., French and English in Canada, Welsh and English in North Wales, Russian and French among prerevolutionary Russian nobility) is a salient, special case of the general phenomenon of linguistic repertoire. No normal person, and no normal community, is limited to a single way of speaking, to an unchanging monotony that would preclude indication of respect, insolence, mock seriousness, humor, role distance, and intimacy by switching from one mode of speech to another.

Given the universality of linguistic repertoires, and of switching among the ways of speaking they comprise, it is not necessary that the ways be distinct languages. Relationships of social intimacy or of social distance may be signaled by switching between distinct languages [Spanish: Guarani in Paraguay (Rubin 1962, 1968)]; between varieties of a single language (standard German: dialect), or between pronouns within a single variety (German *Du:Sie*). Segregation of religious activity may be marked linguistically by a variety whose general unintelligibility depends on being of foreign provenance (e.g., Latin, Arabic in many communities), on being a derived variety of the common language [Zuni (Newman 1964)], or on being a manifestation not identifiable at all (some glossolalia). Conversely, shift between varieties may mark a shift between distinct spheres of activity [e.g., standard Norwegian: Hemnes dialect (see Blom and Gumperz, Chapter 14)], or the formal status of talk within a single integral activity [e.g., Siane in New Guinea (Salisbury 1962)], Latin in a contemporary Cambridge University degree ceremony (e.g., *Cambridge University Reporter* 1969).

A general theory of the interaction of language and social life must encompass the multiple relations between linguistic means and social meaning. The relations within a particular community or personal repertoire are an empirical problem, calling for a mode of description that is jointly ethnographic and linguistic.

If the community's own theory of linguistic repertoire and speech is considered (as it must be in any serious ethnographic account), matters become all the more complex and interesting. Some peoples, such as the Wishram Chinook of the Columbia River in what is now the state of Washington, or the Ashanti of Nigeria, have considered infants' vocalizations to manifest a special language (on the Wishram, see Hymes 1966a; on the Ashanti, Hogan 1967). For the Wishram, this language was interpretable only by men having certain guardian spirits. In such cases, the native language is in native theory a second language to everyone. Again, one community may strain to maintain mutual intelligibility with a second in the face of great differentiation of dialect, while another may declare intelligibility impossible, although the objective linguistic differences are minor. Cases indistinguishable by linguistic criteria may thus be now monolingual, now bilingual, depending on local social relationships and attitudes (discussed more fully in Hymes 1968c).

While it is common in a bilingual situation to look for specialization in the function, elaboration, and valuation of a language, such specialization is but an instance of a universal phenomenon, one that must be studied in situations dominantly monolingual as well. Language as such is not everywhere equivalent in role and value; speech may have different scope and functional load in the communicative economies of different societies. In our society sung and spoken communication intersect in song; pure speaking and instrumental music are separate kinds of communication. Among the Flathead Indians of Montana, speech and songs without text are separate, while songs with text, and instrumental music as an aspect of songs with text, form the intersection. Among the Maori of New Zealand instrumental music is a part of song, and both are ultimately conceived as speech. [It is interesting to note that among both the Flathead and Maori it is supernatural context that draws speech and music together, and makes of both (and of animal sounds as well among the Flathead) forms of linguistic communication.]² With regard to speaking itself, while Malinowski has made us familiar with the importance of phatic communication, talk for the sake of something being said, the ethnographic record suggests that it is far from universally an important or even accepted motive (see Sapir 1949i:16, 11). The Paliyans of south India "communicate very little at all times and become almost silent by the age of 40. Verbal, communicative persons are regarded as abnormal and often as offensive" (Gardner 1966:398). The distribution of required and preferred silence, indeed, perhaps most immediately reveals in outline form a community's structure of speaking (see Samarin 1965; Basso 1970). Finally, the role of language in thought and culture (Whorf's query) obviously cannot be assessed for bilinguals until the role of each of their languages is assessed; but the same is true for monolinguals since in different societies language enters differentially into educational experience, transmission of beliefs, knowledge, values, practices, and conduct (see Hymes 1966a). Such differences may obtain even between different groups within a single society with a single language.

What is needed, then, is a general theory and body of knowledge within which diversity of speech, repertoires, ways of speaking, and choosing among them find a natural place. Such a theory and body of knowledge are only now being built in a sustained way. Social scientists asking relevant functional questions have usually not had the training and insight to deal adequately with the linguistic face of the problem. Linguistics, the discipline central to the study of speech, has been occupied almost wholly with developing analysis of the structure of language as a referential code, neglecting social meaning, diversity, and use. There have been notable exceptions (as in the work of Firth, Jakobson, and Sapir), but the main course of linguistic work has been from the then newly captured sector of phonology (before World War II) through morphology and syntax. Now that the inner logic of linguistics itself brings it to deal with semantics and speech acts, and now that the social sciences generally in the United States are engaged in the sort of cross-cultural and educational research that makes language differences of concern, there has emerged something tantamount to a movement to redress the situation. The movement is commonly called *sociolinguistics*, especially when seen as relating lan-

² These examples draw on a study by Judith Temkin Irvine (1968).

guage to sociological categories, or as mediating between linguistics and social science as a whole.

It is not necessary to think of sociolinguistics as a novel discipline. If linguistics comes to accept fully the sociocultural dimensions, social science the linguistic dimensions, of their subject matters and theoretical bases, sociolinguistic will simply identify a mode of research in adjacent sectors of each. As disciplines, one will speak simply of linguistics, anthropology, and the like (see Hymes 1964b, 1966b, 1970a, b, c). But, as just implied, the linguistics, anthropology, etc., of which one speaks will have changed. In order to develop models, or theories, of the interaction of language and social life, there must be adequate descriptions of that interaction, and such descriptions call for an approach that partly links, but partly cuts across, partly builds between the ordinary practices of the disciplines. This is what makes sociolinguistics exciting and necessary. It does not accept, but it is a critique of the present partitioning of the subject of man among the sciences of man. Its goal is to explain the meaning of language in human life, and not in the abstract, not in the superficial phrases one may encounter in essays and textbooks, but in the concrete, in actual human lives. To do that it must develop adequate modes of description and classification, to answer new questions and give familiar questions a novel focus.

The Case for Description and Taxonomy

For some of the most brilliant students of language in its social setting, the proper strategy is to select problems that contribute directly to current linguistic and social theory. A primary concern is relevant to particular problems already perceived as such in the existing disciplines, although the modes of work of those disciplines must often be transformed for the problems to find solutions. Field studies in societies exotic to the investigator, where strong control over data and hypothesis testing cannot easily be maintained, are not much valued. A concern to secure reports from such societies is thought pointless since it suggests a prospect of endless descriptions which, whatever their quantity and quality, would not as such contribute to theoretical discovery.

My own view is different. I accept an intellectual tradition, adumbrated in antiquity, and articulated in the course of the Enlightenment, which holds that mankind cannot be understood apart from the evolution and maintenance of its ethnographic diversity. A satisfactory understanding of the nature and unity of men must encompass and organize, not abstract from, the diversity. In this tradition, a theory, whatever its logic and insight, is inadequate if divorced from, if unilluminating as to, the ways of life of mankind as a whole. The concern is consonant with that of Kroeber, reflecting upon Darwin:

anthropologists . . . do not yet clearly recognize the fundamental value of the humble but indispensable task of classifying—that is, structuring, our body of knowledge, as biologists did begin to recognize it two hundred years ago (1960:14).

Even the ethnographies that we have, though almost never focused on speaking, show us that communities differ significantly in ways of speaking, in patterns of repertoire and switching, in the roles and meanings of speech. They indicate differences with regard to beliefs, values, reference groups, norms, and the like, as these enter into the ongoing system of language use and its acquisition by children. Individual accounts that individually pass without notice, as familiar possibilities, leap out when juxtaposed, as contrasts that require explanation. The Gbeya around the town of Bossangoa in the western Central African Republic, for example, are extremely democratic, and relatively unconcerned with speech. There is no one considered verbally excellent even with regard to traditional folklore. Moreover,

Gbeya parents and other adults focus little attention on the speech of children. No serious attempt is made to improve their language. In fact, a child only uncommonly takes part in a dyadic speech event with an adult . . . . Among the Gbeya "children are seen and not heard." Finally, there appears to be very little interest in reporting *how* a person speaks . . . (Samarin 1969).

The Anang (Nigeria) received their name from neighboring Ibo, the term meaning "ability to speak wittily yet meaningfully upon any occasion."

The Anang take great pride in their eloquence, and youth are trained from early childhood to develop verbal skills. This proverb riddle [not quoted here, but see discussion] instructs young people to assume adult duties and responsibilities as early as possible, even if doing so is difficult and unpleasant at times. As the vine must struggle to escape growing into the pit [the riddle], so must the child strive to overcome his shyness and insecurity and learn to speak publicly [the proverbial answer], as well as perform other adult roles (Messenger 1960:229).

Or, to consider the word and the sword, among the Araucanians of Chile the head of a band was its best orator, and his power depended upon his ability to sway others through oratory. Among the Abipon of Argentina no desired role or status depended upon skill in speaking; chiefs and members of the one prestigious men's group were selected solely on the basis of success in battle. The Iroquois value eloquence in chiefs and orators as much as bravery in war; the two are usually mentioned together and with equal status. A chief could rise equally quickly by either.

Since there is no systematic understanding of the ways in which communities differ in these respects, and of the deeper relationships such differences may disclose, we have it to create. We need taxonomies of speaking, and descriptions adequate to support and test them.

Such description and taxonomy will share in the work of providing an adequate classification of languages. If the task of language classification is taken to be to place languages in terms of their common features and differences, and if we consider the task from the standpoint of similarities, then four classifications are required. Languages are classified according to features descended from a common ancestor (genetic classification), features diffused within a common area (areal classification), features manifesting a common structure or structures, irrespective of origin or area (typological classification), and features of common use or social role (as koine, standard language, pidgin, etc.) (functional classification) (see Hymes 1968c; Greenburg 1968:133–135). The processes underlying the classifications (various kinds of retention, divergence, convergence) all can be viewed in terms of the adaption of languages to social contexts, but the forms of classification in which the dependence on social processes can be most readily excluded (genetic, typological) are the forms that have been most developed. Sociolinguistic research reinforces the intermittent interest that areal classification has received, and can properly claim the most neglected sector, functional classification, the interaction between social role and features of languages, for its own. The natural unit for sociolinguistic taxonomy (and description), however, is not the language but the speech community.

Of course, sociolinguistic taxonomy is not an end in itself, any more than is language classification. A taxonomy is not in itself a theory or explanation, though it may conceal or suggest one. There will indeed be a variety of taxonomies, answering to a variety of significant dimensions, as well as taxonomies of whole communities, societies, and social fields. (For a step in the latter direction, see Ferguson 1966.) The work of taxonomy is a necessary part of progress toward models (structural and generative) of sociolinguistic description, formulation of universal sets of features and relations, and explanatory theories. (I shall say something about each of these later.) Just the demonstration that the phenomena of speaking are subject to comparative study may help end the obscuring of actual problems by descant on the function of language in general. Those who do so should be received as if they were continuing to discuss physics in terms of the Ionian controversies as to the primordial element.[3]

---

[3] For recent examples of uncritical praise and intransigent indictment of language, see J. O. Hertzler 1965 and Brice Parain 1969. On "high and low evaluations of language" as an integral part of the history of philosophy and human culture, see Urban 1939:12, 23–32.

An Illustration

As an indication of what can be done, as well as of how much there is to be done, let me briefly consider the grossest, and most likely to be reported, aspect of speech, quantity. Contrasts were drawn already in antiquity, although amounting only to folk characterization, as when the Athenian says to his Spartan and Cretan interlocutors,

But first let me make an apology. The Athenian citizen is reputed among all the Hellenes to be a great talker, whereas Sparta is renowned for brevity, and the Cretans have more wit than words. Now I am afraid of appearing to elicit a very long discourse out of very small matter (Plato, *Laws* 641E).[4]

One could extract a dimension with three points of contrast, naming the types according to the dialogue (as kinship systems are named after societies in which they are identified, Crow, Omah, and the like):

i

Dimension:	*verbose*	*laconic*	*pithy*
Type:	ATHENIAN	SPARTAN	CRETAN

A number of analytically different dimensions are probably confounded within gross observations as to quantity of speech, length and frequency of speech, and the like; and there are qualitative characteristics vital to the interaction of language with social life in the particular societies. Something of this appears in the quotation from Plato, and becomes explicit in the following contrast:

ii

Dimension:	*voluble*	*reserved, reticent*	*taciturn*
Type:	BELLA COOLA	ARITAMA	PALIYAN

BELLA COOLA (British Columbia). Fluent, interesting speech is valued, and a common, if not a requisite, part of social life. Essential roles in ceremonial activity, and an important spirit impersonated in the Kusiut initiation, had to have the ability to talk constantly, keeping up a flow of witty and insulting remarks. The ethnographer McIlwraith found that if he could not joke with them constantly, people lost interest. When groups talked, one was sure to hear bursts of laughter every few minutes.

---

[4] According to Sandys (1920, 1:4), the noun *philología* is first found in Plato, and its adjective, *philólogia,* is used in this passage to contrast "lover of discourse" with "hater of discourse." Plato, *Laws* 641E, quoted from Benjamin E. Jowett's translation of *Dialogues* (New York; Random House, 1937, Vol. 2, p. 423).

ARITAMA (Colombia).
People in Aritama are not much given to friendly chatting and visiting. They are controlled and taciturn,[5] evasive and monosyllabic . . . . This reserve . . . is not only displayed toward strangers, but characterizes their own interpersonal contacts as well. There is a front of ready answers and expression, of standard affirmations and opinions, and there is always, in the last resort, the blank stare, the deaf ear or the sullen *no se* . . . . Such behavior . . . leads frequently to a highly patterned type of confabulation (Reichel-Dolmatoff 1961:xvii).

PALIYAN (south India). See previous quotation from Gardner (1966). According to Gardner, the many hunting-and-gathering societies of the world should be divided into two types, of one of which the Paliyans are a perhaps extreme representative.
The dimensions may, of course, apply within, as well as between, societies, as to groups, cultural content, verbal style, and situations. As to groups,

iiia

Dimension:	*voluble*		*taciturn*
Type:		ARAUCANIAN	
Subcategory:	*Men*		*Women*

ARAUCANIAN (Chile). The ideal Araucanian man is a good orator, with good memory, general conversationalist, expected to speak well and often. Men are encouraged to talk on all occasions, speaking being a sign of masculine intelligence and leadership. The ideal woman is submissive and quiet, silent in her husband's presence. At gatherings where men do much talking, women sit together listlessly, communicating only in whispers or not at all. On first arriving in her husband's home, a wife is expected to sit silently facing the wall, not looking anyone directly in the face. Only after several months is she permitted to speak, and then, only a little. Sisters-in-law do not speak much to each other. The one means by which women can express their situation is a form of social singing (*ulkantun*) in which mistreatment, disregard, and distress can be expressed. The one approved role for a woman to be verbally prominent is a shamanistic intermediary of a spirit (Hilger 1957). [Silence is expected of a bride in her new home in a number of cultures, e.g., traditional Korea. The restriction of women's expression of grievances to certain occasions and a musical use of voice also is widespread, as in Bihar (India).]

[5] Although the Reichel-Dolmatoffs use "taciturn" here of the Aritama, the subsequent term "reserved" characterizes them well, while "taciturn" is specifically apt for the Paliyans. As taxonomy and description develop, careful explication of technical terms will be increasingly important. Note that the three groups are also respectively "now-coding," "then-coding," and "non-coding" (cf. footnote 7).

As to situations,

iiib
Dimension: *discursive disclosure   reticent quotation*
Type: WISHRAM-WASCO CHINOOK
Scene: (See discussion)

WISHRAM-WASCO CHINOOK (Washington, Oregon). Recitation of myths in winter, public conferal of personal name, and disclosure of an adolescent guardian spirit experience upon approaching death are three major communicative events. In each event, discursive disclosure (of the myth as a whole, the identification of name and person, or the verbal message of the vision) comes only when an implicit relationship (of culture to nature, person to reincarnated kin-linked "title," or person to personal spirit) has been validated. Each is part of a cycle—the annual round of society, a cycle of reinstituting names of deceased kin, an individual life cycle from adolescence to death. At other times during the cycle there may be quotations (of a detail in a myth, a name in address, a song from one's vision in winter spirit dance), but the substance of the relationship must not be explicitly stated. In each case of discursive disclosure the speaker is a spokesman, repeating words previously said, this being the rule that constitutes formal speech events. (See Hymes 1966a.)
   As to cultural content,

iv
Dimension: *verbal elaboration   verbal sparseness*
Type: HIDATSA   CROW

HIDATSA (North Dakota). CROW (Montana). According to Lowie (1917:87–88), "The culture of the Hidatsa differs from that of the Crow not merely by the greater number and elaboration of discrete features but also in a marked trait of their social psychology—the tendency towards rationalization and systematization." Lowie illustrates the contrast in four domains: formal instruction; accounting for cultural phenomena; individual interpretation and conception of names, myths, and prayer; and kinship nomenclature. In each domain the Hidatsa use language to systematize and stabilize the cultural universe to an extent greatly in contrast to the Crow. (It was the Crow that Lowie knew more intimately; hence his sense of greater Hidatsa elaboration is trustworthy). Of particular interest here is the following:

The Crow child . . . seems to have grown up largely without formal instruction. Even on so vital a matter as the securing of supernatural favor, the adolescent Crow was not urged by his elders but came more or less automatically to imitate his associates . . . . With the Hidatsa everything seems to have been ordered and prearranged by parental guidance; the father repeatedly admonished his sons, at the same time giving them specific instructions.[6]

As to verbal style,

v
Dimension: *elaborate, profuse*   *restrained, sparse*
Type: ENGLISH   YOKUTS

ENGLISH, YOKUTS (California). A contrast with regard to the limits of acceptable use of syntactic possibilities has been drawn by Newman, who tries to sketch each from the standpoint of the other. Sparseness and restraint are found to characterize Yokuts narrative style as well (Gayton and Newman 1940).

Work in societies, with the goals of taxonomy and descriptive models in mind, is interdependent with detailed work in one's own society. Each provides insight and a test of universality and adequacy for the other. It has been suggested, for example, that there is only a class-linked British relevance to Bernstein's sociological model of elaborated vs. restricted coding, governed by personal vs. positional types of social control.[7] While some Americans indeed have misapplied Bernstein's two types to ethnic and class differences in the United States, from the standpoint of taxonomy and description, the model takes on a new scope. It suggests a set of universal dimensions, and possibly polar ideal types, isolable and applicable to the description and comparison of situations and whole communities, as well as particular groups.

Thus Margaret Mead has analyzed the Arapesh and Iatmul of New Guinea as contrasting types of society in which the adult patterns seem appropriately interpreted as *personal* and *positional,* respectively. In the ARAPESH type (which includes the Andamanese, Ojibwa, and Eskimo), societies depend, for impetus to or inhibition of community action in public situations, upon the continuing response of individuals. The point

---

[6] As the initial quotation indicates, Lowie did not relate the contrast explicitly to the role of language in social life. A major task and methodological challenge is to go beyond superficial presence or absence of overt mention of speech, in order to restate existing ethnographic analyses, wherever possible, in terms of speaking, just as it is often possible to find in earlier accounts of languages evidence permitting restatement in terms of contemporary phonological and grammatical models. Such restatement is more than an exercise; it contributes to the range of cases for comparative studies.

[7] Elaborated codes are largely *now-coding,* and adaptive in lexicon and syntax to the ad hoc elaboration of subjective intent, while restricted codes are largely *then-coding,* and adaptive to the reinforcement of group solidarity through use of preformulated expressions. Personal social control appeals to individual characteristics, role discretion, and motivation; positional social control bases itself on membership in categories of age, sex, class, and the like. See Bernstein's chapter in this volume. Mead (1937) places Zuni also as a type intermediate between Iatmul and Bali (cf. also footnote 5).

of communication is to excite interest and bring together persons who will then respond with emotion to whatever event has occurred. In the IATMUL type the societies depend upon formal alignments of individuals, who react not in terms of personal opinions but in terms of defined position in a formal sociopolitical structure.

At the same time the comparative perspective extends the model. Mead identifies a third type of society, such as that of BALI, which does not depend on situations in which individuals express or can be called upon to express themselves for or against something, so as to affect the outcome regarding it, but which functions by invoking participation in and respect for known impersonal patterns or codes, and in which communicators act as if the audience were already in a state of suspended, unemotional attention, and only in need of a small precise triggering of words to set them off into appropriate activity. Mead interprets the differences as ones in which political feeling depends on "How do I (and A, B, and C) feel about it?" (Arapesh); "How does my group (their group) feel about it?" (Iatmul); and "How does this fit in?" (Bali). Such a type as Bali seems appropriately labeled one of *traditional* social control and communication. (Obviously, only a subset of the societies lumped together as "traditional" by some social scientists can be said to be so in a useful way.) (See Mead 1937, 1948; the latter article discusses Manus as well.) Keesing and Keesing (1956:258) suggest Samoa as a type combining Iatmul and Bali characteristics, but distinctive, so that one might have:

vi

Dimension:	*personal*	*positional*[8]	*traditional*	*positional, traditional*
Type:	ARAPESH	IATMUL	BALI	SAMOA

Comparative ethnographic examples show the need to separate sometimes the dimensions joined together in Bernstein's model. Iatmul is a society with important development of oratory, which might seem an instance of elaboration which should go with personal control. If the oratory is then-coding, employing largely preformulated expressions, there is, in fact, no discrepancy. Positional and personal social control do, however, cross-cut then-coding and now-coding to define four types of cases, not just two. Cat Harbour, Newfoundland, as described by Faris (1966, 1968), shows positional social control and restriction of personal expression in speech and other normally scheduled activities. As in most societies, there are certain situations marked as reversals of normal conduct (e.g., legitimated stealing of food); and, as if to compensate for

---

[8] Mead (1937) places Zuni also as a type intermediate between Iatmul and Bali.

plainness of life and to satisfy the great interest in "news" of any kind, while remaining within normal restraints, there has arisen a genre known as the "cuffer." A "cuffer" may arise spontaneously, or someone may be asked to start one. It consists of developing an intense argument over an unimportant detail (such as how many men actually were lost in a boat-wreck some decades back); but to show personal emotional involvement brings shame and exclusion. We thus find elaborated now-coding, indeed, extensive invention, in a positional setting. There can be then-coding in a situation of ad hoc subjective intent as well, as when Ponapeans arrive at the status of mutual lovers through manipulating a long sequence of verbal formulas which allow for role discretion at each step (Paul Garvin, personal communication), or when a traditional saying is used precisely because its impersonal, preformulated character grants role discretion to another that direct rebuke would not (e.g., the Chaga of Central Africa use proverbs to children in this way).[9]

Relevant Features and Types. The examples just presented show that it is essential to isolate the dimensions and features underlying taxonomic categories. These features and dimensions, more than particular constellations of them, will be found to be universal, and hence elementary to descriptive and comparative frames of reference. This is not to consider universal features and dimensions the only goal. Explanation faces two ways, toward the generic possibilities and general constraints, on the one hand (Chomsky's "essentialist" form of explanatory adequacy), and toward the types that are historically realized and their causes (an "existential" or "experiential" form of explanatory adequacy), on the other. The heuristics of description require an etics of types as well as of elements, for insight into the organization intrinsic to a case, as against a priori or mechanical structuring of it.

By both defining some universal dimensions of speaking and proposing explanation within social theory of certain constellations of them, Bernstein has shown the goal toward which sociolinguistic work must proceed.

---

[9] The contrast between Hopi and Zuni, on the one hand, and the Wishram Chinook (Hymes 1967:12) was incorrectly drawn. Among both socialization pressure is initially withheld with regard to toilet training and the like until the child can talk (Dennis 1940, Eggan 1948 [1943]; on the significance of early socialization pressure, though without reference to ways of speaking, Whiting and Child 1953:254 ff.). The sudden shift from indulgence to control among the Hopi apparently came after the first few years of life (Eggan 1948 [1943]:232–233). It is the subsequent difference between "positional" (Hopi) and "personal" social control that would seem to fit with the differences in adult religious experience, together with the shock of public disillusion in the kachinas for Hopi children at an age (7–10) when Wishram children were training for private spiritual encounters of which they themselves would be individually the interpreters and eventual disclosers. It remains that such contrasts as that between Hopi and Chinookan relations to the supernatural, and as between prayer as beseeching petition (e.g., the Delaware) and prayer as "compulsive word" (e.g., the Navaho) need to be related to speech socialization.

The total range of dimensions and of kinds of explanation, to be sure, will be more varied. Indeed, the fact that present taxonomic dimensions consist so largely of dichotomies—restricted vs. elaborated codes, transactional vs. metaphorical switching, referential vs. expressive meaning, standard vs. nonstandard speech, formal vs. informal scenes, literacy vs. illiteracy—shows how preliminary is the stage at which we work. With regard to ways of speaking, we are at a stage rather like that of the study of human culture, as a whole, a century ago, when Tyler, Morgan, and others had to segregate relevant sets of data, and give definiteness and name to some of the elementary categories on which subsequent work could be built (on Tylor, see Lowie 1937:70–71; Tylor 1871, Chapter 1).

Like Tylor and Morgan, we need to establish elementary categories and names. Among the Bella Coola of British Columbia, for instance, there is a genre such that at the investiture of an inheritor of a privilege validated by a myth, someone tells a public audience kept outside just enough of the recited myth to be convincing as to the validation, but not so much as to give it away (knowledge of the myth itself being part of the privilege) (McIlwraith 1948). Among the Iatmul of New Guinea knowledge of the correct version of a myth may also be proof of a claim, in this instance to land and group membership. In public debate a speaker refers to his myth in clichés that fragment the plot. In this way "he demonstrates his membership in a group and at the same time keeps outsiders in the dark as to the esoteric matrix of the story" (Mead 1964b:74). We lack a name for this recurrent way of speaking. Identifying it would increase the chances that others will notice and report it in ways that will lead to knowledge of the conditions under which it occurs in various parts of the world.

Anthropological contributions to this branch of comparative research are almost nonexistent. Even a list of terms lacking careful definition is to be noted (Keesing and Keesing 1956); careful description and analysis of named concepts is remarkable (Calame-Griaule 1965; Abrahams and Bauman 1970). There are no books on comparative speaking to put beside those on comparative religion, comparative politics, and the like. In the major anthropological collection of data for comparative studies, the Human Relations Area Files, information on ways of speaking is only sporadically included and is scattered among several categories. Existing manuals and guides for ethnography, or for specific aspects, such as socialization, largely neglect speech.

The first break in this neglect is the pioneering field manual prepared by a group at Berkeley (Slobin 1967). The manual has already contributed to (and benefited from) the research of a number of fieldworkers. It is important to note that it is *acquisition* of the *structure* of language with regard to which the manual can be most detailed. The linguistic code takes pride of place as to topics, procedures, and specific questions and hypotheses, even though the acquisition of linguistic codes is in principle recognized as but part of the acquisition of communicative competence as a whole. It is recognized that "before a description of the child's language acquisition can be undertaken, the conventions of the adult members of the group must be described" (Slobin 1967:161), but it has not been found possible to make such description the initial matrix of research, nor to show what such description would be like, beyond sketching a conceptual framework with illustrations.

An ethnographic guide, focusing on the acquisition of speaking as a whole (prepared by a group initially at the University of Pennsylvania), is now in press (Hymes et al., 1972). An outline is included as an appendix to this volume. The full form will have queries in considerably more detail, together with ethnographic examples and sketches of cultural types.

The need for etics (Pike 1967, Chapter 2) of terms and types, as an input to description, is clear from the frequency with which fieldworkers have let observations of great interest lie fallow, lacking precedent and format for their presentation. There is need to show ethnographers and linguists a way to *see* data as ways of speaking. At this juncture we are still attempting to achieve "observational adequacy" in the sense of being able to adequately record what is there in acts of speech.

For an adequate etics we of course most need field studies of the sort the manual and guide just cited encourage. We can also make useful ethnographic accounts not obtained with analysis of speaking in mind, by a procedure that can be called "sociolinguistic restatement" (see Hymes 1966a; Hogan 1967; Sherzer 1970). We must draw as well on the accumulated insight of all the fields that deal with speech, rhetoric, literary criticism, and the like. To be sure, the terminologies of rhetoric and literary criticism fall short of the range to be encompassed. Terminology for ways of speaking seems not to have developed much since the heyday of rhetorical education in the Renaissance—the recent revival of interest in rhetorical analysis indeed returns to the starting point (see Joseph 1962; Lanham 1968; Sonnino 1968). But treatments of verbal art of necessity draw distinctions and make assumptions as to notions with which a descriptive model of speaking must deal, as does much work in philosophy, most notably in recent years "ordinary language" philosophy and the work of J. L. Austin, John Searle, and others on "illocutionary acts," or performatives. Several philosophers, psychologists, and literary critics, as well as linguists, have proposed classifications of the components of the functions served in them (Karl Bühler, Kenneth Burke, Roman Jakobson, Bronislaw Malinowski, Charles Morris, C. K. Ogden and I. A. Richards, B. F. Skinner, William Soskin, and Vera John). Much is to be hoped from the growing interest of folklorists in the analysis of verbal performance (see Hymes 1970b). A systematic explication of these contributions is greatly to be desired. These lines of work provide concepts and insights from which much can be learned, and for which a comparative ethnography of speaking can perform anthropology's traditional scientific role, testing of universality and empirical adequacy.

In sum, just as a theory of grammar must have its universal terms, so must a theory of language use. It can indeed be argued that the notions of such a theory are foundational to linguistics proper (see Hymes 1964b, where the theory is called "(ethno)linguistic"). The fundamental problem—to discover and explicate the competence that enables members of a community to conduct and interpret speech—cuts deeper than any schema any of us have so far developed.

Toward a Descriptive Theory

The primary concern now must be with descriptive analyses from a variety of communities. Only in relation to actual analysis will it be possible to conduct arguments analogous to those now possible in the study of grammar as to the adequacy, necessity, generality, etc., of concepts and terms. Yet some initial heuristic schema are needed if the descriptive task is to proceed. What is presented here is quite preliminary— if English and its grammarians permitted, one might call it "toward toward a theory." Some of it may survive the empirical and analytical work of the decade ahead.

Only a specific, explicit mode of description can guarantee the maintenance and success of the current interest in sociolinguistics. Such interest is prompted more by practical and theoretical needs, perhaps, than by accomplishment. It was the development of a specific mode of description that ensured the success of linguistics as an autonomous discipline in the United States in the twentieth century, and the lack of it (for motif and tale types are a form of indexing, distributional inference a procedure common to the human sciences) that led to the until recently peripheral status of folklore, although both had started from a similar base, the converging interest of anthropologists, and English scholars, in language and in verbal tradition.

The goal of sociolinguistic description can be put in terms of the disciplines whose interests converge in sociolinguistics. Whatever his questions about language, it is clear to a linguist that there is an enterprise, description of languages, which is central and known. Whatever his questions about society and culture, it is clear to a sociologist or an anthropologist that there is a form of inquiry (survey or ethnography) on which the answers depend. In both cases, one understands what it means to describe a language, the social relations, or culture of a community. We need to be able to say the same thing about the sociolinguistic system of a community.

Such a goal is of concern to practical work as well as to scientific theory.

In a study of bilingual education, e.g., certain components of speaking will be taken into account, and the choice will presuppose a model, implicit if not explicit, of the interaction of language with social life. The significance attached to what is found will depend on understanding what is possible, what universal, what rare, what linked, in comparative perspective. What survey researchers need to know linguistically about a community, in selecting a language variety, and in conducting interviews, is in effect an application of the community's sociolinguistic description (see Hymes 1969). In turn, practical work, if undertaken with its relevance to theory in mind, can make a contribution, for it must deal directly with the interaction of language and social life, and so provides a testing ground and source of new insight.

Sociolinguistic systems may be treated at the level of national states, and indeed, of an emerging world society. My concern here is with the level of individual communities and groups. The interaction of language with social life is viewed as first of all a matter of human action, based on a knowledge, sometimes conscious, often unconscious, that enables persons to use language. Speech events and larger systems indeed have properties not reducible to those of the speaking competence of persons. Such competence, however, underlies communicative conduct, not only within communities but also in encounters between them. The speaking competence of persons may be seen as entering into a series of systems of encounter at levels of different scope.

An adequate descriptive theory would provide for the analysis of individual communities by specifying technical concepts required for such analysis, and by characterizing the forms that analysis should take. Those forms would, as much as possible, be formal, i.e., explicit, general (in the sense of observing general constraints and conventions as to content, order, interrelationship, etc.), economical, and congruent with linguistic modes of statement. Only a good deal of empirical work and experimentation will show what forms of description are required, and of those, which preferable. As with grammar, approximation to a theory for the explicit, standard analysis of individual systems will also be an approximation to part of a theory of explanation.

Among the notions with which such a theory must deal are those of speech community, speech situation, speech event, speech act, fluent speaker, components of speech events, functions of speech, etc.

SOCIAL UNITS

One must first consider the social unit of analysis. For this I adopt the common expression *speech community*.

Speech Community. Speech is here taken as a surrogate for all forms of language, including writing, song and speech-derived whistling, drumming, horn calling, and the like. Speech community is a necessary, primary term in that it postulates the basis of description as a social, rather than a linguistic, entity. One starts with a social group and considers all the linguistic varieties present in it, rather than starting with any one variety.

Bloomfield (1933) and some others have in the past reduced the notion of speech community to the notion of language (or linguistic variety). Those speaking the same language (or same first language, or standard language) were defined as members of the same speech community. This confusion still persists, associated with a quantitative measure of frequency of interaction as a way of describing (in principle) internal variation and change, as speculatively postulated by Bloomfield. The present approach requires a definition that is qualitative and expressed in terms *norms for the use* of language. It is clear from the work of Gumperz, Labov, Barth, and others that not frequency of interaction but rather definition of situations in which interaction occurs is decisive, particularly identification (or lack of it) with others. [Sociolinguistics here makes contact with the shift in rhetorical theory from expression and persuasion to identification as key concept (see Burke 1950:19–37, 55–59).]

Tentatively, a *speech community* is defined as a community sharing rules for the conduct and interpretation of speech, and rules for the interpretation of at least one linguistic variety. Both conditions are necessary.

The sharing of grammatical (variety) rules is not sufficient. There may be persons whose English I can grammatically identify but whose messages escape me. I may be ignorant of what counts as a coherent sequence, request, statement requiring an answer, requisite or forbidden topic, marking of emphasis or irony, normal duration of silence, normal level of voice, etc., and have no metacommunitative means or opportunity for discovering such things. The difference between knowledge of a variety and knowledge of speaking does not usually become apparent within a single community, where the two are normally acquired together. Communities indeed often mingle what a linguist would distinguish as grammatically and as socially or culturally acceptable. Among the Cochiti of New Mexico J. R. Fox was unable to elicit the first person singular possessive form of "wings," on the grounds that the speaker, not being a bird, could not say "my wings"—only to become the only person in Cochiti able to say it on the grounds that "your name is Robin."

The nonidentity of the two kinds of rules (or norms) is more likely to be noticed when a shared variety is a second language for one or both parties. Sentences that translate each other grammatically may be mistakenly taken as having the same functions in speech, just as words that translate each other may be taken as having the same semantic function. There may be substratum influence, or interference (Weinreich 1953) in the one as in the other. The Czech linguist J. Neustupny has coined the term *Sprechbund* "speech area" (parallel to *Sprachbund* "language area") for the phenomenon of speaking rules being shared among contiguous languages. Thus, Czechoslovakia, Hungary, Austria, and southern Germany may be found to share norms as to greetings, acceptable topics, what is said next in a conversation, etc.

Sharing of speaking rules is not sufficient. A Czech who knows no German may belong to the same *Sprechbund,* but not the same speech community, as an Austrian.

The *language field* and *speech field* (akin to the notion of social field) can be defined as the total range of communities within which a person's knowledge of varieties and speaking rules potentially enables him to move communicatively. Within the speech field must be distinguished the *speech network,* the specific linkages of persons through shared varieties and speaking rules across communities. Thus in northern Queensland, Australia, different speakers of the same language (e.g., Yir Yoront) may have quite different networks along geographically different circuits, based on clan membership, and involving different repertoires of mutilingualism. In Vitiaz Strait, New Guinea, the Bilibili islanders (a group of about 200–250 traders and potmakers in Astrolabe Bay) have collectively a knowledge of the languages of all the communities with which they have had economic relations, a few men knowing the language of each particular community in which they have had trading partners.

In sum, one's speech community may be, effectively, a single locality or portion of it; one's language field will be delimited by one's repertoire of varieties; one's speech field by one's repertoire of patterns of speaking. One's speech network is the effective union of these last two.

Part of the work of definition obviously is done here by the notion of community, whose difficulties are bypassed, as are the difficulties of defining boundaries between varieties and between patterns of speaking. Native conceptions of boundaries are but one factor in defining them, essential but sometimes partly misleading (a point stressed by Gumperz on the basis of his work in central India). Self-conceptions, values, role structures, contiguity, purposes of interaction, political history, all may be factors. Clearly, the same degree of linguistic difference may be associated with a boundary in one case and not in another, depending on social factors. The essential thing is that the object of description be an integral social unit. Probably, it will prove most useful to reserve the notion of speech community for the local unit most specifically characterized for a person by common locality and primary interaction (Gumperz 1962: 30–32). Here I have drawn distinctions of scale and of kind of linkage within what Gumperz has termed the *linguistic community* (any distinguishable intercommunicating group). Descriptions will make it possible to develop a useful typology and to discover the causes and consequences of the various types.

Speech Situation. Within a community one readily detects many situations associated with (or marked by the absence of) speech. Such contexts of situation will often be naturally described as ceremonies, fights, hunts, meals, lovemaking, and the like. It would not be profitable to convert such situations en masse into parts of a sociolinguistic description by the simple expedient of relabeling them in terms of speech. (Notice that the distinctions made with regard to speech community are not identical with the concepts of a general communicative approach, which must note the differential range of communication by speech, film, art object, music.) Such situations may enter as contexts into the statement of rules of speaking as aspects of setting (or of genre). In contrast to speech events, they are not in themselves governed by such rules, or one set of such rules throughout. A hunt, e.g., may comprise both verbal and nonverbal events, and the verbal events may be of more than one type.

In a sociolinguistic description, then, it is necessary to deal with activities which are in some recognizable way bounded or integral. From the standpoint of general social description they may be registered as ceremonies, fishing trips, and the like; from particular standpoints they may be regarded as political, esthetic, etc., situations, which serve as contexts for the manifestation of political, esthetic, etc., activity. From the sociolinguistic standpoint they may be regarded as speech situations.

Speech Event. The term *speech event* will be restricted to activities, or aspects of activities, that are directly governed by rules or norms for the use of speech. An event may consist of a single speech act, but will often comprise several. Just as an occurrence of a noun may at the same time be the whole of a noun phrase and the whole of a sentence (e.g., "Fire!"), so a speech act may be the whole of a speech event, and of a speech situation (say, a rite consisting of a single prayer, itself a single invocation). More often, however, one will find a difference in magnitude: a party (speech situation), a conversation during the party (speech event), a joke within the conversation (speech act). It is of speech events and speech acts that one writes formal rules for their occurrence and characteristics. Notice that the same type of speech act may recur in different types of speech event, and the same type of speech event in different contexts of situation. Thus, a joke (speech act) may be embedded in a private conversation, a lecture, a formal introduction. A private conversation may occur in the context of a party, a memorial service, a pause in changing sides in a tennis match.

Speech Act. The *speech act* is the minimal term of the set just discussed, as the remarks on speech events have indicated. It represents a level distinct from the sentence, and not identifiable with any single portion of other levels of grammar, nor with segments of any particular size defined in terms of other levels of grammar. That an utterance has the status of a command may depend upon a conventional formula ("I hereby order you to leave this building"), intonation ("Go!" vs. "Go?"), position in a conversational exchange ["Hello" as initiating greeting or as response (perhaps used when answering the telephone)], or the social relationship obtaining between the two parties (as when an utterance that is in the form a polite question is in effect a command when made by a superior to a subordinate). The level of speech acts mediates immediately between the usual levels of grammar and the rest of a speech event or situation in that it implicates both linguistic form and social norms.

To some extent speech acts may be analyzable by extensions of syntactic and semantic structure. It seems certain, however, that much, if not most, of the knowledge that speakers share as to the status of utterances as acts is immediate and abstract, depending upon an autonomous system of signals from both the various levels of grammar and social settings. To attempt to depict speech acts entirely by postulating an additional segment of underlying grammatical structure (e.g., "I hereby X you to . . .") is cumbersome and counterintuitive. (Consider the case in which "Do you think I might have that last bit of tea?" is to be taken as a command.)

An autonomous level of speech acts is in fact implicated by that logic of linguistic levels according to which the ambiguity of "the shooting of the blacks was terrible" and the commonality of "topping Erv is almost impossible" and "it's almost impossible to top Erv" together requires a further level of structure at which the former has two different structures, the latter one. The relation between sentence forms and their status as speech acts is of the same kind. A sentence interrogative in form may be now a request, now a command, now a statement; a request may be manifested by a sentence that is now interrogative, now declarative, now imperative in form.

Discourse may be viewed in terms of acts both syntagmatically and paradigmatically; i.e., both as a sequence of speech acts and in terms of classes of speech acts among which choice has been made at given points.

Speech Styles. Style has often been approached as a matter of statistical frequency of elements already given in linguistic description, or as deviation from some norm given by such description. Statistics and deviations matter, but do not suffice. Styles also depend upon qualitative judgments of appropriateness, and must often be described in terms of selections that apply globally to a discourse, as in the case of honorific usage in Japanese (McCawley 1968:136), i.e., there are consistent patternings of speaking that cut across the components of grammar (phonology, syntax, semantics), or that operate within one independently of the selectional restrictions normally described for it. Whorf adumbrated as much in his conception of "fashions of speaking"; Joos has made and illustrated the point with regard to English; Pike (1967) has considered a wide variety of contextual styles as conditions on the manifestation of phonological and morphological units. Besides the existence of qualitatively defined styles, there are two other points essential to sociolinguistic description. One is that speech styles involve elements and relations that conventionally serve "expressive" or, better, stylistic, as well as referential function (e.g., the contrast in force of aspiration that conventionally signals emphasis in English). The second point is that speech styles are to be considered not only in terms of cooccurrence within each but also in terms of contrastive choice among them. Like speech acts, they have both syntagmatic and paradigmatic dimensions. (Ervin-Tripp treats rules of cooccurrence and of alternation in detail in Chapter 7.) The coherence, or cohesion, of discourse depends upon the syntagmatic relation of speech acts, and speech styles, as well as of semantic and syntactic features.

Ways of Speaking. Ways of speaking is used as the most general, indeed, as a primitive, term. The point of it is the regulative idea that the communicative behavior within a community is analyzable in terms of determinate ways of speaking, that the communicative competence of persons comprises in part a knowledge of determinate ways of speaking. Little more can be said until a certain number of ethnographic descriptions of communities in terms of ways of speaking are available. It is likely that communities differ widely in the features in terms of which their ways of speaking are primarily organized.

Components of Speech. A descriptive theory requires some schema of the components of speech acts. At present such a schema can be only an etic, heuristic input to descriptions. Later it may assume the status of a theory of universal features and dimensions.

Long traditional in our culture is the threefold division between speaker, hearer, and something spoken about. It has been elaborated in information theory, linguistics, semiotics, literary criticism, and sociology in various ways. In the hands of some investigators various of these models have proven productive, but their productivity has depended upon not taking them literally, let alone using them precisely. All such schemes, e.g., appear to agree either in taking the standpoint of an individual speaker or in postulating a dyad, speaker-hearer (or source-destination, sender-receiver, addressor-addressee). Even if such a scheme is intended to be a model, for descriptive work it cannot be. Some rules of speaking require specification of *three* participants [addressor, addressee, hearer (audience), source, spokesman, addressees; etc.]; some of but *one,* indifferent as to role in the speech event; some of *two,* but of speaker and audience (e.g., a child); and so on. In short, serious ethnographic work shows that there is one general, or universal, dimension to be postulated,

that of *participant*. The common dyadic model of speaker-hearer specifies sometimes too many, sometimes too few, sometimes the wrong participants. Further ethnographic work will enable us to state the range of
actual types of participant relations and to see in differential occurrence
something to be explained.

Ethnographic material so far investigated indicates that some sixteen or
seventeen components have sometimes to be distinguished. No rule has
been found that requires specification of all simultaneously. There are
always redundancies, and sometimes a rule requires explicit mention of a
relation between only two, message form and some other. (It is a general
principle that all rules involve message form, if not by affecting its shape,
then by governing its interpretation.) Since each of the components may
sometimes be a factor, however, each has to be recognized in the general
grid.

Psycholinguistic work has indicated that human memory works best
with classifications of the magnitude of seven, plus or minus two (Miller
1956). To make the set of components mnemonically convenient, at least
in English, the letters of the term SPEAKING can be used. The components can be grouped together in relation to the eight letters without
great difficulty. Clearly, the use of SPEAKING as a mnemonic code
word has nothing to do with the form of an eventual model and theory.

1. *Message form*. The form of the message is fundamental, as has just
been indicated. The most common, and most serious, defect in most reports of speaking probably is that the message form, and, hence, the rules
governing it, cannot be recaptured. A concern for the details of actual
form strikes some as picayune, as removed from humanistic or scientific
importance. Such a view betrays an impatience that is a disservice to
both humanistic and scientific purposes. It is precisely the failure to unite
form and content in the scope of a single focus of study that has retarded
understanding of the human ability to speak, and that vitiates many attempts to analyze the significance of behavior. Content categories, interpretive categories, alone do not suffice. It is a truism, but one frequently
ignored in research, that *how* something is said is part of *what* is said. Nor
can one prescribe in advance the gross size of the signal that will be crucial to content and skill. The more a way of speaking has become shared
and meaningful within a group, the more likely that crucial cues will be
efficient, i.e., slight in scale. If one balks at such detail, perhaps because it
requires technical skills in linguistics, musicology, or the like that are
hard to command, one should face the fact that the human meaning of
one's object of study, and the scientific claims of one's field of inquiry, are
not being taken seriously.

Especially when competence, the ability of persons, is of concern, one
must recognize that shared ways of speaking acquire a partial autonomy,
developing in part in terms of an inner logic of their means of expression.
The means of expression condition and sometimes control content. For

members of the community, then, "freedom is the recognition of necessity"; mastery of the way of speaking is prerequisite to personal expression. Serious concern for both scientific analysis and human meaning requires one to go beyond content to the explicit statement of rules and features of form.

While such an approach may seem to apply first of all to genres conventionally recognized as esthetic, it also applies to conversation in daily life. Only painstaking analysis of message form—how things are said—of a sort that indeed parallels and can learn from the intensity of literary criticism can disclose the depth and adequacy of the elliptical art that is talk.

2. *Message content.* One context for distinguishing message form from message content would be: "He prayed, saying '. . .' " (quoting message form) vs. "He prayed that he would get well" (reporting content only).

Content enters analysis first of all perhaps as a question of *topic*, and of change of topic. Members of a group know what is being talked about, and when what is talked about has changed, and manage maintenance, and change, of topic. These abilities are parts of their communicative competence of particular importance to study of the coherence of discourse.

Message form and message content are central to the speech act and the focus of its "syntactic structure"; they are also tightly interdependent. Thus they can be dubbed jointly as components of "act sequence" (mnemonically, A).

3. *Setting.* Setting refers to the time and place of a speech act and, in general, to the physical circumstances.

4. *Scene.* Scene, which is distinct from setting, designates the "psychological setting," or the cultural definition of an occasion as a certain type of scene. Within a play on the same stage with the same stage set the dramatic time may shift: "ten years later." In daily life the same persons in the same setting may redefine their interaction as a changed type of scene, say, from formal to informal, serious to festive, or the like. (For an example of the importance of types of scene to analysis of speech genres, see Frake's contrast of the Subanun and Yakan at the end of Chapter 3.) Speech acts frequently are used to define scenes, and also frequently judged as appropriate or inappropriate in relation to scenes. Settings and scenes themselves, of course, may be judged as appropriate and inappropriate, happy or unhappy, in relation to each other, from the level of complaint about the weather to that of dramatic irony.

Setting and scene may be linked as components of act situation (mnemonically, S). Since scene implies always an analysis of cultural definitions, setting probably is to be preferred as the informal, unmarked term for the two.

5. *Speaker,* or *sender.*

6. *Addressor.*

7. *Hearer,* or *receiver,* or *audience.*

8. *Addressee.*

These four components were discussed in introducing the subject of components of speech. Here are a few illustrations. Among the Abipon of Argentina -*in* is added to the end of each word if any participant (whatever his role) is a member of the Hocheri (warrior class). Among the Wishram Chinook, formal scenes are defined by the relationship between a source (e.g., a chief, or sponsor of a ceremony), a spokesman who repeats the source's words, and others who constitute an audience or public. The source whose words are repeated sometimes is not present; the addressees sometimes are (spirts) of the surrounding environment. In the presence of a child, adults in Germany often use the term of address which would be appropriate for the child. Sometimes rules for participants are internal to a genre and independent of the participants in the embedding event. Thus male and female actors in Yana myths use the appropriate men's and women's forms of speech, respectively, irrespective of the sex of the narrator. Use of men's speech itself is required when both addressor and addressee are both adult and male, "women's" speech otherwise. Groups differ in their definitions of the participants in speech events in revealing ways, particularly in defining absence (e.g., children, maids) and presence (e.g., supernaturals) of participation. Much of religious conduct can be interpreted as part of a native theory of communication. The various components may be grouped together as participants (mnemonically, P).

9. *Purposes—outcomes.* Conventionally recognized and expected outcomes often enter into the definition of speech events, as among the Waiwai of Venezuela, where the central speech event of the society, the *oho-chant,* has several varieties, according to whether the purpose to be accomplished is a marriage contract, a trade, a communal work task, an invitation to a feast, or a composing of social peace after a death. The rules for participants and settings vary accordingly (Fock 1965). A taxonomy of speech events among the Yakan of the Philippines (analyzed by Frake, Chapter 3) is differentiated into levels according jointly to topic (any topic, an issue, a disagreement, a dispute) and outcome (no particular outcome, a decision, a settlement, a legal ruling).

10. *Purposes—goals.* The purpose of an event from a community standpoint, of course, need not be identical to the purposes of those engaged in it. Presumably, both sides to a Yakan litigation wish to win. In a negotiation the purpose of some may be to obtain a favorable settlement, of others simply that there be a settlement. Among the Waiwai the prospective father-in-law and son-in-law have opposing goals in arriving at a marriage contract. The strategies of participants are an essential determinant of the form of speech events, indeed, to their being performed at all (see Blom and Gumperz 2, Chapter 14).

With respect both to outcomes and goals, the conventionally expected or ascribed must be distinguished from the purely situational or personal, and from the latent and unintended. The interactions of a particular speech event may determine its particular quality and whether or not the expected outcome is reached. The actual motives, or some portion of them, of participants may be quite varied. In the first instance, descriptions of speech events seek to describe customary or culturally appropriate behavior. Such description is essential and prerequisite to understanding events in all their individual richness; but the two kinds of account should not be confused (see Sapir 1949h:534, 543).

Many approaches to communication and the analysis of speech have not provided a place for either kind of purpose, perhaps because of a conscious or unconsciously lingering behaviorism. [Kenneth Burke's (1945) approach is a notable exception.] Yet communication itself must be differentiated from interaction as a whole in terms of purposiveness (see Humes 1964e). The two aspects of purpose can be grouped together by exploiting an English homonymy, *ends* in view (goals) and *ends* as outcomes (mnemonically, E).

11. *Key.* Key is introduced to provide for the tone, manner, or spirit in which an act is done. It corresponds roughly to modality among grammatical categories. Acts otherwise the same as regards setting, participants, message form, and the like may differ in key, as, e.g., between *mock: serious* or *perfunctory: painstaking.*

Key is often conventionally ascribed to an instance of some other component as its attribute; seriousness, for example, may be the expected concomitant of a scene, participant, act, code, or genre (say, a church, a judge, a vow, use of Latin, obsequies). Yet there is always the possibility that there is a conventionally understood way of substituting an alternative key. (This possibility corresponds to the general possibility of choosing one speech style or register as against another.) In this respect, ritual remains always informative. Knowing what should happen next, one still can attend to the way in which it happens. (Consider, for example, critics reviewing performances of the classical repertoire for the piano.)

The significance of key is underlined by the fact that, when it is in conflict with the overt content of an act, it often overrides the latter (as in sarcasm). The signaling of key may be nonverbal, as with a wink, gesture, posture, style of dress, musical accompaniment, but it also commonly involves conventional units of speech too often disregarded in ordinary linguistic analysis, such as English aspiration and vowel length to signal emphasis. Such features are often termed *expressive,* but are better dubbed *stylistic* since they need not at all depend on the mood of their user. Revill (1966:251) reports, for instance, that "some forms have been found which *cannot* [emphasis mine] be described as reflecting feelings on the part of the speaker, but they will be used in certain social situations" (for emphasis, clarity, politeness).

12. *Channels.* By choice of channel is understood choice of oral, writ-

ten, telegraphic, semaphore, or other medium of transmission of speech. With regard to channels, one must further distinguish modes of use. The oral channel, e.g., may be used to sing, hum, whistle, or chant features of speech as well as to speak them. Two important goals of description are accounts of the interdependence of channels in interaction and the relative hierarchy among them.

13. *Forms of speech.* A major theoretical and empirical problem is to distinguish the verbal resources of a community. Obviously, it is superficial, indeed misleading, to speak of the language of a community (Ferguson and Gumperz 1960). Even where there is but a single "language" present in a community (no cases are known in the contemporary world), that language will be organized into various forms of speech. Three criteria seem to require recognition at the present time: the historical provenience of the language resources; presence or absence of mutual intelligibility; and specialization in use. The criteria often do not coincide. *Language* and *dialect* are suggested for the first; *codes* for the second; and *varieties* and *registers* for the third. One speaks normally of the English language, and of dialects of English, wherever forms of speech are found whose content is historically derived from the line of linguistic tradition we call "English." The different dialects are not always mutually intelligible (see Yorkshire and Indian English), and their social functions vary considerably around the world, from childhood vernacular to bureaucratic lingua franca. "Code" suggests decoding and the question of intelligibility. Unintelligibility may result when speech is in a language historically unrelated to one's own, but also from use of a simple transformation of one's own speech, e.g., Pig Latin, or "op" talk. In short, some forms of speech derive from others by addition, deletion, substitution, and permutation in various combinations. Finally, forms of speech are commonly specialized to uses of various sorts. *Register* has become familiar in English linguistic usage for reference to specific situations; varieties, or "functional varieties," has been used in American linguistics in relation to broad domains (e.g., vernacular vs. standard).

For sociolinguistics, *varieties* has priority as a standpoint from which to view the forms of speech of a community. The criteria of provenience and intelligibility have to do with sources and characteristics of the criterion of use with the functional organization, of the forms of speech. Channels and forms of speech can be joined together as means or agencies of speaking and labeled, partly for the sake of the code word, partly with an eye on the use of the term *instrumental* in grammar, as *instrumentalities* (mnemonically, I).

14. *Norms of interaction.* All rules governing speaking, of course, have a normative character. What is intended here are the specific behaviors and proprieties that attach to speaking—that one must not interrupt, for example, or that one may freely do so; that normal voice should not be

used except when scheduled in a church service (whisper otherwise); that turns in speaking are to be allocated in a certain way. Norms of interaction obviously implicate analysis of social structure, and social relationships generally, in a community. An illustration follows:

The next morning during tea with Jikjitsu, a college professor who rents rooms in one of the Sodo buildings came in and talked of koans. "When you understand Zen, you know that the tree is really *there*."—The only time anyone said anything of Zen philosophy or experience the whole week. Zenbos never discuss koans or sanzen experience with each other (Snyder 1969:52).

15. *Norms of interpretation*. An account of norms of interaction may still leave open the interpretation to be placed upon them, especially when members of different communities are in communication. Thus it is clear that Arabic and American students differ on a series of interactional norms: Arabs confront each other more directly (face to face) when conversing, sit closer to each other, are more likely to touch each other, look each other more squarely in the eye, and converse more loudly (Watson and Graves 1966:976–977). The investigators who report these findings themselves leave open the meanings of these norms to the participants (p. 984).

The problem of norms of interpretation is familiar from the assessment of communications from other governments and national leaders. One often looks for friendliness in lessened degree of overt hostility. Relations between groups within a country are often affected by misunderstandings on this score. For white middle-class Americans, for example, normal hesitation behavior involves "fillers" at the point of hesitation ("uh," etc.). For many blacks, a normal pattern is to recycle to the beginning of the utterance (perhaps more than once). This black norm may be interpreted by whites not as a different norm but as a defect. (I owe this example to David Dalby.)

Norms of interpretation implicate the belief system of a community. The classic precedent in the ethnographic analysis of a language is Malinowski's (1935) treatment of Trobriand magical formulas and ritual under the heading of *dogmatic context*. (Malinowski's other rubrics are roughly related to these presented here in the following way: His *sociological context* and *ritual context* subsume information as to setting, participants, ends in view and outcome, norms of interaction, and higher level aspects of genre; *structure* reports salient patterning of the verbal form of the act or event; *mode of recitation* reports salient characteristics of the vocal aspect of channel use and message form.)

The processes of interpretation discussed by Garfinkel (Chapter 10), including "ad hocing" generally, would belong in this category. These two kinds of norms may be grouped together (mnemonically, N).

(16. *Genres*. By genres are meant categories such as poem, myth, tale,) proverb, riddle, curse, prayer, oration, lecture, commercial, form letter, editorial, etc. From one standpoint the analysis of speech into acts is an analysis of speech into instances of genres. The notion of genre implies the possibility of identifying formal characteristics traditionally recognized. It is heuristically important to proceed as though all speech has formal characteristics of some sort as manifestation of genres; and it may well be true (on genres, see Ben-Amos 1969). The common notion of "casual" or unmarked speech, however, points up the fact that there is a great range among genres in the number of and explicitness of formal markers. At least there is a great range in the ease with which such markers have been identified. It remains that "unmarked" casual speech can be recognized as such in a context where it is not expected or where it is being exploited for particular effect. Its lesser visibility may be a function of our own orientations and use of it; its profile may be as sharp as any other, once we succeed in seeing it as strange.

Genres often coincide with speech events, but must be treated as analytically independent of them. They may occur in (or as) different events. The sermon as a genre is typically identical with a certain place in a church service, but its properties may be invoked, for serious or humorous effect, in other situations. Often enough a genre recurs in several events, such as a genre of chanting employed by women in Bihar state in India; it is the prescribed form for a related set of acts, recurring in weddings, family visits, and complaints to one's husband (K. M. Tiwary, personal communication). A great deal of empirical work will be needed to clarify the interrelations of genres, events, acts, and other components (mnemonically, G).

As has been shown, the sixteen components can be grouped together under the letters of the code word SPEAKING: settings, participants, ends, act sequences, keys, instrumentalities, norms, genres. That the code word is not wholly ethnocentric appears from the possibility of re-labeling and regrouping the necessary components in terms of the French PARLANT: *participants, actes, raison (resultat), locale, agents* (instrumentalities), *normes, ton* (key), *types* (genres).

Rules (Relations) of Speaking. In discovering the local system of speaking, certain familiar guidelines are, of course, to be used. One must determine the local taxonomy of terms as an essential, though never perfect, guide. A shift in any of the components of speaking may mark the presence of a rule (or structured relation), e.g., from normal tone of voice to whisper, from formal English to slang, correction, praise, embarrassment, withdrawal, and other evaluative responses to speech may indicate the violation or accomplishment of a rule. In general, one can think of any change in a component as a potential locus for application for a "sociolinguistic" commutation test: What relevant contrast, if any, is present?

The heuristic set of components should be used negatively as well as positively, i.e., if a component seems irrelevant to certain acts or genres, that should be asserted, and the consequences of the assertion checked. In just this way Arewa and Dundes (1964) discovered additional aspects of the use of proverbs among the Yoruba: Channel had seemed irrelevant (or rather, always spoken). Pressing the point led to recognition of a change in the form of proverbs when drummed, in keeping with a pattern of partial repetition particular to drumming. Again, the status of participant (user) as adult seemed invariant. Pressing the point by stating it as a rule led to discovery of a formulaic apology by which a child could make use of proverbs.

Many generalizations about rules of speaking will take the form of statements of relationship among components. It is not yet clear that there is any priority to be assigned to particular components in such statements. So far as one can tell at present, any component may be taken as starting point, and the others viewed in relation to it. When individual societies have been well analyzed, hierarchies of precedence among components will very likely appear and be found to differ from case to case. Such differences in hierarchy of components will then be an important part of the taxonomy of sociolinguistic systems. For one group, rules of speaking will be heavily bound to setting; for another primarily to participants; for a third, perhaps to topic.

Experimentation with the formal statement of rules of speaking has only recently begun. (See Tyler's informal examples in Chapter 8, and Ervin-Tripp's pioneering survey, with many original points, in Chapter 7.) Work of Joel Sherzer and myself with some ethnographic data suggested the possibility of adapting a syntactic mode of statement. In such a format, features holding throughout a speech event are stated at the outset in a sort of "lexicon" of components. The sequential structure of the act itself is stated in a sort of "syntax" by means of rewriting rules (Chomsky 1965). When prose descriptions of events have been so restated, there has been a considerable gain in understanding of structure; or, one might say, a considerable clarification of what one understood to be the structure has been demanded. The form of the event is disengaged, as it were, from the verbal foliage obligatory in prose sentences, and can be more readily *seen*. In order to compare events within a society, and across societies, some concise and standard formats are needed. Comparison cannot depend upon memorization or shuffling of prose paragraphs vastly different in verbal style. And it is through some form of formal statement that one can commit oneself to a precise claim as to what it is a member of society knows in knowing how to participate in a speech act.

Abipon "Scoring" (= G)

1. *Event: shaman's retribution (minor offense)*

Components:	S	⟶	shaman's house
	P	⟶	(1) shaman, (2) offender

shaman ⟶ [−female]
offender ⟶ person identified by shaman as responsible for a misfortune

	E	⟶	$\begin{bmatrix} \text{to punish offender} \\ \text{to test courage?} \end{bmatrix}$
	K	⟶	ritual seriousness
	I	⟶	Abipon language, fish (*palometa*) jaw
	N	⟶	$\begin{bmatrix} -\text{speech} \\ +\text{speech} \end{bmatrix} = \begin{bmatrix} \text{courage} \\ \text{cowardice} \end{bmatrix}$

Sequence:		⟶	call + scoring
	Call	⟶	?
	Scoring	⟶	(P1) $\begin{Bmatrix} \text{piercing} \\ \text{response} \end{Bmatrix}$ + (P2) response
	(P2) Response	⟶	$\begin{bmatrix} -\text{avoidance, }-\text{speech} \\ +\text{avoidance, }+\text{speech} \end{bmatrix}$
	(P1) Response	⟶	$\begin{bmatrix} \text{R1} \\ \text{R1 + R2} \end{bmatrix} \Big/ \begin{bmatrix} -\text{avoidance, }-\text{speech} \\ +\text{avoidance, }+\text{speech} \end{bmatrix}$
	R1	⟶	reproach in name of ancestral spirit and traditions for initial offense
	R2	⟶	Reproach in name of ancestral spirit for offense of cowardice

2. *Event: girl's puberty rite*

Components:	S	⟶	shaman's house
	P	⟶	(1) shaman, (2) girl

shaman ⟶ [+female, +old]
girl ⟶ [+female, +marriageable age (ca. 20)]

	E	⟶	$\begin{bmatrix} \text{to identify girl as marriageable} \\ \text{to beautify girl} \\ \text{to test/manifest girl's courage} \end{bmatrix}$
	K	⟶	ritual seriousness
	I	⟶	Abipon language, thorns
	N	⟶	$\begin{bmatrix} -\text{speech} \\ +\text{speech} \end{bmatrix} + \begin{matrix} \text{courage} \\ \text{cowardice} \end{matrix}$

Sequence:		⟶	(?call) + scoring
	Scoring	⟶	(P1) $\begin{Bmatrix} \text{pricking} \\ \text{response} \end{Bmatrix}$ + (P2) response
	(P2) Response	⟶	$\begin{bmatrix} -\text{avoidance, }-\text{speech} \\ +\text{avoidance, }+\text{speech} \end{bmatrix}$
	(P1) Response	⟶	$\begin{bmatrix} (?) \\ \text{R2 + R2} \end{bmatrix} \Big/ \begin{bmatrix} -\text{avoidance, }-\text{speech} \\ +\text{avoidance, }+\text{speech} \end{bmatrix}$
	R2	⟶	reproach in name of ancestral spirit and traditions for cowardice

R3 $\longrightarrow$ taunt of future spinsterhood

3. *Event: testing of children*

Components: S	$\longrightarrow$	parent's home?
P	$\longrightarrow$	(P1) parent, (P2) child
E	$\longrightarrow$	to teach receiver's role in ritual taunting to teach, test courage (?)
K	$\longrightarrow$	?
I	$\longrightarrow$	Abipon language
N	$\longrightarrow$	$\begin{bmatrix} -\text{speech} \\ +\text{speech} \end{bmatrix} + \begin{bmatrix} \text{courage} \\ \text{cowardice} \end{bmatrix}$

Sequence:	$\longrightarrow$	(?) + scoring
"Scoring"	$\longrightarrow$	(P1) $\left\{ \begin{array}{l} \text{taunt} \\ \text{response} \end{array} \right\}$ + (P2) response
Taunt	$\longrightarrow$	??
(P2) Response	$\longrightarrow$	$\begin{bmatrix} -\text{speech} \\ +\text{speech} \end{bmatrix}$
(P1) Response	$\longrightarrow$	$\begin{bmatrix} ?\ (\text{praise?}) \\ \text{R2} \end{bmatrix} \Big/ \begin{bmatrix} -\text{speech} \\ +\text{speech} \end{bmatrix}$

It was the explicit analysis of the more formally defined events that led Sherzer to notice features of the same sort in the casual mention by the source of an informal use of speech by parents. More than one mode of formal (explicit) statement obviously might be attempted—the format used here differs from that in Sherzer (1967) and also in minor details from the revised format of Sherzer (1970). The point is that to put the analysis in such a format forces one to confront what prose may let escape: Just exactly what does one's information specify, and what does it fail to specify, about those features? The task of presentation in a format—something that can take a good deal of time to do consistently and exhaustively—forces attention to structure, and brings out the parallelism in organization of these events, as well as the revealing differences—the relative hierarchy, e.g., of piercing with a fish jaw, pricking with thorns, and purely verbal taunting, covarying with the relative hierarchy of the initiator's response to silence, single reproach (R1), silence, and perhaps praise, in keeping with the general ends in view, punishment, initiation, and training. The parallel structure suggests the exploitation of the several sense of the English word "scoring" for the initiator's first action, and would direct attention (were the Abipones still extant) to behavior equivalent to the call of the shaman's retribution that might be found with the other two events.

The labeling of the acts is unavoidably somewhat arbitrary. We cannot now determine how the Abipones would have translated "taunting" and "reproach," e.g., nor whether they would have distinguished the two as is done here. While the terms overlap in their senses in English, it is reasonable to use "reproach" with regard to offenses (cause of a misfortune, offense against traditions by replying to "scoring"), and "taunting" otherwise, while following Sherzer in choosing "taunting" for the general category. Information from other indigenous South American cultures, and general theory of speech acts, may later support or change the interpretation.

The analysis has been from the "syntactic" standpoint of the component of act sequence. The analysis also makes possible the standpoint of categories or a "lexicon" of acts. The first participants acts of scoring and response can be somewhat as subcategorization in the context either of the event or the component of the second participant:

> Scoring $\longrightarrow$ [piercing]/[Shaman's retribution] *or* [offender]
> [pricking]/[Girl's puberty rite] *or* [marriageable girl]
> [taunting]/[training of child] *or* [child]
>
> Taunting $\longrightarrow$ [R1 + (R2)]/[as above] *or* [as above]
> (P1)Response [(R2 + R3)]/
> [(R2)]/

We do not know the message form of the initial taunting or response which might lead to further specification. The second participant's response is constant throughout the three events on the level at which we have information, but again, might be subcategorized if message form were known.

All three kinds of acts can also be seen as entries in a communicative lexicon, where the familiar formulation $X \rightarrow$ (is rewritten, or realized, as) Y/(in the context) $W–Z$, can be adapted to read, X (has the value) Y/(in the context) $W–Z$.

> Scoring $\longrightarrow$ [punishment]/[shaman's retribution] [offender]
> [initiation]/[girl's puberty rite] *or* [marriageable girl]
> [training]/[testing of child] [child]

The second participant's alternative responses have the same meaning throughout: courage/cowardice. Perhaps it is not accidental that the one insight into verbal socialization that we have from Dobrizhoffer fits with a society in which no valued adult role depended upon verbal skill.

Such a mode of analysis permits formal treatment of many of the acts of speech. The conventional means of many such functions can indeed be analyzed as relations among components, e.g., message form, genre, and key in the case of the $-y$ form of the accusative plural of masculine nouns in Polish, which has the value "solemn" in the genre of poetry, and the value "ironic, pejorative" in the genres of nonpoetic speech. Functions themselves may be statable in terms of relations among components, such that poetic function, e.g., may require a certain relationship among choice of code, choice of topic, and message form in a given period or society.

It would be misleading, however, to think that the definition of functions can be reduced to or derived from other components. Such a thought would be a disabling residue of behaviorist ideology. Ultimately, the functions served in speech must be derived directly from the purposes and needs of human persons engaged in social action, and are what they are: talking to seduce, to stay awake, to avoid a war. The formal analysis of speaking is a means to the understanding of human purposes and needs, and their satisfaction; it is an indispensable means, but only a means, and not that understanding itself.

Explanation

Beyond description is the task of devising models of explanation. The many kinds of act and genre of speech are not all universal; each has a history, and a set of conditions for its origin, maintenance, change, and loss. All the questions that attach to explanation in social science— questions of primacy of factors (technology, social structure, values, and the like), considerations of areal patterning, diffusion, independent development, and evolution, will impinge. If the kind of explanatory adequacy discussed by Chomsky (1965) is recognized as "essential," i.e., as concerned with what is internal to language, and beyond that, internal to human nature, we can see the need for an "existential" or "experiential" explanatory adequacy, a kind of explanation that will link speaking with human history and praxis (Petrovich 1967:111–118, 126–127, 171–172; LeFebvre 1968:34, 45–46). To do this is not only to see languages as part of systems of speaking but also to see systems of speaking from the standpoint of the central question of the nature of sociocultural order—a theory of the maintenance of order being understood as implying a corresponding theory of change, and conversely.[10]

Each case, or each type of case, to be sure, may be valued in its own

[10] See Cohen 1968. His cogent, penetrating account takes explanation as fundamental to theory and social order as central to what is to be explained (pp. x, 16, Chapter 2). Cohen speaks simply of "social order." I use "sociocultural order" to make explicit the inclusion of symbolic or cognitive order (see Berger 1967). On the relevance of sociolinguistics, note the introduction by Donald MacRae (center p. x). On an adequate theory of linguistic change, see Weinreich, Labov, and Herzog 1968, especially pp. 100–101: "The key to a rational conception of language change—indeed, of language itself—is the possibility of describing orderly differentiation in a language serving a community . . . native like command of heterogeneous structures is not a matter of multidialectalism or "mere" performance, but is part of unilingual linguistic competence . . . in a language serving a complex (i.e., real) community, it is *absence* of structured heterogeneity that would be dysfunctional" (101). The conclusions (187–188) make clear that an adequate theory must be sociolinguistic and be based on sociolinguistic description.

right as an expression of mankind. My own work stems in part from a desire to understand the meanings of language in individual lives, and to work toward ending the frequent alienation from human beings of something human beings have created (see Berger 1967, Chapter 1, especially pp. 12–13, and notes 1, 2, and 11; Lefebvre 1966: Chapter VIII, and 1968:72–74; and Merleau-Ponty 1967). Individuating, interpretive, and phenomenological motives are consistent with a concern for general, causal explanation. Each case and type is valuable, enlarging and testing general knowledge, and it is only with a general view of conditions and possibilities that the value of individual ways of speaking can be accurately assessed.

We require a widely ranging series of descriptions, whatever the motives that severally produce them. Neither a descriptive model nor an explanatory theory is convincing if it has not met the test of diverse situations, of a general body of data. Recall that Darwin's exposition of natural selection, and Tylor's (1871, Chapter I) of exposition of a science of culture, were convincing in part for such a reason. We require some initial ordering of the diversity, although the ordering need not be conceived as either historical or unique. Sociolinguistic description and taxonomy are joint conditions of success for understanding and explaining the interaction of language and social life.

2

Culture Patterning of Speech Behavior in Burundi[1]

ETHEL M. ALBERT

Ethel M. Albert is Professor of Anthropology and Speech at Northwestern University. She received her doctorate in philosophy at the University of Wisconsin and taught logic and philosophy of science at Brooklyn College, Wisconsin, and Syracuse. As Research Associate of the Comparative Study of Values in Five Cultures at Harvard, she concentrated on Navaho values with fieldwork among the Ramah Navaho. This chapter, revised from a paper included in Gumperz and Hymes' "The Ethnography of Communication" (Albert 1964), draws on two years of fieldwork on values and world view in Burundi. Dr. Albert's main interests are in "macrosemantics" as a theory of verbal and cultural contexts and cultural logics and ethnoepistemology.

A comprehensive account of speech behavior, such as Dr. Albert provides here, is rare. To it she adds a discussion of the problems of fieldwork on speech behavior that is also of great value. Most ethnographers obtain information on speech behavior through the sheer necessity of learning how to comport themselves and to obtain information, whatever their principal subject of study. Few make that process an object of reflection and report in itself, as Dr. Albert does here. Both ethnography and

A revision of "'Rhetoric,' 'Logic,' and 'Poetics' in Burundi: Cultural Patterning of Speech Behavior," reproduced by permission of the American Anthropological Association and the author from *American Anthropologist*, Vol. 66, No. 6, 1964.

[1] The research upon which this paper is based was carried out in Burundi, Central Africa. It was supported by a Ford Foundation Overseas Study Fellowship (1955–1957) and materially facilitated by the assistance of I.R.S.A.C. (Institut pour la Recherche Scientifique en Afrique Centrale).

sociolinguistics would benefit if more researchers were to do so.

Notice that while social structure is discussed first, its role in speech is seen by Dr. Albert as following from the underlying beliefs and values that are her main concern. Here cultural outlook is the explanatory starting point rather than social structure itself (as with Bernstein in Chapter 17). Among the many individual points of interest in this rich paper, notice particularly the "competence of incompetence" required of peasants in the presence of aristocrats (recalling the defensive image of "shuffling" and Steppinfechit imposed on American Negroes); the differential speech training of men and women; the example of switching from formal to informal interaction between an aristocrat and servant, indicating that other aspects of speaking are predictable from the social position of the participants and the topic; the inverse relationship between the manner ("key") in which an instruction is accepted by a servant and the likelihood of its being carried out; the prevalence of indirect reference; the simultaneous concealment and invitation to disclosure of allusive narrative songs; the invention and interpretation of figurative and allusive speech as a general cultural skill; the pervasive valuing of both esthetic and instrumental aspects of speech. The paper is especially valuable for its portrayal of the relations between cultural patterns of speaking and personal strategies. Another unique feature is the discussion of fieldwork problems. Albert lists in detail the possibility for misunderstanding arising from Rundi verbal strategies and gives practical suggestions for the ethnographer of speaking. Many of the problems of interpretation that Garfinkel alludes to in Chapter 10 are exemplified here. For another important discussion of ethnography in a similar vein, see Moerman (1968b). Seitel (1969 and 1971) gives a highly suggestive analysis of how pronouns are used to convey meaning. Additional related readings are provided by Calame-Griaule (1965), Hogan (1967), Hymes (1966a), and Samarin (1967).

Like other universal categories of human behavior, speech is the object of diverse, complementary specializations. In the context of the ethnography of speaking, not only the language spoken but also the uses of speech may be assumed to have distinctive culture patterns. Ideally, a complete anthropological description of the pattern of a culture would include the rules and uses of speech, their implementation and violation, and relevant sanctions, positive and negative. Conversely, when inquiry is focused on cultural patterns of speech behavior, the optimum context is the whole culture pattern. Major intracultural variations in the uses of speech may be assumed to be systematically related to the constituents of culture patterns, including aspects of the social structure, cultural definitions of the situations of action, the cultural philosophy and value system, and their patterned interrelations.

The traditional kingdom of Burundi[2] is a particularly fortunate case study of culture patterning of speech behavior. Speech is explicitly recognized as an important instrument of social life; eloquence is one of the central values of the cultural world-view; and the way of life affords frequent opportunity for its exercise. Sensitivity to the variety and complexity of speech behavior is evident in a rich vocabulary for its description and evaluation and in a constant flow of speech about speech. Argument, debate, and negotiation, as well as elaborate literary forms, are built into the organization of society and the content of the world-view as means of gaining one's ends, as social status symbols, and as skills enjoyable in themselves.

A highly secularized, sophisticated feudal kingdom with a population of approximately two million, traditional Burundi has well-defined criteria of rhetoric, logic, and poetics, and well-developed ideas about their uses and interrelations. The norms governing the uses of speech are explicitly differentiated according to caste, sex, and age so that the relations of speech behavior to social structure are easily grasped by observers. Formalization and stylization of speech situations are extensive and elaborate, suggesting ways in which the uses of language are conditioned by culturally distinctive conceptions of situational appropriateness. Esthetic criteria are well developed and have an extensive range of relevance. Explicit concern with the values of truth and falsity and their situational relativism connect concepts governing the uses of speech to the premises of the cultural world-view and value system.

The primary intention of this paper is to explore concepts and categories that may be useful for constructing cultural patterns of speech behavior. The descriptive data presented were provided by informants'

---

[2] "Burundi" is the post-independence form of the name of the kingdom earlier included in the joint designation, Ruanda-Urundi. The Bantu form will be retained for the name of the people, viz., Barundi (singular, Murundi); "Kirundi" for the language; but for the adjective, only the stem will be used, viz., Rundi.

verbalizations, spontaneous or by elicitation, and checked by observation and the comparison of the interview protocols of a variety of informants. Space does not permit an exhaustive account of all the relevant data. Organization of the material is only in small part a reflection of explicit informant statements about speech as such.

Adoption of the terms "rhetoric," "logic," and "poetics" from Western culture is necessarily tentative and obviously entails the risk of culture-bound distortion. Conventional denotative meanings will be used: "rhetoric" designates the norms and techniques of persuasion, as well as the criteria governing styles of delivery in public speaking; "logic" refers to the rules and uses of evidence and inference; and "poetics" refers to the esthetic criteria that govern discourse. The referents of these terms are neither precise nor unambiguous in their native cultural habitat. "Poetics" overlaps with "rhetoric" insofar as public address and persuasion are governed by esthetic rules; the line between rhetoric and sophistry is so fine that it not infrequently disappears when persuasion is contrasted with the strict rules of logic and the ideals of literal, descriptive truth. Admittedly of limited utility, the terms "rhetoric," "logic," and "poetics" nevertheless call attention to a significant and large but often neglected body of data constitutive of culture patterns of speech behavior. They are also potentially useful for cross-cultural comparisons.

Many of the components of Rundi patterns for the uses of speech are familiar to Western observers. Some of the key terms and concepts are close or equivalent in referential meanings to their English translations. However, contextual meanings—meanings that arise out of the relationships among the constituent elements of discourse—vary with specific cultural sets of assumptions and values. The allocation of intellectual resources in Burundi is controlled by a hierarchy of values far removed from Western ideals or a scientific approach to discourse, though very close to that of other African cultures and many Mediterranean societies. Practical and esthetic values take precedence over logical criteria in all but a few classes of communication situation. A well-brought-up Murundi would suffer agonies of shame in the presence of the naked truth and would hasten to provide the esthetic coverings called for by the cultural value system. Reliance upon appeals to the emotions as the chief technique of rhetoric is taken for granted as right and natural and indeed the whole ground of its utility. There are no reservations about the desirability of flattery, untruths, taking advantage of weakness of character or profiting from others' misfortune. Whatever works is good, and esthetic-emotive values are higher in the hierarchy than moral or logical principles in speech and other behavior. The implications for fieldwork of culture patterning of speech behavior will be discussed in the conclusion.

Social Structural Definitions of Speech Situations

BACKGROUND: HIERARCHICAL ORDER IN THE UNIVERSE AND SOCIETY

The importance of speech to survival and success and the primacy of esthetic-emotive values in speech behavior follow directly from Rundi causal theory. In the universe at large and in society, personal power is the sole or chief causal force; it is conceived as directed by the actor's free choice; choice is viewed as dependent on emotional dispositions, assumed to be unstable and changeable. There is a steady diminution of power, hence of freedom of self-determination, and proportionally an increase in subjection to the whim and will of superiors in the hierarchy, from the high god (*Imana*), to the king (*mwami*), the princes (*baganwa*), the nobles (*abafasoni*), the herders (*Batutsi*), the farmer-peasant caste (*Bahutu*), to the lowborn pariahs (*Batwa*).

In a voluntaristic-emotive universe, no event is predictable. What actually happens depends on the good pleasure of the determining superior power. Since emotion is the source of action and is much affected by esthetic factors, manipulation of emotions by esthetic devices is the principal business of speech behavior. To procure a gift and protection from a superior, to obtain a favorable judgment in a court case, to defend oneself against calumny or accusations of wrongdoing, to oust a rival—in short, to survive and to succeed—is everybody's concern. The particularities of esthetic criteria vary in content and in degree or rigor of application with subject matter, situation, and social roles. The primacy of esthetic-emotive values gives the impression that there is more poetry than truth in the flow of discourse.

SPEECH TRAINING

Socialization patterns reveal the main lines of social role differentiation as relative to caste, age, and sex. *Ubukuru,* seniority or superiority, is the guiding principle of all behavior: caste order is known; the older are superior to the younger; men are superior to women. The ideal of good breeding and aristocracy, *imfura,* includes "speaking well" as one of its principal elements. From about the tenth year, boys in the upper social strata are given formal speech training. The "curriculum" includes composition of impromptu speeches appropriate in relations with superiors in age or status; formulas for petitioning a superior for a gift; composition of *amazina,* praise-poems; quick-witted, self-defensive rhetoric intended to deflect an accusation or the anger of a superior. Correct formulas for addressing social inferiors, for funeral orations, for rendering judgment in a dispute, or for serving as an intermediary between a petitioner and one's feudal superior are learned in the course of time as, with increasing age and maturity, each type of activity becomes appropriate. Training includes mastery of a suitable, elegant vocabulary, of tone of voice and its modulation, of graceful gestures with hand and spear, of general posture and appropriate bodily movements, of control of eye-contacts, especially with inferiors, and above all, of speedy summoning of appropriate and effective verbal response in the dynamics of interpersonal relations.

Girls in the upper caste are also carefully trained, but to artful silence and evasiveness and to careful listening that will enable them to repeat nearly verbatim what has been said by visitors or neighbors. Faithful wives and daughters, servants, and feudal dependents are expected to recount to the men of the family anything they have heard that might be construed as inimical to husband, father, or brother, or as helpful in combatting a real or potential enemy of the head of the household. Public speaking is unseemly for women. The proper pattern of the *imfura* female requires shyness and delicacy. However, maturity brings with it the development of highly effective bargaining and negotiating skills for use behind the scenes. There are many women who in fact make the decisions presented publicly by their husbands, or who become politically or economically powerful through skillful though discreet and private use of intellectual and verbal talents. Except at the extreme top and bottom of the social scale, each individual learns verbal formulas and styles appropriate to a variety of roles, some those of a social superior, some those of an inferior. For example, a herder of good family must know how to show subservience and obedience to his elders and princely superiors and also how to address and control the peasantry; peasants develop speech behavior patterns to deal with their immediate and remote superiors but also with their younger relatives, with men of their own age and station, with the pariah Batwa, and with any dependents they may have.

FORMS OF PETITION

Petitioning for gifts or favors is one of the most frequent and significant situations of interpersonal communication. It is, then, predictably, highly stylized. When a man asks for cattle or a bride or a wife or a son asks the head of the household for permission to smoke or drink beer or to pay a visit to a neighbor or relative, a physical position of submission is assumed by the petitioner. Kneeling in the presence of the superior is usual if the matter is intrafamilial. In the formal business of requesting cattle or a bride, the petitioner assumes a formal stance, often rising from a seated position to stand during the delivery of the formal request. His speech has probably been carefully composed in advance. To follow the general formula, one refers to the gift one has brought, a prescribed number of pots of banana beer serving as a clue to the purpose of the visit; one expresses love, admiration, and respect for the excellent qualities (real, imagined, and hoped-for) of the superior; one expresses the hope that the affection is reciprocated; one again refers to the gift, this time as a token of affection; one promises further gifts in the future; one states one's wish; one closes with a repetition of the praise of the superior and an expression of hope that the wish will be granted. Seeking cattle or a wife entails a series of visits, each formal, but graded as to the number of pots of beer presented and the verbal formulas used as negotiations proceed.

Cues that indicate the intention to refuse requests are sometimes delayed. Superiors thereby gain pots of beer or services without compensating the petitioners, but suffer a loss of reputation through gossip that directs potential petitioners away from them to more profitable patrons. A reputation for generosity is a necessity of high status since it attracts followers and augments political power. Negative publicity is a sanction at the disposal of social inferiors, not only frustrated petitioners for cattle but also disgruntled wives and overworked servants. Verbalization of the rules of the petitioning process and the forms of petition are easily elicited from persons of high and low rank.

Choice of vocabulary and of gestures and other paralinguistic elements tends toward the ideal set by the aristocratic superior, but realization of the ideal varies, expectably, with the background, training, and social and personal characteristics of the petitioner. Humble peasant women are often capable of a very good approximation to the ideal, their speech flowing gracefully and smoothly, their gestures fitting the words, and compliments framed in poetic figures of speech. On the other hand, some members of upper caste patrilineages lack the wit or the character to learn their speech manners. They are privately and sometimes publicly mocked for behaving like peasants. Appropriate speech behavior for peasants in intercaste relations is that of an inferior; their words are haltingly delivered or run on uncontrolled, their voices are loud, their gestures wild, their figures of speech ungainly, their emotions freely displayed, their words and sentences clumsy. As will appear below in the description of respect patterns, the appropriate style for inferiors is attached to roles and situations, not to persons. The speed and apparent ease with which individuals switch speech behavior patterns is likely to be disconcerting to observers trained to expect "consistency" or socialized in a system of low contrast among role-relative speech patterns.

FORMULAS FOR VISITING,
FORMAL AND INFORMAL

The notion of idle talk has little place in Rundi conceptions of verbal behavior. So too, the notion of a social call without a definite purpose is not entertained, except in rare instances, e.g., visits among old friends who are also close neighbors. Self-interest is assumed natural and universal. Purposive behavior, especially speech behavior, is its assumed natural complement. Visiting is categorized according to the visitor's purpose and is subject to a variety of formulas which must be learned. A distinction appears to be made between formal and informal visiting. Formal visitis include those made to a feudal superior to request favors, to give formal thanks for favors received, to remind him of one's continuing loyalty, and to improve the occasion by listening to whatever gossip may be available. Arranging marriages and funerals and conducting other social transactions have their own rules. Distinguished neighbors expect to be waited upon by their inferiors and occasionally confer upon their inferiors the honor of a visit. In either case, it is necessary to send at least one pot of beer in advance, both to announce one's intention to visit and also to insure that the host or hostess will "have something to offer." Hospitality, understood as offering drink and food, is a key value in social life. Visiting, even when formal, need not preclude some quiet talk of a political nature, calumny or lesser gossip, plans for cooperation in effecting the downfall of some common enemy, probing for cues as to possible gifts, and other everyday concerns of a very politically and economically alert people.

Family visits follow prescribed sets of proper formulas for verbal and other behavior. The heaviest constraints of formality govern visits between a father and a married daughter, separated by a nearly total avoidance taboo. In the event of important business to be transacted, e.g., if the daughter wishes to break up her marriage and hence impose upon the father the necessity to receive her again in his household and to return the bride-price, intermediaries must be used, usually the girl's mother or some other female relative. A slightly less rigid avoidance relation obtains between mother-in-law and son-in-law. He is obliged to pay visits of respect, but he is forbidden to seek her out at her hearth; joking and levity are proscribed; each addresses the other as *mufasoni*, noble, irrespective of their actual caste position. Nephews and nieces visiting a paternal aunt are bound by a strict respect pattern, tempered by the fact that the home of the paternal aunt is a quasi-scared sanctuary from an angry father or paternal uncle. Diminishing degrees of formality may be traced through the kinship system to the open, joking relations between cross-cousins and the spouses of cross-cousins and between grandchildren and grandparents. These call for rough sexual joking. Occasionally, young people take umbrage at the sexual jokes of older relatives, but there is open, strong disapproval of so inappropriate a response. More in keeping with custom is a young grandson's teasing his grandmother by telling her he will not go to bed with her because she is wrinkled and ugly, to which a suitable response would be an offer of references of excellence of performance based on long experience.

Family attendance at funerals is expected even of those residing some distance away. They are expected to comfort the bereaved and to take over household and other chores which the bereaved are too grief-stricken to perform. Visitors also keep an eye on the execution of the last will and testament when it is a head of a household being mourned. After the burial, there are formal orations and pledges of help, and calves or cattle are led through the corral in silent acknowledgment that debts and obligations incurred by the dead man will be honored by his heirs. Quarreling among the heirs is so common as to be almost part of the prescribed behavior. The "manifest content" of disputes is often some trivial goods not specified in the will. To quote one Murundi, "Brothers will fight almost to the death over a basket of beans." The outcome is far from trivial: quarrels test the power of the father's heir and set up a pecking order among siblings. Departures from the family homestead may occur if one of the sons is dissatisfied with the new order.

Quarreling is also a semiformalized part of another prescribed family affair, the wedding. Quarrels between representatives of the two families start as a symbolic abduction struggle. With the help of many pots of beer, the symbolic fight not infrequently becomes quarreling in earnest. However, in these as in other situations where quarreling is virtually inevitable, some members of the family will probably have kept sober so as to act as sergeants-at-arms and prevent matters from getting too far out of hand.

Relatives and neighbors are expected to make a formal call upon anyone who has just been through a ritual cleansing ceremony, e.g., a woman after the birth of twins. The visit signifies that they can now "ask for fire from that house," the symbol that normal and friendly social relations may safely be resumed.

A limited amount of informal dropping-in on neighbors occurs, more often than not the visitor being led to his destination by the news that there is a supply of beer available. Gossip flows freely in proportion to the flow of beer, sometimes too freely for the peace of mind of participants suffering morning-after second thoughts. As in most other cultures, drinking parties tend to end in fighting, also cause for misgivings in retrospect.

The form appropriate to a neighborly or friendly social call is sometimes used for a mission customarily assumed on behalf of friends or relatives, viz., looking over a family into which the friend's or relative's son or daughter may marry. Semiformal in pattern, such missions bear all the signs of being to some purpose. Each party knows at what discount to take the other's questions and assertions. An experienced eye can distinguish authentic from assumed industriousness and modesty in the potential bride, recognize the signs of a potential brutally excessive wife-beater or glutton in the would-be bridegroom, size up the temperament of the potential mother-in-law who controls the life of a new wife. Details of the relevant skills and signs could not or would not be presented by informants.

A long list of amenities, conventions, and rules are part of the Barundi's pattern of polite interpersonal relations and conversation. In the old days, age-mates greeted each other in a lengthy ceremony of sung greetings, embraces, and stylized gestures; children knelt before parents or grandparents to pay respect and to receive blessings; feudal inferiors greeting a superior proceeded through the numerous steps of an elaborate assurance of affection and respect that involved verbal formulas accompanied by touching the superior with both hands, literally from head to foot.

RULES OF PRECEDENCE
AND GOOD SPEECH MANNERS

The order in which individuals speak in a group is strictly determined by seniority. However, if the eldest present is lower in social rank than some other individual, age gives way before social status. Thus, a nephew may be older than his uncle but the uncle is of higher rank and will speak before him. A prince or chief may be younger than others present but speaks first by virtue of his higher rank. There is apparently no recorded confusion or conflict in the matter of determining order of precedence, even in very large groups. A question intended to discover what would occur in the event of confusion was rejected by all to whom it was presented as irrelevant and improbable.

The rule for servants, females, and other inferiors for behavior in the presence of outsiders is to speak when spoken to but otherwise to maintain silence. Nevertheless, the pattern is so arranged that younger or socially inferior males are in due course able to express their views in public. At the opening stage of talk, strict order of seniority is observed. After the first or second round of remarks, the senior person will still speak first; the next in order of rank opens his speech with a statement to the effect, "Yes, I agree with the previous speaker, he is correct, he is older and knows best, etc." Then, depending on circumstances and issues, the second speaker will by degrees or at once express his own views, and these may well be diametrically opposed to those previously expressed. No umbrage is taken, the required formula of acknowledgment of the superior having been used. If the *umukuru,* senior person, is aged and weak, his son may speak first, initiating his utterance by explaining his departure from the rules: "My father is old, his memory is not good, he wishes me to speak for him," or some other appropriate excuse is given. It is not unusual for the formal order of precedence to be abandoned in the latter part of a protracted discussion and for loud voices to be heard even among upper-class individuals.

Caste stereotypes represent those in the upper strata of society as never raising their voices or allowing anger or other emotions to show. It is said that the Batutsi herders prefer to bear a grudge silently and to take revenge when opportunity permits, even if it comes twenty years after the affront has been suffered. This applies to dealings with individuals of their own class. Communication with inferiors involves a different approach that includes a kind of stylized "reverse signaling." If an underling quietly accepts an order, there is a good chance that he is showing respect but has no intention of carrying out the order. On the other hand, if he gets his resentments out of his system by shouting protest and refusal and by drawing his superior into a noisy quarrel, he is almost certain at the end to do as he has been told. Explicit references to the positive value of an inferior's outburst take various forms and appear to be an upper caste "in" thing to say.

It is assumed that the peasants express their emotions and opinions freely, do not bear grudges, and are generally warmer, more open and forthright, and friendler than herders. Generally, the Batutsi herders live up to their reputation for dignity in public situations. They are also expert in applying as a very effective rhetorical technique the rule that silence is golden. Good rhetoricians, they appreciate the utility of refraining from comment, reply, or rejoinder. The total, glacial silence of a perfectly immobile Mututsi who has chosen not to speak has to be experienced to be appreciated. To all appearances, the silence can be maintained indefinitely and in the face of every known technique of provocation, domestic or imported. In family conclave or political caucus, silence or avoiding the topic intended for discussion on the part of the ranking person present effectively cancels the proceedings. It is understood by all attending as total disapproval. Also, it can directly block discussion. Application of the principle of seniority is such that a superior's silence or evasion of the issue effectively silences all his social inferiors. At the very top of the social hierarchy, all the skills and patterns of refined behavior are fully controlled, but they are modified by the value of princely magnanimity and benevolence. A prince of the blood may unbend, a Tutsi rarely if ever.

Respect Patterns
and Role Relativism

An intelligent man must measure the character of his interlocutor and select style and content for his speech accordingly. It would be an unforgivable blunder for a peasant-farmer, no matter how wealthy or able, to produce a truly elegant, eloquent, rapid-fire defense before a herder or other superior. However, the same peasant who stammers or shouts or forces a smile from a superior by making a rhetorical fool of himself when his adversary is a prince or herder may, with a change in the situation involving his superiors, or as a judge in a local or family affair, in a council, or in making a funeral oration, show himself an able speaker, a dignified man who speaks as slowly and as intelligently as ever a highborn herder could. The accent will be different; the figures of speech will more likely be drawn from agriculture than from herding and only in the rare instance reflect knowledge of courtly life; the gestures of the muscular arms and heavyset body and the facial expressions will not be like those of the long-limbed, slim-boned, narrow-headed "Hamitic" Batutsi herders, but they will not lack studied grace and dignity.

In his role as rhetorician, the fortunate peasant is skillful and not at all the humble, mumbling fool he plays before his caste superiors. He is in control of alternative, appropriate patterns. Or, if he cannot make a fine speech, he has a legitimate excuse in his inherited caste inferiority. There are highborn men who speak badly, either because nature failed to endow them with the intelligence, innate verbal ability, and grace assumed to be the biological inheritance of the herders or because drink, disease, or private disaster have destroyed their character. Failure to speak clearly and well, clumsy and wild gestures and allowing emotions to show, earn such unfortunates the epithet *muhutu,* peasant, whose socially stereotyped speech pattern they employ for want of the power to do better.

In Kirundi, as in French and other languages, the second person singular is the familiar, the second person plural is the respect form. In addressing a superior, the plural must be used. Thus, to thank an inferior, one may say *urakoze,* but to thank a superior, it must be *murakoze.* The nonverbal signs of respect are numerous. In effect, they consist of the whole set of signs defining the characteristics of social inferiority. The inferior walks behind the superior, drinks and eats after the superior has begun or only after he has finished. If the superior is of princely rank, nobody may be present during mealtimes, the taster remaining but squatting with his back to his master. The inferior talks only after the superior has spoken. He inclines his head in respect, and the body, too, must signal humility, obedience, and respect.

A highly formal respect situation, once official business is completed, may abruptly change into easy, informal discussion. The redefinition of the situation may be presumed to follow some sign from the superior, probably a change from the formal stance prescribed for official business to "at-ease." In response, the social inferior drops the plural form of address, and the bodily stance and use of voice are transformed from "humble respect" to "relaxed." Particularly if the subject of discussion is cattle, the Barundi's favorite subject for bull-sessions, informality prevails. Voices rise higher as differences of opinion are defined and defended, the expression of various emotions being permitted and even expected for this topic. The debating pair may easily be constituted of a highborn prince and lowborn cowherd in his employ, but once the signal for informal discussion has been given, the respect pattern becomes not merely irrelevant but improper. However, it was pointed out by both upper- and lower-caste persons that a judicious inferior will not allow himself the liberty of too enthusiastic disagreement despite the permissiveness, nor overlook any cues to future opportunities for requesting a gift or otherwise assuring or improving his position. Batutsi, male and female, also adjust their speech behavior up and down the situational scale. A gracious, silent lady of good family may be obliged to excuse herself to attend to an emergency in the corral. Her voice rings loud and sharp as she chastises the offending herder or servant girl, and there may be an accompaniment of sharp slaps. Returned to her visitors and hostess role, she resumes the ladylike pattern, the transitions apparently effortless and expected. By contrast, if a peasant girl imitates too closely the speech and manner of the upper caste, she must put up with teasing and the accusation of absurd affectation.

AMENITIES AND CONVENTIONS

A full inventory of the amenities and conventions that govern verbal communication would properly include numerous minor rules for speech. There are few word taboos. It is forbidden to tell what one has eaten for dinner, or to mention the name of a dead person in the presence of relatives, and euphemisms are in order when referring to excretion. Violations of the rules are breaches of good taste, and verbal bad manners are likely to be condemned by a graceful gesture and the expression *n'ishano,* "how shocking!" The Rundi technique for avoiding an unwanted visitor is familiar: a child or servant is sent to announce that nobody is home. It is perfectly proper for a servant or child to enter a room where company is being entertained and to whisper some message to the host or hostess. It is understood that something has gone wrong or that another visitor has arrived. (An outside observer trained to a different and negative evaluation of whispering in company has to make an adjustment to local mores—perhaps more of a strain than learning the meaning of some totally new element.)

As in other communities, there are polite formulas for numerous occasions, e.g., greetings, thanks, apologies, or terminating a visit. Men usually offer thanks for hospitality and leave. Women will offer their excuses: "I must go home now, there is nobody watching the house," or "I must go home now, or my husband will beat me." Rundi women may not properly leave their homes without permission from their husbands, so that reference to the common and socially-accepted practice of wife-beating means simply that permission to leave the house had not been requested. It is as likely to be offered as an excuse by a peasant woman as by a lady so distinguished for her gentility that she has been selected as governess in a princely residence. (Again, an outside observer may have to overcome a certain "culture shock" the first few times the threat of a beating is daintily offered in farewell.)

PARALINGUISTIC
AND KINESIC SIGNS

To comprehend Rundi communication fully also requires knowledge of conventional gestures, sometimes replaced by statements, e.g., the action or phrase, "I pull up grass for you" is a sign of subservience and gratitude. Among the nonlinguistic vocal signals is one that in the United States is the Indian war cry, in Iran the populace's cheer for the shah, but in Burundi, the cry of alarm sent out into the hills to solicit help when animal or human marauders threaten a household.

Paralinguistic and kinesic signs have been indicated above as intrinsic to specific speech situation behavior. Possibly the radical, highly visible physical differences among the several castes of Barundi facilitate explicit naming and explaining of non-verbal signs, and categorizing them as "Tutsi" or "Hutu." For the outsider learning the culture, however, the subtleties are not so easily or quickly mastered. For example, open mockery was the corrective initial treatment applied to the error of assuming that anyone over six feet tall was a Mututsi. Detailed accounts of speech and gesture patterns used as cues by the Barundi were offered as aid to the ignorant foreigner. Not only authentic Batutsi and Bahutu, short and tall, but also several Bahutu who came by their elegant Tutsi manners honestly as servants in upper-caste households, were introduced as visual aids. Instruction continued throughout the fieldwork period. The initial error apparently seriously traumatized the staff and neighbors. Presumably their own pride required that the observer, fitted into the social system as a member of the upper caste, learn to recognize and to use the appropriate role patterns. Again, the extraordinary sensitivity of Barundi to speech behavior and the ease of verbalization associated with their socialization and social control patterns not only brought into prominence the fact of cultural patterning of speech behavior but also much facilitated the research.

SUMMARY OF SOCIAL
STRUCTURAL VARIABILITY

The patterning of speech behavior in Burundi in relation to social structure involves rules governing the specific relationships among those present in a speech situation according to caste, age and sex, kinship, friendship, contiguous residence, or political-economic ties. Distinctions are made according to the social roles of those present; the degree of formality, publicity or privacy; and the objectives of the speech situation. Together, social role and situational prescriptions determine the order of precedence of speakers, relevant conventions of politeness, appropriate formulas and styles of speech, including extralinguistic signs, and topics of discussion. Socialization and sanctions are also determined by the social role-situational complexes within which discourse occurs.

Ubgenge: The Allocation of Intellectual Resources

ETHNOEPISTEMOLOGICAL VALUES

The conceptual context of the uses of intellectual resources, among which speech ranks high in many societies, is the cultural world-view and value system. Understanding the patterning of the content and style of speech in Burundi depends in part upon awareness of the cultural conceptions of truth, falsehood, and fiction and of their value priorities and interrelations. The key concept to the norms and values associated with the uses of language is *ubgenge,* "successful cleverness." *Ubgenge* chiefly applies to intellectual-verbal management of significant life-situations. Situational adaptability is a permanent condition of action. Hence, the specific manifestations of *ubgenge* are numerous and diverse. The cleverness of a rogue; the industriousness of a virtuous man whose overlord gives him a cow as a reward for virtue; the skill of a good psychologist-rhetorician in persuading a generous, impulsive—or inebriated—superior to give him a cow, although he had done nothing to earn it; the skill of a medical curer; the success of a practical joker who has victimized a simple-minded peasant or feeble-minded boy; the wise and just judgments of the *abashingantahe,* the "elders," in courts and councils; and the technological accomplishments of Europeans are equally good examples of *ubgenge* —for they all succeed in bringing something good to their designers. In effect, success is beautiful and good, and the beautiful is more likely to succeed than the inelegant. Factual accounts of the use of *ubgenge* and fables and legends of successful cleverness evoke strong, positive, esthetic appreciation.

In the Rundi vocabulary, the distinctions made between fact and fiction, knowledge and conjecture, truth, error, and falsehood, are close equivalents to those of Western culture. Their hierarchical order and situational relativity, however, reflect Rundi interpretations of the values of survival, esthetics, and the satisfaction of desire. Lexical distinctions are made between literal truth and fact, outright lies, errors, misleading others and being misled or ill-informed, offering a hypothesis without sufficient prior knowledge, foolishly offering an explanation despite ignorance in order to seem knowledgeable, and formulating a hypothesis or making a judgment on the basis of satisfactory evidence. Oriented more to persons and personalities than to abstract principles, the Barundi also name these degrees of difference of reliability in substantives designating types of persons. Context distinguishes shades of meaning of *kuvuga,* to speak; *kumva,* to hear, to understand, to conceive of; and *kumenya,* to know, to observe, to perceive. Culturally distinctive referents have also to be noted. Labeling a man a liar does not reflect a tendency to falsify factual statements, but rather denotes an individual guilty of breaking a promise to give a gift or to do a favor. Of especial emotional impact is calumny. The calumniator who reports evil of a man, with or without good grounds, is perhaps more feared than any social threat, even witchcraft in some instances, since it may lead to deprivation of property, protection of a superior, or loss of life itself.

The cultural requirement of the fine rhetorical style applies to all public speaking, though methods and techniques vary with objectives. Logic is the correct method for the *umushingantahe,* whose goal is to arrive at a sound judgment—as a judge presiding in a formal court of law or informally adjudicating a family dispute, offering counsel at the behest of a political superior, or decision-making and problem-solving generally in the conduct of life's serious business. Sophistic rhetoric is the natural and acceptable resort of self-interested individuals, whether they are seeking to win a lawsuit or to procure a gift or protection from a superior or to satisfy a desire or to fulfill a need. The usual techniques include evasions, falsehoods, flattery, and other calculated appeals to and attempted manipulations of the emotions.

Adults of both sexes in all caste and age groups learn both logical and rhetorical techniques and criteria and the situations in which they are applicable. A well-developed ethnopsychology is as pervasive through all types of speech situation as is the esthetic. The emotive and esthetic are twin necessities of discourse. The relative frequencies of logic-oriented and rhetoric-oriented speech situations and their specific objectives depend on age and position in the social structure. The higher a man is placed, the less often need he defend himself, for the fewer are his superiors. On the other hand, they are more likely to be highly intelligent and powerful and therefore dangerous. Defenses against numerous clever inferiors competing for favor have also to be mounted with greater frequency, the higher the individual's place in the social-political-economic hierarchies.

UMUSHINGANTAHE: LOGICAL AND RHETORICAL IDEAL VALUES

The highest ideal of public speaking is associated with the role of *umushingantahe*. Informants of different age, caste, and social roles agree on the criteria and can verbalize them without hesitation. A good judge is intelligent, in complete command of the arts of logic, a fine speaker— i.e., he speaks slowly and with dignity, in well-chosen words and figures of speech; he is attentive to all that is said; he has a good memory, enabling him to compare different reports of events; he cannot be bribed; and he is an able analyst of logic, empirical evidence, and the vagaries of the human psyche. Initiation as *umushingantahe* comes late—usually not before forty-five. It is restricted to men of means who can pay for the costly initiation party and who have demonstrated their ability, usually in a prolonged apprenticeship of attendance at cases conducted by those reputed to be good judges. The qualifications stipulated for judges are explained as indispensable to the resolution of conflicts. It is assumed that the self-interest and emotional involvements of disputants and witnesses will lead them to falsify evidence, to exaggerate accounts of damage or make excessive claims for compensation, and even to perjure themselves. Testimony is likely to be contradictory. All human relationships involve matching wits, but in law cases and political strategy councils, there is a premium on good judgment based on clear logic and control of reliable information.

Principles for the analysis of testimony are readily verbalized by court judges. They closely resemble the principles in use in the Western world. Contradictory statements cannot both be true, so a choice must be made; the discovery of the truth depends upon evidence; in its evaluation, the credibility of witnesses has to be weighed; eyewitness testimony is the most reliable. So insistent is the demand for direct evidence that where it is possible and relevant, a judge may adjourn court and go in person to verify statements, e.g., respecting the location of a boundary marker between properties. Usually, however, such direct examination is not possible. To get at the truth, judges will subject principals and witnesses one at a time in closed interrogation sessions to repeated questioning if contradictory testimony has been given. After sifting and winnowing to come to a conclusion as to the actual facts, the judge will probably recall each one who has testified, confront him with his own contradictions or the heavy weight of probability against him, and usually contrive to get an admission as to the true state of affairs.

The use of psychological observation and principles is part of the judge's apparatus, an adjunct to logical analysis and fact-finding. Rules for detecting lies, exaggerations, and other departures from fact, and for spotting subtle cues to distinguish guilty from innocent nervousness or eloquence, are easily and even proudly verbalized by experienced elders. In addition, the judges have mastery over appropriate rhetorical techniques for wearing down stubborn witnesses, quieting overexcited ones, browbeating by silence or scorn, and various other devices that experience has shown will give the judge, hence the truth, the upper hand. There is no tolerance for the technique of "strategic obfuscation" used by many Barundi to the despair of trial lawyers and judges during European trusteeship government, viz., calculated inconsistencies in accounts of events directed (often with great success) to so obscuring the truth that no case could be made.

In dealing with domestic disputes, judges are concerned primarily with psychological and social factors and proceed to fact-finding only if it is relevant. For example, a judge must discover from the spoken words and the general demeanor of a couple demanding a divorce whether a divorce is in keeping with their wishes and best interests or whether in truth they wish to save face by having the court order them back together again. In settling quarrels between father and son, a judge has a doubly difficult task. Custom has it that the elder is never wrong. The judge must discover what really happened. If in fact the father is at fault, he must find a way to tell him so and to impose a suitable mild penalty on the son without openly stating that it is the father who is in the wrong.

Determination of appropriate principles and techniques for each case is an integral part of *ubgenge,* as much for the cleverness of a judge as for the wisdom of any mature person in the conduct of life's business. Each one must make judgments—to decide whether a wife should be kept or be sent back to her father and the bride-price refunded; to choose as the heir the son who will be best able to carry on the responsibility of head of the family; to select spouses for sons and daughters; to choose or dismiss feudal inferiors; to choose or to abandon a feudal superior. Truth, as fact tied into a web of sound logical organization, is indispensable where sound judgment is the objective.

THE SURVIVAL VALUE OF
DISCRETION AND FALSEHOOD

Though truth is necessary for judgment, it is not useful for survival or practical success. The Barundi make no bones about this. The proverb is often quoted, "The man who tells no lies cannot feed his children." Another proverb warning against truth reveals further the awareness of the Barundi that speech is not simply an instrument of social life but is often a weapon: "Truth is good, but not all that is true is good to say." Truth is not valuable in itself but is relative to other values. It is positively required when judgment is needed, positively dangerous when a person must defend himself or wishes to maintain or better his position.

The need for discretion, a halfway house between literal truth and bald lie, is understood as either not speaking at all about delicate matters or as refurbishing facts so that they wear an innocent face. Discretion is appropriate to a wide variety of situations in life. Its specific character depends on specific situations and actors. In political matters (probably the chief concern of Barundi at every level of the society) discretion is necessary as a self-defensive measure. Information about the misbehavior or the faults of a political superior is best concealed, at least until such time as he has lost status and is thereby deprived of power to harm. Loyalty to a superior is defined largely in terms of what is said about him. If one spreads praises abroad—and *amazina,* poems based on praise-names composed for a superior are one of the formalized means of demonstrating loyalty—then one may hope for a reward. The formula "I shall sing your praises" is an often spontaneous response to a gift and a significant token of devotion. It has already been mentioned that social inferiors can use as a sanction against superiors publicizing his lack of generosity or other defects. However, if one speaks ill of a superior or plots against him, the disloyalty will bring down heavy punishment on the guilty one if it reaches the superior's ears.

Among socio-political "equals," that is, those seeking favor with the same political superior, calumny is the chief weapon, discretion the best shield. Given the importance and quantity of verbal report in gossip and in calculated calumny and praise that may reach the ears of the superior, safety absolutely requires concealing faults and devising means to counteract calumny, whether or not it has a basis in fact. No one is so high or low in the social scale, no one so secure in the affections of a superior or inferior, as to be able to afford the luxury of speaking the unedited truth. Few if any individuals are so lacking in intelligence and in an esthetic sense of graceful, appropriate discourse as to blurt out truths without restraint or to reply truthfully to questions from the inquisitive. In relations between husband and wife and in family relations generally, verbal discretion is a serious matter. A lazy wife or a sterile one may or may not be sent back home. A disloyal woman, by definition, one who speaks ill of her husband, will surely be severely punished and rejected. A disobedient son may be tolerated and even procure his share of the inheritance, but a disloyal one may be disinherited.

In lesser matters than life and property and position, discretion still has its place. One may discuss with close friends and neighbors the problems created by a spouse who is a bit slow-witted, but not broadcast the fact far and wide. If one suspects that a neighbor is a witch, one refrains from mentioning it in his presence. There is no point in accusing him, it is said, for he will say, "Death is not afraid to come, whether you speak of it or not," or, "Whom have I killed? Have you caught me at it?" There are, then, some truths not to be spoken aloud to anyone; some to a faithful spouse or a blood brother but nobody else; some to close relatives or neighbors. Only rarely is any statement so innocent that it is not necessary to consider the possibility that it will bring trouble. That words are powerful realities is a fundamental truth of the Rundi system of belief and behavior.

There is a premium, practical and esthetic, on rapid, graceful, and more-than-plausible falsehood. Especially if anyone is directly accused of wrongdoing, on-the-spot composition of an effective defense is necessary. In general, a man is safer when he thinks quickly and lies, mixing the right amount of flattery for his superior with the other ingredients of his discourse, than when he tells the truth, good though the truth may be in some situations. There seems no anxiety, where lies are told or false accusations made, as to the possible consequences of subsequent discovery of the facts. If one survives the critical moment, it is explained, one may find a way to deal with an ungainly or inconvenient truth if and when it appears. The time gained by on-the-spot inventions of defense is associated with an optimistic interpretation of the uncertainty of the future. Escape to another part of the country; a generous gift to the right person; a change in mood of the feudal protector or accuser; in fact, anything may happen.

A cool head counts for more than a high I.Q. in realizing the practical-esthetic-emotive values of effective speech. Everyone knows the rules. Everyone plays the game of matching wits through verbal parry and thrust. Differences of individual skills, the likelihood of fortuitous circumstances, and the inherent instability of emotions make it certain that there will be few dull moments. Uncertainty of the outcomes of verbal manipulations of one's affairs is built into the system and is part of the game, enjoyed when the outcome is favorable, lamented when it is not.

AN ILLUSTRATION OF
UBGENGE IN ACTION

A full account of rhetorical styles and techniques and of situations in which they are to be used would be necessary to a full description of the role of *ubgenge* in speech behavior. A single illustration must suffice to indicate the way in which Rundi values, esthetic and practical, operate in behavior. It is contemporary in theme, traditional in form, and enjoyed equally for its success and elegance of design. For what such assurance may in fact be worth, the narrative was sworn to as having actually occurred—but, of course, not to the narrator. A Murundi chief, who will remain nameless, of course, was very rude to a young Murundi agricultural officer. Instead of doing as he was told, viz., collecting a labor force to start a coffee plantation, the chief went off to drink with one of his favorite tenants. His delinquency discovered, the chief was roundly scolded by the agricultural officer and assured that a report would be made to the higher authoritities, i.e., to the Belgian senior agricultural officer of the region. In due course, the summons came. The chief ordered his wife to fill three huge baskets with food and he dressed in his finest robes. With his porters carrying the baskets, he proceeded to the office of the Belgian administrator. He was accused of refusing to provide workers to plant coffee, of rudeness as well as disobedience to the junior officer present, of permitting his cattle to browse on the plot designated for the coffee plantation. On hearing the accusation, the chief looked very grieved and surprised. "Sir," he said, with all the respect and elegance his education enabled him to muster, "I have never seen this person. Since he knows my lands, perhaps he is the one about whom my tenants complained a few weeks back as demanding beer and getting drunk and disorderly." He waited for a moment for his statement to take effect, counting on the suspicion of a national weakness for beer and tendency to false report to be transferred from him to the junior officer. He then went on, "I am here because I have heard that you are suffering from famine. Here are the few humble baskets of food I could assemble in haste, but do not fear, there are many more on the way. I wish you all health." Of course, the administrator was furious with his junior officer and very favorably impressed by the chief. The officer was punished, the chief courteously released. On the way home the chief passed a church. Being a good Christian, he stopped to pray. He addressed himself to God, confessing his false accusation of the young agricultural officer, a fellow-Murundi and a fellow-Christian. He explained to the Lord that he knew he had sinned, but he begged forgiveness. "O God, surely you will pardon me. Since you did not save me, I had to save myself."

Literary Form and Literal Truth

THE ESTHETIC HIERARCHY
OF SPEECH FORMS

Practicality, esthetic values, and literal truth in different proportions characterize most Rundi discourse that satisfies cultural criteria for speech. Descriptive precision and literal description are relevant not only in the fact-finding situation of judgment but also in discussion of objects of central interest. Kinship, economic matters, and social control—especially where they involve the ownership and inheritance of land and cattle—as well as speech itself, are matters in which direct, precise discourse is called for. Literal descriptions of cattle and agriculture involve vocabularies of minutely detailed discriminations beyond the capacities of an outsider to appreciate. Barundi are intensely interested in human psychology, and the extensive vocabulary and shrewd generalizations of the ethnopsychology supply linguistic evidence of the cultural concern with motives, emotions, intelligence levels, and personality types.

Although the demand for esthetic composition and delivery applies to descriptive discourse as to all speech, factual accounts are at the bottom of a culturally defined series of steps of esthetic complexity. Public address may be placed at the midpoint. At the top of the esthetic scale is the rich tradition of oral literature. The various types of literary composition have well-defined social and practical functions and communication content often of great significance, but esthetic criteria are most stringent for poetry, prose (including the narration of historical events), songs, proverbs, and stylized conversational formula. While criteria for everyday conversation are near the bottom of the scale, elegance of composition and delivery, figures of speech, and the interpolation of stores and proverbs are expected and employed.

THE PREEMINENCE OF
INDIRECT REFERENCE

Praise-poems (*amazina,* literally "names," figuratively, "praise-names," are composed to honor a generous superior or the author's valor in battle. Highly refined literary-rhetorical skills, composition and delivery of *amazina* are included in the speech training of young boys of good family. The form is fixed but the contents are created impromptu. The naturally alliterative character of Kirundi as a Bantu language is reinforced by conscious selection of assonant words in the construction of praise-names and figures of speech. There are slight though perceptible modifications in wording and number of verses as authors repeat their steadily increasing store of *amazina* on appropriate occasions. Nobody borrows the *amazina* of others, except to learn composition, but each must demonstrate his own abilities. For some, virtuosity earns wide fame. An elderly man with a long history of bravery and gifts of cattle may fill three of four hours with his chanted recitation.

The *amazina* in fact are repositories of Rundi history. This is not immediately evident from their content. The chief requirement for esthetic accomplishment in literature is indirect reference. The value and delicacy of a composition depends on the remoteness and subtlety of the allusion. Composition of *amazina* is primarily for the upper castes, where in any event the criteria for elegant speech behavior are determined. However, there are also farmers' *amazina* of sorts, praise-poems to honor hoes, bees, and other things of interest to them. A prosperous peasant may compose praises for the patron who has given him cattle. Clever cow thieves, much-dreaded members of the community, may compose *amazina* in self-praise: since the punishment for stealing cattle is immediate crucifixion if the thief is caught in the act and since precautions against stealing are elaborate, a cow thief who lives to tell the tale has earned the right to his *amazina*.

A large stock of traditional figures of speech and inventions of new ones are used in *ibicuba* (songs composed by cowherds in praise of their herds), in hunting songs, lullabies, tales, fables, and riddles. Thousands of proverbs, old and new, are in some cases direct, but in others more or less subtly allusive. Cultural skill in inventing and interpreting figurative speech and allusions is general, but indirect reference also operates to define boundaries between in-groups and out-groups in various situations. At a princely court, a man may sing a tale full of allusions understood only by the prince himself or only by a few of those present. The incomprehensibility of the allusions is in itself meaningful. Listeners know something is in the wind, and they are not slow to inquire and to find out. If the information were not intended to be made public, it would not have been presented at all; if it were common knowledge, the allusions would not have been incomprehensible. Like the rhetorical technique of strict silence, the poetic technique of not quite telling all has positive information content of great significance.

News is carried from one neighborhood to another by individuals on various types of business, but especially by a sort of self-appointed minstrel who sings the news, accompanying himself on a seven-string zither. Great humor, sly and stinging in many cases, is part of the performance, and indirect reference is characteristic. Indirectness of reference through figures of speech is a popular device in polite social intercourse. Gratitude for a gift of beer and cigarettes, both much enjoyed, requires more than a simple word of thanks, e.g., from a visitor who had been ill at the time such a gift was given to him: "I know a man who named his child *Inzokira*, 'I shall be saved'. For, first he received beer and then he received tobacco. Through these, his spirits and his health were restored." Discussing the hardships of life, an old gentleman may remark: "Once I was strong, and now I am weak. Indeed, in the daytime, the sun shines strongly, but at night it is gone. And for me, it is now night."

A request to a superior for a trifling gift, e.g., a new pair of shoes, does not take the form, "I am a poor man, you are rich; please give me money for a new pair of shoes; as you see, these I have are torn to shreds." Rather: "One does not hide one's misfortunes; if one tries to hide them, they will nevertheless soon be revealed. Now, I know a poor old man, broken in health and ill; there is a spear stuck in his body and he cannot be saved." A terminal gesture directs attention to a pair of ragged old tennis shoes, one of the pair held together by means of a "spear," i.e., a safety pin.

In addition to idioms, i.e., locutions that are incomprehensible if taken literally, there are in Rundi discourse a number of stylistic conventions that would make statements incomprehensible or misleading if taken literally. Speaking of a revolutionary (there was much domestic political disturbance in the 1920s), it is conventional to say, "Nobody knows who he is; nobody knows his family." The speaker knows perfectly well and will go on to tell in great detail the history of the patrilineage in question, its alliances, successes and failures, and ultimate destruction: the conventional introduction is a negative value judgment or outright insult. If anyone says of a man, "He has no children, there will be nobody to bury him," this must not be taken literally, especially if it is said in the presence of the man's sons. It means that some of his sons have died, literally, "He fathered many, but many have died." In a somewhat lighter vein, the statement, "I went to X's house but there was no beer," means in fact that only a few quarts were downed, but either the total available supply was small or the number of visitors great, or the reception was not friendly enough, so there was no point in staying on, one's thirst would not be quenched. The name traditionally given to an eleventh or twelfth child is *Bujana,* "Hundreds," signifying that the family is a large one. Stylized exaggeration is also common in practical contexts, notably in economic or political negotiations, claims for damages, and in praises—a generous person may be called *mwami,* king, or *Imana,* God.

FICTIONAL FORMS FOR FACTUAL
DATA: AN ILLUSTRATION

Generally, what men must understand is other men. All else is fit at best for *imigani,* tales, fables, and proverbs. The deity is far above man and beyond human comprehension. There are tales of Imana's creation of the universe and of his benevolent dispositions toward men, but it is futile to wonder about his nature or why he created things as he did.

The natural environment is a passive instrument of various powers. Storms, lightning, midday sun, and heavy rain tend to be unfriendly to man and hence require ritual attention. Otherwise, nature is not important. Techniques and commodities introduced from European culture are warmly welcomed and much admired, but they are not human and therefore do not stir intellectual curiosity.

Life is here and now, so the past and future are of little interest. Older men may entertain the younger generation with family history or accounts of wars and political events of the past in which they have participated or to which they have been eyewitness. These automatically become fiction to the listeners because of the remoteness of the events and the requirement for literary embellishment, especially allusiveness and figures of speech, in the style of narration. A single illustration may suffice to indicate the way in which historical events are likely to be presented.

The leader of the Abadagi was a man named Gahezeri Binyori Dagi. He asked Mwongereza for one of his daughters in marriage. This was a trick, for he only wanted to obtain passage through the property of Mwongereza. Once he had married the girl, he asked for permission to hunt elephants. Mwongereza asked him to pay the hunting tax, but Dagi refused. Dagi then went to Mbiligi to ask him for a place on which to settle. While they were talking, Mwongereza appeared. He asked Mbiligi, "What did Dagi say to you?" Mbiligi answered, "He has asked me for a place on which to settle." "Be careful," warned Mwongereza, "he is deceiving you. He wants to take over all your property and then chase you away." After that, Dagi fought with Mwongereza, whom Mbiligi helped. They killed Dagi, and after that Mwongereza and Mbiligi became good friends.

Once a few indirect references and some Africanized eponyms are understood, the tale is a fairly straightforward though condensed account of World War I in Central Africa. *Dagi* is the Rundi version of *Deutsch* and means *"the German."* The plural prefix, *aba-*, makes of Abadagi "the Germans," who were in control of Burundi prior to World War I. *Mwongereza* is "the English," the word composed of the singular personal prefix *mu-*, modified to *mw-* before a vowel, and *-Ongereza,* the Rundi rendering of "English," reflecting the interchangeability of "*r*" and "*l*" in intermediate positions. *Mbiligi,* with *mu-* reduced for euphony to *m-*, is "the Belgian." The rest is history. The Germans are represented by Dagi, an eponymous treacherous adventurer; the marriage is a simple symbol of alliance; European interest in the ivory trade is suggested by the reference to elephant hunting; "killing," in the story and in other literary forms, is stylized exaggeration for reference to inflicting damage or defeat; the subsequent shift in alliance that excluded Germany but made England and Belgium friends is also a familiar process in Rundi history and needed no comment. It is taken for granted that each narrator will invent his own way of telling a story and, if he can, a new way for each telling. Multiple versions of historical events are common. The same is true of other nonvital types of discourse, e.g., origin tales or descriptions of nature and of natural events.

IMPLICATIONS FOR FIELDWORK

Attention to at least the most salient and accessible features of the cultural patterning of speech behavior in Burundi was in part a necessity imposed by the speech-oriented content of the pattern, in part a by-product of field research directed to the cultural philosophy, especially the value system. Consequently, the description offered above is in many respects defective. It is incomplete descriptively, and the analytic model reflects an inelegant mixture of informants' and observer's categories and information. The methods and techniques of ethnophilosophy by which the fieldwork research was conducted are resistant to orderly, complete specification, but even if explicated would not be applicable without modification to a study intended primarily to describe the cultural patterning of speech behavior. Nevertheless, even a rough approximation to such a pattern is useful as a starting point for exploring the potential instrumental utility of knowledge of the speech behavior pattern of the culture for the conduct of ethnographic research generally and for projecting possibilities for substantive studies in the ethnography of communication which are focused directly on speech behavior.

The potential for misunderstanding verbal behavior in Burundi and consequently for misperceiving other behavior is obviously high. There is a proportionately high necessity for understanding the uses of language in the context of the culture's social structure, world-view, and value system. Awareness of radical discrepancy between expected and observed verbal behavior came early in the fieldwork. Specifically, earlier research on values had proceeded on the assumption that the relevant data were not easily accessible. For example, it was assumed that value judgments and evaluations were relatively infrequent and obscure in discourse and their elucidation by informants problematic. However, it was immediately obvious that the Barundi habitually terminated descriptions of events or persons or observations about cattle or the weather with an appropriate moral proverb or other evaluative statement. In general, no utterance or discussion seemed complete until a value judgment had been rendered. By contrast, seemingly innocuous questions, for example about child-rearing or food, were often met with silence or evasion. Apparently, there are no intrinsically innocent or taboo topics for all societies. Preoccupation with speech as an instrument of survival and success and as an identifying criterion of social status was evident if not intrusive in general discussion. The assumptions and values expressed and the techniques described and observed bore a startling resemblance to those of Plato's enemies, the Sophists. Clearly, a revision of expectations and constant awareness of the cultural assumptions of the observer were in order.

Reasonable progress in fieldwork became possible only as the local speech behavior pattern was learned. To obtain a reasonably clear, correct, and comprehensive set of data, it was necessary to find ways around the high cultural evaluation of clever lies and evasions and to devise means to penetrate the elegant but often incomprehensively subtle literary allusions. For Barundi (and possibly for a number of similar societies in Africa and the Mediterranean countries), the rules of procedure for data gathering included: (1) avoiding direct questions, except in such matters as asking which road leads to Kitega or Nyabikere; (2) learning the cues by which individuals signal an intention to use sometimes lengthy disquisitions superficially concerned with religion or custom merely as a request for a gift; (3) locating verbal and other cues by which individuals unconsciously signal either ignorance of the subject on which they are pretending to give information or intentional distortion—for example, one elderly gentleman, the easiest to deal with, invariably told a whopping lie each time he volunteered his assurance that he did not lie; (4) seeking and comparing alternative accounts of institutions, customs, or events since only rarely do different individuals lie about or conceal the same facts; (5) learning good language manners to minimize interpersonal friction and incomprehension; and (6) more generally, learning in detail the patterns of language use and specific meaning—in effect, playing the game of matching wits with informants, albeit against high odds.

"LEARNING THE LANGUAGE" AS
LEARNING SPEECH BEHAVIOR

A culture pattern of speech behavior is in principle easily researched. As we know, however, it must be made an object of inquiry since neither data nor patterns insist upon being observed. In the normal course of research, language and its accompanying signs are used instrumentally to obtain information on whatever subject we are researching, whether kinship or political behavior, world-view or linguistic structure, even semantic fields and taxonomies. As an instrument of research, it does not attract our attention. To make it an object of early, intensive study as part of learning the language imposes a special strain. It is a condition of normal, instrumental language use that language behavior be or become unconscious.

The analogy between enculturation of the young and the anthropological fieldworker's induction into the ways of the culture he is studying, though of limited utility, is instructive with respect to some of the problems of speech behavior study. For the ethnographer, as for the young members of society, the language is the chief means of communication and enculturation. Command of the language and culture requires far more than control of lexicon and syntax, and more than control of paralinguistic and kinesic signs. Good speech manners may be more useful than technical control of the linguistic features of language, in much the same way that native speakers' intonation contours are more conducive to efficient communication than an extensive vocabulary or impeccable grammar.

To all appearances, language learning is the medium by which the young learn not only the social roles which they will have to perform or to recognize but also the conceptual and value system. Inculcating speech behavior patterns is part of the process. Only some parts of the enculturation processes to which the young are subject are verbally explicit or in the form of such easily observed behavioral signs as spankings for punishments or sweetmeats for rewards. It is here that the analogy between child language learning and ethnographer's language learning begins to break down. Ethnographers are not children and cannot be taught as children are. Rather, they are adult strangers and can expect to be treated as members of that category. Not only are sanctions different but also exposure to nonexplicit instruction is limited. Further, unlike the child in process of learning his mother tongue, the ethnographer already has his native language and the complex of behavioral and conceptual patterns acquired with it. These complicate further the usual difficulties of mastering even the mechanics of a second language acquired relatively late in life. To some extent, beliefs and values and role-playing directives appropriate to the new language may be unconsciously absorbed in the course of learning it. For a full representation or awareness of the speech behavior pattern, such unconscious learning of culture with language has to be shifted to the level of consciousness. Errors resulting from extension of our native-speaker habits of thought to the new language are pointed and easy lessons in correct speech behavior.

DENOTATIONS FOR TRANSLATING

Knowledge of local patterns of speech use is necessary even for the mundane business of correct literal interpretation of discourse. In studying kinship or color terminology, we are now far too wise to look for equivalents to the terms found in the investigator's language and culture. The difficulties presented when the observer's language lacks an equivalent term to one in the culture being studied are readily overcome by circumlocution. Such difficulties have the merit of being immediately evident to the observer. By contrast, as various anthropologists have pointed out, when an equivalent word exists in the language of the observer, there is a genuine threat to reliability. Each specific instance must be discovered and dealt with. Not only is the cultural-contextual meaning likely to be different but also the "same" words may not have the "same" referents. There is no apparent obstacle to asking a literal Kirundi equivalent to the English question, "How many children do you have?" But if a man answers, he will state only the number of his sons, if a woman, only the number of daughters. There are distinct words for children (*abana*), sons (*abahungu*) and daughters (*abakobwa*), but custom has it that only the same-sexed offspring will be counted. Further, paternity and maternity are highly valued, and their value is numerically determined. "Total" offspring (*abana bose*) includes the stillborn and those who died in infancy or childhood as well as the living. For accurate census data or merely to keep track of the living, it is necessary to ask a different question in Kirundi, viz., "What is the number of both sons and daughters now alive?" In principle, the idiomaticity of apparently straightforward discourse has to be kept in the forefront in language-use learning.

NAMING CATEGORIES
OF DISCOURSE

Seemingly familiar forms and ideas, it should be reiterated, are potentially a threat to reliable perception and reporting. That literary form is not a reliable index to the functions of discourse is one of the generalizable implications for theory and method of the examination of Rundi speech behavior. The priority of esthetic and practical values over literal truth and the explicit situational relativism of criteria governing the uses of language and intellect reflect that culture's social system and ethno-epistemology. The necessity for culturally specific interpretation of what is habitually identified as literary form is indicated by scattered data on many cultures. For example, poetry cannot properly be classed as exclusively or even primarily an esthetic phenomenon when, as is so often the case, its main significance is religious. Styles of forensic and political rhetoric vary widely. The demand for fiery oratorical style is strong in Burundi and many other places, but is explicitly deplored elsewhere, for example, among Navaho and Zuni Indians and in many parts of the present-day United States. Appropriate subjects and situations for literal description, as well as the hierarchy of interest in different types of knowledge—e.g., psychological, natural, supernatural—are also cultural variables that enter into the patterning of speech behavior. The uses and values of truth, although the concept of truth may be highly uniform, show variations other than those encountered in Burundi. For example, among Navaho Indians, the value of truth-telling is very high. A sharp line is drawn between in-group and out-group. Truth is for the in-group.

Lying to outsiders or performing other negative acts toward them will either be given different names or different evaluations, or both.

Literary style can be misleading to the researcher. That a curer or rain-maker uses ritual formulas and a collection of bones or feathers is not a relevant datum for evaluating the *empirical* efficacy of the totality of his procedures. The same holds when customary technology is explained as a gift of the gods or of culture heroes. These rationales are not "scientific" in form or content. Nevertheless, trial and error have in every society produced reasonably and sometimes highly reliable empirical sciences. To infer from the ritualistic procedures and literary form that the procedures are so much hocus-pocus is to be misled by appearances and is contrary to scientific criteria, which call for suitable technical training, laboratory facilities, and observation of the behavioral complexes and actual consequences of the uses of mythical or ritual formulas. This is not to say that all ritual formulas are science in disguise but rather to emphasize the culture-bound distortion introduced by treating style as a universal clue to the referential significance of terms or statements or formulas.

Multiple versions of the "same" events cannot be interpreted as though the Western rationalistic demand for strict consistency and uniform, standard description were universal. Different versions of origin tales or so-called mythopoeic history may well be the product of conscious art and effort as in Burundi, not signs of confusion about facts. Many types of discourse regarded as nonfiction in the West, on religious and secular subjects, are found in multiple versions and literary form in many societies. Before we know with what name to label samples of discourse, we need to know the cultural assumptions about the nature of truth and its range of relevance, as well as the prescribed literary forms for communicating different types of subject matter in different situations. Informants may be relied upon to know about matters of such importance and wide dispersion in their culture.

In principle, anthropological inquiry is free from invidious comparison with the observer's culture, where it does not bend over backwards to make kindly interpretations. Yet, it is not improbable that some sense of obligation to play fair or to show a culture in a favorable light affects the selection, naming, and presentation of materials in what is intended as objective reporting. Here, it seems a courtesy due the Barundi to state that we are all well aware that although our highest ideals are different from theirs, the practices in their explicit system of rhetoric and in our actual practice bear a close resemblance. In Western culture, the tricks of the rhetorician's trade, altering or concealing truths, hatching plots, and various other aspects of practical speech behavior would perhaps be called sophistry rather than rhetoric. It is a happy accident that the

Barundi make explicit and accept as right a set of rhetorical norms diametrically opposed to the ideals but excellently descriptive of the practices found in Western culture. The contrast makes for high visibility and suggests that for the sake of objectivity and in the interest of full description, knowledge of cultural values governing the uses of speech should be treated as intrinsic to the method and theory of studies of speech behavior.

Omitted from the description of Rundi speech behavior were several special languages (court language and a variety of formalized "talking with tongues" used in an obsolescent possession cult); oaths, insults, and curses; and speech situations not open to strangers (e.g., political caucuses, some illegal religious and curing ceremonies, and story-telling sessions after dark within the houses). The full list of types of discourse and speech situations discriminated in any culture has in all likelihood to be sought within the culture and degrees of publicity and privacy discovered.

SPEECH AS BEHAVIOR:
DATA COLLECTION

Speech is usually an adjunct to or instrument of other behavior, but it is the primary identifying characteristic of such phenomena as oratory, story telling, gossiping, and joking. Studies of speech behavior require data on both adjunct and primary speech events and theory and methods appropriate to behavioral research. Looking beyond accidental and trial-and-error discoveries, we may suggest some types of data and techniques relevant to study of the cultural patterning of speech behavior.

Speech is so important and pervasive in any society that at least those with the reputation for wisdom or success are probably capable of stating the norms that govern the uses of speech. Moreover, enculturation includes instruction of the young not only in the mechanics of speaking but also in the patterns of speech behavior. Hence, virtually any adult and probably many young people are potential sources of relevant information, direct or inferential. With speech behavior, as with other phenomena, once alerted to the subject, we perceive it with increased frequency and attention. It is probably easiest to start with observation of primary speech events, i.e., formal speech making, recitations of oral literature, courtroom proceedings, and whatever situations bear the extra-linguistic signs that define the role of "a speaker" in contrast to "an audience." In due course, an inventory could be made of the cultural answers to such questions as, "On what occasions—and of whom—are formal speeches expected?" "When are tales, or poems, or riddles in order?" "Who is qualified or permitted to tell myths and legends?" Observation and questioning would normally be directed not only to language but also to conventional paralinguistic and kinesic signs. Comments about gestures, voice loudness, and voice control are pertinent data. Value judgments, spontaneous or elicited, should yield cultural criteria governing each class of speech and related extra-linguistic signs.

In general, fixed verbal formulas—conventional phrases, idioms, spells —though part of the record, are not rewarding as information about speaking. Their literal meaning may be lost, or their significance as "things" in their own right may overshadow their significance as verbal phenomena. Even the most literate or literary speaker of English would be in difficulties if asked to say more about "good-bye" than that it is a contraction of "God be with you," or to account for the malicious power inherent in reciting the Lord's Prayer backwards.

Examination of adjunct speech behavior is more complex. It is embedded in nonspeech situations, is far greater in quantity, and though far more varied in type than primary speech situations, is less likely to be neatly categorized either in the local lexicon for speaking behavior or in any existing external analytic schemes.

Socialization and social control explicitly directed to language use are probably easiest to begin work with. Nevertheless, practical difficulties must be expected. Only rarely in any culture is even a small part of speech instruction explicit, systematic, and localized in time and place. Similarly, occasions for criticism or correction are not easily predictable. Principally, we must observe speech events in which positive or negative comments are addressed to or made about an inexperienced or inexpert speaker. "Don't mumble!" and "Speak when you are spoken to!" are typical of the inglorious stuff of which we must construct our pattern. The criticism that someone is speaking too much, when it occurs, must be checked against the language being spoken since, not infrequently, even a laggard may be condemned as verbose if he is speaking a dialect or language in which the listener is not fluent. Consistent criticism of an individual for speaking too little probably reflects a cultural norm of correct quantity of speech for the occasion and social role. It is both relevant information and a basis for further questioning. "Talking out of turn" may also be noticed and criticized. In short, talk about talk should be noted and inquiry directed to its explanation.

Observations about the speech components of behavior of any kind may be useful in themselves and as cues to additional information. For example, an aside offered during the conduct of a law case in Burundi gave useful hints: "His aunt is speaking for him. He is too young to plead his own case." Inquiry into the ways in which pleading skills are acquired and criteria for ascertaining maturity in their use is then obviously in order, especially since adults of both sexes serve as their own advocates. Proverbs, axioms, or advice about good or correct speech will probably turn up in the course of time and can be used as a basis for eliciting more detailed information about the importance of speech, its powers, and its limitations.

Some of the norms governing speech, characteristically for norms in general, may be violated only at the risk of negative sanctions, while others may be violated with impunity. It is therefore desirable to pursue inquiry beyond discovery of the contents of the norms that define good speech, correct speech, elegant speech, or whatever criteria are employed in the culture. Barundi know and say that a well-brought-up woman (*imfura*) does not shout at or beat a disobedient servant. She corrects him gently, as a mother corrects a wayward child. But when specific violations are discussed, it is stated that the ideal is rarely if ever carried out in practice, excepting in the disagreeable sense that by and large mothers systematically shout at and beat their disobedient children. Such a rule belongs in the presentation of the pattern, but as an ideal which few if any persons are expected to realize. Alertness to cultural concessions to ideals and rules is appropriate not only for language behavior as such but also for other types of institutionalized signs. For example, a law case in Burundi is officially closed when the judge, plaintiff, defendants, and witnesses drink beer together. The accompanying verbal form asserts that all are now friends, that none will hold a grudge against the judge, and that the plaintiff and defendant will resume friendly relations. According to informants who know about or have been directly involved in litigation, this is a sham. It is only the battle that has ended; the war goes on. The principals will sooner or later find a fresh cause for litigation. The loser will probably slander the judge by asserting that his decision was influenced by a bribe, and he will quarrel with the witnesses for having failed to support him more effectively.

SAMPLING AND PATTERNING

Observation of speech behavior, noting spontaneous statements that are obviously or potentially about speaking, systematic questioning, and confirmatory observation should produce the data required for a comprehensive view of speech behavior. Construction of the culture pattern from the data, however, requires some principle of simplification and selection, as well as a model for organizing the data. In the nature of the case, adjunct speech behavior situations are nearly as numerous and varied as the totality of situations. Appreciation of their significance depends on understanding the general characteristics of the situations in which speech occurs. Since no individual controls an entire culture, a well-chosen sample of persons and situations is needed to construct the over-all pattern.

Ideally, the observer will uncover the speech patterns associated with all the social roles and speech situations distinguished in the culture. Simplification of the task is afforded by the complementarity between behavioral or institutional definitions of social roles and modes of speech as indicators of variability of social roles. Systematic shifts in lexicon or syntax, extra-linguistic signs, style, and permitted or appropriate topics and types of comment are among the defining characteristics of social role variation. They are also cues for differential definitions of situations, as distinguished by the persons in the culture. Complementarity between speech behavioral indices and nonlinguistic defining characteristics of social differentiation may be assumed to hold in any culture, but it is obvious that the descriptive details and actual categories will vary with each culture.

Somewhat more difficult to demonstrate and to characterize is interdependence between speech behavior patterns and the cultural worldview and value system. Far less is known about cultural logics and epistemology than about social structure. The exploration of the relationship between the allocation of intellectual resources and the uses of speech in Burundi suggests that there are deep-lying interdependencies between the world-view and value system on one side and patterns of speech behavior on the other. Research in ethnophilosophy requires attention to language in as many of its aspects as knowledge and time allow. In the course of such research, language use, almost of its own weight, moves out of the status of instrument to the status of a distinctive and substantive subpattern in its own right. This is perhaps only to say that speaking is behavior, and like other types of behavior, it is internally patterned within the general pattern of the culture.

Ethnophilosophy offers only one avenue of approach to the study of culture patterns of speech behavior. Refinement of methods and concepts is obviously needed. Moreover, not until more is known of each of the many aspects of speech behavior can specific linkages among the research results of different specializations be reliably established, e.g., between the lexicon and morphology of a language and the characteristics of the world-view of its speakers, or between the universal features of cognition or learning and the specific patterns of cultures and personalities, or between semantic fields or taxonomies and conceptual systems, or between patterns of speech behavior and related patterns of nonverbal behavior. Since the flow of human speech fills a reservoir of nearly infinite capacity, its study does not lack for materials with which to work.

3

Struck by Speech: The Yakan
Concept of Litigation[1]

CHARLES O. FRAKE

Charles Frake is Professor of Anthropology at Stanford
University. He received his doctorate at Yale University
and has taught at Harvard. His fieldwork in the Philippines, first with the Subanun of Mindanao and currently
among the Yakan, has been the basis for analysis of
several spheres of cultural behavior and cognition, including kinship, ecology, and religion. His current interests include the development and structure of Philippine creole Spanish. The present paper is reprinted from
an original appearing in *Law in Culture and Society*
(Nader 1969).

Frake's study exemplifies what has variously been
called the "ethnoscience," "ethnographic semantics," or
"new ethnography" approach to anthropological analysis
(Frake 1964c; Conklin 1962; Sturtevant 1964). It utilizes
the heuristic principles of descriptive linguistics in order
to improve the validity of ethnographic field investigations. The aim is to discover the ways in which members
of a community themselves categorize their own behavior and thus to overcome the tendency to superim-

Reprinted from Laura Nader, editor, *Law in Culture and Society*
(Chicago: Aldine Publishing Company, 1969); copyright © 1969 by
the Wenner-Gren Foundation for Anthropological Research, Inc.

[1] Field work among the Yakan in 1962, 1963–1964, and 1965–1966 was supported by a
United States Public Health Service Grant under the National Institute of Mental Health
and by an auxiliary research award from the Social Science Research Council. The statements in this paper are at a level of generality applicable to the Basilan Yakan as a whole and
represent knowledge that any adult Yakan could be expected to have. Yakan expressions
are represented by a linguistically motivated orthography, but certain canons of traditional
phonemic analysis are ignored ("a," for example, represents both /a/ and /e/ where this
contrast is neutralized). This practice enables dialect differences to be accounted for by
special rules applicable to a uniform orthography. /q/ is a glottal cathc, /e/ a mid-front
vowel, /j/ a voiced, palatal affricative.

pose one's own analytical categories, while aiming at a description that goes beyond mere observation and recording.

The methodological influence of linguistics appears in the attention to segmenting and classifying events within the stream of behavior. The informal nonfestive nature of the relevant Yakan situation or *scene*, e.g., means that the occurrence of litigation could not be recognized from the physical setting but only from the content and structure of the talk itself. The natural starting point for the analysis is, therefore, the Yakan's own legal terminology. The relevant named speech events are classified by the method of focusing on contrast within a frame to determine what counts as "the same" and "different." In this litigation is found to be definable within a set of four contrasting, successively inclusive speech events. These events constitute a set in virtue of being instances of the native category of "talking to each other." These speech events themselves were defined in response to a query such as "What are they doing?" The dimensions that underlie the set of speech events are identified as focus, purpose, role, and integrity of the event. Focus denotes the topic of the discussion. Integrity denotes the distinctiveness of the event and its occurrence in relation to others of the same or different scale (i.e., whether it includes or is included in others, is interruptible, is clearly bounded, etc.).

Having placed litigation as one kind of Yakan talk, Frake describes the nature and structure of litigation itself. From one standpoint, the description is an example of the ethnography of law. But note that it differs from more conventional ethnographies in that it concentrates on the *forms* of litigation, how members recognize that grounds for a case exist. As Frake puts it, "What we are trying to formulate are the conditions under which it is congruous, neither humorous nor deceitful, to state that

---

The ethnographic record upon which this description is based includes the investigator's observations of court sessions, transcriptions of forty-three tape-recorded trial sessions at all jurisdictional levels, and informants' interpretations of the content of these observations and texts. In addition, by living in Yakan households during the entire field period, the investigator was continually exposed to conversations related to litigation. Special acknowledgement is due to Samual Pajarito and Reuben Muzarin for assistance in recording and transcribing court sessions and to Hadji Umar of Giyung for many long discussions at Yakan law.

one is engaged in litigation. These conditions are the semantic features of concept in question." Frake views the Yakan legal system as a system of symbols or a "code for talking." His description attempts to give the rules of interpretation by which speakers evaluate this code. These rules are seen as being of the same abstract nature as the linguists' deep structure. The view of culture implied here is quite similar to that of Goodenough (1964) and Garfinkel (Chapter 10).

Frake's description is also a contribution to the ethnography of speaking, specifying the place of various verbal genres and particular acts of speech within the overall cultural activity, or speech situation, e.g., choice between *complaint* and *gossip* to initiate a charge; *limorok* "to slip through," i.e., to inadvertently tell A in the presence of B about a litigable offense of C, where B is likely to inform C; the dependence for compliance with a ruling on persuasive use of the elaborate verbal trappings that accompany the ruling; *admonition* and *prayer* as two of the three outcomes of a ruling. (A monographic study would, of course, give detailed analysis of each of these in its own right.) Other aspects of speaking enter, as with the forensic ability that is one of the qualifications of a judge, and the specification of norms of interaction governing allocation of speaking time and right to speak.

Ethnographic semantics has an important part in the description, regarding the criteria for an act to be interpretable as an "offense" and two of the three possible defenses against an accusation; each concerns the relation between a concept and instances of it. With regard to lexicon, notice also that it is social prestige, rather than intellectual impact, that accounts for the prevalence of loan words in Yakan legal discourse. The idiom, or semantic structure, of kinship is employed for the relations among the participants on each side of the dispute; the event is under the sign of speech itself, for the article's title refers to the principals on each side, who are "struck by speech."

The concluding comparison between two cultures points to the importance of this type of analysis for the proper interpretation of speech. Although the terms for litigation in Yakan and Subanun are superficially the same, they reflect different speech events and imply different things about the social relationships among participants. Two Yakan engaged in litigation probably are not serious enemies. This is not necessarily the case among the Subanun. The background knowledge furnished by this kind of analysis is thus an essential prerequisite for sociolinguistic work because it deals with basic problems of segmentation in speech events. Abrahams and Bauman (1970) and Faris (1968) provide additional related readings.

For an attempt to apply Frake's procedures to the ethnographic study of drug culture in the United States, see Agar (1971).

> *tiyaq ku tawwaq bissāh.*
> (Here I am struck by speech.)
> (Remark of an accused in a trial.)

The Yakan legal system is manifest almost exclusively by one kind of behavior: talk. Consequently the ethnographer's record of observations of litigation is largely a linguistic record, and the legal system is a code for talking, a linguistic code. In this chapter we focus initially on a small part of this talk, that representing the concept of litigation. Then, without giving a full description, we attempt to illustrate how a definition of this concept guides a description of the legal system, enables us to relate litigation with other activities within Yakan society, and finally, points the way toward meaningful comparisions with legal systems of other cultures.

The Yakan are Philippine Moslems inhabiting the island of Basilan located off the southern tip of Zamboanga Peninsula, a western extension of the island of Mindanao. Southwest of Basilan stretches the Sulu archipelago, a chain of small islands extending some 200 miles to within a few miles of the northeast coast of Borneo. Some 60,000 Yakan share Basilan's 1,282 square kilometers with Christian Filipinos concentrated along the north coast and with Taw Sug and Samal Moslems living mostly in coastal villages all around the island.[2] The Yakan are close linguistic kin of the sea-faring Samal; but, unlike them, practice an exclusively land-oriented economy: diversified grain, root, and tree-crop agriculture on ploughed fields and swiddens, commercial copra production, and cattle raising, Supplementary economic activities include plantation labor, distribution of cigarettes smuggled from Borneo by their Moslem broth-

[2] There are also Yakan speakers on Sakol, Malanipa, and Tumalutab islands just east of Zamboanga City. These communities are beyond the scope of this discussion.

ers, and banditry. These economic activities bring the Yakan into close contact with the Philippine economy, political system, and army. Having been given this much information, the anthropological reader has probably already classed the Yakan as "peasants," which is all right as long as it does not bring to mind a downtrodden, economically exploited, culturally deprived people submerged by the weight of some "great tradition."

Houses, mosques, and graveyards dot the Yakan countryside rarely revealing any obvious patterns of spatial clustering. Each, however, represents the focus of a pattern of social alignment. Houses are occupied by nuclear families, independent units of production and consumption. The family is the unit of membership in a parish, a religious and political unit under the titular leadership of a mosque priest (*qimam*). Parishes are alliances of independent families; affiliation is by choice, not by residence or kinship ties. Parishes comprise only several dozen families and any family has a network of social relations with kin and neighbors extending beyond the parish. Ancestors, buried in conspicuously decorated graves, define networks of cognatic kinship ties among the living. Although these networks are unsegmented by discrete, corporate groups of any kind, the Yakan talk about groupings of kin in ways that would do credit to a social anthropologist. Note, for example, the contrast between *paŋkat baqirah* 'the unrestricted, non-unilineal descent group defined by an ancestor (female) named Baira' and *qusba baqirah* 'the kindred centered around an ego named Baira.' Like the legal expressions we are about to discuss, this talk about social groups must be understood as a part of social behavior as well as a description of it.

Defining Litigation

A description of a culture derives from an ethnographer's observations of the stream of activities performed by the people he is studying. As a first step toward producing an ethnographic statement, the investigator must segment and classify the events of this behavior stream so that he can say, for example, of two successive events, that one is "different" from the other and, of two non-successive events, that they are repetitions of the "same" activity. If the ethnographer claims his people do X three times a week, verification of his statement requires not simply counting occurrences of X but also assessing the criteria for distinguishing X from all the other things people do during the week and for deciding that all the different events construed as instances of X in fact represent the "same" activity. Information about what is the "same" and what is "different" can only come from the interpretations of events made by the people being studied.

Within the stream of behavior observable in Yakan society, there are some events which are difficult to characterize initially except as "a group of people talking together." There seems to be no focus of activity other than talk, no distinctive settings, apparel, or paraphernalia. We might postulate that all such cases are manifestations of the same category of cultural activities, that they are all repetitions of the same scene. At a very general level we could justify this decision. All these activities can be labelled *magbissāh* 'talking to each other' in response to a query such as *magqine siyeh* 'what are they doing?' But, as the English glosses indicate, this categorization is not particularly informative, especially to an observer of the scene. To discover a more refined categorization we must attend to the way the Yakan talk about talking.

Yakan, like English, provides a large number of linguistic expressions for talking about a great variety of aspects of speech behavior. Of these we sort out for consideration the following set of semantically related expressions, all possible responses to the query "What are they doing?" (Only the variable portion of the response is shown.[3] Some of these forms, especially *hukum*, have different, but related, meanings in different contexts. Etymological information is given for later discussion.):

1. *mitin* (< English) "discussion"[4]
2. *qisun* "conference"
3. *mawpakkat* (< Arabic) "negotiation"
4. *hukum* (< Arabic) "litigation"

The structure of inclusion and contrast relations manifest in the use of these terms to denote events is shown in Fig. 3.1. Let A, B, C, D represent situations that can be labelled as *mitiŋ, qisun, mawpakkat,* and *hukum* respectively. Then it is the case that *mitiŋ* can label the set of situations [ABCD], *qisun* the set of situations [BCD], *mawpakkat* the set [CD], whereas *hukum* can only label [D]. Thus these expressions form an ordered series, the situations labelable by a given term including all those labelable by each succeeding term. However, it is also the case that *mitiŋ* can be used to contrast situation A with each of the other situations (A not B, C, or D) as in the exchange:

magqisun qenteg siyeh 'They seem to be conferring'
dumaqin, magmitiŋ hadja qiyan 'No, they're discussing'

The form *hadja* 'just, merely' specifies that *mitiŋ* is to be construed in its minimal sense, but its use is not obligatory to convey this sense. Similarly *qisun, mawpakkat,* and *hukum* can be used to contrast B, C, D respectively with each of the other situations. We have then a case of the

---

[3] In response to *magqine* (< *N* 'active' + *pag* 'mutuality' + *qine* 'what') 'what is the mutual activity or relationship?', the forms cited, all unanalyzable morphemes, replace *qine* 'what': *magqine siyeh* 'What are they doing?' *magqisun* 'Conferring with each other.' Note also: *magqine siyeh* 'How are they related to each other?' *magpoŋtinaqih* 'As siblings.'

[4] Single quotes enclose English glosses. These are to be assigned the meaning given to the Yakan expressions for which they substitute.

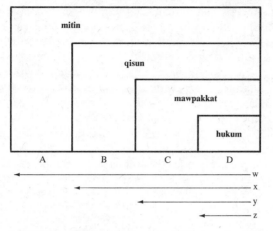

A, B, C, D: Situations represented   w, x, y, z: Features of meaning

figure 3.1

Semantic structure

use of the same forms at different levels of contrast, a situation common in semantic representation (Frake 1964d), and one that has caused some controversy over interpretation (Bright and Bright 1965:258).

In the use of the same expression at different levels of contrast, there is in Yakan a distinction between those cases, such as the present example, in which use at the less inclusive level is specifiable by a deemphatic particle (e.g., *hadja* 'just, merely') and those in which it is specifiable by an emphatic particle (e.g., *teqed* 'very, true, real'). Contrast

  magmitin hadja qiyan 'They're just discussing' (and not 'conferring,' 'negotiating,' etc.)

with

  magpoŋtinaqi teqed qiyan 'They're real siblings' (and not 'half-siblings,' 'cousins,' etc.)

The use of the same term at different levels of contrast results, in the former case, from a *specification* of the basic general sense of an expression. In the latter case it results from an *extension* of the basic specific sense of an expression. Cases of specification, such as the present example, can be interpreted as manifestation of "marking," a phenomenon widespread in linguistic representation in phonology and morphology as well as in semantics (Jakobson 1957; Greenberg 1966). Semantic marking means that given two expressions, A and B, sharing some feature of meaning x but differing with respect to some feature y (and in that sense contrasting), that the difference is not

  term A represents the meaning: xy
  term B represents the meaning: xy

but rather

term A represents the meaning: x

term B represents the meaning: xy

The use of term B necessarily implies feature y, but the use of term A does not necessarily say anything about the presence or absence of y. Term B is marked for y. In our series each term is marked for a feature (or features) not necessarily by its predecessor:

mitiŋ 'discussion': w

qisun 'conference': wx

mawpakkat 'negotiation': wxy

hukum 'litigation': $wxyz$

The next task is to characterize the features of meaning represented above as $w, x, y, z;$ w being what the set has in common and x, y, z being successive increments to this common meaning.

At the outset we should be clear about just what linguistic and cognitive operations of our informants we are trying to account for. It is not simply a case of determining the perceptual cues for distinguishing one object from another. If a Yakan sees some people engaged in mutual speech behavior (that categorization he can make perceptually) and wants to know what they are doing, he will in all probability ask them. In this case the object of categorization, a group of people engaged in some activity, is aware of what it is doing. This awareness is, in itself, an attribute, a necessary one, of the category. Just as in classifying a plant one might apply a test of taste or smell to determine a criterial property, in classifying these speech events one applies a test of eliciting a linguistic response from the performers of the activity. It is impossible for people engaged in 'litigation' or in 'conference' not to be aware of what they are doing and not to be able to communicate their awareness. For people engaged, say, in 'litigation' to be able to state that they are 'litigating' is a necessary condition for the activity to be 'litigation,' but it is not a sufficient condition. They might be lying or, more probable in Yakan life, they might be joking. Being funny is a prominent goal of Yakan speech behavior and semantic incongruity is a standard way of adding humor to speech—but the effect is dependent on the hearer's ability to recognize the incongruity. What we are trying to formulate, then, are the conditions under which it is congruous, neither humorous nor deceitful, to state that one is engaged in 'litigation.' These conditions are the semantic features of the concepts in question. Our evidence for semantic features does not come from informants' statements about the linguistic representations of these concepts (though such explicit definitions of terms are often useful guides for preliminary formulations) but from informants' interpretations of the situations which the concepts represent. Our aim is not to give an elegant formulation of minimal contrastive features but a statement that reflects

the various dimensions of speech behavior revealed in the use and interpretation of these expressions.

Let us consider first the features common to the whole set, those that
distinguish all events construable as *mitiŋ* 'discussion' from other things
Yakans do. This set of events includes the events labelled by the other
expressions. Then we will consider what each successive term adds to
these common features. Four dimensions of speech behavior appear to be
involved in contrasting "discussion" with other activities:

mitiŋ 'discussion'
   1. Focus. The focus of 'discussion' is on the topic of messages. There
is a subject of discussion. Excluded are speech events in which the focus
is on message form: story-telling, riddling, exchanging verses, joking,
prayer (which, being in Arabic, has no semantic content for the Yakan).
   2. Purpose. The purpose of the gathering is to talk. Excluded are activities in which the intent to accomplish something other than talking is
responsible for the gathering of participants.
   3. Roles. Speaking time is distributed among the participants. Each
role in the scene, whatever its other characteristics, is both a speaking
and a listening role. Excluded are monologues in which speaking time is
monopolized by one person.[5]
   4. Integrity. Integrity refers to the extent to which the activity is construed as an integral unit as opposed to being a part of some other activity.
A 'discussion' must have sufficient integrity not to be construable as
incident to or accompanying some other activity. A 'discussion' can
occur within the context of another kind of event, but only as a recognizably bounded interruption, as when participants disengage from some
other activity to talk something over. (This dimension will sound less
fuzzy when we consider its relevance to the contrast between 'litigation'
and other kinds of 'discussion.')

The expression *mitiŋ* 'discussion' necessarily implies only these
features. Each of the succeeding expressions in the series adds some
necessary implications along one or more of these dimensions (Table 3.1).

qisun 'conference'
   1. Focus. The subject of discussion is an *issue,* some topic that presents a problem to be decided: when to plant rice, when to go on a trip,
what price to pay in a transaction.
   2. Purpose. A 'conference' has an expected outcome, a *decision* about
the issue. Participants meet in order to reach a decision, and, if a decision
is made, the conference is concluded.

---

[5] The mutuality of the behavior is represented by the prefix *pag* in the sequence *N* +
pag > *mag.* See footnote 3.

3. Roles. No added implications.
4. Integrity. No added implications.

mawpakkat 'negotiation'
   1. Focus. The issue in 'negotiation' is a *disagreement*, a topic over which participants have conflicting interests.
   2. Purpose. The decision is a *settlement*, a legally binding resolution of the disagreement.
   3. Roles. Participants are divided into two protagonistic sides. Witnesses may be present.
   4. Integrity. No clear added implications. Although *mawpakkat* is more likely to refer to an integral event than *qisun*, and *quisun* than *mitiŋ*, these are not necessary implications.

hukum 'litigation'
   1. Focus. The *disagreement* is a dispute, a disagreement which arises from a charge that an *offense* has been committed. A dispute can also be handled by negotiation, but the topic of litigation is necessarily a dispute. A dispute handled by litigations is a *case*.
   2. Purpose. The settlement takes the form of a legal *ruling* based on precedent and having special sanctions.
   3. Roles. In addition to protagonists and optional witnesses, 'litigation' requires a *court*, a seat of neutral judges who control the proceedings and attempt to effect a ruling.
   4. Integrity. 'Litigation' is always an integral activity. If it is interrupted by a different kind of activity, eating, for example, there is a new instance of litigation, a different court session. 'Discussion,' 'conference,' and 'negotiation,' in their minimal senses, can occur as parts of 'litigation,' but 'litigation' cannot occur as a part of these other activities.

table 3.1
Semantic Features

	Topic	Purpose	Role Structure	Integrity
'discussion'	subject	talk	undifferentiated	mimimal
'conference'	issue	decision	undifferentiated	minimal
'negotiation'	disagreement	settlement	opposing sides	moderate
'litigation'	dispute	ruling	court	maximal

Each expression in our series, except the terminal one, has a maximal and minimal sense, depending on whether the speaker intends to include or exclude the meanings marked by succeeding expressions. 'Mere discussion' (*mitiŋ hadja*), the minimal sense of *mitiŋ*, implies the features listed as common to the whole set, but the topic is simply a subject to discuss, not an issue to be decided, a disagreement to be settled, or a case to be ruled on. The purpose is to talk, but there is no expected outcome which terminates the event, no decision to be reached, no settlement to be negotiated, no ruling to be handed down. Role structure is undifferentiated and integrity minimal, although still greater than that implied by *magbissāh* 'talking to each other.' A *mitiŋ* in its minimal sense more closely resembles an American 'bull session' than what we would call a "meeting."

'Mere conference' applies to situations in which the issue is not a dispute, the decision not a settlement, and role structure remains undifferentiated. 'Mere negotiation' applies to situations in which, though the disagreement may be a dispute, the intended outcome is a settlement that is not a legal ruling and that is reached without the aid of judges.

The flexibility of reference afforded by this semantic structure, the ability to be ambiguous about whether a general or specific sense is intended, reflects the fact that these expressions are used not only to talk about speech behavior, but their use is also a part of the behavior they describe. A Yakan uses terms like *mawpakkat* and *hukum* not simply to give serious answers to probes for information but also to further his own objectives in speech situations by advancing a particular, perhaps ostensibly incongruous, interpretation of an event and by representing this conceptualization linguistically in an effective way. He can, for example, call for a 'conference' without immediately committing himself to an interpretation of the divisiveness of the issue; he can call for a 'discussion' without implying there is an issue at stake.

For these reasons stylistic features of expressions, selections among alternative linguistic representations of a given conceptual distinction, figure importantly in their use and effect their semantic properties. In our set, *mawpakkat* is considered more learned than the other terms, all of which are ordinary, everyday words. Although the word is widely known, it occurs most often during 'litigation' when 'negotiations' are being talked about. In other contexts the notion of 'mere negotiation' is more likely to be referred to as *qisun,* using 'conference' in its general sense. It is probably a consequence of this stylistic difference that the semantic contrast between *mawpakkat* and *qisun* seems less sharply drawn than that between the other pairs of expressions. In direct questioning about the meaning of these terms, many informants have stated offhand that *mawpakkat* and *qisun* mean the same thing. No one has said that of *hukum* and any other term in the set. The same informants will still agree that if, for example, several guests at a festivity get together to decide when to leave, this is a case of *qisun* but not of *mawpakkat.* The two expressions are not synonymous, but the difference between them is somewhat harder to uncover than in the other cases. The concept of 'negotiation' can also

be represented by expressions referring to the distinctive aspects of the
event, for example:

pagsulutan 'agreement, settlement—not including legal rulings
(*hukuman*)'
qalegdah (<Spanish) 'to settle a dispute by any means'
janjiqan (<Malay) 'negotiated contractual promise'

Any citation of Yakan legal terms illustrates another property of these
expressions, that is, the large percentage of forms that are loan words
from the languages of both of the "great traditions" impinging on the
Yakan: Arabic and Malay of the Malaysian-Moslem tradition, English
and Spanish of the Filipino-Western tradition.[6] These loans have been
acquired through contact with intermediary languages (Taw Sug and
Zamboangueño) and their prevalence is not a reflection of a crushing impact of either Moslem or Western legal concepts upon Yakan law but of
the stylistic coups a speaker of Yakan scores by displaying a knowledge
of foreign words. This process apparently has a long history. Many loans,
such as *hukum* (<Arabic), are now completely assimilated and are not
now recognized as foreign. The term *mitiŋ*, currently much more popular
than alternative designations of 'discussion,' seems to be on the verge of
losing its loan-word aura. English loans used in current litigation include:
wantid, holdap, kidnap, wadan ('warrant'), *supenah, pospon, pendiŋ,
qokeh* ('approval'), and *qistodok* ('strategy' from "stroke").

Describing Litigation

Our formulation states that litigation is a kind of topic-focused
mutual speech behavior whose distinctive attributes pertain to the content
and role structure of talking. An observer of Yakan litigation would have
difficulty finding anything else that sets it apart from other activities.
There are no distinctive settings, no courtrooms, for litigation to take
place. A site for a trial should be neutral and should require no one to play
a host role, a role which requires the offering of food. A typical result of
these considerations is to meet on the porch of the house of one of the
judges (in Yakan terms "on" the house but not "within" it). But a wide
variety of other activities take place here as well. There are no distinctive
paraphernalia associated with litigation: no law books, no gavel, no judges'
bench, no witness stand. There is no provisioning of participants. They
may smoke and chew betel, but the rules for soliciting and proffering
smoking and chewing makings are the same as for other informal gather-

---

[6] The source of etymological information on Malay and Arabic loans is Wilkinson's
(1932) dictionary. Yakan expressions are marked as Malay loans only when there are
phonological grounds for distinguishing loans from inherited cognates.

ings. There is no distinctive dress associated with litigation—no judges robes—and participants do not dress up to go to court as they do to go to ceremonies. If one were to make a cut in Yakan activities between festive and nonfestive, formal and informal, litigation would clearly fall on the nonfestive, informal side. As speech-focused activity, litigation is outside the domain of ceremonies, feasts, technological tasks, and other object-focused activities. We must, therefore, organize a description of litigation along those dimensions of speech behavior found to be significant.

CASES

The topic of litigation is a 'case' (*pākalag* < Malay < Sanskrit), a 'dispute' brought to court. A 'dispute' arises when an identified part is 'charged' with an 'offense' and the accused counters the charge. To make a charge is to publicly proclaim a particular interpretation of an act. To counter a charge is to advance another interpretation. Clearly the key descriptive problem is to state the rules for interpreting an act as an offense. Equally clear is that these rules cannot be perfectly consistent in their formulation or straightforward in their application. There must be room for argument if there is to be litigation.

Offenses. 'Offenses' (*salaq*) are a subset of 'wrongs' (*duseh*), those wrongs against persons that can lead to a dispute. There are also wrongs against God (*tuhan*), such as desecrating a Koran; wrongs against this-world supernaturals (*saytan* < Arabic), such as cutting down a tree they inhabit; and wrongs against ancestors (*kapapuqan*) now in the other world (*qahilat* < Arabic), such as selling an heirloom. But these beings need not rely on courts to seek redress.

The Yakan employ a large number of linguistic expressions for talking about different kinds of offenses along a variety of semantic dimensions dealing with the nature and consequences of acts as well as with the social relationships between offender and victim. The saliency of dimensions with respect to one another can vary in different portions of the domain. For example, physical assault with intent to kill (*bonoq*) and sexual assault (*hilap* from Arabic, and many other expressions) are terminologically distinguished unless the offense is also a wrong against God, as is the case if victim and offender are primary kin or primary affines. There is one term, *sumbaŋ*, to cover these grievous sins against both man and God. One might say that the contrast "sex vs. killing" is neutralized when an expression is marked for "interference by God." (It might be noted that sexual relations are often designated euphemistically or facetiously by metaphors based on expressions for killing or fighting. "To make a killing" in Yakan does not refer to business success.) We will state here only a few general inferences about the nature of the concept of 'offense' which have been drawn from Yakan talk about particular kinds of offenses.

At the most general level, for an act to be interpretable as an offense, it must be a threat to a *dapuq* relationship. The term *dapuq* occurs together with a possessive attribute in response to the same query that elicits kinship terms and other relationship expressions. Unlike kinship relations, however, a person may be *dapuq* of an object as well as of another person. Being someone's or something's *dapuq* implies having an economic interest in it and a responsibility for it. The notion includes, but is broader than, that of ownership. To be a *dapuq* of a person in no way implies that the person is one's slave. One is *dapuq* to his children, his legal wards, his spouse, and to himself. To be a *dapuq* of an object does not necessarily imply that one has rights of use, possession, or sale but only that one has a legitimate interest in its use or disposal. A water source, for example, has its *dapuq* (*dapuq boheq*), those who use it and who would suffer economic loss if it were destroyed, but no owner. The *dapuq* of a mosque (*dapuq laŋgal*) is not its owner—there is such a person—but the entire congregation. The *dapuq* of an inheritance (*dapuq pusakaq*) is a potential heir. Any threat to a *dapuq* relationship can be interpreted as an economic threat, a threat whose gravity is expressible in pesos and centavos. All offenses, including murder, can be compensated for by money. The purpose of Yakan litigation is not to mete out punishment but to award compensation for injury.

There are two ways in which an act can be an offense. First, it can challenge a person's status as a *dapuq,* usually in the form of a claim that some other person is properly the *dapuq* of a given object or person. Second, an act can damage an object or person in such a way as to reduce its economic value to its *dapuq* (including, in the case of persons, the victim himself). Since a given object or person is likely to have more than one *dapuq,* an offense generally produces several plaintiffs. A sexual assault, for example, is an offense against the victim (*dapuq badannen* 'dapuq of one's body'), her parents (*dapuq qanakin* '*dapuq* of the child'), and, if married, her husband (*dapuq qandahin* '*dapuq* of the wife').

Charges. It is up to a victim of an offense to make a charge (*tuntut*); all Yakan law is civil law. He must furthermore determine the identity of the offender and assume responsibility for the identification. Offenses in which victim and offender do not meet face to face or in which the victim does not survive are difficult to prosecute. Even though theft, ambush shootings, and murder are among the more common, and certainly the most complained about offenses in Yakan life, they rarely reach the courts. It is largely sex and, to a lesser extent, fights and property disputes that keep court agendas full.

An initial charge can be made in the form of a *complaint* (*diklamuh* < Spanish) to a court or even by directly confronting the accused. More often an accuser will utilize *gossip* channels to make his charge known to the accused. In this way he can feel out the response of his opponent before being irrevocably committed. A way out is left open through denying the truth or serious intent of the gossip. One of the dangers of Yakan life is *limorok* (literally 'slip through'): 'inadvertently instigating a dispute by incautious gossip in the presence of someone who is likely to relay the accusation to be accused.'

There are three strategies available for countering a charge:

1. One can deny the validity of the accuser's definition of the offense in question, disputing the meaning of a concept. Does, for example, the notion of sexual offense include all acts in which a male makes unnecessary physical contact with a female not his spouse or only those acts in which a male has sexual designs on the woman?

2. One can deny that the act in question has the properties to qualify it as an instance of an offense, disputing what really happened. For example, granted any physical contact as described above is an offense, did any such contact actually occur in the particular instance?

3. One can deny responsibility for the act because (a) someone else did it; (b) the accused was provoked by the accuser; (c) the accused was incited by some third party (a much stronger excuse for wrong-doing among the Yakan than among ourselves); (d) the act was unintentional.

To deny a charge is at the same time to make a charge against one's accuser, for a false charge is in itself an offense. It threatens the economic interests of the accused. The set of arguments propounded by one side in a dispute to counter the charges of the other is their *daqawah* (< Arabic) or "case" in the sense of "the defense rests its case."

Disputes. Once a charge has been made and countered, a dispute exists. Disputants may simply decide to live with the dispute, they may attempt to dispose of each other, or they may seek a settlement. If they decide on the last course of action, they may either 'negotiate' or 'litigate.' In 'negotiation' two opposing parties meet to settle a disagreement by mutual agreement. The disagreement need not be a dispute (i.e., the outcome of a charge). Negotiating a contract, property settlements, marriage (which involves all of the preceding) are cases to point. Negotiations are often sufficient to handle minor disputes and are necessary for major disputes difficult to place under the jurisdiction of any Yakan court. An agreement is specific to the negotiating parties and need not derive from legal precedents. The breaking of an agreement, however, is an offense and can result in a dispute taken to court. Marriages are made by negotiation but dissolved by litigation. To settle a dispute by litigation it must be reported to a court at which point the dispute becomes a legal case. The party that considers itself offended against should report first, but often by the time a case reaches court there is such a complex of charges and countercharges that any distinction between plaintiff and defendant becomes obscure.

COURTS

What distinguishes litigation from other methods of settling disputes is the presence of a court (*saraq* < Arabic), a set of persons performing the role of judge, who are ostensibly neutral on the issue and whose task it is to formulate a settlement. The Yakan court has few of the tangible manifestations of its Western counterpart: professional judges holding an office, court houses, explicit and continuous schedules, and well-defined jurisdictions. On the other hand, a set of judges is not recruited ad hoc to try each case that appears. Particular sets of judges meet more than once and may try more than one case in a single session. Furthermore, there is a fundamental difference between a single case appearing again in a subsequent session of the same court—a continuation of a single trial—and a case appearing again in a different court—a retrial of the same case. One may also report to a court when the court is not in session, to file a charge, for example, or to seek asylum. The crucial problems in a description of Yakan courts are those of legal authority and of jurisdiction: How are persons recruited to the role of judge? How are cases assigned to particular courts?

Judges. To act as a judge, a person must be a parish leader with the ability and knowledge to perform the role and sufficient political power at the jurisdictional level of the court to make his voice effective. Parish leadership is not a political office with formal rules of recruitment but a position achieved by accumulating influence and prestige by a variety of means: religious learning, economic success, military prowess, forensic ability, acquisition of a title, pilgrimage to Mecca, election to a local office in the Philippine political system (councilor or barrio captain), or simply growing older. (The most common expression for a leader is *bahiq* 'elder'.) Typically parish leadership is vested in a small group of close kinsmen, each specializing in one or more of these routes to power. One man may be the priest and litigator, another the entrepreneur, another the fighter. Larger political groupings are informal and unstable alliances of parishes. To exert leadership at this wider level, one must also be a leader at the parish level. One does not rise to higher positions; one merely extends the range of his influence. An exceptional position is that of titular tribal chief (*datuq*) of all the Yakan, a hereditary office now held by the Westernized son of a Christian Filipino escaped convict, who, during the latter part of the Spanish regime, fled to Basilan. There he assumed political leadership over the Yakan and achieved formal recognition of his position by both the Spaniards and the Sultan of Sulu.

Jurisdiction. The jurisdiction of a court is a function of the social distance between the judges who comprise it. This distance, in turn, is a response to the need to preserve neutrality with respect to the cases brought before it. The rule for assignment of a case to a court is to maintain minimal social distance between court and protagonists consistent with preserving neutrality. This rule has the effect that the greater the social distance between protagonists and the more serious the case, the higher the jurisdiction of the court that can try the case. If both protagonists belong to the same parish, then one or more of their own parish leaders may be found who, by kinship and other dimensions of social affiliation, are equidistant from both sides. If, however, the protagonists belong to different parishes, the court must comprise representatives of both parishes. The seriousness of a case is measured by the number of active supporters recruited by each disputant. As the number of supporters surrounding each disputant increases, that is, as each party of protagonists grows larger, the further afield one must go to find judges who are not involved on one side or another. Because of these considerations, there is a certain ad hoc nature to the formation of courts as adjustments are made to handle particular cases. Nevertheless, three basic jurisdictional levels can be distinguished: parish, community, and tribal.

The tribal court, composed of leaders appointed by the tribal chief, meets in the yard of the chief's Western-style house in the town of Lamitan. Although in theory it is sort of a supreme court for all the Yakan, handling cases local courts have failed to settle, in practice its jurisdiction and its composition is geographically limited to the side of the island where the court meets. Parish courts are generally formed ad hoc to try relatively trivial disputes—fights among young men, for example,—among parish members. Occasionally a parish trial will be conducted with the absolute minimum personnel: two disputants and one judge. The bulk of litigation occurs at what might be called the community level. In most areas there are regular court sessions about once a week. Adjustments are made in these courts to handle particular cases. Any court intermediate between a regular community court and the tribal court is an ad hoc formation to handle a special case. Before reaching the tribal level, however, there is a limit beyond which jurisdiction cannot be stretched, where judges who are neutral and at the same time sufficiently close socially to act together cannot be found. Disputes at this level may be referred to the tribal court, to government courts, or a settlement by negotiation may be attempted. Frequently, however, disputants resort to violence at this point.

Other roles. Added to the basic role structure of litigations—a court and two opposing sides—there is a further differentiation of roles within each party of protagonists:
1. The principal, the one primarily involved in the original dispute, the person who, as the Yakan say was '*struck*' by speech (*tawwaq bissah*) or who 'collided' with litigation (*lumaŋgal si hukum*).
2. His guardian, the one who assumes responsibility for accepting or rejecting a ruling and complying with it. The guardian may be the principal himself, a parent or parental surrogate, or a spouse.
3. Senior and peer supporters.
The Yakan talk about this role structure in the language of kinship using an ideal model in which the principal is a child, the court his peers, the guardian his parent, and his supporters his senior and peer kin. A final role is that of witnesses, who may be called by either side or by the court.

Rulings. The intended outcome of litigation is a ruling (*hukuman*) on a case handed down by the court. The crucial fact shaping Yakan legal rulings is that the court has no powers of coercion to force compliance with a ruling. It must resort to persuasion. What distinguishes a ruling from an agreement arrived at by negotiation consists largely of the elaborate verbal trappings that go along with a ruling and lend it a sacrosanct aura. The ideology expressed in talking about rulings during the process of proclaiming them should not be taken as an expression of the manner in which rulings are actually derived but as part of the behavior of making a ruling in the most effective way. The basic principle for actually arriving at successful rulings seems to be the same as those for agreements; namely, to give each side somewhat less than full satisfaction but something better than the worst they might expect. In other words, to effect a compromise. The basic objective of both litigation and negotiation is to eliminate a dispute, to reestablish normal social relations between the disputants. It is not to do justice whatever the cost.

A ruling may call for one or more of three acts: payment of a fine (*multah* < Spanish, *qātaq* < Malay < Sanskrit), listening to an *admonition* (*nasihat* < Arabic, *pituwah* < Arabic, *tōqan*) from the court, and performing a *prayer* (*duwaqah* < Arabic) of *reconciliation*. A fine, in turn, has one or more of three components: a compensation for the offense, an amount serving to "wipe away" any sin against God associated with the offense (which the court collects), and a payment to the court the *baytalmāl* (< Arabic 'treasury'). Fines are calculated in ten-peso units (*laksaq*) and paid in Philippine currency (P1 = $.25). In proposing a ruling the court must explain in detail how the amount was arrived at, relating it to traditional fines for the offense and to the particular exigencies of the case at hand. In one case involving two youths who had been in a fight, one side claimed damages for bodily injury and presented a medical bill for the amount of P 180.25 from a Christian Filipino physician. The court suggested a fine of P 100 to be paid to the injured party explaining its decision as follows:

P 120	For paying the medical bill (principle: never give full satisfaction)
− 50	In recognition of the countercharge of collusion between the plaintiff and the physician; The court was careful to state it did not necessarily believe the countercharge but, since there were no witnesses, account must be taken of the possibility
50	For the offense against the plaintiff
− 20	For the plaintiff's responsibility in instigating the fight
P 100	

If an *admonition* is part of the ruling, it is given in the form of a lecture by the court to both sides at the end of the trial. It is designed to make both parties feel their share of responsibility for the dispute, to smooth ruffled feelings, and to warn of the grave consequences of repeating the offense. Admonitions are especially common in rulings over marital disputes and fights among youths.

If a *prayer of reconciliation* is called for, it is performed at a later time as a different scene, a religious ceremony. Its performance involves expenses, instructions for the payment of which is an important aspect of the ruling. The prayer unites the former disputants in a divinely-sanctioned ritual-sibling tie. A call for prayer is especially common in cases of violence.

Upon suggesting a ruling the court argues for compliance, not only by carefully justifying the form of the decision but also by pointing out the dire consequences of refusal to comply. God and the ancestors may mete out sickness upon the offender and his kin. Opponents may resort to violence against the offender and his kin. The offender's kin, under threat from these sanctioning agents, may withdraw support or even disown the offender. Judges threaten to wash their hands of the case and withdraw political support, and finally the case may be referred to Philippine government legal system with its expensive lawyers and prisons. See Fig. 3.2 for a portrayal of these sanctioning forces converging on an offender.

If the litigants agree to the ruling, those who are called upon to hand over money almost never pay in full on demand, this being a rule in all monetary transactions. They ask for *taŋguh,* a deferment of part of the

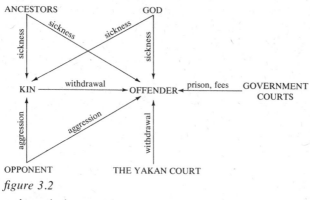

figure 3.2

Sanctions and sanctioning agents

payment until a specified later date. As might be expected, failure to pay *taŋguh* when due is itself a major cause of disputes.

If a court fails to formulate an acceptable ruling, the litigants may attempt to take the case to another Yakan court, seek redress in a government court, or drop attempts to settle the dispute by litigation. Another alternative is to turn the decision over to God. In a religious ceremony, each disputant swears (*sapah*) on the Koran to the validity of his arguments in the case. God decides who is right and announces his decision by inflicting fatal illness (*kasapahan*) upon the person who swore a false oath or upon his kin. *Swearing* is a serious matter, rarely resorted to in fact. The threat of it, however, figures prominently in legal debate. One can protect himself from false charges by challenging his opponent to participate in a swearing ritual. In several recorded cases, young men saved themselves from conviction on charges of sexual assault by this tactic. The fact that God may punish not only the offender but also his kin may seem capricious to Western moralists; yet it greatly increases the effectiveness of the punishment. Support of one's kin is crucial in a dispute, but they will be extremely reluctant to carry this support to the point of swearing unless they are firmly convinced of their kinsmen's innocence. Also, if the disputants are in any way related to each other, as is often the case, this relationship tie must be dissolved before swearing. Consanguineal kinship ties can be formally broken in a religious ceremony. The term for the ritual payments required to disown a kinsman is *tallak* from the Arabic word for the formula spoken by a husband to divorce his wife (Yakan divorce is not that simple).

PROCEDURES AND SCHEDULES

Our formulation of the concept of litigation states that litigation is an integral activity never performed as part of another scene. It is a maximal unit of planning and scheduling. The description of the manifestations of this aspect of the concept requires a statement of the constituent structure of the scene—the sequence of parts that make up the whole—and of the scheduling of litigation with respect to other scenes in the society.

Procedures. Unlike mere negotiation or conference, litigation is conducted according to definite procedural rules. Although these rules are much looser than those of Western courts, they are, by Yakan standards, fairly strict and explicit. During procedings, judges frequently make reference to general rules governing the speech conduct of court sessions such as the following:

1. Speaking time is a free good available in unlimited quantity to any person present as long as what he says is relevant to the case.
2. A speaker has the right to finish before being interrupted.
3. Judges have the right to call on a person to speak, but one may speak without being called upon.[7]
4. Litigants should address all their arguments to the court.
5. Overt expression of anger, and especially any violence, must be avoided. Allowance should be made for the necessity, in litigation, for people to say unkind things about one another. Disputants must be allowed to accuse, judges to admonish.
6. Each party of protagonists, as well as the judges, has the right to confer in private whenever necessary.
7. A continuous period of time should be allotted to each case during a single court session.

Although there is some variation in the type of case, the usual sequence of events is as follows:

1. Presentation of the case by the person to whom it is reported
2. Taking testimony from each side and from witnesses
3. Interrogation by the court
4. Arguments from each side presented together (one side does not present its complete case and then defer to the other side)
5. Private conference of the judges
6. Presentation of a ruling
7. Further argument (optional but inevitable)
8. Private conference of each side (optional)
9. Expression of acceptance or refusal by each side
10. Final decision for disposition of case

---

[7] The question of someone refusing to testify never seems to arise.

11. Payment of fines, listening to courts admonition (if required)
12. Ritual handshaking (*salam* < Arabic) with the judges signalling the termination of a trial session

Steps 2–4 often occur simultaneously. Steps 5–9 may be repeated several times.

Schedules. Fixed timing is not an attribute of litigation as it is, say, of some calendrical religious ceremonies and agricultural activities. Court sessions are fitted into vacancies left by the schedules of other scenes. As a matter of convenience, community courts generally have regular scheduled meetings (Friday afternoon after Mosque service is a favorite time), but these are easily accommodated if schedules conflict. The tribal court meets two afternoons a week. Court sessions must be scheduled between meals with allowance made so participants can return home to eat. The five daily prayers of Islam, performed in most localities only by a few religiously inclined individuals, cause no problem. If someone wants to say a prayer, he can always go off and do so.

Comparisons

In this section we make a few summary comparisons with another Philippine legal system. The purpose is not to offer an explanation of these differences but to demonstrate that the ethnographic approach argued for here, rather than hampering cross-cultural comparison as some critics seem to fear, provides a basis for determining which units are comparable and points up significant dimensions of comparison.

The Eastern Subanun are pagan swidden agriculturists inhabiting the interior of Zamboanga Peninsula on the island of Mindanao.[8] The Yakan and Subanun are not in direct contact but they speak related languages and, along with other central Malaysian peoples, share many basic technological and social-organizational features. Subanun communities are much smaller and more scattered, although the basic principles of settlement pattern are the same: nuclear family household dispersed in individual fields. The difference is that the Yakan practice continual exploitation of privately owned fields and groves. Both groups have long been subject first to Moslem, then to Christian, cultural influence, political authority, and economic exploitation. The Yakan accommodated where necessary and resisted where possible. They became Moslems, they participate in Philippine politics, and they market copra. At the same time

---

[8] Reference is to the Eastern Subanun of the Lipay area of Zamboanga del Norte studied in the field in 1953–1954 and 1957–1958.

they have retained a marked cultural distinctiveness, some freedom to run their own affairs, and, above all, their land. The Subanun, on the other hand, retreated or succumbed entirely. They have remained pagan and retained temporary economic and political independence at the price of increased isolation and loss of land. Perhaps not unrelated to this difference in adaptation to external pressures is a marked difference in the behavior of the two peoples today: the Subanun drink whereas the Yakan fight.

There is among the Subanun a set of activities that, in contrast to other Subanun activities, can be defined in much the same terms as Yakan litigation: an integral speech event concerned with settling disputes by means of a ruling formulated by neutral judges. A brief description of litigation in one Subanun community appears elsewhere (Frake 1963). Here we will restrict ourselves to a few comparisons along the dimensions of topic, role structure, outcome, and integrity.

Topic. Subanun legal cases arise in much the same way as Yakan ones except that they need not be initiated by a plaintiff. A judge can try someone for an offense even if no complaint has been made. It seems ridiculous, however, to call this criminal law since the offenses in question are generally slanderous or flirtatious remarks made by an incautious drinker, often not at all resented by the victim. Otherwise the definitions of particular kinds of offenses are similar. (A major difference is that the Yakan consider sexual relations with an affine as incestuous whereas the Subanun practice levirate and sororate marriage and sororal polygyny.) There are great differences, however, in the kinds of offenses that occur (violence is almost unknown among the Subanun) and the types of cases that reach court. Adultery, for example, fills the agendas of Yakan courts whereas it is rarely the overt basis of a Subanun legal case. This is not a comment on Subanun virtue but on the weakness of their legal sanctions.

Outcome. The rulings of a Subanun court, like those of the Yakan, generally demand financial compensation (but fines are calculated in units of twenty centavos rather than of ten pesos), and may call for admonitions and rituals of reconciliation. But, not only does the Subanun court have no legal sanctions of force to back up a decision, there is also little realistic threat of illegal force it can bring to bear. The Subanun offender may fear a certain amount of social censure—a real enough sanction to be sure—but he need not fear a shotgun blast interrupting his evening meal, the outcome of more than one Yakan dispute. The Subanun also lack an Almighty God to mete out justice when litigation fails. For this reason, "a large share, if not the majority, of legal cases deal with offenses so minor that only the fertile imagination of a Subanun legal authority can magnify them into a serious threat to some person or to society in general"

(Frake 1963:221). Yakan courts too cannot cope with the full range of offenses committed, but the Yakan, by absolute standards, commit much more serious crimes. A Parkinsonian cynic viewing Yakan and Subanun life and law might conclude that the severity of crime increases with the ability of a legal system to cope with it.

Role Structure. Subanun courts are always formed ad hoc to try a particular case. There are no court schedules or regular meeting places. The role of judge is open to any adult male with the ability to formulate successful decisions and performance in the role is largely a route to community leadership rather than a result of it. Unlike the Yakan, where a parish priest is generally a political leader as well, Subanun roles of legal and religious authority are quite distinct and typically filled by separate individuals. Subanun litigation less often musters bodies of kin in support of disputants, partly because there is usually less of common interest at stake, and kin do not share collective responsibility under mortal and divine sanctioning agents.

Integrity. The striking difference between Subanun and Yakan litigation, and one that does not derive from differences in socioeconomic complexity in any obvious way, is the place of the activity in the overall structure of cultural scenes. Subanun activities are sharply divisible into festive and nonfestive scenes, the former always involving feasting and drinking (Frake 1964b). Subanun litigation is festive behavior, performed as part of a larger scene and accompanied by eating, drinking, and merry-making. In this respect it is the same kind of thing as the performance of religious offerings, and the two activities in fact often occur together as parts of the same festivity. Subanun litigation, then, is less of an integral unit of performance and scheduling than the comparable Yakan activity. Subanun legal arguments, as they develop in the course of drinking, exhabit more obvious attention to message form. Litigants and judges employ esoteric legal language often arranged into verse and sung to the tune of drinking songs (Frake 1964a). Thus whereas the Yakan try relatively serious cases in scenes of informal discussion, the Subanun devote themselves to trivial disputes in scenes of formal festivities. This difference is crucial to any functional interpretations of litigation in the two societies. Participation in litigation has different meanings and different consequences in the two societies because of it.

4

The Strategy of Turkish Boys' Verbal Dueling Rhymes

ALAN DUNDES, JERRY W. LEACH, AND BORA ÖZKÖK

Alan Dundes is Professor of Anthropology and Folklore at the University of California, Berkeley. He received his doctorate in folklore at Indiana University, and he has taught at the University of Kansas. Dr. Dundes has played a leading part in the revitalization of folklore as a discipline in the United States. Much of his work has been concerned with the structural definition and analysis of folkloristic genres, such as folktales, superstitions, and riddles. He has also been active in collecting and interpreting folkloristic features of contemporary popular culture. Jerry W. Leach has done graduate work at Cambridge University, England, and at the University of California, Berkeley. Bora Özkök, a native of Turkey, is a graduate student at the University of California, Berkeley.

This chapter focuses on verbal dueling, a well-defined genre of oral art which can be found in many parts of the world. As the authors point out, however, folklorists' accounts of these phenomena tend to be confined to descriptions of content or ad hoc lists of elements or stylistic characteristics. Folklorists have failed to show how the forms in question are used in actual interaction and what they imply about language usage in relationships in the societies in which they occur. This chapter attempts to overcome these limitations. By analyzing Turkish verbal duels within the conceptual framework of the ethnography of communication in terms of the structural relations among constituent factors, it opens up new possibilities for evaluating the communicative devices involved in speech play and comparing them to other more common interaction processes in Turkey and elsewhere. Turkish verbal duels do in fact show most of the characteristics of speech events in general. Interaction typically revolves around a culturally specific range of topics. In this case the topic is homosexuality, including sexual attack on a person's close relatives, manliness, courage, etc. There are rigid constraints on message form, with exchanges consisting of two parts: a challenge and a reply, which are linked both through content and form (rhyme). Similarly, there are limitations on speakers and audiences: Only teenage boys can participate. Like the telephone conversations analyzed by Schegloff (Chapter 12), dueling exchanges in Turkey have clearly defined sequencing rules which determine who gets the floor and under what conditions. There are further stereotyped openings and closings, which function to channel what can be conveyed in a manner similar to that described by Frake in his discussion of Subanun drinking behavior (1964a).

A number of features of communication are illustrated which have clear counterparts in every sequence of the interaction. One of the most important features is the contrast between overt topic or content, on the one hand, and communicative goal, or function, as Ervin-Tripp (Chapter 7) calls it, on the other. Topics such as sexuality, manliness, etc., are not used for the information they convey by themselves. Sexual submission serves as a symbol for interactional inferiority. The actual communicative intent seems to be to put one's opponent down or to test his ability to maintain presence of mind in interaction. Compare the Turkish material with Ervin-Tripp's example of a husband who, upon entering a room, finds his wife talking to a lady friend and is told: "We were talking about our next sewing club meeting." In this case, the husband takes the hint and withdraws. As with sex in Turkish duels, the topic is introduced in that case because of what it implies about restrictions upon participants not because of its inherent content.

Note also the semantic strategy of the duels. The opponent singles out central, potentially ambiguous features of the speaker's challenge and by placing them in a new environment alters their meaning so as to make them reflect on the speaker. There is some similarity with common children's word games such as the following:

A: I love that dog.
B: Why don't you marry it?

In terms of the concepts developed by Sacks in Chapter 11, the change of environment forces the reassignment of an item from one category collection to another.

Participation in verbal duels requires both specific linguistic skills and general cultural knowledge. A competent performer must know a large number of set rhymes, he must display ingenuity in inventing new metaphors and combining them within the constraints imposed by the medium. This suggests that verbal dueling among boys may serve as an important language socialization device. Labov's recent extensive study of verbal behavior in black ghetto peer groups illustrates a similar case of this type of speech play (Labov et al. 1968). Labov's attempt to describe the grammatical competence of peer groups in culturally realistic settings led to the discovery that what folklorists have variously called "sounding" or "playing the dozens" (Abrahams 1964; Kochman 1969) is a daily occurrence in ghetto areas and forms an integral part of interaction within ghetto peer groups. Analysis of transcripts of such sounding sessions show that the very process of competing with others (i.e., the necessity of topping one's opponent's "sound") may cause a speaker to produce highly complex and involved syntactic constructions of the type usually thought to be lacking in lower-class uneducated speech. However, these same black children, when interviewed alone, by white or black interviewers, away from their peers, frequently may seem unresponsive, communicating only in brief and stereotyped statements. When speech performance is investigated only in these contexts, speakers may be considered as lacking in verbal skills. Clearly, failure to respond in formal interviews cannot be understood simply in the framework of linguistic competence, in the way that that term is usually defined. One must also deal with the social meaning which the interview setting carries for respondents. This is a classic illustration of the fact that communicative competence involves more than just grammatical skills.

After analysis of the forms and symbolic content of a number of sequences, the authors turn to the place of verbal dueling in the society in which it occurs. Taboos on obscenity perhaps account for apparent neglect of this genre in previously published work, but grafitti and folktales indicate that it is well known. The authors attempt to explain the involvement of men in the genre and its general meaning by arguing that symbolic sexual dominance is a predominant theme in terms of the enculturation experience in the male life cycle.

An alternate explanation, more in line with the theoretical position taken elsewhere in this volume, would be to turn away from the search for psychological motivation, disregard the literal meaning of the key terms, and view them as symbolic of the community's most deeply ingrained social taboos or notions of boundary. The duel thus tests the performers' ability to manipulate these emotion-charged topics within the constraints imposed by the speech event. By besting his opponent in this dangerous and potentially explosive situation, he demonstrates his fitness as a member of the peer group and ultimately his social communicative skill.

To the student of verbal interaction, the importance of verbal dueling lies in the fact that it illustrates, in ritualized and vivid form, some highly important and, so far, relatively little understood aspects of the communication process, and thus materially contributes to our understanding of the social basis of verbal interaction. For an additional related reading, see Paulhan's (1913) book. Many of the articles in Kochman (in preparation) deal with similar matters within the context of Afro-American culture, especially Labov's "Rules for Ritual Insult." Peter Seitel (1971) gives a highly interesting and suggestive analysis of the communicative uses of proverbs in Africa.

The underlying strategy of specific traditional verbal encounters has not received much attention from anthropologists and folklorists. Anthropologists speak at length of joking or teasing relationships in general, but rarely do they describe in detail actual verbal duels or provide anything remotely resembling *explication de texte*. Folklorists, who tend to be text rather than context oriented, do at least present reasonably complete texts of insults, taunts, retorts, etc. However, more often than not, these texts are presented in no particular order other than the arbitrary one imposed by the collector. Given this presentation of the data, it is virtually impossible to reconstruct even an approximate idea of a live verbal battle in which the texts might appropriately be employed. In Roger Abrahams' valuable study of the dozens, e.g., the classic American Negro example of verbal dueling, he first lists thirty different dozens insults ("raps") and then follows them with a separate list of twelve dozens replies ("caps") (1962). It is conceivable, of course, that it really doesn't matter which reply follows which initial insult. Yet, there is obviously a particular order or sequence in any one actual dueling encounter. For those students who are interested in understanding folk rhetorical strategy (e.g., what strategic factors influence a verbal duel participant to choose one retort rather than another), it seems clear that knowledge of the particular sequence of exchanges is absolutely essential. Thus full transcriptions of observed or at least participant-reported hypothetical verbal duels must be collected if we are ever to attempt to analyze underlying strategies.

The study of strategy in verbal duels is part of what has been termed "the ethnography of speaking folklore" (Arewa and Dundes 1964). The ethnography of speaking folklore refers to the rules governing the use of both whole genres of folklore and particular exemplars of those genres. Thus it is not just a matter of describing the general function of one type of insult but also of describing the particular rationale underlying the use of one particular insult by one particular individual to another particular individual on one particular occasion. Admittedly, the determining factors involved may not be in the conscious mind of the duel participants. Nevertheless, like so many of the "rules" of culture, they may be articulated after careful analysis. If there is to be any fruitful study of the dynamics of the transmission or communication of folklore, then the particulars of the processes in which the folkloristic materials are employed must begin to receive the critical attention of folklorists and anthropologists. If folklore is a code, then folklorists must consider the rules of usage of that code by examining its concrete contexts. As an illustration of "the ethnography of speaking folklore," we shall briefly examine one type of verbal duel found throughout Turkey.[1]

---

[1] Although almost all of the materials in this paper were provided by one of the coauthors, Bora Özkök, who was himself an active participant in the tradition, spotchecking with more than twenty other Turkish students revealed that the same or similar texts were common in Istanbul, Ankara, Adana, Erzurum, and Izmir. Professor Ilhan Basgoz of Indiana University also had personal knowledge of the tradition and we are indebted to him for several useful comments on the paper. The undoubted popularity of the tradition tempts us to speculate about the possibility of its relationship to the alleged sexual indignities suffered by the famed Lawrence of Arabia, when he was captured by Turkish forces at Deraa.

Some General Features of Turkish
Verbal Dueling

Among Turkish boys from about the ages of eight to around fourteen, there is a traditional form of ritual insult exchange which depends upon an individual's skill in remembering and selecting appropriate retorts to provocative insults. While it is possible that some of the initial insults or curses might be known by girls and women, it is quite unlikely that the retorts are similarly known. Moreover, in the absence of evidence to the contrary, it seems doubtful that the elaborate mechanics and tactics of engaging in these linked retort contests are familiar to many Turkish females. For that matter, the very existence of this verbal dueling tradition seems to be little known by professional students of Turkish culture, judging by lack of allusions to it in the Turkish scholarly literature. Most probably, the same obscenity which keeps the tradition out of the reach of most Turkish women has tended to keep it out of the province of scholars. Still it seems incredible that none of the anthropologists who have conducted ethnographic fieldwork in Turkey have so much as mentioned the tradition.

The tradition includes the following general principles:

1. *One of the most important goals is to force one's opponent into a female, passive role.* This may be done by defining the opponent or his mother or sister as a wanton sexual receptacle. If the male opponent is thus defined, it is usually by means of casting him as a submissive anus, an anus which must accept the brunt of the verbal duelists's attacking phallus. A more indirect technique is to disparage or threaten the opponent's mother or sister, which is a serious attack upon his male honor. Thus the victim either has to submit to phallic aggression himself or else watch helplessly as phallic aggression is carried out upon his female extensions: his mother or sister. Of course, the victim normally does not simply remain passive. Rather he tries in turn to place his attacker in a passive, female role. Much of the skill in the dueling process consists of parrying phallic thrusts such that the would-be attacking penis is frustrated and the would-be attacker is accused of *receiving* a penis instead. According to this code, a young boy defends and asserts his virile standing in his peer group by seeing to it that his phallus threatens the anus of any rival who may challenge him. *It is important to play the active role in a homosexual relationship; it is shameful and demeaning to be forced to take the passive role.*

2. *The retort must end rhyme with the initial insult.* This is a critical stylistic principle as opposed to the overall structural or content requirement just noted. It clearly involves a fairly demanding and restrictive

rule. In most instances, there are specific rhymed retorts for given insults, and if one is the victim of such an insult, he is expected to come back with the most appropriate traditional retort. It is thus to an individual's advantage to memorize as many of such traditional retorts as possible inasmuch as such memorization thereby arms him against any sudden attack. Failure to respond in rhyme will almost certainly invite a scathing comment from one's opponent. However, even worse than not answering in rhyme or in what is adjudged good rhyme is not answering at all. If one does not or cannot retort to a phallic insult, one essentially admits that he is reduced to the female receptive role.

Within the general necessary requirements of content (one's phallus must enter one's opponent's anus) and texture (the retort must rhyme with the immediately preceding insult) there is still some room for individual skill. This skill entails making editorial judgments upon the quality of the previous verbal thrust and also making a judicious selection of either another attack formula or a sufficient defense formula from the large fund of available formulas. So long as one fulfills the minimal content and rhyme requirements, one can continue to duel. In some of the fairly lengthy sequences of linked retorts, the participants must often be able to seize upon an actual or alleged "mistake" in the attacker's previous text. Often it is just one word or the quality of the rhyme which forms the basis for the selection of an appropriate traditional response formula. In one sense, an individual is almost honor-bound wherever possible to take part of the previous text as the point of departure for the continuation of the duel. With such a folk esthetic principle, two evenly matched youths may produce quite an extensive series of linked retorts. Frequently, considerable word play may be required to keep the linkage going. In summary then, an important part of the strategy would seem to entail selecting a retort from the repertoire, the selection to be based in part upon one or more "weak" elements of one's opponent's text as well as upon the exigencies of the rhyme requirement. At the same time, the retort should be sufficiently clever so as not to provide that same opponent with potential ammunition for a good thrust in return. In addition, the pace is fast and the retorts are supposed to be quickly and flawlessly delivered.

Brief Exchanges

Before examining some examples of the lengthier strings of linked rhymed retorts, it might be well to consider several brief exchanges (in these and all following examples the first line gives the Turkish text, the second line a literal English translation, and the third, in parenthesis, a full idiomatic English translation, if required):

Speaker A: *Ayı*
                bear

Speaker B: *Sana   girsin   keman yayi*
                you to   enter let it   violin   bow
                (May the bow of a violin enter your anus.)

Ayı meaning 'you bear' is a commonly used insult in Turkey. Bear connotes a clumsy, big, and supposedly stupid animal. The conventional reply 'May the bow of a violin enter your ass' illustrates the rhyme requirement. *yayı* ('bow' in the possessive form) rhymes with *ayı* ('bear'). In theory, there are many other word forms which rhyme with *ayı* and which could have been used. However, there are in fact only two traditional retorts that we know of to the *ayı* insult. The bow of a violin is particularly appropriate because of its length, its smoothness, its unusualness in this context, and perhaps even because the nuances of the repeated bowing motion suggest the possibility of repeated penetrations of the opponent's anus. The motion of the bow thus gives it an advantage over more stationary potential phallic symbols such as a winnowing fork or a hoe. (Of course, the latter are ruled out by the rhyming pattern.) One informant, when asked to comment on the violin bow image, suggested that the most habitual homosexuals—i.e., the ones with larger or extended anuses—would "require the longest and biggest instruments."

Another traditional retort to *ayı* is:

     Sana   koysun   (*speaker's own first name*)   *dayı*
     you to   put let him   mother's brother
     [Let a real man like (*B's name*) put his penis in your anus.]

Incidentally, *dayı*, the mother's brother, in terms of the quality of the relationship is the *familiar* uncle, the uncle with whom one can joke. This is in contrast with *amca,* the father's brother, the more formal uncle, to whom one must invariably show respect.

                Speaker A: *Hıyar*
                              cucumber

                Speaker B: *Götüne   uyar*
                              ass your to   fits
                              (It fits your ass.)

Hıyar meaning 'you cucumber' is a pithy insult. There are, as a matter of fact, a number of idiomatic usages involving the cucumber.

> *Hıyara   bak!*
> cucumber to   look at
> (Look at that cucumber!)
>
> *Hıyarlık   etme!*
> cucumberness   act not
> (Don't act like a cucumber!)

'Look at that cucumber' or 'Don't act like a cucumber!' are representative. Cucumber is an insult not because of any literal sense but rather because of its fancied resemblance to the male organ. Cucumber basically implies stupidity. A speaker who is called a cucumber (which would be somewhat analogous to being called a "prick" in American argot) must reply under pain of admitting that he is indeed a cucumber. By using the traditional retort *Götüne uyar*, he neatly turns the insult back upon his opponent inasmuch as he has asserted that the "cucumber" *fits* the insulter's ass. At this point B, the second speaker, having rhymed *uyar* with *hıyar*, and having placed his phallus deftly in his opponent's anus, has earned the advantage of the verbal duel.

Although most of the brief exchanges do not involve a great deal of choice on the part of the boy trying to retort, there are some insults which may be answered by quite a variety of standard responses. For example, if speaker A tells speaker B

> *Has   siktir*
> Come on   penised get
> (Get fucked.)

B may choose one of a number of possibilities. While *has siktir* literally refers to "getting penised," i.e., fucked, figuratively, it is normally used to tell someone to "get the hell out of here." However, the second speaker will normally use the literal sense as the basis of his comeback. He might say:

> *Siktirdiğin   yere   mum   diktir*
> penised got that you   place to   candle   set up
> (Put a candle at the spot where you got yourself fucked.)

The second speaker thus implies that his opponent has already been sexually assaulted and he specifically tells him furthermore that the place where this occurred, e.g., a particular room, a clearing in the woods, or wherever, should be memorialized by placing a lighted candle there. This mockingly sanctifies the "holy" place. The brief exchange may end at this point, but the first speaker could reply

> *Ablan   varsa   bana   siktir!*
> older sister you   there is   if me to penised get
> (If you have an older sister, let me fuck her.)

Here the first speaker wishes to avoid the passive role as signaled by having a lighted candle mark the spot where he was supposedly in the habit of accepting a male phallus. So instead he launches a would-be phallic attack against the older sister of the second speaker. A verbal sexual attack on a speaker's mother or older sister is a tactic commonly resorted to in these duels.

It should be noted that not all the traditional retorts to *has siktir* are in strict rhyme. One such alternative response is

> *Has   sik   istiyorsan   Istanbula   git!*
> good   penis   want if you   Istanbul to   go
> (If you want a good penis go to Istanbul.)

This retort informs the initial speaker that if he wants a good prick, he should go to Istanbul, the latter presumably being the hometown of the second speaker. Once again, the obvious principle is that when one is confronted with the threat of being sexually assaulted, one attempts to sexually assault the attacker in turn.

Still another possible retort to *Has sikter* is

> *Tabii   siktir*
> Of course   penis it is
> (Of course it's a prick!)

> *paçacı*   kemiği   mi   zannettin?*
> butcher's   shinbone   (question marker)   think did you
> (Did you think it was a sheep's shinbone?)

* *Paçacı, kemigi* is the sheep's shinbone, obtained from a butcher, used to make broth.

In this case, there is a play on the word *siktir,* which can mean 'get fucked' as the causative form of the verb *sikmek* ('to penis'), but which can also mean 'Indeed it is a prick.' The second speaker pretends to ignore the first and more usual meaning in favor of the second meaning. By so doing, the second speaker implies that the first speaker is stupidly unable to recognize a penis when he sees one.

It is perhaps worth noting that the retort tradition is so well entrenched that sometimes routine innocuous statements are converted into excuses for an exchange:

Speaker A: *Hayrola*
              What's going on?

Speaker B: *Gotune   girsin   karyola*
              Ass your to   enter let it   bedstead
              (Stick a bedstead up your ass.)

In this instance, the simple innocent question 'What's going on?' is answered with 'Stick a bedstead up your ass.' However, this is almost a play on the whole retort convention, and it probably would not be taken seriously as an invitation to duel by either participant. In true duels, there is a serious atmosphere of jousting insult. In this case, there was absolutely no offense meant by the initial remark, and its utilization as an excuse for a retort is facetious. Nevertheless, the rules of the convention are observed *karyola* ('bedstead') rhymes with *Hayrola* ('What's going on?'), and a large, unlikely object is shoved up the victim's anus. Boys familiar with the retort tradition must always be alert for playful traps of this kind. In practice, almost any word or phrase can lead an unwary boy into committing himself to the dupe's role. When one of the authors of this paper wrote to one of his friends in Turkey for examples of the retort tradition, e.g., he was victimized. The friend, after giving some examples of the tradition, ended his letter by asking, "Bora, you know this airplane that is bringing you this letter?" Bora naturally said yes to himself, expecting some comment about the airplane. The next line in the letter was:

Sana   girsin!
you to   enter let it
(May it enter your anus.)

meaning 'May that stick up your ass.' In casual conversation, the same danger prevails. The only defense is not to say *evet* ('yes' or 'yeah') when someone says, "Do you know the car we're driving in?" "Do you know the weather today?" etc. If one silently nods rather than saying, "Yeah," the attacker cannot shove the car, weather, etc., up the prospective victim's anus.

Before proceding now to the extended exchanges, it should be mentioned that in a few instances the second speaker simply buries the first speaker with a list of rhymes. In these cases, the first speaker is not given an opportunity to reply at all. He must stand and take the punishment. One such example is afforded by the use of the precipitating insult *Inek*, one of the many Turkish insults involving an animal term of abuse.

Speaker A: *Inek*
              cow

Speaker B: *Üstüne*   *binek*
top your to   ride let's
(Let me ride you.)

Dagā   *gidek*
mountain to   go let's
(Let's go to the mountain.)

Seni   *sikek*
you   penis let's
(Let me fuck you.)

This exchange involves speaker A calling B a cow—a *female* animal—followed by B's reply, 'Let me ride you. Let's go to the mountain. And there let me fuck you.' In a variant from Adana, the retort is:

Üstüne   *binek*
top your to   ride let's
(Let me ride you.)

Halebe   *gidek*
Aleppo to   go let's
(Let's go to Aleppo.)

Halep   *yıkıldı*
Aleppo   flattened
(Aleppo was flattened.)

İçine   *tıkıldı*
inside your   to stick in
[It (Aleppo) was crammed inside (your ass).]

This implies that the opponent's anus is so large that not only could an entire city fit in it but a city totally flattened with all of its ruins (e.g., collapsed walls) could be accommodated. Whether or not the flattening of Aleppo is supposed to be caused by the severity of A's sexual assault on B is open to question.

The burying or overwhelming of an initial attacker may consist of more than four lines. A fairly elaborate response of this type is the following reply to still another domestic animal insult:

Speaker A: *Esolesek*
son of a donkey

Speaker B: *Eşşoḡlu*   *eşşek*   *baban*
(Your father is the son of a donkey.)

Seni   *siken*   *çoban*
you   penising   shepherd
(The shepherd who fucks you.)

Çoban   *da*   *ben*
shepherd   so   me
(That shepherd is me.)

Aldın   *mı*   *ağzının*   *payını*
get did you   (question marker)   mouth your's   share
(Did you get your mouth's share? (i.e., You sure got the
answer you deserved)?)

Yedin   *mi*   *kıllı*   *dayım*
eat did you   (question marker)   hairy   mother's brother my
(Did you eat my hairy prick?)

O   *sözlerini*   *atlatırım*
that   words your   make jump I
(Your words don't get to me.)

Götünü   *patlatırım*
ass your   explode I
[I burst your ass (i.e., by means of a massive ejaculation).]

O   *sözlerin*   *havaya*
that   words your   air to
(Those words that you gave me go to the air (mean nothing
to me).)

Götün   *tavaya*
ass your   frying pan to
(Your ass goes into the frying pan.)

Köprü   *altı*   *cam*   *cam*
bridge   below   glass   glass
(Beneath the bridge is lots of broken glass.)

Seni   *siken*   *amcam*
you   penising   paternal uncle my
(My paternal uncle fucks you.)

Köprü   *altı*   *boy boy*
bridge   below   length length
(Underneath the bridge are varying lengths.)

Seni   *siken*   *kovboy*
you   penising   cowboy
(The cowboy fucks you.)

First of all, it should be noted that although the whole retort can be used
as a single reply, it actually consists of separate sections. Speaker B might
well have paused after 'Did you eat my hairy prick?' to see if A had anything to say. The following *atlatırım/patlatırım* couplet could be held in

abeyance to squelch anything A did say. The same is true for the *havaya/ tavaya* lines and for the final four lines concerned with *köprü* ('bridge'). On the one hand, B might elect not to use so much ammunition at once but rather to save some of his salvos for the duel which may ensue. On the other hand, B's rattling off such a list of retorts might, tactically speaking, be the most effective course of action.

In this elaborate retort sequence are a large number of allusions which are not clear at first glance. The shepherd, for instance, seems to have special significance because he lives his life alone, often far from human society. Frequently, he has only animals for companionship. According to one informant, it is the shepherds' presumed sexual relations with donkeys and dogs which are thought to make their penises larger than normal. Thus speaker B, by assuming the identity of a shepherd, takes on super-phallic characteristics. (The same informant also indicated that it was a sin to have sexual relations with animals that one eats. Hence there was supposed to be no intercourse with cattle or sheep. Donkeys and dogs, however, are not eaten and thus may serve as possible sexual partners. Assuming that intercourse with any animal is in some sense a "sin," the distinction between animals one eats and animals that one does not eat is a most interesting one.)

The reference to 'mouth's share' in 'Did you get your mouth's share?' refers to an answer in kind. In other words, your mouth issued a verbal challenge or insult; now it is being paid back in kind. It may or may not also refer to fellatio. Certainly, the next line 'Did you eat my hairy prick?' does suggest oral-genital contact. However, the informant said that it was the ass which "ate" the hairy phallus. The allusion to bursting the victim's ass is a self-congratulatory bit of hypermasculinity. One's phallus is so large and so powerful that the opponent's passive anus cannot contain it and, consequently, the poor anus quite simply falls apart. The explosion *patlaırım* implies orgasm, and, more precisely, it is the power of the orgasm or ejaculation which destroys/bursts the victim's anus.

The broken glass under the bridge is somewhat obscure. Possibly, broken glass *cam cam* was introduced primarily for rhyming purposes. However, the area under bridges in Turkey—as elswhere—is often a favorite trysting place for homosexuals, and homosexual activities do occur there. The broken glass may suggest certain physical danger (castration?) to the body. Probably, the varying lengths "under the bridge" refer to various sized phalluses, which might also cause pain. The reference to the U.S. cowboy may be like the reference to the shepherd. The cowboy, like the shepherd, spends much of his time alone with animals with whom he is thought to enjoy sexual intimacies. A cowboy is tough; he carries a gun; he has a large phallus. Thus B heaps ignominies upon A by having A submit to sexual attacks from shepherds, cowboys, and B's father's brother.

Extended Duels

Having sampled several short examples of rhymed retorts, one may be better able to appreciate what is involved in an extended duel. Here is an example of such a duel. Individual A, angered at individual B, says to him,

> *Ananın   amı*
> mother your's   cunt
> (Your mother's cunt.)

This is a serious insult and B, the addressee, may respond in one of several ways. He may go and physically strike A, or he may reply using exactly the same words or he may elect to respond with a retort. If he chooses the latter alternative, he has to end rhyme with *ami*. B could reply to A,

> *Babamın   kıllı   damı*
> father my's   hairy   roof
> (My father's hairy roof.)

This retort stresses the role of B's father as the protector of B's mother. The parts of the retort which carry meaning are 'father' and 'hairy.' Together they mean that the retorting person has a father with a hairy prick and that this father, acting as the protector of the mother, will sexually assault the first speaker as a matter of revenge. The word *damı* ('roof' in the possessive) is used primarily for the sake of rhyme. However, in the context of this retort, *damı*, following as it does the words *Babamın kıllı*, takes on the meaning of 'phallus'. (Also, since a roof covers a house, the implicit reference may even be to A's having been "covered" by B's father, that is, that A has submitted to a phallic attack by B's father.)

Now A is on the spot. Having started by mentioning the vagina of B's mother, he suddenly finds himself attacked by the hairy phallus of B's father. He must try to retort in turn. Examining B's rhyme, he quickly realizes that one part of it makes little sense. B said *damı*, which *literally* means 'roof,' and this gives A an opportunity to criticize B's retort. A could say:

> *Onu   öyle   demezler*
> that   this way   say don't they
> (They don't say it that way.)
>
> *Peynir   ekmek   yemezler*
> cheese   bread   eat don't they
> (They don't eat bread and cheese.)

Ben   de   seni   sikmezsem
I   too   you   penis don't if I
(If I don't fuck you)

Bana   (speaker's name)   demezler
me to   (speaker's name)   say don't they
[They won't call me *Ahmet* (or whatever the speaker's name is).]

A tense and fast-moving duel is now in progress. B must now come up with another answer. He realizes that now he himself as well as his mother is under possible sexual attack. A has criticized his preceding retort and has articulated the guiding principle of the dueling code: If I, A, don't fuck you, B, they, the other males, our peers, will not honor me by calling me by my name. B, sizing up the situation, spots the weak point of A's rhyme. 'They don't eat bread and cheese,' as a part of A's retort, has little to do with the context. It apparently has neither literal nor figurative relevance and is there perhaps only because *yemezler* ('they don't eat') provides a rhyming base for *demezler* ('they won't call') in this particular rhyme scheme, which involves end rhyming in lines 1, 2, and 4. With this potential weak spot in mind, B mounts a new assault:

Uyduramadın   yan   gıttı
make up couldn't you   side   went it
(You couldn't fit in the rhyme; it/what you said
went to the side/missed the target.)

Ananın   amūna (or amından)   kan   gitti
mother your's   to (or from) cunt   blood   went
(And blood went to or came from your mother's
cunt in the process.)

This is a good thrust and a good rhyme. The only problem is that the same word *gitti* is used at the end of each line to produce the rhyme. Here is a good point upon which A might base his counterattack. A's retort, using the 1, 2, and 4 line end-rhyme scheme, could be:

Uyduramadın   yancığına
make up couldn't you   side its to of it
(You didn't make a very good rhyme.)

Bin   devenin   kancığına
ride   camel's   female to
(You ride a female camel.)

Anan   çamaşır   yıkarken
mother your   laundry   washing while
(While your mother was washing clothes)

Sabun   kącmiş   amcığına
soap   escapes   cunt her to
(Soap slipped into her cunt.)

First, A tells B that his rhyme is inferior (referring to the double use of *gitti*). Then he insults him further by saying that he, B, is not even able to ride a *male* camel, only a female one. The subsequent reference to B's mother implies that her cunt is so large that anything—even the soap used in washing clothes, can gain access to it!

At this point, B cannot argue about the quality of A's rhyme. It is clear that the rhyme in B's previous retort (which used *gitti* twice) was not up to par and that A has used a very good rhyme *yancığına, kancığına,* and *amcığına* in *his* last retort. B therefore changes tactics and retorts as follows:

O   lafları   atlattık
that   words   make jump did we
(Those words don't have any effect on me.)

Ananın   amını   patlattık
mother your's   cunt   blew up we
(We blew up your mother's cunt.)

It would appear that B is on the defensive. He may be running out of rhymes and he is seemingly helpless against the onslaught of a good rhyme from A. This may be why, instead of basing his rhyme upon a selected aspect of A's previous rhyme, B retreats to the position that A's entire retort doesn't make sense, taking care to rhyme *atlattık* and *patlattık*. B does, however, attempt to burst A's mother's vagina. A, in replying to the challenge that his words don't make any sense and to the phallic attack on his mother, might offer the following:

O   laflar   havaya
that   words   air to
(Those words have no meaning.)

Taşaklar   tavaya
testicles   frying pan to
(Testicles go into the frying pan;)

Bir   göt   ver   bana
One   ass   give   me to
(You give a piece of your ass)

Ahmet (speaker's name)   *ağaya*
Ahmet (or speaker's name) Mr. to
[To me, *Mr. Ahmet* (or speaker's name).]

Note the high quality of the rhyme in this retort: lines 1, 2, and 4 with *havaya, tavaya,* and *ağaya.* A implies that B is no good and is so unmasculine that he does not need his testicles. B might therefore just as well cut off his testicles and put them in a frying pan and cook them. A thereby castrates B. Having emasculated B, A then completes the humiliating process by asking B to present his anus for penetration. A has thereby converted B from a male to a female. If B is unable to reply in kind to this excellent rhyme, then in some sense A is the "winner" of the verbal duel.

Let us now turn to the strategy of another extended verbal duel. Suppose A calls B *Ïbne,* which means passive homosexual. It is extremely important to note that the insult refers to *passive* homosexuality, not to homosexuality in general. In this context there is nothing insulting about being the active homosexual. In a homosexual relationship, the active phallic aggressor gains status; the passive victim of such aggression loses status. This distinction between homosexual roles in which it is only the passive, female role which brings discredit is not limited to Turkish culture. It is found, e.g., in rural Mexican verbal dueling known as *albures* (Ingham 1968:236). In any event, B might respond to A's calling him *Ïbne* as follows:

Speaker A: *Ïbne*
                       passive homosexual

Speaker B: *Sen   ibneysen   bana   ne?*
                       you   a queer if you   me to   what
                       (What is it to me if you are a passive homosexual?)

B could answer A's 'You queer' with 'What is it to me if *you* are a queer?' Note that B ends with *ne*, thereby rhyming with A's initial *Ïbne*. As described earlier, the individual attacked tries to make the initial attacker the *victim* of an attack instead. It is analogous to children's disputes in American culture in that the rhetorical device consists of repeating the initial insulter's pronoun so as to refer back to him. One child says to another, "you're crazy." The second might reply, "That's right, you're [or *you are*] crazy," pretending that the first child's exact words are correct, but correct only when uttered by the second child in reference to the first child. The device is not terribly sophisticated, but it is apparently reasonably effective. In this case, B says, if it is A who is the one who is queer, what is that to me? In other words, B not only calls A a passive homosexual, but he completely disassociates himself from A's problem. It is then A's turn. He might well, with a new tack not really connected to the preceding couplet, insult B by using one of the many animal insults such as:

İt   oğlu   it
dog   son of   dog
(son of a dog)

A calls B a 'son of a dog.' If B is alert, he may reply,

İti   Allah   yaratmıs
dog the   God   created
(God created the dog.)

Ananın   amını   kim   kanatmıs?
mother your's   cunt   who   made bleed
(Who made your mother's cunt bleed?)

The logic of B is that a dog is certainly (like all of us) a god-created, legitimate animal. There is nothing wrong with a dog. A dog is a legitimate being and the son of a dog is likewise a legitimate being. But while it is perfectly all right for Allah to make a dog, it is obviously *not* all right for anyone to make A's mother's cunt bleed. The cunt bleeds presumably because of the great phallic force applied to it. The implication is that A's mother is a prostitute who sleeps with anyone who comes along. A could parry this insult in the following way:

Anamın   sahibi   var
mother my's   owner   there is
[My mother has an owner (i.e., A's father).]

Bacının   da   amı   dar
sister your's   so   cunt tight
(Your sister has a tight cunt.)

Bahceden   balcan   getirip
garden from   eggplant bring and
(They bring eggplant from the garden.)

Bacının   amına   sokarlar
Sister your's   cunt to   stick they
(They stick it in your sister's cunt.)

First of all, we can see that A has duplicated the technique employed by B in B's last retort. Remember that B had responded to A's initial 'son of a dog' insult in two steps. He began by setting the record straight with respect to being a son of a dog and he ended by going on to attack A's mother. In this retort, A does much the same. He starts by correcting the record with respect to the question of the ownership of or access to his mother's vagina. A points out that his father is the one and the only one who "owns" A's mother and her sexual parts. Having answered B's attack, A goes on to an attack of his own, in this case, an attack on the virginity of B's sister.

The virginity of a male's sister is almost sacred in terms of Turkish family norms. The honor of the family depends upon it. A penis enters her *only* when she marries and the penis is that of her husband. When A refers to B's sister's tight vagina, he is referring to her virginity, but when he mentions that an "eggplant," i.e., phallus (the eggplant which grows in Turkey is long and thin), has entered B's sister's vagina, he is saying that B's sister is no longer a virgin. B's allusion to A's sister's initial virginity is not so much a compliment as a means of underlining the contrasting ruthless violation of that virginity. B must now defend the honor of his family. Perhaps he can only muster the following rather mediocre retort:

> *Bacıyı   karıştırma*
> sister the   mention don't
> (Don't mention my sister.)

> *Ananın   amına   koydurma*
> mother your's   cunt   place cause to don't
> (Don't force me to enter your mother's cunt.)

This is almost an indirect admission by B of his acceptance of defeat. He asks A not to mention his sister. Still, he does make a last effort to insult A by saying that if A does mention his (B's) sister, then he, B, will be forced to retaliate by having intercourse with A's mother.

One final example of an extended series of linked retorts should suffice to demonstrate the nature of this extraordinary tradition. In this example, there are especially instructive instances of the use of metaphor and allusion. Frequently in verbal duels, it is the nuance which is most important. It is the connotation, not the denotation, which may cause the greatest concern. Unfortunately, these subtleties are not always obvious from an examination of the text alone. This is why informants must be encouraged wherever possible to spell out "oral literary criticism," that is, *their* interpretations and understandings of particular words and phrases (Dundes 1966b).

In this example of an extended verbal duel, there are not only cryptic suggestive metaphorical descriptions which the uninitiated will probably not easily comprehend but there are allusions to other specific verbal dueling routines as well. In other words, one of the duel participants may test his opponent's knowledge of the entire tradition by referring to one or more of the shorter discrete retort sequences, several of which have been discussed here. Readers of the following verbal duel may decide for themselves how much or how little they could understand from just the texts alone.

Two young boys, say about twelve years of age, are talking. The subject is their penises. One claims that his penis is big (an obvious point of pride among both boys and men). The other boy contends that his penis is just as big. Now the first boy, A, should say something else, something more about his penis, something "impressive." So he says,

Kara   kaslı
black   eyebrowed

A says 'black eyebrowed' meaning that his penis has black hair around it. The acquisition of abundant or at least sufficient pubic hair is another point of phallic pride among young boys. "Eyebrow" is immediately understood by the second boy, B, to refer to the hair around A's penis. He may be a little overwhelmed, but his answer, which rhymes with the first boy's boast, is just as impressive. He says,

Soğan   başlı
onion   headed

This refers to another desirable phallic attribute, namely, that the head of a penis is just as big as an onion. B has thereby matched A's boast with a boast of his own. It is worth noting here that there is a well-known boys' song which lists these phallic characteristics:

ba–şi so gan gi bi or–tasi yi lan gi bi di–bi or man gi–bi bam bili   bili   bili   bom

figure 4.1

Başı   soğan   gibi
head its   onion   like

Ortası   yılan   gibi
middle its   snake   like

Dibi   orman   gibi
bottom its   forest   like

Bam bili bili bili bom

Here is a valuable insight into Turkish body esthetics. The head of a penis should resemble an onion. The middle of the penis should be as round and as smooth as a snake. The bottom should have a 'forest' of pubic hair around it. (The last line *Bam bili bili bili bom* is nonsense, but it does connote happiness. In this case, the happiness is that of a boy attaining the three stated requisite attributes of an ideal penis.) This boys' song thus confirms the appropriateness of the terms of the verbal duel.

In any case, A, realizing that B has matched his boast *kara kasli* with *soğan başlı,* tries a new gambit:

> *Ağzını   açtı*
> mouth its opened
> (opened its mouth)

'Opened its mouth' in this context means that the second speaker's female sex organ has opened its mouth as a gesture inviting sexual intercourse. Since the second speaker, B, is a male, the retort reverts to his wife. However, since B is too young to be married, the insult indirectly applies to his mother or sister. B immediately answers,

> *İçine   kaçtı*
> inside its to escaped it
> (penis enters open mouth)

The retort means that the second boy suddenly sticks his penis into the 'open mouth.' He thereby changes the intended meaning of A's retort by making it sound as though A had said that his (A's) own mother's sexual organ had opened its mouth to him (B). A realizes that he is obligated to impress B with a new rhyme. He offers

> *Dedi   hastayım*
> said   sick I
> (I am sick.)

Dedi 'said' is a semiliterary word, a kind of formal quotative. It is especially used by wandering minstrels at the begining of sentences in their poems. Here it has no significance other that that of a child imitating an elder. By saying 'I am sick,' A means that he is "sick" with love or, as we might put it in American slang, sexually "hot" for B's mother or sister. However, B is quick to counter with

> *Dedi   ustayım*
> said   expert I
> (I am an expert.)

Note that the rhyme requirement is strictly observed: *ustayım* rhymes with *hastayim.* B, by stating that he is the expert, tells A that he, B, is a great lover and that he would accordingly be greatly appreciated by A's mother or sister. One should realize that even though 'mother' and 'sister' are *not* specifically mentioned, they are definitely implied.

Duels as Tests of Verbal Skills

At this point, the duel may cease to be a matter of strategy and become more a matter of memory testing. In this form of the duel there is no absolute winning or losing per se. Nevertheless, there are some governing unwritten rules with respect to gauging the outcome. It is the first boy who is the aggressor. He begins with an initial boast or insult. The second boy must come up with an appropriate rhymed retort *or an acceptable portion thereof.* The first boy can only "win" if the second boy fails to respond with a rhyming retort. So long as the second boy succeeds, the first boy must go on proposing other retorts, each time posing a different word which the second boy must counter with a proper rhyming word. The first boy is, however, obliged to use only traditional retort sequences. He cannot make up new retorts. Thus, in effect, the first boy tests the second boy's knowledge of the verbal dueling tradition. The *Dedi* routine might continue in the following manner with A saying,

> *Dedi   inek*
> said   cow
> (you cow)

A, by calling B a cow, is testing B's familiarity with the standard retort(s) to the cow insult (see p. 141). If B knows a retort, he will simply say;

> *Dedi   binek*
> said   ride let's
> (Let's ride.)

The 'Let's ride' (*binek*) is the crucial rhyming portion of the traditional retort to the *inek* insult. B has "won" that portion of the match. A may continue,

> *Dedi   siktir*
> said   penised get
> (Get fucked.)

Again, if B knows one of the usual retorts, he may reply,

> *Dedi   mum   diktir*
> said   candle   set up
> (set up a candle)

In this unusual form of the duel, the retort need not be linked. In fact, the order of the retort couplets may be quite loose. In essence, A is simply testing B's knowledge of the whole tradition. So what B needs at this point is a good memory rather than a good sense of tactics and strategy. Presumably, only boys very familiar with the tradition and very well armed with a considerable repertoire would conduct the duel in this fashion. The fact that one boy can, in the course of a duel, test a second boy's knowledge of the different retort traditions supports the notion that these traditions are well established and well known. To be sure, there may be some Western-educated Turkish youths who are not familiar with this type of verbal duel, but there is evidence that the tradition has permeated Turkish male youth culture and this includes urban youth. For instance, the tradition finds expression in the graffiti found on bathroom walls, that is to say, in what has been termed "latrinalia" (Dundes 1966a). Interestingly enough, the same kind of verse linkage so prominently characteristic of the oral encounters occurs in the latrinalia. A common latrinalia verse in Turkey, found written in various boys' public school bathrooms is as follows:

> *Banu   yazan   Tosun*
> this   writing one   Tosun
> (This was written by Tosun.)

> *Okuyana   kosun*
> writing one to   place let him
> (Anybody who reads it is fucked by him.)

This boasting taunt 'This was written by Tosun: anybody who reads it is fucked by him,' has both the rhyme and content features of the oral insult. Tosun is a man's name as well as a word for young male ox. It implies masculinity but it also has a slightly humorous connotation. Naturally, the key reason for using Tosun is that it conveniently rhymes with *kosun*.

Now if someone enters the men's rooms and reads the insult, he will, if he is well versed (pun intended!) in the tradition, be tempted to reply. He would almost certainly write the following traditional retort:

> *Okudu bunu Molla*
> read   this   Molla
> (This was read by Molla.)

> *Tosun   gotunu   kolla*
> Tosun   ass your   watch for
> (Tosun, watch out for your own ass.)

Here are the familiar elements. The first verse contained the phallic attack. The reply warned the attacker that the attacker's ass might be the ass which is attacked. It is clearly the my-penis-up-your-anus strategy, and furthermore, like the oral duel, it may continue. A third person may enter the bathroom and take note of the exchange thus far. Assuming the role of the first writer and addressing a retort to Molla, the second writer, he might write,

> *Oğlum   Molla   sen   toysun*
> son my   Molla   you   inexperienced
> (My son Molla, you are so inexperienced;)
>
> *Tosun sana   yine   koysun*
> Tosun you to   again   place let him
> (Let Tosun fuck you again.)

This gives the advantage back to the initiator of the exchange. Notice the skillful word play. The original rhyme was on *Tosun* and *kosun*. This third verse rhymes *toysun* and *koysun*. Note also that the third person does not add a new name. Rather, since the duels are almost invariably dyadic and it is "Tosun's" turn to answer, the third person speaks on behalf of Tosun.

Still another indication of how well-known the verbal duel rhyming tradition is may be found in a Hodja folktale. The Hodja figure is, of course, *the* national character of Turkish folklore, and there are scores of tales about him. In a striking example of metafolklore (Dundes 1966b), the very nature of the dueling rhyme tradition becomes the subject of the following humorous folktale:

One day Hodja was coming home, riding his donkey from the forest, with wood he had cut for the day. A friend of his stops him and asks him what he is carrying. Hodja answers, "*Odun*" ('wood'). The friend immediately replies with a rhyme:

> *Ben   de   sana   kodum*
> I   so   you to   placed I
> (So I fucked you.)

Hodja is really mad at his friend. But he just can't come up with a rhyme like his friend's in order to put *him* down. So finally he says,

> *Bugün   günlerden   ne?*
> Today   days from   what
> (What day of the week is it today?)

His friend answers, "Parzaetesi" (Monday). "*Ben de sana kodum*" ('so I fucked you'), says the Hodja. The friend protests, "But Hodja, the rhyme doesn't fit." Hodja, red with anger, answers,

> *Uysada   kodum   uymasada   kodum*
> fit if even   place I   fit not if even   placed I
> [I fuck you if it fits; I fuck you (even) if it doesn't fit!]

As in so many of the Turkish Hodja tales, the Hodja, in childlike or fool fashion, is unable to operate successfully in the adult world. Yet he is no ordinary fool; he is a wise fool, as are so many trickster figures. Although he is slow-witted (he couldn't think of a rhyme), he is also quick-witted (he made a good retort anyway). The opposition is exemplified with respect to the rules of verbal dueling. On the one hand, the Hodja takes it upon himself to ignore or violate the established norms: He forgets about the rhyming requirement. On the other hand, when questioned about this breach, the Hodja has the last word by which means he in fact conforms to the norm, i.e., he successfully threatens placing his penis in the anus of his friend! Perhaps this suggests that the phallic thematic principle takes priority over the stylistic rhyme principle.

The Hodja narrative also tempts us to speculate that there may be a symbolic parallel between the rhyme requirement and the entire penis-in-anus image. One has to place his penis in his opponent's anus, but he has to make this threat in rhyme form. The rhyme form, like the opponent's anus, are the limiting boundaries into which the phallic thrust must go. Just as the penis must be bounded by the anus, so the verbal insult must be couched in rhyme form. With this reasoning, there does seem to be precedent for Hodja's violating the rhyme rule. Judging from some of the verbal duel texts previously cited, one can see that a particularly strong phallus is capable of bursting the anus. If bursting one's opponent's anus is an assertion of hypermasculinity, then the Hodja's breaking the rhyme convention may possibly be similarly construed. On the one hand, he is so phallic that he penetrates his opponent whether *it* (*it* being the content in the rhyme scheme and/or perhaps the presumably large phallus itself) fits or not! On the other hand, the apparent violation of formal rhyming contraints on form of content may be nothing more than an intentional sort of clumsiness.

At this point, regardless of the validity of the suggestion that the rhyme scheme may be symbolically parallel to the anus with respect to containing or restricting phallic thrusts, there can be no doubt whatsoever that the verbal dueling tradition exists in modern-day Turkey. In fact, there is evidence that a similar if not cognate tradition thrives in modern Greek folklore and northern African Arabic cultures. Most probably, this form of male verbal dueling occurs throughout the Near East. It also shares some features in common with verbal dueling in Africa generally (Mayer 1951) and also with the African-derived form of verbal dueling found in the United States known as "playing the dozens," among other terms. It is, however, apparently more similar to the Mexican *albures* (Ingham 1968:231–236) than to the American Negro dozens. But the question of the distribution of verbal dueling among the peoples of the world is another matter altogether. Even if verbal dueling as a form were universal, the specific content would surely vary with individual cultures. The issue thus is the significance of the tradition as it is found in Turkish culture.

What cultural/psychological needs does the tradition attempt to fill? Here we must enter the ever-treacherous area of interpretation. The empirical evidence of the tradition's existence is clear enough; we are similarly confident about our analysis of verbal strategies; the meaning of the tradition in the context of Turkish culture is not as obvious and may, of course, be controversial. Nevertheless, we assume that the thematic content of the linked rhyming retorts must be intimately related to Turkish male psychology.

Cultural Meaning of the Tradition

One of the most curious features of Turkish psychology or personality concerns an apparent paradox. On the one hand, Turkish world view is said to be fatalistic such that individuals are almost totally dependent upon the wishes and whims of a higher power, e.g., the Will of Allah and the inevitability of Kismet (fate). On the other hand, there appears to be a very positive attitude toward aggression. Courage and strength are highly valued male ideals. One of the most popular national sports is wrestling, and military deeds are greatly esteemed. Many Turkish boys look forward with great anticipation to their military service. The question is whether Turks are fatalistic dependent, or whether they are actively aggressive, or whether they are both. Is it possible for an individual to be docile and obedient, often to the point of what Westerners would regard as obsequiousness, to seniors and at the same time be actively engaged in proving his manliness through various socially sanctioned forms of aggression? Is there, in fact, a culturally caused insoluble problem arising from any attempt to reconcile these seemingly contradictory behavior patterns?

We believe that one of the origins of or, should we say, one of the contributing factors to the formation of specific world-view paradigms is the enculturating experience implicit or explicit in the dominant parent-child sets of relationships in any given culture. If the childhood experience is relevant to the study of world view, then it is logical to look into the Turkish boy's childhood for possible precursors for the "dependent-aggressive" conflict. In the Turkish childhood experience, it is clear that sex and age are critical social factors. In Turkish culture, there is considerable sex segregation. Furthermore, men decidedly dominate women. Publicly women are definitely subordinate to men. There is also the factor of age. The young are subordinate to the old; children are subordinate to parents. How does all this affect the young Turkish boy?

The Turkish boy learns that since men dominate women, he can assert himself with respect to his sisters and even his mother. In the world of women, even a little boy has status. But just as soon as this little boy leaves the world of women to join the segregated society of men, he suddenly finds that he has junior, very junior, status. He is at the bottom of the social pecking order. He discovers that men do rank one another. In the rural *oda,* the room in some village houses where men and only men congregrate, for example, he learns that ranking oneself with regard to one's peers is crucial and that even the seating order in the *oda* may reflect the public evaluation of any one individual's status (Stirling 1953:35). Thus, though the boy wants status, he finds he doesn't have much.

It is possible that the boy's extremely low status in the men's society is essentially equivalent or analogous to the low status of women. In other words, little boys have learned that men should be aggressive and forceful with regard to male-female relations, and so the little boys were while they lived in the world of women. But once having entered the world of men, the little boys soon realize that their own relationships to older men must, in fact, entail the assumption of passive, deferential roles quite similar to what they understand are the roles of women vis-à-vis men. Yet there is an additional critical feature of Turkish boyhood which may well bear upon the specific nature of the verbal duel pattern. This feature is circumcision.

The circumcision of boys was traditionally performed without anesthesia, typically when the boy was in the four- to eight-year age range (Öztürk 1964:346). It is, in this light, entirely appropriate for Pierce to have begun his *Life in a Turkish Village* (1964:4–8) with an account of a circumcision. It has been suggested that circumcision performed at this age may be perceived by the child as an aggressive attack (Cansever 1965:322, 326). Cansever, in his interesting study of the psychological effects of circumcision on Turkish boys, suggests further (pp. 322, 325) than circumcision, perceived by the child as symbolic castration, may lead to confusion concerning sexual identity such that boys may later tend to assume feminine traits. Cansever also indicated that some boys regarded females rather than males as the perpetrators of the castrative circumcision (although circumcision is in fact performed by a male—in villages it is often the barber). Cansever explained (p. 328) that the Turkish child's initial close contact with the mother, in contrast with the child's relationship with a distant father—Bradburn's study (1963:464) indicates that Turkish males find their fathers to be "stern, forbidding, remote, domineering, and autocratic"—may partially explain why a female rather than a male is perceived as the primary castrator. The great trust in the mother has been betrayed. She is blamed for having allowed the "castration" to take place. But whether it is the father or mother who is blamed for the traumatic ritual, the fact remains that the "higher powers" upon whom the child depended have betrayed his trust, and they have betrayed this trust with respect to a particular part of the body: the boy's phallus.

If circumcision is regarded by the young boy as a serious aggressive attack, and this is precisely what Cansever found from the results of standard psychological tests, then it is not illogical for the young boy to focus upon this part of the body as a means of combating future forms of aggression. In fact, from psychological data alone, one might well be led to hypothesize that boys would want to punish attacking males by demonstrating to these males their considerable priapic prowess. Thus to gain status among one's male peer group, one would need to prove that one's phallus was in perfect working order and in fact was sufficiently powerful to place one's opponents in the passive, feminine position. In addition, if some old men as practicing pederasts demand that young boys assume the female position, then as these young boys become older and seek to attain a man's status, they must insist, in turn, upon the active, male role. In other words, the shift from the *boy's* female passive role to the *man's* male active role is an intrinsic part of the process of becoming an adult male.

There is another facet of the circumcision experience which may be related to the verbal dueling tradition. If Cansever is correct—and he does have supporting data—in stating (1965:328) that it is frequently females who are perceived as the castrators, then it would be perfectly appropriate for a young male to perform some act of retaliatory damaging mutilation upon an analogous portion of the female anatomy. One such technique might be causing a vagina to burst or fall apart. Another might be to have the original injured party, the phallus, cause the vagina to bleed. After all, the bleeding of the newly circumcized phallus of the young boy was thought to have been caused by the castrating mother! Certainly, the repeated references to making mother's cunt bleed can be more logically explained by this than by, say, references to menstruation.

Circumcision does, then, appear to be a critical factor in the boyhood of Turkish males. And one cannot help but notice that it usually occurs at an age immediately preceding the initial participation in the verbal dueling tradition. Cansever puts the problem caused by circumcision among Turkish youth in this way: "The Turkish male, with his strivings towards, on the one hand, bravery, courage and endurance to pain, and on the other hand total submission to authority, particularly father figures, might represent a good example of the conflict between masculinity and homosexuality" (1965:329).

In the light of all this, there does seem to be some basis for maintaining that the verbal dueling pattern among young Turkish males is a vivid dramatization of the whole dilemma. It is in quasi-ritual form a concretization, an externalization, of what is undoubtedly a crucial internal psychological dilemma for most young boys. The problem is that to belong to the world of men in Turkish culture, a boy needs to prove that he is a man, not a woman, and one of the ways of proving this is to demonstrate through act or symbolic words that one has a powerful, aggressive phallus.

Yet the difficulty is that such existence in the world of men necessarily involves the danger of being put in the female position by a more powerful male. Just as women in a male-dominated society can do little more than serve as passive victims of male aggression, so boys and weak men may be forced by the same society into similar passive roles. Young boys, under the threat of having been castrated, a threat caused by a culturally induced misreading of circumcision, must do their best to avoid being like women in serving as helpless victims of male phallic aggression. In this sense, Turkish male personality is not unlike that of Algerian males as described by Miner and De Vos (1960). In analyzing the psychological characteristics of Algerians, Miner and De Vos remark that "The fear of retreating into passive homosexuality is one of the dangers besetting an individual who retreats from genital masculinity in the face of subconscious castration threat," and they also comment on the Algerian males' unconscious fear of being penetrated, as would be the case of one assumed a passive homosexual role (1960:141, 138; cf. Ingham 1968:236).

Turkish male verbal dueling serves in part as a kind of extended rite of passage. Like most if not all puberty initiation rites, the duel allows the young boy to repudiate the female world with its passive sexual role and to affirm the male world with its active sexual role. The fact that the repudiation of the female role seems to involve the partial enactment of that role by males is in accord with Bettelheim's general theory of initiation rites in which males, envious of female organs, seek to usurp female sexual powers and activities (1962:45; cf. Burton and Whiting).

The verbal duel, then, offers the opportunity of penetrating one's fellow male but also the danger of being penetrated in turn by that same fellow male. The homosexual relationship involves dependence coupled with mistrust: dependence upon friends who will not attack but mistrust in the fear that they might attack. Just as the higher powers upon whom the young boy depended suddenly launched an emasculating attack (circumcision), so one's peers upon whom one depends may suddenly threaten one's masculinity. In the verbal duel, a boy must try to aggressively hand out at least as much as—and hopefully a bit more than—he is forced to take. To the extent that Turkish world view contains an oppositional contrast between fatalistic, passive dependence *and* individualistic, active aggression, the presence of both kinds of behavior in the verbal dueling situation makes sense. The Turkish proverb "Some said he was *deli, some said he was *veli*" says much the same. *Deli* 'insane' refers to destructive, aggressive behavior, while *veli* 'saint' has connotations of passivity and stability (Öztürk 1964:349). The point is that an individual must be both. The inconsistency is consistent. Each Turkish male must be both *deli* and *veli*.

One last detail concerns the Turkish male concept of friendship. The most commonly used word for 'friend' is *Arkadaş*. Without presuming etymological expertise in Turkish, one is nevertheless tempted to remark that *arka* means among other things the backside of the body and *daş* is a suffix implying fellowship or participation. A friend is thus literally a back participant or a "backfellow." It is, in short, someone who is trustworthy and who can therefore be allowed to stand behind one. One must be careful who one allows to enter one's back zone. A nonfriend might take advantage of such a position to initiate an aggressive attack. Only a true friend or "back" can be trusted not to do so. To trust to the protection of someone is:

> *Birine   arka   vermek*
> One to   back   give to
> (to give one's back to someone)

This and many other traditional metaphors involving the *arka* root suggest that friendship is semantically related to a safe backside.[2] If these philological materials are relevant, as they would seem to be, they would tend to support the idea that an active penis attacking a passive anus has been a critical psychological configuration in Turkish culture for some time.

In any event, whether the ritual phallic penetration of an opponent's anus is a long-standing tradition or not, it seems safe to conclude that as the verbal dueling technique exists in twentieth-century Turkey, in city and in village, it is hardly an isolated, unimportant bit of esoterica. Rather it is a dynamic functioning element of Turkish culture, an element which provides a semipublic arena for the playing out of common private problems. The duel affords the young Turkish boy an opportunity to give appropriate vent to the emotional concomitants of the painful process of becoming a man.

In the spirt of this essay, we should like to close by asking the reader: "Do you know the chapter you just read?" (Reader: Yes.)

> *Sana   girsin*
> you to   enter let it

---

[2] Among the traditional words and phrases found in A. D. Alderson and Fahir Iz, eds., *The Concise Oxford Turkish Dictionary* (Oxford, 1959) and Mehmet Ali Ağakay, ed., *Türkçe Sözlük* (Ankara, 1966) which we might cite in support of our hypothesis are: (1) *arkasıpek*—literally, he has a lot of back; figuratively, one who has protectors or one who trusts somebody or one who trusts in a strong place. (2) *arkalamak*—literally, to back, to support, or to back up someone; figuratively, to help by giving trust to someone. (3) *arkadaş değil, arka tası*—literally, he's not a friend, he's a back stone (a stone in the back); figuratively, he's hardly a friend. This might be said about friends who do one harm. (4) *ardına kadar açik*—literally, open up to the backside; figuratively wide open. (5) *birinin arkasını sıvamak*—literally, to plaster (as in construction) someone's back; figuratively, to flatter someone insincerely, to butter up.

5

Signifying and Marking: Two Afro-American Speech Acts

CLAUDIA MITCHELL-KERNAN

Claudia Mitchell-Kernan is assistant professor of anthropology at Harvard University. She received her B.A. and M.A. degrees from Indiana University, her Ph.D. from the University of California, Berkeley, and has done fieldwork in the urban United States and Samoa. As one of a group of anthropologists and psychologists who have recently embarked on a long-term cross-cultural study of the development of communicative competence, she is a coauthor of the field manual prepared to guide this study (Slobin et al. 1967). The present chapter, which is adapted from her dissertation, reports on her ethnographic work in a northern California urban black community.

The last few years have seen a growing concern with Afro-American dialects on the parts of linguists concerned with descriptive and historical problems (Stewart 1967; Labov 1969b; Wolfram 1969) and educators interested in improved language and reading instruction (Barat and Shuy, 1969). These studies have made important contributions to our understanding of black speech. It has been shown, e.g., that the language of urban blacks is not, as some have implied, simply a random collection of features deviating from the standard but rather an independent dialect of English. Like other dialects of English, it has its own rules of grammar and pronunciation, rules which are explainable in terms of the history of its speakers in much the same way as rules of other English language dialects. The educator's notions of "linguistic deprivation" have also been discredited. These notions, which are based almost entirely on responses to formal questionnaires and psychological tests which assume a knowledge of middle-class white culture, have led some educators to characterize ghetto children as linguistically underdeveloped and lacking in verbal abilities. Ethnographic studies which deal with black speech behavior in terms of the culture's own conceptual system show quite different results. As Mitchell-Kernan suggests, the exceptionally rich terminological system including such folk concepts as "sounding," "rapping," "running it down," "signifying," and "marking," all referring to verbal skills, testifies to the importance which black culture assigns to verbal skills.

The American urban situation is thus best regarded as a system of multilingualism and multiculturalism characterized by the coexistence of a variety of distinct ethnic groups, each with its own body of traditions, values, and rules of speaking. To understand this complex system, it is, of course, first of all necessary to identify and describe its constituent components. But mere description of subsystems is not enough if we are to learn how the plurality of cultures operates in everyday interactions and how it affects everyday speech behavior. Members of ethnic minority groups spend much of the day in settings where dominant norms prevail. Even those individuals whose behavior on the surface may seem quite deviant tend to have at least a passive knowledge of the dominant culture. What sets them off from others is not simply the fact that they are distinct but that their own private language and life styles are juxtaposed with those of the public at large as well. Mitchell-Kernan deals with juxtaposition of values and its effect on everyday speech behavior through her analysis of signifying the marking.

Her study builds on the work of folklorists such as Abrahams and Kochman (1969), and her discussion also shows some similarity to Dundes discussion of verbal dualing (Chapter 4). Note the similarity of the skills involved in choosing topics appropriate to the context, building on weaknesses in opponents argument, and relying on shared cultural knowledge.

While folklorists, however, deal with their material in its own terms, emphasizing description and structural analysis, Mitchell-Kernan is primarily concerned with the way folk themes are used in natural conversations to convey special culture-specific meanings. All her ex-

amples are taken from tape recordings in everyday settings. She also devotes considerable discussion to the
value of signifying and marking as communicative strategies, discussing the condition under which a speaker
might find it advantageous to rely on such indirect means
of getting across his point rather than making his point
directly.

Mitchell-Kernan also illustrates many of the features of
communication discussed elsewhere in this volume, such
as the discrepancy between surface meaning and communicative function referred to by Ervin-Tripp (Chapter
7) and Sacks (Chapter 11), the notion of culture as background knowledge (Garfinkel, Chapter 10; Sacks,
Chapter 11; etc.). Of particular importance is the way in
which she relates choice of linguistic code to content and
function. Basing her ideas on Hymes's (Chapter 1) notion
of the speech event as a structured whole, she shows how
these components of speech events combine to convey
meaning. Her view of black dialects is thus quite different
from that of the other traditional dialectologists, who deal
with black dialects purely on the level of syntax and reference. For Mitchell-Kernan, these formal features of the
linguistic code are merely signals of culturally based
communicative strategies, strategies which reflect the
Afro-American concern with speaking as a skill and an
art.

Like many of the chapters in this volume, Mitchell-
Kernan's work constitutes a departure from previous
academic tradition and must be read not for its solid
research results but for the suggestions it implies for further work. Nevertheless, it would seem that her point of
view has several important implications for educational
policy. Some of these implications are discussed by
Gumperz (1970b). See also the works of Frederick Williams (1969) and Henrie (1969). For a historical discussion of Afro-American speech patterns, see Dalby 1970,
as well as his article in Kochman (in preparation).

In a linguistic community which is bilingual or bidialectal, the
code in which messages are conveyed is likely to be highly salient both to
members of the community and to the ethnographer. The languages
spoken tend to be named, and individual speakers, who speak one or the

other dialect in particular settings, identified as belonging to one or more groups. The fact that more than one language is spoken, that various social categories of people use specific languages in certain settings when discussing particular topics with members of other social categories, is a significant point of departure.

Aside from language or grammar *per se,* there are, however, other aspects of the communicative competence of such a group which require analysis. The appropriate beginning point for an investigation may be the analysis of the components which are emphasized by elaboration in a variety of speech forms. Well-elaborated components comprise a basis for selection among alternates. The pattern of such selection reveals crucial social information.

Hymes (1967) notes that precedence of components may differ from case to case, and such differences may be a basis for the classification of sociolinguistic systems. Such hierarchies of precedence may depend not simply on apparent causal direction in the interrelationships between components but also on the cultural focus (salience-emphasis) upon one or more of the components.

The artistic component is significant in black English. The salience of consideration of the artistic characteristics of speech acts in black English is evidenced by both the proliferation of terms which deal with aspects of verbal style and the common occurrence of speech routines which may be labeled by these terms. The artistic characteristics of a speech act are the characteristics that have to do with the *style* of the speech act, i.e., with the way in which something is said rather than with such components as the topic or the interlocutors. Moreover, the very term art carries connotations of value or judgment of appreciation (or nonappreciation).

The speech acts which will be described here are among the many which are given labels in black English. The terms themselves are sometimes descriptive of the style of the speech act. A partial list of such terms is: *signifying, rapping, sounding, playing the dozens, woofing, marking, loud-talking, shucking,* and *jiving.* Some of these terms are variants used in particular geographic areas. Undoubtedly, other variants exist.

I shall deal in detail two of these speech acts, treat their stylistic aspects, and attempt to relate the artistic characteristics to the other components which together comprise the speech act. I will describe how these speech acts are used and demonstrate that concern with style and value of artistic merit on the part of speakers of black English influences' the other components. Specifically, I will show that this concern has a direct effect upon the choice of the linguistic code in certain conversational settings and frequently explains the use of black dialect forms.

Value regarding verbal art in black English is evident not only from the high frequency of occurrences of nameable artistic variants but also from the comments on such variants in ongoing conversations, including stated values regarding speech use and judgments of the ability of particular speakers that are based upon considerations of artistic merit and style. Concern with verbal art is a dominant theme in black culture, and while these speech acts do not have style as their sole component, style is nevertheless the criterion which determines their effective use.

Signifying

A number of individuals interested in black verbal behavior have devoted attention to the "way of talking" which is known in many black communities as *signifying* (see Abrahams 1964; Kochman, 1969). Signifying can be a tactic employed in game activity—verbal dueling—which is engaged in as an end in itself, and it is signifying in this context which has been the subject of most previous analyses. Signifying, however, also refers to a way of encoding messages or meanings in natural conversations which involves, in most cases, an element of indirection. This kind of signifying might be best viewed as an alternative message form, selected for its artistic merit, and may occur embedded in a variety of discourse. Such signifying is not focal to the linguistic interaction in the sense that it does not define the entire speech event. While the primacy of either of these uses of the term *signifying* is difficult to establish, the latter deserves attention due to its neglect in the literature.

The standard English concept of signifying seems etymologically related to the use of this term within the black community. An audience, e.g., may be advised to signify "yes" by standing or to signify its disapproval of permissive education by saying "aye." It is also possible to say that an individual signifies his poverty by wearing rags. In the first instance we explicitly state the relationship between the meaning and the act, informing the audience that in this context the action or word will be an adequate and acceptable means of expressing approval. In the second instance, the relationship between rags and poverty is *implicit* and stems from conventional associations. It is in this latter sense that standard English and black usage have the most in common.

In the context of news analyses and interpretation we hear the rhetorical question, "What does all of this signify?" Individuals posing this question proceed to tell us what some words or events mean by placing major emphasis on the implications of the thing which is the subject of interpretation and, moreoften than not, posing inferences which are felt to logically follow. Such interpretations rely on the establishment of context, which may include antecedent conditions and background knowledge as well as the context in which the event occurred.

The black concept of *signifying* incorporates essentially a folk notion that dictionary entries for words are not always sufficient for interpreting meanings or messages, or that meaning goes beyond such interpretations. Complimentary remarks may be delivered in a left-handed fashion. A particular utterance may be an insult in one context and not in another. What pretends to be informative may intend to be persuasive. Superficially, self-abasing remarks are frequently self-praise. The hearer is thus constrained to attend to all potential meaning carrying symbolic systems in speech events—the total universe of discourse. The context embeddedness of meaning is attested to by both our reliance on the given context and, most importantly, our inclination to construct additional context from our background knowledge of the world. Facial expression and tone of voice serve to orient us to one kind of interpretation rather than another. Situational context helps us to narrow meaning. Personal background knowledge about the speaker points us in different directions. Expectations based on role or status criteria enter into the sorting process. In fact, we seem to process all manner of information against a background of assumptions and expectations. Thus, no matter how sincere the tone of voice affected by the used car salesman, he is always suspect.

Labeling a particular utterance as signifying thus involves the recognition and attribution of some implicit content or function, which is potentially obscured by the surface content or function. The obscurity may lie in the relative difficulty it poses for interpreting (1) the meaning or message the speaker is adjudged as intending to convey; (2) the addressee—the person or persons to whom the message is directed; (3) the goal orientation or intent of the speaker. A precondition for the application of the term *signifying* to some speech act is the assumption that the meaning decoded was consciously and purposely formulated at the encoding stage. In reference to function the same condition must hold.

The following examples of signifying are taken from natural conversations recorded in Oakland, California. Each example will be followed by interpretations, intended to clarify the messages and meanings being conveyed in each case.

1. The interlocutors here are Barbara, an informant; Mary, one of her friends; and the researcher. The conversation takes place in Barbara's home and the episode begins as I am about to leave.

BARBARA:	What are you going to do Saturday? Will you be over here?
R:	I don't know.
BARBARA:	Well, if you're not going to be doing anything, come by. I'm going to cook some chit'lins. [Rather jokingly] Or are you one of those Negroes who don't eat chit'lins?
MARY:	[Interjecting indignantly] That's all I hear lately—soul food, soul food. If you say you don't eat it you get accused of being saditty [affected, considering oneself superior].
	[Matter of factly] Well, I ate enough black-eyed peas and neck-

bones during the depression that I can't get too excited over it. I eat prime rib and T-bone because I like to, not because I'm trying to be white. [Sincerely] Negroes are constantly trying to find some way to discriminate against each other. If they could once get it in their heads that we are all in this together maybe we could get somewhere in this battle against the man.

[Mary leaves.]

BARBARA: Well, I wasn't signifying at her, but like I always say, if the shoe fits, wear it.

While the manifest topic of Barbara's question was food, Mary's response indicates that this is not a conversation about the relative merits of having one thing or another for dinner. Briefly, Barbara was, in the metaphors of the culture, implying that Mary (and/or I) is an assimilationist.

Let us first deal with the message itself, which is somewhat analogous to an allegory in that the significance or meaning of the words must be derived from known symbolic values. An outsider or nonmember (perhaps not at this date) might find it difficult to grasp the significance of eating chit'lins or not eating chit'lins. Barbara's "one of those Negroes that" places the hearer in a category of persons which, in turn, suggests that the members of that category may share other features, in this case, negatively evaluated ones, and indicates that there is something here of greater significance than mere dietary preference.

Chit'lins are considered a delicacy by many black people, and eating chit'lins is often viewed as a traditional dietary habit of black people. Changes in such habits are viewed as gratuitous aping of whites and are considered to imply derogation of these customs. The same sort of sentiment often attaches to other behaviors such as changes in church affiliation of upwardly mobile blacks. Thus, not eating or liking chit'lins may be indicative of assimilationist attitudes, which in turn imply a rejection of one's black brothers and sisters. It is perhaps no longer necessary to mention that assimilation is far from a neutral term intraculturally. Blacks have traditionally shown ambivalence toward the abandonment of ethnic heritage. Many strong attitudes attached to certain kinds of cultural behavior seem to reflect a fear of cultural extermination.

It is not clear at the outset to whom the accusation of being an assimilationist was aimed. Ostensibly, Barbara addressed her remarks to me. Yet Mary's response seems to indicate that she felt herself to be the real addressee in this instance. The signifier may employ the tactic of obscuring his addressee as part of his strategy. In the following case the remark is, on the surface, directed toward no one in particular.

2.   I saw a woman the other day in a pair of stretch pants, she must have weighed 300 pounds. If she knew how she looked she would burn those things.

Such a remark may have particular significance to the 235-pound member of the audience who is frequently seen about town in stretch pants. She is likely to interpret this remark as directed at her, with the intent of providing her with the information that she looks singularly unattractive so attired.

The technique is fairly straightforward. The speaker simply chooses a topic which is selectively relevant to his audience. A speaker who has a captive audience, such as a minister, may be accused of signifying by virtue of his text being too timely and selectively apropos to segments of his audience.

It might be proposed that Mary intervened in the hope of rescuing me from a dilemma by asserting the absence of any necessary relationships between dietary habits and assimilationist attitudes. However, Barbara's further remarks lend credence to the original hypothesis and suggest that Mary was correct in her interpretation, that she *was* the target of the insinuation.

BARBARA: I guess she was saying all that for your benefit. At least, I hope she wasn't trying to fool me. If she weren't so worried about keeping up with her saditty friends, she would eat less T-bone steak and buy some shoes for her kids once in a while.

Although Mary never explicitly accuses Barbara of signifying, her response seems tantamount to such an accusation, as is evidenced by Barbara's denial. Mary's indignation registers quite accurately the spirit in which some signifying is taken.

This brings us to another feature of signifying: The message often carries some negative import for the addressee. Mary's response deserves note. Her retaliation also involves signifying. While talking about obstacles to brotherhood, she intimates that behavior such as that engaged in by Barbara is typical of artificially induced sources of schism which are in essence superficial in their focus, and which, in turn, might be viewed as a comment on the character of the individual who introduces divisiveness on such trivial grounds.

Barbara insulted Mary, her motive perhaps being to injure her feelings or lower her self-esteem. An informant asked to interpret this interchange went further in imputing motives by suggesting possible reasons for Barbara's behavior. He said that the answer was buried in the past. Perhaps Barbara was repaying Mary for some insult of the past, settling a score, as it were. He suggested that Barbara's goal was to raise her own self-esteem by asserting superiority of a sort over Mary. Moreover, he said that this kind of interchange was probably symptomatic of the relationship between the two women and that one could expect to find them jockeying for position on any number of issues. "Barbara was trying to *rank* Mary," to put her down by typing her. This individual seemed to be defining the function of signifying as the establishment of dominance in this case.

Messages like the preceding are indirect not because they are cryptic (i.e., difficult to decode) but because they somehow force the hearer to take additional steps. To understand the significance of not eating chit'lins, one must voyage to the black social world and discover the characteristics of social types referred to and the cultural values and attitudes toward them.

The indirect message may take any number of forms, however, as in the following example:

3. The relevant background information lacking in this interchange is that the husband is a member of the class of individuals who do not wear suits to work.

WIFE:	Where are you going?
HUSBAND:	I'm going to work.
WIFE:	(Your're wearing) a suit, tie, and white shirt? You didn't tell me you got a promotion.

The wife, in this case, is examining the truth value of her husband's assertion (A) "I'm going to work" by stating the obvious truth that (B) he is wearing a suit. Implicit is the inappropriateness of this dress as measured against shared background knowledge. In order to account for this discrepancy, she advances the hypothesis (C) that he has received a promotion and is now a member of the class of people who wear suits to work. B is obviously true, and if C is not true, then A must also be false. Having no reason to suspect that C is true, she is signifying that he is not going to work and moreover, that he is lying about his destination.

Now the wife could have chosen a more straightforward way of finding an acceptable reason for her husband's unusual attire. She might have asked, e.g., "Why are you wearing a suit?" And he could have pleaded some unusual circumstances. Her choice to entrap him suggests that she was not really seeking information but more than likely already had some answers in mind. While it seems reasonable to conclude that an accusation of lying is implicit in the interchange, and one would guess that the wife's intent is equally apparent to the husband, this accusation is never made explicit.

This brings us to some latent advantages of indirect messages, especially those with negative import for the receiver. Such messages, because of their form—they contain both explicit and implicit content— structure interpretation in such a way that the parties have the option of avoiding a real confrontation [Brown (1958:314) provides a similar discussion]. Alternately, they provoke confrontations without at the same time exposing unequivocally the speaker's intent. The advantage in either case is for the speaker because it gives him control of the situation at the receiver's expense. The speaker, because of the purposeful ambiguity of his original remark, reserves the right to subsequently insist on the harmless interpretation rather than the provocative one. When the situation is such that there is no ambiguity in determining the addressee, the addressee faces the possibility that if he attempts to confront the speaker, the latter will deny the message or intent imputed, leaving him in the embarrassing predicament of appearing contentious.

Picture, if you will, the secretary who has become uneasy about the tendency of her knee to come into contact with the hand of her middle-aged boss. She finally decides to confront him and indignantly informs him that she is not that kind of a girl. He responds by feigning hurt innocence: "How could you accuse me of such a thing?" If his innocence is genuine, her misconstrual of the significance of these occasions of body contact possibly comments on her character more than his. She has no way of being certain, and she feels foolish. Now a secretary skilled in the art of signifying could have avoided the possibility of "having the tables turned" by saying "Oh, excuse me Mr. Smith, I didn't mean to get my knee in your way." He would have surely understood her message if he were guilty, and a confrontation would have been avoided. If he were innocent, the remark would have probably been of no consequence.

When there is some ambiguity with reference to the addressee, as in the first example, the hearer must expose himself as the target before the confrontation can take place. The speaker still has the option of retreating and the opportunity, while feigning innocence, to jibe, "Well, if the shoe fits, wear it." The individual who has a well-known reputation for this kind of signifying is felt to be sly and, sometimes, not man or woman enough to come out and say what he means.

Signifying does not, however, always have negative valuations attached to it; it is clearly thought of as a kind of art—a clever way of conveying messages. In fact, it does not lose its artistic merit even when it is malicious. It takes some skill to construct messages with multilevel meanings, and it sometimes takes equal expertise in unraveling the puzzle presented in all of its many implications. Just as in certain circles the clever punster derives satisfaction and is rewarded by his hearers for constructing a multisided pun, the signifier is also rewarded for his cleverness.

4.   The following interchange took place in a public park. Three young men in their early twenties sat down with the researcher, one of whom initiated a conversation in this way:

I: Mama, you sho is fine.
R: That ain' no way to talk to your mother.

[Laughter]

I: You married?
R: Um hm.
I: Is your husband married?

[Laughter]

R: Very.
      [The conversation continues with the same young man doing most of the talking. He questions me about what I am doing and I tell him about my research project. After a couple of minutes of discussing "rapping," he returns to his original style.]
I: Baby, you a real scholar. I can tell you want to learn. Now if you'll just cooperate a li'l bit, I'll show you what a good teacher I am. But first we got to get into my area of expertise.
R: I may be wrong but seems to me we already in your area of expertise.

[Laughter]

I: You ain' so bad yourself, girl. I ain't heard you stutter yet. You a li'l fixated on your subject though. I want to help a sweet thang like you all I can. I figure all that book learning you got must mean you been neglecting other areas of your education.
II: Talk that talk! [Gloss: *Olé*]
R: Why don't you let me point out where I can best use your help.
I: Are you sure you in the best position to know?

[Laughter]

I: I'mo leave you alone, girl. Ask me what you want to know. Tempus fugit, baby.

[Laughter]

The folk label for the kind of talking engaged in by I is *rapping,* defined by Kochman as "a fluent and lively way of talking characterized by a high degree of personal style," which may be used when its function is referential or directive—to get something from someone or get someone to do something. The interchange is laced with innuendo—signifying because it alludes to and implies things which are never made explicit.

The utterance which initiated the conversation was intended from all indications as a compliment and was accepted as such. The manner in which it was framed is rather stylized and jocularly effusive, and as such makes the speaker's remarks less bold and presumptuous and is permissive of a response which can acknowledge the compliment in a similar and jokingly impersonal fashion. The most salient purpose of the compliment was to initiate a conversation with a strange woman. The response served to indicate to the speaker that he was free to continue; probably any response (or none at all) would not have terminated his attempt to engage the hearer, but the present one signaled to the speaker that it was appropriate to continue in his original style. The factor of the audience is crucial because it obliges the speaker to continue attempting to engage the addressee once he has begun. The speaker at all points has a surface addressee, but the linguistic and nonlinguistic responses of the other two young men indicate that they are very aware of being integral participants in this interchange. The question "Is your husband married?" is meant to suggest to the hearer, who seeks to turn down the speaker's advances by pleading marital ties, that such bonds should not be treated as inhibitory except when one's husband has by his behavior shown similar inhibition.

The speaker adjusts his rap to appeal to the scholarly leanings of his addressee, who responds by suggesting that he is presently engaging in his area of virtuosity. I responds to this left-handed compliment by pointing out that the researcher is engaging in the same kind of speech behavior and is apparently an experienced player of the game—"I' ain't heard you stutter yet."—which is evidenced by her unfaltering responses. At the same time he notes the narrowness of the speaker's interests, and states the evidence leading him to the conclusion that there must be gaps in her knowledge. He benevolently offers his aid. His maneuvers are offensive and calculated to produce defensive responses. His repeated offers of aid are intended ironically. A member of the audience interjects, "Talk that talk!" This phrase is frequently used to signal approval of some speaker's virtuosity in using language skillfully and colorfully and, moreover, in using language which is appropriate and effective to the social context.

The content of the message is highly directive. Those unfamiliar with black cultural forms might in fact interpret the message as threatening. But there are many linguistic cues that suggest that the surface meaning is not to be taken seriously. Note particularly the use of such expressions as "scholar," "cooperate," "area of expertise," "fixated on your subject," and "neglecting other areas of your education." All these relatively formal or literary expressions occur in sentences spoken with typically black phonology and black grammar (e.g., "I ain't heard . . ." and "Are you sure you in the best position to know?"). By his code selection and by paralinguistic cues such as a highly stylized leer, the speaker indicates that he is parodying a tête-à-tête and not attempting to engage the researcher in anything other than conversation. He is merely demonstrating his ability to use persuasive language, "playing a game," as it were. The researcher signals acknowledgment by her use of black forms such as "That ain' no way no way . . .", and " . . . we already in . . .". The speaker indicates that the game is over by saying, "I'mo leave you alone," and redirects the conversation. The juxtaposition of the lexical items "tempus fugit" and "baby," which typically are not paired, is meant to evoke more humor by accentuating the stylistic dissonance of the speech sequence.

Signifying as a Form of Verbal Art

All other conditions permitting, a style which has artistic merit is more likely to be selected than on which does not because of positive cultural values assigned to the skillful use of speech. Having discussed some of the characteristics of signifying, I would now like to examine briefly the artistic characteristics of signifying.

No attempt will be made here to formulate an all-encompassing definition of art. That individuals may differ in their conceptions of art is made patently clear, e.g., by Abrahams's (1964:54) summarizing statement that signifying is "many facets of the smart-alecky attitude." That my appreciation differs has, more than likely, been communicated in these pages. For present purposes, what is art is simply what native speakers judge witty, skillful, and worthy of praise. This is a working definition at best. It nevertheless serves to limit our field of discourse and, more importantly, to base our judgments on the native speaker's own point of view.

It is true that poor attempts at signifying exist. That these attempts are poor art rather than non-art is clear from comments with which some of them are met. Needless and extreme circumlocution is considered poor art. In this connection, Labov has made similar comments about sounding (Labov et al. 1968). He cites peer group members as reacting to some sounds with such metalinguistic responses as "That's phony" and "That's lame." Signifying may be met with similar critical remarks. Such failures, incidentally, are as interesting as the sucesses, for they provide clues as to the rules by violating one or more of them while, at the same time, meeting other criteria.

One of the defining characteristics of signifying is its indirect intent or metaphorical reference. This indirection appears to be almost purely stylistic. It may sometimes have the function of being euphemistic or diplomatic, but its art characteristics remain in the forefront even in such cases. Without the element of indirection, a speech act could not be considered signifying. Indirection means here that the correct semantic (referential interpretation) or signification of the utterance cannot be arrived at by a consideration of the dictionary meaning of the lexical items involved and the syntactic rules for their combination alone. The apparent significance of the message differs from its real significance.

Meaning conveyed is not apparent meaning. Apparent meaning serves as a key which directs hearers to some shared knowledge, attitudes, and values or signals that reference must be processed metaphorically. The words spoken may actually refer to this shared knowledge by contradicting it or by giving what is known to be an impossible explanation of some obvious fact. The indirection, then, depends for its decoding upon shared knowledge of the participants, and this shared knowledge operates on two levels.

It must be employed, first of all, by the participants in a speech act in the recognition that signifying is occurring and that the dictionary-syntactical meaning of the utterance is to be ignored. Second, this shared knowledge must be employed in the reinterpretation of the utterance. It is the cleverness used in directing the attention of the hearer and audience to this shared knowledge upon which a speaker's artistic talent is judged.

Topic may have something to do with the artistic merit of an act of signifying. Although practically any topic may be signified about, some topics are more likely to make the overall act of signifying more appreciated. Sex is one such topic. For example, an individual offering an explanation for a friend's recent grade slump quipped, "He can't forget what happened to him underneath the apple tree," implying that the young man was preoccupied with sex at this point in his life and that the preoccupation stemmed from the relative novelty of the experience. A topic which is suggested by ongoing conversation is appreciated more than one which is peripheral. Finally, an act of *signifying* which tops a preceding one, in a verbal dueling sense, is especially appreciated.

Kochman cites such an example in the context of a discussion of *rapping:*

A man coming from the bathroom forgot to zip his pants. An unescorted party of women kept watching him and laughing among themselves. The man's friends hip (inform) him to what's going on. He approaches one woman—"Hey, baby, did you see that big Cadillac with the full tires, ready to roll in action just for you?" She answers, "No, mother-fucker, but I saw a little gray Volkswagen with two flat tires" (1969:27).

As mentioned earlier, signifying may be a tactic used in rapping, defined by Kochman as "a fluent and lively way of talking, always characterized by a high degree of personal style" (1969:27).

Verbal dueling is clearly occurring; the first act of signifying is an indirect and humorous way of referring to shared knowledge—the women have been laughing at the man's predicament. It is indirect in that it doesn't mention what is obviously being referred to. The speaker has cleverly capitalized on a potentially embarrassing situation by taking the offensive and at the same time, displaying his verbal skill. He emphasizes the sexual aspect of the situation with a metaphor that implies power and class. However, he is, as Kochman says, "capped." The woman wins the verbal duel by replying with an act of signifying which builds on the previous one. The reply is indirect, sexual, and appropriate to the situation. In addition, it employs the same kind of metaphor and is, therefore, very effective.

Motherfucker is a rather common term of address in such acts of verbal dueling. The term *nigger* also is common in such contexts, e.g., "Nigger, it was a monkey one time wasn't satisfied till his ass was grass" and "Nigger, I'm gon be like white on rice on you ass."

These two examples are illustrative of a number of points of good signifying. Both depend on a good deal of shared cultural knowledge for their correct semantic interpretation. It is the intricacy of the allusion to shared knowledge that makes for the success of these speech acts. The first refers to the toast "The Signifying Monkey." The monkey signified at the lion until he got himself in trouble. A knowledge of this toast is necessary for an interpretation of the message. "Until his ass was grass"—meaning "until he was beaten up"—can only be understood in the light of its common use in the speech of members of the culture and occurs in such forms as "His ass was grass and I was the lawnmower." What this example means is something like: You have been signifying at me and, like the monkey, you are treading on dangerously thin ice. If you don't stop, I am likely to become angry and beat you!

"Nigger, I'm gon be like white on rice on your ass" is doubly clever. A common way of threatening to beat someone is to say, "I'm gonna be all over your ass." And how is white on rice?—all over it. Metaphors such as these may lose their effectiveness over time due to overuse. They lose value as clever wit.

The use of the term *nigger* in these examples is of considerable linguistic interest. It is often coupled with code features which are far removed from standard English. That is, the code utilizes many linguistic markers which differentiate black speech from standard English or white speech. Frequently, more such markers than might ordinarily appear in the language of the speaker are used. Thus participants in these speech acts must show at least some degree of bidilectalism in black and standard English. They must be able to shift from one code to another for stylistic effect. Note, e.g., that the use of the term *nigger* with other black English markers has the effect of "smiling when you say that." The use of standard English with *nigger,* in the words of an informant, represents "the wrong tone of voice" and may be taken as abusive.

Code selection and terminological choice thus have the same function. They highlight the fact that black English is being used and that what is being engaged in is a black speech act. More is conveyed here than simple emphasis on group solidarity. The hearer is told that this is an instance of black verbal art and should be interpreted in terms of the subcultural rules for interpreting such speech acts.

Code and content serve to define the style being used, to indicate its tone, and to describe the setting and participants as being appropriate to the use of such an artistic style. Further, such features indicate that it should be recognized that a verbal duel is occurring and that what is said is meant in a joking, perhaps also threatening, manner. A slight switch in code may carry implications for other components in the speech act. Because verbal dueling treads a fine line between play and real aggression, it is a kind of linguistic activity which requires strict adherence to sociolinguistic rules. To correctly decode the message, a hearer must be finely tuned to values which he observes in relation to all other components of the speech act. He must rely on his conscious or unconscious knowledge of the sociolinguistic rules governing this usage.

Marking

A common black narrative tactic in the folk tale genre and in accounts of actual events is the individuation of characters through the use of direct quotation. When in addition, in reproducing the words of individual actors, a narrator affects the voice and mannerisms of the speakers, he is using the style referred to as *marking* (clearly related to standard English 'mocking'). Marking is essentially a mode of characterization. The marker attempts to report not only what was said but the way it was said, in order to offer implicit comment on the speaker's background, personality, or intent. Rather than introducing personality or character traits in some summary form, such information is conveyed by reproducing or sometimes inserting aspects of speech ranging from phonological features to particular content which carry expressive value. The meaning in the message of the marker is signaled and revealed by his reproduction of such things as phonological or grammatical peculiarities, his preservation of mispronounced words or provincial idioms, dialectal pronunciation, and, most particularly, paralinguistic mimicry.

The marker's choice to reproduce such features may reflect only his desire to characterize the speaker. It frequently signifies, however, that the characterization itself is relevant for further processing the meaning of the speaker's words. If, e.g., some expressive feature has been taken as a symbol of the speaker's membership in a particular group, his credibility may come into question on these grounds alone.

The marker attempts to replay a scene for his hearers. He may seek to give the implications of the speaker's remarks, to indicate whether the emotions and affect displayed by the speaker were genuine or feigned, in short to give his audience the full benefit of all the information he was able to process by virtue of expressive or context cues imparted by the speaker. His performance may be more in the nature of parody and caricature than true imitation. But the features selected to overplay are those which are associated with membership in some class. His ability to get his message across, in fact, relies on folk notions of the covariance of linguistic and nonlinguistic categories, combined, of course, with whatever special skill he possesses for creating imagery.

The kind of context most likely to elicit marking is one in which the marker assumes his hearers are sufficiently like himself to be able to interpret this metaphoric communication. Since there is, more likely than not, something unflattering about the characterization, and the element of ridicule is so salient, the relationship between a marker and his audience is likely to be one of familiarity and intimacy and mutual positive affect.

An informant quoted a neighbor to give me an appreciation of her dislike for the woman. She quoted the following comment from Pearl in a style carefully articulated to depict her as "putting on the dog," parodying gestures which gave the impression that Pearl is preposterously affected: "You know my family owns their own home and I'm just living here temporarily because it is more beneficial to collect the rent from my own home and rent a less expensive apartment." "That's the kind of person she is," my informant added, feeling no need for further explanation. This is, incidentally, a caricature of a social type which is frequently the object of scorn and derision. The quote was delivered at a pitch considerably higher than was usual for the informant, and the words were enunciated carefully so as to avoid loss of sounds and elision characteristic of fluid speech. What was implied was not that the phonological patterns mimicked are to be associated with affectation in a one-one relationship but that they symbolize affectation here. The marker was essentially giving implicit recognition to the fact that major disturbances in fluency are indexes of "monitored" speech. The presence of the features are grounds for the inference that the speaker is engaged in impression management which is contextually inappropriate. Individuals who are characterized as "trying to talk proper" are frequently marked in a tone of voice which is rather falsetto.

A marker wishing to convey a particular impression of a speaker may choose to deliver a quotation in a style which is felt to best suit what he feels lies underneath impression management or what is obscured by the speaker's effective manipulation of language. In the following example, the marker departs radically from the style of the speaker for purposes of disambiguation. The individuals here, with the exception of S_1, had recently attended the convention of a large corporation and had been part of a group which had been meeting prior to the convention to develop some strategy for putting pressure on the corporation to hire more blacks in executive positions. They had planned to bring the matter up at a general meeting of delegates, but before they had an opportunity to do so, a black company man spoke before the entire body. S_2 said, "After he spoke our whole strategy was undermined, there was no way to get around his impact on the whites."

S_1:   What did he say?

S_2:   [Drawling] He said, "Ah'm so-o-o happy to be here today. First of all, ah want to thank all you good white folks for creatin so many opportunities for us niggers and ya'll can be sho that as soon as we can git ourselves qualified we gon be filin our applications. Ya'll done done what we been waiting for a long time. Ya'll done give a colored man a good job with the company."

S_1:   Did he really say that?

S_3:   Um hm, yes he said it. Girl, where have you been. [Put down by intimating S_1 was being literal]

S_1:   Yeah, I understand, but what did he really say?

S_4:   He said, "This is a moment of great personal pride for me. My very presence here is a tribute to the civil rights movement. We now have ample evidence of the good faith of the company and we must now begin to prepare ourselves to handle more responsible positions. This is a major step forward on the part of the company. The next step is up to us." In other words, he said just what [S_2] said he said. He sold us out by accepting that kind of tokenism.

S_2 attempted to characterize the speaker as an Uncle Tom by using exaggerated stereotyped southern speech coupled with content that was compromising and denigrating. It would certainly be an overstatement to conclude that southern regional speech is taken by anyone as a sign of being an "Uncle Tom," but there is an historical association with the model of this sterotype being southern.

The characterization of individuals according to the way they speak is, of course, not peculiar to black people, although the implicit association of particular ways of speaking with specific social types may be more elaborated than elsewhere.

The parodying of southern regional black speech may sometimes serve as a device for characterizing a speaker as uneducated or unintelligent, and sometimes it is used to underscore the guilelessness of the speaker. The marker encodes his subjective reactions to the speaker and is concerned with the expressive function of speech more than its referential function.

Because marking relies on linguistic expression for the communication of messages, it is revealing of attitudes and values relating to language. It frequently conveys many subtleties and can be a significant source of information about conscious and unconscious attitudes toward language. An individual, on occasion, may mark a nonblack using exaggerated black English, with the emphasis clearly being on communicating that the subject was uneducated and used nonstandard usages. Perhaps more than anything, marking exhibits a finely tuned linguistic awareness in some areas and a good deal of verbal virtuosity in being able to reproduce aspects of speech which are useful in this kind of metaphorical communication.

Conclusion

Signifying and marking exemplify the close relationship of message form to content and function which characterizes black verbal behavior. Meaning, often assumed by linguists to be signaled entirely through code features, is actually dependent upon a consideration of other components of a speech act (cf. Gumperz 1964b). A remark taken in the spirit of verbal dueling may, e.g., be interpreted as an insult by virtue of what on the surface seems to be merely a minor change in personnel, or a minor change in code or topic. Crucially, paralinguistic features must be made to conform to the rules. Change in posture, speech rate, tone of voice, facial expression, etc., may signal a change in meaning. The audience must also be sensitive to these cues. A change in meaning may signal that members of the audience must shift their responses, and that metalinguistic comments may no longer be appropriate.

It is this focus in black culture—the necessity of applying sociolinguistic rules, in addition to the frequent appeal to shared background knowledge for correct semantic interpretation—that accounts for some of the unique character and flavor of black speech. Pure syntactic and lexical elaboration is supplemented by an elaboration of the ability to carefully and skillfully manipulate other components of the speech act in order to create new meanings.

6

Riddles: Expressive Models of Interrogation[1]

JOHN M. ROBERTS AND MICHAEL L. FORMAN

John M. Roberts is Professor of Anthropology at Cornell
University. He received his doctorate from Yale University and has taught at Harvard and the University of
Nebraska. His principal fieldwork has been with the Zuni
and Navajo Indians of the American Southwest, emphasizing values and laws. His concern has been to develop
fresh approaches to the description of cultural behavior
in terms of information storage and management (see
Roberts 1964 and references therein). Roberts' major
research currently deals with the investigation of expressive culture as it is refflected in this paper. He has also
been actively concerned with the development of formal
analysis of anthropology.

Michael Forman, a linguist specializing in Philippine
languages, has done graduate work at Cornell University.
He is currently affiliated with the Pacific and Asian
Linguistic Institute, University of Hawaii.

This previously unpublished study of riddling suggests
the complexities encountered when any one of the many
genres of speech activity—such as oath taking, verbal
dueling, praying, cursing, and punning—found in human
cultures are studied. First, there is the problem of description—how the genre may be described, in both general and specific terms. Any serious study is confronted

[1] This research was supported in part by PHS Research Grant MH 08161-03. The
authors are particularly indebted to William W. Lambert and Brian Sutton-Smith for help in
dealing with the theory of riddles. They are grateful to Sheila Forman for her aid in conducting the Tagalog study and to Cynthia Burton and Maureen Liebl for assistance. They
must also thank Donn V. Hart, Gerald B. Kelley, Bernard Lambert, Terence S. Turner, and
numerous students and informants for help and suggestions.

at present, as Roberts and Forman point out, by lack of agreed definitions on precisely what is being studied, by inadequate reporting in comparative ethnographic literature, and other problems. Second, there is the problem of explanation. Here lies the special interest of the approach taken in this chapter.

In virtue of a general hypothesis relating genres of speech to socialization, Roberts and Forman are able to use comparative data as a preliminary approximation (a point they stress), and to seek to confirm an explanation in more fine-grained experimentation in their own society. This approach opens up the possibility of both of generality for results obtained only in one society and of continued relevance and validation of reports from societies no longer accessible, as a result of extinction or change.

Notice that the key to the method is that it is able to deal with not only the presence or absence of a trait but also with the frequency of occurrence of that trait, and with the strength or weakness of commitment or motivation. The method can be seen as one realization of Edward Sapir's view that "it is only through an analysis of variation that the reality and meaning of a norm can be established at all" (1949f:576). Sapir called for "an investigation into living speech" (1949a:593). Robert's approach shows one way that Sapir's concern with the concrete, with personally realized meanings in actual networks of communicative experience, can be linked to theories of human culture as a whole. Notice also that variation in order to validate pattern is essential to the methodology developed by Labov (Chapter 19).

Roberts and Forman had initially thought that riddling shows a relationship mainly with the presence of a strong interest in strategy (Abrahams 1968); instead, their preliminary cross-cultural survey displays a primary relationship with strong training for responsibility (note the parallels with Dundes', verbal dueling Chapter 4). The Tagalog inquiry confirms this latter link. At the same time it indicates a shift in principle settings for riddling, from wakes and courtship to schools. It also suggests a possible difference between men and women in the kinds of riddling preferred, and it links riddling with the socially important role of intermediary in marriage arrangements. The study of American students further substantiates the fact that strategy is not the answer, and it brings out new

associations between high interest in riddling and the importance of chores (responsibility) and the absence of
nagging in childhood, as well as with a balanced or positive attitude toward oral questioning. The paper concludes with a sketch of the further lines of inquiry that
are needed for an adequate theory.

One point of general methodological importance
touched on is the study by fieldworkers of the relation
between their own modes of questioning and those native
to the community. Both Hymes (1969) and Grimshaw
(1969) provide discussions of cross-cultural variations in
modes of questioning. Goffman (1967) discusses involvement in conversational terms.

In the United States riddling is largely a children's recreational
activity, although many adults retain an interest. If riddling is not particularly salient, then, it is still so general that everyone, other than quite small
children has some familiarity with it. (It will be assumed here that the
reader has this general familiarity.)

Riddles thus have a place in American culture, just as they do, often
more importantly, in many other cultures throughout the world. Riddles,
however, do not occur in all cultures; and within the cultures in which
they occur, individuals and groups differ, both in their involvement in
riddles and riddling and in their control of them. There is something here
to be explained. An adequate theory must account for the uneven distribution of the genre in time and space, both in culture-historical and in
functional terms, for differential involvement and cognitive control of the
patterns of the genre, and for the structure and meaning of the patterns
themselves. No such theory of riddling now exists, but the research
reported here suggests a view point from which such a theory may be
developed.

Our general approach has been developed through the study of games
and similar phenomena and is embodied in a number of publications.[2] In
the main these studies have been concerned with explaining the interest
and competence that persons acquire in what may be called *expressive
models*. By 'model' is meant simply a representation of something. Here
we are concerned with the *natural models* found in cultures, such as
games, portraits, maps, etc., rather that with the formal models of mathe-

[2] Roberts, Arth, and Bush 1959; Roberts and Sutton-Smith 1962; Roberts, Sutton-Smith,
and Kendon 1963; Sutton-Smith, Roberts, and Kozelka 1963; Sutton-Smith, and Roberts
1964; Sutton-Smith, Roberts, and Rosenberg 1964; Roberts 1965; Roberts, Hoffmann, and
Sutton-Smith 1965; Roberts and Sutton-Smith 1966; Roberts, Thompson, and Sutton-Smith
1966; Sutton-Smith and Roberts 1967; and Roberts and Koenig (1968).

matics and science. Every such natural model has both expressive and cognitive components, but usually one of the two is the more important. Thus chess, regarded as a model of war, emphasizes the expressive component, while an aerial photograph, as a model of terrain, emphasizes the cognitive (or instrumental) component. Both chess and aerial photographs are surrogates, but normally the photograph is primarily a means to an end whereas chess, like other expressive models, becomes an end in itself, whose relation to other ends may be hidden. It seems natural to us that people should enjoy games and related expressive involvements. It is only when we ask why they should foster some and not others, that we see that these phenomena may be not only expressive but models as well.

The investigations noted previously (see footnote 2) have supported a hypotheses as to personal involvement in models that may be termed *conflict-enculturation*. Two earlier statements of a *conflict enculturation* hypotheses, as it pertains to game playing by American adults, are the following:

These relationships suggested a *conflict-enculturation* hypothesis of model involvement which stated . . . that conflicts induced by social learning in childhood and later (such as those related to obedience, achievement, and responsibility) lead to involvement in expressive models, such as games, through which these conflicts are assuaged and as a result of which a process of buffered learning occurs which has enculturative value for the competences required in the culture (such as acquiring the competitive styles of strategy, physical skill, or chance).

In sum, the conflict-enculturation hypothesis says that child training induces conflict which leads to curiosity about representations (as in expressive models) of the dimensions of this conflict. Involvement in models follows because their microcosmic representation reduces the conflict's complexities to cognitive and emotional comprehensibility and because the participant can learn about the cognitive and emotional aspects of winning in a model in a way that he cannot do outside of it, and because his successes give him increased confidence that he can manage the achievement pressures in full-scale cultural participation. The models thus have the general cultural function that they contribute to the learning and adjustment of persons who must maintain a high level of achievement motivation if the general cultural norms are to be sustained (Sutton-Smith, Roberts, and Kozelka 1963:15, 28).

These statements will need to be revised to take into account three kinds of results of further research: (a) There are relevant differences between interest and competence; (b) the scale, representativeness or verisimilitude, and complexity of the model are important variables; (c) most importantly, new research into the psychology of conflict must be taken into account. For the present we rely on Berlyn's definition: "when two or more incompatible responses are aroused simultaneously in an organism, we shall say that the organism is in conflict (Berlyne 1960:10). Relationships between conflict and arousal, curiosity, and other relevant matters are discussed by Berlyne (1960). The subject has also been approached from an anthropological standpoint (Roberts 1965; Roberts and Koening 1971; Roberts, Strand, and Burmeister, in press; Meyers and Roberts 1968), but the findings are preliminary. For the present, we simply say that conflict can be measured and described, and that it leads to involvement and curiosity.   The place of riddling in the general body of research can be indicated in this way. Many of the papers cited here deal with contests or contesting (games, folktales which represent contests, etc.). One deals with testing in the form of oaths and autonomic ordeals (Roberts 1965), and one with expressive self-testing (Roberts, Thompson, and Sutton-Smith 1966). The present discussion deals with expressive testing, but testing of a nature which can be transformed into contesting (riddling contests occur in a number of cultures) or self-testing (as when an individual reads printed riddles and attempts to guess the answer before he turns to the printed answer).

The interpretation of riddling that has emerged from the present research is this: Riddles may be regarded as natural models which represent interrogation, i.e., riddles represent an instrumental (nonexpressive) activity in a expressive way. More specifically, riddles will be regarded here as expressive models, or representations, of the serious and even formal interrogation of subordinates by superordinates. Such interrogation occurs when a parent questions a child, a teacher a pupil, an employer an employee, a judge a defendant, an officer a soldier, and so on. In these situations the subordinate usually is deemed to have less knowledge and power, and the superordinate to have more, at least with regard to the specific context of a given interrogation. (The extent to which written interrogation should be considered part of the antecedent cultural question which riddles model is not clear. Certainly, for riddles the basic pattern of questioning is an oral one.)

For our purposes a dictionary definition of riddle can be accepted: "*riddle:* a mystifying, misleading, or puzzling question posed as a problem to be solved or guessed often as a game" (*Webster's Third New International Dictionary* 1967:1952). More technical definitions exist,[3] but the advantage of the dictionary definition is its focus on the riddle as a question, this being the heart of the matter so far as the present inquiry is concerned. Also, the definition describes a riddle as a game, thus bringing out its expressive character. (The relationship between expressive and nonexpressive questioning will be considered throughout the discussion.)

[3] See especially the important study by R. A. Georges and Alan Dundes (1963). They survey definitions of the riddle from Aristotle to Archer Taylor and then provide one of their own, which has been used since by others, e.g., Hart (1964:25). Another such survey has been provided by C. T. Scott (1965:14–22). Insofar as classification implies a kind of definition, we might also note here that the Human Relations Area Files (HRAF) lists riddles under category 524, "Games," under the subhead "Problem Games." *Notes and Queries* orders riddles under "Knowledge and Tradition": "Proverbs, traditional sayings and riddles may be education or a form of intellectual recreation" (1951:206).

Questions, of course, are linguistic phenomena. Unfortunately, linguists have not provided us with a formal definition of question suitable for universal or cross-cultural use. Recent discussions of linguistic universals touch on interrogation (Weinreich 1963:150–151) (Greenberg, 1966:50, 70), yet never quite state the question as a language universal. Perhaps the most used definition is that of Fries: Questions are the largest group of those utterances (calls, greetings, and questions) which regularly elicit oral responses (Fries 1952:47; see also 53:142–172). Other work by linguists asserts that neither phonological nor grammatical charateristics have proven adequate for identifying phrases as questions (Pike, 1945:168; Bolinger, 1958:3). Transformational work discusses such questions as permutational transforms, but the assumption is made that the reader can identify questions. As our study moves "outward into the exploration of speech behavior and use" (Hymes 1962:18), we too must be content for the present to use our cultural judgment. We all recognize questions.

The recognition of settings of interrogation poses a similar problem. A relatively rare offering from linguistics is found in Samarin's guide to field linguistics (1967:144–145):

Sustained questioning (or what we call in English interrogation) is probably restricted in all societies to a limited number of settings. In our own we can imagine being questioned by a physician, highway patrolman, income tax controller, census taker, personnel manager, bank mortgage representative, and so on. This list of interrogators points out a significant fact about these settings: That the person opposite us is in some official capacity: his role is formally defined within a legal, occupational, or other context. In this setting we are passive and vulnerable. This is no less true when the questions are put by those with whom we are otherwise on intimate terms, our parents or our spouses, for example.

Anthropologists have given little explicit attention to informal and formal interrogation as cultural phenomena. Like sociologists, however (cf. Hyman 1954), anthropologists have been concerned with interviewing. Frake has recently argued for a new approach to "queries in ethnography." The investigator's ethnographic record has traditionally been a list of questions and answers, Frake says, the questions being brought from home and the answers sought in the field. The ethnography Frake argues for

also includes lists of queries and responses, but with this difference: both the queries and their responses are to be discovered in the culture of the people being studied. The problem is not simply to find answers to questions the ethnographer brings into the field, but also to find the questions that go with the responses he observes after his arrival (Frake 1964c:132).

This is done at least partly by listening for:

queries in use in the cultural scenes he observes, giving special attention to query-rich settings, e.g., children querying parents, medical specialists querying patients, legal authorities querying witnesses, priests querying the gods (1964c:143).

Work of the sort which Frake seeks to encourage obviously would be of great value, indeed would ultimately be essential, to the theory of riddling proposed here. The concern with questioning in this particular study stems from examination of the formal interrogation associated with use of judicial oaths and ordeals (Roberts 1965) and with the development of a field technique of dyadic elicitation (Roberts and Arth 1966).[4] The design of the present study is very simple, and the study must be regarded as an exploratory, low-cost venture. First, a preliminary cross-cultural study was conducted in the Human Relations Area Files.[5] Next, a small study of Tagalog riddling was made, from literature on the Tagalog and by working with Tagalog informants available in Ithaca, New York. Finally, several small surveys were made of American students at Cornell. In the pages which follow each of these substudies will be discussed in turn, and then the overall conclusions and implications to be drawn from this research will be given in a final section.

A Preliminary Cross-Cultural View

Despite the facts that a substantial comparative literature exists on riddles and a few anthropologists have made brilliant contributions to the study of riddles,[6] the cross-cultural literature is so uneven that riddles are not a good subject for conventional cross-cultural investigation. The interest in riddles and riddling has not been general enough to insure standard anthropological coverage. A great deal of intensive and extensive scholarship would be required to produce a cross-cultural study of riddles and riddling which would be definitive in its own right; the authors have lacked the resources to produce such a study. Yet it can be argued that a preliminary and admittedly inadequate cross-cultural survey can be most uesful in putting riddles into cross-cultural perspective, testing preliminary hypotheses, and framing revised hypotheses for further testing. This

[4] The senior author of this chapter has also profited from discussions on this subject with Lindsey Churchill, who is currently studying questioning.

[5] The Human Relations Area Files at Cornell University were searched in the fall of 1966. Since new materials are steadily added to the files, it is always necessary to give the date of the search.

[6] Archer Taylor's work is perhaps the best known. The outstanding structural study is that by Georges and Dundes (1963). T. R. Williams (1963), D. Simmons (1958), and B. M. du Toit (1966) have made notable functional studies. Potter (1950) and Hart (1964; Chapters III, IV, and V) provide general surveys. See also the linguistic study by C. T. Scott (1965).

use of the cross-cultural survey to provide a first approximation of a problem has not received the attention that it deserves from the cross-cultural methodologists, largely because most of them (with the outstanding exception of Whiting) have failed to consider the possibilities of sub-system replication and validation.[7] In any event, this is the method which is used here.

Initially, it was thought that riddles were expressive models of strategy. This led to the hypothesis that riddles should occur in the same cultural environments as games of strategy. Since it was not convenient to compare the riddling variables with the numerous additional variables published in the literature, the authors used a series of variables selected for relevance to the hypothesis. Later the initial hypothesis was modified, as the relation to interrogation emerged, but the same variables still have interest, and the results of these comparisons will be given here.

In the fall of 1966 students who had been trained to judge the presence and absence of riddles surveyed the material in the Human Relations Area Files. Each reviewed only a limited number of cultures, but the survey was made in such a way that every culture had two judges. An attempt was made to correct their file-based entries where they disagreed or where the findings did not make sense, but after a few corrections were made, this attempt was abandoned because of lack of time for additional research. This judging technique is not ideal, but it may have been adequate for the present preliminary or exploratory view.

The survey had other limitations which ought to be mentioned. Clearly, the most advanced requirements for ethnographic sampling have not been met, and a purist might argue that the use of the simple statistics used here is not appropriate (riddles, e.g., are clearly concentrated in the Old World). Practical experience has shown, however, that work with unacceptable samples is often robust in the sense that acceptable predictions can be made for single system or subsystem replication. Undoubtedly, there was error in the judging, but there was even more error in the filed literature.

A few cultures lacking riddles may have been reported as having them. Much more importantly, cultures having riddles have been reported as lacking them or, more probably, as not containing information on them. If we treat no information as indicating absence, as we do, we are undoubtedly introducing a substantial amount of error into the study. This latter source of error stems from the facts that riddles are a minor interest for many ethnographers, with the result that they are not reported even when they exist and that riddles are often reported in obscure, highly specialized articles which are too specific for general inclusion in the files. Again

[7] This method was used by Roberts and Sutton-Smith in several studies (c.f. Roberts and Sutton-Smith 1962; Sutton-Smith, Roberts, and Kozelka 1963).

few ethnographers state that riddles are definitely absent even when they are genuinely absent. All of these errors are compounded, of course, when riddles are compared with other ethnographic variables, for the judgments used in producing the other variables are also subject to error. Still it is argued that the robustness of the findings is great enough to permit the toleration of a substantial amount of error.

Turning now to the riddles, the following cultures were reported as definitely having riddles: Afgan, Amharic, Apayao, "Arabic," Austrian, Aymara, Bemba, Bhil, Bisayan (central), Bulgariam, Bush Negro, Callinago, Cambodian, Chagga, "Chinese," Cornish, Cuna, Czechoslovakian, Dard, Dhegiha, Eskimo (central), Estonian, Fang, Fellahin, (modern) "Formosan," Gondi, Greek, Gujerati, Hausa, Hottentot, Hungarian, Iban, Ila, Indonesian, Iranian, Irish (rural), Kashmiri, Kikwyu, Kol, Korean, Kurdish, Lapp, Lithuanian, Lovedu, Malays, Maori, Masai, Mayan (Yucatan), Mbundu, Mongolian, Ngondi, Ngoni, Nuer, Polish, Rumanian, Rundi, Rwala, Samoan, Serbia, Somali, Soviet Union, Syrian, Thonga, Tibet, Tiv, Toda, Ukrainian, Wolof, Yao, Yakut, and Yugoslavian.

The following cultures were reported as being indeterminate (hereafter they will be classed with the riddles-present group): Aden, Burmese, Chukchee, Iraqi, Jordanian, Kuwait, Lebanese, Nahane, Nootka, Saudi Arabian, Thailand, Tuareg, Yemen.

The following cultures are those in which riddles were reported as being definitely absent: Manus, Miao, and Pukapuka.

The following cultures are those in which the presence of riddles is unreported: Ainu, Albanian, Aleut, Andamans, Azandi, Aztec, Bahrain Islands, Bambara, Bedouin, Bellacoola, Burusho, Bushman, Caingang, Carib, Caucasian, Cayapa, Choroti, Comanche, Creek, Crow, Delaware, Dorobo, Easter Islands, Eskimo (Copper), Gandian, Georgian, Goajiro, Gros Ventre, Guana, Hadhramut, Ifugao, Incan, Indian, Iroquois, Jivaro, Kachin, Kamchadal, Kapauku, Katab, Kazak, Khasi, Koryak, Laotian, Lepcha, Lolo, Luo, Manchurian, Mandan, Marquesas, Massachusetts (historical), Mende, Micmac, Mongo, Monguor, Montagnais, Mosquito, Mossi, Munduracu, Murgnin, Nambicuara, Navaho, New Ireland, Nupe, Ojibwa, Orokaiva, Paiute (northern), Papago, Pawnee, Pomo, Punjab (east), Rif, Russian (great), Samoyed, Semang, Senegal, Seri, Siberian, Sinkiang, Sino-Tibetan border, Shilluk, Sirono, Siwan, Talamanca, Tallensi, Tanala, Tapirape, Tarahumara, Tarasco, Tehuelche, Tepoztlan, Tewa, Tikopia, Timpira, Tiwi, Tlingit, Tubatulabal, Tucuna, Turkestan, Tupinamba, Twi, Uttar Pradesh, Yahgan, Yokut, Yoruba, Yuman (plateau), Yuman (river), Yurok, Vedda, Wogeo, and Zuni.

In the tables which follow, those societies in which riddles are definitely and probably absent are compared with all others. For any one comparison, though, the full range of societies may not be used since the entries for other cultural variables may not exist.

In 13 of the 38 cases where it could be studied, riddling was true game, and in 13 of the 28 cases where the matter could be judged, there were riddling contests. The relationship between riddling and gaming clearly merits more examination than it will receive here.

In 22 of 33 judgeable cases riddles were regarded as being important in the culture, and in 22 of 29 cases the frequency of riddling was judged to be high. In general, importance and frequency could not be judged.

In all of the 18 cases where the presence of rote learning and riddles could be judged, rote learning was present. In 15 of these cases, rote learning had a religious connection. It proved to be exceptionally difficult to judge rote learning.

Comparisons were made with variables from the "Ethnographic Atlas" (as it existed in the fall of 1966)[8] (see Murdock 1967). There is, e.g., an obvious relationship between levels of political integration, the presence or absence of authority, and the presence of riddles. This distribution speaks

table 6.1

Level of Political Integration

	Absent	Autonomous Local	Peace Groups	Depen- dent	Minimal State	Little State	State
Riddles absent	9	40	2	3	16	6	25
Riddles present	0	8	2	2	10	7	16

for itself, but if we omit the possibly ambiguous "peace group" and "dependent" categories, $x^2 = 13.92$, $p < .01$, with four degrees of freedom. Note that the riddle-absent-state cell almost certainly contains a large number of erroneous entries, but these work against the hypothesis that riddles will be associated with institutionalized interrogation. Again, if we contrast the "absent" and "autonomous local" categories against all others (e.g., simple against complex), $x^2 = 11.10$, $p < .001$, $G = .627$. Riddles appear to be associated with political integration.

The higher the level of political integration, the more likely the presence of institutionalized interrogation. Probably, some interrogation occurs in all courts, so if we compare the presence or absence of riddles with the number of levels in the jurisdictional hierarchy beyond the local community, we can again see the predicted association. The distribution speaks for itself (Table 6.2). $x^2 = 10.81$, with four degrees of freedom, $p < .05$. Again if the societies with no and one level are compared with all others, $X^2 = 8.90$, $p < .01$, $G = .553$. The more elaborate the jurisdictional hierarchy, the more likely the presence of riddles.

[8] The atlas as it was published in *Ethnology* was used, but the complete summary is cited for the reader's convenience.

table 6.2

Number of Levels in Jurisdictional
Hierarchy Transcending Local Community

	0	1	2	3	4
Riddles absent	47	28	13	9	2
Riddles present	7	11	14	4	2

Oaths and ordeals are associated with formal judicial interrogation, although they can occur in other settings. Table 6.3 shows the asso-

table 6.3

Riddles and Oaths and Ordeals

	Riddles				
	Absent	Present	x^2	$p^<$	G
Oaths absent	70	15			
Oaths present	28	20			
			7.94	.01	.538
Ordeals absent	78	17			
Ordeals present	18	20			
			10.70	.01	.672

ciation. The association is somewhat stronger with ordeals than it is with oaths, and this is not surprising.

There is also an association with domestication, as Table 6.4 illustrates.

table 6.4

Riddles and Domesticated Animals

	Riddles				
	Absent	Present	x^2	$p^<$	G
Domesticated animals absent	36	4			
Domesticated animals present	53	35			
			10.14	.01	.712
Domesticated animals other than large animals (cows, camels) present	65	12			
Domesticated large animals present	34	27			
			12.4	.001	.612

This is probably an important association, and its relevance will emerge when the child-training variables are considered.

Finally, there is an association between the presence of games of strategy and the presence of riddles (see Table 6.5). Table 6.5 has $x^2 = 4.45$,

table 6.5		
Riddles and Games of Strategy		
	| Riddles	
	Absent	*Present*
Games of strategy absent	47	11
Games of strategy present	21	16

$p < .05$, $G = .530$. It will be noted that this association is not as strong as the associations with either ordeals or cows and camels. Originally, this particular association had been predicted to be exceptionally strong. It is present, but it is weak. The Barry, Bacon, and Child mimeographed child-training ratings were also used. These have since been published in corrected form (Barry, Bacon, and Child 1967). Here the samples are even smaller, but the results presented in Table 6.6 have obvious interest.

This brief preliminary view suggests that riddling is associated with (1) strong responsibility training, (2) large domestic animals, (3) high political integration, (4) more than one level of jurisdictional hierarchy beyond the local community, (5) oaths, (6) ordeals, and (7) games of strategy. No doubt a more elaborate survey would reveal other associations, but these findings constitute a pattern which is consistent and which will be interpreted after the evidence of the other studies has been presented. It would appear, though, that responsibility training is more important than the hypothesis had originally predicted and that the strategy component is less important.

The Tagalog Study

In order to gain more insight into riddles and riddling, it was decided to study riddles in Tagalog culture. The Tagalog are an ethnolinguistic subclass of Philippine people found chiefly in the central and southern parts of Luzon. The decision to study Tagalog riddling was made in part because native speakers were available on the Cornell University campus, in part because of the stimulation of the recent anthropological analysis of Filipino riddles (Hart 1964), and in part because of the saliency of riddling in Tagalog culture. The material presented here is

table 6.6

Riddles and Child-Training Practices

Child-Training Variable	Sex (male, M; female, F)	Contingency Table Cells				x^2	$p<$	G
		(Riddles absent)		(Riddles Present)				
		a (Low CT rating)	b (High CT rating)	c (Low CT rating)	d (High CT rating)			
Responsibility								
Reward for performance	M	19	16	3	12	3.95	.05	.652
Anxiety over nonperformance	M	25	9	3	12	10.09	.01	.713
Anxiety over performance	M	26	8	6	9	4.61	.05	.660
Frequency of performance	M	24	8	4	11	8.00	.01	.784
Frequency of performance	F	23	11	4	10	4.67	.05	.679
Obedience								
Reward for performance	F	17	15	2	12	4.56	.05	.744
Independence								
Anxiety over performance	M	20	15	3	12	4.43	.05	.684
Nurturant agent								
Constancy of presence of		16	18	11	1	5.56	.02	−.850

based on independent field work by the junior author, work with informants, and a survey of the specific literature.

A Filipino psychologist, Jaime Bulatao, using a thematic analysis of stories collected from 90 subjects, has described four principle values for the Tagalog: family solidarity, authority, economic sufficiency, and patience (1962:52–75). Under these values were found recurrent themes such as the need for parents or older children to make sacrifices for the younger family members, or the necessity of respecting and obeying authority figures, although only within limits. When not discussed explicitly, responsibility is interwoven in the discussion of family solidarity, authority, and reciprocity. This is true as well of other studies (such as those by Hollensteiner 1962 and Lynch 1962a) in the same volume (Lynch 1962b).

Clearly, there is an emphasis on responsibility. Guthrie and Jacobs describe

the whole area of responsibility into which the child is gradually initiated. Depending on the particular family situation and the age he has reached, there are always errands to run, household jobs to do, and younger siblings to be cared for. There are chickens and pigs to feed, goats or a carabao to pasture, yard corners to weed, dead leaves to sweep up and burn, and water and firewood to carry to the house (1966).

Children who are not old enough to do these chores prepare for them by playfully imitating their elders (Abasolo-Domingo 1961:150–157).

When a Tagalog child fails to meet the expectations of his elders in the performance of these tasks, he can expect a punishment, usually a verbal one, rarely in the form of nagging. Some of the main verbal punishments are teasing, joking, and the threat of sundry witches. Tagalog children are extremely sensitive to ridicule.[9] That these facts are relevant to riddling seems apparent. It is interesting to note that in nearby Borneo, Dusun men riddle in a tone otherwise reserved for teasing children (Williams 1963:97).

If a culture has (1) *an authority system* (e.g., high political integration) and (2) *heavy responsibility training,* conjoined with (3) *oral questioning,* then it has the conditions which favor riddling. That Tagalog culture contains the first two conditions we have illustrated from the literature. It is more difficult to do this for the third condition. Ethnographic work on the Tagalog does not differ from other anthropological literature in lacking discussion of oral questioning. But there are settings in Tagalog culture

---

[9] Compare the similar sensitivity to ridicule and use of verbal punishments in other areas of the Philippines: Ilokos (Nydegger and Nydegger 1966:167), Leyte (Nurge 1965:79), and Sulu (Eslao 1962:87). Abasolo-Domingo (1961) supports the conformity of Tagalog practices to this basic pattern.

which might be described as "query rich" (Frake 1964c:143). A full discussion of these would likely require monograph treatment. Only a few can be mentioned here. Our Tagalog informants report that parents often questioned them on their behavior. When they visited their baptismal godparents on the traditional feast days (e.g., Christmas), they were also subjected to many questions. Perhaps more important is the oral interrogation throughout a marriage negotiation, a questioning which is often couched in metaphoric language and managed by a "go-between" (Malay 1957:79).

Most Tagalogs are at least nominally Roman Catholics. Within the context of the Church, oral interrogation exists in association with baptism, catechism, and confession. In the baptism ceremony there is ritual interrogation by the priest of the person being baptized, or in the more common case of infant baptism, of the infant's godparent sponsors. The interrogation associated with catechism is obvious. Perhaps less obvious is the interrogation in confession, but Hart has provided us with a Filipino view in the words of one Cebuano (the same could have been said by a Tagalog): "Before the wedding ceremony I was led to the confessionario and before long the padre began bombarding me with questions" (Hart 1956:275). Phelan has described the missionary confessors' technique: "In order to overcome the Filipinos' fear and embarrassment, the missionaries developed a simple question and answer technique. Brief questions were phrased . . . , [but], placing no faith in the veracity of their parishoners . . . , the confessors asked the same question in a variety of ways" (1959:66–67).

The present Philippine undersecretary of education has pointed out the tie between Spanish friar-dominated education and the current practice of rote recitation in the schools (Corpuz 1965:49–50). Beside this form of question and answer, there are national examinations and periodic inspections in the school system which subject both teachers and pupils to interrogation.

The Tagalogs have a rich legal culture which is filled with interrogation. Apparently, this was also the case prior to Spanish contact. "In 1599 the Audiencia defined as customary law for the whole archipelago Tagalog usages as codified by Friar Juan de Plasencia" (Phelan 1959:129). In some ways Tagalog interrogative culture is epitomized in the social role of the go-between, a person of great verbal skill. Within this context, the political function of the *fiscal,* a role that might ordinarily be viewed as legal, is particularly interesting. When the Spanish introduced the role, the *fiscal* was at the national level a member of the court of the Inquisition, and at the local level he was an assistant to the parish priest with the task of serving as intermediary between the priest and the people. His special duty was drilling of the children in their catechism. Today, the role of the *fiscal* has been shifted from the arena of religion to that of the public courts and politics. As of the coming of the American system, the *fiscal* is the public defender at the provincial level; but in addition, *fiscal* is a special title used to honor a politician who functions as oppositionist. All in all, he must be a man of great verbal skill, adept at questioning and answering.

It seems clear that there is formal interrogation of subordinates by superordinates in Tagalog culture. Now we can turn to Tagalog riddling. The Filipino folklorist Manuel states,

While the bugtungan [Tagalog term for contest in riddle making] is chiefly the pastime of children, adults are not unknown to have indulged in it. In fact it is from the old folks that boys and girls learn some of the enigmatic riddles. Young women and men are observed to enjoy it as practised in night vigils over the dead, baptismal parties and other social gatherings (1955:152).

Although content analysis is a common concern of riddle studies, it is not our concern to apply this method to Tagalog riddles. Nevertheless, before we get too far away from the discussion of query-rich settings, we wish to mention an observation by Frake in his review of Harts (1964) analysis. "Certain prominent aspects of Central Philippine cultures are weakly represented: malevolent supernaturals, politics, birth, marriage, sickness, crime, and cats" (Frake 1966:245; Hart 1964:70–72). The subject matter of Tagalog riddles is seldom that of the serious interrogations. Malevolent supernaturals figure in the interrogations linked with disease and death. The serious interrogations linked with politics, crimes birth, and marriage have already been noted. We suspect that the taboo on cats relates to their part in witchcraft beliefs introduced by the Spanish, but we may be wrong. It is noteworthy that the intermediary or go-between serves in all of these situations.

Against this background then, it was decided to study riddle competence and associated attitudes possessed by 20 Tagalog informants. These informants came from the Greater Manila area or from Laguna, a Tagalog-speaking province south of Manila. All the informants had spoken Tagalog as their first language; this language was the current language of their homes and was the language of their childhood.

With a lone exception all our Tagalog informants had engaged in riddling while in elementary school. Some of them had also heard riddles at wakes, and three of the better riddlers mentioned using riddles in their courtship. It would appear, however, that the locus of riddling is steadily shifting away from the older settings of the wake and courtship and settling in the school. Although interest in riddling may be declining (not one of our informants engages in riddling now), still riddling remains salient enough in Tagalog culture that our riddling instrument induced nostalgia and brought tears to the eyes of a number of our informants. Riddles are still relatively more important than they are in American culture.

These Taglog informants were given the riddle test discussed here. In constructing the test 26 riddles were selected from a popular collection entitled *Isang Libo at Isang Bugtong* (Santos 1958). This collection of riddles was read very carefully by an intelligent and highly motivated bilingual assistant, who selected riddles she felt would have maximum generality (any Tagalog speaker would feel that he should have known the answer to a riddle once given it). The maximally general riddles were then judged for degree of difficulty, and a matching set of easy and difficult riddles, 26 in all, was chosen.[10]

An example of a riddle (#724) considered easy is

> *Aling bunga ang palibot ng mata?*   *pinya*
> Which fruit (is) the one surrounded by eyes?   pineapple

An example of a difficult riddle (#777) is

> *Sapagka't lahat na ay nakahihipo*
> Since everybody handles it
>
> *Walang kasindumi't kasimbaho*
> Nothing is dirtier or smellier
>
> *Bakit mahal nati't ipinakatatago?*   *salaping papel*
> Why do we love and treasure it?   paper money

In the interest of approximating the proper setting, the instrument was administered in the Tagalog language, even though all the informants were bilinguals. A score was computed by giving an informant one point for each correctly answered riddle. The most successful informant answered 17 of 26. The least successful answered 7 riddles. The average for the 20 informants was 12.3 and the median was 13.

From this group of 20, all those who had previously played ticktacktoe (18) were given the Tick Tack Toe test described in Sutton-Smith and Roberts (1967) as a rough measure of strategic competence.[11] Results are indicated in Table 6.7.

Unfortunately, 8 of the 20 informants returned to the Philippines before

[10] The riddles used in this instrument are to be found as follows in the book by Santos (1958) (they are listed in the order in which we presented them): #953, #724, #556, #442, #377, #383, #266, #91, #75, #37, #5, #60, #57, #68, #777, #661, #673, #427, #379, #277, #497, #418, #323, #314, #324, #295.

[11] Scores on the first stripe were judged more competent than those on the second, and so on. X scores were used for ordering within each stripe. Otherwise no attention was paid to the x and y scores in and of themselves (c.f. Roberts and Sutton-Smith 1966).

table 6.7

Tagalog Riddle and Strategic Competence*

	High Strategic Competence	Low Strategic Competence
High riddle competence	8	1
Low riddle competence	1	6

*$p < .01$.

the study was completed, but the 12 remaining subjects were given the following questions:

Try to remember, if you will, back to the time in your elementary school when you were learning the multiplication table. Now imagine that one day the academic supervisor (a province-level official in the Philippine school system) makes a surprise visit—and this is one of those rare times when it really catches your teacher by surprise. The supervisor—and notice well, it is the supervisor and not your teacher—calls on you to multiply two numbers for him. If your answer is correct, how HAPPY would you be, giving a score of 1 for *completely indifferent* and a score of 7 for *very happy?*

Completely Indifferent 1 2 3 4 5 6 7 Very Happy

How HIYA [ashamed] would you be if you got confused and your answer was wrong?

The responses to the two questions were added, and the 12 informants were ranked in terms of the resultant score. It was thought that those who scored high on both would have the antecedent conflict necessary for riddle involvement in that they had both high approach and high avoidance attitudes.

The basic ranks by informants are given in Table 6.8. It is interesting to note that the rank order correlation between the ranks of the riddling competence scores and the Tick Tack Toe competence scores was .406, using Kendall's Tau ($p = .033$). The rank order correlation between the riddle competence scores and the interrogational conflict scores was .600 ($p = .004$), and the rank order correlation between the Tick Tack Toe test scores and the interrogational conflict scores was .460 ($p = .0188$). Use of the Kendall Partial Rank Correlation Coefficient showed that the correlation between riddle competence and interrogational conflict was relatively independent of strategic competence.

Riddling in modern Tagalog society, then, conforms with the basic complex suggested by the cross-cultural study: Riddles are related to training for responsibility and the maintenance of a complex society with its associated interrogation. Today, however, the locus of Tagalog rid-

table 6.8

Rank Order

Riddle Rank	Question Rank	TTT (Tick Tack Toe) Rank
1	1	6.5
2	2.5	2
3	10.5	9
4	2.5	1
5.5	5.5	8
5.5	5.5	11
7	5.5	3.5
8	9	3.5
9	8	5
10	5.5	6.5
11	12	10
12	10.5	12

dling is shifting from the settings of wakes and courtship to the setting of schools, and this shift raises the matter of time perspective.

Over an area of islands in Southeast Asia broader than the Philippines, and back through time, riddling has been associated with wakes and harvests. To answer a riddle at other times meant risking danger from malevolent supernaturals. Crops too were subject to such dangers, but rituals existed for warding off this danger to the spirit of the rice or millet. Perhaps riddling models success or failure at harvesting. Harvest time provided the possibility of other successes, for the harvest was a time of opportunity for young men and women to court. Courtship, we have noted, remains to some extent one of the settings for riddling. And today, as fewer people are involved in harvesting, more and more the road to success in general and the opportunities for courtship has become the school. It seems not without significance that the setting of riddling has shifted toward the schools. Clearly, the total pattern is not well understood but would merit further examination.

Evans (1951, 1954, 1955) Thomas R. Williams (1963) have reported differences in male and female riddling for one Southeast Asian group, the Dusun. Women are reported as showing a preference for those riddles which use archaic words or syllables not usually meaningful in the language, a form suggestive of religious ritual. Men seem not to share the preference; their riddles are the more simply metaphoric type. Women too bear the heavier responsibilities for the chores of wakes. Perhaps this involvement is of significance for explaining the component of obscure words in women's riddles. If, however, men are more interested in harvest riddling, this may be related to the possibility that a successful harvest courtship can lead to new chores for men, for bride service is a not uncommon prelude to marriage in this area of the world.

In any case, although we have not studied the matter, it seems particularly significant to note the metaphoric nature of most riddle questions and to consider this in the light of Malay's description of the intermediary: a person verbally skilled in the use of metaphoric language. We offer the hypothesis that riddling functions as training for the role of intermediary, a role of great importance to the maintenance of solidarity in many Southeast Asian societies.

The American Study

The Tagalog study suggests that involvement in riddles might well be linked with attitudes toward oral interrogation. Some additional exploratory surveys were made with Cornell students to examine this relationship in greater detail.

As a pretest, members of a large undergraduate class in sociology were asked to estimate their general interest in riddles on a scale ranging from 1 (low interest) to 7 (high interest) and to answer a number of questions dealing with oral interrogation. The general level of reported interest in riddles was so low, however, that it was decided to measure this interest more precisely.

With the members of a large undergraduate class in anthropology, a different measure of riddle involvement was used. Here 20 riddles were selected randomly (through the use of a random number table) from a general book on riddles (Withers and Benet 1954).[12] The 20 randomly selected riddles were then arranged in a random order for presentation in a written instrument. Each student was asked to judge his interest in each riddle on a scale of 1 (low interest) to 7 (high interest). An average of the 20 riddle interest scores was used to arrive at the average interest of each student in riddles. These average scores ranged from 1.00 (the absolute minimum) to 5.40, with the next highest score being 4.80 (well short of the 7.00 possible highest score). Clearly, the general level of interest was low. For purposes of the study the 69 students with riddle interest scores of 2.89 or less were placed in a "low riddle interest" group, while the 73 students with scores of 2.90 or higher were placed in a "high riddle interest" group.

Each student was also asked 4 questions designed to elicit positive atti-

---

[12] The specific riddles selected were the following [in each instance the page number in the Withers and Benet volume (1954) is given together with the number of the riddle counting from the top of the page; in addition each riddle is lettered in order of presentation in the test]: p. 14 (4), K; p. 18 (7), D; p. 26 (2), H; p. 28 (6), 0; p. 30 (5), T; p. 31 (2), P; p. 44 (5), Q; p. 45 (1), R; p. 47 (5), M; p. 65 (2), F; p. 76 (6), S; p. 87 (3), G; p. 92 (1), A; p. 92 (2), C; p. 104 (1), 1; p. 110 (7), E; p. 111 (6), L; p. 116 (8), j; and p. 118 (5), B.

tudes toward oral questioning and 4 questions designed to elicit negative attitudes. Each of the 8 questions was preceded by the phrase, "In the generalized classroom of your childhood (no earlier than the fifth or sixth grade)." With the exclusion of this phrase, the questions were the following:

1,2. how (eager) (uneager) were you to answer a question when the teacher selected you to answer a moderately difficult oral question in class?

3,4. how (happy) (unhappy) were you when you answered a moderately difficult oral question when it was asked by the teacher in class?

5,6. how (proud) (ashamed) were you when you (answered) (failed to answer) a moderately difficult oral question asked by the teacher in class?

7,8. how (comfortable) (uncomfortable) were you when you answered an oral question correctly which other students in the class had failed to answer?

After each question the student was asked to circle the appropriate number indicating his attitude ranging from 1 (low) to 7 (high). Hindsight allows us to say that these questions could have been improved, but still the 4 positive questions were held to be indicative of approach attitudes toward oral questioning and the 4 negative questions were held to be indicative of avoidance attitudes toward oral questioning.

Various types of analysis were used, But Table 6.9 summarizes the general findings. The division of the respondents into "high riddle interest" and "low riddle interest" groups has already been described. The distribution of scores for each of the 8 oral interrogation questions was plotted, and the responses to each question were divided into a high and a low group, as nearly in half as the distribution permitted. Each respondent, then, was given a score ranging from 0 to 4 for the number of approach questions to which his answers were above the median; similarly, each respondent was given a like score based on the avoidance items. The distribution of these scores is given in Table 6.9. Note that all entries to the left of line A fall in the approach < avoidance category; the entries falling between lines A and B are in the approach = avoidance category; and entries to the left of line B are in the approach > avoidance category.

It is our provisional formulation that the greatest competence at riddling and the greatest interest in riddles should be displayed by respondents falling in the approach < avoidance category, that the intermediate competence and interest should be displayed by the respondents falling in the approach = avoidance category, and that the least competence and interest should be displayed by the respondents falling in the approach > avoidance category. Subsequent tables, therefore, have been arranged with the three categories listed in that order, and they have been treated as an ordinal scale.

table 6.9

Attitudes toward Oral Interrogation and Riddle Interest

Approach < Avoidance Approach = Avoidance

	High Approach Score				
High Avoidance Score	0	1	2	3	4
4	2LoR 2HiR	3LoR 1HiR	1LoR 1HiR	1LoR 0HiR	0LoR 0HiR
3	2LoR 4HiR	4LoR 3HiR	7LoR 3HiR	3LoR 2HiR	1LoR 3HiR
2	5LoR 0HiR	5LoR 3HiR	2LoR 7HiR	3LoR 10HiR	4LoR 6HiR
1	2LoR 1HiR	3LoR 2HiR	5LoR 5HiR	9LoR 9HiR	3LoR 3HiR
0	0LoR* 1HiR	1LoR 2HiR	1LoR 3HiR	1LoR 1HiR	1LoR 1HiR

Line A Line B

Approach = Avoidance   Approach > Avoidance

* LoR, low riddle interest (2.89 or less); HiR, high riddle interest (2.90 or more).

The relationship between high and low riddle interest and the three approach-avoidance categories can be seen in Table 6.10.

table 6.10

Riddles and Oral Interrogation Attitudes

	Approach = Avoidance	Approach > Avoidance	Approach < Avoidance
High riddle interest	12	43	18
Low riddle interest	8	29	32

$x^2 = 7.44$, $p < .05$, $G = .352$. If approach < avoidance is compared with the other two categories, $G = .451$.

Although these findings indicate that avoidance attitudes are associated with low interest in riddling, an examination of the male and female distributions shows that this is largely true of the male, not the female, respondents (see Table 6.11). It should be noted that when males and

table 6.11

Male and Female Interest in Riddles and
Attitudes toward Oral Interrogation

	Oral Interrogation			
	$Ap = Av$*	$Ap > Av$	$Ap < Av$	x^2 p G
Male high riddle interest	5	15	7	
Male low riddle interest	2	9	19	$x^2 = 7.55 < .05$
Total, male	7	24	26	$G = .598$
Female high riddle interest	7	28	11	nonsignificant
Female low riddle interest	6	20	13	
Total, female	13	48	24	

* Ap, approach; Av, avoidance.

females are compared without regard to riddle interest in terms of the approach-avoidance category, as against the other two categories combined, males clearly show relatively more avoidance, $x^2 = 3.79$, which is almost significant at the .05 level.

Each of the respondents was asked to list his favorite game. Later these games were classified into games of physical skill and strategy and games of strategy (cf. Roberts, Arth, and Bush 1959). The basic distribution is given in Table 6.12. Although it was thought that the high riddlers would favor games of strategy, there is no general relationship of this kind. How-

table 6.12

Male and Female Interest, Oral Interrogation, and Preferred Game

| | Female | | | | Male | | | |
| | Physical Skill | | Strategy | | Physical Skill | | Strategy | |
Oral Interrogation	High Riddle	Low Riddle	High Riddle	Low Riddle	High Riddle	Low Riddle	High Riddle	Low Riddle
Approach = avoidance	4	4	2	2	4	1	1	0
Approach > avoidance	15	11	9	7	9	8	6	0
Approach < avoidance	4	3	4	9	2	12	3	6

ever, males preferring games of physical skill are less likely to have high interest in riddles than males preferring games of strategy ($G = -.40$, $p <$ .01). There is a directional relationship between the Ap = Av, Ap > Av, Ap < Av ordinal scale and the ordinal scales of physical skill and strategy ($G = .320$), which suggests that relatively more of the strategists are avoiders of oral interrogation.

When the female distributions were plotted, it could be seen that the majority of the high riddle interest responses for females preferring games of physical skill occurred at four data points (2 Ap, 1 Av), (3 Ap, 1 Av), (2 Ap, 2 Av), and (3 Ap, 2 Av). When the distribution of responses in these cells (15 high and 5 low riddle interest) was compared with all others combined (8 high and 13 low interest), it could be seen that the four cells mentioned were the locus of high riddle interest ($X^2 = 4.27$, $p < .05$). Notice that in these particular cells there is a balance between approach and avoidance, but that all extreme balances are not represented. The same comparisons were nonsignificant for female strategists, male potent strategists, and male strategists.

Indeed, the female strategists, male potent strategists, and male strategists can be combined to produce the same relationship given for males ($G = 6.02$) as far as riddle interest and oral interrogation are concerned. Yet there is no obvious reason why the female potent strategists should differ from the others. When they are compared with the female strategists in terms of average responses to the individual questions, the female potent strategists display slightly greater approach and slightly lesser avoidance than the female strategists, but the differences are not great. Clearly, this is a problem for future study.

Finally, a very small survey was made of the students in an introductory linguistics class in which the same instrument was administered together with some additional questions. The same relationships of riddle interest and oral interrogation appeared to hold. More importantly, however, this group was asked the following questions. Each question was rated: Very Little   1 2 3 4 5 6 7   A Great Deal.

Most children are expected to perform certain tasks or chores for which they are held accountable by adults. These tasks can include things such as performing homework or doing household chores ranging to such things as milking the cows.

A.   What is your estimate of the amount of such work that you were expected to do as a child?
B.   How much importance did the adults who assigned the work place on your responsible completion of it?
C.   To what extent was your performance of these tasks monitored through persistent questioning or nagging by adults?
D.   To what extent do you think that you were nagged in general?

The responses to these questions provide new insight into involvement in riddles.

Interestingly enough, there was no correlation between the responses to question A and to question B. Only question B was used, with entries of 6 and 7 counting as "high importance." The questions C and D were combined to produce a single nagging score with respondents who had entries of 3 or more for each of the two questions being placed in the high-nagging group. Table 6.13 shows the results. The same grouping of riddle

table 6.13

Responsibility (Chores), Nagging, and Riddle Interest

Responsibility (chores) and Nagging	*High Riddle Interest*	*Low Riddle Interest*
High importance of chores with low nagging	9	2
High importance of chores with high nagging	1	11
Low importance of chores with low nagging	3	7
Low importance of chores with high nagging	3	4

involvement responses into high and low used for the larger survey was used. Note in this table that there is an association between low nagging and high riddle interest, $X^2 = 4.01$, $p < .05$. High riddle interest, however, is particularly associated with low nagging when chores are important (as against the other three categories combined) ($X^2 = 8.78$, $p < .01$, $G = .868$). If we consider only the group with high importance of chores, there is a definite association of high riddle interest with low nagging ($X^2 = 9.57$, $p < .001$, $G = .960$). There were no sex differences of importance.

In the American college student study, high riddle interest was associated with balanced or positive attitudes toward oral questioning, with low nagging, and particularly with the high importance of chores conjoined with the presence of low nagging. The relationship of riddle interest to sex and to game involvements is intriguing, but not clear from the present inquiry.

Discussion

Each of the three successive exploratory studies reported in this chapter is too modest to be publishable in its own right, but taken together as a series of reinforcing and related inquiries, they merit consideration. Certainly, they serve to identify cultural and psychological variables which ought to be considered when a general theory of riddles and riddling is finally framed. We will now discuss some of these variables.

Pattern. This chapter does not deal with the linguistic forms of riddles, but both the Tagalog and American studies suggest the importance of such analysis. Our collection of Tagalog riddles, e.g., seems to be separable into a number of types, at least some of which are marked linguistically by patterns of stress and rhyme. Some exploratory work with the American data suggested that the conundrum, in contrast to other riddles, has appeal for respondents with high-approach–low-avoidance attitudes toward oral interrogation and with a slight preference for games of physical skill, but this relationship, if it exists, must be tested in further research. In any event, it is highly probable that riddles with different patterns have different psychological and cultural significance within a single culture and that these differences can be mapped with profit.

Culture history. Riddles appear to be primarily an Old World phenomenon, and such riddles as do occur in the New World may be largely the result of acculturation. There are undoubtedly cultural environments in the New World where riddles are not found, but where riddles would have been accepted if they had diffused there or if they had been invented independently in these settings. Perhaps there are functional equivalents to riddles in such settings, and this is a problem which ought to be studied. Again, some riddles may be peculiar to single communities or to small groups, but others are systemic patterns with very wide cultural and geographical distributions. The culture history of both types is interesting.

Pattern load. The patterns of riddles and riddling may be nearly the same descriptively in two different cultures without having the same salience or weight in each. The pattern of riddling is more heavily loaded in Tagalog culture than it is in the United States, although admittedly the two patterns are not the same. The frequency of riddling, intensity of interest and evaluation, differing competence, differing behavioral settings, and other variables contribute to differences in pattern loading. The study of such loading is a task for the future.

Cultural complexity. It would appear that cultures must have attained a minimal level of cultural complexity if riddling is to exist as a form of expressive behavior. This conclusion is supported by the associations reported in this chapter of riddles with the higher levels of political integration, the number of levels in the jurisdictional hierarchy transcending the local community, and oaths and ordeals. More indirectly, the links with games of strategy, large domestic animals, and certain patterns of child training have a similar significance. It would not be difficult to produce other associations with traits indicative of cultural complexity. In complex cultures, too, there is more likely to be institutionalized formal interrogation in the court, schoolroom, temple, and elsewhere. Here superordinates do question subordinates.

Responsibility. Cross-culturally the presence of riddles is associated with several child-training variables, but the most striking of these are the associations with high responsibility training (see Table 6.6). The large-animal and rote-learning findings are also pertinent. Remarkably enough, the same variable seems to be relevant at the intracultural level in the United States (see Table 6.13). Perhaps the responsible performance of chores may be linked with the responsible answering of questions, both expressively and nonexpressively. In all probability it is not accidental that judicial oaths and ordeals also have associations with responsibility training (Roberts 1965:204). Clearly, the definition and the measurement of this variable should be improved.

Oral socialization. Nagging which involves persistent questioning and scolding must be one form of oral socialization. This study suggests that high nagging leads to high-avoidance and low-approach attitudes toward oral interrogation and to a low interest in riddles. A lesser amount of nagging, however, may contribute to the conflict over oral interrogation, which contributes to high involvement in riddles. Other techniques of oral socialization, such as teasing, praising, ridiculing, rebuking, and the like, may be more relevant to a positive interest in riddles. At least teasing is important in Tagalog culture. Further information is needed on this group of variables.

Oral interrogation. The Tagalog study suggests that high-approach attitudes toward oral interrogation balanced by high-avoidance attitudes toward oral interrogation are linked with high riddling competence. In the second game study (Roberts and Sutton-Smith 1962) and in the later work dealing with games and other expressive models, much has been made of the conflict-enculturation hypothesis for game involvement which has already been described. This same general hypothesis may hold for competent involvement in such expressive models as riddles.

A high interest in riddles, however, is not the same as a high competence at riddling, for a man may enjoy responding to riddles, listening to riddles, and reading riddles without being able to ask riddles effectively in genuine riddling situations or even to tell them in any number. Admittedly, someone who is highly competent at riddling is likely to be highly interested in them. In contrast to the Tagalog study, the American investigation dealt with interest and not with competence. Here, at least, the conflict-enculturation hypotheses must be modified.

The American study shows that there is an approach-avoidance field insofar as attitudes toward oral questioning are concerned. In this field, despite the scoring used in Table 6.9, there is probably conflict throughout in that there is always some approach and there is always some avoidance. Still approach balanced by avoidance is linked with high riddle interest, as is approach where it is greater than avoidance. When, approach is less than avoidance, however, there is low riddle interest. In other words, in addition to the link between conflict over oral interrogation and high riddle interest predicted by the hypothesis, riddle interest is also found where approach attitudes outweigh avoidance ones. Perhaps the hypothesis should now be termed the conflict approach and enculturation hypothesis, for two motivational principles seem to be at work: (1) conflict and (2) simple approach. The extremes may be handled by a conflict theory, but simple reinforcement may account for lower levels of motivation.

Work with the happiness, unhappiness, pride, and shame questions showed that there was a high conflict group characterized by high approach and high avoidance (type-1 interest) and a low conflict group characterized by high approach and low avoidance (type-2 interest). The type-2 respondent seemed to prefer conundrums and games of physical skill, while the type-1 respondent seemed to prefer the other riddles and games of strategy. Further work must be done here before anything can be said, but there is a possibility, at least, that two types of interest can be distinguished. Possibly, the type-1 individuals are the active riddlers (i.e., players) and the type-2 people are less actively involved (in effect, spectators). This must be tested.

It would appear in any case that interest in riddles is associated with attitudes toward oral interrogation. Also if interest is to be considered broadly, the narrow interpretation of the conflict-enculturation hypothesis must be modified.

Strategy. A strategic component exists in riddles and riddling. Cross-culturally, there was the predicted association between the presence of riddles and the presence of games of strategy. Within American culture, however, it was not determined that people who like games of strategy in preference to other games of physical skill are also more likely to have a high interest in riddles. Since most of the games of physical skill listed were games of the "physical skill and strategy" subtype, it is probable that even those involved with games of physical skill had some interest in strategy. It may be more interesting to consider the game interest and the power styles which they indicate. Clearly, the female potent strategist must be placed in a different category. This power-style question will be considered in another study.

Competence. The level of competence among the Tagalog riddlers was high, and it was obviously low among the American college students. This variable also merits more quantitative study.

Enculturation. Again it is argued that participation in riddling as an expressive activity entails some valuable learning, possibly about how to handle oneself under interrogation and how to interrogate others. This important variable was not studied at all.

Other variables. There were interesting sex differences, and it is certain that the child training is varied in terms of sex, that game involvement varies with sex, and that patterns of oral interrogation may vary with sex. It was not possible in this study to do enough research to say something meaningful about this variable, but it must be considered in future research. There are other variables, as well, including those which contribute to uncertainty in interactive situations (is, e.g., teasing more ambiguous than nagging?), but these will not be discussed here.

Theory of riddle involvement. We assert here that riddles are expressive models of oral interrogation. Such models should occur in cultures sufficiently complex to provide patterns of formal or serious oral interrogation to be modeled. Furthermore, there should be high responsibility training which both contributes to an individual's caring about his performance in oral interrogation situations and to his interest in such situations (particularly if he is in conflict about responsibility). If with these antecedent conditions an individual's attitudes toward oral interrogation are balanced between approach and avoidance, or if his attitudes are such that approach outweighs avoidance, he is likely to be interested in a representation of the area of conflict (i.e., a riddle), but if avoidance attitudes are stronger than approach attitudes, he should not be interested in such a model. Possibly, the more nearly approach is balanced by avoidance, the more likely he is to be competent at riddling and to have high interest. Finally, participation in riddling should provide useful learning to the participants in that they may improve their ability to ask and answer oral questions in a variety of situations and they may learn to deal with enigmatic situations. In a sense it is to the advantage of the society to provide models which assuage conflict-induced motivation and which contribute to learning.

Future research. Additional work is needed, and it is probable that multivariant statistical techniques should be used in the data analysis rather than the very simple statistics used here. Riddles and riddling must be studied in the field in cultures where they are important, as among the Tagalog, and at the childhood level within American culture. Additional research into the theory of expressive models in general should also contribute to our understanding of the place of riddles and riddling in expressive behavior and in expressive culture.

part two

DISCOVERING
STRUCTURE
IN
SPEECH

7

On Sociolinguistic Rules: Alternation and Co-occurrence[1]

SUSAN ERVIN-TRIPP

Susan Ervin-Tripp is a professor in the Department of Rhetoric and lecturer in psychology at the University of California, Berkeley, and a member of the Committee on Sociolinguistics of the Social Science Research Council. She received her doctorate in social psychology from the University of Michigan, and has done fieldwork on bilingualism among French residents of the United States, the Navaho, and Japanese-Americans in San Francisco. She has recently completed a long-term investigation of child language development, and is currently engaged in the cross-cultural study of language socialization.

   The first two parts of Ervin-Tripp's chapter each deal with a major type of sociolinguistic rule. As the terms suggest, *alternation* concerns choice among alternative ways of speaking, *co-occurrence* concerns interdependence within an alternative. These two types of rules are the sociolinguistic analogues of the paradigmatic and syntagmatic axes long recognized in linguistics (cf. Jakobson

[1] A longer and slightly different version of this chapter appeared as a paper entitled "Sociolinguistics" (Ervin-Tripp 1969). I am deeply indebted to William Labov, William Geoghegan, and the editors for detailed commentaries on drafts of this work and to other members of the Sociolinguistic Committee of the Social Science Research Council and our work group in Berkeley for discussions which have radically altered my views. Wallace Lambert and Richard Tucker very generously lent their working tables and draft manuscripts. Elizabeth Closs-Traugott was a consultant on British address. Dan Slobin provided Soviet data. This paper was written with the support of the Institute of Human Development and aid from the Language-Behavior Research Laboratory of the University of California. Student work contributing to generalizations in the text included studies by Renee Ackerman, Lou Bilter, Camille Chamberlain, Judith Horner, Andrea Kaciff, Jane Logan, Dana Meyer, Elaine Rogers, Elisabeth Selkirk, and Billi Wooley.

214 Discovering Structure in Speech

and Halle 1956). Ervin-Tripp shows that the two principles, while simple, are of great scope, serving to integrate
a wide variety of studies. She begins with an illustration
of how much can be at stake in the choice of an alternative in address. The case is not isolated.

The fact that a journeyman artisan accorded a student *Er*
aroused such protest at the University of Göttingen that a great
part of the student body left town. . . . A similar incident in
Mainz created such disorder that the elector was forced to call
in troops.

Metcalf (1938:4) is here referring to the late eighteenth
century, when the third person singular form *Er*, having
attained a relatively high position as a form of address in
the seventeenth century, first in co-occurrence with titles
and *Herr* _____, then independently of them, had generally sunk again in status, being mainly used to subordinates.

Ervin-Tripp proceeds to show how a formal analysis
based on the theory of information processing developed by William Geoghegan (1971a) can serve to make
explicit the involuntary processes underlying selection
rules. In surveying other systems of address, she points
both to specific contrasts (e.g., consequences of added
age, ways of realizing a value) and to universal characteristics (e.g., the point at which the greatest number of
choices may be found and some of the dimensions that
may underlie choice). Ervin-Tripp's analysis is tentative,
yet it offers highly interesting insights into human interaction processes. Note, e.g., the discussion of communication problems arising from the fact that speakers
of the same language may have different sociolinguistic
rule systems and thus may misread each others' intentions. One wonders whether such differences may acer-
bate ethnic tensions in modern contemporary societies.
Kohl's (1967) and Gumperz and Hernandez (1971) account of ghetto children's communication problems in
schools and studies of American Indian children (Polgar
1960; Philips 1970) suggest that they do. Bateson's work
(Jackson, Haley, and Weakland 1956) on the communicative basis of schizophrenia is also relevant here
(1968).
From consideration of rules for specific linguistic alternatives, Ervin-Tripp turns to social variables, such as

deference, as a more general starting point. She notes that in both respects analyses take the standpoint of predicting choice by speaker, and that the relation of this to comprehension and interpretation by others largely remains to be studied.

In the second part of the essay two kinds of co-occurrence rules are distinguished, (a) those operating within a single level, or sector, of linguistic structure and (b) those operating between levels or sectors. The first are termed "horizontal," the second "vertical." Thus lexical selection would be horizontally inconsistent in mixing an informal form into a formal sequence in "You may rest assured that His Excellency is most seriously considerin' your suggestion." A striking case of vertical selection is found in Surinam (former Dutch Guiana), whose two main languages are Dutch and the English-based creole, Sranan. To speak Dutch with a Dutch pronunciation is considered affected, but to speak grammatically and lexically perfect Dutch with a Sranan pronunciation is praised. In some circles, however, to speak Sranan with a Dutch pronunciation is prestigious.

Ervin-Tripp points out that the existence of normal co-occurrence allows departures from it to take on, or invite, social meaning. These questions lead into the very broad area commonly designated as that of *style*. (On work in stylistics in relation to literature, but with implications for sociolinguistics, see Guiraud (1961) and the collections edited by Chatman and Levin (1967), Sebeok (1960), and Steinmann (1967). The common distinction between formal and informal style is discussed with some reference to slang, elaboration, and ellipsis. Interpretation of the selections made by the speaker implicates the general study of *linguistic repertoires,* the range of alternative ways of speaking available, and thus broaches some of the questions dealt with in Part III.

The concepts discussed under the heading of *switching within discourse,* particularly *speech act* and *function,* and also *topic* and *episode,* are at the core of modern sociolinguistics and are referred to either explicitly or implicitly in this volume (see Blom and Gumperz, Chapter 14; Friedrich, Chapter 9). Ervin-Tripp first mentions alternation between one situation and another (situational shifting). When that to which an alternation rule applies is itself defined by co-occurrence rules, one has the relationship singled out in much of the British work in sociolinguistics by the term *register* (Halliday, McIntosh, and Strevens 1964), a register being a way of speaking that stands in a one-to-one relationship to a situation. By definition, if the register is different, then so is the situation, and conversely. More fundamental is the notion of metaphoric alternation of ways of speaking within a situation. It is in such alternations that the meaning of ways of speaking, and the rule-governed creativity entailed in their use, are most revealed. Here one requires the notion of *speech act,* such that the sequence of conversation can be identified as a sequence of such acts. Ervin-Tripp notes that most studies so far have dealt with the more patent routines that mark the boundaries of conversation (greeting, taking leave), or with "set pieces," as it were (narrating a tale, telling a joke, playing the dozens), and goes on to explore the difficult, yet essential, notion of *topic.* Since speakers are able to identify change and recurrence of topic within a conversation, it must be possible to characterize what is involved in doing so.

Notice that the focus of concern has shifted. At the outset alternation rules concerned particular terms. In considering entire ways of speaking, one may find alternation rules at a different level. Not only may alternation rules deal with styles themselves defined by co-occurrence rules but one may find rules for choosing between different sets of alternations—e.g., choice between the alternatives of address offered by one language and those offered by another, or choice of one language rather than another because oneself or one's interlocutor was more master of the alternation rules within it.

With regard to *messages,* Ervin-Tripp makes an important distinction between manifest and latent content. It is sometimes thought that sociolinguistic questions, particularly those of function, require one to deal with communication in its totality, including intent, and thus are unmanageable. As if in order to consider some aspect of the function of sentences one had to embrace every aspect at once. In fact, reasonably orderly progress is possible; in particular, a great deal of work can and must be done to identify the speech acts recognized in a community, work which is formal in the same sense as phonology and syntax. Such work makes explicit criteria for recognizing recurrences of particular acts of speech or tactics, parallel to criteria for recognizing phonological and syntactic sameness or difference; in dealing with this additional aspect of the form of an utterance, socio-linguistic research begs the question of ultimate intent just as much or as little as phonology and syntax. One can, e.g., identify "May I help you?" as, say, interrogative in sentence form, in message form, an offer; one may even be able to specify (from paralinguistic features, probably) that there is a functional component (elocutionary force) of ingratiation ("Please let me . . ."), matter-of-fact per-formance of duty, warning ("You are not unobserved"), or rebuff ("Are you certain you are the sort of person who belongs here?"). That is, one can know these things, perhaps only from hearing (apart from seeing) the utter-ance, through a knowledge of shared means of com-munication, without necessarily ascertaining the entire intent or state of mind of the speaker (e.g., without acer-taining the extent to which there is expression of sponta-neous attitude, to what extent a rehearsed manner). In sum, there is a shared competence here—it can be learned, for example, by actors, and we can judge how adequately an actor manifests it, independently of his state of mind while so doing.

Ervin-Tripp takes the position that a theory of func-tions served in speech is itself outside sociolinguistics. Her discussion, however, would seem to support the dis-tinction between function as private intent and function as the communicative status or value that a speech act is conventionally recognized as having. She indeed goes on to consider criteria for determining functional status, and to discuss study of the functional category of what Skinner calls *mands,* in some detail. If sociolinguistics must turn to other social-science fields for theories of functions (as of institutions, values, and the like), it is clear that it must itself develop the connection between such theories and specification of their realization in speech.

The essay concludes with recognition of the problem of different conceptions of the notion of "rule," and of the problem of the relation between behavior and reports of behavior, reports themselves being one of the kinds of behavior to be studied. One's first impression of this survey must be that there is so much to be learned and done; sociolinguistics is in its infancy. If one considers what was available before, the essay is seen to stand as a path-breaking integration of diverse lines of work, and to reveal more concretely than ever before the presence of a coherent field in which one can identify cumulative lines of research. Searle (1969) and Ervin-Tripp (1970a, 1970b) provide additional related readings. For a more recent treatment of Geoghegan's address rules, see Geoghegan 1971b.

Alternation Rules

AMERICAN RULES OF ADDRESS

A scene on a public street in the contemporary United States:

"What's your name, boy?" the policeman asked. . . .
"Dr. Poussaint. I'm a physician. . . ."
"What's your first name, boy? . . ."
"Alvin."

(Poussaint 1967:53)

Anybody familiar with American address rules can tell us the feelings reported by Dr. Poussaint: "As my heart palpitated, I muttered in profound humiliation. . . . For the moment, my manhood had been ripped from me. . . . No amount of self-love could have salvaged my pride or preserved my integrity. . . . [I felt] self-hate." It is possible to specify quite precisely the rule employed by the policeman. Dr. Poussaint's overt, though coerced, acquiescence in a public insult through widely recognized rules of address is the source of his extreme emotion.

Brown and Ford (Hymes, 1964b) have done pioneering and ingenious research on forms of address in American English using as corpora American plays, observed usage in a Boston business firm, and reported usage of business executives. They found primarily FN (first name) reciprocation, or TLN (title plus last name) reciprocation. However, asymmetrical exchanges were found where there was age difference or occupational rank difference. Intimacy was related to the use of multiple names.

Expanding their analysis to account for details from my own rules of address, I have found the structure expressed in the diagram in Fig. 7.1. The advantage of formal diagramming is that it offers precision greater

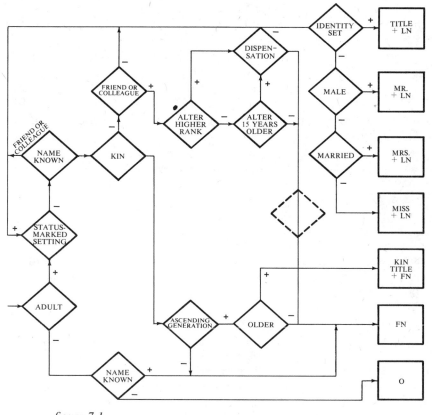

figure 7.1

American address

than that of discursive description (Hymes 1967). The type of diagram presented here, following Geoghegan (1971a), is to be read like a computer flow chart. The entrance point is on the left, and from left to right there is a series of binary selectors. Each path through the diagram leads to a possible outcome, that is, one of the possible alternative forms of address.

Note that the set of paths, or the rule, is like a formal grammar in that it is a way of representing a logical model. The diagram is not intended as a model of a process, of the actual decision sequence by which a speaker chooses a form of address or a listener interprets one. The two structures may or may not correspond. In any case, the task of determining the structure implicit in people's report of what forms of address are possible and appropriate is clearly distinct from the task of studying how people, in real situations and in real time, make choices. The criteria and methods of the two kinds of study are quite different. Just as two individuals who share the same grammar might not share the same performance strategies, so two individuals might have different decision or interpretation procedures for sociolinguistic alternatives but have the identical logical structure to their reports of behavior.

The person whose knowledge of address is represented in Fig. 7.1 is assumed to be a competent adult member of a Western American academic community. The address forms which are the "outcomes" to be accounted for might fit in frames like "Look, _____, it's time to leave." The outcomes themselves are formal sets, with alternative realizations; for example, first names may alternate with nicknames, as will be indicated in a later section. One possible outcome is no-naming, indicated in Fig. 7.1 by the linguistic symbol for zero [Ø].

The diamonds indicate selectors. They are points where the social categories allow different paths. At first glance, some selectors look like simple external features, but the social determinants vary according to the system, and the specific nature of the categories must be discovered by ethnographic means. For example, "Older" implies knowledge by the range of age defined as contemporary. In some southeast Asian systems, even one day makes a person socially older.

The first selector checks whether the addressee is a child or not. In face-to-face address, if the addressee is a child, all of the other distinctions can be ignored. What is the dividing line between adult and child? In my own system, it seems to be school-leaving age, at around eighteen. An employed sixteen-year-old might be classified as an adult.

Status-marked situations are settings such as the courtroom, the large faculty meeting, and Congress, where statuses are clearly specified, speech style is rigidly prescribed, and the form of address of each person is derived from his social identity, e.g., "your honor" or "Mr. Chairman." The test for establishing the list of such settings is whether personal friendships are apparent in the address forms or whether they are neutralized (or masked) by the formal requirements of the setting. There are, of course, other channels by which personal relations might be revealed, but here we are concerned only with address alternations, not with tone of voice, connotations of lexicon, and so on.

Among nonkin the dominant selector of first-naming is whether alter is to be classified as having the status of a colleague or social acquaintance. When introducing social acquaintances or new work colleagues, it is necessary to employ first names so that the new acquaintances can first-name each other immediately. Familiarity is not a factor between dyads of the same age and rank, and there are no options. For an American assistant professor to call a new colleague of the same rank and age "Professor

Watkins" or "Mr. Watkins" would be considered strange, at least on the American west coast.

Rank here refers to a hierarchy within a working group, or to ranked statuses like teacher-pupil. In the American system, no distinction in address is made to equals or subordinates since both receive FN. The distinction may be made elsewhere in the linguistic system, for example, in the style of requests used. We have found that subordinates outside the family receive direct commands in the form of imperatives more often than equals, to whom requests are phrased in other ways, at least in some settings.

A senior alter has the option of dispensing the speaker from offering TLN by suggesting that he use a first name, or tacitly accepting the first name. Brown and Ford (Hymes, 1964b) have discussed the ambiguity that arises because it is not clear whether the superior, for instance a professor addressing a doctoral candidate or younger instructor, wishes to receive back the FN he gives. This problem is mentioned by Emily Post: "It is also effrontery for a younger person to call an older by her or his first name, without being asked to do so. Only a very underbred, thick-skinned person would attempt it" (Post 1922:54). In the American system described in Fig. 7.1, age difference is not significant until it is nearly the size of a generation, which suggests its origins in the family. The presence of options, or dispensation, creates a locus for the expression of individual and situational nuances. The form of address can reveal dispensation, and therefore be a matter for display or concealment in front of third parties. "No-naming" or 0, is an outcome of uncertainty among the options.[2]

The *identity* set refers to a list of occupational titles or courtesy titles accorded people in certain statuses. Examples are "Judge," "Doctor," "Professor," and so on.[3] A priest, physician, dentist, or judge may be addressed by title alone, but a plain citizen or an academic person may not. In the latter cases, if the name is unknown, there is no address form

---

[2] *Reference rules* involve additional considerations such as the relation of the addressee and referent. If the addressee is of lower rank or age than both the referent and the speaker, e.g., then the speaker in Fig. 7.1 employs the addressee's address term—e.g., Mrs. Jones may refer to her husband to addressees who know him as "Charles" to a friend, "Mr. Jones" to a servant, or "Daddy" to his young child (Ervin-Tripp 1969).

[3] English occupational titles usually neutralize sex. The first woman appointee to the British High Court of Justice produced an address crisis because the traditional occupational titles contained terms that in other contexts are selected by sex. Mrs. Lane, like the other justices, were by the lord chancellor's decree to be called "My Lord" and Mr. Justice Lane." His lordship, Mr. Justice Lane, is also entitled by ancient judicial tradition to a bachelor knighthood" (*Time*, August 27, 1965). Justices in British law wear wigs and robes, elaborating the status marking of the settings in which they act. The decision shows that to members the terms are not sex indicators, and that the alternatives, "My Lady" and "Mrs. Justice Lane" would be sex marked rather than neutral, just as "chairwoman" is.

(or zero, Ø) available, and we simply "no-name" the addressee. The parentheses used here refer to optional elements, the bracketed elements to social selectional categories.

[Cardinal]: Your excellency
[U.S. President]: Mr. President
[Priest]: Father (+ LN)
[Nun]: Sister (+ religious name)
[Physician]: Doctor (+ LN)
[Ph.D., Ed.D.], etc.: (Doctor + LN)
[Professor]: (Professor + LN)
[Adult] etc.: (Mr. + LN)
          (Mrs. + LN)
          (Miss + LN)

Wherever the parenthetical items cannot be fully realized, as when LN is unknown, and there is no lone title, the addressee is no-named, by a set of rules of the form as follows: Father + Ø → Father, Professor + Ø → Ø, Mr. + Ø → Ø, etc. An older male addressee may be called "sir" if deference is intended, as an optional extra marking.

These are my rules, and seem to apply fairly narrowly within the academic circle I know. Nonacademic university personnel can be heard saying "Professor" or "Doctor" without LN, as can schoolteachers. These delicate differences in sociolinguistic rules are sensitive indicators of the communication net.

The zero forms imply that often no address form is available to follow routines like "yes," "no," "pardon me," and "thank you." Speakers of languages or dialects where all such routines must contain an address form are likely in English either to use full name or to adopt forms like "sir" and "ma'am," which are either not used or used only to elderly addressees in this system.

One might expect to be able to collapse the rule system by treating kin terms as a form of title, but it appears that the selectors are not identical for kin and nonkin. A rule which specifies that *ascending generation* only receives title implies that a first cousin would not be called "cousin" but merely FN, whereas an aunt of the same age would receive a kin title, as would a parent's cousin. If a title is normally used in direct address, and there are several members of the kin category, a first name may also be given (e.g., Aunt Louise). Frequently, there are additional features marked within a given family, such as patrilineal vs. matrilineal, near vs. distant. Whenever the address forms for an individual person's relatives are studied, this proves to be the case, in my experience.

Presumably, the individual set of rules or the regional dialect of a reader of this chapter may differ in some details from that reported in Fig. 7.1; or a better formulation is possible. Perhaps sociolinguists will begin to use a favorite frame of linguists—"In my dialect we say . . ."—to illustrate such differences in sociolinguistic rules. For example, I have been told that in some American communities there may be a specific status of familiarity beyond first-naming, where a variant of the middle name is optional among intimates. This form then becomes the normal, or unmarked, address form to the addressee.

> "What's your name, boy?"
> "Dr. Poussaint. I'm a physician."
> "What's your first name, boy?"
> "Alvin."

The policeman insulted Dr. Poussaint three times. First, he employed a social selector for race, in addressing him as "boy," which neutralizes identity set, rank, and even adult status. Addressed to a white man, "boy" presumably would be used only for a child, youth, or medial regarded as a nonperson.

Dr. Poussaint's reply supplied only TLN and its justification. He made clear that he wanted the officer to suppress the race selector, yielding a rule like Fig. 7.1. This is clearly a nondeferential reply since it does not contain the FN required by the policeman's address rule. The officer next treated TLN as failure to answer his demand, as a nonname, and demanded FN; third, he repeated the term "boy," which would be appropriate to unknown addressees.

According to Fig. 7.1, under no circumstances should a stranger address a physician by his first name. Indeed, the prestige of physicians even exempts them from first-naming (but not from "Doc") by used-car salesmen, and physicians' wives can be heard so identifying themselves in public so as to claim more deference than "Mrs." brings. Thus the policeman's message is quite precise: "Blacks are wrong to claim adult status or occupational rank. You are children." Dr. Poussaint was stripped of all deference due his age and rank.

Communication has been perfect in this interchange. Both were familiar with an address system which contained a selector for race available to both blacks and whites for insult, condescension, or deference, as needed. Only because they shared these norms could the policeman's act have its unequivocal impact.

COMPARATIVE RULE STUDIES

The formulation of rules in this fashion can allow us to contrast one sociolinguistic system with another in a systematic way. We can assume that a shared language does not necessarily mean a shared set of sociolinguistic rules. For instance, rules in educated circles in England vary. In upper-class boarding schools, boys and girls address each other by last name instead of FN. In some universities and other milieux affected by the public school usage, solidary address to male acquaintances and colleagues is LN rather than FN. To women it is Mrs. or Miss + LN by men (not title + LN), and FN by women. Thus sex of both speaker and addressee is important.

In other university circles the difference from the American rule is less; prior to dispensation by seniors with whom one is acquainted, one may use Mr. or Mrs. rather than occupational title as an acceptably familiar but deferential form. Note that this is the usage to women by male addressees in the other system. The two English systems contrast with the American one in allowing basically three, rather than two, classes of alternatives for nonkin: occupational title + LN, M + LN, and FN/LN. M + LN is used for intermediate cases, the familiar person who must be deferred to or treated with courtesy.

Two Asian systems of address have been described recently. The pioneering work of William Geoghegan (1971a) describes the naming system of a speaker of Bisayan, a Philippine language. As in most systems, children routinely receive the familiar address form. The Bisayan system, like the American and English, chooses on the basis of relative rank, relative age, and friendship. But there are important differences. In the United States, all adult strangers are addressed with deference; in the Bisayan system, social inferiors do not receive titled address. In the American system for nonkin, added age, like higher rank, merely increases distance or delays familiar address; in the Bisayan system inferiors or friends who are older receive a special term of address uniting informality and deference.

The Korean system is more unlike the American (Howell 1967). In Korea, relative rank must first be assessed. If rank is equal, relative age within two years is assessed, and if that is equal, solidarity (e.g., classmates) will differentiate familiar from polite speech. This system differs both in its components and its order from the American and Bisayan rules. Both inferiors and superiors are addressed differently from equals. Many kinds of dyads differ in authority—husband-wife, customer-tradesman, teacher-pupil, employer-employee. In each case, asymmetrical address is used. Addressees more than two years older or younger than the speaker are differentially addressed, so that close friendship is rigidly age graded. Solidary relations arise from status, just as they do between equal colleagues in the American system, regardless of personal ties. There are more familiar address forms yet to signal intimacy within solidary dyads. If the English system has three levels, there are even more in the Korean system. Since the criteria were multiple in the Howell study, not a single frame, the comparison is not quite exact.

As Howell points out, the Korean system illustrates that the dimension of approach that Brown and Gilman (1960) called solidarity may in fact have several forms in one society. In the Korean system intimacy is separable from solidarity. This separation may also exist in the American system, but in a different way. One is required to first-name colleagues even though they are disliked. As Brown and Ford (Hymes 1964b) showed, however, nicknames may indicate friendship more intimate than the solidarity that requires or is shown by FN. They found that various criteria of intimacy, such as self-disclosure, were related to the *number* of FN alternates, such as nicknames and sometimes LN, used to an addressee, and proposed that greater intimacy creates more complex and varied dyadic relations which speakers may opt to signal by a greater number of address variants. Thus in the American system two points of major option for speakers exist: the ambiguous address relation between solidary speakers of unequal age or status and intimacy. We can expect that systems will vary in the points where address is prescribed or where options exist; Brown and Ford suggest a universal feature, however, in saying that in all systems relatively more frequent interaction should be related to more address variation. This they suggest is related to a semantic principle of greater differentiation of important domains.[4]

TWO-CHOICE SYSTEM

The brilliant work of Brown and Gilman which initiated the recent wave of studies of address was based on a study of T and V, their abbreviation for familiar vs. formal second person verbs and pronouns in many European languages. In English the same alternation existed before "thou" was lost. The contrast is realized in German by *du* and *sie,* in French by *tu* and *vous,* and in Russian by *ty* and *vy.*

One might expect two-choice systems to be somewhat simpler than a system like Bisayan, which in Geoghegan's (1971a) description gives nineteen output categories.[5] But the number of outcomes can be few, though the number of selectors is many or the kinds of rules relating them

[4] In the system shown in Fig. 7.1, it is possible to create asymmetrical address by using FN to a familiar addressee who cannot reciprocate because of rank or age difference and lack of dispensation, e.g., a domestic servant. E. Hughes has noted a shift from TLN to FN by physicians whose patients moved from private fees to Medicare. This usage is hard to accommodate in Fig. 7.1.

[5] William Geoghegan has pointed out that in the community he studied in the Philippines, there was probably a higher degree of familiarity than that reached by Brown and Ford's students at the Massachusetts Institute of Technology. In this condition, shifts were not realized lexically, so he would not expect extreme familiarity to be related to multiple address, only moderate familiarity. Note that extreme familiarity makes available interpretability of paralinguistic and other subtle cues, which are particularly likely to be employed for signalling emotion and function shifts in "restricted code" groups (Bernstein 1964a).

complex. Figure 7.2 gives a description of the nineteenth-century rules of the Russian gentry, as I derive them from the excellent analysis by Friedrich (Chapter 9), which gives sufficiently full detail to permit resolution of priorities. *Special statuses* refers to the tsar and God, who seem not to fit on any status continuum. *Status-marked settings* mentioned by

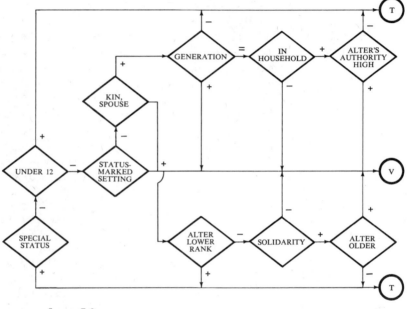

figure 7.2

Nineteenth-century Russian address

Friedrich were the court, parliament, public occasions, duels, and examinations. *Rank* inferiors might be lower in social class, army rank, or ethnic group or be servants. *Solidarity* applied to classmates, fellow students, fellow revolutionaries, lovers, and intimate friends. Perhaps it is more properly called familiarity or intimacy since there does not seem to be the prescription present in the Korean and American solidary relation. A feature of the system which Friedrich's literary examples illustrate vividly is its sensitivity to situational features. Thus T means "the right to use *ty*" but not the obligation to do so. Within the kin group, household is of considerable importance because of the large households separated by distance in traditional Russia.

A slightly later eastern European system described by Slobin (1963) is given in Fig. 7.3. The Yiddish system, as described by immigrants, is

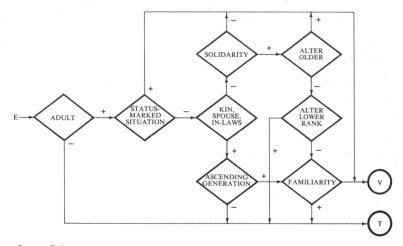

figure 7.3
Yiddish address

somewhat more like the American than like the Russian system in that deference is always given adult strangers, regardless of rank. However, an older person received deference, despite familiarity, unless he was a member of the kin group. In the American system familiarity can neutralize age.

How have these systems changed? We have some evidence from the Soviet Union. The Russian revolutionaries, unlike the French, decreed V, implying that they wanted respect more than solidarity. The current system is identical to the old with one exception: Within the family, asymmetry has given way to reciprocal T, as it has in most of western Europe, at least in urbanized groups. For nonkin in ranked systems like factories, superiors receive *vy* and give *ty:*

When a new employee is addressed as *"ty,"* she says, "Why do I call you '*vy*' while you call me '*ty*'?" "Kormilitzyn gleefully shoots back a ready answer:" "If I were to call everyone '*vy*' I'd never get my plan fulfilled. You don't fulfill plans by using '*vy*'" (Kantorovich 1966:30).

Evidently, the upper-class habit of using *vy* until familiarity was established (a system reflecting the fact that the T/V contrast itself came in from above as a borrowing from French) has seeped downward. "A half-century ago even upon first meeting two workers of the same generation would immediately use '*ty*.' Today things are different. Middle-aged workers maintain '*vy*' for a long time, or else adopt the intermediate form which is very widespread among people within a given profession: '*ty*' combined with first name and patronymic" (Kantorovich 1966:81).

Kantorovich, true to the 1917 decree, complains about three features of the current system: *ty* to inferiors regardless of age, *ty* to older kin, and first names alone among young acquaintances. Thus he favors the more deferential alternative in each case. Social change in Russia has been relatively slow in sociolinguistic rules, has affected family life more than public life, and has spread the practices of the gentry among the workers.

The Puerto Rican two-choice system shown in Fig. 7.4 is quite simple,

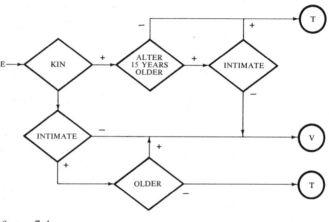

figure 7.4

Puerto Rican address

either because it is a system of children or because my analysis is based on statistical tables not individual interviews. The data were generously supplied by Wallace Lambert and his collaborators from a large-scale study of comparative address systems in several cultures. Elementary and high school students filled in questionnaires about the forms of address given and received. In this chart, interlocale and intersubject differences have been suppressed. The striking feature of this system is that it requires only three discriminations. It is likely, of course, that adult informants would elaborate further details. Intimacy in this system refers to close ties of friendship, which can occur with others of widely varying age, e.g., with godparents, and is quite distinct from solidarity, which arises from status alone. Adolescent girls, for example, do not give *tu* to a classmate unless she is a friend.

Lambert and his collaborators have collected slightly less detailed data from samples of schoolchildren in Montreal, from a small town in Quebec, from Mayenne, France, and from St. Pierre et Michelon, an island colony with close ties to France, much closer than to nearby Canada.

The system of kin address varies considerably. In both Mayenne and St. Pierre, all kin and godparents receive *tu*. In Quebec, the urban middle class is moving in this direction, but the urban lower class and the rural regions from which it derives retain an address system like Puerto Rico's in which distance (including age) with the family is important. In some families, even older siblings receive *vous*. For kin address, of course, the sanctions are intrafamily, so one would expect between-family differences to be greater during social change than in nonkin address. Generally, "intimate" means parents, then aunts, uncles, and godparents, then grandparents. Some interfamily differences might be accounted for by finding which family members live in the household, which nearby, and which far away.

Sex of addressee appears to be a feature of adult systems, or may influence the probabilities of intimacy where there is a selector. In Quebec, adults generally give *tu* to children and young men regardless of familiarity. In St. Pierre (except with upper-class girls, who are less likely to receive *tu* under any conditions) acquaintance legitimizes *tu* and is necessary even in addressing children. In Mayenne, middle-class little boys said they received *tu* from everyone (and reported often reciprocating to strangers), but otherwise familiarity seems to be required, as in Puerto Rico, in the Mayenne system. Boys generally receive T from employers, and in the country and the urban lower class they receive T from service personnel. It should be noted that the analysis from the children's standpoint of what they think they receive is an interesting reflection of the fact that people know what they should say themselves, and they also expect some standard form from others. In analyzing the adult rule systems, however, the children's data are not the best; the adults of rural or lower-class background may have different rules (e.g., service personnel?) than others.

Elsewhere Lambert (1967b) has discussed the development of address rules with age. There are several interesting problems in the learning of these systems, such as the visibility of the various social selectors. One can assume the rank gradations in an adult system might be learned late (at least in terms of generalizability to new addressees), as would generation differentiations not highly related to age.

A second problem emphasized by Lambert is the structure of alternation itself. Children in most language communities learn fairly early to employ the asymmetry of first and second person (for a case study, see McNeill 1963). Thus if they always received T and gave V, there might be less difficulty; however, they see others exchanging reciprocal V and T as well as asymmetrical address, and they give T to some alters. Comparative research should be done in natural language communities where the language structure provides different category systems and social selectors (Slobin 1967).

The compressed presentation here of Lambert's work has indicated several directions for research on social criteria of address selection. Lambert has shown that these rules are sensitive indicators of differences between social groups, and of social change. One must look beyond the address system for independent social features correlated with address systems of a defined type. In order to do such studies, a clear-cut formal system for typologizing properties of address systems (like language typologies) is necessary.

Brown has already suggested that the dimensions of power and solidarity are likely to be present in all address systems since they are the basic dimensions of social behavior. If these are universals, we can look elsewhere for ways of typologizing systems, as suggested here, according to

1. The order of universal selectors in the rule

2. The location of personal options (such as dispensation, located at rank in the rule on Fig. 7.1)

3. Outcome types (for a given social selector, what linguistic or paralinguistic features most commonly realize the contrast?)

4. Formal features of the informational system (e.g., the relation of input alternatives to outcomes, or the amount of neutralization)

5. Formal type of rule for realizing insults, condescension, deference, and so on by operations on the output of rules for normal, unmarked address (or on the rules themselves) (see the last section of this chapter)

SOCIALIZATION

Adults entering a new system because of geographical or occupational mobility may have to learn new sociolinguistic rules. A contrastive analysis of formal rules, in combination with a theory of social learning, would allow specification of what will happen.

First, we can predict what the speaker will do. We can expect, on the basis of research on bilinguals, that the linguistic alternatives will at first be assimilated to familiar forms, to "diamorphs." Thus a Frenchman in the United States might start out by assuming that monsieur = Mr., madame = Mrs., and so on.

However, the rules for occurrence of these forms are different in France. In polite discourse, routines like *"merci," "au revoir," "bonjour,"* and *"pardon"* do not occur without an address form in France, although they may in the United States. One always uses *"Au revoir, madame*" or some alternative address form. *Madame* differs from "Mrs." in at least two ways. Unknown female addressees of a certain age are normally called *madame,* regardless of marital status. Further, Mrs. $+ \emptyset = \emptyset$; *madame* $+ \emptyset = madame$. As a matter of fact, the rule requiring address with routines implies that when LN is not known, there cannot be a "zero alternant"—some form of address must be used anyway, like the English "sir." As a result of these differences in rules, we can expect to hear elderly spinsters addressed: "Pardon me, Mrs."

How do listeners account for errors? Shifting at certain points in sociolinguistic rules is regularly available as an option. Normally, it is interpreted as changing the listener's perceived identity, or his relation to the speaker. The result may be complimentary, as "sir" to an unknown working-class male, or insulting, as "Mommy" to an adolescent male. If the learner of a sociolinguistic system makes an error that falls within this range of interpretable shifts, he may constantly exchange predictably faulty social meanings. Suppose the speaker, but not the listener, has a system in which familiarity, not merely solidarity, is required for use of a first name. He will use TLN in the United States to his new colleagues and be regarded as aloof or excessively formal. He will feel that first-name usage from his colleagues is brash and intrusive. In the same way, encounters across social groups may lead to misunderstandings within the United States. Suppose a used-car salesman regards his relation to his customers as solidary, or a physician so regards his relation to old patients. The American using the rule in Fig. 7.1 might regard such speakers as intrusive, having made a false claim to a solidary status. In this way, one can pinpoint abrasive features of interaction across groups.

Another possible outcome is that the alternative selected is completely outside the system. This would be the case with "excuse me, Mrs.," which cannot be used under any circumstances by rule 1. This behavior is then interpreted by any additional cues available, such as the face, dress, or accent of a foreigner. In such cases, if sociolinguistic rules are imperfectly learned, there may be social utility in retaining an accent; wherever the attitude toward the group of foreigners is sufficiently benign, it is better to be so designated than to risk insulting or offending addressees.

INTEGRATED SOCIOLINGUISTIC RULES

The rules just given are fractional. They are selective regarding the linguistic alternations accounted for. They define only specific linguistic entries as the universe of outcomes to be predicted. If one starts from social variables, a different set of rules might emerge. This is the outlook of William Geoghegan (1971a), Ward Goodenough (1965a), and Dell

Hymes (1964b), who suggests taking "a specific or universal function, such as the distinguishing of the status or role of man and woman, derogation, respect, or the like, and investigating the diverse means so organized within the language habits of the community, . . . [rather than] looking for function as a correlative of structure already established." This is the point of view taken in the last section of this paper.

Using such an approach, Goodenough examined behavior toward a range of statuses and found that it was possible to rank both the statuses and the forms of behavior into Guttman scales and equivalent classes, grouped at the same scale point (1965a). In this way, various kinds of verbal and nonverbal behavior can be shown to be outcomes of the same social selectors.

Deference, the feature studied by Goodenough, may be indicated by pronoun alternations, names or titles, tone of voice, grammatical forms, vocabulary, and so on (Capell 1966:104ff; Martin, in Hymes 1964d). Rubin suggests even language change may serve the same purpose (1962). Deferential behavior as in the Spanish-Guarani choice in Paraguay may in some systems only be realized in special situations such as in introductions or in making requests. If one compares an isolated segment of two sociolinguistic systems, it cannot legitimately be concluded that a given social variable is more important in one system than the other. It may simply be realized through a different form of behavior.

It is not clear how the different realizations of social selectors might be important. Language, address, terms, pronominal selection, or consistent verb suffixing (as in Japanese) can be consciously controlled more readily, perhaps, than can intonation contours or syntactic complexity. Frenchmen report "trying to use *tu*" with friends. Such forms can be taught by rule specification to children or newcomers. Forms which allow specific exceptions, or which have options so that too great or too little frequency might be conspicuous, cannot be taught deliberately so easily. Such rules can be acquired by newcomers only by long and intense exposure rather than formal teaching.

Some alternations are common and required; others can be avoided. Howell reports that in Knoxville, Tennessee, Negroes uncertain whether or not to reciprocate FN simply avoided address forms to colleagues (Howell 1967:81–83), just as Brown and Ford noted in the academic rank system. In a pronominal rank system, like French or Russian, such avoidance is nearly impossible. Among bilinguals, language switching may be employed to avoid rank signaling (Howell 1967; Tanner 1967). The avoidable selector can be considered a special case of the presence of options in the system. Tyler (1965) has noticed that morphological deference features (like the Japanese) are more common in societies of particular kinship types, such as lineage organization.

This description is primarily made from the standpoint of predicting a speaker's choice of alternatives in some frame. It is also possible to examine these rules from the standpoint of comprehension or interpretation, as have Blom and Gumperz (Chapter 14) in their discussion of *social meaning*. Just as one can comprehend a language without speaking it, as actors we can interpret the social meaning of the acts of others without necessarily using rules identical to our own. The relation between production and comprehension rules remains to be studied.

Co-occurrence Rules[6]

TYPES OF RULES

"How's it going, Your Eminence? Centrifuging OK? Also have you been analyzin' whatch'unnertook t'achieve?" The bizarreness of this hypothetical episode arises from the oscillations between different varieties of speech. It violates the co-occurrence rules that we may assume English to have.

In the preceding section, we were concerned with the selection of lexical items, pronouns, or inflectional alternatives. We conceived of each instance as involving social selectors. Once a selection has been made, however, later occurrences within the same utterance, conversation, or even between the same dyad may be predictable. Whenever there is predictability between two linguistic forms, we can speak of co-occurrence rules (Gumperz 1967).

Co-occurrence rules could be of two kinds. The instance of predictability through time might be called horizontal since it specifies relations between items sequentially in the discourse. Another type might be called vertical, specifying the realization of an item at each of the levels of structure of a language. For instance, given a syntactical form, only certain lexicon may normally be employed, and a particular set of phonetic values may realize the lexicon. If one has learned political terms in New York and gardening terms in Virginia, the phonetic coloring of the lexicon may reflect their provenance in the individual's history. The most striking case lies in the well-practiced bilingual who uses French syntax and pronunciation for French vocabulary and English syntax and pronunciation for English vocabulary.

In the example, the following are violations of vertical co-occurrence:

---

[6] Many of the concepts covered in this and the preceding section were discussed from a slightly different perspective by Gumperz (1964b).

a. "How's it going" is a phrase from casual speech, but the suffix "-ing" is used, rather than "-in'," which is normal for casual speech

b. An elliptical construction is used in the second utterance, which contains only a participle, but the formal "-ing" appears again

c. A technical word, "centrifuge," is used in the elliptical construction

d. The "-in'" suffix is used with the formal "analyze"

e. Rapid informal articulation is used for the pedantic phrase "undertook to achieve"

Horizontal co-occurrence rules refer to the same level of structure, and might be lexical or structural. The vocabulary in the example oscillates between slang and technical terms, the syntax between ellipsis and parallel nonellipsis. In bilingual speech one may find structural predictability independent of lexicon, as in an example of Pennsylvania German:

> Di kau ist over di fens jumpt.

Here the syntax and grammatical morphemes are German, lexicon English. Horizontal co-occurrence rules governing selection of grammatical morphemes are common, with lexical switching and phrase switching allowed. Diebold (1963) also gives examples in which Greek-Americans who can speak both Greek and English with "perfect" co-occurrence rules, if they employ English loan words in the Greek discourse, realize them in the Greek phonological system. This would suggest that for these speakers horizontal, or syntagmatic, phonological rules override vertical realization rules.

One of the startling aberrations in the example is the use of slang to a cardinal. We would expect to find that deferential address forms would be co-occurrent with formal style. One pictures a cardinal in a microbiology laboratory addressed by a janitor who knows technical terms but cannot fully control formal syntax and phonology! Like ungrammatical sentences, sociolinguistically deviant utterances become normal if one can define setting and personnel to locate them. This, of course, is the point. Wherever there are regular co-occurrences, deviant behavior is marked and calls attention to its social meaning.

The most extreme forms of sanctions for co-occurrence specification are likely to be found in ritualized religious speech in traditional societies. Here it would be blasphemous to utter the wrong speech. Indeed, Gumperz has suggested that linguistics first began with the Sanskrit scholars' efforts to identify the formal features of religious texts and transmit them unchanged. Thus from the special social constraint on alternations sprang the concept of "language."

At the opposite extreme are the conditions in American college lecturing, where technical terms, slang, and informal and formal syntax alternate to some extent. Friedrich also gives examples (Chapter 9) of delicate communication of changing relationships by shifts within conversations.

STYLE

Formal Style. Style is the term normally used to refer to the co-occurrent changes at various levels of linguistic structure within one language. The vertical properties of such shifts have been pointed out by Joos (1962). Hymes (1964d) has commented that probably every society has at least three style levels: formal or polite, colloquial, and slang or vulgar.

If Hymes is right about a polite style which contrasts with the unmarked or "normal" colloquial, it might be proposed that this is the style preferred in public, serious, ceremonial occasions. Co-occurrence restrictions are particularly likely because of the seriousness of such situations. The style becomes a formal marker for occasions of societal importance where the personal relationship is minimized. We would expect that the distant or superior form of address and pronoun is universally employed in public high style. In Fig. 7.1 and 7.2 "status-marked situations" which call for titles and V may also call for polite style. Thus speakers who exchange colloquial style normally might change to this style in certain public occasions such as funerals or graduation ceremonies.

It might in general be the case in English that in otherwise identical situations, an alter addressed with TLN receives polite style more than one addressed with FN. Howell (1967:99) reported such correlations in Korean.

In Geertz' (1960) analysis of *prijaji* speech etiquette in Java, a distinction is made between affixes and function morphemes controlled by co-occurrence rules, and honorific vocabulary (like "sir"), which is sporadic and which is governed in effect by rules of frequency rather than categorical co-occurrence. Since a single selection is made in the first case, he refers to a "styleme."

Formal lexicon and "-ing" should be related. Fischer (Hymes 1964d) found that criticizing, visiting, interesting, reading, and correcting and flubbin', punchin', swimmin', chewin', and hittin', occurred in a single speaker's usage. It is not clear here whether it is lexical style or topic that is at issue since there were no examples of denotative synonyms realized through different vocabulary. Such examples, of the sort given in Newman (Hymes 1964d) and found plentifully in English lexicon for body functions (e.g., urinate vs. weewee), provide clearer evidence for co-occurrence restrictions between lexicon and structure.

Labov (1966b) did include the "-ing" vs. "-in'" variation in his study of style contrasts in different social strata, and found it worked precisely as did the phonological variables. Polite style in a speaker might require a certain higher frequency (Figs. 7.5 and 7.6) of postvocalic [r], or [ð] rather

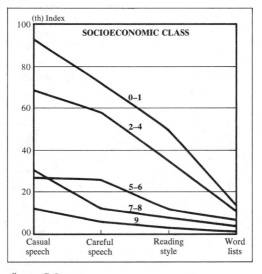

figure 7.5

Class and style stratification of 'th' in 'thing,' 'three,' etc., for adult native New York City speakers (Labov 1966).

than [d] in, e.g., "this," and of "-ing." While the variables differentiating polite from casual style tended to be the same in different classes, the precise frequency reached for each variable was a function of class too (Labov 1966). Thus his evidence suggests co-occurrence rules for grammatical morphemes and phonology. Labov (1966b) and Klima (1964) consider the formal description of phonological and syntactic style features, respectively.

Informal Style. In trying to sample different styles while interviewing, Labov made the assumption that speakers would use a more formal style during the interview questioning than at other times. He used several devices for locating such shifts contextually: speech outside the interview situation, speech to others usually in the family, rambling asides, role playing (specifically, getting adults to recite childhood rhymes), and

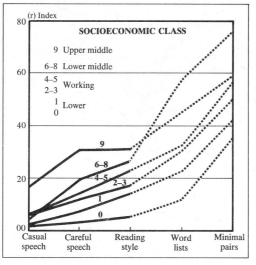

figure 7.6

Class stratification of 'r' in 'guard,' 'car,' 'beer,' 'beard,' etc., for native New York City adults (Labov 1966).

answers to a question about a dangerous experience. He found that when "channel cues" (changes in tempo, pitch range, volume, or rate of breathing) indicated a change to casual or spontaneous speech within a speech episode, the phonological features changed. In the examples illustrating the shifts, lexicon and syntax changed too.

It is commonly the case that as one moves from the least deferent speech to the most, from the informal to the ceremonial, there is more structural elaboration and less abbreviation. Probably, this difference is a universal, for two reasons. One is that elaboration is a cost, and is therefore most likely in culturally valued situations or relationships (Homans 1958). The other is that a high degree of abbreviation is only possible in in-group communication. While ceremonials may be confined to a sacred few, wherever they have a public function and must communicate content, we assume that this principle of elaboration holds. Elaboration could be defined with respect to a surface structure, or to the complexity of imbedded forms in the syntax, or some such criteria. A very brief poem might, in fact, in terms of rules and "effort" of compression, be more complex than a discursive report of the "same" content. Some forms are unambiguous: suffixed versus unsuffixed forms, as in Japanese honorifics or polite verb suffixes; titles versus nontitles; and so on.

From a formal grammatical standpoint, ellipsis is more complex than nonellipsis since the grammar must contain an additional rule. It is not clear how ellipsis might be handled in a performance model. However, ellipsis in the syntactical sense is clearly more common in informal speech.

From Soskin and John's (1963) text of a married couple we find the following:

> Bet you didn't learn it there.
> Your name?
> Want me to take it . . .
> Wanna take your shoes off?
> Not that way!
> Directly into it.

The formal rules for sentence contractions and ellipsis are readily written.

Another form of ellipsis is that used in conversational episodes in second-speaker forms or to complete one's own earlier utterances. From Soskin and John (1963):

> That fish, Honey.
> Like this?
> Undulating!
> Towed!
> With both of them!
> Well, I could.

These forms of ellipsis are learned. Brent and Katz (1967) found that anaphoric pronominalization is rare in young children; it is obligatory in second-speaker rules. Bellugi (1967) found also that contractions occur later than uncontracted forms in children, except as unanalyzed morphemes.

Semantic compression is also available, in casual speech among intimates (see Ervin-Tripp 1968). In *slang* the alternates are primarily lexical. As Newman (Hymes 1964d) has pointed out, the actual forms used are not necessarily different, but in sacred or slang contexts they take on a different meaning, so in speaking of slang vocabulary one must include both form and its semantic features. Since slang is highly transitory by definition, it will be understood and correctly used only within the group or network where it developed or to which it has moved at a given time. Thus one might predict that the selection rules for slang should restrict it to addressees to whom one claims a solidary relation. Thus a college lecture laced with slang is a claim on the identification of the audience.

Phonetically, a form which occurs in casual speech more than in polite styles is rapid speech, which entails horizontal changes.

What are you doing?	[hw ədar ju 'duwiŋ]
Whaddya doing?	[*hw*ədji 'duwiŋ]
Whach doon?	[wəč 'dun]

There are regular phonetic alternations related to rate, e.g.,

1. Retention of syllable of major stress and peak pitch
2. As degree of speeding increases, loss of weakest stress
3. Loss or assimilation of semivowels
   [r] in postvocalic position lost
   [d] + [y] → [j]   e.g., Whadja do?
   [t] + [y] → [č]   e.g., Whaca doin?
4. Possible loss of marginal phonological distinctions like /hw/ vs. /w/, perhaps as part of casual speech style
5. Centralization of unstressed vowels

There is a *reverse* set of rules available to speakers used to these alternations. The extra-slow style may be employed in sounding out for a dictionary or over the telephone. Thus normal "school" may become slow [sɨkuwɨl]. Many of these rules derive from the rules of English stress (Chomsky and Halle 1968).

Styles Related to Occupation. Language changes related to work arise for three reasons. One is that any activity brings with it objects, concepts, and values which are talked about by specialists in that activity, and indeed may be known only to them. Another is that whatever solidarity an interacting work group may achieve, or whatever identification a reference group (e.g., psychologists or transformational linguists) may stimulate, it can be alluded to by selection of appropriate alternatives in speaking or writing. Many instances of abbreviations in factories, or of work-group slang, or of technical terminology synonymous with colloquial vocabulary, must have this second feature. Further, the particular communicative conditions might give rise to some features—signal tower communication, headline style, the special syntax of short-order restaurant speech. While the slang and lexical features of restaurant speech can be found in kitchens, fast unambiguous oral communication needed between waiter and cook alone may lie behind the special syntax Brian Stross reported (see Ervin-Tripp 1969). Examples are the structure (number) + (category) + (modifier) which he found in such orders as "two bacon and" for bacon and eggs and "LT plain" for lettuce and tomato sandwich. Virtually all registers, including that of social-science writing, have syntactic as well as lexical features. The details of the co-occurrence rules for such styles remain to be studied.

Baby Talk. In many languages a special style is employed in talking to infants, which changes its features with the age of the child. A cross-linguistic comparison has been made by Ferguson (1964b). In English, baby talk affects all levels of structure.

Most speakers are likely to be conscious of baby-talk lexicon, as they often are of the lexical features of styles. Baby lexicon includes words like potty, weewee, bunny, night-night, mommy, and daddy. Many other words in adult speech become appropriate for speaking to infants when the suffix "-ie" is added. Drach and his colleagues (1969) found that speech to children is syntactically simpler and more repetitious, and contains fewer errors and hesitation pause and more ellipsis resulting in shorter sentences than speech to adults.

Phonological effects and paralinguistic features are especially conspicuous. Samples of talk to infants show certain general phonetic changes such as palatalization. Most striking is the higher pitch the younger the infant, and the use of a singsong, wide-ranging intonation. Observations of the social distribution of this style show it more common in addressing other people's children than one's own. For instance, nurses use the paralinguistic features at least in persuading children; and in cooperative nurseries, comparison of own-child and other-child addressees indicates a distinct shift to more age attribution with own child.

Children themselves use many of the features of adult baby talk very early. In addressing younger siblings they may adopt lexical and paralinguistic features of the adult baby talk as early as age two. In role play they use phrases and address terms from baby talk, e.g., "Goo-goo, little baby," and freely employ the sing-song intonation in addressing "babies." In other respects their role play is stereotyped rather than strictly imitative, for example in the frequent use of role names, and it may be that the use of the intonational and lexical features of baby talk may function simply as role markers in their play.

Linguistic Repertoire. Co-occurrence rules refer to the selection of alternates within the repertoire of a speaker in terms of previous or concomitant selections. The range of possible alternates should be known in such a study. In an American monolingual, the range is likely to include the styles just discussed, and perhaps an occupational register. Labov has pointed out, however, that it is rare to control a very wide stylistic range unless one is a speech specialist and that upwardly mobile persons usually lose the "ability to switch 'downwards' to their original vernacular" (1964b:92).

In many parts of the world, a code that is relatively distinct from the casual vernacular is used in formal situations. This condition, called "diglossia" in Ferguson's (Hymes 1964d) classic article, may, because of the greater code difference, be accompanied by more co-occurence restriction than is style shifting, where the common features of the styles may outweigh their differences. Examples where the codes are related are Greece, German Switzerland, Haiti, and Arab countries. Standard languages coexisting with local dialects are somewhat less perceptually separable; historically, the dialect does not usually maintain itself except phonetically, though there may be ideological resistance to borrowing from the standard (Blom and Gumperz, Chapter 14). Differential access to the everyday use of the standard, in combination with valued social meanings of a dialect, as in the case of nonstandard urban English or creoles such as those of Hawaii and Jamaica, may preserve variation.

Where diglossia takes the form of bilingualism (Fishman 1967), one might at first assume that the co-occurrence rules would primarily govern situations requiring the high form. Such a condition exists in many American bilingual communities, with English as the high form. However, these are not usually pure cases since English is the vernacular if there are casual contacts outside the immigrant community. Under these conditions there can be considerable interpenetration (Gumperz 1967).

Co-occurrence rules in common-sense terms refer to "language mixing." Some bilingual communities have strong attitudinal opposition to switching (usually they mean lexical co-occurrence). Blom and Gumperz (Chapter 14) found that in a Norwegian village speakers were unconscious of the use of standard forms and were very upset to hear tapes showing lack of co-occurrence restrictions in behavior. In practice, the maintenance of coordinate or segregated systems depend on social factors. Coordinate bilingualism is possible if there is a complete range of equivalent lexicon in both systems, and social support for the bilingualism. If this is not the case, some topics cannot be discussed, some emotions cannot be conveyed, and borrowing, perhaps surrounded by a routine disclaimer frame, will occur. The other social condition permitting such segregation in diglossia are the closed network circumstances reported by Blom and Gumperz (Chapter 14) where certain topics and transactional types simply would not occur in casual discourse. Thus American researchers can find rich grounds for the study of behavioral support or loss of co-occurrence rules, either in English style, registers, dialects, or multilingualism.

Shifting within Discourse

Situational Shifting. The social features alluded to in the alternation rules so far discussed have primarily been features of situations or personnel present. Sociolinguistic alternations based on these kinds of "situational shifting" (Blom and Gumperz, Chapter 14) can be seen in the two-year-old's use of baby-talk intonation to his baby sister, the multilingual child's selection of language for a new servant, the slum Afro-American child's loss of classroom copulas when on the playground, the Hawaiian college boy's selection of standard lexicon when a mainland stranger arrives, and replacement, in addition, of the creole's intonation if the stranger is a girl. These consistent behavioral shifts may or may not be related to normative rules of the type shown in Figs. 7.1 to 7.4 derived from informant's reports.

Speech Acts. In addition, however, such shifts can occur *within* occasions. They might be related to functions, speech acts, or topics. "What did he say?" "He asked her for a match." "Why did he do that?" "He wanted to meet her, talk with her." The first characterization describes a speech act, request. The second refers to the *function* of the act. We assume that all members of social groups can identify speech acts, that they are units in the cultural system. "What are you talking about?" "We were just saying hello." "We were telling jokes." "I was introducing Joe." *Saying hello, telling jokes,* and *introducing* are speech acts subordinate to organized exchanges like parties and joint work, often located within them by sequencing rules (Schegloff, Chapter 12) or rules of propriety (e.g., one introduces guests at a formal dinner, but not the waitress).

In these examples, the speech acts are labeled units. It is possible that some consistencies in rules of behavior imply the existence of a unit, though it may not appear in the folk taxonomy of speech acts. For example, suppose that one cannot say to a stranger on the street, "My name is George Landers. What time is it?" or "Hello, sir. Where is the post office?" Then to formulate the rule, one needs a category of information requests addressed to strangers in order to indicate that greetings and self-introductions are excluded. Another indication that such units may exist is that they commonly occur in bilingual interaction; there may be a language shift between two different speech acts.[7]

There is no reason to assume that speech acts are the same everywhere. Certain special forms of discourse, like poetry and speechmaking, may have components known only to specialists. Whether and why there are labels used in the teaching of these performances is itself an interesting cultural study.

Speech acts in English include greetings, self-identification, invitations, rejections, apologies, and so on. The ones identified so far tend to be rou-

---

[7] Recent work in transformational grammar has specified certain speech acts as performative verbs in the deep structure of sentences. Then the syntactic rules would have to contain the rules for neutralization or ambiguity I allude to later.

tines, but we can expect to find other more abstract units as research proceeds.

Topics. When conversations have an explicit message with informational content, they can be said to have a *topic.* "What are you talking about?" "Nothing." "Gossip." "Shop talk." "The weather." "The war." "We were having an automobile discussion about the psychological motives for drag racing in the streets." In everyday discourse, the question of topic is most likely to occur in invitations or rejections so that the answers are such as to exclude a new arrival or give him enough information to participate. Besides selecting personnel for participation, topics may be governed by a continuity rule. In a formal lecture in a university there is a constraint on continuity and relevance, just as there is in technical writing, where editing can enforce the constraint. Evidences of constraint are apologies for deviation: "That reminds me . . ." "Oh, by the way . . ." "To get back to the question . . ." "To change the subject . . ." Cultural rules regarding speech events may include constraints as to the grounds for relevance.

Kjolseth (1967) has found in analysis of some group interaction that topical episodes are key factors in speakers' tactics.

A performer's tactic may be to direct his episode as a probe into the preceding episode. In contrast, in another situation his tactic may be to extend and elaborate some antecedent episode. On still another occasion his tactic may be to close off and limit a previous episode. . . . These tactical types are based on, or defined in terms of, two qualities abstracted from the performances: (a) the episode locus of relevances drawn from the existent conversation resource, and (b) the purpose of the episode with respect to surrounding episodes.

The three examples given by Kjolseth would involve topical continuation, recycling, or change, respectively. These general features of speech events require that members be able to identify relevance but not necessarily to label topics.

There is yet a third form of evidence that topic may be a cultural unit. Bilinguals can frequently give reliable accounts of topical code switching, and their behavior often corresponds in general to their accounts (Ervin-Tripp 1964).

We can thus argue that topic, like speech act, must be a basic variable in interaction on the grounds that speakers can identify topical change as generating code shift, that speakers can sometimes report what they are talking about, and that topical continuity, recycling, and change may be normative features of speech events, or at least relevant to values about good conversations. One might, in fact, find that there are rules for topic selection just as there are for address.

Messages. The analysis of messages refers to two-term relationships, whereas topic is a single term allowing for simple taxonomies. Here we intend to refer only to the manifest or explicit message. Our reason for the distinction is that latent content categories typically refer to intent (see, e.g., Dollard and Auld 1959; Katz 1966; Leary 1957; Marsdo 1965). Our position here is that intent or function is part of the constellation of social features out of which interaction is generated. It can be realized in a variety of ways, of which verbal interaction is only one. We seek regular rules by which one can relate underlying categories to their formal realizations, or the formal features of interaction with their social meanings. Failure to discover such rules has led to considerable discouragement with the evident arbitrariness of content classifications in studies of natural discourse.

The manifest message, however, is the product of the social features of the situation as well as of intent, and is therefore inseparable from the interaction product. All the selections made in realization of the functions of communication can carry some kind of information, whether about the speaker, the situation, the hearer, or the topic. In detail, given alternations cannot do all at once, though they may be ambiguous as to which is intended. In this case, we intend the message only to refer to what is said or implied about the topic. There have been numerous summaries of ways of classifying messages (e.g., Pool 1959). A recent innovation is logical analysis (Veron et al. 1965). The underlying structure of logical linkages between terms in utterances was analyzed, then semantic relations were described in terms of logical relations between pairs of units (e.g., equivalence, inference, conjunction, specification of conditions, sequential relations, explanation, opposition, causes, . . .). A Markov semantic analysis revealed very large and consistent differences between subject groups, which were, in the study reported, clinical categories, but could be texts in a different society.

FUNCTION OF INTERACTION

Criteria. If sociolinguistic alternation rules have intents or functions as their input, then one strategy in identifying such rules is to isolate a functional category and examine its realizations. We assume that the theory of functions itself must lie outside of sociolinguistics, in another social science. However, an examination of the various functions realized by speech is of considerable importance in view of the evidence that these functions change with age and vary with culture.

Firth (Hymes 1964d) was among many who sought to identify the functions of speech. He included phatic communion (creating solidarity or alluding to it); pragmatic efficiency (accompanying work); planning and guidance; address; greetings, farewells, adjustment of relations, and so on; speech as a commitment, (courts, promises). Primarily, his view of function was the social value of the act.

Function is likely to be viewed by a psychologist from the standpoint of the interacting parties, either the sender or the receiver. Soskin has played tapes to listeners and asked them to report what they would *say* and what they would *think*. This method assumes that function is effect. It is close to Blom and Gumperz' (Chapter 14) criterion of social meaning.

A second method is to analyze actual instances of acts, and infer whether the receiver's response satisfied the speaker, either from his overt behavior or by questioning him. This method includes action, response, and reaction. It is derived from Skinner's (1957) theory that speech is operant behavior which affects the speaker through the mediation of a hearer. Feedback and audience consistency presumably "shape" effective speech in the normal person. In this method, function is identified by classes of satisfactory listener responses.

If intent is imputed to a speaker on the basis of some features of the content or form of his speech, a third form of functional analysis appears. This, of course, is the method of latent content analysis (e.g., Katz 1966).

A set of function categories was devised to account for the initiation of dyadic interaction, on the basis of a corpus of instances of action, response, and reaction (Ervin-Tripp 1964). The list includes eliciting goods, services, and information; implicit requests for social responses; offering of information or interpretations; expressive monologues; routines, and speech to avoid alternative activities.

Mands. One of the simplest functional categories to examine is one which Skinner (1957) called the mand since it is defined by the fact that normally it elicits goods, services, and information. One could broaden the definition by specifying that the intent is to obtain these since it is clear that under some conditions, the actor does for himself.

Soskin and John (1963) devised a category system, intermediate between the strata suggested here, which will serve to illustrate the breadth of possible realizations of mands. Suppose the actor wants the loan of a coat:

> "It's cold today" (structone).
> "Lend me your coat" (regnone).
> "I'm cold" (signone).
> "That looks like a warm coat you have" (metrone).
> "Br-r-r" (expressive).
> "I wonder if I brought a coat" (excognitive).

It is immediately obvious that these ways of getting a coat are socially distributed in a nonrandom way and would be quite ineffective under many circumstances.

If we look at the category which most explicitly realizes a mand, and can be said to be pragmatically unambiguous, the regnone, we find that there are a variety of speech acts that might be regnones, including *requests* and *orders:* "Ask him to close the window" vs. "Tell him to close the window." "Shut the window!" vs. "Would you mind closing the window?"

At a lower stratum, the syntactical, the request often involves some kind of speech act neutralization. For example, one can joke by misinterpreting a speech act, by saying "yes" to "Would you mind closing the window?" or to "Do you have a match?" or "Do you know where the post office is?" or to "Is George there?" on the phone, and doing nothing further. In each of these cases, the request is realized through a yes/no question. From the standpoint of syntax, such a response is quite appropriate. Under specifiable social conditions, however, these become the normal, unmarked form for realizing requests in the mature speaker. When one does not in fact want to speak to George but merely to know whether or not he is home, some other form must be chosen, or a fast footnote added.

These instances are highly stabilized cases of an apparent neutralization which has become the normal form for request and therefore would in fact be described by many speakers as "asking X to close the window" and so on, if they were told to convert these into indirect speech.

In addition, one finds many instances of the selection of the normal form for realization for some other function to represent a mand. Quite possibly, of course, in closed networks these become as usual as the "asking" examples.

In a term paper, Bessie Dikeman and Patricia Parker (1964) found that within some families mands were neutralized between equals most of the time, less than half the time from seniors to juniors, and in a minority of cases when juniors spoke. Examples from their papers were these

"Where's the coffee, Dremsel?" (it is visible) (to wife) [gloss: bring me the coffee].
"Is that enough bacon for you and Thelma?" (to husband) [gloss: save some for Thelma].
"It's 7:15 (to daughter) [gloss: hurry up].
"Mother, you know I don't have a robe. Well, we're having a slumber party tomorrow night" [gloss: buy me a robe].
"Oh dear, I wish I were taller" (to adult brother) [gloss: get down the dishes].

In factory settings, subordinates usually received commands, sometimes requests. Carol Pfuderer (1968) found that in a university office commands were reserved for familiar peers. Within this category of addressee, however, if the speaker was within the territory of the receiver, requests were used instead. If distance separated them, a command might be altered by a tag question making it a request ("Ask Marcy, why don't you?"), "please," address terms, or rising pitch. If the addressee was not a peer, requests, pragmatic neutralizations, or displacement of addressee occurred. Pragmatic neutralizations included information questions ("Has anyone gone to the accounting this week?" "Whose turn is it to make coffee this week, Ruby?") and statements "(It's stuffy in here." "Someone has to see Dean Smith."). In cases where the obvious receiver was much higher in rank, there might be displacement to a peer addressee but use of a highly deferent request form ("Joan, would you please get the stapler for me?"). In this example the nearest person to the stapler was a standing senior professor, not Joan, who was seated farther away.

Mands require action on the part of the alter so that the obligations and privileges inherent in the social relations of the personnel are likely to result in different linguistic realizations of the same function. We might expect displacement where possible in cases of extreme deference, perhaps pragmatic neutralization allowing the receiver an option of interpretation. In situations of high mutual nurturance where intimacy makes interpretability likely, as in many families, the basis for pragmatic neutralization may be quite different, perhaps serving to mask mands outside the normal duties of the receiver. In the same way, Stross (1964) found that "please" was used only for requested acts extraneous to duties.

We can expect that where variant address forms exist, they might alternate in minds. Milla Ayoub (1962), in a discussion of bipolar kin terms in Arabic, points out that in addition to proper names, a mother can call her son by either of two terms that also can mean "my mother." When a parent wishes to cajole or placate a child, but not command him, he uses these bipolar terms. This is particularly the case with sons. They are never used in direct commands.

In discussing current address practices in the Soviet Union, Kantorovich (1966) mentions that friends might switch from *ty* to *vy* with first name and patronymic when help is asked for.

Episodes. Watson and Potter (1962) used the term *episode* as a unit of analysis, which can terminate whenever there is a change in the major participants, the role system of the participants, the focus of attention, and the relationship toward the focus of attention. This term, rather than topic, was chosen to differentiate cases where a similar apparent topic might be within a person's own experience, part of an ongoing activity, or an abstract referential category, as in a discussion.

The different episodes that Watson and Potter's units identify probably will find some reflections in formal changes. These shifts arise from:

a. Sequencing rules concerning speech acts within a speech event.

b. Changes in the activity, if any, accompanying the interaction (e.g., a ball game or dinner preparation).

c. Disruptive events such as the arrival of new personnel, accidents like bumps or sneezes, and phone calls which require routines to right the situation.

d. Shifts arising from unexpected responses of alter, leading to changes in function.

e. Function satiation. Presumably, functions oscillate in patterned ways in stable groups.

f. Topic-evoked shifts in functions. Under the impact of instructions or of associative dynamics, the topic may change in the course of the conversation. These changes can alter the available resources for the participants and thereby change their intent. If the topic shifts from child rearing to economics, e.g., a bachelor may find he has greater resources for displaying knowledge and receiving recognition. He may speak more, use more technical vocabulary, perhaps even to the point that listeners do not understand. There were many such instances in studying the speech of bilinguals, in which topic and language were controlled by instructors (Ervin 1964; Ervin-Tripp 1964, 1967).

Blom and Gumperz (Chapter 14) found that among university-trained villagers, many features of standard Norwegian appeared when topics shifted from local to nonlocal. In the offering of information, speakers with a large repertoire of speech alternatives can maximize credibility by adopting the most suitable role. Thus discussion of university structure might elicit use of more standard Norwegian forms than would gossip about instructors, where student speech features would be adopted, especially those shared with addressees.

As functions change, address too may change through a conversation. David Day described in a term paper changes when an argument occurred in a class regarding an instructor's views of a student's beliefs. Address progressed from FN to Dr. LN to Professor LN. In comments with other students as addressee, LN was used in reference to the instructor, in front of him. Concurrently, slang decreased.

When there is agreement about the normal, unmarked address form to alters of specified statuses, then any shift can convey intent. Friedrich (Chapter 9) gives convincing cases of momentary shifts at times of personal crises. He points out that in a public setting friends would mask their intimacy with V; in talking of personal topics they would invoke their friendship with *ty* and remove it for impersonal topics with *vy*.

Kantorovich (1966:43) gives similar examples in current practice:

I say "*ty*" to my subordinates, but certainly don't do this in order to belittle them. I know that they'll answer me with "*vy*," but this isn't grovelling—it's a mark of respect. . . . Somebody I call "*ty*" is somehow closer to me than someone I have to call "*vy*." . . . If I get mad at one of my workers, and he needs a bawling out, I frequently switch to "*vy*." When cursing, many people who customarily use "*ty*" suddenly switch to "*vy*," and many who are on a mutual "*vy*" basis switch to "*ty*" (Kostomarov 1967).

In systems with age or rank asymmetrics of address, the use of the more deferential form to an equal or subordinate can either mean that they are receiving respect or being put off at a distance. To account fully for the interpretation of such actions by the receivers, we need to know the other signals, such as tone of voice, other address features, and the available ambiguities of the relationship. In the case of courtship, e.g., the important dimension is closeness or distance, and address changes would be so interpreted.

Rules for Switching. I have emphasized throughout this chapter that linguistic interaction is a system of behavior in which underlying functions are realized through an organized set of output rules within a social situation. If the function requires conveying an explicit message with informational content, some semantic information is presented in the alternatives selected. Other alternatives require the representation of social information.

In addressee-dominated rules like those in Figs. 7.1 to 7.4, effects of function switching can be represented as transformations upon the unmarked outputs of the addressee rules. They may take the form of simple replacements, e.g., if familiarity exists, different names may be employed as a direct representation of varied functions. Thus a node or selector for familiarity and for function is added to the branching rules. Tyler's (1966) rules are of this type.

Blom and Gumperz (Chapter 14) have suggested that metaphorical switching simply consists of treating the addressee as though his social features were different. In this case, the rule acts upon the selection points. In the case of Dr. Poussaint, hostile intent was represented in the selection of "adult"—rather than "adult +"—at the first selection point. Presumably, this possibility suggested itself by the existence of a traditional southern system of address to Blacks in which all but the very old (aunty) were addressed as children. When Harvey Sacks asked his UCLA students to play the role of boarders with their families in vacation, their silence, politeness of address and requests, and withdrawal from gossip and semantic ellipsis in conversation were interpreted by their families as evidence of sickness or hostility.

The Russian example implies that a simple transformation upon the output forms can express hostility; however, the inversion may be a consequence of transformation of selection features, making the friend a nonfriend, and the formal associate an inferior. Such general rules are a necessity if familiarity is absent since they permit the interpretation of new instances on the basis of the hearer's general knowledge of the system of sociolinguistic rules.

"Rules" could refer to structures for generating or interpreting speech, to reports of beliefs about practices, or to standards of correctness. We have given examples of all three kinds of rules, not always clearly distinguishing them. Labov's (1966b) index of linguistic insecurity compared the last two.

Behavioral rules and reports about behavior are likely to be systematically different. If the norms contain a probability or frequency factor, speaker's beliefs are, instead, categorical (Labov 1966b). Beliefs about the social selectors in sociolinguistic rules are more likely to include features of personnel, since categorization devices realize these (Sacks in press) features, than to note functional variation. Syntactical variables are not remembered (Sachs 1967) beyond the time needed for decoding unless they are markers, helping us classify the speaker. In multilingual communities phonological, syntactic, and semantic shifting is often not observed (Gumperz 1964a, 1967). Even borrowed vocabulary is unnoticed by members if values oppose borrowing (Blom and Gumperz, Chapter 14). Some speakers cannot remember the language in which they just spoke, let alone report it to an interviewer.

These phenomena are not merely grounds for distrusting members' reports. Just as reference to a relative (Tyler, Chapter 8) is affected by more than the semantic dimensions of reference, so the act of describing, even to oneself, is a product which could realize a variety of functions. Member's reports are likely to be as sensitive to social variation as any speech act mentioned in this chapter, and therefore prove as amenable to study. We expect then that rules based on report will have a systematic relation to behavioral consistencies, but not a one-to-one correspondence.

8

Context and Alternation in Koya Kinship Terminology[1]

STEPHEN A. TYLER

Stephen A. Tyler is associate professor of anthropology at Tulane University. He received his doctorate from Stanford University and has taught at Tulane and the University of California, Davis. The present chapter is a slightly revised version of an original paper first published in the *American Anthropologist* (Tyler 1966) and draws on several years of fieldwork among the Koya in central India. Tyler's current interests center on formal analysis of culture, kinship, language, and social structure.

Tyler himself puts his chapter in context in the following words:

"The analysis of kinship terminologies has traditionally operated only with the genealogical denotata of the nominal stems of kin terms, with little reference to the social and linguistic contexts in which kin terms are used. Such analysis has usually resulted in the delineation of a single, unitary structure. Problems of

Revision of "Context and Variation in Koya Kinship Terminology" by Stephen A. Tyler. Reproduced by permission of the American Anthropological Association from the *American Anthropologist*, Vol. 68, pp. 693–707 (June, 1966).

[1] The research on which this chapter is based was carried out in India in 1962–1963, supported by a Foreign Area Training Fellowship from the Ford Foundation. An earlier version of this chapter was presented at the Timber Cove Conference on "Approaches to Interpersonal Relations in South and Southeast Asia," April 9–12, 1965, sponsored by the Institute of International Studies, University of California, Berkeley. It has benefitted from the conference discussion, and from specific suggestions made by David M. Schneider, Gene Hammel, John Gumperz, and Alan Beals. Yehudi Cohen and David Olmsted read earlier drafts and provided useful comments, and some suggestions by Dell Hymes are incorporated in the present formulation, revised from the original paper (Tyler 1966).

alternation are seldom systematically accounted for; one reason for this failure is that an explanation of it requires information on the social and linguistic environments as well. Focusing on alternation indicates that there is no single, unitary structure of kin terms defined solely on the basis of genealogical components. This implies that typological analysis or formal analysis is based on genealogical criteria (Hammel 1965) alone is apt to obscure important data. It also indicates that the traditional "genealogical method" is an inadequate field method—if the ethnographic aim is to predict "who will be called what" (abstract provided with the original publication).

This is a point which has been made by several social anthropologist critics of the earlier componential analyses (Schneider 1968, 1969).

This chapter thus focuses on the speech event as source of data for analysis and on the rules of alternation. The subject matter is central to social life, and to social anthropology. Formal analysis of kinship terminology (often called *componential analysis*) is a subject of controversy to those who equate it with a highly abstract linguistic approach that neglects social realities. Tyler shows here that there need be no conflict. Indeed, he adapts a standard device of formal analysis in linguistics (use of rules involving a slant line to indicate the particular environment in which a form or structure occurs) in order to deal with social diversity in use of terms. Formal analysis is a way of being explicit and succinct. Tyler shows that because of their explicitness and succinctness, the operations involved in such analysis may lead to unanticipated discoveries. Whether the final analysis is adequate or not depends on the adequacy of the elicitation questions and on the use of data obtained by the investigator who employs it. An interest in *context-sensitive rules* (as the kind of statement employed by Tyler is known in linguistics) is indeed likely to be a major avenue for more adequate integration of linguistic and social analysis. Geoghegan (1970) provides a similarly ethnographically realistic formal analysis of address terminology.

Tyler cites variations in kinship terminology that can be ascribed to dialect differences but focuses on alternate terms which, although pertaining to two different languages, are part of the repertoire (Gumperz 1964a) of a single speaker. The error of limiting analysis to a material of a single language is clear from the outset. Nor is the relationship between the terms in the two languages a simple one of use, now of one language, now of the other. Rather, choice of terms from one language or the other (and, in certain interesting cases, choice of semantic structure) depends more specifically on social features; in this case, on the religious, as well as ethnic, identity of the speaker and hearer.

Within any one language's set of terms, there are alternative subsets of terms, depending upon such features of context as formality, coresidence in a patrilaterally extended household, and intimacy; and choices apply not only to the part of the term that designates a relative but also to pronouns and suffixes that occur with it. Among the contextual factors determining choice are joking relationships, composition of audience (e.g., presence or absence of the one referred to), major cultural scenes such as weddings and festivals, and a particular genre of wedding songs sung in competing rounds between the parties of bride and groom. Age of the speaker, use in the home, relative status, and friendship are also noted. The derivative suffixes are closely tied to formality and respect. Interesting here are the correlation of frequency of use with those audiences containing the relatives most likely to be critical of lack of respect, and the tying of formal behavior to only certain phases and participants in a wedding. As Tyler observes, a complete analysis would entail analysis of all those conditions that define scenes and relationships as formal, etc. (see Frake, Chapter 3). The present chapter serves to show that formal analysis of terms can be extended into a systematic relationship between the full range of cultural contexts. Additional related readings are provided by Romney and D'Andrade (1964), Tulisano and Cole (1965), Geoghegan (1971a), and Passin (1966).

Kinship terminologies, like most other linguistic phenomena, are usually analyzed as a single unitary structure. Alternate forms may not be altogether excluded, but they are seldom explained, either formally or functionally. The following is a typical example:

the language is particularly prolific in terms of endearment . . . for the formal "father," Sinhalese has *appa, appocci,* and *tatta* as alternatives for *piyā* . . . . When *complications* of this sort are ignored, the structural pattern of Sinhalese kinship terminology is identical to that of the Tamil . . . . Practical usage does not correspond strictly to this formal design . . . the terms *ayiyā* (elder brother) and *malli* (younger brother) may be used *indiscriminately,* even of individuals who should, according to formal principles, be classed as *massinā* (cross-cousin) (Leach 1960:125–126, English italics mine).

There is no mention of the environment in which these alternate forms occur, nor is there any indication that the kin types denoted by these alternate forms are structurally equivalent. Aside from notable exceptions (Schneider 1953, 1955; Frake 1960; Fischer 1964), anthropologists seem to have remained content with the simple environmental differentiation of terms of reference and terms of address. Other than this rather rudimentary classification, interest in alternate forms has been expressed in terms of historical reconstruction (Spoehr 1947) or culture change (Bruner 1955). This is not to denigrate these approaches; for as long as one is concerned only with typology, historical reconstruction, or culture change, the methods may be adequate. But in the realms of functional and formal analysis many significant data are neglected by these methods. For example, it is the boast of formal analysts that formal analysis will provide the minimum information for deciding "who will be called what" in any given kinship system (Lounsbury 1964:352). Yet I know of no formal analysis that has dealt adequately with the problems of alternate usage. To be sure, problems of synonymy and homonymy have been discussed (cf. Wallace and Atkins 1960:64–65, 67–68), but no system has been fully analyzed to account for these factors. To some extent this failure may be attributed to the fact that most formal analysis has been concerned with lexical items or, more appropriately perhaps, with the nominative stems of kin terms. It is my contention that, so construed, formal analysis does not provide the minimum information for deciding who will be called what in any kinship system (cf. also Swartz 1960:397; Hymes 1964a:26; 1964b:97–98).

Elsewhere I have argued that a part of the variation occurring in kinship terminologies can be explained by the contradictions entailed in the role systems of the class of kinsmen denoted by a given term (1967; cf. also Schneider 1955:17). In this chapter I want to explore further implications of role specificity for variations in terminology. Specifically, I will attempt to relate terminological variation to the contexts in which terms of reference are used. In essence, the problem of variation here is the same as that, for example, in phonology. What are the restrictions on the occurrence of a given form, and/or in what environments does a given form occur? My general aim is to provide a statement of the contexts in which variant forms occur, and thus to fulfill one part of the minimum requirement of the ethnography of kinship—the prediction of who will be called what.

The Ecology of the Speech Community

Following Gumperz (1962, 1964b), the delimitation of the "natural unit" to be used is based on patterns of communication. Within any given geographical area it is possible to arrive at any number of such units, depending on the level of abstraction desired; but for the purposes of this chapter the communication matrix is limited to direct face-to-face contacts among people who are socially defined as kinsmen. Justification for this procedure lies in the fact that such a limitation partially obviates the necessity for a rigorous definition of communication networks on the basis of frequency counts.

Starting from any ego in a Koya village it is possible to trace a widely ramifying group of people who are classed as kinsmen (*cuTTaaku*).[2] In this particular region the class of kinsmen may include people who are non-Koya. It may include members of various Telugu-speaking castes and Koya- and Telugu-speaking members of the Christian caste.

Members of all these groups are resident in villages along the banks of the Godavari River and in close proximity to the road from Bhadrachallam to Nugur. Within the villages, it is common for each group to be physically separated into distinct hamlets, which are named for the subgroup occupying them. All the constituent groups of the population are further segmented by occupational specializations and kin-group alignments. Occupational specialists include blacksmiths, stoneworkers, and religious performers and practitioners; kin-group alignments include clans, lineages, phratries, and castes.

Types of Alternation

At the level of abstraction that refers to the whole Koya tribe, it is possible to demonstrate that alternations in the use of terms of reference for kinsmen occur at the phonological, morphological, and lexical levels. For example, the term *aaNe* (sister's son) among the Gommu

---

[2] The transcription is broadly phonetic. Long vowels are marked by double vowels, retroflex consonants by upper case letters.

Koyas is realized in another dialect area as *aaNDe*. In still other area there is an isogloss D/R, especially in pronominal endings. Thus, *GuTTa* Koya has *eelaaRi* (younger sister) and Gommu Koya has *eelaaDi*. Other variants occur in morphology, particularly with reference to the distribution of plurals. More important, however, for present purposes, are the variations occurring within a communication network where dialect differences are minimal.

Within a group of socially defined kinsmen and, further, within the subset that interacts with some frequency, there exist lexical and morphological variations inexplicable by simple reference to dialect differences. Table 8.1 records a set of alternate lexemes used by a single informant for the group of people classed by him as kin.

Lexical Alternation—1

Taken in traditional terms, the items in list 1 are Telugu and the items in list 2 are Koya. Isolating the terms in this fashion, however, is misleading, for all forms occur in the linguistic repertory of a single speaker. Considered as such, certain complications arise. For almost the entire set of kinsmen there would appear to be alternate lexemes. The problem would be simple if a bilingual Koya used items from list 1 when speaking Telugu and items from list 2 when speaking Koya. We would then have a simple case of code switching in which a Koya speaker employs the Koya terms when speaking to a Telugu. Since most Telugus know little if any Koya, the relationship would be asymmetrical. In a given linguistic interchange involving the use of kin terms, the speaker's choice of the appropriate term would be determined by: (1) the kin relation obtaining between the speaker and hearer (or between the speaker or hearer and the person referred to), and (2) the linguistic repertoires of both speaker and hearer. Thus, given a Koya speaker and a Telugu hearer, the term chosen would be Telugu. Such switching would be facilitated if the semantic structures of the two codes were identical. The situation to be described, however, is somewhat more involved.

The semantic distance between the two kinship codes is relatively slight. A componential analysis reveals the structure of the two codes, outlined in Table 8.2. The components are: (1) sex; (2) generation; (3) cross versus parallel; (4) relative age. For convenience, the component of relative sex of speaker is omitted and the relative age of linking relative is subsumed under relative age. The relative effectiveness of each component is indicated in the preceding table. It will be noted that the parallel-cross distinction does not obtain in the Telugu system at the $+2$ and -2 generations. In

table 8.1

Generation	Telugu	Koya
Grandparental (+2)		
FaFa	*taata*	*daadaal*
MoFa	*taata*	*taataal*
FaMo	*avva*	*emma*
	avva	*kaako*
Parental (+1)		
Fa, FaBr, MoSiHu	*ayya,*	*eyya,*
	taNDri,	*tappe*
	nayana,	
	naana	
MoBr, FaSiHu, WiFa, HuFa	*maama*	*maamaal*
Mo, MoSi, FaBrWi	*aama,*	*evva,*
	talli	*talluru*
FaSi, MoBrWi, WiMo, HuMo	*atta*	*pooye*
Own (0)		
EBr, Emale parallel cousin	*anna*	*enna*
Emale cross cousin, ESiHu	*baava*	*baaTaal*
ESi, Efemale parallel cousin	*akka*	*ekka*
Efemale cross cousin, EBrWi	*vodina*	*enge*
YBr, Ymale parallel cousin	*tammuDu*	*tammuNDu*
Ymale cross cousin YSiHu	*baamaaradi*	*eruNDu*
YSi, Yfemale parallel cousin	*cellelu,*	*eelaaDi*
	celli	
Yfemale cross cousin, YBrWi	*maradalu*	*eendaaDi*
Children's (−1)		
So, (x)BrSo, (o)SiSo	*koDuku,*	*marri*
	kummaruDu,	*peeka*
	abbayi	
(x)SiSo, DaHu, (o)BrSo	*alluDu*	*aaNe*
Da, (x)BrDa, (o)SiDa	*ammayi,*	*mayyaaDi*
	kuturu,	*piikiDi*
	biDDA	
(x)SiDa, SoWi, (o)BrDa	*kooDalu*	*koDiyaaDi*
Grandchildren (−2)		
SoSo	*manamaDu*	*tammuNDu*
DaSo	*manamaDu*	*eruNDu*
xDaDa	*manamaraal*	*eelaaDi*
SoDa	*manamaraal*	*eendaaDi*

Note: These are minimal ranges of application of the terms to kin. For a fuller treatment, as well as formal analysis and discussion of morphology, see Tyler 1964, 1965, 1967. (x) indicates male speaker; (o) indicates female speaker. E and Y denote elder and younger respectively. The remaining abbreviations are standard: Br Brother, Da Daughter, Fa Father, Hu Husband, Mo Mother, Si Sister, So Son, Wi Wife. A parallel cousin is a child of one's mother's sister (MoSi) or father's brother (FaBr); a cross cousin is a child of one's mother's brother (MoBr) or father's sister (FaSi); i.e., in the chain of consanguineal kin through whom one is related, the sex of the links remains the same ("parallel") or changes ("cross").

table 8.2

Telugu

	Male		Female	
	Parallel	Cross	Parallel	Cross
+2		taata		avva
+1	ayya	amma	maama	atta
0	anna	akka	baava	vodina
	tammuDu	cellelu	baamaaradi	maradalu
−1	koDuku	kuturu	alluDu	kooDalu
−2		manamaDu		manamaraal

Koya

	Parallel	Cross	Parallel	Cross
+2	daadaal	taataal	emma	kaako
+1	eyya	maamaal	evva	pooye
0	enna	baaTaal	ekka	enge
	taamuNDu	eruNDu	eelaaDi	eendaaDi
−1	marri	aaNe	mayyaaDi	koDiyaaDi
−2	tammuNDu	eruNDu	eelaaDi	eendaaDi

Note: Certain aspects of morphology have been omitted. For details, see Tyler 1967. In Koya *tammuNDu* in 0 and −2 generations is analyzed as a pair of homonyms, and similarly for the other pairs (*eruNdu, eelaaDi, eendaaDi*) in the younger sibling/cousin and grandchild generations (cf. Tyler 1964). As indicated with Table 8.1, "parallel" indicates that the consanguineal links in the relationship are all of the same sex, and "cross" that this is not so; thus *ayya* (Fa, FaBr, MoSiHu) is +1, Male, Parallel; *amma* (Mo, MoSi, FaBrWi) is +1, Female, Parallel; *maama* (MoBr, FaSiHu, WiHu, HuFa) is +1, Male, Cross; etc.

all other respects, the two systems are coordinate. Hence, in terms of semantic structure, the transform (for a Koya speaker) from one system to the other is fairly simple. It entails only the following rules.[3]

1. [Koya] $\begin{cases} \text{FaFa} \\ \text{MoFa} \end{cases}$ ⟶ [Telugu] Parent's Fa

2. [Koya] $\begin{cases} \text{FaMo} \\ \text{MoMo} \end{cases}$ ⟶ [Telugu] Parent's Mo

3. [Koya] $\begin{cases} \text{SoSo} \\ \text{DaSo} \end{cases}$ ⟶ [Telugu] Child's So

4. [Koya] $\begin{cases} \text{SoDa} \\ \text{DaDa} \end{cases}$ ⟶ [Telugu] Child's Da

[3] The notation system used is that developed by Romney (1964). *m* indicates male, *f* female, *a* any sex, ± an ascendant link, −*a* descendant link, *o* a sibling link. Since grandson is the reciprocal of grandfather, the reciprocal operation (*) says to read * as ±. The first member of an expression is ego; e.g., English *father* would be a + m.

These relationships can be restated in a notation system developed by Romney (1964), in which the first member of any expression is ego; *a* indicates person of any sex; *m* indicates male, *f* female; + indicates an ascending link, − a descending link, and 0 a sibling link. English *father* would thus be a + m, *daughter* a − f.

1. $\begin{cases} a + m + m \\ a + f + m \end{cases}$ $\longrightarrow$ a + a + m

2. $\begin{cases} a + m + f \\ a + f + f \end{cases}$ $\longrightarrow$ a + a + f

3. $\begin{cases} a - m - m \\ a - f - m \end{cases}$ $\longrightarrow$ a − a − m

4. $\begin{cases} a - m - f \\ a - f - f \end{cases}$ $\longrightarrow$ a − a − f

The individual rules show little or no advantage to the formal notation system. An advantage does appear, however, when we try to state the generalization that underlies the individual rules. Notice that the rules apply just in the case of relatives two generations removed from the speaker (ego). Rules 1 and 3, and likewise rules 2 and 4, thus could and should be united. In words,

5. [Koya] male lineal relative, two generations removed, through a male link, and male lineal relative, two generations removed, through a female link [Telugu] male lineal relative, two generations removed.
6. [Koya] female lineal relative, two generations removed, through a male link, and female lineal relative, two generations removed, through a female link [Telugu] female lineal relative, two generations removed.

Since grandson and grandfather are reciprocals of each other, that is, the same except for the direction in which generation is counted, it is possible to define a symbol, *, for a reciprocal operation (that is, read * as ±), and to state the generalizations of 5 and 6 much more economically and clearly:

5. $\begin{cases} a * m * m \\ a * f * m \end{cases}$ $\longrightarrow$ a * a * m

6. $\begin{cases} a * m * f \\ a * f * f \end{cases}$ $\longrightarrow$ a * a * f

The simplification takes advantage, not only of reciprocal * but also of the symbol *a*, representing either sex. Indeed, taking further advantage of *a*, all the rules can be expressed in a single succinct statement:

$$7. \begin{cases} a * m * a \\ a * f * a \end{cases} \longrightarrow a * a * a$$

In words, wherever two terms for a lineal relative two generations removed are differentiated in Koya by the sex of the lineal link, they are not so differentiated in Telugu.

To complete the statement of the rules, it is necessary to provide data on the environment in which this transform is permissible. Since we have said that such a transform occurs when a Koya speaker refers to a kinsman in a linguistic interchange with a Telugu-speaking kinsman, this can be formulated as follows:[4]

$$8. \begin{cases} a * m * a \\ a * f * a \end{cases} \longrightarrow [a * a * a/K - T]$$

This is to be read: the kin types comprise under a * m * a and a * f * a are realized as a * a * a in the environment of a Koya speaker and Telugu hearer.

For all significant environments, the distributional statement is:

$$9. \begin{bmatrix} a * m * a \\ a * f * a \end{bmatrix} \longrightarrow \begin{cases} \begin{matrix} a * a * a \\ a * a * a \\ \begin{bmatrix} a * m * a \\ a * f * a \end{bmatrix} \\ a * m * a \\ a * f * a \end{matrix} \end{cases} \begin{matrix} -T \\ \\ -t \\ \\ \text{elsewhere} \end{matrix}$$

That is, to take the particular case of reference to a grandfather (a + a + m), the kin types father's father and mother's father are realized as parent's father in the environment of a Koya speaker and Telugu hearer; they are realized as either parent's father or as father's father and mother's father (separately) in the environment of a Koya speaker and a Telugu Christian hearer; in all other environments they are realized as father's father and mother's father (separately). (The parallel statement, *mutatis mutandis,* would hold for grandmother (a + a + f), grandson (a − a − m), and granddaughter (a − a − f).

---

[4] The notation / denotes "in the environment of." Thus,

$$a + f + m\text{—}a + a + m/k\text{-}t$$
$$a + m + m$$

indicates that a + m + m and a + f + m are both realized as a + a + m in the environment of a Koya speaker and a Telugu hearer.

The added variation with regard to −t requires a further restriction of the social environment. To my knowledge, this alternation occurs only where a Koya Christian male is married to a Telugu Christian female. In these cases, the linguistic repertories of husband and wife in kinship terminology tend toward isomorphy, and code switching probably occurs only when the presence of his wife's relatives, for example, the husband would use the appropriate Telugu term in speaking to her.

In general, at the level of semantic structure these two transform rules plus the accompanying distributional statement enable one to predict the appropriate denotata of a term. Once these operations have been performed, the lexical realization of the remaining categories involves only a simple process of substitution, or word-for-word translation, for example, *aaNe-aalDu*/k − T. Realization of the appropriate lexeme can be predicted on the basis of the foregoing rules, with the exception of a Koya Christian speaking to another Christian (k − k, k − t). For k − k, the following additional statements are necessary:

$$\left. \begin{array}{l} \text{a} - \text{f} - \text{m}-manamaDu \\ \text{a} - \text{f} - \text{f}-manamaraal \end{array} \right\rvert \text{k} - \text{k}$$

That is, when referring to a daughter's child (son or daughter), Koya Christians use the term from the Telugu list in Table 8.1.

Lexemic realization for these categories when a Koya Christian's addressee is a Telugu Christian (k − t) is dependent on the transform occurring in rule 9, above:

The rules are to be read: (1) when father's father and mother's father are merged as parents' father, and son's son are merged as child's son, one's daughter's son is called *manamaDu* in the environment of a Koya Christian speaker and a Telugu Christian hearer; under the same circumstances one's daughter's daughter is called *manamaraal;* when the merger does not occur, then (in the same environment) one's daughter's son is called *eruNDu,* one's daughter's daughter *koDiyaaDi.* That is, in the one case a Telugu, in the other a Koya term is used.

Since Koya and Telugu are both Dravidian languages, many of the kin terms are cognate. Some are related by quite simple sound changes, for example, Telugu *a-,* Koya *e-* (*avva, evva*); Telugu *-D,* Koya *-ND-* (*tammuDu, tammuNDu*). Note, however, that the semantic range of these cognate forms varies. *amma* in Telugu denotes Mo, while Koya *emma* denotes FaMo; Telugu *taata* denotes FaFa amd MoFa, while Koya *taataal* denotes only MoFa. Given the phonological similarity of these terms, one might expect a certain amount of interference. This does not seem to be the case here—although it could be argued that in other areas, where differences occur in the extent to which Koyas dominate the ecology of the speech community, interference stemming from these sources could be a cause of changes in the terminological system. This, however, is outside the domain of this chapter.

Lexical Alternation—II

The second type of lexical alternation relates more to situational alternates within a kinship code than it does to varieties of codes. In the preceding schedule of terms, it will be noted that within each of the codes certain categories have alternate lexemes. These occur with terms for father, mother, younger sister, son, and daughter in the Telugu code, and for father, mother, son, and daughter in the Koya code. There are two problems involved here: (1) Are the denotata of all variant forms equivalent; (2) if so, are there environments that limit the distribution of some variants?

In the case of *taNDRi/nayana/ayya/naana*, the first two denote father and father's brothers, with appropriate morphemes denoting relative age, that is, $a + m(om)^{0,1}$.[5] *naana*, however, denotes only an actual father $(a + m)$, and *ayya* denotes father's brothers $(a + mom)$, but not father. In summary:

taNDRi/nayana denotes $a + m(om)^{0,1}$	[Fa(FaBr)]
naana	denotes $a + m$	[Fa]
ayya	denotes $a + mom$	[FaBr]

Since *ayya* and *naana* are not structually equivalent to the other terms, they need no longer concern us here. *taNDRi* is generally regarded as the more formal and respectful term; *nayana* is less respectful and more informal. The major variable for these two then is the extent to which one wishes to confer respect on the referent. In summary statement:

$$a + m(om)^{0,1}//F/taNDRi$$
$$//If/nayana$$

F indicates formal and If informal. The set of situations in which informality is permissible for this range is unrecorded.

For *eyya/tappe:*	*eyya* denotes $a + m(om)$	Fa (FaBr)
	tappe denotes $a + m$	Fa
For *evva/talluru:*	*evva* denotes $a + f(of)$	Mo (MoSi)
	talluru denotes $a + f$	Mo

---

[5] Parentheses indicate an optional expansion; superscript numbers indicate the number of times the expansion may be employed. Thus $a + m(om)^{0,1}$ will generate $a + m$ and $a + mom$.

For *anna/talli* I have been unable to isolate significant differences in either denotata or environment, other than a general impression that *talli* more frequently denotes a + f and may be more formal than *amma*. For lack of better data, these two will be considered synonymous in the domain of kinship reference.

It should be noted that all these structural differences have the effect of transforming the system at the +1 consanguineal level from bifurcate merging to bifurcate collateral.

cellelu/celli differentiate at both structural and environmental levels. *cellelu* denotes younger sister and younger female parallel relatives $(f^y)^5$ that is $a(+a_i)^{0,1} o(aj-)^{0,1}f^y$, $(i = j)$, while *celli* denotes only YOUNGER SISTER (aof^y) unless one's female parallel relatives reside in the same patrilaterally extended household. In this case the structural differentiation is negated. *celli* in reference to a younger sister is further differentiated from *cellelu* as "sweet" (*tiyyani*) usage. I have little data on the specific environments in which "sweet" usage is permissible, but believe its use is restricted to the home among consanguineal kin. In terms of the speaker's intention, *celli* denotes an intimate relation between speaker and younger sister. These distributions are formulated as:

$$a(+a_i)^{0,1} o(aj-)^{0,1}f^y \quad celli/\text{In}$$
$$celli/\text{PEH}$$
$$celli/\text{H}$$
$$cellelu/\text{elsewhere}$$

PEH indicates patrilateral extended household, *In* intimacy, *H* in the home. The ordering of rules is as given. Both parenthetical expressions must be expanded or not expanded together.

Note that the highest frequency of alternation occurs among categories of kin who are apt to be members of the same household. This is in line with the general expectation that maximum differentiation occurs in areas of high interest and interaction. Further, for the population being discussed, it is precisely between the reciprocals Fa/Ch and Mo/Ch that the greatest role inconsistencies occur. (For further discussion of this point, see Tyler 1964.)

Morphological Variation

Both in Koya and Telugu, the referential use of kin terms involves not only the selection of the appropriate noun stem but also the selection of appropriate possessive pronouns and derivative suffixes. (Thus, in Koya and Telugu a kin term may consist of possessive pronoun + noun stem ± derivative suffixes.) It can be argued that this is in the domain of syntactic function, but it is easier in the present context to treat the whole problem under morphology. Whether syntactic or morphological, the main point is that the mere knowledge of the appropriate noun stem and its denotata is not sufficient to generate acceptable statements of kinship reference.

The distribution and use of possessive pronouns and derivative suffixes in first person reference have previously been discussed for Koya (Tyler 1967). The first and second person possessive pronouns in Koya and Telugu do not differ. They are: *maa-* "our, my" formal; *naa-* "my" informal. Second person possessive pronouns are *nii-* "your" informal, *mii-* "your" formal. The derivative suffixes occurring with kin terms for Telugu are: *-ayya,* "sir"; *-gaaru,* "sir, madam"; for Koya: *-aal,* "mature male."[6] Table 8.3 indicates the distribution of first person possessives and derivative suffixes for Telugu.

Possessive Pronouns

For Koya, the distribution of possessives is similar to that in Table 8.3 with the exception that *maa-* and *naa-* alternate for elder female relatives.

The alternation of *naa-/maa-* for *baava* and *vodina* is paralleled in Koya, and the reasons for the alternation seem to be identical. On the one hand, these are elder relatives whom one should respect, but on the other hand, they are people with whom a joking relation is permissible. Since a female is given somewhat more latitude in a joking relation, sex of speaker is a determinant. The next determinant is audience composition. This involves two factors: (1) The presence or absence of the referent, and (2) the presence or absence of the speaker's elder consanguineal relatives and/or the presence or absence of non-kin. If the referent is absent, *maa-* is used; if present, *naa-*. The latter is abandoned when the speaker's elder consanguineal relatives or elder non-kin are present. The major situational determinants are weddings and a festival, the *Bhima paNDum.* One phase in a wedding ceremony involves a form of group singing in which the bride's party and the groom's party sing competing rounds. As the songs frequently refer to the sexual attributes of a *baava* or *vodina,* these terms occur in the songs with the informal possessive *naa-.* Since Christians no longer use the Koya ceremony, the significant environments for this variation are K – T and, with the appropriate semantic transform, K – K. During the Bhima festival a mock marriage

---

[6] There are others, for example, *-Du, -Di, -a(a)/(u),* and so forth; but for the most part these are not optional in the same sense as *-aal, -gaaru, -ayya.* The English glosses are only handy approximations.

table 8.3

(Telugu) Stem	First Person Possessive		Derivative Suffix	
	maa—	naa—	—ayya	—gaaru
taata*	+	+	+	+
avva	+	+		+
naana	+		+	+
nayana	+			+
taNDRi	+			+
ayya	+			+
amma	+			+
talli	+			+
maama	+		+	+
atta	+			+
anna	+		+	+
tammuDu		+		
baava	+	+	+	+
vodina	+	+		+
akka	+		+	+
cellelu		+		
baamaaradi		+		
maradalu		+		
koDuku		+		
abbayi	+	+		
kummaruDu		+		
ammayi	+	+		
kuturu		+		
biDDa		+		
alluDu		+		
kooDalu		+		
manamaDu		+		
manamaraal		+		

* Where *maa*—and *naa*—alternate, derivative suffixes do not occur when *naa*—is used. This differs substantially from the system in T-T and t-t, and wherever T—to t—is speaker. In these cases *maa*—does not alternate with *naa*—.

is performed. At this time the distribution of *maa-/naa-* is the same as for a real wedding.

These distributions may be formulated as:

$$a + a_i o a_j - a^e, (i \neq j), PP^1 \quad \begin{aligned} &naa\text{-}/f \\ &naa\text{-}/R \\ &naa\text{-}/WS \\ &maa\text{-}/elsewhere \end{aligned}$$

f denotes female speaker, R referent present, WS wedding songs, and PP[1] first person possessive pronoun.

Alternation of *maa-/naa-* with terms in the +2 generation is largely a function of the age of the speaker. Between grandparents and grandchildren there is usually a close, intimate relationship. The care of children is frequently entrusted to elder grandparents who are no longer able to work actively in the fields. Consequently, young children use *naa-* when referring to these relatives. The social setting and audience composition may also be important here. It is my general impression that mature speakers use *naa-* in reference to these kinsmen in the home among other household members. My principal informant asserted that this was the case, but since my access to Koya homes was limited, I have little to substantiate this. These rules may be summarized as:

PP[1]   *naa-*/I

      naa-/H

      naa-/elsewhere

I denotes an immature speaker, H inside the home.

The alternation of *maa-/naa-* for *ammayi* and *abbayi* is unexplained.

The use of possessive pronouns in second person kinship reference, unlike that in first person reference, confers status or respect on the hearer, not on the referent of the term. The pronouns in question are: *mii-* "your" formal; *nii-* "your" informal. The pronouns are the same for both Telugu and Koya. The following example should indicate the process involved here.

K-T: *mii tammuDu ee pani ceestunnaaDu,* "what work is your younger brother doing (now)?" Since a younger brother is low status, one might expect agreement between the possessive pronoun and the noun stem, that is, *nii tammuDu* rather than *mii tammuDu*. Because *nii tammuDu* occurs in other situations, *nii-* and *mii-* are not inalienable in the sense that *naa-* and *maa-* are. The important variable here concerns the relative statuses of speaker and hearer. Briefly, the sources of status are education, wealth, occupation, categorical membership in kin groups, and personal characteristics. Since all sources of status are not isomorphically distributed in specific population segments or kin categories, the use of possessive pronouns in second person reference cannot be predicted simply on the basis of categorical membership in K, k, T, t groups or from knowledge of the kin relation obtaining between speaker and hearer. The precise details of this system cannot be delineated in this brief discussion. Suffice it to say that when the speaker's status is lower than the hearer's, *mii-* occurs; when higher, *nii-* occurs. If the status of speaker and hearer are approximately equivalent, *mii-* and *nii-* are in free variation. Between old or ritual friends, *nii-* is used irrespective of status differences. This may be formulated as:

PP²/*mii-*/   L-H
/*nii-*/   H-L
/*nii-*/   F-F
/*nii-, mii-*/ E-E

L indicates low status, H high status, E equivalent status, F friends, and PP² second person possessive pronouns.

Derivative Suffixes

Derivative suffixes in Koya and Telugu differ in the lack of a Koya equivalent for *-gaaru*. Where *-gaaru* occurs for females in Telugu, Koya has ϕ. With the exception of its occurrence with Esi, Telugu *-ayya* is identical in distribution to Koya *-aal*.

Unfortunately, data are not at all certain here, but the most important variable seems to be the definition of the situation. In part, this is determined on the basis of audience composition. First, if the referent of a given term is present, derivative suffixes are used; when the referent is absent, they are used less frequently. Second, if the audience consists of people whom the speaker wants to impress by his knowledge of respectful behavior, the derivative suffixes will be used. The strength of this situation is such that one of the most disparaging comments one can make about another is that he is not respectful. Since one of the most critical audiences consists of one's elder affines, the presence or absence of elder affines is usually sufficient to predict the appropriate use of derivative suffixes. Further, among affines, those who are related to ego by only a single affinal link (in contradistinction to those with whom a series of such affinal links may be traced) are apt to be more critical. These distributions may be formulated as follows:

DS   DS/R
      DS/A¹
      ϕ, DS/A²
      ϕ/elsewhere

DS denotes derivative suffixes, R referent present, A¹ single link affines, A² multiple link affines, and ϕ no DS.

In more general terms, certain social gatherings are considered to be more formal than others. Marriages, for example, are formal occasions. Formal behavior, however, is required only in specific phases of the wedding ceremony, or only from the central actors. The rules of formal behavior are not enjoined for peripheral actors—in fact, the reverse is usually the case. Analysis of these situations is too complex for brief summary, but enough has been said to indicate that a general rule may be formulated:

$$DS \quad /DS/F$$
$$\phi/\text{elsewhere}$$

F denotes a formal situation.

Conclusion

This paper does not conclude that the rules presented are sufficient to predict who will be called what in entirety. There are too many gaps, both in data and in analysis. Yet, sketchy and incomplete as this analysis is, it should at least indicate that the appropriate use of Koya kin terms cannot be predicted solely on the basis of a formal analysis predicted on the assumption of genealogical reckoning. There are many contextual factors to be taken into consideration. Among these are: social setting, audience composition, sex and age of speaker/hearer, linguistic repertoires of speaker/hearer, and—most difficult of all—something that might be called the speaker's intention. Many of these and others have been previously discussed (Ervin-Tripp 1964:86–94; Gumperz 1964b: 143–147; Hymes 1964e:15–25) and need not receive further comment here. The important point is that this chapter demonstrates the possibility of extending formal rules to these contextual factors. It is not an argument against the validity of formal analysis; rather, it is an argument for the extension of formal analysis to include extra-genealogical factors.

Even though the Koya case may seem rather extreme, it should demonstrate that less complex types of variation can probably be easily handled by analysis of the sort used in this chapter. In addition, it should emphasize that problems of variation (or of general ethnography) call for somewhat different field techniques than those that have traditionally been used. There must, for example, be a greater emphasis on the recording of kin terms as they are used in concrete and/or simulated ethnographic situations (cf. Conklin 1964; Hymes 1964e:11). The anthropologist armed only with a genealogy and an informant or informants and using traditional methods of questioning cannot hope to cope with the problem of variation. This is not intended as a blanket condemnation of such methods. They are useful in collecting some kinds of data and can provide a base of information on which it is possible to build, but it should be abundantly clear from other publications (e.g., Frake 1962; Metzger and

Williams 1963) that if our aim is ethnographic description, then field methods must be adequate to the task.

Finally, these data show that much of what has usually been simply regarded as unimportant variations on the basic structural pattern of a terminological system consists of highly important differentiations, not only in denotata but in role expectations as well. The structural pattern of a system emerges as an ordered relation between these differentiations and contextual features.

9

Social Context and Semantic Feature: The Russian Pronominal Usage

PAUL FRIEDRICH

Paul Friedrich is professor of anthropology at the University of Chicago. He received an M.A. degree in Russian at Harvard before taking his doctorate at Yale, and has since taught structural linguistics and cultural anthropology at Harvard, the University of Michigan, and the University of Pennsylvania. In addition to two years of fieldwork among the Tarascan Indians of Mexico, he has done research on Russian semantics, on the Malayalam language (along the Malabar coast in India), and in the reconstruction of Proto-Indo-European semantic systems.

Friedrich himself sums up neatly the interest of pronominal usage: "Just two short words, operating in all speech events that involve two interlocutors, signaled the relative position of each pole in hundreds of dyadic relationships." There is good precedent for use of a historical-philological approach in anthropology, but its application to a major literary tradition may seem unusual. Literature, however, is well established as a source for analysis of address (see Metcalf 1938; Brown and Ford 1961), and Friedrich makes clear the value of nineteenth-century novels in particular. Not only are they rich in indications of common usage but they also bear witness to dynamics of use and implicit meanings. Friedrich points to a conscious awareness in Russian society of extralinguistic signaling as sharing the same dimensions as pronouns, for example, the seduced girl whose eyes say *ty* while her words are *vy* (in Tolstoy's *Resurrection*). Here, as so often where the two conflict, the nonlinguistic modality overrides the linguistic (see the concluding remarks on "latent *ty*"). And, Friedrich suggests, use of such data, by grappling with inner as well as overt speech, may enable one better to understand personal strategies and to anticipate linguistic change (cf. Howell 1968).

The pronouns are linked with other sets of terms which would have to be taken into account in a complete study of address. Pronominal selection is therefore merely a special case of the type of sociolinguistic selection discussed by Ervin-Tripp (Chapter 7), Blom and Gumperz (Chapter 14), and Passin (1966). As Friedrich points out, however, focus on pronouns is nevertheless specially advantageous. They are as frequent, easily noted, obligatory categories linking grammar with social categories. Here in address, he suggests, may be a surer connection of grammar with culture than in attempts to link grammar with world view.

Ten components serve to indicate the features necessary to account for the Russian usage: social context (setting, scenes); characteristics of participants, i.e., age, generation, sex, genealogical distance, relative authority, group membership; the tone (or key) underlying a relationship or brought to expression in it (principally solidarity but also, later, sarcasm and irony); topic of discourse; and language variety itself, i.e., dialect. The same discriminations underlie the symbolism of kinship terminology and, one may suspect, the other forms of sociolinguistic choice and switching within the society. Friedrich suggests that some six to a dozen such components may be found to underlie all such systems; he implies that further research might establish such a limited set of dimensions or universals for sociolinguistic symbolism (social meanings) generally (see Buchler and Freeze 1966). The present dimensions meet the test of accounting for nearly all the Russian evidence and of predicting the usage in new texts.

Notice that the discriminations are made with regard to the social situation and relationship with which the pronouns are used. The two pronouns themselves are diacritic directly of social distance (its presence or absence, or greater or lesser degree). Whether the absence of social distance signaled by *ty* is affectionate or contemptuous, whether the presence of social distance signaled by *vy* is respectful or rejecting, emerges from the interaction between the meaning of the pronoun and the meanings of pronouns in the twin contexts of previous discourse and present event (including, as noted, facial and paralinguistic accompaniment).

The Russian usage is presented first from the standpoint of patterns of exchange within dyadic relationships rather than, as with the Koya in the preceding chapter, from the standpoint of rules for a given speaker. (But notice that to specify interlocutors, or their relevant characteristics, in the context to which rules are sensitive, can accomplish the same thing). After symmetrical and asymmetrical patterns for both *vy* and *ty* are described, Friedrich turns to the dynamics of what he felicitously calls a stable though not static system. Having observed earlier that context may determine usage, but that usage may also define context, he presents several instances of pronominal "switching" and "breakthrough," including temporary and persistent deviance, and covert attitudes. Paralinguistic signaling aside, the pronominal system itself provides for an expressive counterpoint within relationships.

This and the preceding chapter complement each other, each broaching an essential aspect of research into rules of use. Both are concerned with the social context of linguistic forms, the one to bring it within the scope of formal rules, the other to interpret the texture of use as well. Additional related readings are provided by Conklin (1962), Friedrich (1964, 1966), Goodenough (1965b), Hymes (1964c), Hymes (typescript), Jain (1969), Martin (1964), and Nuestupný (1968).

Introduction

Studies in the relation between language and culture have sometimes focused on how a way of life is categorized through words. The results are often of enormous value, as in the case of a dictionary of contextual definitions. But lexicographical inventories typically lack theoretical explication.

A second kind of study may focus on the connections between obligatory grammatical categories in the linguistic system and axiomatic distinctions in the abstract thought of a people. Controlled demonstrations are sometimes possible, and the conclusions may be intellectually challenging, but one often finds on closer inspection that the causal relationships are little more than suggested or asseverated (Jakobson 1959:142–43).

In short, language and culture studies tend to oscillate between comparatively descriptive correlations of "words and things" and comparatively tenuous correlations between grammar and metaphysics. Just as fruitful as the lexicographic and philosophical extremes have been the attempts to relate *either* speech behavior *or* the inferred linguistic structure to *either* the societal regularities *or* the patterns of a culture.[1] In what follows I shall attempt to demonstrate how speech usage is determined by cultural principles. More concretely, I shall try to show how second person pronouns were selected and understood in nineteenth century Russia. To do this I will first evaluate the evidence for pronominal usage. Then I will show how pronominal usage covaried with genealogical distance, emotional solidarity, and eight other variables. The patterns governing the three types of symmetrical and asymmetrical usage of the pronoun will be considered in detail, leading directly to five cases of pronominal switching and what I call "breakthrough," notably in *Crime and Punishment*. A final section deals with the expressive and latent functions of the pronoun *ty*. The conclusions concern the relative advantages and disadvantages of this kind of semantic analysis.

Background

The evidence on the society and culture of the Russia of the last century happens to be excellent, largely due to three brilliant *magna opera* of one to two volumes each, composed by three very different men: a German baron and economist (von Haxthausen), a French sociologist and man of letters (Leroy-Beaulieu), and a peripatetic Scotch journalist (Wallace). Their picture is rounded out by other sociological, ethnographic, and belletristic articles and books written over the past hundred years.

The information on pronouns is similarly full. But first a historical note. Until about 1700 only *ty* had been employed, whereas ". . . the French manner of address to one person in the plural number appeared in eighteenth century and rapidly became current among educated circles" (Isachenko 1960:414).[2] By the Napoleonic era French was already a passport to high society. The use of Russian *vy* as a formal and respectful singular had become firmly established and launched on its independent

---

[1] "Society" in this slightly technical sense refers to the regularities that may be observed, measured, or otherwise determined as relating the individuals and groups of some bounded population. "Culture," on the other hand, refers to the structured set of historically derived explicit and implicit norms, values, attitudes, feelings, and ideas that are shared and transmitted by the members of a society.

[2] References for Russian literature cited are appended at the end of this chapter.

course, although subsequently reinforced and subtly influenced by the pervasive French bilingualism of the upper classes and their constant exposure to the *tu/vous* system of French novels and plays.

The Russian realistic novel gives full and balanced evidence on pronominal usage. For example, Tolstoy depicts the high aristocracy, Dostojevsky, the patterns of the intermediate urban classes. Gorki unfolds a panorama of proletarian and artisan customs, Leskov covers the clergy, and Zlatovratsky and Sholokhov provide truly ethnographic detail on the peasants and Cossaks, respectively. All authors—particularly Tolstoy and Dostojevsky—include contacts between persons of diverse background; their status conflicts and rapidly fluctuating emotions are often symbolized through pronominal usage, which, needless to say, is one of the serious losses in any English translation. The Russian novel was realistic, not only in its concern with status differences, with burning moral issues, and with human nature but because it referred to the culture of the readers themselves, or to that of groups such as the peasantry which they had come to know through personal experience; ethnographic accuracy was an aesthetic imperative.[3] In the Russian novel and any similar text the pronouns are both frequent and very free in their distribution; in my sample of over eight thousand pages the pronoun must at least be implied every time a verb refers to an addressee. Pronouns belong to what linguists of the Prague School call "background phenomena," and cannot be artificially employed any more than any other grammatical paradigm; no matter how original his wording or syntax, a creative writer must use the obligatory, covert categories of language and culture in conformity with the generally held norms. The figures in Gogol and Chekhov, for all their uniqueness, do not jar the reader in their use of pronouns *qua* pronouns. In fact, the originality of a protagonist cannot be evaluated without reference to the larger context of cultural norms and values.

The second person pronouns functioned, not in isolation, but interrelated with other sets, notably kinship terms, proper names, official ranks, words reflecting occupation, relative age, and similar categories. Numerous kinship terms of address and many other quasi-kinship terms such as *kum* (ritual co-parent) were frequent in conversation, particularly among the peasants. All classes of Russians interjected "brother," "little mother," and other terms when consciously or subconsciously trying to create an informal, congenial atmosphere with non-relatives. And there were numerous combinations of proper names, ranging from nicknames, to diminutives, to the first name alone, to the first name plus a fixed

---

[3] As Gerald Kelly has pointed out in a personal communication, this contrasts with the United States, where much of the literature functions to inform the reader, to create expectations of usage and behavior in subcultures not known through personal experience. The critical notion of "realism" is hardly adequate as a cover term for the Russian novel. In the present context, suffice it to say that the literature did provide a wealth of insight into society and character.

epithet ("Mikhail the Wolf"), to the name plus an informal or formal patronymic (Ivanych as against Ivanovich), and so on up the line. These means of address had to be calibrated with each other. For example, "Aren't *ty* joking, Foma?" "In the first place, I am not *ty* . . . but *vy*, and don't forget it; and not Foma, but Foma Fomich" (Dostojevsky, *Stepanchikovo Village,* 472). Finally, all the terms of address covaried with the partly independent and equally copious terms of reference. The total number of combinations was astronomical. Gogol was literally correct when he wrote facetiously in *Dead Souls* (35–36):

It should be said that if we in Russia have not yet caught up with the foreigners in some things, we have long overtaken them in the means of address. It is impossible to count all the shades and niceties of our means of address. The Frenchman or the German will never grasp or understand all the particularities and differences; with almost the same voice and language he will start to speak with a millionaire, and with a petty tobacco vendor although, of course, in his soul he is appropriately base to the first. It is not like that with us. Among us there are wise fellows who will speak altogether differently with a landlord having two hundred serfs than with one who has three hundred, and with one who has three hundred they will not speak as they would with one having five hundred, and with one having five hundred, again, not as with one having eight hundred; in a word, although you go to a million, they will always find shades (or difference).

Second person pronouns have been analyzed from various points of view. Social psychologists have shown how pronominal usage is connected with attitudes and behavior (Brown and Gilman 1960). Philologists have produced accurate and carefully documented histories of the usage in German, French, and other languages (e.g., Fay 1918–20). Linguists such as Jesperson have inferred the distinctive attributes shared by pronouns, such as their degree of abstraction and freedom of distribution. In fact, the second person pronouns are of singular theoretical interest because they link the abstract properties of a basic grammatical paradigm to a second matrix of culturally specific components that are both very frequent and of major emotional and social significance. In other words, pronominal usage affords us an analytically accessible link between the obligatory categories of grammar and a second domain of obligatory semantic categories related to the social culture: second person pronouns occupy a boundary zone between "deep grammar" and the deep levels of attitude and norm by which a society is organized. For this reason their study may emerge as a comparatively fruitful ground, a felicitous case, for explorations of the hypotheses advanced by von Humbolt, Boas, Whorf, Sapir, and others.[4]

---

[4] Norman McQuown has been emphasizing the sociolinguistic significance of substitutes for several years. I have profited from several discussions with him on this subject. Otherwise, I retain hope but extreme skepticism about demonstrating any pervasive causal relation between social structure and grammatical patterns (e.g., Russian aspect), à la Whorf.

Discriminations Underlying
Pronominal Usage

Cultural systems are roughly of two kinds: those which are explicit and understood by the native speaker, as against those primarily inferred and understood by the analyst. It is true that most Russians occasionally would have to hesitate or reflect over their usage and that exceptionally sophisticated persons such as Leo Tolstoy were largely aware of the basic determinants. But in general it seems that the discriminations underlying pronominal usage were subconscious and were not conceptualized as a system by the Russian. This was even more true of the evaluation which had to intervene between the discriminations and one's pronominal response, and between one's hearing of a pronoun and one's classification of the speaker's discriminations. Such evaluation was largely subconscious.[5] In sum, what follows is a system that has been inferred by one analyst.

The ten components symbolized by Russian pronominal usage were: the topic of discourse, the context of the speech event, then age, generation, sex, and kinship status, then dialect, group membership, and relative jural and political authority, and, finally, emotional solidarity—the sympathy and antipathy between the two speakers.

First, two discriminations are implied by all acts of speech. The speaker had mentally to associate the selection of pronouns with the *topic of discourse;* two officers might exchange *vy* while discussing military tactics, but revert to *ty* when chatting about women back in their quarters. A large number of such culturally defined topics—kinship, former school experiences—tended to suggest informality, whereas business and professional affairs and certain lofty (*torzhestvennyje*) themes would encourage one to select *vy.* Of course, many subjects were relatively neutral and did not predispose the speaker in any particular direction.[6]

Pronominal usage was also determined by the context, especially the *social context* of the speech event; an august judge would use *vy* to a tramp during proceedings in court. The social context and the topic of discourse were logically related and are often hard to separate analytically.

---

[5] I am indebted to Larry Krucoff for this point.

[6] In the transliteration of Russian words and passages the apostrophe stands for a "soft sign" (softening or palatalization of the preceding consonant); *kh* stands for a letter in the Russian alphabet that, in turn, stands for a sound that resembles the final *ch* of German *ach; zh* is similarly related to a sound that resembles the middle consonant in English *azure; j* is so related to the y-like front semi-vowel called "short i" and to the initial element of the so-called "soft vowels"; *e* initially is so related to a hard front midvowel, but elsewhere to a soft front midvowel. The names of familiar authors and books have been transliterated less exactly and more or less in accordance with the conventions in English language sources.

Nonetheless, instances of clearly independent variation are not too hard to find; a daughter might use *vy* to her mother during a masked ball, but revert to *ty* when whispering about the same boy later in her mother's bedroom.

Next come four discriminations that are "biological" in a sense, although defined in terms of the culture. Relative *age* within the same generation was not too important, but could tip the scales between distant blood relatives, or in cases where relative authority and affection led to ambiguity. Relative *generation,* on the other hand, was frequently decisive, as in the automatic asymmetry between any two gentryfolk relatives separated by one or more generations. Relative *sex* could also decide usage in the sense that two speakers of the same sex were normally more prone to use familiar terms, whereas speakers of the opposite sex would exercise greater restraint. Finally, *genealogical distance,* of which all Russians were keenly aware, provided highly specific rules and many general ones, such as that siblings of the same age at all social levels reciprocated *ty*. Age, generation, sex and genealogical distance were also important components underlying the use of Russian kinship terms.

The third set of discriminations includes various social and group phenomena. To begin with, *relative authority* depended on differences in the distribution of rights and obligations; for example, the father or house chief held many economic and legal rights, whereas the position of the son could be largely defined through his obligations in this patriarchal culture. Such jural relationships, since they involved individual statuses, could and often did vary independently of group membership. In other cases, the relative authority had to be backed by the ability or readiness of the individual to exercise the raw power available. Relative authority often represented the resolution of conflict between several sets of dimensions—above all, between the formal authority of the bureaucracy as against the local leadership and political values of the peasants and Cossaks. Clearly, relative authority and other discriminations had many more specific jural and political implications.

Group membership subsumed, above all, the notion of household; for instance, cousins or affines of about the same age would exchange *ty* if they were residing in the same household but would not necessarily do so if they were living widely separated. The prestige of a family name also influenced pronominal usage among the gentry. Village membership could be decisive for the peasants, as in the regions where the elders addressed each other informally but used *vy* to elders from other villages. Finally, class or caste membership determined usage; workers, peasants, and Cossaks of about the same age normally employed *ty* even at the outset of a conversation, whereas two gentrymen would have to begin with *vy*.

Dialect refers to grammatical and semantic patterns marking a particular variety of Russian. Dialect lines were not clear among many merchant families and members of other transitional classes, but thick bundles of isoglosses did distinguish the gentry from the workers, Cossaks and peasants; all of the latter lived in what amounted to a quasi-familial *ty* universe. The comparative homogeneity of the lower classes, while not congruous with the many divergences in their way of life, did reflect their constant interaction and the recency of their differentiation. The independence of dialect as a variable was demonstrated neatly when, for example, a bilingual, blue-blooded aristocrat became so inured to *vy* that he used it even to peasant children, although receiving *ty* from their parents (Tolstoy 1960a *Resurrection:*218–20).

Finally, there is the psychological dimension of "solidarity," of emotional affinity or antipathy. Emotional distance and certain negative feelings went together with the formal pronoun. Contrariwise, close friends, lovers, and persons joined in some common purpose would tend to use *ty*, and *ty* in some contexts could symbolize the dislike or deprecation bred of familiarity. In brief, the correlation between pronouns and solidarity was complicated, and difficult to predict in terms of a simple continuum between the *ty* of "like-mindedness" (Brown and Gilman 1960) and the *vy* of weak solidarity.

The foregoing summary suggests the conclusion that pronominal usage implied complex concatenations of discriminations that reinforced each other often enough to make speech predictable. The rough breakdown of the society inferred from such usage is congruous with the sociological map arrived at by external criteria. In a larger, cross-cultural sense, the ten components inferred for Russian probably underlie most usage in other languages where second person pronouns are differentiated by authority and solidarity; they may be as universal for pronominal usage as Kroeber's nine components have turned out to be for kinship nomenclatures (Kroeber 1909).

Let us now turn to the types of dyadic relationship, beginning with the symmetrical use of *vy*.

The Dyadic Pairs:
The Symmetrical Vy

Vy was mandatory in certain unambiguously formal occasions. Thus, elder peasants of probity and worth (*blagomyslennyje*) would exchange the formal pronoun when meeting on the street after Sunday mass, and peasant parents and matchmakers would tend to the same usage during the formalities of negotiation and the wedding.[7] But such

---

[7] In both cases, there would be a greater use of the name plus patronymic (*poimenovat' po otechestvu;* Zlatovratsky 1947:153).

obligatory reciprocation was largely confined to non-peasants. For example, all participants used the formal pronoun in a large category of public occasions in the cities, such as a parliamentary meeting, a court session, university examinations, or, for that matter, an open, public altercation between a factory manager and leaders of the workers (Gorki 1946, *Mother:*134). A special poignancy could be created when, for example, former comrades-in-arms or drinking partners switched to formal terms during the challenge and execution of a duel (Lermontov 1948, *A Hero of Our Time:*192–210). While usage was thus dictated by context, the process of feedback common to all communication also meant that the usage itself might symbolize an august and ceremonial atmosphere (*torzhestvennost'*). By the same token, obligatory usage could create peculiar stresses or types of ambiguity when the speaker was conversing with a close friend. In such cases, *vy* might signal the artificiality of the social distance being maintained.

In the second place, *vy* was reciprocated between any two persons desiring to show respect or deference, regardless of their relative status. While such personal motivation was secondary or redundant to many socially determined usages, it also functioned independently in other cases where asymmetrical or even informal usage might have been expected, or at least permitted. Thus, at one point a student and a policeman offer to help a young woman, very drunk, who has apparently been violated or mistreated and is stumbling through the streets (Dostojevsky 1951, *Crime and Punishment:*57); their sympathy and pity is partly conveyed by *vy*. In another case, a Russian officer and a surgeon of German background decide to room together in a resort town in the Caucasus. They become confidants and good friends. Their elective affinity—to translate Goethe's precise phrase—is congruous with a continued reciprocation of an affectionate but respectful *vy*.

The role of pronominal signals for the individual's self-image is brought out in the following exchange between a proud young worker and an arrogant officer who is leading a search party (Gorki 1946:127). The officer begins with:

"This is *ty*, Andrew Nakhodka."
"I," answered Nicholas, moving forward. Andrew stretched out his hand, took Nicholas by the shoulder, and thrust him backwards.
"He made a mistake! I am Andrew!"
The officer, raising his hand and threatening Vesovshchik with his finger, said:
"You look out with me!"
He began to dig in his papers.
"Nakhodka, were *ty* ever brought before an inquiry on political grounds?" he asked.
"I was summoned in Rostov, and in Saratov . . . only there the policeman said *vy* to me."

The officer winked his right eye, wiped it and, baring his small teeth, began to say:

"But isn't it known to *vy*, Nakhodka, precisely to *vy*, just who are the rascals who are distributing criminal proclamations in the factory, aah?"

Here we see a factory worker insisting—with admittedly ambiguous success—that an inspecting officer show him the proper personal respect.

This and other cases in my data point to important discriminations not covered by my system: those of sarcasm and irony. Under certain circumstances the opposite of the expected usage could confuse, humiliate, or affront an addressee. Such inverse usage was especially devastating before a group of people who were more aware even than the victim of the disparity between the verbal symbolism and the underlying social realities. This is illustrated by a passage from the twentieth chapter of Tolstoy's *Childhood.*

Grandmother had a singular gift of expressing her opinion about people under certain circumstances by using the plural and singular pronouns of the second person together with a certain tone of voice. She used *vy* and *ty* contrary to general custom, and on her lips these shades of meaning acquired an entirely different significance. When a young prince walked up to her she said a few words calling him *vy* and looked at him with an expression of such contempt that if I had been in his place I would have become utterly confused. . . .

(An ancient countess would normally use *ty* to a young prince.) In contrast to sarcasm, humor does not appear to have been significantly related to pronominal usage.

We have discussed formal occasions and the particular needs to show or receive deference. *Vy,* in the third place, was determined by a large set of contexts that can be defined exclusively through the relative status of the participants within the larger context of the society. The higher the individual in the social system, the more he tended to both receive and use *vy* with persons of lower standing, including lackeys. Such usage to almost all except one's siblings and spouse was largely a carry-over from the patterns of the French high aristocracy, probably the most formal in Europe. Such bilingual blue-bloods lived in what approximated a *vy*-universe.[8]

Relative status within the larger society was also symbolized by automatic formality on first encounter or casual acquaintance between all officials and gentryfolk who were not lovers, close friends, or certain types of kinsmen. In one novel a petty official receiprocates *vy* with a long series

[8] Roger Brown, writing in 1960, reported a French aristocrat who could remember using *tu* only to an old woman who had been his nurse (Brown and Gilman 1960:270).

of rustic landlords with whom he is often cordial or even pseudo-intimate (Gogol 1947, *Dead Souls:*102–103). The Russian officers and non-coms usually stayed on formal terms, just as did gentryfolk with the tutors and governesses of their children, and also prison officials with political prisoners of the educated classes. Moving yet further down the ladder, a wealthy peasant would normally exchange *vy* with older peasants in the village he was visiting (Zlatovratsky 1947, *The Foundations:*459), and elders from neighboring villages might do the same under certain circumstances. In all the instances just discussed, we find formality between persons who do not know each other well and whose social status was felt to be significantly coordinate.

Among the gentry, at least, the formal pronoun was enjoined between certain categories of actual and potential relatives, such as a man and the consanguines of a girl he was wooing (Dostojevsky 1951:218), and between cousins who were strangers, and between parents-in-law and their children-in-law. Man and woman held to *vy* during a formal courtship until entering upon marriage, or sexual relations, or some comparably intense experience. Women tended to use *vy* more than men, among the gentry because of their greater concern for propriety, among all classes because of their partially subordinate status. In one intriguing case that cuts across class lines, two women held to the formal term while they passed through three relative statuses: landlord's niece as against the same landlord's maid, a provincial actress as against the landlord's concubine, and finally, a broken prostitute as against the village wanton. The persisting use of *vy* despite considerable emotional affinity and, toward the end, approximately equal power, lends unique flavor to this evolving bond (Saltykov-Shchedrin 1958, *The Golovlyov Family:*265, 289)— social status proving dominant over both personal feelings and the general situation.

The Asymmetrical Relationship

In the patriarchal society of Russia deference and obedience were widely accorded to age. Among the gentry, a child would reciprocate *ty* with the mother until about school age, but older children and adolescents used the formal pronoun to their parents. These patterns did not hold for some aristocratic families, and there may well have been marked differences between parents, with less formality toward the mother, particularly between mother and daughter. Similarly asymmetrical were the ties between married daughters and either parent, and between such distant consanguines as a man and his cousin's son's wife (Aksakov 1958, *A Family Chronicle:*82, 157, 188). Step-relatives and affines separated by one or more generations were also on *vy/ty* terms. Two concrete examples must suffice for genealogical distance. In one case, an adult prince received *ty* from an aunt thirty years his senior, although both were exchanging the French *vous*. In another, singular instance, an elderly landlord and his niece retained the asymmetrical terms even after he had become a psychotic and disreputable miser and she had returned home from a career as an actress and prostitute, broken through drink and tuberculosis (Saltykov-Shchedrin 1958:181, 267). At one point the miser even suggests that his niece become his mistress. Among the gentry and wealthier merchant classes, then, usage was necessarily asymmetrical between relatives of any sort, including those by adoption, who were separated by one or more generations.

Among peasants and Cossaks asymmetrical usage was occasional or regional, but was not generally obligatory between the household head and his younger house-mates, with one major exception: in most of the larger households of the urban lower classes and of the peasants of the central "industrial" zones, the household head normally received *vy* and addressed all as *ty*; these were precisely the two social groups and the geographical area where Great Russian patriarchy reached its acme, and where the influence of the *vy*-using gentry was most deeply felt. Asymmetrical usage also set off a peasant from his parents-in-law, particularly a girl from her father-in-law. In sum, asymmetrical usage tended to emerge between two peasants when they were separated by two or more dimensions, such as generation, community, extreme authority, or the solemnity of the situation.

Superior and inferior authority within the established officialdom was pronominally symbolized in the relation between a teacher and pupils, law officers and criminal prisoners, and officers or non-commissioned officers with their soldiers; the last of these three usages was congruous also with the gentry or middle class origin of almost all officers, as against the proletarian or peasant background of almost all soldiers. The Cossaks, despite their strong egalitarianism, reflected their common experience as members of a military caste by scrupulously using *vy* to non-coms, officers, gentryfolk, and all government officials.[9]

One well-known short-story of Pushkin's illustrates how pronouns could symbolize authority. A young hussar feigns illness while *en route* in order to seduce the adolescent daughter of a fifty-year-old stationmaster and war veteran. The brokenhearted father makes his way into the large house in the capital where his daughter is being kept as a mistress, but, during a final, climactic scene, is literally thrown out by the irate young aristocrat.

---

[9] One of the first acts of the Provisional Government in 1917 was to force all commissioned officers to use *vy* to privates, but the Red Army reintroduced *ty*, eventually extending it to all subordinates.

Neither man ever deviates from asymmetrical usage. Thus, a low-ranking official could be subordinate to any member of the high aristocracy. The frequency with which social differences over-rode age demonstrates the strength of class cleavage in the first part of the century.

Perhaps of greater psychological interest than the school, prison, army, and officialdom were the domains such as the gentry household and the landed estate where asymmetry was enjoined and often automatically ascribed for the members of an entire group. Any patriarch or matriarch with the abilities and motivation to realize his or her power would eventually use *ty* to all, and receive *vy* from all except the spouse (Saltykov-Shchedrin 1958:6, 15, 71), and sometimes even from the spouse; such gentry patterns emphasizing the formal or secular aspect of the father's or husband's authority, became models for the peasant and lower class households mentioned above. As a rule, landlords and their estate managers were on *vy/ty* terms, although both kinds of symmetrical relationship might occur for personal reasons. Country squires usually remained on a *vy/ty* basis with their peasant concubines, although genuine affection and isolation could lead to a mutual *ty* within the rustic privacy of the home.

Pronominal usage between peasants and other classes entailed surprises. For example, a wealthy, respectable, and urbanized serf in Moscow would still use *vy* and receive *ty* from the dissolute and disgraced son of his distant proprietor, ascribed status taking precedent over both age and actual power. In a second case, a fully mature huntsman and house serf would be pronominally subordinate to the little son of his landlord. A third instance comes from the *Childhood* of Tolstoy, always so sensitive to status. As a boy he was cared for by a beloved elderly peasant woman who, incidentally, was on *vy/ty* terms with his mother. At one point this nurse scolded him, saying, "Don't *ty* soil the tablecloth." Little Tolstoy gets furious and exclaims, sputtering, "How . . . Natal'ja is saying *ty* to me. . . ." at which she apologizes with, "That's enough, daddy [*batjushka*], don't *vy* cry. . . ." at which he is comforted. Here a small boy is literally calling an elderly woman into line on her usage.

Other, obvious differences in social rather than administrative status could determine usage. With the exceptions already noted, all persons used *ty* to small children and would use *ty* and expect *vy* with pre-adolescent children. Any member of the gentry tended to use *ty* to a lower-class servant, typically the valet, or lackey, or the waiter in a tavern. The strength of the combination of age and class differences is shown by a gentleman-landlord and his peasant boarder, who automatically entered upon an asymmetrical relationship and held to it even when the youth was demanding the return of a large sum that the old codger had borrowed and squandered (Zlatovratsky 1947:288, 350). *Ty* was used downwards to the members of minority groups whose poverty and ethnic status were clear, as between a middle-aged landlord and a Jewish watchman (Dostojevsky 1951:544–45). Any person with education and with civil or military rank would immediately enter into *vy/ty* terms with some irregular semi-legal person, such as a professional thief, a gypsy, a beggar, or a criminal. In sum, asymmetrical relationships were automatic when social differences were wide and mutually felt.

The Symmetrical Ty

Within and between all social classes children under about age eleven or twelve exchanged *ty*. In one delightful scene, an aloof, isolated, and already psychotic eight-year-old is approached by three adventurous, arrow-shooting little "Mohicans" who are also on vacation, and immediately begin using *ty* (Sologub 1961, *In Bondage:*241–243). The apparent assumption was that children were essentially equal and potentially solidary. The status of child overwhelmed or obscured that of class. Childhood informality also created the frequent comradeship between the offspring of peasants and landlords, and contributed to the peculiar nostalgia for an irretrievable past that was felt by so many of the gentry in their adult years.[10]

Second, the informal pronoun was exchanged with certain non-humans, such as God, the Devil, demons, and other objects, animals, spirits, and essences that might be addressed; the folklore and the texts containing fantasy show that the usage was returned. The conversations between Gorki's grandmother and God reveal the intimacy of such relations with non-humans and the supernatural.

In the third place, all members of the lower classes strongly tended to reciprocate *ty*, even among total strangers. In one case, a proletarian woman exchanges the informal pronoun with an elder peasant from another community, whereas her son and the same man are on formal terms. In a second instance, a wealthy *kulak* and his impoverished body servant express through *ty* their sense of common peasant origin and their personal affinity (Zlatovratsky 1947:520). In some northern, northeastern, and Siberian regions, lacking landlords and far from the urban centers, *ty* was probably the only functional pronoun.[11]

Membership in the same community was often decisive. Thus relations—irrespective of age—were mutually informal between proletarian

---

[10] It is psychologically intriguing that the *ty* was primarily associated with infant experiences and, for the aristocracy, was a symbol of intimate personal identity; in psychiatric terms, it may correspond to the so-called "ego-id" (Silverberg 1940:511).

[11] I am indebted to Howard Aronson for this point.

neighbors in the squalid factory towns. The villages of Cossaks and Great Russian peasants were pronominal in-groups of a sort, the members conceiving of each other as relatives and addressing even the village elder informally. In one revealing case, the peasants in a small commune start on formal terms with a young visiting Muscovite, but after they have ascertained his friendship with a local son their whole attitude and their pronominal usage shift, as is summed up by one matron, "So *ty*, my dear (kinsman), are on friendly terms with him" (Zlatovratsky 1947:153).

Until the middle of the century, peasants usually said *ty* to the landlord, but not to his wife; this was part of their tendency toward informality but, in a perhaps more important sense, it symbolized their conceptual grouping of persons of supreme authority; the landlord's rights over his serfs included purchase and marital arrangements. With the partial exception noted above, the household chief, the landlord, Tsar, and God were all addressed with *ty* and the quasi-kinship term, *batjushka* ("little father"). Thus a striking feature of authority in Russia as against the West was that *vy* generally did symbolize greater power, but that when the greatness passed a certain point the speaker switched back to what might be called the *ty* of total subordination or of an intimacy that could not be jeopardized.[12] From another point of view, *ty* to God, Tsar, and squire emphasized the fatherly aspect of their jural authority.

In addition to the social categories just discussed, pan-Russian patterns enjoined a mutual *ty* between brothers and sisters. This was related to the norms of cooperation and loyalty between brothers and, in addition, was extended to many kinds of comrades and associates. Peasants, Cossaks, and artisans banded together into brotherhoods, and there was considerable overlap both in sentiment and usage between the words for commune (*mir*) and cooperative (*artel'*). In addition, ritual brotherhood, sealed by exchanging crosses worn around the neck, was important at all levels. Students, officers, and other members of the educated classes had a ritual of "drinking to *ty*," but this foreign *brudershaft* appears to have been rare in the last century and is not evidenced in my texts. In any case, fraternal solidarity of many kinds was a pervasive and integrating theme in Russian culture and was partly symbolized by the reciprocal *ty*.

The informal pronoun was usual between spouses at all social levels, as would be congruous with the balance of rights between man and woman that underlay the symbols of male dominance. In many merchant families and lower-middle class families, however, the wives addressed their husbands with *vy* plus the name and patronymic. Among the bilingual gentry

[12] As Julian Pitt-Rivers points out, total subordination implies intimacy whereas formal social usage implies social distance which obtains where respect might conceivably be denied.

the mutual informality ran counter to pressures toward a reciprocal *vy* on the model of French.[13] And conjugal usage could be poignantly ambiguous, as when estranged or even hostile spouses persisted with *ty*. Even among the high aristocracy, lovers held to informal terms long after the liaison had cooled (Lermontov 1948:141).

Aside from siblings and spouses, *ty* was reciprocated between more distant kinsmen under certain conditions; for example, gentryfolk cousins who knew each other reasonably well would be on informal terms. Second degree relatives through marriage, such as the spouse's siblings or the sibling's spouses, would usually reciprocate *ty* with a speaker of about the same age, although this could produce conflicts if they were personally antipathetic; in one case, a man and his sister's husband "tried to use *ty*" after the sister's marriage, "but remained on *vy* terms" (Tolstoy 1960a:332). In general, usage between affines varied considerably. As a final point, the growth of the individual at all social levels was critically affected by the grandmother, who was both a nurse, and a storyteller, and a repository of norms and traditions; she varied from the peasant *babushka* of Gorki's *Childhood* to the august and matriarchal *babushka* of Leo Tolstoy. Throughout life most Russians remained on informal terms with at least one grandmother, although among the high aristocracy she might be addressed with *vy*, while a peasant nurse filled many of the more intimate and homely roles.

The informal pronoun was also reciprocated between members of the gentry who had been joined through shared experiences, such as regular participation in card games or a common revolutionary ideology. Classmates from the same secondary school and alumni of the same privileged school, such as the Corps of Pages, were formally linked by *ty*. As a rule, men who had moved in the same circles as university students would continue with *ty* throughout life, although reunion with an old chum might entail conflicts and pronominal gaucherie. In one case, a prince and an old army comrade use *ty* although the former is embarrassed by the implied closeness he no longer feels (Tolstoy 1960a:245–246).[14] The informal usage between friends and students generally expressed a certain affection or *esprit de corps,* but at a more profound level it was the felt extension of a kinship bond just as, conversely, the use of *vy* within the peasant village—which was an extended kinship group—was often associated with the introduction of external standards by government bureaucrats.

[13] Indeed, one of the most fascinating problems, barely hinted at in this chapter, was the degree of congruity between French and Russian usage; both languages functioned as largely independent systems for classifying the same set of actual and potential addressees.

[14] This contrasts with many other languages, such as German, where the *Du* to a former classmate is clearly not felt to necessarily imply anything more than the former group membership.

The Dynamics of Pronominal Usage: Eight Cases of "Switching" and "Breakthrough" 同時 vs. 進化

Crucial to linguistics and social anthropology is the distinction between studies of synchronic systems as they presumably operate in the mind of speakers during at least one generation, as against the study of historical sequences and cultural evolution. But despite the value of keeping the two approaches apart to some extent, they can be rigidly separated only at great cost to our understanding. This is because the second or "diachronic" framework always sheds light on the synchronic system; by following replacement, loss, and rearrangement through time the dynamic relations of units can be inferred. In addition to historical and evolutionary change, any synchronic system shows alternation, variation, and various kinds of rapid and often erratic option which can lead to inferences about the functional and hierarchical relations between elements. Let us review eight extended cases of pronominal "switching" and "breakthrough" with the end of indicating and illustrating some of the more obvious dynamic relationships.

COMRADESHIP BETWEEN PECHORIN AND MAXIM MAXIMYCH IN LERMONTOV'S *A HERO OF OUR TIME*

An arrogant, aristocratic lieutenant and a grizzled, older captain find themselves thrust together as the only officers on an isolated outpost in the Caucasus. Reciprocal formality at first seems appropriate to both. But while the latter is sitting on the young lieutenant's bed and discussing a confidential matter he switches to *ty*. When the lieutenant appears to suggest insubordination, however, the captain reverts to *vy* as he issues a peremptory demand; for the older man, the power of military rank is in delicate balance with the emotions uniting the two lonely comrades in the Caucasus.

In the following scenes the lieutenant uses *vy* at all times, partly because he is almost thirty years younger, partly because he comes from the high aristocracy, partly because, as is borne out by several episodes, he is emotionally incapable of warm, positive attachments to other people; as is so often the case, the relative power of the three determinants cannot be ascertained. On the other hand, I would deduce that in some contexts the young lieutenant would have used *ty* or that at least after their separation the older man thought of him as employing the more in-

timate pronoun. During the final scene the two friends accidentally meet
again at an inn. The affectionate and simple-hearted captain rushes
forward impulsively, but is countered with, "How delighted I am, dear
Maxim Maximych! Well, how are *vy*?" (Lermontov 1948:88).
"'But . . . *ty* . . . *vy*?' muttered the old man with tears in his eyes."
The wrenching quality of the passage turns on the binary and here
ironic choice between two pronouns.

CHICHIKOV AND KOROBOCHKA
IN GOGOL'S *DEAD SOULS*

Chichikov, a well-bred, petty official, gets lost at night in a snow storm,
and finally knocks on the door of the unknown proprietress of a small estate. Both he and the maid at first use *ty*, reflecting their mutual surprise
and the spontaneity of the situation. But after hearing a few words, she
switches her pronouns, apparently in reaction to his urban accent: "But
who are *vy*?"

Later that night Chichikov and the proprietress reciprocate *vy* as they
converse over tea, although repeatedly interjecting the kinship terms, *ma-
tushka* (derived from "mother"), and *batjushka*. The proprietress
switches to the informal *ty* when expressing sympathy over his carriage
accident, and when bidding him goodnight she calls him not only *batjushka* but literally "my father" (*moj otets*), and tenderly offers to scratch
his heels, a soporific comfort her deceased husband had habitually
required (1947:34). By this time both Chichikov and his hostess feel
themselves to be approximately on a par.

The following day finds our guest, who is about forty, addressing his
hostess in familiar terms; because of her seemingly small estate, "he
didn't stand at all on ceremony." He soon inquires after her last name,
and is told, "Korobochka (the wife of), a collegiate secretary," and that,
on further inquiry, her name and patronymic is Nastas'ja Petrovna. The
official title impresses Chichikov, and from then on he is careful to
address her respectfully. He begins to importune her to sell him the title of
such of her serfs as have passed away since the last census. As soon as
this extraordinary intention becomes clear, Korobochka switches from *vy*
to *ty*. By this time (pp. 37–42) the asymmetrical relationship is coming to
symbolize their mutual and increasingly clear-cut awareness that she is an
established owner of serfs and land, a true *pomeshchitsa*, whereas he is
materializing into a rather suspicious sort of solicitor. The function of *ty*
as an expression of Korobochka's growing wariness comes out in several
strongly felt utterances: "What are they (the dead souls) to *ty*?" or "Are
ty deceiving me, *batijushka?*" or "What terrible things *ty* say!" The
unequal quality of the relationship is underscored by his combination of
vy plus Nastas'ja Petrovna, whereas she mentions no proper name at all

(partly because he had dodged her original question about it). But both continue to interlard kinship terms.

Chichikov finally persuades Korobochka to sell her dead souls by implying that he is taking government contracts and may be in a position to buy some of her vegetables. In the last scene, after a rich dinner for the "contractor," she switches to *vy* when asking if he will buy some pork lard, but then goes right back to *ty* when discussing his carriage and road conditions (p. 41).

In ten of the most masterful pages in *Dead Souls* the dyadic relationship evolves from *vy/vy,* to *ty/vy* to *vy/vy* to *ty/vy* to *vy/vy,* and finally to *ty/vy.* This illustrates the frequency and rapidity of pronominal switching as total strangers adjusted to each other. More particularly, it illustrates the complexity of covariation between pronouns and various sorts of "kinship terms." Thus, *ty* plus a kinship term of address occurred quite normally among the gentry. But less redundant and more interesting was the conjunction of the formal pronoun with a kinship term such as *matjushka,* enabling the speaker such as Chichikov to partially cross the gap between himself and his interlocutor.

A PROLETARIAN MOTHER, HER SON,
AND HER SON'S FRIENDS
(GORKI'S *MOTHER*)

After the death of her brutal husband, a mother somewhere in her forties is left with an adolescent son who soon turns to private study and underground revolutionary activities. More and more books appear on his shelves and, to signal his growing cultivation, ". . . he said *vy* to her and called her *mamasha,* but sometimes, suddenly, he would address her tenderly:

'Ty, mother, please don't worry. I will be coming home late . . .'" (Gorki 1946:113). And later:

"He said 'mother' and '*ty*' to her, as was his wont only when he drew closer to her. . . ."

About the time of the conversations just described, the son brings home a worker about twenty-eight years old to live with the family. At first the mother calls him *vy* plus the respectful name plus patronymic (Andrej Anisimovich), plus the respectful and affectionate kinship term that literally means "dear little father" (*batjushka*). But they grow more intimate as the weeks pass, as is clear from the following scene.

"Andrjusha, you ought to mend your shoes, or you will catch cold." To which he responds, "You are almost like a true mother to me" (*a, mozhet, vy i est' rodnaja mat' moja*). They remain on a formal basis, while exchanging the "kinship terms," *batjushka* and *nenka.* But after the young friend confesses to the murder of a political informer (pp. 166, 168), the mother switches to *ty* although he continues with *vy*. At this point her son actually comments on the pronominal usage:

"'*Ty* know, *ty* did well, that *ty* began to say '*ty*' to him after that.' She looked at him with surprise and said. 'Yes, but I didn't even notice how it happened! He has become so close to me—I can't say how!'"

The mother's relations to her son's other revolutionary friends were generally formal, even in the case of women, such as her son's sweetheart, whom she got to know rather well. She remained on formal terms with an educated school teacher though living in her house, and emotionally very close (p. 247). The main exception to such reciprocal formality was the relation between the mother and a young revolutionary in his thirties before the hour of his death, when she becomes a loving nurse to him and he is a hero to her (p. 201). But I hasten to add that even in such critical relations between two proletarians fused by a common ideology, one could not predict a switch to *ty* with absolute certainty.

THE PRINCE AND THE PROSTITUTE IN *RESURRECTION*

The heroine of Tolstoy's novel *Resurrection* (1960a) was born the daughter of a wandering gypsy and the village wanton. She was then adopted and reared in the cultivated home of an elderly, aristocratic lady. When the eighteen-year-old nephew of her patroness comes home from school on vacation, he unselfconsciously starts out using *ty*. She responds with the respectful *vy* (p. 47), except when he steals a kiss from her during a game, and even then her *vot tebe raz* is part of a fairly frozen, exclamatory expression. The contrast between their asymmetrical address comes out neatly when he is leaving for the university and they bid farewell: *Proshchaj, Katjusha*, as against, *Proshchajte, Dmitryj Ivanovich*. During their first, idyllic acquaintance their usage reflects caste status more or less as one would predict.

Three years later the prince returns as a pleasure-seeking officer. She still uses *vy* (p. 54), whereas he vacillates before finally settling on the same form. Both the young people are soon in love, but continue on formal terms; when they meet after the moving Easter service their usage is apparently reinforced by the solemnity of the occasion (p. 60). But a few hours later on the same Sunday he switches to *ty* while trying to embrace her in a corridor, and this is conjoined with the diminutive of her first name. She sticks to *vy* and the congruously respectful first name plus patronymic, as above. During the physical seduction that evening he repeatedly says *ty*, whereas she says *vy* while her eyes say *ty*, "I am yours (*tvoja*)"; the physical conquest of a woman appears to have been inseparably connected with a switch to *ty*, at least by the man; the woman might use *vy*, while her gestures, intonation and so forth indicated that she was thinking and feeling *ty*.

Twelve years later the same prince finds himself in the juror's box and asked to pass judgment on an attractive, young prostitute who has been accused of poisoning and robbing a client. He recognizes her as the village girl he seduced long ago. Feeling remorse about his role in precipitating her downfall, he visits her later in jail. As he begins to speak (p. 1953) he uses *ty*, possibly in recognition of the enormous social distance between them, possibly to express his impulsive love toward her. But following an interruption in the conversation, he reverts to *vy* as part of the desire to increase the propriety of their relationship.

Soon afterwards he returns to the jail and declares his resolve to marry her. At this her instant reaction is to recall the degrading scene the morning after the seduction when he tried to thrust one hundred rubles into her hand. With a sort of ironic reference she therefore erupts with: "There is your (*tvoja*) price." The prince also switches pronouns with, "I won't leave *tebja!*" For a brief period thereafter she reiterates a *ty* of anger and contempt: "*Ty* are a prince . . . (*ty*) go away!" (pp. 173–74). But after a second, brief interruption by the warden she returns to *vy* although the prince continues with *ty*, as in, "*Ty* don't believe me." As the interview draws to a close both interlocutors grow colder, and he finally switches back to *vy* himself, saying, "*Vy* think it over." Here we see the pronoun functioning as a sort of exclamatory particle, a two-phoneme signal of rapid emotional shifts.

Shortly afterwards, Kat'ja is convicted. When the ill-matched couple meet again they at first reciprocate *vy*, but when he proposes to her for the second time, it is with, "I am asking *tebja* to marry me." She rejects him using the formal pronoun, and he almost immediately switches back to *vy* himself. Eight pages later, when he dreams of her, she says, "I am a female convict, but *vy* are a prince."

Later the prince returns from St. Petersburg after an unsuccessful attempt to appeal her sentence. He is chagrined to learn that she has been accused of gratifying one of the sergeants and, as a result, has been fired from an advantageous job in the prison hospital. During the ensuing dialogue he feels ambivalent, and Kat'ja is mortified. Both use *vy* and they never deviate from it for the rest of the story, during their long trek to Siberia (pp. 357, 406), nor at their last meeting (p. 453), when her moral redemption has been largely achieved through the influence of the political prisoners, to one of whom, a psychotic terrorist, she is already promised in marriage.

The particular value of the *Resurrection* lies in the interaction between persons from opposite ends of the social continuum. In Prague School terms, at either end of the continuum one of the two pronouns was unmarked, while the second was marked and conveyed more precise information. Thus, for a prince *vy* was the more frequent and the less marked pronoun, whereas for a prostitute *ty* was comparatively unmarked; in either case a switch to or a maintenance of the marked pronoun implied special hostility, affection, or ambivalence.[15]

RASKOLNIKOV AND SON'JA IN *CRIME AND PUNISHMENT*

Raskolnikov, an undernourished and idealistic student in his early twenties, is obsessed with the theoretical implications of willfully breaking a fundamental moral law. He is living in a small garret that adjoins a room filled with two half-crazed parents and their hungry children. One daughter, a shy, nervous girl of about eighteen, has turned as inconspicuously as possible to prostitution in order to help support her impoverished but originally upper-class family.

These two young people reciprocate *vy* during their casual first contacts. But after his brutal ax-murder of the old usuress and her niece, Raskolnikov is torn by guilt and needs a confidant. He goes to visit the girl in her lodgings. As the conversation develops, they increasingly sense their need for each other. His voice becomes "quiet and tender." But Son'ja remains formal while talking about the suffering of her family, and even her first professional experiences; once she affixes the hyperrespectful particle /-s/. As they continue to draw closer, Raskolnikov realizes with more terrible clarity the conflict between her degrading profession and her innocent, generous nature. He falls to his knees and kisses her feet (*nogi*). Son'ja cries out, "What are *vy* doing?" (precisely: *chto vy, chto vy eto! Peredo mnoj!*), and Raskolnikov immediately arises and answers, "I did not bow down to *ty*, I bowed down to all human suffering" (Dostojevsky 1951:343). This scene, deservedly one of the most renowned in all Russian literature, owes its drama in no small measure to the profound, kaleidoscopic reorganization within Raskolnikov's mind; Son'ja is elevated to a vast symbol, an abstract, metaphysical idea, and her shift in status is signaled at the critical moment by a switch in pronouns.

But let us continue. The asymmetrical relationship is held during a subsequent discussion and while Son'ja is reading the story of Lazarus: ". . . I am the resurrection and the life. . . ." and then ". . . the stub was already burning low in the candleholder, murkily lighting up in a beggarly room the murderer and the prostitute who had been strangely

---

[15] I am grateful to Milka Ivič for this point.

united through a reading of the Holy Book" (p. 350). Raskolnikov, realizing that Son'ja is also half insane, asks her to go with him "along the same road," and announces that he has chosen to tell her who murdered the niece of the usuress. Son'ja, terrified by his wild-eyed conduct, and not understanding his motives, persists with *vy*, and so they part.

Shortly afterwards, in a humiliating scene, Son'ja is accused of theft, and stoutly defended by Raskolnikov. He again visits her lodgings, and they start out reciprocating *vy*. Their relationship soon grows very tense as Raskolnikov poses a terrible if hypothetical moral question, and Son'ja breaks down, sobbing and appealing to Providence: ". . . did you indeed come only to torture?" at which Raskolnikov, feeling a burst of remorse, switches his pronouns, while answering, "But of course *ty* are right, Son'ja" (*a ved' ty prava*). His voice "weakens" and his entire manner alters as he confesses that he has come to ask her forgiveness. They sit together on her bed and he gradually begins his confession, at first by giving her hints and asking her to guess. (At one point she fleetingly reminds him of the murdered niece.) Son'ja finally gets his message, that he himself was the ax-murderer, and recoils in horror, and then throws herself to her knees before him and cries out, "*Vy*, what have *vy* done to yourself!" (*chto vy, chto vy eto nad soboj sdelali*). Raskolnikov responds with, "How strange you are!" (*strannaja kakaja ty*). It is at this critical juncture that Son'ja at last switches her pronouns, "No, there is no one in the entire world more unhappy than *ty*" (p. 439); (*net, net tebja neschastnee nikogo v tselom tsvete*), and she immediately repeats *ty* in several sentences while venting her own compassion, and pledging her willingness to follow him anywhere. Son'ja's pronominal switch, just like her kneeling, exactly parallels the earlier scene, and is reminiscent of the eruption of *tu* at the most climactic moments in *Phedre* and other plays of Racine.

After her rush of commiseration, however, Son'ja thinks of the murder, of the fact that Raskolnikov has bludgeoned her friend, the niece of the usuress. She pulls away, and also switches back to *vy*, "Yes, but what are *vy* (p. 440; *Da kak vy, vy takoj*). Raskolnikov then explains that he may have killed in order to steal, at which Son'ja's love comes flooding back, with a switch to *ty*, "*Ty* were hungry. *Ty* . . . in order to help your mother. . . ." But when he denies this, Son'ja, again horrified, reverts back to *vy*: ". . . how do *vy* give away your last money, but kill . . . ?" At this point Raskolnikov is torn between his growing affinity and sympathy for Son'ja and his desperate need to be frank about his own cynicism and immorality. He becomes agonized, wonders out loud why he has come to confess at all, and exclaims that they are two very different (*roznyje*) people. Here Son'ja, again seeming to sense his loneliness and despair, switches back to the pronoun of intimacy with "(*Ty*) speak, speak!"

(p. 442). This exhortation precipitates Raskolnikov into his theory of the Napoleonic hero: would Napoleon have murdered in defiance of the moral law? Son'ja, confused and irritated, switches back again to the formal pronoun, "*Vy* better speak to me plainly, without examples" (p. 443). At this Raskolnikov launches into a third line of explanation: he might have murdered to help his mother and sister, but the genuine reason was that he wanted to dare (*osmelit'sja*). Son'ja is yet more estranged and cries out, "*Vy* have left God, and he has struck you down" (*ot boga vy otoshli, i vas bog porazil*) and "*Vy* be quiet! Don't *vy* dare, blasphemer" (p. 446), and "Do *vy* have the right to kill?" Raskolnikov, persisting in the exposition of his philosophy, states that he just wanted to try something out (*poprobovat'*), but soon realizes the hollowness of his position. He appeals to her for advice. True to her character, Son'ja responds to him, and changes pronouns for the seventh and last time in only nine pages of dialogue, "(*Ty*) rise up . . . (*ty*) bow down at the crossroads . . . (*ty*) confess to all the world" (p. 448). This unforgettable scene of the gradual union of two human beings ends with Raskolnikov's agreement to go to the police eventually, and of Son'ja's gift of a cross to be worn around the neck (*natel'nyj krest*), which had been presented to her by the murdered niece. As when urging him to confess at the crossroads, Son'ja's offer of the cross, a symbol of ritual siblinghood, links this novel of intellectuals and outcasts to some of the most enduring and profound dimensions of Russian peasant culture. Just as in *The Idiot* and *The Brothers Karamazov,* the theme of solidarity between brothers and ritual siblings underlies much of Dostojevsky.

Toward the end of the book (e.g., pp. 556–558), the two young people use only *ty* to one another. Thus, an elective affinity gradually guides them through many stages of pronominal usage with a frequency and rapidity of change that is at times difficult to follow. Starting fairly close, as destitute and demoralized individuals of good family, they have been drawn yet closer, as a guilt-ridden murderer and an unwilling prostitute, and, at last, as husband and wife about to share the rigors and deprivation of a protracted exile in Siberia. Their relation differs profoundly from that depicted in *Resurrection* between a status-conscious blue-blood and a practiced whore.

A Special Kind of Switching:
The Expressive and the Latent Ty

The present study, while primarily concerned with the cognitive aspects of culture, also touches at many points on sentiment and feeling, both as they were regularly patterned, and in their idiosyncratic manifestations. Some mood, whim, or mental state could make the speaker play with or altogether ignore the usual rules, depending, of course, on his emotional makeup and social sensitivity. In such instances the pronoun often had latent or purely expressive functions.

To begin with, the second person pronouns—notably when in rapid-fire alternation—could express idiosyncratic impulses or the peculiarities of a situation. The shift to *ty*, both more frequent and more charged with emotion, was often an unconscious slip or outburst that, because of its transitory or covert character, did not necessarily evoke or reflect a mutual restructuring of the relationship. For example, *ty* was simply part of many petrified phrases of surprise, fear, or other strong emotion; thus, a country squire on fairly formal terms with a visiting gentleman, might burst out momentarily with a grateful, "Ah, *ty* are my benefactor" (Gogol 1947:89). A maid normally on asymmetrical terms with her master might cry out, on bumping into him in a dark corridor, "*Ty*, my lord, watch out!" The informal pronoun was part of many frozen expressions such as, "The devil take you (*tebja*)!" Such exclamations often did little more than express the speaker's sentiments about a touchy or startling situation but, at another level of contrast, they at least implied a fleeting and superficial shift in his relation to his interlocutor.

In the second place, personal derangement was also signaled by the excessive use of *ty*. Many persons when drunk grew familiar to all and sundry. In one striking scene from Lermontov a drunken and berserk Cossak *ty*'s an officer while cutting him down with a saber. More permanent disorganization was often associated with a readiness to use *ty*. An aristocratic woman, the daughter of a general, is gradually dying of tuberculosis in a squalid one-room apartment, surrounded by her starving children. Half-crazed and hysterical, she turns on the companion of her alcoholic husband with, "From the tavern! *Ty* were drinking with him! (*Ty*) get out!" (Dostojevsky 1951:32). Later, at the husband's funeral, both go back to their usual *vy*. But a few pages later her maternal instincts are exacerbated by the guilt she feels over her daughter's condition (p. 421), and she lashes out with *ty* no less than six times on half a page, and many times more if one counts the verbal forms that imply the pronoun. When she is lacerating a vicious gentleman who has accused her daughter of theft, she goes, "*Ty* look then! (*Ty*) look, (*ty*) look, now (*ty*) look!" These exclamatory pronouns symbolize her abject despair. The extreme use of the *ty* of pronominal instability was part of hysteria, or, in Prague School terms, the onset of insanity was signaled by a neutralization or canceling out of the distinction that set off the two pronouns from each other. I accept as apparently sound the theory of Jakobson (1942:83) that in aphasia, extreme senility, and so forth, individuals generally revert to the unmarked, generic form of their childhood years.

The informal pronoun could also serve as the unilateral, one-sided expression of an extreme ideology which, from one point of view, is a lack of contact with "reality." One handsome and egregiously chaste young woman "was on *ty* terms with everybody" (Tolstoy 1960a:416) as part of her revolutionary posture. An old wanderer and anarchist, who had been jailed once for "insanity," "believed only in himself" and used *ty* to all (Tolstoy 1960a: 437–438). Speaking more generally, the exclusive use of the informal pronoun often symbolized an outlook on man and society characteristic of the insane, the senile, hermits, and extreme revolutionaries, notably terrorists.

The "second person singular" was also used by normal persons in normal states to express involuntary or transient feelings of contempt, hostility, and the like, often quite independent of the social class of the speakers. In one instance, a poor village priest consistently reciprocates *vy* with the niece of a powerful landlord until questioning her about life as an actress, when he says ". . . sometimes with a spitty snout—one ought to be forbidden to even look at him—but *ty* have to proffer your lips." His switch of pronouns here was apparently unintentional, but the effect on his listener of the message and the pronoun itself was devastating. In another case, a doorman thinks to himself while turning away an undesirable gentleman, "Just the same, if they chase *ty* away from the threshold, then *ty* must be some sort of rascal" (Gogol 1947:153). Similarly, a young lackey, when nagged at about fixing some blinds, thinks to himself with reference to the princess, "But the devil take *ty* if I know what *ty* need" (Tolstoy 1960a:100). Finally, Gorki's grandmother does use *vy* to her husband, the patriarch, but during crises such as the great and ruinous fire she switches to *ty*. Later, when he is losing relatives and sinking into abject poverty, she uses nothing but the informal pronoun.

Such shifts in pronouns could explicitly mark a shift toward contempt coupled with vilification. The big trading houses had special agents known as "nephews" to make false bids at auctions, among other things. When a nephew fell into disfavor and was about to be booted downstairs, "the director would begin to interlard his speech ever more with the pronoun *ty*, and with polite epithets in the nature of 'rascal,' 'good-for-nothing' . . ." (Zlatovratsky 1947:297). In another, better known case, a young woman, finding herself locked in a man's room, shifts to *ty*: "(*Ty*) open the door immediately, immediately, base man . . . so this (means) rape!" Later she draws a miniature revolver and accuses her tormentor of having poisoned his wife: "*Ty! Ty* hinted it to me yourself; *ty* spoke to me of the poison . . . I know, *ty* made a trip to get it . . . *ty* had it ready . . . it was *ty* . . . it was decidedly *ty*, lout!" (Dostojevsky 1951:528). Here the pronoun is repeated seven times in two and a half lines of Russian, illustrating how a woman might switch to *ty* as a partial expression of her terror, or contempt, or some other underlying antipathy, and more generally, how a pronoun could function as an exclamation and a symbol of feelings about the addressee. In another case, a housemaid has been forced into concubinage. She directs her frustrated emotions into maternal love for an illegitimate child, until it is torn away and sent off. From then on she thinks only *ty* to her master, although sticking to *vy* in face-to-face conversations (Saltykov-Shchedrin 1958:232). Let us take a last example. Toward the close of the famous cross-examination Raskolnikov's interrogator, who had never deviated from the formal pronoun, thinks *ty* toward the man whom he has broken with his questions. In sum, a low opinion or even hatred could be mentally expressed through an unarticulated and therefore unreciprocated *ty*.

Affection and love could also be related to the covert or idiosyncratic thinking of *ty*. For instance, one aristocrat, when passing through the initial stages of what might become a liaison with a seductive St. Petersburg lady, finds himself conversing with *ty* "in the language of the eyes. The eyes said, 'Can *ty* love me?' and the answer was 'Yes'" (Tolstoy 1960a:265, 300, 314). A woman might be the first to make the shift with her eyes, although a man would normally take the initiative with the articulate form. Such intuitions, shared by all normal Russians, were made delightfully explicit by Pushkin in a verse entitled "Ty and Vy."

> пред ней задумчиво стою;
> Свести очей с нее нет силы;
> и говорю ей: как вы милы!
> и мыслю: как тебя люблю!

This last quatrain may be translated as:

> Pensive I stand before her now
> And cannot tear my eyes away.
> "How dear *vy* are," I say,
> And think, "How I do love *tebja*."

Practically all Russians, particularly of the gentry class, were potentially or mentally on *ty* terms with a larger number of persons than could be deduced from their overt linguistic behavior.

Such latent usage also mattered among the lower classes, except, perhaps, for the peasants in their communes. In one instance, a proletarian mother in her forties says, "Farewell," to a young female worker, but, looking after her from the window, she thinks, "Comrade! . . . ah, you dear, may God give *tebe* an honorable (*chestnogo*) comrade for all your life" (Gorki 1946:153). The same proletarian mother-image regularly thinks *ty* but says *vy* to her son's sweetheart, an educated girl of vaguely middle-class background. She "felt a desire to say to her, '(*Ty*) my dear, indeed, I know that you love him. . . .' But she could not make up her mind to it" (*ne reshalas'*). And then later, "she pressed the extended hand and thought, '(*Ty*) my unhappy one.' " But soon thereafter she says aloud, "*Vy* speak truly" (Gorki 1946:196).

The foregoing data demonstrate some of the functions of the latent or mental *ty*, and this relates to a more general point. One of the fallacies of behavioristic descriptive linguistics and of behavioristic social psychology is that, by a sort of convention, the evidence is artificially limited to the overt, actually articulated forms. Such an approach, while usually valid for phonemics or many kinds of sociometrics, is apt to lead to distortion in semantics, because so much of meaning is private and never made explicit during the act of speech. On the one hand, such inner life is often maximally expressive, although barely reciprocated unless the addressee picks up the cue of gesture, intonation, and so forth. On the other hand, some of the most trenchant communication involves the combination of one spoken pronoun with paralinguistic features of body movement and intonation that would normally accompany the covert unspoken pronoun; thus, an explicit *vy* combined with paralinguistic *ty* (warmness of tone, and so forth), could often signal a felicitous union of personal respect and an affection whose strength was not mitigated by overt restraint; spoken *vy* when conjoined with the modulations and gestures usual for certain *ty* bonds could often signal revilement and disgust in the most painful manner. Unfortunately, the evidence being considered here does not permit many inferences of this sort, but, by the same token, the singular value of novels is that, unlike plays or psychological experiments, or most field work, they do provide evidence of what speakers would *think* in a variety of situations and status relationships.

Conclusions

Pronouns display unusual properties of emotional expressiveness, logical abstraction, and frequency in dialogue. Pronominal sets, like those of kinship terminology, are Janus-faced because linked into both the linguistic matrix of grammatical paradigms and the cultural matrix of social statuses and group categories. Among the many symbols of status in Russian, the second person singular pronouns were the most pervasive, frequent, and profound in their implications. Just two short words, operating in all speech events that involved two interlocutors, signaled the relative position of each pole in hundreds of dyadic relationships. Analysis of a representative sample of pronominal usage leads to the inference of a relational system of positional slots in the status system, and of other culturally specific categories. For Russian the categories which have to be postulated in order to predict pronominal usage more or less correlate with those inferred on the basis of external sociocultural evidence. The same, ego-oriented analysis of pronominal usage leads to the inference of discriminations or components that had to be controlled by the Russian in order to speak and understand. In the nineteenth century, at least, ten discriminations underlay the overwhelming mass of pronominal usage: topic of discourse, the context of the speech event, then age, generation, sex and kinship status, then dialect, group membership, and relative jural and political authority, and finally, emotional solidarity. All these discriminations, in modified form, also underlay the equally important symbolism of the kinship terminology. Such overlap of components in even these two semantic subsystems suggests that a continuing analysis of social structure would lead to an ever diminishing margin of discoveries of discriminations, which are probably quite limited in number. Also, about six to a dozen such discriminations probably underlie most systems with two pronouns. The ten discriminations with their patterns of combination constitute the stable—though not static—system that accounts for nearly all the evidence and predicts with accuracy the usage in new texts.

The Russian usage was further characterized by a great deal of switching, by sudden changes of pronoun during a conversation or new encounter. Precisely because it depends on addition, loss, or realignment of discriminations, switching gives invaluable evidence on relative or hierarchical order. But while many important relationships between discriminations can be inferred, the total network is less accessible. This is partly just because some evidence is lacking. Moreover, a decision as to the relative status of any two discriminations can only be made within realistic contexts that involve several others; the total number of such possible combinations is very high. In addition, graphs of the relations between discriminations would only be valid if made for precisely defined dyadic pairs in precisely defined contexts; the axes would have to specify many subdivisions of the ten discriminations used above.

Switching and what I have called "pronominal breakthrough" was interesting also because motivated by an interplay of the aforementioned cultural principles with what were essentially psychological forces of hostility, affection, ambivalence, mental derangement, and the like; the role of emotion was comparatively great in Russian life. Insight into the psychology of pronominal usage may be had, not only from switching, but from the expressive or latent use of *ty*, particularly when the speaker reverts to the informal pronoun. In many cases provided by the realistic novel and experienced by any normal Russian, the informal pronoun was encoded mentally, often embedded in phrases of love or hate, even while the formal pronoun was being articulated in a more or less different context. I take this to be but an accessible instance of the more general phenomenon whereby people think or feel one continuous message while enunciating a second string of overt forms. The content of the two messages can range from virtual identity to total divergence. A linguistic theory which boldly exploits all available evidence and intuitions about such concomitant inner speech and other "psychological" phenomena will not only have grappled with some of the most challenging experience but be capable as well of predicting future events more fully and realistically.[16]

References to Russian Sources

Akskov, Sergej T., 1958, *Semejnaja Khronika* ("A Family Chronicle"). Moscow:Gos. Iz. Khud Lit.

Dahl, V., 1880–1882, *Tolkovyj Solvar' Russkogo Jazyka*. Petersburg, Moscow.

Dostojevsky, Fedor M., 1951, *Prestuplenije i Nakazanije* ("Crime and Punishment"). *Selo Stepanchikogo i ego Obitateli* ("Stepanchiko Village"), pt. I. Cambridge: University Press.

Gogol, Nikolaj V., 1947, *Mertvyje Dushi* ("Dead Souls"). Poema. Moscow: Ogiz Goslitizdat.

Gorki, Maksim, 1947, *Detstvo* ("Childhood"). Moscow, Leningrad: Gos. Iz. Det. Lit.

———, 1946, *Izbrannyje Sochinenija* ("Selected Works," including "Mother"). Moscow: Ogiz. Gos. Iz. Khud. Lit.

Isachenko, A. V., 1960, *Morfologicheskij Stroj Russkogo Jazyka,* vol. II. Bratislavo.

Lermontov, Mikhajl Ju., 1948, *Geroj Nashego Vremeni* ("A Hero of Our Time"). Moscow, Leningrad: Gos. Iz. Det. Lit.

Pushkin, Aleksandr S., 1949, 'Stantsionnyj Smotritel' ("The Station Master"), pp. 86–97 in *Polnoe Sobranie Sochinenij v shesti tomakh*. Moscow: Gos. Iz. Khud. Lit.

Saltykov-Shchedrin, M. E., 1958, *Gospoda Golovlevy* ("The Golovlyov Family"). Moscow: Gos. Iz. Khud. Lit.

Sholokhov, Mikhajl, 1959, *Tikhij Don* ("The Quiet Don"). 2 vols. Moscow: Gos. Iz. Khud. Lit.

Sologub, Fjodor, 1961, *V Plenu* ("In Bondage"). In *Russian Stories—Russkije Rasskazy,* Gleb Struve (ed.). New York: Bantam Books.

Tolstoy, Lev, 1960a, *Voskresenije* ("Resurrection"). Moscow: Gos. Iz. Khud. Lit.

———, 1960b, *Detstvo. Ostrochestvo. Junost'* ("Childhood," "Boyhood," "Youth"). Leningrad: Gos. Iz. Det. Lit.

Zlatovratsky, N N., 1947, *Izbrannyje Proizvedenija* ("Selected Works"). Moscow: O. Giz.

[16] I stand gratefully indebted to Roger Brown and Albert Gilman, whose brilliant article (Brown and Gilman 1960) inspired the present effort, and to Joshua Fishman for valuable points of method, to Marlys Wendell for stylistic criticisms, and to Gertrude Vakar for many comments on both style and content. Above all, I wish to thank Julian Pitt-Rivers and Nicholas Vakar for their pervasive comments at all levels. Earlier versions of this chapter were presented to the Chicago Society for Slavic and South Asian Linguistics and Poetics, to Milton Singer's class on the Philosophy of Culture, and to the Los Angeles Conference on Sociolinguistics; many persons in these audiences provided helpful points. Finally, the present research was partly supported by a grant from the Department of Health, Education and Welfare under the National Defense Education Act.

10

Remarks on Ethnomethodology[1]

HAROLD GARFINKEL

Harold Garfinkel is a professor of sociology at the University of California, Los Angeles. He received his doctorate from Harvard University. His research for many years has been concerned with "common sense" knowledge of social structure, and with practical reasoning, as found in a variety of experimental and institutional settings. The material discussed here is drawn from a paper, much of which is incorporated in the first chapter of his book *Studies in Ethnomethodology* (1967). It outlines some of the basic assumptions about communication and social science methodology which underlie the work of Sacks and Schegloff in the following two chapters.

As the first part of the name suggests, ethnomethodology has ties both with ethnology and linguistics and with philosophy. In some respects, it is the counterpart within sociology of ethnographic semantics and ethnoscience (see Frake, Chapter 3; Sturtevant 1964; Colby 1966; Tyler 1969). The second part of its name indicates the point of difference. Ethnography and ethnomethodology share a methodological stance in that both give primacy to explicating the competence or knowledge of members of a culture, the unstated assumptions which determine their interpretation of experience.

[1] The investigations were supported by Senior Research Fellowship SF-81 from the U.S. Public Health Service, Grant Q-2 from the Research Section of the California State Department of Mental Hygiene, and project AF-AFOSR-757-65 of the Behavioral Sciences Division of the Air Force Office of Scientific Research. I am indebted to Michael Mend and Patricia Allen, graduate students, for their aid with the clinic studies; to Eleanor B. Sheldon for suggesting the format of and for her interest in the reliability study; and to Lindsey Churchill and Harvey Sacks for conversations about these materials. Obviously, they are not responsible for the chapter's deficiencies.

Like the descriptive linguists of the 1930s or 1940s, both insist on the need for more intensive and systematic empirical research into the nature of basic cognitive processes, and by implication they are critical of social science measurement which neglects to show how the researcher's categories relate to the actor's perceptions of what takes place. But whereas ethnographic semanticists deal with members' knowledge primarily through folk terminologies (as does Frake in Chapter 3), Garfinkel takes a much broader and, consequently, also less formal approach to communicative acts. His main concern is with the interpretative processes which underlie these acts, be they verbal or nonverbal. Meaning for him is "situated meaning," that is, meaning constructed in specific contexts by actors who must actively interpret what they hear for it to make sense. Garfinkel points out that humans everywhere, whether in foreign cultures or our own, whether laymen or social scientists, rely on the fundamental procedures he illustrates. Methodology for him, therefore, is more than the way the study is done; it is part of what there is to study as well.

The two case studies, each concerned with demonstrating a kind of impossibility, make the distinctive character of ethnomethodology clear. In one sense, the first study, concerned with coding procedures in a psychiatric clinic, is a straightforward study in ethnographic semantics. What are the categories by which those in the clinic, as well as those studying the clinic, segment the universe in question; what are the criteria by which instances are assigned to the categories? For Garfinkel, the essential point is that the categorization is not automatic but an open-ended process that entails operations not provided for in the classification or, indeed, in any stated set of procedures for using the classification. These apparently "ad hoc" operations (called here "ad hocing") are commonly invoked unconsciously. When they are brought to attention, the ordinary response is to consider them defects to be remedied or removed. (The clinic was distressed at the investigation's resulting specification of procedures actually used in classifying patients, and would not allow it to be reproduced as part of the study, except with a clear warning on its cover that it was not the official specification, and not to be consulted in place

of it). Garfinkel contends that the ad hoc operations cannot be remedied or removed (although they can be ignored). Similarly, those engaged in coding from the clinic records (i.e., translating the language of these records into social science categories suitable for formal statistical analysis), found it impossible to follow their coding instructions without resorting to ad hocing.

The second study set students the task of explaining a brief conversation reported by one of them. The students became convinced that each successive attempt at description was insufficient and, finally, that no total description could be made. Again there is a tie with ethnography, specifically the ethnography of speaking; Garfinkel explains that the students found the task impossible because, as would most social scientists, they took the task to be one of remedying the sketchiness of the conversation by elaborating its contents, by appealing outside the speech event to what became, under prodding, an infinite regress of context. Their error was to assume a theory of signs in which the way something is said is divorced from what is being said (form vs. content), and in concentrating on the "what," neglecting the "how." In fact, the conversation (like any conversation) was an instance of one or more alternative ways of speaking; it was intelligible to its participants not because of some shared infinity of substantive knowledge as to what was being talked about but in the first instance because they agreed at the time on how the talking was being done and how it was to be interpreted. The fact that such momentary agreements can be reached, however, does not mean that content can be reconstructed later under different conditions.

The insistence that speaking has a form beyond that of grammar; that a simple semantic, or referential, perspective is inadequate to explaining intelligibility; that intelligibility depends upon the way in which something is said, inseparable from what is being said; in short, that members of a speech community share knowledge of ways of speaking as well as of grammar, that communication requires sociolinguistics as well as semantics—all this is common ground. Garfinkel, however, again goes beyond an ethnographic approach. While recommending the study of ways of speaking (and listing illustrations, such as narrating, lying, and gossiping), he does not stop to consider them in detail. For him the essential point is that rules of speaking also ultimately run afoul of "the essential incompleteness of *any* set of instructions." Common understanding is never simply *recognition* of shared contents or rules, but it is always open-ended, brought about in any given case because participants bring it about as their "artful (if unconscious) accomplishment." Ad hocing remains the ultimate concern. People understand each other because "for the while" they assume the reasonableness of each other's statements and impute and construct reasonableness, where needed, out of often fragmentary data.

Here is the fundamental contention of Garfinkel's work: that the orderliness, rationality, accountability of everyday life is, as he puts it, a "contingent, ongoing accomplishment," a kind of "work," or "doing." Any occasion whatsoever provides material. "Methodology" thus refers to modes of practical reasoning *used by researcher and subject alike*. It is these modes of reasoning that should be the first order of business in social research. The basis of culture, Garfinkel suggests, is not shared knowledge, but shared rules of interpretation; not common substantive information, already acquired, but "common sense" knowledge of what can count as reasonable, factual, related, and the like. [Cf. Wallace's (1961) related view of culture as not "replication of uniformity" but "organization of diversity." See also Goodenough 1964]

The emphasis on culture as interpretative rules shows a certain parallel to transformational-generative grammar, a parallel which is made explicit by Cicourel (1970), who sees social structure as akin to deep structure (see also Blom and Gumperz, Chapter 14). Just as speakers are held to be masters of a grammatical knowledge that they employ, fluently and largely unwittingly, a kind of "rule-governed creativity," largely free from stimulus control (Chomsky 1968), so here speakers are held to be masters of a speaking knowledge, employed fluently, unwittingly, and creatively. For Garfinkel, indeed the common sense knowledge with which he is concerned is that of "members," *member* being used as a technical term to refer to mastery of a natural language, where language includes not only grammar but also its use. And, just as for Chomsky, the resolution of other questions in linguistics is held to depend on characterizing the grammatical competence of speakers, if not, in fact, on discovering its basis in universal human nature. Garfinkel's project might be said to be the discovery of the human world view, at least its epistemological component.

There are differences from generative grammar as well. Ethnomethodology might agree that the partial or "degenerate" nature of much of the speech encountered by the child argues against sheer learning as an explanation of the child's rapid acquisition of grammatical structure; it would agree in rejecting the empiricist or descriptivist view that "text signals its own structure"; but it would not see the ancillary character of speech as merely an obstacle but rather as part of the knowledge the child must acquire. What, for grammarians, may be data not worth saving—clipped, elliptical, incomplete sentences— may be for the ethnomethodologist the precise way of accomplishing some particular thing that is being said. One reason for this is the ethnomethodologists' contextual emphasis (i.e., the concern with the dependence of data on contexts created both by participants and by the investigator, which is lacking in most linguistics). For an anthropological view of communication akin to that of Garfinkel, see Bateson's Cybernetic Explanation (1967).

A further difference, between this approach and linguistic and ethnographic theory, may lie in the relation between particular studies and universal properties. At the particular level a parallel would hold, as we have seen, inasmuch as the data are understood as underlaid by mental capacities of the participants, and as being the product of these capacities. In linguistic theory, the adequacy of particular descriptions is tied to the adequacy of a general theory of the nature of language ["explanatory adequacy" (Chomsky 1965)]. Ethnomethodology also bases itself in a conception of the nature of language (recall the definition of the key term *members*), but it is not clear, at least at this time, that for it the study of universal properties might undergird particular studies, constraining the number of alternative analyses possible, and even deciding among them—in short, discovering behind the infinity of possible sentences and the diversity of languages a finite mechanism. The universality envisaged in ethnomethodology would seem to underlie particular studies in two not clearly compatible ways.

On the one hand, it is argued that investigators themselves make unwitting use of processes that are intrinsic to that which they study. The recommendation here would seem to be that to avoid a vicious circularity, one must make ways of speaking and practical reasoning objects of explicit simultaneous study. Ethnographers, for example, obtain and interpret information by learning ways of communicating appropriately in a community. Those ways of speaking are normally regarded as means to an end and forgotten, except in anecdotes, but should be described. Rather than take what is said only as a sign of a content somewhere else (in some ethnological category), ethnographers should learn the lesson of Garfinkel's students and study the ways of speaking on which their verbal information depends. One might envisage some general theory of ways of speaking to which ethnographers would contribute and on which they would draw.

However, the universality and ubiquity of methodological phenomena leads to the view that it is not possible to remedy or repair the presence of practical reasoning in investigations. One gains the impression that all the investigator can do is to collect and exhibit instances. Quite possibly, this posture of extreme empiricism—reminiscent of the descriptive linguists—is merely a passing phase, which will disappear with the accumulation of more properly documented case studies.

While pointing out, on the one hand, that the task of formulating ways of speaking is infinite, Garfinkel calls attention, on the other hand, to some highly general and most probably universal processes through which meaning is conveyed in natural conversation. These are: that ways of speaking are essentially *indexical* (like pronouns), in the sense that part of their meaning and intelligibility always will lie in the situation in which they occur and in the association this situation evokes in the participants' minds; they are *reflexive*, in the sense that the operations in question are part of all speaking and making sense, so that an inquiry into them is itself always a new, as yet unanalyzed instance—the student of the "glossing practices" of others himself must employ some; and they are *open-ended* in that the sense that what is happening now can always be taken to depend upon, be revisable in the light of, what happens later. Instances of this last property, indeed, are favorite "representative anecdotes" to use Kenneth Burke's (1945:59–61, 323–325) apt term; e.g., "Rose's gloss": In this practice Professor Rose, visiting a city for the very first time, while being driven from the airport by his host, "does" [looking ahead] and [watching something go by], and then remarks, "It certainly has changed." His host's reply tells Rose what he has been talking about. [The quotation marks and brackets adapt conventions established by Garfinkel and Sacks (1969)]. Analogous practices indeed are known in the interpretation of literature, as in I. A. Richard's (1955:17–56) proposal that question marks be used to bracket some initial piece of talk or text (e.g., ?analogous practices?) as indication that how it is to be comprehended is to be left for decision or review later. A related practice is known in biblical studies as *typology,* referring to the procedures by which New Testament writers interpret the Old Testament past in the light of the present, "for now they see clearly the true significance of what had formerly been discerned only dimly," and by which Old Testament writers as well "had interpreted the meaning of God's action in the past in the light of their understanding of later events" (Richardson 1964:178–179). For ethnomethodology, this family of practices is essential to the rationality of everyday life.

The spirit of ethnomethodology is exactly that of the sociolinguistics with which we are concerned in many respects—the insistence that the number and kinds of ways of speaking are problematic and to be discovered; that analysis begin within the data of speech events themselves; and that a person's speaking competence is not passive or mechanical, but part of strategies for the encompassing of situations (cf. Burke 1941).

Garfinkel's ultimate concern with common sense knowledge and practical reasoning is invaluable in making one realize that the study of speaking entails issues central to contemporary philosophical perspectives. It is work stimulated by phenomenology through Alfred Schutz (1962, 1966, 1967), and has recognized affinity with the later Wittgenstein (1953), as well as with the late Scot philosopher Sinclair (1951), who has also influenced Kenneth Pike's (1967) approach to an integrated view of language as part of behavior. The concern with what is known and the conditions of knowing it in the human sciences is of a kind with methodological questions raised from a variety of starting points—ordinary language philosophy [e.g., Hare 1963; Hampshire 1967; cf. 114, 234; Marxist existentialism (or existentialist Marxism) in Sartre 1963 (and cf. LeFebvre 1966); Protestant and Catholic theology (Ebeling 1966; Kaspar 1969; Mascall 1968)]. Each shares with ethnomethodology a concern to deal with human thought and action as concrete, situated, yet going beyond the situation; each examines received categories and practices found inadequate to human experience; but each, while recognizing human experience as necessarily outrunning determinate knowledge, is concerned with a structure of knowledge that can be established, as, in its own field, is sociolinguistic study of ways of speaking.

Rose's gloss provides an illustration. Whether or not it is an adequate "representative anecdote," it is clear that it would not work in the same way in all situations. In some, as in the one described, it would pass unremarked; in some, it would be remarked as unusual, odd, or specially expressive; in some it would not be regarded as interpretable at all—at least it would be taken as not related to the situation at all. In the first case, it would be odd to remark on what had been said; in the second, what has been said would be literally remarkable (i.e., worth retelling); in the third, response might range from open questioning to silent head shaking. A fourth possibility, of course, is absence of response because the remark, being uninterpretable, goes unnoticed. (These categories are adapted from work of William Labov.) Even if the remark could always be potentially "glossed" [given the (good) will], by finding some explanation for an unrelated or uninterpretable remark to have been made, existence of the possibility does not mean it will be acted upon.

To pass over these four kinds of relation between

speaking and situation is to overshoot the heart of sociolinguistic research into the structure of discourse. It is in
terms of such research, indeed, that recourse to a particular glossing practice, e.g., one of last resort ("Well, he
must have some reason for saying that, though now's no
time to ask what it is"), could be accounted for. Two
things must be stressed: (1) Rules of interpretation (including glossing practices) can always be used to tran-
scend determinate rules of speaking in the narrower
sense, but need not be; and it is essential to discover
where the boundary lies in a community, such that to find
some particular thing interpretable in part puts one outside the community's norms of interpretation, (2) Rules
of interpretation apply through, or incorporate, determinate rules of speaking, and use of one is not intelligible
without knowledge of the other. In short, ethnomethodology goes beyond most sociolinguistic research, but presupposes and stimulates it, as Sacks and
Schegloff (Chapters 11 and 12) will show. Though its notion of social categories is akin to semantic rules, it also
offers a potentially highly useful methodological framework for integrating linguistic and social phenomena.
Additional related readings are provided by Duncan
(1968), Hill and Crittenden (1968), Postal (1968), Sapir
(1949c), Kramer, Goldstein, Israel, and Johnson (1956),
and Quentin Skinner (1970).

I use the term *ethnomethodology* to refer to various policies,
methods, results, risks, and lunacies with which to locate and accomplish
the study of the rational properties of practical actions as contingent
ongoing accomplishments of organized artful practices of everyday life.
Given strongly enforced limitations of space and stronger ones on patience, I found the peaks of recommending these studies with detailed,
descriptive arguments beyond my skill. I therefore took as the limited
purpose of this chapter to characterize ethnomethodology.[2] I have done
this by presenting two studies and a concluding recitation of policies. It is

[2] For detailed studies, see Garfinkel (1967), and Garfinkel and Sacks (in press); a further
characterization of ethnomethodology, with introduction to detailed studies, is in Garfinkel
and Sacks (1969).

possible to develop the central theme if the reader treats each section as a guide to deepen and point up the others. The first study deals with following coding instructions; the second with common understanding.

Following Coding Instructions

Several years ago we undertook to analyze the experience of the UCLA Outpatient Psychiatric Clinic in order to answer the question: "By what criteria are its applicants selected for treatment?" To formulate and answer this question, we used a variation of a method of cohort analysis that Kramer and his associates (1956) had recommended to describe load and flow characteristics of patients in mental hospitals. Successive activities of "contact," "intake interview," "psychological testing," "intake conference," "in-treatment," and "termination" were conceived with the use of the tree diagram of Fig. 10.1. Any path from first contact

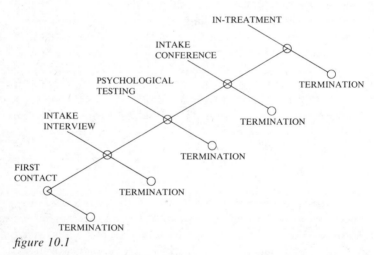

figure 10.1

Career paths of patients of a psychiatric clinic.

to termination was called a "career." We wished to know what characteristics of patients, of clinic personnel, of their interactions, and of the tree were associated with which careers. Clinic records were our sources of information, the most important of which were intake application forms, and contents of case folders. In order to obtain a continuing record of patient-clinic transactions from the time of a patient's initial contact until he terminated, a "Clinic Career Form" was designed and inserted into case folders. Because clinic folders contain records that clinic personnel provide of their own activities, almost all of these sources of data were the results of self-reporting procedures.

Two graduate students in sociology at UCLA examined some 1500 clinic folders for the information to complete the items of a coding sheet. A conventional reliability procedure was designed and run with the aim of determining the amount of agreement between coders and between successive trials of their coding. According to conventional reasoning, the amount of agreement furnishes one set of grounds for lending credence to coded events as actual events of clinic activities. A critical feature of conventional reliability assessments is that the agreement between coders consists of agreement on the end results.

To no one's surprise, preliminary work showed that in order to accomplish the coding, coders were assuming knowledge of the very organized ways of the clinic that their coding procedures were intended to produce descriptions of. More interestingly, such presupposed knowledge seemed necessary and was most deliberately consulted whenever, for whatever reasons, the coders needed to be satisfied that they had coded "what really happened" *regardless of whether or not they had encountered "ambiguous" folder contents.* Such a procedure undermined any claim that actuarial methods for interrogating folder contents had been used, no matter how apparently clear coding instructions were. Agreement in coding results was being produced by some other contrasting procedure with unknown characteristics.

To find out more about it, the reliability procedure was treated as a problematic activity in its own right. The "reliability" of coded results was addressed by asking how the coders had actually brought folder contents under the jurisdiction of the coding sheet's item. Via what practices had actual folder contents been assigned the status of answers to the researcher's questions? What actual activities made up coders' practices called "following coding instruction"?

A procedure was designed that yielded conventional reliability information so that the original interests of the study were preserved. At the same time the procedure permitted the study of how any amount of agreement or disagreement had been produced by the actual ways that the two coders had gone about treating folder contents as answers to the questions formulated by the coding sheet. But, instead of assuming that coders, proceeding in whatever ways they did, might have been in error, in greater or lesser amount, the assumption was made that *whatever* they did could be counted correct procedure in *some* coding game. The question was, what were these "games"? How *ever* coders did it, it was sufficient to produce whatever they got. How did they do it to get what they got?

We soon found the essential relevance to the coders of such considerations as: "et cetera," "unless," "let it pass," and "factum valet."[3]

For convenience call these considerations "ad hoc," and call their use in the coder's work of interrogating contents for answers to their questions "ad hocing." Coders used these same ad hoc considerations in order to recognize the relevance of the coding instructions to the organized activities of the clinic. Only when this relevance was clear were the coders satisfied that the coding instructions did analyze actually encountered folder contents in such a way as to permit the coders to treat folder contents as reports of "real events." Finally, ad hoc considerations were an invariant ineradicable part of "following coding instructions." Attempts to suppress them while retaining an unequivocal sense to the instructions produced coders' bewilderment.

Various facets of the "new" reliability study were then developed, at first, in order to see if these results could be firmly established, and after it was clear, to my satisfaction, that they could, to exploit their consequences for the general sociological character of the coders' methods of interrogation (as well as contrasting methods) as well as for the work that is involved in recognizing or claiming that something had been done by rule—that an action had followed or had been "governed" by instructions.

Ad hoc considerations are invariably relevant considerations in deciding the fit between what could be read from the clinic folders and what the coder inserted into the coding sheet. No matter how definitely and

---

[3] These considerations are quite generally found when professionals—sociologists, anthropologists, linguists, whosoever—make use of instructions, formulas, rules, and the like. There is always an implicit additional section to such statements, one that might be headed: "practical advice to whomsoever might seek to insure the usefulness of the instructions (formulas, etc.) to analyze the situations." Professionals in effect claim the right to make out a situation so as to see that a rule, or description, or the like is right. They claim such rights and assign them to each other by reason of common membership in a profession. This implicit practical advice consists of the things that need not be stated, yet are expected, and which to ask about may define one as *not* a member of the profession, the things that anyone (in the profession) knows.

"Et cetera" refers to the piece of implicit practical advice that runs: "Read it like this, '. . .' *and so forth*", i.e., to see the rule, if you understand the rule, you presumably can recognize other circumstances and cases of its application without all of them being stated here. "Unless" refers to a second piece of advice: "Read the rule so as to include, as part of what it is talking about, any and all considerations of *unless,* considerations which any member knows need not and cannot be cited before they are needed, though no member is at a loss when the need is clear. That is, you presumably can recognize circumstances and cases to which no one in their right (professional) mind would take the rule as applying, though not stated." "Let it pass" refers to the advice that runs: "In the course of seeing that a rule applies, the use of *and so forth* and *unless* can introduce any matter whatsoever, thereby raising questions of where any of it ought appropriately to begin or end. Read the rule, therefore, with the proviso, 'Let it pass,' or 'Enough is enough, as anyone knows,' we have to get done." Finally, *factum valet* is, I understand, a medieval term that means that an action that is otherwise prohibited by a rule is to be treated as correct; it happens nevertheless. (Based on Garfinkel 1966.)

elaborately instructions had been written, and despite the fact that strict actuarial coding rules[4] *could* be formulated for every item, and with which folder contents *could* be mapped into the coding sheet, insofar as the claim had to be advanced that coding sheet entries reported real events of the clinic's activities, then in every instance, and for every item, "et cetera," "unless," "let it pass," and *"factum valet"* accompanied the coder's grasp of the coding instructions as ways of analyzing actual folder contents. Their use made it possible as well for the coder to read a folder content as a report about the events that the coding sheet provided and formulated as events of the processing tree.

Ordinarily researchers treat such ad hoc procedures as flawed ways of writing, recognizing, or following coding instructions. The prevailing view holds that good work requires researchers, by extending the number and explicitness of their coding rules, to minimize or even eliminate the occasions in which "et cetera" and the others would be used.

To treat instructions as though ad hoc features in their use was a nuisance, or to treat their presence as grounds for complaint about the incompleteness of instructions, is very much like complaining that if the walls of a building were only gotten out of the way, one could see better what was keeping the roof up.

Our studies show that ad hoc considerations are essential features of coding procedures. Ad hocing is required if the researcher is to grasp the relevance of the instructions to the particular and actual situation they are intended to analyze. For every particular and actual occasion of search, detection, and assignment of folder contents to a "proper" category— which is to say, over the course of actually coding—such ad hoc considerations have irremediable priority over the usually talked about "necessary and sufficient" criteria. Rather than it being the case that the "necessary and sufficient" criteria are procedurally defined by coding instructions, and rather than it being the case that ad hoc procedures are controlled in their presence, use, number, or occasion of use by making coding instructions as definite as possible, ad hoc considerations are consulted by coders, and ad hocing practices are used in order to recognize what the instructions are definitely talking about. Ad hoc considerations are consulted by coders in order to recognize coding as "operational definitions" of coding categories. They operate as the ground for and as methods to advance and secure researchers' claims to have coded in accordance with "necessary and sufficient" criteria.

We do not have strong evidence, though we do have some demonstrable grounds for pursuing the hunch, that the work of ad hocing occurs without possibility of remedy whenever the coder assumes the position of

---

[4] David Harrah's (1961) model of an information-matching game was taken to define the meaning of "strict actuarial method for interrogating."

a socially competent member of the arrangement that he seeks to assemble an account of, and from this "position" treats actual folder contents as standing in a relationship of trusted signification to the "system" in the clinic activities. We think that it is because the coder assumes the "position" of a competent member to the arrangements that he seeks to give an account of, and that he can "see the system" in the actual content in something like the way that we must know the orderly ways of English usage in order to recognize an utterance as a work-in-English or know the rules of a game to make out a move-in-a-game—given that alternative ways of making out an utterance or a board play are always imaginable. Thereby the coder recognizes the folder content for "what it actually is," or can "see what a note in the folder is really talking about."

Given this, then the coder, if he has to be satisfied that he has detected a real clinic occurrence, must treat actual folder contents as standing proxy for the social-order-in-and-of-clinic-activities. Actual folder contents stand to the socially ordered ways of clinic activities as *representations* of them; they do not describe the order, nor are they evidences of the order. It is the coder's use of folder documents as *sign functions* to which I mean to be pointing in saying that the coder knows the order of the clinic's activities that he is looking at to be able to recognize the actual content as an appearance-of-the-order. Once the coder can "see the system" in the content, it is possible for the coder to extend and to otherwise interpret the coding instructions—to ad hoc them—so as to maintain the relevance of the coding instructions to the actual contents, and in this way to formulate the sense of actual content so that its meaning, even though it is transformed by the coding, is preserved in the coder's eyes as a real event of the clinic's actual activities.

There are several important consequences of this.

1. Characteristically, coded results are treated as if they were *disinterested descriptions* of clinic events, and coding rules are presumed to back up the claim of *disinterested description*. But if the work of ad hocing is required to make such claims intelligible, it can always be argued—and so far I do not see a defensible reply—that the coded results consist of a *persuasive version* of the socially organized character of the clinic's operations regardless of what the actual order is, perhaps independently of what the actual order is, and even without our having detected the actual order. This is to say that instead of our study of patients' clinic careers, as well as the multitude of studies of various social arrangements that have been carried out in similarly conventional ways, having described the order of the clinic's operations, the account may be argued to consist of a socially invented, persuasive, and proper way of talking about the clinic as an orderly enterprise since "after all" the account was produced by "scientific procedures." The account would be itself part of the actual

order of the clinic's operations in much the same way that one might treat a person's report on his own activities as a feature of his activities. The actual order would remain to be described.

2. Another consequence arises when we ask what is to be made of the care that nevertheless is too assiduously exercised in the design and use of coding instructions for interrogating actual contents and transforming them into the language of the coding sheet? If the resulting account is a feature of the clinic's activities, then one ought not perhaps to read the coding instructions as a way of obtaining a scientific description of the clinic's activities since this assumes that the coding language, in what it is talking *about,* is independent of the interests of the members that are being served in using it. *Coding instructions ought to be read instead as consisting of a grammar of rhetoric; of furnishing a "social science" way of talking to persuade consensus and action within the practical circumstances* of the clinic's organized daily activities, a grasp of which members are expected to have as a matter of course. By referring to an account of the clinic that was obtained by following coding instructions, it is possible for members with different interests to persuade each other and to reconcile their talk about clinic affairs in an impersonal way, while the matters that are really being talked *about* retain their sense for the "discussants" as a legitimate or illegitimate, a desirable or undesirable, an advantaged or disadvantaged state of affairs for the discussants in their occupational lives. It furnishes an impersonal way of characterizing their affairs without the members relinquishing important organizationally determined interests in what the account, in their eyes, is "after all" all about. What it is all about is the clinic order whose real features, as any member knows that "anyone knows," are always none of somebody-else-in-that-organization's business.

Common Understanding and Ways of Talking

Sociologists distinguish the "product" from the "process" meanings of a common understanding. As "product," a common understanding consists of a shared agreement on substantive matters; as "process," it consists of various methods whereby something that a person says or does is recognized to accord with a rule. With his concepts of *Begreifen* and *Verstehen,* each with its distinct character as method and knowledge, Weber provided sociologists an authority for this distinction.

An analysis of students' experiences in reporting commonplace conversation suggests that for either case, for product or process, a common understanding consists of an inner-temporal course of interpretive work. Their experiences suggest some strange consequences of the facts that *in either case* a common understanding has necessarily an *operational* structure. (See the last paragraph of this section.)

Students were asked to report common conversations by writing on the left side of a sheet what the parties actually said and on the right side what they and their partners understood that they were talking about. A student reported the following colloquy between himself and his wife:

HUSBAND:	Dana succeeded in putting a penny in a parking meter today without being picked up.	This afternoon as I was bringing Dana, our four-year-old son, home from the nursery school, he succeeded in reaching high enough to put a penny in a parking meter when we parked in a meter zone, whereas before he had always had to be picked up to reach that high.
WIFE:	Did you take him to the record store?	Since he put a penny in a meter that means that you stopped while he was with you. I know that you stopped at the record store either on the way to get him or on the way back. Was it on the way back, so that he was with you or did you stop there on the way to get him and somewhere else on the way back?
HUSBAND:	No, to the shoe repair shop.	No, I stopped at the record store on the way to get him and stopped at the shoe repair shop on the way home when he was with me.
WIFE:	What for?	I know of one reason why you might have stopped at the shoe repair shop. Why did you in fact?
HUSBAND:	I got some new shoe laces for my shoes.	As you will remember I broke a shoe lace on one of my brown oxfords the other day so I stopped to get some new laces.

WIFE:	Your loafers need new heels badly.	Something else you could have gotten that I was thinking of. You could have taken in your black loafers which need heels badly. You'd better get them taken care of pretty soon.

Students filled out the left side of the sheet quickly and easily, but found the right side incomparably more difficult. When the assignment was made, many asked how much I wanted them to write. As I progressively imposed accuracy, clarity, and distinctness, the task became increasingly laborious. Finally, when I required that they assume I would know what they had actually talked about only from reading literally what they wrote literally, they gave up with the complaint that the task was impossible.

Although their complaints were concerned with the laboriousness of having to write "more," the frustrating "more" was not made up of the large labor of having to reduce a mountain with buckets. It was not their complaint that what was talked about consisted of bounded contents made so vast by pedantry that they lacked sufficient time, stamina, paper, drive, or good reason to write "all of it." Instead, the complaint and its circumstances seemed to consist of this: *If* for whatever a student wrote I was able to persuade him that it was not yet accurate, distinct, or clear enough, and *if* he remained willing to repair the ambiguity, then he returned to the task with the complaint that the writing itself developed the conversation as a branching texture of relevant matters. The very *way* of accomplishing the task multiplied its features.

What task had I set them, such that it required that they write "more"; such that the progressive imposition of accuracy, clarity, and literalness made it increasingly difficult and finally impossible; and such that the way of accomplishing the task multiplied its features? If a common understanding consisted of shared agreement on substantive matter, their task would have been identical with one that professional sociologists supposedly address. The task would have been solved as professional sociologists are apt to propose its solution, as follows:

Students would first distinguish *what* was said from *what* was talked about, and set the two contents into a correspondence of sign and referent. *What the parties said* would be treated as a sketchy, partial, incomplete, masked, elliptical, concealed, ambiguous, or misleading version of *what the parties talked about*. The task would consist of filling out the sketchiness of what was said. What was talked about would consist of elaborated and corresponding contents of what the parties said. Thus the format of left- and right-hand columns would accord with the "fact" that the contents of what was said were recordable by writing what a tape recorder would pick up. The right-hand column would require that something "more" be "added." Because the sketchiness of what was said was its defect, it would be necessary for students to look elsewhere than to what was said in order (a) to find the corresponding contents, and (b) to find the grounds to argue for—because they would need to argue—the correctness of the correspondence. Because they were reporting the actual conversation of particular persons, they would look for these further contents in what the conversationalists had "in mind," or what they were "thinking," or what they "believed," or what they "intended."

They would need further to be assured that they had detected what the conversationalists actually and not supposedly, hypothetically, imaginably, or possibly had in mind, which is to say that they would need to cite observed actions—observed ways that the parties conducted themselves —in order to furnish grounds for the claim of "actually." This assurance would be obtained by seeking to establish the presence in the conversationalists' relationship of warranting virtues such as their having spoken honestly, openly, candidly, sincerely and the like. All of which is to say that students would invoke their knowledge of the community of understandings, their knowledge of shared agreements, in order to recommend the adequacy of their accounts of what the parties had been talking about, i.e., what the parties understood in common. Then, for anything the students wrote, they could assume that I, as a competent comember of the same community (the conversations were after all commonplace) should be able to see the correspondence and its grounds. If I did not see the correspondence or if I made out the contents differently than they did, then as long as they could continue to assume my competence—i.e., as long as my alternative interpretations did not undermine my right to claim that such alternatives needed to be taken seriously by them and by me—I could be made out by the students as insisting that they furnish me with finer detailing than practical considerations required. In such a case, they should have charged me with blind pedantry and should have complained that because "anyone can see" when, for all practical purposes, enough is enough, none are so blind as those who *will* not see.

This version of their task accounts for their complaints of having to write "more." It also accounts for the task's increasing laboriousness when clarity and the like were progressively imposed. But it does not account very well for the final impossibility, for it explained one facet of the task's "impossibility" as students' unwillingness to go any further, but it does not explain an accompanying sense, namely, that students somehow saw that the task does not explain at all their complaint that the way of accomplishing the task multiplied its features.

An alternative conception of the task may do better. Although it may at first appear strange to do so, suppose we drop the assumption that in order to describe a usage as a feature of a community of understandings,

we must at the outset know of what the substantive common understanding consists. With it, drop the assumption's accompanying theory of
signs according to which a "sign" and "referent" are, respectively, properties of something said and something talked about, and that in this fashion proposes sign and referent to be related as corresponding contents.
By dropping such a theory of signs we drop thereby as well the possibility
that an invoked shared agreement on substantive matters explains a
usage.

If these notions are dropped, then what the parties talked about could
not be distinguished from how the parties were speaking. An explanation
of what the parties were talking about would then consist not of an account of what the parties had intended and not said entirely of describing
how the parties had been speaking; of furnishing a method for saying
whatever is to be said, like talking synonymously, talking ironically,
talking metaphorically, talking cryptically, talking narratively, talking in a
questioning or answering way, lying, glossing, double-talking, and the
rest.

In the place of, and in contrast to, a concern for a difference between
what was said and what was talked about, the appropriate difference is
between a speech-community member's recognition that a person is
saying something, i.e., that he was *speaking,* on the other hand, and *how*
he was speaking, on the other. Then the recognized sense of what a
person said consists only and entirely in recognizing the method of his
speaking, of seeing *how he spoke.*

I suggest that one not read the right-hand column as corresponding contents of the left, and that the students' task of explaining what the conversationalists talked about did not involve them in elaborating the contents
of what the conversationalists said. I suggest instead that their written
explanations consisted of their attempts to instruct me in how to use what
the parties said as a method for saying what the conversationalists said. I
suggest that I had asked the students to furnish me with instructions for
recognizing what the parties were actually and certainly saying. By persuading them of alternative "interpretations," by persuading them that
ambiguity remained, I had persuaded them that they had demonstrated to
me only what the parties were supposedly, or probably, or imaginably, or
hypothetically saying, *which they took to mean that their instructions
were incomplete; that their demonstrations failed by the extent to which
their instructions were incomplete; and that the difference between claims
of "actually" and "supposedly" depended on the completeness of the instructions.*

We now see what the task was that required them to write "more," that
they found increasingly difficult and finally impossible, and that became
elaborated in its features by the very procedures for doing it. I had set
them the task of formulating these instructions so as to make them

"increasingly" accurate, clear, distinct, and finally literal where the meanings of "increasingly" and of clarity, accuracy, distinctness, and literalness were supposedly explained in terms of the properties of the instructions themselves and the instructions alone. I had required them to take on the impossible task of "repairing" the essential incompleteness of *any* set of instructions no matter how carefully or elaborately written they might be. I had required them to formulate the method that the parties had used in speaking as rules of procedure to follow in order to say what the parties said. The rules were thus rules that would withstand every exigency of situation, imagination, and development. I had asked them to describe the parties' methods of speaking as if these methods were isomorphic with actions in strict compliance with a rule of procedure that formulated the method as an instructable matter. To recognize *what* is said *means* to recognize *how a person is speaking,* e.g., to recognize that the wife, in saying, "Your shoes need heels badly," was speaking narratively, or metaphorically, or euphemistically, or double-talking.

They stumbled over the fact that the question of how a person is speaking, the task of describing a person's method of speaking, is not satisfied by and is not the same as showing that what he said accords with a rule for demonstrating consistency, compatability, and coherence of meanings.

For the conduct of their everyday affairs, persons take for granted that what is said *will be made out* according to methods that the parties use to make out what they are saying for its clear, consistent, coherent, understandable, or planful character, i.e., as subject to some rule's jurisdiction —in a word, as rational. To see the "sense" of what is said is to accord to what was said its character "as a rule." "Shared agreement" refers to various social methods for accomplishing the member's *recognition* that something was said according to a rule and not the demonstrable matching of substantive matters. The appropriate image of a common understanding is, therefore, an *operation* rather than a common intersection of overlapping sets.

A person doing sociology—lay or professional—can treat a common understanding as a shared agreement on substantive matters by taking for granted that what is said will be made out in accordance with methods that need not be specified, which is to say that need only be specified on "special" occasions.

Given the discovering character of what the husband and wife were talking about, its recognizable character for both entailed the use by each and the attribution by each to the other of work whereby what was said is or will have been understood to have accorded with their relationship of interaction as invokable rule of their agreement, as an intersubjectively used grammatical scheme of analyzing each other's talk whose use provided that they *would* understand each other in ways that they *would* be understood. It provides that neither one was entitled to call upon the other to specify how it was being done, i.e., without either being entitled to claim that the other needed to "explain" himself.

In short, a common understanding, entailing as it does an "inner" temporal course of interpretive work, has necessarily an operational structure. To disregard its operational structure is to use common sense knowledge of the society in exactly the way that members use it when they must decide what persons are really doing or really "talking about," i.e., to use common sense knowledge of social structures as both a topic and a resource of inquiry. An alternative is to assign to the study of the methods of concerted actions and methods of common understanding exclusive priority. Not *a* method of understanding but immensely various methods of understanding are the professional sociologist's proper and hitherto unstudied and critical phenomena. Their multitude is indicated in the endless list of ways that persons speak. Some indication of their character and their differences occurs in the socially available glosses of a multitude of sign functions as when we take note of marking, labeling, symbolizing, emblemizing, cryptograms, analogies, anagrams, indicating, miniaturizing, imitating, mocking-up, simulating—in short, in recognizing, using, and producing the orderly ways of cultural settings from "within" those settings.[5]

Ethnomethodology

That practical actions are problematic in ways not so far seen; *how* they are problematic; how to make them accessible to study; what we might learn about them—these are proposed tasks. I use the term *ethnomethodology* to refer to the study of practical actions according to policies such as the following, and to the phenomena, issues, findings, and methods that accompany their use.

1. An indefinitely large domain of appropriate settings can be located if one uses a search policy that *any occasion whatsoever* be examined for the feature that "choice" among alternatives of sense, facticity, objectivity, cause, explanation, and communality *of practical actions* is a project of members' actions. With its use, inquiries of every imaginable kind from divination to theoretical physics thereby claim our interest as

---

[5] This note was touched off by Monroe Beardsley's remark (1962) to the effect that we do not decide that a word is used metaphorically because we know what a person is thinking; rather we know what he is thinking because we see that a word is used metaphorically. Taking poetry for his case, Beardsley points out that "the clues to this fact must somehow be in the poem itself, or we should seldom be able to read poetry."

socially organized artful practices. That the social structures of everyday activities furnish contexts, objects, resources, justifications, problematic topics, etc., to practices and products of inquiries establishes the eligibility for our interest of every way of doing inquiries without exception.

None can be excluded no matter where or when they occur, no matter how vast or trivial their scope, organization, cost, duration, consequences, whatever their successes, whatever their repute, their practitioners, their claims, their philosophies or philosophers. Procedures and results of water witching, divination, mathematics, sociology—whether done by lay persons or professionals—are addressed according to the policy that every feature of sense, of fact, of method for every particular case of inquiry without exception is the managed accomplishment of organized settings of practical actions, and that particular determinations in members' practices of consistency, planfulness, relevance, or reproducibility of their practices and results—from witchcraft to topology—are acquired and assured only through particular, located organizations of artful practices.

2. Members to an organized arrangement are continually engaged in having to decide, recognize, persuade, or make evident the rational, i.e., the coherent, or consistent, or chosen, or planful, or effective, or methodical, or knowledgeable character of such activities of their inquiries as counting, graphing, interrogation, sampling, recording, reporting, planning, decision making, and the rest. In order to describe how actual investigative procedures are accomplished as recognizedly rational actions *in actual occasions,* it is not satisfactory to say that members invoke some rule with which to define the coherent or consistent or planful, i.e., rational, character of their actual activities. Nor is it satisfactory to propose that the rational properties of members' inquiries are produced by members' compliance to rules of inquiry. Instead, "adequate demonstration," "adequate reporting," "sufficient evidence," "plain talk," "making too much of the record," "necessary inference," "frame of restricted alternatives," in short, every topic of "logic" and "methodology," including these two titles as well, are glosses for organizational phenomena. These phenomena are contingent achievements of organizations of common practices, and as contingent achievements, they are variously available to members as norms, tasks, and troubles, and only in these ways rather than as invariant categories or as general principles do they define "adequate inquiry and discourse."

3. Thus, a leading policy is to refuse serious consideration to the prevailing proposal that efficiency, efficacy, effectiveness, intelligibility, consistency, planfulness, typicality, uniformity, reproducibility of activities—i.e., rational properties of practical activities—be assessed, recognized, categorized, described by using a rule or a standard obtained

from somewhere outside actual settings within which such properties are recognized, used, produced, and talked about by settings' members. All procedures whereby logical and methodological properties of the practices and results of inquiries are assessed in their general characteristics by rule are of interest as *phenomena* for ethnomethodological study but not otherwise. Instead, structurally differing organized practical activities of everyday life are to be sought out and examined for the production, origins, recognition, and representations of rational practices. All "logical" and "methodological" properties of action, every feature of activity's sense, of its facticity, of its objectivity, of its accountability, of its communality, without exception is to be treated as a contingent accomplishment of socially organized common practices. In short, they are not given, but accomplished.

4. The policy is recommended that any setting be viewed as self-organizing with respect to the intelligible character of its own appearances as either representations of or as evidences-of-a-social-order. Any setting organizes its activities to make its properties as an organized environment of practical activities detectable, countable, recordable, reportable, tell-a-story-aboutable, analyzable—in short, *accountable*.

Organized arrangements consist of various methods for accomplishing the accountability of a settings' organizational ways as a concerted undertaking. Every claim by practitioners of effectiveness, clarity, consistency, planfulness, or efficiency, and every consideration for adequate evidence, demonstration, description, or relevance, obtains its character as a *phenomenon* from the corporate pursuit of this undertaking and from the ways in which various organizational environments by reason of their characteristics as organizations of activities "sustain," "facilitate," "resist," etc., these methods for making their affairs accountable-matters-for-all-practical-purposes.

In exactly the ways that a setting is organized, it consists of members' methods for making evident that settings' ways as clear, coherent, planful, consistent, chosen, knowable, and uniform, with reproducible connections—i.e., rational connections. In exactly the way that persons are members to organized affairs they are engaged in the serious and practical work of detecting, demonstrating, persuading through displays in the ordinary occasions of their interactions the appearances of consistent, coherent, clear, chosen, planful arrangements. In exactly the ways in which a setting is organized, it consists of methods whereby its members are provided with accounts of the setting as countable, storyable, proverbial, comparable, picturable, representable—i.e., accountable—events.

5. Every kind of inquiry without exception consists of organized, artful practices whereby the rational properties of proverbs, partially formulated advice, partial description, elliptical expressions, passing remarks,

fables, cautionary tales, and the like are made evident, are demonstrated. The demonstrable rationality of occasional expressions and occasional actions is an ongoing achievement of the organized activities of everyday life. Here is the heart of the matter. The managed production of this phenomenon in every aspect, from every perspective, and in every stage retains the character for members of serious, practical tasks, subject to every exigency of organizationally situated conduct.

11

On the Analyzability
of Stories by Children

HARVEY SACKS

Harvey Sacks is an associate professor of sociology at
the University of California, Irvine. He received his doctorate from the University of California, Berkeley, and has
taught at the University of California, Los Angeles. His
research has been concerned with natural conversation,
analyzed to discover how its structure and resources
reflect speakers' social knowledge. In the present
chapter, which contains material to be incorporated in
more detailed form in his recent book (Sacks 1971), he
develops a conceptual apparatus for the empirical study
of the specific ways in which what Garfinkel calls practical reasoning is used in everyday discourse.

   The initial observation is quite like that of grammar:
We understand sentences rapidly and unreflectingly in
terms of relationships that are not overtly expressed.
There must, therefore, be implicit kinds of knowledge in
terms of which this ability can be explained. Sacks deals
with material on which linguists have also worked—the
coherence of texts [how it is that sentences are heard as a
connected text and not as an arbitrary list (Hassan 1968)]
and the delimitation of semantic fields. But unlike the
linguists, who in their concern with literary style tend to
be concerned with texts per se, Sacks focuses specifically
on verbal exchanges between speakers. He studies the
semantic and theoretical strategies by which speakers
identify themselves or react to others, his analysis concentrates on the use of particular nouns or verbs such as
'mother,' 'baby,' 'shortstop,' 'baseball team,' 'hairstylist,'
or activities such as 'crying,' 'doing fashions,' or 'having
sexual problems,' which serve as markers of social rela-

tionships. His aim is to show how listeners must utilize their own knowledge of the social system to interpret the juxtaposition of these terms in conversation. Members are seen as using social knowledge in three ways: (a) to recognize particular strings of sentences as possible or potentially valid instances of descriptions, stories, conversations, etc.; (b) to achieve certain social effects: to elicit a response, to get the floor, to induce somebody to gain a favor, etc.; (c) to communicate affect such as praise, criticism, humor, etc.

Notice two points of perspective shared with linguistics and ethnoscience. There is, first, the view that analysis of human sciences need not wait for results from other sciences and that communicative sequences can be analyzed as entities in themselves without reference to actual events depicted therein. Sacks argues that members can identify "possible descriptions" solely on the basis of formal features such as those he describes. What is rejected here are views like that of Bloomfield (1933), who holds that semantic analysis had to wait for other sciences to analyze those phenomena to which words referred, as if description of meaning was the same as description of denotata. Only with recognition that one could, and must, deal with meaning independently, proceeding in terms of just those attributes of phenomena relevant (criterial) for members of the language community, could the recent development of semantic analysis take place (see Haugen 1957; Weinreich 1963, 1968). The issue is the same as with the beginnings of modern phonology. Phonology began with the realization that one could, and must, analyze speech sounds in terms of a level of features criterial for members of the language community, beyond that of a purely physical (phonetic) description (see Sapir 1949g). Second, there is the recognition of a qualitative structure in the stream of behavior, as implied by the distinction between "items" and "slot," and the singling out, as a key feature, the possibility of validly specifying that something is absent, has *not* occurred. The importance of this is brought out in detail by Schegloff (Chapter 12).

Sacks characterizes the differences between his own approach to social norms and those of most of his colleagues as follows:

In the sociological and anthropological literature, the focus on norms is on the conditions under which and the extent to which they govern, or can be seen by social scientists to govern, the relevant actions of those members whose actions they ought to control. While such matters are, of course, important, our viewer's maxim suggests other importances of norms, for members. Viewers use norms to provide some of the orderliness, and proper orderliness, of the activities they observe.

It has been common social-science practice to assume that social norms, like jural rules, exist somewhere outside communicative acts. Many investigators accept norms as given and consider actions simply from the standpoint of whether their content conforms to or deviates from independently given norms. For this point of view, Sacks' choice of data seems trivial: If it is a social norm that mothers should pick up babies, there is nothing remarkable in a mother who does just that—though if a mother did not, there might be a cause to seek out. Sacks, however, is not at all concerned with the "why" of the action in question, but with how the action is made intelligible and interpretable in the first place. *Social norms to him are part of the communicative code which governs our perception of events in somewhat the same way as grammar governs our perceptions of speech.* Other social scientists accept without question that the two sentences that Sacks quotes will be understood in the same way by everybody, whereas Sacks makes these processes of comprehension problematical. He argues that it is our knowledge of social structure which makes such passages intelligible. To the extent that Sacks succeeds, his work is crucial for the study of cross-cultural communication problems raised by Ervin-Tripp in Chapter 7.

A precondition for the study of social categories along Sacks' lines is a knowledge of lexical systems. It is necessary to be familiar with the total range of alternate terms that the speaker has available for expressing a certain kind of message in order to evaluate the significance of his choice. Sacks' analysis therefore bears some similarity to ethnoscience (see Frake, Chapter 3). However, in attempting to relate lexical domains to the use of specific terms in conversations, Sacks goes considerably beyond normal ethnoscience practices. He points out, e.g., that words such as "baby" can form part of two "category collections" or semantic domains: "stage of life" and "family." Additional relevance rules are needed to specify which one of the possible categories applies in this particular case. These relevance rules have functions similar to some linguists' semantic rules. They determine which of a number of possible interpretations holds in a particular instance. But whereas the linguists' rules apply only to relationships within sentences, Sacks' rules typically apply to the semantic ties between terms in different sentences, or sometimes, as in the passage quoted in footnote 2, between two sections of conversation which are separated by long intervening passages.

Further points of interest are that the rules of interpretation go beyond speech. There is a viewer's maxim precisely the same as the hearer's maxim. Interpretation is also related to the structuring of narrative genres in terms of proper beginnings and endings, a feature of natural conversation which is examined in more detail by Schegloff in the following chapter.

Sacks' analysis may seem to proceed overlaboriously for the material at hand. Yet although only two sentences are subjected to detailed analysis, the apparatus developed (specifically, such concepts as *categorization device, duplicative organization, category-bound activity, consistency rules,* etc.) is a highly general one and promises to be applicable to analysis of all verbal interaction. If we want to understand what a speaker seeks to achieve with a particular utterance (as apart from the overt content of what he says), it is necessary to be familiar with the social categories he uses and the cultural associations they carry for him. Assigning others to these categories, and ascribing to them certain category-related activities, are important ways of expressing his intention.

The Turkish verbal dueling described by Alan Dundes (Chapter 4) forms a case in point. The strategy of these duels is to assign the opponent either to the social category of passive homosexual or to the category of a person who allows his mother or sister to undergo sexual attack. Both of these categories carry cultural connotations of cowardliness and lack of manliness and inferiority in comparison to the speaker, who is presumably the attacker. The end effect is that of a put down, but a put down which is understandable only to one who knows the relevant Turkish social categories and their cultural implications. The referential meaning of a word here is less important than the associations it conveys through its membership in a culturally determined category collection. Apparently, in this verbal dueling context, words such as *'cow'* and *'donkey'* are both part of the category collection passive homosexual, whereas words such as *'cowboy,'* or expressions such as *"my father's hairy roof,"* are part of the category collection associated with manliness.

Of special importance from the standpoint of sociolinguistic analysis is the view that social phenomena are of the same order as linguistic phenomena. The same linguistic corpus can be used for both the analysis of linguistic form and the analysis of social categories, and instead of attempting to correlate linguistic forms with social information collected elsewhere, the choice of linguistic forms can be seen simply as a realization of the social meanings and categories in somewhat the same way the pronunciation of a word is a realization of its semantic structure. Additional related readings are provided by Frake (1964c), Gunter (1966), Halliday (1967–1968), Labov and Waletsky (1967), Wheeler (1967). For an application of Sacks' approach to problems of urban education, see Gumperz and Hernandez (1971).

In this chapter I intend, first, to present and employ several of the more basic concepts and techniques which I shall be using. Since most of those I shall use at this point may also be found in the paper "An Initial Investigation of the Usability of Conversational Data for Doing Sociology" (Sacks 1970), the discussion here may be seen as reintroducing and extending the results developed there.

Second, I shall focus on the activity "doing describing" and the correlative activity "recognizing a description," activities which members may be said to do, and which therefore are phenomena which sociologists and anthropologists must aim to be able to describe. It will initially be by reference to an examination of instances of members' describings that my attempts to show how sociologists might solve their own problem of constructing descriptions will be developed.

Proceeding in the fashion I have proposed will permit a focus on several central and neglected issues which social science must face, most particularly, the problem of members' knowledge and the problem of relevance. Let us then begin.

Problems in Recognizing
Possible Descriptions

The initial data are the first two sentences from a "story" offered by a two-year-and-nine-month-old girl to the author of the book *Children Tell Stories.*[1] They are: "The baby cried. The mommy picked it up." I shall first make several observations about these sentences. Before doing so, however, let me note: If these observations strike you as a ranker sort of subjectivism, then I ask you to read on just far enough to see whether it is or is not the case that the observations are both relevant and defensible. When I hear "The baby cried. The mommy picked it up," one thing I hear is that the 'mommy' who picks the 'baby' up is the mommy of that baby. That is a first observation. (You will, of course, notice that the second sentence does not contain a genitive. It does not read, "Its mommy picked it up," or variants thereof.) Now it is not only that *I* hear that the mommy is the mommy of that baby, but I feel rather confident that at least many of the natives among you hear that also. That is a second observation. One of my tasks is going to be to construct an apparatus which will provide for the foregoing facts to have occurred; an apparatus, i.e., which will show how it is that we come to hear the fragment as we do.

Some more: I take it we hear two sentences. Call the first S_1 and the second S_2; the first reports an occurrence O_2 and the second reports an occurrence O_2. Now, I take it we hear that as S_2 follows S_1, so O_2 follows O_1. That is a third observation. And also: We hear that O_2 occurs because of O_1:i.e., the explanation for O_2 occurring is that O_1 did. That is a fourth observation. I want the apparatus to show how we come to hear those facts also.

If I asked you to explain the group of observations which I have made, observations which you could have made just as well—and let me note, they are *not* proposed as sociological findings, but rather do they pose some of the problems which social science shall have to resolve—you might well say something like the following: We hear that it is the mommy of the baby who picks the baby up because she's the one who ought to pick it up, and (you might eventually add) if she's the one who ought to

---

[1] Pitcher and Prelinger, *Children Tell Stories: An Analysis of Fantasy.* (New York: International Universities Press, 1963.)

pick it up, and it was picked up by somebody who could be her, then it was her, or was probably her.

You might go on: While it is quite clear that not any two consecutive sentences, not even any consecutive sentences that report occurrences, are heard, and properly heard, as reporting that the occurrences have occurred in the order which the sentences have, if the occurrences ought to occur in that order, and if there is no information to the contrary (such as a phrase at the beginning of the second, like "before that, however"), then the order of the sentences indicates the order of the occurrences. And these two sentences do present the order of the occurrences they report in the proper order for such occurrences. If the baby cried, it ought to have started crying before the mother picked it up, and not after. Hearing it that way, the second sentence is explained by the first; hearing them as consecutive or with the second preceding the first, some further explanation is needed, and none being present, we may suppose that it is not needed.

Now let me make a fifth observation: All of the foregoing can be done by many or perhaps any of us without knowing what baby or what mommy it is that might be being talked of.

With this fifth observation it may now be noticed that what we've essentially been saying so far is that the pair of sentences seems to satisfy what a member might require of some pair of sentences for them to be recognizable as "a possible description." They "sound like a description," and some form of words can, apparently, sound like a description. To recognize that some form of words is a possible description does not require that one must first inspect the circumstances it may be characterizing.

That "possible descriptions" are recognizable as such is quite an important fact, for members, and for social scientists. The reader ought to be able to think out some of its import for members, e.g., the economies it affords them. It is the latter clause, "and for social scientists," that I now wish to attend to.

Were it not so both that members have an activity they do, "describing," and that at least some cases of that activity produce, for them, forms of words recognizable as at least possible descriptions without having to do an inspection of the circumstances they might characterize, then it might well be that social science would necessarily be the last of the sciences to be made do-able. For, unless social scientists could study such things as these "recognizable descriptions," we might only be able to investigate such activities of members as in one or another way turned on "their knowledge of the world" when social scientists could employ some established, presumptively correct scientific characterizations of the phenomena members were presumably dealing with and knowing about.

If, however, members have a phenomenon, "possible descriptions" which are recognizable per se, then one need not in the instance know how it is that babies and mommies do behave to examine the composition of such possible descriptions as members produce and recognize. Sociology and anthropology need not await developments in botany or genetics or analyses of the light spectra to gain a secure position from which members' knowledge, and the activities for which it is relevant, might be investigated.

What one ought to seek to build is an apparatus which will provide for how it is that any activities, which members do in such a way as to be recognizable as such to members, are done, and done recognizably. Such an apparatus will, of course, have to generate and provide for the recognizability of more than just possible descriptions, and in later discussions we shall be engaged in providing for such activities as "inviting," "warning," and so forth, as the data we consider will permit and require.

My reason for having gone through the observations I have so far made was to give you some sense, right off, of the fine power of a culture. It does not, so to speak, merely fill brains in roughly the same way, it fills them so that they are alike in fine detail. The sentences we are considering are after all rather minor, and yet all of you, or many of you, hear just what I said you heard, and many of us are quite unacquainted with each other. I am, then, dealing with something real and something finely powerful.

Membership Categorization Devices

We may begin to work at the construction of the apparatus. I'm going to introduce several of the terms we need. The first term is *membership categorization device* (or just *categorization device*). By this term I shall intend: any collection of membership categories, containing at least a category, which may be applied to some population containing at least a member, so as to provide, by the use of some rules of application, for the pairing of at least a population member and a categorization device member. A device is then a collection plus rules of application.

An instance of a categorization device is the one called 'sex': Its collection is the two categories (male, female). It is important to observe that a collection consists of categories that "go together." For now that may merely be seen as a constraint of the following sort: I could say that some set of categories was a collection, and be wrong. I shall present some rules of application very shortly.

Before doing that, however, let me observe that 'baby' and 'mommy' can be seen to be categories from one collection: The collection whose device is called 'family' and which consists of such categories as ('baby,' 'mommy,' 'daddy,' . . .) where by " . . ." we mean that there are others, but not any others, e.g., 'shortstop.'

Let me introduce a few rules of application. It may be observed that if a member uses a single category from any membership categorization device, then they can be recognized to be doing *adequate reference* to a person. We may put the observation in a negative form: It is not necessary that some multiple of categories from categorization devices be employed for recognition that a person is being referred to, to be made; a single category will do. (I do not mean by this that more cannot be used, only that for reference to persons to be recognized more need not be used.) With that observation we can formulate a "reference satisfactoriness" rule, which we call "the economy rule." It holds: A single category from any membership categorization device can be referentially adequate.

A second rule I call "the consistency rule." It holds: If some population of persons is being categorized, and if a category from some device's collection has been used to categorize a first member of the population, then that category of other categories of the same collection *may* be used to categorize further members of the population. The former rule was a reference satisfactoriness" rule; this latter one is a "relevance" rule (Sacks, in press).

The economy rule having provided for the adequate reference of 'baby,' the consistency rule tells us that if the first person has been categorized as 'baby,' then further persons may be referred to by other categories of a collection of which they are a member, and thus that such other categories as 'mommy' and 'daddy' are relevant given the use of 'baby.'

While in its currently weak form and alone, the consistency rule may exclude no category of any device, even in this weak form (the "may" form—I shall eventually introduce a "must" form), a corollary of it will prove to be useful. The corollary is a "hearer's maxim." It holds: If two or more categories are used to categorize two or more members of some population, and those categories can be heard as categories from the same collection, then: Hear them that way. Let us call the foregoing "the consistency rule corollary." It has the following sort of usefulness. Various membership categorization-device categories can be said to be ambiguous. That is, the same categorial word is a term occurring in several distinct devices, and can in each have quite a different reference; they may or may not be combinably usable in regard to a single person. So, e.g., 'baby' occurs in the device 'family' and also in the device 'stage of life' whose categories are such as 'baby,' 'child,' . . . 'adult'). A hearer who can use the consistency rule corollary will regularly not even notice that there might be an ambiguity in the use of some category among a group which it can be used to hear as produced via the consistency rule.

It is, of course, clear that the two categories 'baby' are sometimes combinably referential and sometimes not. A woman may refer to someone as "my baby" with no suggestion that she is using the category that occurs in the 'stage of life' device; her baby may be a full-fledged adult. In the case at hand that problem does not occur, and we shall be able to provide the bases for it not occurring, i.e., the bases for the legitimacy of hearing the single term 'baby' as referring to a person located by reference both to the device 'family' and to the device 'stage of life.'

With this, let us modify the observation on the consistency rule as follows: The consistency rule tells us that if a first person has been categorized as 'baby,' the further persons may be referred to by categories from either the device 'family' or from the device 'stage of life.' However, if a hearer has a second category which can be heard as consistent with one locus of a first, then the first is to be heard as *at least* consistent with the second.

Given the foregoing, we may proceed to show how the combined reference of 'baby' is heard for our two sentences, and also how 'the mommy' is heard as 'the mommy of the baby.' We shall deal with the latter task first, and we assume from now on that the consistency rule corollary has yielded at least that 'baby' and 'mommy' are heard as from the device 'family.' We assume that without prejudice to the further fact that 'baby' is also heard as 'baby' from the device 'stage of life.'

The device 'family' is one of a series which you may think of by a prototypical name 'team.' One central property of such devices is that they are what I am going to call "duplicatively organized." I mean by the use of that term to point out the following: When such a device is used on a population, what is done is to take its categories, treat the set of categories as defining a unit, and place members of the population into cases of the unit. If a population is so treated and is then counted, one counts not numbers of daddies, numbers of mommies, and numbers of babies but numbers of families—numbers of 'whole families,' numbers of 'families without fathers,' etc. A population so treated is partitioned into cases of the unit, cases for which what properly holds is that the various persons partitioned into any case are 'coincumbents' of that case.

There are hearer's maxims which correspond to these ways of dealing with populations categorized by way of duplicatively organized devices. One that is relevant to our current task holds: If some population has been categorized by use of categories from some device whose collection has the "duplicative organization" property, and a member is presented with a categorized population which *can be heard* as 'coincumbents' of a case of that device's unit, then: Hear it that way. (I will consider the underscored phrase shortly.) Now let it be noticed that this rule is of far more general scope than we may seem to need. In focusing on a property like duplicative organization it permits a determination of an expectation (of social scientists) as to how some categorized population will be heard independently of a determination of how it is heard. It is then formal and predictive, as well, of course, as quite general.

Now, by the phrase "can be heard" we mean to rule out predictions of the following sort. Some duplicatively organized devices have proper numbers of incumbents for certain categories of any unit. (At any given time a nation-state may have but one president, a family but one father, a baseball team but one shortstop on the field, etc.) If more incumbents of a category are proposed as present in the population than a unit's case can properly take, then the 'can be heard' constraint is not satisfied, and a prediction would not be made.

Category-Bound Activities

The foregoing analysis shows us then how it is that we come to hear, given the fact that the device 'family' is duplicatively organized, and the "can be heard" constraint being satisfied, 'the mommy' to be 'the mommy of the baby.' It does, of course, much more than that. It permits us to predict, and to understand how we can predict, that a statement such as "The first baseman looked around. The third baseman scratched himself." will be heard as saying "the first baseman of the team on which the third baseman is also a player" and its converse.

Or, putting the claim more precisely, it shows us how, in part—"in part" because for the materials at hand it happens that there are other means for providing that the same hearing be made, means which can operate in combination with the foregoing, otherwise sufficient ones, to further assure the hearings we have observed. That will be done in the next section. Let us now undertake our second task, to show how 'the baby' is heard in its combined form, i.e., as the category with that name from both the 'stage of life' device and from the 'family' device.

Let me introduce a term which I am going to call *category-bound activities*. While I shall not now give an intendedly careful definition of the term, I shall indicate what I mean to notice with it and then in a while offer a procedure for determining that some of its proposed cases are indeed cases of it. By the term I intend to notice that many activities are taken by members to be done by some particular or several particular categories of members where the categories are categories from membership categorization devices.

Let me notice then, as is obvious to you, that 'cry' is bound to 'baby,' i.e., to the category 'baby' which is a member of the collection from the 'stage of life' device. Again, the fact that members know that this is so only serves, for the social scientist, to pose some problem. What we want is to construct some means by reference to which a class, which proposedly contains at least the activity-category 'cry' and presumably others, may have the inclusion of its candidate-members assessed. We will not be claiming that the procedure is definitive as to exclusion of a candidate-member, but we will claim that it is definitive as to inclusion of a candidate-member.

It may be observed that the members of the 'stage of life' collection are 'positioned' ('baby' . . . 'adolescent' . . . 'adult' . . .), an observation which, for now, we shall leave unexamined. I want to describe a procedure for praising or degrading members, the operation of which consists of the use of the fact that some activities are category bound. If there are such procedures, they will provide one strong sense of the notion "category-bound activities" and also will provide, for any given candidate activity, a means for warrantably deciding that it is a member of the class of category-bound activities.

For some positioned-category devices it can be said as between any two categories of such a device that A is either higher or lower than B, and if A is higher than B, and B is higher than C, then A is higher than C.

We have some activity which is a candidate-member of the class 'category-bound activities' and which is proposedly bound to some category C. Then, a member of either A or B who does that activity may be seen to be degrading himself, and may be said to be 'acting like a C.' Alternatively, if some candidate activity is proposedly bound to A, a member of C who does it is subject to being said to be acting like an A, where that assertion constitutes "praising."

If, using the 'stage of life' categories, we subject 'crying' to such a test, we do find that its candidacy as a member of the class "category-bound activities" is warrantable. In the case of 'crying' the results are even stronger. For, it appears, if a 'baby' is subject to some circumstances which would for such a one warrant crying, and he does not, then his 'not crying' is observable, and may be used to propose that "he is acting like a big boy," where that assertion is taken to be "praise."[2]

The foregoing procedure can, obviously enough, be used for other devices and other candidate activities. Other procedures may also be used; e.g., one way to decide that an activity is category bound is to see whether, the fact of membership being unknown, it can be "hinted at" by naming the activity as something one does.[3]

---

[2] Consider e.g., the following: "These children are highly aware that they have graduated from the rank of 'baby' and are likely to exhibit considerable scorn of babies, whether a neighbor's child or a younger sibling. This feeling of superiority is the residue of the parents' praise for advance behavior and their inciting the child by remarks like "Only *babies* do that. *You're* not a baby." The frequency of these remarks at this age, however, suggest that in adult minds, at least, there is concern lest the children lapse into babyish ways" (Fischer and Fischer in Whiting 1963:949).

[3] The following data is from a telephone call between a staff member (S) and a caller (C) to an emergency psychiatric clinic. Note the juxtaposition of "hair stylist" in item 4 with suspected homosexuality in the last item.

Having constructed a procedure which can warrant the candidacy of some activity as a member of the class "category-bound activities," and which warrants the membership of 'cry' and provides for its being bound to 'baby,' i.e., that category 'baby' which is a member of the 'stage of life' collection, we move on to see how it is that 'the baby' in our sentence is heard in the combined reference we have proposed.

We need, first, another "hearer's maxim." If a category-bound activity is asserted to have been done by a member of some category where, if that category is ambiguous (i.e., is a member of at least two different devices) but where, at least for one of those devices, the asserted activity is category bound to the given category, then hear that *at least* the category from the device to which it is bound is being asserted to hold.

The foregoing maxim will then provide for hearing "The baby cried." as referring to at least 'baby' from the 'stage of life' device. The results obtained from the use of the consistency rule corollary, being independent of that, are combinable with it. The consistency rule corollary gave us at least that 'the baby' was the category from the device 'family.' The combination gives us both.

If our analysis seems altogether too complicated for the rather simple facts we have been examining, then we invite the reader to consider that our machinery has intendedly been "overbuilt." That is to say it may turn out that the elaborateness of our analysis, or its apparent elaborateness,

---

S: So, you can't watch television. Is there anything you can stay interested in?
C: No, not really.
S: What interests did you have before?
C: I was a hair stylist at one time. I did some fashions now and then. Things like that.
S: Then why aren't you working?
C: Because I don't want to, I guess. Maybe that's why.
S: But do you find that you just can't get yourself going?
C: No. Well, as far as the job goes?
S: Yes.
C: Well, I'll tell you. I'm afraid. I'm afraid to go out and look for a job. That's what I'm afraid of. But more, I think I'm afraid of myself because I don't know. I'm just terribly mixed up.
S: You haven't had any trouble with anyone close to you?
C: Close to me. Well, I've been married three times and I'm—Close, you mean, as far as arguments or something like that?
S: Yes.
C: No, nobody real close. I'm just a very lonely person. I guess I'm very—
S: There's nobody who loves you.
C: Well, I feel that somebody must someplace, but I don't know where or who.
S: Have you been having some sexual problems?
C: All my life.
S: Uh huh. Yeah.
C: Naturally. You probably suspect—as far as the hair stylist and—either go one way or the other. There is a straight or homosexual, something like that. I'm telling you, my whole life is just completely mixed up and turned over and it's just smashed and I'm not kidding.

will disappear when one begins to consider the amount of work that the very same machinery can perform.

In the next section I will attempt to show that the two sentences "The baby cried. The mommy picked it up." constitute a possible description.

Identifying Possible Descriptions

I shall focus next on the fact that an activity can be category bound and then on the import of there being a norm which provides for some second activity, given the occurrence of a first, considering both of these with regard to the "correctness," for members, of "possible description."

Let me for the moment leave aside our two sentences and consider some observations on how it is that I see, and take it you see, describable occurrences. Suppose you are standing somewhere, and you see a person you don't know. The person cries. Now, if I can, I will see that what has happened is that a baby cried. And I take it that you will, if you can, see that too. That's a first pair of observations. Suppose again you are standing somewhere and you see two people you don't know. Suppose further that one cries, and the other picks up the one who is crying. Now, if I can, I will see that what has happened is that a baby cried and its mother picked it up. And I take it that you will, if you can, see that too. That's a second pair of observations.

Consider the first pair of observations. The modifying phrases, to deal with them first, refer simply to the possibility that the category 'baby' might be obviously inapplicable to the crier. By reference to the 'stage of life' collection the crier may be seen to be an adult. And that being so, the 'if . . . can' constraint wouldn't be satisfied. But there are certainly other possible characterizations of the crying person. For example, without respect to the fact that it is a baby, it could be either 'male' or 'female,' and nonetheless I would not, and I take it you would not, seeing the scene, see that "a male cried" if we could see that "a baby cried."

The pair of observations suggest the following "viewer's maxim": If a member sees a category-bound activity being done, then, if one can see it being done by a member of a category to which the activity is bound, then: See it that way. The viewer's maxim is another relevance rule in that it proposes that for an observer of a category-bound activity the category to which the activity is bound has a special relevance for formulating an identification of its doer.

Consider the second pair of observations. As members you, of course, know that there is a norm which might be written as: A mother ought to try to soothe her crying baby. I, and you, not only know that there is such a norm but, as you may recall, we used it in doing our hearing of "The baby cried. The mommy picked it up." In addition to the fact of duplicative organization, the norm was relevant in bringing us to hear that it was the mommy of the baby who did the picking up. While we would have heard that it was the mommy of the baby for other pairs of activities in which the two were involved (but not any pair), the fact that the pair were relatable via a norm which assigns the mother of the baby that duty may have operated in combination with the duplicative organization to assure our hearing that it was she who did it.

Leaving aside the hearing of the sentence, we are led to construct another viewer's maxim: If one sees a pair of actions which can be related via the operation of a norm that provides for the second given the first, where the doers can be seen as members of the categories the norm provides as proper for that pair of actions, then: (a) See that the doers are such members and (b) see the second as done in conformity with the norm.

This second viewer's maxim suggests an observation about norms. In the sociological and anthropological literature, the focus on norms is on the conditions under which and the extent to which they govern, or can be seen by social scientists to govern, the relevant actions of those members whose actions they ought to control. While such matters are, of course, important, our viewer's maxim suggests other importances of norms, for members.

Viewers use norms to provide some of the orderliness, and proper orderliness, of the activities they observe. Via some norm two activities may be made observable as a sequentially ordered pair. That is, viewers use norms to explain both the occurrence of some activity given the occurrence of another and also its sequential position with regard to the other, e.g., that it follows the other, or precedes it. That is a first importance. Second, viewers use norms to provide the relevant membership categories in terms of which they formulate identifications of the doers of those activities for which the norms are appropriate.

Now let me observe, viewers may use norms in each of the preceding ways, and feel confident in their usage without engaging in such an investigation as would serve to warrant the correctness of their usages. This last observation is worth some further thought.

We may, at least initially, put the matter thus: For viewers, the usability of the viewer's maxims serves to warrant the correctness of their observations. And that is then to say, the usability of the viewer's maxims provides for the recognizability of the correctness of the observations done via those maxims. And that is then to say, "correct observations" or, at least, "possible correct observations" are "recognizable."

(Members feel no need in warranting their observation, in recognizing its correctness to do such a thing as to ask the woman whether she is the mother of the baby,[4] or to ask her whether she picked it up because it was crying; i.e., they feel no such need so long as the viewer's maxims are usable.)

In short: "Correctness" is recognizable, and there are some exceedingly nice ties between recognizably correct description and recognizably correct observations. One such tie which is relevant to the tasks we have undertaken is: A string of sentences which may be heard, via the hearer's maxims, as having been produced by use of the viewer's maxims, will be heard as a "recognizably correct possible description."

Sequential Ordering

The rest of this chapter will be devoted to two tasks. I shall try to develop some further rewards of the analysis so far assembled, some consequences it throws off; and to show also how it is that the two sentences ("The baby cried. The mommy picked it up.") can warrantably be said to be from "a story." I start with the latter task.

It ought to be apparent that the fact that the children whose talk is reported in *Children Tell Stories* were asked to tell a story is not definitive of their having done so. It is at least possible that the younger ones among them are not capable of building stories, of building talk that is recognizable as a "story," or, at least, as a "possible story."

It happens to be correct, for Western literature, that if some piece of talk is a possible description it is also, and thereby, a possible story or story part. It appears, therefore, that having established that the two sentences are a possible description, I have also, and thereby, established that they are possibly (at least part of) a story. To stop now would, however, involve ignoring some story-relevant aspects of the given sentences which are both interesting and subjectable to analysis. So, I go on.

Certain characteristics are quite distinctive to stories. For example, there are characteristic endings ("And they lived happily ever after") and characteristic beginnings ("once upon a time"). I shall consider whether the possible story, a fragment of which we have been investigating, can be said (and I mean here, as throughout, "warrantably said") to close with what is recognizable as "an ending" and to start with what is recognizable as "a beginning."

In suggesting a difference between "starts" and proper "beginnings," and between "closes" and proper "endings," I am introducing a distinction which has some importance. The distinction, which is by no means

---

[4] "A late child was at times embarrassing to one woman who, while enjoying him, found that in public places she often overheard people saying, 'They must be his grandparents'" (Fischer and Fischer in Whiting 1963:934).

original, may be developed by considering some very simple observation.

1. A piece of talk which regularly is used to do some activity—as "Hello" is used to do "greeting"—may not invariably be so used, but may do other activities as well—as "Hello" is used to check out whether another with whom one is talking on the phone is still there or has been cut off—where it is in part its occurrence in "the middle" and not "the start" of a conversation that serves to discriminate the use being made of it.

2. Certain activities not only have regular places in some sequence where they do get done but may, if their means of being done is not found there, be said, by members, to not have occurred, to be absent.

For example, the absence of a greeting may be noticed, as the following conversation, from field observation, indicates. The scene involved two adult women, one the mother of two children, ages six and ten. The kids enter and the following ensues:

WOMAN: Hi.
BOY: Hi.
WOMAN: Hi, Annie.
MOTHER: Annie, don't you hear someone say hello to you?
WOMAN: Oh, that's okay, she smiled hello.
MOTHER: You know you're supposed to greet someone, don't you?
ANNIE: [Hangs head] Hello.

3. Certain activities can only be done at certain places in a sequence. For example, a third strike can only be thrown by a pitcher after he has two strikes on a batter.

Observations such as these lead to a distinction between a "slot" and the "items" which fill it, and to proposing that certain activities are accomplished by a combination of some item and some slot.

The notion of slot serves for the social scientist to mark a class of relevance rules. Thus, if it can be said that for some assertable sequence there is a position in which one or more activities properly occur, or occur if they are to get done, then: The observability of either the occurrence or the nonoccurrence of those activities may be claimed by reference to having looked to the position and determined whether what occurs in it is a way of doing the activity.

An instance of the class of relevance rules might run: To see whether a conversation included "greetings," look to the first utterance of either party and see whether there occurs in it any item which passes as a greeting; items such as ('hello,' 'hi,' 'hi there,'. . .). The fact that the list contains the ellipsis might be deeply troublesome were it not the case that while we are unable to list all the members of the class "greeting items," we can say that the class is bounded, and that there are some utterables which are not members of it, perhaps, for example, the sentence now being completed. If that and only that occurred in a first utterance, we might feel assured in saying that a greeting did not occur.

Consider just one way that this class of relevance rules is important. Roughly; it permits the social scientist to nontrivially assert that something is absent. Nontrivial talk of an absence requires that some means be available for showing both the relevance of occurrence of the activity that is proposedly absent and the location where it should be looked for to see that it did not occur. Lacking these, an indefinite set of other activities might equally well be asserted to be absent given some occurrence, and the assertion in question not being discriminable from the (other) members of that indefinite set, it is trivialized.

It does seem that for stories it is correct to say that they can have beginnings, and we can then inspect the items that occur at their start to see whether they can be seen to make a beginning. Given further that stories can have endings, we can inspect the items that occur at their close to see whether they can be seen to make an ending.

While my main interest will be with the story's start as a possible proper beginning, let me briefly consider its close: "She went to sleep." With this the speaker would seem to be not merely closing but closing making a proper ending. It so seems by virtue of the fact that such a sentence reports an occurrence, or can be heard as reporting an occurrence, which is a proper ending to something for which endings are relevant and standardized, that very regularly used unit of orientation, the day. A day being recognized as ending for some person when they go to sleep, so a story may be recognized as closing with an ending if at its close there is a report of the protagonist's having gone to sleep. This particular sort of ending is, of course, not at all particular to stories constructed by young children; it, and other endings like it, from "the last sleep" death unto the shutting down of the world, are regular components of far more sophisticated ventures in Western literature.

Let me turn then to the start, to consider whether it can be said to be a beginning. I shall attempt to show that starting to talk to adults is for small children a rather special matter. I shall do that by focusing on a most characteristic way that small children, of around the age of the teller of the given story, characteristically open their talk to adults, i.e., the use of such items as "You know what?" I shall offer an analysis of that mode of starting off, which will characterize the problems such a start can be seen to operate as a methodical solution to.

The promised analysis will warrant my assertion that starting to talk is, for small children, a special matter. That having been established, I shall turn to see whether the particular start we have for this story may be seen as another type of solution to the same problem that I will have shown to be relevant.

If I can then show that another solution is employed in our problematic utterance (the sentence "The baby cried"), I will have shown that the story starts with something that is properly a beginning, and that therefore, both start and close are "proper" beginning and end. Such, in any event, are my intentions.

I begin, roughly and only as an assumption (though naively, the matter is obvious), by asserting that kids have restricted rights to talk. That being the case, by assumption, I want to see whether the ways that they go about starting to talk, with adults, can be most adequately seen to be solutions to the problem which focuses on needing to have a good start if one is going to get further than that. Starts which have that character can then be called beginnings.

Now, kids around the age of three go through a period when some of them have an almost universal way of beginning any piece of talk they make to adults. They use things like: "You know what, Daddy?" or "You know something, Mommy?"

I will introduce a few rules of conversational sequencing. I do that without presenting data now, but the facts are so obvious that you can check them out easily for yourself; you know the rules anyway. The sequencing rules are for two-party conversation; and, since two-party conversation is a special phenomenon, what I say is not intended as applying for three- or more party conversation.

One basic rule of two-party conversation concerns a pair of objects, questions and answers. It runs: If one party asks a question, when the question is complete, the other party properly speaks, and properly offers an answer to the question and says no more than that. The rule will need considerable explication, but for now, it will do as it stands.

A second rule, and it's quite a fundamental one, because by reference to it the, in principle, infinite character of a conversation can be seen as: A person who has asked a question can talk again, has, as we may put it, "a reserved right to talk again," after the one to whom he has addressed the question speaks. *And,* in using the reserved right he can ask a question. I call this rule the "chaining rule," and in combination with the first rule it provides for the occurrence of an indefinitely long conversation of the form Q-A-Q-A-Q-A-. . . .

Now, the characteristic opener that we are considering is a question (e.g., "You know what?"). Having begun in that way, a user who did not have restricted rights to talk would be in a position of generating an indefinite set of further questions as each question was replied to, or as the other otherwise spoke on the completion of some question.

But the question we begin with is a rather curious one in that it is one of those fairly but not exceptionally rare questions which have as their answer another question, in this case the proper and recurrent answer is

"What?". The use of initial questions of this sort has a variety of consequences. First, if a question which has another question as its proper answer is used and is properly replied to, i.e., is replied to with the proper question, then the chaining rule is turned around, i.e., it is the initial answerer and not the initial questioner who now has the reserved right to speak again after the other speaks. The initial questioner has by his question either not assumed that he can use the chaining rule or has chosen not to. (Note that we are not saying that he has not chosen to invoke the chaining rule but rather that he has instead given the choice of invoking it to the initial answerer. There are two different possibilities involved.)

Second, the initial questioner does not only not make his second speech by virtue of the chaining rule but he makes it by virtue of the first sequencing rule, i.e., by reference to the fact that a person who has been asked a question properly speaks and properly replies to it. His second speech is then not merely not made as a matter of either the chaining rule or his choice by some other means of making a second speech but it is something he makes by obligation, given the fact that he has been asked a question and is therefore obliged to answer.

Third, the question he is obliged to answer is, however, "an open one" in the sense that what it is that an answer would be is something that its asker does not know, and further is one that its answerer by the prior sequence should know. What an answer is then to the second question is whatever it is the kid takes to be an answer, and he is thereby provided with the opportunity to say whatever it is he wanted to say in the first place, not now, however, on his own say-so but as a matter of obligation.

In that case then—and the foregoing being a method whereby the production of the question "You know what?" may be explicated—we may take it that kids take it that they have restricted rights which consist of a right to begin, to make a first statement and not much more. Thereafter they proceed only if requested to. And if that is their situation as they see it, they surely have evolved a nice solution to it.

With the foregoing we can say then that a focus on the way kids begin to talk is appropriate, and we can see whether the beginnings of stories, if they are not made of the culturally standardized beginnings (such as "once upon a time"), might be seen to be beginnings by virtue of the special situation which kids have vis-à-vis beginning to talk.

We may arrive at the status of "The baby cried" as a proper beginning, in particular as a start that is a beginning by virtue of being a proper opener for one who has restricted rights to talk, by proceeding in the following way. Let us consider another solution to the problem of starting talk under restricted rights. I'll begin by introducing a word, 'ticket.' I can show you what I mean to point to with the word by a hypothetical example. Suppose two adults are copresent and lack rights to talk to each other; e.g., they have never been introduced, or whatever. For any such two persons there are conditions under which one can begin to talk to the other. And that those conditions are the conditions used to in fact begin talk is something which can be shown via a first piece of talk. Where that is done we will say that talk is begun with a ticket. That is, the item used to begin talk is an item which, rights not otherwise existing, serves to warrant one having begun to talk. For example, one turns to the other and says, "Your pants are on fire." It is not just any opening, but an opening which tells why it is that one has breached the correct silence, which warrants one having spoken. Tickets then are items specially usable as first items in talk by one who has restricted rights to talk to another. And the most prototypical class of tickets are "announcements of trouble relevant to the other."

Now it is clear enough (cf. the discussion of norms earlier) that the occurrence of a baby crying is the occurrence of a piece of trouble relevant to some person, e.g., the mother of the baby. One who hears it gains a right to talk, i.e., to announce the fact that it has occurred, and can most efficiently speak via a ticket, i.e., "The baby cried." That being so, we can see then that the opener "The baby cried" is a proper beginning, i.e., it is something which can serve as a beginning for someone whose rights to talk are in the first instance restricted.

With the foregoing we have established that the story we have been examining has both a proper beginning and a proper end, and is thus not only a story by virtue of being a possible description but also by virtue of its employing, as parts, items which occur in positions that permit one to see that the user may know that stories have such positions, and that there are certain items which when used in them are satisfactory incumbents.

12

Sequencing in Conversational Openings[1]

EMANUEL A. SCHEGLOFF

Emanuel A. Schegloff is an assistant professor of sociology at Columbia University. He received his doctorate from the University of California, Berkeley. His research has concentrated on rules of everyday behavior, especially as disclosed in natural conversation.

In this chapter Schegloff begins with an American answer to a universal communicative problem: who speaks first, and what does the first speaker say? Less crudely, the question is, what rules govern conversational openings, and, as Schegloff puts it, secure "coordinated entry" (i.e., what rules determine the orderliness and intelligibility of what takes place)? The opening segment of conversation is perhaps everywhere especially advantageous for sociolinguistic research, being continually in evidence and continually revealing. What one can say to anyone, and how one must deal with anyone with whom one speaks, may imply fundamental assumptions about the rights and obligations mutually felt by

Reproduced by permission of the author and the American Anthropological Association from *American Anthropologist,* Vol. 70, No. 6, 1968.

[1] The research on which the present discussion is based was supported in part by the Advanced Research Projects Agency, Department of Defense, through the Air Force Office of Scientific Research under contract number AF 49 (638)–1761. I want to acknowledge, as well, the assistance of the Bureau of Applied Social Research, Columbia University, and its director, Allen Barton. For much of the general approach taken here I am indebted to Harold Garfinkel and Harvey Sacks, and for specific suggestions, doubts, critical remarks, and suggestive additions I am grateful to Erving Goffman, Alan Blum, Michael Moerman, and especially to David Sudnow and Harvey Sacks. Responsibility is, of course, entirely mine.

This discussion is a shortened and modified version of chapters two and three of the

members of a society—perhaps any human beings—are felt to owe to each other. (In parts of Africa whole languages may be evaluated in terms of the greeting patterns.)

Work such as Schegloff's calls attention to the possibility and necessity of deriving a formal analysis of such sequences (closings would be also important). Cross-cultural work is needed to place the American rules in perspective. No one is able now to say what is universal or what is culturally specific. Nor can we do more now than guess as to the evolutionary and historical factors that explain the virtual absence of stereotyped verbal greeting in some societies, its elaboration in others, or the particular form it takes if any.

The nature of the argument in Schegloff's discussion is important. Familiar in linguistics, it is unusual in sociology. Faced with an exception among some hundreds of cases, Schegloff neither dismisses it nor explains it ad hoc. He reconsiders his previous analysis in the light of the exception, seeking a deeper generalization that will account for both. A "distribution rule" for question-answer sequences is incorporated in a more general rule that treats the opening of telephone conversations in terms of rules for summons-answer sequences; and this rule is "structural" in the sense of being qualitative rather than quantitative, being usually out of awareness, yet deeply binding.

This kind of reasoning is in the spirit of Sapir's pioneering conception of the unity of patterning in all behavior, verbal and nonverbal (1949). As with Sacks' analysis of hearer's and viewer's maxims, Schegloff's analysis of summons and answer comprises nonverbal as well as verbal phenomena—most centrally here, the ringing of the phone itself as a summons, but notice also the contrast between summons and greeting that depends upon

author's Ph.D. dissertation (Schegloff 1967). It is based on the analysis of tape-recorded phone calls to and from the complaint desk of a police department in a middle-sized Midwestern city. References to the "data" in the text should be understood as references to this corpus of materials. Names have been changed to preserve anonymity; numbers preceding citations of data identify calls within the corpus. I wish to thank the Disaster Research Center, Department of Sociology, The Ohio State University, for the use of this recorded material, which was obtained in connection with studies of organizational functioning under stress, especially disaster conditions. The views expressed and the interpretations of the data, of course, are those of the author and not necessarily those of the center.

whether a term of address is not, or is, accompanied by a wave.

The findings bring out an essential methodological point. Analysis of speech acts, or, more generally, communicative acts, is not at a level super-added and simply parallel to the more familiar levels of phonology and syntax. Communicative acts cut across the familiar levels, showing new relationships among their contents, and showing relationships between their contents and other modalities of communication, such as gesture, the ringing of a phone, knocking on a door. A level of communicative acts is necessary to account for some of the properties of purely linguistic elements, as in the different distribution of proper names when serving as terms of address and when serving as summons, and their different consequences, regarding recycling, for sentence sequence (points 1 and 3 under the section "Summons-Answer Sequences"). At the same time act categories unite quite diverse linguistic material (Schegloff notes that a turn may range from a single "mm" to a string of complex sentences), and, as we have seen, nonlinguistic material as well.

Notice that Schegloff's central body of data allows him to control for the nonverbal modalities involved, here, exclusively the telephone ring, while his deeper generalization depends upon including that nonverbal signal in the sequence analyzed. It would be most unfortunate if sociologists, discovering the fascination of verbal data, were to forget such points, and to become as word bound as most linguists.

As does Sacks, Schegloff relates his formal analysis of a portion of "social syntax" to norms of interaction, and to the strategies of interaction persons employ (this time, e.g., mothers' strategies vis'-à-vis children in employing them). Structure, interpretation, and use are united in one analysis.

Schegloff himself brings out the close relation of his work to that of Goffman and Sacks. Besides references cited with Sacks (Chapter 11) there are several observations of interest in Kiparsky (1968) and a body of important work with conversations from a people of northeastern Thailand in Moerman (in press) and Douglas (1971).

ויאמר אליו אכדהם, ויאמר ה.נג.

"And He said, Abraham; and he said, Behold, I am here."
Genesis XXII:1

My object in this paper is to show that the raw data of everyday conversational interaction can be subjected to rigorous analysis. To this end, I shall exhibit the outcome of one such analysis, confined to one limited aspect of conversation. The aspect is sequencing, in this case sequencing in two-party conversations, with attention directed to the opening of such conversations (although only one kind of opening is considered). The chapter proceeds by suggesting a first formulation—referred to as a "distribution rule"—to analyze materials drawn from telephone conversation. The first formulation is found deficient, and the search for a more adequate analysis leads to a second formulation not limited to telephone conversations alone, but able to deal with them, and subsuming the "distribution rule" as a special case. Some properties of the second formulation—called "summons-answer sequences"—are detailed, and consideration is given to the uses of the interactional mechanism that has been analyzed.

This work may have relevance for anthropologists for several reasons. First, there is a possible direct interest in the materials under investigation; second, the developing interest in the ethnography of communication (Gumperz and Hymes 1964); and third, what I take to be a prevailing interest of anthropologists in the possibility of direct analysis of the "stuff of everyday life" so as to discover its orderly or methodical character.

I cannot say for what domain my analysis holds, but, as the biblical citation in the heading and references to settings other than the contemporary United States should indicate, I do not think the findings are limited to America today. Since cross-cultural variability and invariance are of abiding interest to anthropologists, information on this question will have to be sought from them. Whether this sort of analysis is possible or practical on materials from societies of which the analyst is not a member is also not clear, and again it may remain for anthropologists to supply the answer. [See, for example, Moerman (1968b).]

Introduction

I use "conversation" in an inclusive way. I do not intend to restrict its reference to the "civilized art of talk" or to "cultured interchange" as in the usages of Oakeshott (1959) or Priestly (1926), to insist on its casual character thereby excluding service contacts (as in Landis and Burtt 1924), or to require that it be sociable joint action, identity related, etc. (as in Watson and Potter 1962). "Dialogue," while being a kind of conversation, has special implications derived from its use in Plato, psychiatric theorizing, Buber, and others, which limits its usefulness as a general term. I mean to include chats as well as service contacts, therapy sessions as well as asking for and getting the time of day, press conferences as well as exchanged whispers of "sweet nothings." I have used "conversation" with this general reference in mind, occasionally borrowing the still more general term "state of talk" from Erving Goffman.

It is an easily noticed fact about two-party conversations that their sequencing is alternating. That is to say, conversational sequence can be described by the formula *ababab,* where "a" and "b" are the parties to the conversation. [I am indebted to Sacks (n.d., ms.) for suggesting the significance of this observation, and some of its implications.] The *abab* formula is a specification, for two-party conversations, of the basic rule for conversation: *one party at a time.* The strength of this rule can be seen in the fact that in a multi-party setting (more precisely, where there are four or more), if more than one person is talking, it can be claimed not that the rule has been violated, but that more than one conversation is going on. Thus, Bales can write:

The conversation generally proceeded so that one person talked at a time, and all members in the particular group were attending the *same conversation.* In this sense, these groups might be said to have a "single focus," that is, they did not involve a number of conversations proceeding at the same time (Bales et al. 1951:461).

When combined with an analytic conception of an utterance, the *abab* specification has a variety of other interesting consequences, such as allowing us to see how persons can come to say *"X is silent,"* when no person in the scene is talking. (For a psychiatric usage, see Bergler 1938.)

The problem I wish to address is the following: the *abab* formula describes the sequencing of a two-party conversation already underway. It does not provide for the allocation of the roles "a" and "b" (where "a" is a first speaker and "b" is a second speaker) between the two persons engaged in the conversation. Without such an allocation, no ready means is available for determining the first speaker of the convention. The *abab* sequence makes each successive turn sequentially dependent upon the previous one; it provides no resources when who the first speaker might be is treated problematically. I should like to examine the ways in which coordinated entry by two parties into an orderly sequence of conversational turns is managed. (This general area has been considered from a somewhat different perspective in Goffman 1953, Chapter 14; see also Goffman 1963:88–95).

Notice that I do not mean to identify a "turn" necessarily with any syntactic or grammatical unit or combination of units, nor with any activity. In the former case, it should be clear that a turn may contain anything from a single "mm" (or less) to a string of complex sentences. In the latter, it is crucial to distinguish a single turn in which two activities are accomplished from two turns by the same party without an intervening turn of the other. An example of the latter occurs when a question must be repeated before it is heard or answered; an example of the former is the line, following the inquiry "How are you," "Oh I'm fine. How are you." A "turn," as I am using the term, is thus not the same as what Goffman refers to as a "natural message," which he describes as "the sign behavior of a sender during the whole period of time through which a focus of attention is continuously directed at him" (Goffman 1953:165). There are, of course, other views of the matter, such as using a period of silence or "appreciable pause" to mark a boundary (as in Stephen and Mishler 1952:600 or Steinzor 1949:109). But unanalyzed pauses and silences are ambiguous (theoretically) as to whether they mark the boundary of a unit, or are included in it (as the very term "pause" suggests).

Telephone Conversation: The Distribution Rule

A first rule of telephone conversation, which might be called a "distribution rule for first utterances," is: *the answerer speaks first.* Whether the utterance be "hello," "yeah," "Macy's," "shoe department," "Dr. Brown's office," "Plaza 1–5000," or whatever, it is the one who picks up the ringing phone who speaks it.

This rule seems to hold in spite of a gap in the informational resources of the answerer. While the caller knows both his own identity and, typically, that of his intended interlocutor (whether a specific person or an organization is being phoned), the answerer, at least in most cases, knows only who he is and not specifically who the caller is. That is not to say that no basis for inference might exist, as, for example, that provided by time of day, the history of a relationship, agreed upon signaling arrangements, etc. To the question "whom are you calling?" a caller may give a definitive answer, but to the question "who's calling?" the answerer, before picking up the phone, can give only a speculative answer.

Without developing a full analysis here, the import of the gap in the answerer's information ought to be noted. If, in this society, persons uniformly used a single standardized item to open a conversation without respect to the identity of the other party or the relationship between the two, then the informational lack would have no apparent import, at least for the opening. This, however, is not the case. A variety of terms may be used to begin conversation and their propriety is geared to the identity, purposes, and relationships of either or both parties. Intercom calls, for example, are typically answered by a "yeah" or "yes" while incoming outside calls are seldom answered in that way (In citations of data in which the police receive the call, "D" refers to the police "dispatcher" and "C" refers to the caller.):

#68

D: Yeah.
C: Tell 85 to take that crane in the west entrance. That's the only entrance that they can get in.
D: O.K. Will do.
C: Yeah.

#88

D: Yes.
C: Uh Officer Novelada.
D: Yes, speaking.
C: Why uh this is Sergeant ———
D: Yes Sergeant.
C: And uh I just talked to [etc.]

#123

D: Yeah.
C: If you can get ahold of car 83, go'm tell him to go to [etc.]

Full consideration of the problem that this answerer's information gap presents, and some solutions to it, requires reference to aspects of conversational openings other than sequencing, and cannot be adequately discussed here (see Schegloff 1967, Chapter 4).

It may help to gain insight into the working of the distribution rule to consider, speculatively, what might be involved in its violation, and the reader is invited to do so. (For the illumination of normal scenes produced by considering disruption of them, I am indebted to Harold Garfinkel; see Garfinkel 1967.) One possible violation would involve the following: The distribution rule provides that the answerer normally talks first, immediately upon picking up the receiver. To violate the rule and attempt to have the other person treated as the one who was called, he would not talk, but would remain silent until the caller spoke first. Suppose after some time the caller says "Hello?" This might be heard as an attempt by the caller to check out the acoustic intactness of the connection. In doing so, the caller employs a lexical item, and perhaps an intonation, that is standardly used by called parties in answering their home phones. This would provide the violator (i.e., the answerer acting as a caller) with a resource.

Given the identity of the lexical items used by persons to check out and to answer in this case, the violater may now treat the checking out "hello" as an answering "hello." Continuing the role reversal, he would be required to offer a caller's first remark.

We may note that, without respect to the detailed substance of their remarks, it is a property of their respective utterances that the answerer typically says just "hello," whereas the caller, if he says "hello," typically then adds a continuation, e.g., "this is Harry." Our hypothetical violator, in having to make a caller's first remark to achieve the role reversal, must then say "hello" with a continuation.

To be sure, a caller might say only "hello," so as to invite the called person to recognize who is calling. This is a common attempt to establish or confirm the intimacy or familiarity of a relationship. To cite one instance from our data, in which a police complaint clerk calls his father:

#497

OTHER:	Hello
POLICE:	Hello
OTHER:	Hello, the letter, you forgot that letter
POLICE:	Yeah but listen to me, the _____ just blew up, [etc.]

The "intimacy ploy." however, is available only to a "genuine" caller, and not to the hypothetical violator under consideration. If the violator says it, the genuine caller might hear it as a correct answerer's first remark that was delayed. The attempted violation would thereupon be frustrated.

In saying "hello" with a continuation, however, the would-be violator would encounter trouble. While trying to behave as a caller, he does not have the information a genuine caller would have. In having to add to the "hello" to play the caller's part, the choice of an appropriate item depends on his knowing (as a genuine caller would know) to whom he is speaking. We may give three examples of what this bind might consist of:

1. One common addition to a caller's "hello" involves the use of a term of address, for example: Answerer: "Hello?"; Caller: "Hello, Bill." Not knowing to whom he is speaking, the violator can obviously not employ such an addition.

2. Another frequent addition is some self-identification appended to the "hello." Self-identification involves two parts: (a) a frame and (b) a term of identification. By "frame" is meant such things as "this is _____," "my name is _____," or "I am _____."[2] Terms of identification

---

[2] The latter framing item "I am . . ." is not normally used on the telephone as the frame for a name, although it may be used in a next item, as when an organizational affiliation is offered to provide further identification. In face-to-face interaction, "This is . . ." is not typically used for self-identification but only for introducing a third party. "My name is . . ." is usable in both face-to-face and in telephone interactions.

include, among others, first names, nicknames, or title plus last name. We may note that the choice both of appropriate frames and appropriate self-identification terms varies with the identity and relationship of the two parties. For example, the frame "My name is ———" is normally used only in identifying oneself to a stranger. Similarly, whether one refers to oneself as Bill or Mr. Smith depends upon the relationship between the two parties. Our imagined violator would not have the information requisite to making a choice with respect to either determination. Although these two examples are not exhaustive of the variety of caller's continuations, a great many calls proceed by use of one or more of them, and in each case a masquerading caller, not having the simple information a genuine caller would have, would have trouble in using such a continuation.

3. An alternative continuation for a caller, whether used in combination with one of the foregoing continuations or as the caller's next turn, suggests another rule of opening conversations: the caller provides the first "topic" of conversation. This rule would confront a violator with the problem of formulating a topic of conversation that could serve appropriately without respect to to whom he is speaking. Whether there are such topics is unclear. A promising candidate as a general first topic might seem to be the ritual inquiry "How are you?" or some common variant thereof. This inquiry is usable for a very wide range of conversational others, but not for all conversational others. For example, telephone solicitors or callers from the Chamber of Commerce would not be typically greeted in this way. As formulated here, the rule "The caller provides the first 'topic'" is not nearly as general as the distribution rule. There are obvious occasions where it is not descriptive, as when the "caller" is "returning a call." A formulation that would hold more generally might be "The initiator of a contact provides the first topic." But this alternative is no better in providing a continuation to "hello" that is usable for all conversational others. (It may be noted here that much of the analysis in this section will be superseded below.)

Other violations of the distribution rule are readily imaginable, and need not be enumerated here. My interest is chiefly in exploring the operation and constraints provided by the distribution rule, as well as the resources it provides for keeping track of the developing course of a conversation. I found, in attempting to imagine violations, that without the proper operation of the simple distribution rule, it was difficult to keep track of who was who, who the genuine caller and who the violator, the order of events, what remarks were proper for whom, etc. Although I have attempted to describe the hypothetical violation clearly, I fear, and trust, that the reader will have been sore-pressed to follow the "play-by-play" account and keep the "players" straight. It may be noted, then, that not only does the distribution rule seem to be routinely followed in the actual practice of telephone conversationalists but it provides a format by which observers maintain a grasp of the developing activity.

Finally, consider as evidence of the binding character of the distribution rule the following personal anecdote recounted by a student. At one time, she began receiving obscene phone calls. She noted that the caller breathed heavily. She, therefore, began the practice of picking up the receiver without speaking. If she heard the heavy breathing, she would hang up. The point she wanted to make in relating this anecdote was that she encountered considerable irritation from her friends when it turned out that it was they calling and she had not made a first utterance upon picking up the receiver. She took this to be additional evidence for the correctness of the rule "the answerer speaks first." However, she has supplied an even more pointed demonstration than she intended. It is notable that she could avoid hearing the obscenities by avoiding making a first utterance; however obscene her caller might be, he would not talk until she had said "hello," thereby obeying the requirements of the distribution rule.

A DEVIANT CASE

The distribution rule discussed above holds for all but one of the roughly 500 phone conversations in the entire corpus of data. In the vast majority of these, the dispatcher, when calls were made to the police, or others, when calls were made by the police, spoke first. In several cases the tape recordings contained instances of simultaneous talk at the beginning of the interchange (often because the caller was still talking to the switchboard operator when the dispatcher "came on the line"). In these cases, a resolution occurred by the callers withdrawing in favor of the called. That is, either the caller stopped and the dispatcher continued, or both stopped and the dispatcher went on.

#364

D: Police Desk. } Simultaneous
C: First aiders with me.
D: Police Desk.
C: Hello?
D: Yes.
C: Uh this is [etc.]

#66

D: Police Desk.
C: (Simultaneously giving phone number in background to operator)
D: Hello
C: I am a pharmacist. I own [etc.]

#43

D: Police Desk.
C: Say, what's all the excitement . . .   } Simultaneous
D: Police Desk?
C: Police Headquarters?
D: Yes.
C: What's all the excitement [etc.]

Simultaneous talk is of special interest because it is the converse of *abab*, which requires that only one party talk at a time. If simultaneous talk could be shown to be regularly resolved via the distribution rule, at the beginning of telephone conversations, then its status as a solution to the problem of coordinated entry would be more general. A fully adequate demonstration might involve giving somewhat stronger explication of the notion of one party's "withdrawal," perhaps by reference to some utterance unit, e.g., a sentence, begun but not finished. (For this last point, I am indebted to Harvey Sacks.)

One case clearly does not fit the requirements of the distribution rule:

#9 (Police make call)

(Receiver is lifted, and there is a one second pause)

POLICE: Hello.
OTHER: American Red Cross.
POLICE: Hello, this is Police Headquarters . . . er, Officer Stratton [etc.]

In this case the caller talks first, while the distribution would require that the first line be "American Red Cross," the statement of the called party.

While indeed there is only one such violation in my data, its loneliness in the corpus is not sufficient warrant for not treating it seriously. Two alternatives are open. We might focus exclusively on this case and seek to develop an analysis particular to it that would account for its deviant sequencing. This would constitute an ad hoc attempt to save the distribution rule, using a technique commonly used in sociology—deviant case analysis. Alternately, we might reexamine the entire corpus of materials seeking to deepen our understanding of the opening sequencing. We might ask: Is this best treated as a deviant case, or would a deeper and more general formulation of the opening sequencing reveal properties of the initiation of talk that the distribution rule glosses over. Analysis of the case reveals that the distribution rule, while it holds in most cases, is in fact best understood as a derivative of more general rules. As we shall see, the additional sequencing rules, which this case forces us to examine, clarify properties of talk in nontelephone communication as well as in telephone communication. The rules discussed below do not make the distribution rule superfluous, but concern more finely grained aspects of the opening sequence. They require that we analyze aspects of the opening structure that the distribution rule does not handle. The distribution rule is but one, if indeed a most typical, specification of the formulation to follow, and the deviant case is another specification. As Michael Moerman has suggested, the distribution rule is no less a "special case" for having many occurrences, nor the latter more so for having only one (in my corpus of materials). Not number of occurrences but common subsumption under a more general formulation is what matters. It will be shown that, in broadening the formulation of the opening sequence, a set of more interesting and formal properties of the opening sequencing structure are exposed.

Summons-Answer Sequences

Originally we spoke of two parties to a telephone interaction, a caller and an answerer. The distribution rule held that the answerer spoke first. One of the activities in the material under examination seems to be "answering," and it is appropriate to ask what kind of answering activity is involved and what its properties are.

Let us consider for a moment what kinds of things are "answered." The most common item that is answered is a question, and a standardized exchange is question-answer. At first glance, however, it seems incorrect to regard the "called" party as answering a question. What would be the question? A telephone ring does not intuitively seem to have that status. Other items that are answered include challenges, letters, roll calls, and summonses. It seems that we could well regard the telephone ring as a summons. Let us consider the structure of summons-answer sequences.

It can be noted at the outset that a summons—often called an "attention-getting device"—is not a telephone-specific occurrence. Other classes besides mechanical devices, such as telephone rings, include:

1. Terms of address (e.g., "John?," "Dr.," "Mr. Jones?," "waiter,"[3] etc.)

---

[3] We may note here several special classes of occupational titles. Most occupational titles cannot be used as terms of address or to summon persons of whom they are descriptive. So, for example, one would not introduce into a sentence as a term of address, nor seek to get attention via the term "secretary." There is a small collection of occupational titles that can be used, under appropriate circumstances, as terms of address or to summon their possessors. For example, one may either address or summon by way of "Doctor," "Rabbi," "Officer," "Nurse," etc. There is a still smaller class of occupational titles which, while not usable as terms of address, are usable as summons items. For example, "cabby," or "ice cream man," etc. About this collection we may note that aside from their referential uses, e.g., "He is a cabby," they seem to be used only as summons items.

2. Courtesy phrases (e.g., "Pardon me," when approaching a stranger to get his attention)

3. Physical devices (e.g., a tap on the shoulder, waves of a hand, raising of a hand by an audience member, etc.)

It is to be noted that a summons occurs as the first part of a two part sequence. Just as there are various items that can be used as summonses, so are there various items that are appropriately used as answers, e.g., "Yes?," "What?," "Uh huh?," turning of the eyes or of the body to face the beckoner, etc. Some typical summons-answer sequences are: telephone ring—"hello"; "Johnny?"—"yes"; "Excuse me"—"Yes"; "Bill?"—looks up.

The various items that may be used as summonses are also used in other ways. "Hello," for example, may be used as a greeting; "Excuse me" may be used as an apology; a name may be used as a term of address only, not requiring an answer. How might we differentiate between the summons uses of such terms and other uses? Taking as an example items whose other use is as terms of address, it seems that the following are ways of differentiating their uses:

1. When addressing, the positioning of a term of address is restricted. It may occur at the beginning of an utterance ("Jim, where do you want to go?"), at the end of an utterance ("What do you think, Mary?") or between clauses or phrases in an utterance ("Tell me, John, how's Bill?"). As summons items, however, terms of address are positionally free within an utterance. [This way of differentiating the usages has a "one-way" character; that is, it is determinative only when an item occurs where terms of address (as nonsummons items) cannot. When it occurs within the restrictions on placement of terms of address, it clearly is nondifferentiating.] As a mere address term, an item cannot occur between a preposition and its object, but as a summons it may, as in the following telephone call from the data:

#398

C: Try to get out t'—Joe?
D: Yeah?
C: Try to get ahold of [etc.]

2. Summons items may have a distinctive rising terminal juncture, a raising of the voice pitch in a quasi-interrogative fashion.[4] This seems to

---

[4] Bolinger (1958). We say, with Bolinger, "quasi-interrogative" because there is in American English apparently no definitive interrogative intonation, such that anything so intoned is a question, or if not so intoned cannot be a question.

be typically the case when a summons occurs after a sentence has already begun, as in the above datum. It need not be the case when the summons stands alone, as in "Jim," when trying to attract Jim's attention.

3. A term of address is "inserted" in an utterance. By that I mean that after the term of address is introduced, the utterance continues with no break in its grammatical continuity; e.g., "Tell me, Jim, what did you think of. . . ." When a summons occurs in the course of an utterance, it is followed by a "recycling" to the beginning of the utterance. The utterance is begun again, as in the datum cited in point 1 above. Although in that datum the original utterance is altered when started again, alteration is not intrinsic to what is intended by the term "recycling."

It is an important feature of summonses and answers that, like questions and answers, they are sequentially used. This being so, the unit of our analysis is a sequence of summons and answer, which shall henceforth be abbreviated as "SA" sequence. Question-answer sequences shall be referred to as "QA." We now turn to an examination of two major and several subsidiary properties of SA sequences.

NONTERMINALITY OF SA SEQUENCES

By nonterminality I mean that a completed SA sequence cannot properly stand as the final exchange of a conversation. It is a specific feature of SA sequences that they are preambles, preliminaries, or prefaces to some further conversational or bodily activity. They are both done with that purpose, as signaling devices to further actions, and are heard as having that character. This is most readily noticed in that very common answer to a summons "What is it?" Nonterminality indicates that not only must something follow but SA sequences are specifically preliminary to something that follows.

Is the continuation upon the completion of an SA sequence constrained in any way, e.g., in which party produces it? The very property of nonterminality is furnished by the obligation of the summoner to talk again upon the completion (by the summoned) of the SA sequence. It is he who has done the summoning and by making a summons incurs the obligation to talk again. With exceedingly rare exceptions, some of which will be noted below, the summoner fulfills this obligation and talks again. It is the fact of the routine fulfillment of the obligation to talk again that produces data in which every conversation beginning with an SA sequence does not terminate there.

It may be noted in passing that the structure of SA sequences is more constraining than the structure of QA sequences. It seems to be a property of many QA sequences that the asker of a question has the *right* to talk again but not an obligation to do so.[5] SA sentences more forcefully constrain both contributors to them. One way to see the constraining character of nonterminality as a normative property of an SA sequence is by observing what regularly occurs when the summoner, for whatever reason, does not wish to engage in whatever activity the SA sequence he originated may have been preliminary to. Here we characteristically find some variant of the sequence: "Sam?" "Yeah?" "Oh, never mind." Note that in the very attempt to appropriately withdraw from the obligation to continue after a completed SA sequence, an original summoner must in fact conform to it and not simply be silent. Even in telephone conversations between strangers, where maintaining the intactness of some relationship would not seem to be at issue, the obligation to continue talk upon an SA sequence has been observed to hold. For example, in calling an establishment to learn if it is open, that fact may sometimes be established positively when the ringing phone (summons) is lifted and "hello" or an establishment name is heard. Rather than hang up, having obtained the required information, many persons will continue with the self-evidently answered question "Are you still open?" (although note here the common tendency to append to it a more reasonable inquiry, one not rendered superfluous by the very act, as "How late are you open?" even though that might not, on the given occasion, be of interest). The limited rule "the caller supplies the first topic" advanced earlier may be seen to be one partial application of the obligation of a summoner to talk again.

A property directly related to the nonterminality of SA sequences is their nonrepeatability. Once a summons has been answered, the summoner may not begin another SA sequence. A contrast is suggested with QA sequences where a questioner, having a *right* to talk again after an answer is given, may fill his slot with another question. Although a questioner may sometimes be constrained against asking the same question again (e.g., in two-person interaction: A: "How are you?" B: "Fine." A: "How are you?"), he may choose some question to fill the next slot. A summoner is not only barred from using the same summons again but from doing any more summoning (of the same "other"). If, as occurs on occasion, a summoner does not hear the answer of the other, and repeats the summons, should the answerer hear both summonses he will treat the second one as over-insistent. This is most likely to occur in those situations where physical barriers make it difficult for the summoned person to indicate his having received the summons and having initiated a course of

---

[5] I am indebted to Harvey Sacks for the first part of this observation. Some questions may, to be sure, obligate their askers to talk again. The statement in the text may, therefore, reflect a stage in the analysis of questions where such questions have not yet been closely examined.

answering. Continued knocking on the door is often met with the complaint as the answerer is on his way, "I'm coming, I'm coming." To sum
up, the summoner's obligation to talk again cannot be satisfied by initiating another SA sequence to the same other. This does not mean, however, that one might not have, in a transcript of the opening of a conversation, two SA sequences back-to-back. As we shall shortly see, if the
nonterminality property is not met, i.e., should the summoner not fulfill
his obligation to talk again, the answerer of the first SA sequence may, in
turn, start another with a summons of his own, as in the first line below (E
has called M—the initial S):[6]

M: MacNamara (pause). Hello? (A # S)
E: Yeah uh John? (A . . .)
M: Yeah.
E: I uh just trying to do some uh intercom here in my own set up and get
      ahold of you at the same time.

We may further see the operation of the nonterminality property in a
common misunderstanding of the use of a name. Names may serve, as
suggested above, both as simple terms of address or as summoning terms
of address. Should a name intendedly uttered as a simple term of address be
heard as a summons, the hearer will expect a continuation while the
speaker will not be prepared to give one. While not a particularly frequent
occurrence, when found, it usually occurs in the following way: *X* uses
Y's name, and in so doing waves. This is a typical way to perform a greeting, part of which is verbally accomplished and part gesturally accomplished. The lexical item perceived alone, i.e., where the gesture is
not seen, may be heard as a summons, and one who hears it in this way
will then answer it and await the activity to which it was expectably preliminary. The misinterpreted sender, like he who calls merely to find out
information that the answer conveys, may feel obligated to say "I was just
saying 'hello.'"
    It is worth noting about such occurrences that misinterpreted persons
can see how they were misinterpreted. Being able to see the kind of error
involved rather than having to investigate its character, allows immediate
correction. Such availability of the nature of an error may be quite important. One consequence may be the following. That the systematic ambiguity of the term (i.e., its use to do more than one activity—here "summoning" and "greeting") is available when invoked by the second party,
suggests that the summoner can see how the error could be made; he can

---

[6] The datum is from a collection of calls to and from a public agency other than the one
from which the bulk of the data are drawn. The first two SA sequences are indicated in
parentheses.

see its methodical character. Members may be able, then, not only to methodically detect which of two activities a term is being used for but also to detect methodical errors in such determinations. The hope may, therefore, be warranted that investigators will be able to describe methods for differentiating "term of address" usages from "summons" usages, even if the three suggestions offered earlier prove wrong.

Nonterminality is an outcome of the obligation of the summoner to talk again. Corollary to that obligation is the obligation of the answerer, having answered the summons, to listen further. Just as the summoner, by virtue of his summons, obligates himself for further interaction, so the answerer, by virtue of his answer, commits himself to staying with the encounter. More will be said about this matter and some of its ramifications in the discussion of what I term the problem of "availability." For the present it may suffice to give an example of a common situation under which the power of this reciprocality makes itself felt. Compare, for example, two ways in which a mother may seek to call her child to dinner from a play area. One way would involve the use of his name as a term of address with the request that he return home, e.g., "Johnny, come home. It's time for dinner." It is not an anomalous experience in this culture that such calls may elicit no response from the parties to whom they are directed. It may be claimed, upon complaint about this nonresponse, that the call was not heard. Contrast with this, however, a sequence in which the child is summoned prior to a statement of the summoner's intention. If the child answers the summons, he is estopped from ignoring what follows it, e.g., "Johnny," "Yes?" "Come home for dinner." Children may resist answering the summons, knowing what may follow it, and realizing that to answer the summons commits them to hearing what they do not want to hear. Although they may nonetheless not obey the commandment, claiming they have not heard, it is more difficult if they have answered the summons.[7]

---

[7] The same phenomenon is presented in a rather more exalted setting in the following excerpt from Kafka's *The Trial:*

He had almost passed the last of the pews and was emerging into the open space between himself and the doorway when he heard the priest lifting up his voice. A resonant, well-trained voice. How it rolled through the expectant Cathedral! But it was no congregation the priest was addressing, the words were unambiguous and inescapable, he was calling out: "Joseph K.!"

K. started and stared at the ground before him. For the moment he was still free, he could continue on his way and vanish through one of the small, dark wooden doors that faced him at no great distance. It would simply indicate that he had not understood the call, or that he had understood it and did not care. But if he were to turn round he would be caught, for that would amount to an admission that he had understood it very well, that he was really the person addressed, and that he was ready to obey. Had the priest called his name a second time K. would certainly have gone on but since there was a persistent silence, though he stood waiting for a long time, he could not help turning his head a little just to see what the priest was doing. The priest was standing calmly in the pulpit as before, yet it was obvious

It is to be noted that the nonterminality of an SA sequence and the obligations that produce it are mutually oriented to by the parties to the interaction and may affect the very choice of an answer to the original summons. A prospective answerer of a summons is attuned to the obligation of the summoner to respect the nonterminality of the sequence (i.e., to continue the interaction, either by talk or bodily activity) once the answer is delivered. He is likewise attuned to his obligation, having answered, to be prepared to attend the summoner's obligated next behavior. Should he not be in a position to fulfill this listener's obligation, he may provide for that fact by answering the summons with a "motion to defer," e.g., "John?" "Just a minute, I'll be right there." Of course, such deferrals may, in fact, serve to cancel the interaction, as when a "just a minute" either intendedly or unwittingly exhausts the span of control of the summons. More will be said below about deferrals, and their appropriateness, in our consideration of the issue of availability to interact. [Compare Goffman (1953:197): "sometimes the reply may contain an explicit request to hold off for a moment . . . ." The present analysis is intended to explicate why this should be needed (its occurrence being independently establishable) by reference to the temporal organization of the opening sequence.]

We now turn to a consideration of another property of SA sequences, one that will allow us to examine not only the relationship between completed SA sequences and their sequels but the internal structure of the sequences themselves.

CONDITIONAL RELEVANCE IN SA SEQUENCES

The property of conditional relevance is formulated to address two problems. [The term and some elements of the idea of "conditional relevance" were suggested by Sacks (1969).] The first of these is: How can we rigorously talk about two items as a sequenced pair of items, rather than as two separate units, one of which might happen to follow the other? The second problem is: How can we, in a sociologically meaningful and rigorous way, talk about the "absence" of an item; numerous things are not present at any point in a conversation, yet only some have a relevance

---

that he had observed K.'s turn of the head. It would have been like a childish game of hide-and-seek if K. had not turned right around to face him . . . "You are Joseph K.?" said the priest, lifting one hand from the balustrade in a vague gesture. "Yes," said K., thinking how frankly he used to give his name and what a burden it had recently become to him; nowadays people he had never seen before seemed to know his name. How pleasant it was to have to introduce oneself before being recognized: "Yes," said K., "so I have been informed." "Then you are the man I seek," said the priest. "I am the prison chaplain" (© copyright, 1956 by Alfred A. Knopf, Inc.).

that would allow them to be seen as "absent." Some items are, so to speak, "officially absent." It is to address these problems that the notion of conditional relevance is introduced. By conditional relevance of one item on another we mean: given the first, the second is expectable; upon its occurrence it can be seen to be a second item to the first; upon its nonoccurrence it can be seen to be officially absent—all this provided by the occurrence of the first item.

We may begin to explicate conditional relevance in SA sequences by employing it to clarify further some materials already discussed. The property of "nonterminality" may be reformulated by saying that further talk is conditionally relevant on a completed SA sequence. In such a formulation we treat the SA sequence as a unit; it has the status of a first item in a sequence for which further talk becomes the second item, expectable upon the occurrence of the first. As noted, the specific focus of this expectation is upon the summoner, who must supply the beginning of the further talk. Within this reformulation, if he fails to do so, that fact is officially noticeable and further talk is officially absent. It is by orienting to these facts that an answerer may find further talk coming fast upon him and, if unprepared to fulfill his obligation to attend to it, may seek to defer it by answering "Just a minute," as was noted above.

My main interest in conditional relevance at this point does not, however, have to do with that of further talk upon a completed SA sequence but with the internal workings of the sequence itself. Simply said, *A is conditionally relevant on the occurrence of S.*

We can see the conditional relevance of A on S most clearly in the following sort of circumstance. If one party issues an S and no A occurs, that provides the occasion for repetition of the S. That is to say, the nonoccurrence of the A is seen by the summoner as its official absence, and its official absence provides him with adequate grounds for repetition of the S. We say "adequate grounds" in light of the rule, previously formulated, that the summoner may *not* repeat the S if the sequence has been completed. As long as the sequence is not completed, however, the S may be repeated.

Two qualifications must be introduced at this point, one dealing with the extendability of repetitions of S, the other with the temporal organization of those repetitions relative to the initial S. To take the second point first: In order to find that an A is absent, the summoner need not wait for posterity. In principle, unless some limitation is introduced, the occurrence of S might be the occasion for an indefinite waiting period at some point in which an A might occur. This is not the case. In noting this fact, a subsidiary property of the conditional relevance of A on S may be formulated—the property of immediate juxtaposition.

The following observations seem to hold: In QA sequences, if one asks a question, a considerable amount of silence may pass before the other speaks. Nonetheless, if certain constraints on the content of his remarks (having to do with the relation of their substantive content to the substantive content of the question) are met, then the other's remark may be heard as an answer to the question. Secondly, even if the intervening time is filled not with silence but with talk, within certain constraints some later utterance may be heard as the answer to the question (e.g., X: "Have you seen Jim yet?" Y: "Oh is he in town?" X: "Yeah, he got in yesterday." Y: "No, I haven't seen him yet.").

By contrast with this possible organization of QA sequences, the following may be noted about SA sequences. The conditional relevance of an A on an S must be satisfied within a constraint of *immediate juxtaposition*. That is to say, an item that may be used as an answer to a summons will not be heard to constitute an answer to a summons if it occurs separated from the summons. While this point may seem to imply that temporal ordering is involved, it is far from clear that "time" or "elapsed time" is the relevant matter. An alternative, suggested by Harvey Sacks, would make reference to "nextness" plus some conception of "pacing" or of units of activity of finer or coarser grain by reference to which "nextness" would be located.

We may now note the relevance of this constraint to the formulation of the absence of an A. When we say that upon A's absence S may be repeated, we intend to note that A's absence may be found if its occurrence does not immediately follow an S. The phenomenon is encountered when examining occurrences in a series such as S-short pause-S-short pause, or "Dick" . . . no answer . . . "Dick" . . . , etc. In this mechanical age it may be of interest to note that the very construction and operation of the mechanical ring is built on these principles. If each ring of the phone be considered a summons, then the phone is built to ring, wait for an answer, if none occurs, to ring again, wait for an answer, ring again, etc. And indeed, some persons, polite even when interacting with a machine, will not interrupt a phone, but wait for the completion of a ring before picking up the receiver.

The other qualification concerning the repeatability of an S upon the official absence of an A concerns a *terminating rule*. It is empirically observable that S's are not repeated without limitation, until an A is actually returned. There is, then, some terminating rule used by members of the society to limit the number of repetitions of an S. I cannot at this point give a firm formulation of such a terminating rule, except to note my impression that S's are not strung out beyond three to five repetitions at the most. However, that some terminating rule is normally used by adult members of the society can be noted by observing their annoyance at the behavior of children who do not employ it. Despite the formulation in numerical terms, a similar reservation must be entered here as was entered with respect to time above. It is not likely that "number" or "counting" is the relevant matter. Aside from contextual circumstances (e.g., location), the requirement of "immediate juxtaposition" discussed above may be related to the terminating rule(s). It may be by virtue of a telephone caller's assumption of the priority or "nextness" of a response, given the ring of the phone, that the telephone company finds it necessary to use the phone book to advise callers to allow at least ten rings to permit prospective answerers time to maneuver their way to the phone.

One further observation may be made at this point about repetitions of S. "Repetition" does not require that the same lexical item be repeated; rather, successive utterances are each drawn from the class of items that may be summonses, although the particular items that are used may change over some string of repetitions. For example, "Mommy . . . Mommy" may then shift to "Mom . . . Mom" or "Mother . . ."; "Jim" may shift to "Mr. Smith," or "Jim Smith" (as, for example, when trying to attract someone from the rear in a crowded setting). A ring of a doorbell may shift to a knock on the door, the mechanical ring of a phone is replaced by some lexical item, such as "hello" when the caller hears the receiver lifted and nothing is said (as with the deviant case introduced earlier to which I shall return later).

While I am unable to formulate a terminating rule for repetitions of S when no A occurs, it is clear that we have a terminating rule when an A does occur: *A terminates the sequence.* As noted, upon the completion of the SA sequence, the original summoner cannot summon again. The operation of this terminating rule, however, depends upon the clear recognition that an A has occurred. This recognition normally is untroubled. However, trouble sometimes occurs by virtue of the fact that some lexical items, e.g., "Hello," may be used both as summonses and as answers. Under some circumstances it may be impossible to tell whether such a term has been used as summons or as answer. Thus, for example, when acoustic difficulties arise in a telephone connection, both parties may attempt to confirm their mutual availability to one another. Each one may then employ the term "Hello?" as a summons to the other. For each of them, however, it may be unclear whether what he hears in the earpiece is an answer to his check or the other's summons for him to answer. One may, under such circumstances, hear a conversation in which a sequence of some length is constituted by nothing but alternatively and simultaneously offered "hellos." Such "verbal dodging" is typically resolved by the use, by one party, of an item on which a second is conditionally relevant, where that second is unambiguously a second part of a two-part sequence. Most typically this is a question, and the question "Can you hear me?" or one of its common lexical variants, regularly occurs.

We may note that the matters we have been discussing are involved in problems having to do with the coordinated character of social interaction, whether they be coordinated entry into a conversation, coordinated re-entry into an interrupted conversation, or the coordination of the activity in its course. In particular, we will shortly turn to a consideration of the bearing of SA sequences on coordinated entry.

The power of the conditional relevance of A on S is such that a variety of strong inferences can be made by persons on the basis of it, and we now turn to consider some of them. We may first note that not only does conditional relevance operate "forwards," the occurrence of an S providing the expectability of an A, but it works in "reverse" as well. If, after a period of conversational lapse, one person in a multi-person setting (and particularly when persons are not physically present but within easily recallable range) should produce an item that may function as an A to an S, such as "What?," or "Yes?," then another person in that environment may hear in that utterance that an unspoken summons was heard. He may then reply "I didn't call you." (This, then, is another sort of circumstance in which we find an immediately graspable error, such as was remarked on earlier.) The connection between a summons and an answer provides both prospective and retrospective inferences.

A further inferential structure attached to the conditional relevance of A on S can lead us to see that this property has the status of what Durkheim (1950) intended by the term "social fact"; i.e., the property is both "external" and "constraining." When we say that an answer is conditionally relevant upon a summons, it is to be understood that the behaviors referred to are not "casual options" for the persons involved. A member of the society may not "naively choose" not to answer a summons. The culture provides that a variety of "strong inferences" can be drawn from the fact of the official absence of an answer, and any member who does not answer does so at the peril of one of those inferences being made.

[Terms such as "casual option," "naively choose," and "strong inference" are used here in a fashion that may require explanation. Although not supplying a fully adequate explication, the following suggestion may be in order. By "may not naively choose" is meant that the person summoned cannot deny that *some* inference may legitimately be made. If some *particular* inference is proposed, then in denying *it* the summoned offers a substitute, thereby conceding the legitimacy of *an* inference, though not perhaps of a *particular one*. If questioned as to the warrant for his inference, the summoner may refer to the absence of an answer, and this stands as an adequate warrant. A sequence constructed to exemplify these remarks might be:

SUMMONER: Are you mad at me?
SUMMONED: Why do you think that?
SUMMONER: You didn't answer when I called you.
SUMMONED: Oh. No, I didn't hear you.

Conversely, the following observed exchange may suggest what is intended by "casual option" (or "native choice"):

WIFE: What are you thinking about?
HUSBAND: Who says I'm thinking?
WIFE: You're playing with your hair.
HUSBAND: That doesn't mean anything.

The activity "playing with one's hair" is a "casual option" (or "naive choice") in this interaction and, therefore, the claim can be made that no inference is warranted.]

What sorts of inferences are involved? A first inference is "no answer–no person." When a person dials a number on the telephone, if the receiver on the other end is not picked up, he may say as a matter of course "there is no one home"; he does not typically announce "they decided not to answer." A person returning home seeking to find out if anyone else is already there may call out the name of his wife, for example, and upon not receiving an answer, may typically take it that she is not home or, while physically home, is not interactionally "in play" (e.g., she may be asleep. The term is from Goffman 1963). If one person sees another lying on a couch or a bed with eyes closed and calls their name and receives no answer, he takes it that that person is asleep or feigning sleep. He does not take it that the person is simply disregarding the summons. Or, to use a more classical dramatic example, when Tosca, thinking that her lover has been only apparently and not really executed, calls his name, she realizes by the absence of his answer that he is not only apparently dead but really so. She does not take it that he is merely continuing the masquerade.

It is this very structure of inferences that a summoner can make from the official absence of an answer that provides a resource for members of the society who seek to do a variety of insolent and quasi-insolent activities. The resource consists in this: The inference from official absence of an answer is the physical or interactional absence of the prospective answerer. Persons who want to engage in such activities as "giving the cold shoulder," "sulking," "insulting," "looking down their noses at," etc., may employ the fact that such inferences will be made from "no answer" but will be controverted by their very physical presence and being interactionally in play (they are neither asleep nor unconscious). So, although members can, indeed, "choose" not to answer a summons, they cannot do so naively; i.e., they know that if the inference of physical or interactional absence cannot be made, then some other inference will, e.g., they are cold shouldering, insulting, etc.

We may note what is a corollary of the inferential structure we have been describing. The very inferences that may be made from the fact of the official absence of an answer may then stand as accounts of the "no answer." So, not only does one infer that "no one is home," but also "no one is home" accounts for the fact of no answer. Not only may one see in the no answer that "he is mad at me" but one can account for it by that fact. More generally then, we may say that the conditional relevance of A on S entails not only that the nonoccurrence of A is its official absence but also that that absence is "accountable." Furthermore, where an inference is readily available from the absence of an answer, that inference stands as its account.

However, where no ready inference is available, then no ready account is available and the search for one may be undertaken. Something of this sort would seem to be involved in an incident such as the following (field notes): A husband and wife are in an upstairs room when a knock on the door occurs; the wife goes to answer it; after several minutes the husband comes to the head of the stairs and calls the wife's name; there is no answer and the husband runs down the stairs. If the foregoing analysis is correct, we might say that he does so in search of that which would provide an account for the absence of the wife's answer. The point made here does not follow logically, but empirically. From the relationship of the availability of an inference to its use as an account, it does not logically follow that the absence of an inference entails the absence of an account and the legitimacy of a search. An account may not be needed even if absent. It happens, however, that that is so although not logically entailed.

We have now introduced as many of the features of conditional relevance as are required for our further discussion. While the discussion of conditional relevance in this section has focused on the relations between A and S, these features are intrinsic to conditional relevance generally, and apply as well to the relations between completed SA sequences, as a unit, and further talk. If a called person's first remark is treated as an answer to the phone ring's summons, it completes the SA sequence, and provides the proper occasion for talk by the caller. If the conditional relevance of further talk on a completed SA sequence is not satisfied, we find the same sequel as is found when an A is not returned to an S: repetition or chaining. In our data:

#86

D: Police Desk (pause). Police Desk (pause). Hello, Police Desk (longer pause). Hello. (A#AA#A)
C: Hello. (S)
D: Hello (pause). Police Desk? (A#A)
C: Pardon?
D: Do you want the Police Desk?

We turn now to a consideration of the problem of the availability to talk that provides the theoretical importance of SA sequences and opening sequences in general. In doing so we return to the concerns with the coordinated entry into an encounter, and the deviant case that required the reformulation of the distribution rule.

The Availability to Talk

After having formulated a simple description for the opening sequence of telephone calls, we encountered a deviant case that was not described by that formulation. Rather than developing a deviant case analysis we set out to try to deepen the formulation of the opening sequence so that it would encompass with equal ease the vast majority of cases already adequately described and the troublesome variant. It will be recalled that the datum that gave us trouble read as follows:

#9

(Police make call—receiver is lifted and there is a one-second pause.)

D: Hello.
Other: American Red Cross
D: [etc.]

In that piece, the caller made the first remark, whereas the distribution rule requires that the called party makes the first remark. The foregoing analysis provides for this occurrence as being as rule-governed a phenomenon as other interchanges are. Treating the ringing of the phone as a summons and recalling the conditional relevance of an answer on it, we find that after the receiver has been lifted, the expectation of an answer is operative. In this piece of data, what occurs after the receiver is picked up would have passed as a normal case of the distribution rule had it not been noted that it was the caller, not the called, who uttered it. The SA formulation gives us the circumstances under which it is not unusual for that remark to be uttered by the caller: treating the ring of the phone (which the distribution rule disregards) as a summons to which no answer is returned. As was noted in our discussion of conditional relevance, A is conditioned upon the occurrence of an S, and should it not occur it is officially absent and warrants a repetition of the S. Hearing, now, the "Hello" as such a repetition provides for its status as a second summons in such an occurrence. The structure of the datum thus is seen to be S, no answer, S, A.

Likewise, all the cases easily handled by the distribution rule are handled with equal ease by the SA formulation, so long as the telephone ring is regarded as a summons. Thus, the rule "the called talks first" follows clearly from the conditional relevance of an A upon the occurrence of an S; and the less general rule, the "caller provides the first topic," follows from the conditional relevance of further talk upon a completed SA sequence. The distribution rule's operation is incorporated within the structure of SA sequencing.

We will now discuss the work SA sequences do by elaborating some properties of the component summons and answer items. The remainder of the present discussion, on the availability to talk and the coordinated entry into the sequence, will be devoted to further explicating the opening interactional structure.

Many activities seem to require some minimum number of participants. For thinking or playing solitaire, only one is required; for dialogue, at least two; and for "eristic dialogue," at least three.[8] When an activity has as one of its properties a requirement of a minimal number of parties, then the same behavior done without that "quota" being met is subject to being seen as an instance of some other activity (with a different minimum requirement, perhaps), or as "random" behavior casting doubt on the competence or normality of its performer. (This is so where the required number of parties is two or more; it would appear for any activity to get done, one party at least must be available.) Thus, one person playing the piano while another is present may be seen to be performing, while in the absence of another he may be seen to be practicing. Persons finding themselves waving to no one in particular by mistake may have to provide for the sense of their hand movement as having been only the first part of a convoluted attempt to scratch their head.

Conversation, at least for adults in this society, seems to be an activity with a minimal requirement of two participants. This may be illustrated by the following observations.

Buses in Manhattan have as their last tier of seats one long bench. On

---

[8] I touch here only tangentially on a larger area—what might be termed "*n*-party properties and problems." What is suggested by that term is that for activities with a common value for *n* (i.e., two-party activities, three-party activities, etc.), there may be, by virtue of that common feature, some common problems or properties. For example, two-party activities may share some problems of coordination, or some properties as compared to three-party activities. Alternatively, activities that have a minimum-number-of-parties requirement may have common properties as compared to those whose relevant parameter is a maximum number of participants. It is the latter possibility that is being touched on here.

On "eristics," see Perelman:

Were there any need for a clear sign enabling one to contrast the criterion of eristic dialogue with that of the other kinds, it would be found in the existence of a judge or arbitor charged with giving the casting vote between the antagonists, rather than in the intentions and procedures of the adversaries themselves. Because the purpose of the debate is to convince not the adversary but the judge; because the adversary does not need to be won over to be beaten; for this very reason the eristic dispute is of no great interest to the philosopher (1963:166).

one occasion two persons were observed sitting on this last bench next to one another but in no way indicating that they were, to use Goffman's term (1963:102–103), "with each other." Neither turned his head in the direction of the other and for a long period of time, neither spoke. At one point, one of them began speaking without, however, turning his head in the direction of the other. It was immediately observed that other passengers within whose visual range this "couple" were located, scanned the back area of the bus to find to whom that talk was addressed. It turned out, of course, that the talk was addressed to the one the speaker was "with." What is of interest to us, however, is that the others present in the scene immediately undertook a search for a conversational other. On other occasions, however, similar in all respects but one to the preceding, a different sequel occurred. The dissimilarity was that the talker was not "with" anyone and, when each observer scanned the environment for the conversational other, no candidate for that position, including each scanner himself, could be located. The observers then took it that the talker was "talking to himself" and the passengers exchanged "knowing glances." The issue here could be seen to involve what Bales (1951:87–90) has called "targeting," and, to be sure, that is what the persons in the scene appear to have been attending to. It is to be noted, however, that it is by reference to the character of conversation as a minimally two-party activity that the relevance of seeking the target is established in the first place. In this connection, it may be remarked that such phenomena as "talking to the air" (Goffman 1953:159) or glossing one's behavior by "talking to oneself," are best understood not as exceptions to the minimal two-party character of conversation but as special ways of talking to others while not addressing them, of which other examples are given in Bales (1951:89–90).

On another occasion, two persons were observed walking toward one another on a college campus, each of them walking normally. Suddenly one of them began an extremely pronounced and angular walk in which the trunk of his body was exaggeratedly lowered with each step and raised with the next. The one encountering him took such a walk to be a communicative act and immediately turned around to search the environment for the recipient of the communication. In the background a girl was approaching. The two males continued on their respective paths and after some fifteen to twenty paces the one looked back again to see if, indeed, it was to the girl in the background that the gesture was directed.

We have said that conversation is a "minimally two-party" activity. The initial problem of coordination in a two-party activity is the problem of availability; that is, a person who seeks to engage in an activity that requires the collaborative work of two parties must first establish, via some interactional procedure, that another party is available to collaborate. It is clear that a treatment of members' solutions to the problem of availability might, at the same time, stand as a description of how coordinated entry into an interactive course of action is accomplished. Our task is to show that SA sequences are, indeed, germane to the problems both of availability and coordinated entry, and how they provide solutions to both these problems simultaneously.

We must show how the working and properties of SA sequences *establish* the availability of the two parties to a forthcoming two-party interaction (and, in the absence of a completed sequence, foreclose the possibility of the activity) and how they, furthermore, ensure that availability, both at the beginning and in the continuing course of the interaction. We noted before that the absence of an answer to a summons led strongly to the inference of the absence of a party or claimed the other's unavailability to interact. Conversely, the presence of an answer is taken to establish the availability of the answerer; his availability involves, as we have seen, his obligation to listen to the further talk that is conditionally relevant upon the completion of the sequence. In sum, the completion of a sequence establishes the mutual availability of the parties and allows the activity to continue, and failure to complete the sequence establishes or claims the unavailability of at least one of them and perhaps undercuts the possibility of furthering that course of action.

We may note, in qualification, that a distinction must be made between a party's "presence" and his "availability" to interact (as we shall later distinguish between his "availability" to interact and his "commitment" to do so). In our earlier discussion, we pointed out that the resource that members of the society draw upon in doing such activities as "cold shouldering," "insulting," "sulking," etc., involves the joint observability of physical presence, social presence (that is, consciousness and awareness) and the absence of an answer to a summons, indicating or claiming unavailability for interaction. For the insolent activity to be accomplished via such a contrast, obviously enough, requires the distinctness of the items so contrasted. Several additional illustrations may serve to extend the scope of our sense of this difference.

Those who can remember their adolescence may recall occurrences such as the following in their high schools. In the morning, quite often as a first piece of official business, the teacher would "call the roll." In that case, a student, when his name was called, would respond by answering "present" or by raising his hand. Neither party then expected that further interaction between them would occur. Mere presence was being established. If they went to a "proper" high school, they may have been required to respond to a teacher's calling of their name in a recitation period by jumping to their feet, and awaiting some further behavior by the teacher. In that situation, their presence already established, they were being summoned to be available for some interaction, typically some examination. Teachers who saw a student physically present but not attentive to the official environment might make that fact observable to the public there assembled by calling a student's name and allowing all to see that he did not answer by standing up and establishing his availability. In that way then, the properties of a summons-answer sequence could be employed not only to establish availability or unavailability but to proclaim it to all who could see.

In telephone interactions, the lifting of a receiver without further ado serves to establish the presence of a person at the called number. It does not, however, establish the availability of that person for further conversation. Indeed, the deviant case that was introduced earlier presents precisely this set of circumstances, and was met by further summoning by the caller to elicit some demonstration of availability, i.e., some answering remark.[9] In this age, in which social critics complain about the replacement of men by machines, this small corner of the social world has not been uninvaded. It is possible, nowadays, to hear the phone you are calling picked up and hear a human voice answer, but nevertheless not be talking to a human. However small its measure of consolation, we may note that even machines such as the automatic answering device are constructed on social, and not only mechanical, principles. The machine's magnetic voice will not only answer the caller's ring but will also inform him when its ears will be available to receive his message, and warns him both to wait for the beep and confine his interests to fifteen seconds. Thereby both *abab* and the properties of SA sequences are preserved.

While the machine's answer to a summoning incoming call is specifically constructed to allow the delivery of the message by the summoner, and is mechanically constructed with a slot for its receipt, the fact that it is a machine gives callers more of an option either to answer or not than they

---

[9] Note that the French may answer the phone with a remark specifically oriented to their availability—"*j-écoute*"; while the British may respond to an interlocutor's failure to answer a summons or question by inquiring if the "no answer—no person" inference is correct—"Are you there?"

After this paper had been completed, Miss Gail Ziferstein brought to my attention the following datum (from another corpus of materials) that is relevant here and at other points in the analysis:

OPERATOR:	Hello, Mister Lehrhoff?
LEHRHOFF:	Mh hm . . .
OPERATOR:	Mister Savage is gon' pick up an' talk to ya.⎫ simultaneous
LEHRHOFF:	Alright. ⎭

(52 seconds intervening)

OPERATOR:	Hello.
LEHRHOFF:	Yes.
OPERATOR:	Did Mistuh Savage ever pick up?
LEHRHOFF:	If he did, he didn't say "hello."
OPERATOR:	Oh, o alright, smarty, just hold on.⎫ simultaneous
LEHRHOFF:	heh! heh heh heh heh heh heh ⎭
OPERATOR:	hhh!

have when the voice emanates from a larynx and not a loudspeaker. One thing that is specifically clear and differentiated between a human and mechanical answerer is that although both may provide a slot for the caller to talk again, the human answerer will then talk again himself whereas currently available machines will not. We have previously provided for the obligation of the answerer to listen to that talk, but we have not yet provided for the possibility that the answerer may then talk again, and it is to that we now turn.

One hitherto unnoticed and important fact about answers to summonses is that they routinely either are, or borrow some properties of, questions.[10] This is most obviously so in the case of "what?" but seems equally so of "yeah?," and "yes?," which three terms, together with glances of the eyes and bodily alignments, constitute the most frequently used answer items. The sheer status of these items as questions, and the particular kinds of questions that they are, allow us to deepen the previous analysis of the obligation of the summoner to talk again upon the completion of the sequence, the obligation of the answerer to listen, and what may follow the talk he listens to.

The obligation of the summoner to talk again is not merely a distinctive property of SA sequences. In many activities similar to the SA sequence, where, for example, someone's name may also be called, the caller of it need not talk again to the person called. Such activities as indicating someone's "turn to go," as in a discussion or game, share with "signaling" by rings of the telephone the fact that they are prearranged or invoke some shared orders of priority and relevance. Such activities much more directly can be seen to be pure signaling devices and not summoning devices. That an activity starting, for example, with the enunciation of a name, is a summons, is provided by its assembly over its course. The obligation of the summoner to talk again is, therefore, not merely "the obligation of a summoner to talk again"; it is the obligation of a member of the society to answer a question if he has been asked one. The activity of summoning, is, therefore, not intrinsic to any of the items that compose it; it is an assembled product whose efficacious properties are cooperatively yielded by the interactive work of both summoner and answerer. The signaling devices accomplish different outcomes. By not including questions as their second items, they do not constrain the utterers of their first items to talk again. Rather, they invoke prearrangements, priorities, and shared

---

[10] I am indebted here to David Sudnow. The notion of "borrowing properties of questions" is a difficult one. How one might prove that some item, while not a question, borrowed some property of questions is not clear, in part because it is not clear how one would prove that some item was or was not a question. The discussion that follows may, therefore, be read as being limited to items that are, intuitively, "clearly" questions, e.g., items that have "interrogative intonation," or that are lexically question items (e.g., "what?"), deferring the issue of "borrowing properties."

relevances as matters to which the addressed party must now direct his attention.

We now see that the summons is a particularly powerful way of generating a conversational interaction. We have seen that it requires, in a strong way, that an answer be returned to it. By "in a strong way" we intend that the strong set of inferences we described before attend the absence of an answer, e.g., physical absence, social absence (being alseep or unconscious), or purposeful ignoring. Moreover, it seems to be the case that the answer returned to it has the character of a question. The consequence of this is two-fold: (1) that the summoner now has, by virtue of the question he has elicited, the obligation to produce an answer to it, and (2) the person who asked the question thereby assumes an obligation to listen to the talk he has obligated the other to produce. Thus, sheerly by virtue of this two-part sequence, two parties have been brought together; each has acted; each by his action has produced and assumed further obligations; each is then available; and a pair of roles has been invoked and aligned. To review these observations with specific reference to the two steps that are their locus:

SUMMONER:	Bill? (A summons item; obligates other to answer under penalty of being found absent, insane, insolent, condescending, etc. Moreover, by virtue of orientation to properties of answer items, i.e., their character as questions, provides for user's future obligation to answer, and thereby to have another turn to talk. Thus, preliminary or prefatory character, establishing and ensuring availability of other to interact.)
SUMMONED:	What? (Answers summons, thereby establishing availability to interact further. Ensures there will be further interaction by employing a question item, which demands further talk or activity by summoner.)

We may notice that in relating our observations to the first two steps of the sequence we have dealt not only with two steps but with the third as well. We may now show that the span of control of the first two items extends further still. Not only is it the case that a question demands an answer and thereby provides for the third slot to be filled by the summoner, but also one who asks a question, as we noted above, has the right to talk again. The consequence of this is that after the summoner has talked for the second time, this talk will have amounted to the answer to the answerer (of the summons), and the latter will have a right to take another turn. This provides for the possibility of four initial steps following from the use of a summons, which thus emerges as an extraordinarily powerful social item.[11] We have not yet exhausted its power.

We may note that the item the summons elicits in the second slot is not adequately described as merely "a question." It is a question of a very special sort. Its special characteristic may become observable by contrast with other kinds of questions. One not unusual type of question has the property that its asker knows the specific content of the answer that must be returned to it. So, for example, radio interviewers acquainted with the person they are interviewing and perhaps long and intimate friends of theirs may nonetheless ask such a question as was heard posed to one musician by another who doubles as a disk jockey: "Tell me, Jim, how did you first break into music?" In a second type of question, while the asker does not know the specific content of the answer, he knows, if we may use a mathematical analogy, the general parameters that will describe it. So, for example, while the doctor in an initial interview may not know specifically what will be answered to his "What seems to be the trouble?" he very readily takes it that the answer will include references to some physical or psychic troubles.

The character of the question that is returned to a summons differs sharply from either of these. Its specific feature seems to be that the asker of "what?" may have little notion of what an accomplished answer may look like, both with respect to its substantive content and with respect to the amount of time that may be necessary for its delivery. This property— the specific ambiguity of what would constitute an answer—is clearly seen in the use that is often made of it by those persons in the society who may have restricted rights to talk. Thus, we may understand the elegance

---

[11] That conversational oaks may out of conversational acorns grow is a frequent theme in folklore. One version of such a story, starting from a somewhat different acorn, is the following:

On the express train to Lublin, a young man stopped at the seat of an obviously prosperous merchant.

"Can you tell me the time?" he said.

The merchant looked at him and replied: "Go to hell!"

"What? Why, what's the matter with you! I ask you a civil question in a properly civil way, and you give me such an outrageous rude answer! What's the idea?"

The merchant looked at him, sighed wearily, and said, "Very well. Sit down and I'll tell you. You ask me a question. I have to give you an answer, no? You start a conversation with me—about the weather, politics, business. One thing leads to another. It turns out you're a Jew—I'm a Jew, I live in Lublin—you're a stranger. Out of hospitality, I ask you to my home for dinner. You meet my daughter. She's a beautiful girl—you're a handsome young man. So you go out together a few times—and you fall in love. Finally you come to ask for my daughter's hand in marriage. So why go to all that trouble. Let me tell you right now, young man, I won't let my daughter marry anyone who doesn't even own a watch!!" ("To Save Time," in Ausubel 1948:404–405).

involved in a standardized way in which children often begin conversations with adults. A phrase such as "You know what, Mommy?," inviting a "what?" as its return, allows the child to talk by virtue of the obligation thereby imposed upon him to answer a question while retaining a certain freedom in his response by virtue of the adult's inability to know in advance what would have been adequate, complete, satisfactory, or otherwise socially acceptable answer. (For these points I am indebted to Harvey Sacks.)

Such an open-ended question does not expand what can be said beyond the constraints of the categorical relationship of the parties. But as compared with other kinds of answers to summonses, it does not introduce additional constraints. Additional constraints may, of course, be introduced by modifications on "what?," such as intonation or addition (e.g., "what now?"). [Other lexical items used as answers are (on the telephone) "hello" or some self-identification (e.g., "Macy's"). For a discussion of the ways the latter items impose additional constraints, see Schegloff (1967, Chapter 4).]

In other words, there are constraints on the "contents" of a speaker's remarks once a conversational course is entered into and some conversational "line" is already present to be coordinated to. At the beginning of a conversation, however, no such "line" is already present, and the open-endedness of the answer that "what?" allows is a reflection of that fact and the requirement that if there is to be a conversation, it must be about something. The fact of open-endedness, however, does not necessarily imply the absence of all constraint. How much constraint is to be put, or can be put, on the content of some opening substantive remark may depend strongly on the relationship of the parties to one another, and that includes not only their relationship as it may turn out to be formulated but their relationship as it develops from moment to moment. While two parties who are about to be joined by an interaction medium may later be properly categorized as father and son, for them, as the phone rings, and indeed when it is picked up and the "hello" is uttered, they may be strangers. Their relationship to one another may have to be "discovered," while interactional work must precede the "discovery." Under such a circumstance, given that strangers have restricted rights to talk to one another and restricted topics about which they may talk, then a completely open-ended "what" may be a "hazardous" opening for a phone conversation in which, at the moment of its utterance, the other may be a stranger. The consequences of such matters for the infrequency of answers such as "what" or "yes" on the phone, and for the alternatives that may be employed in their stead, are matters that cannot be gone into here.

To conclude the present discussion, it may be noted that provision is made by an SA sequence not only for the coordinated entry into a conversation but also for its continued orderliness. First, we may note that in the very doing of the two items that constitute SA sequences, and in the two turns these items specifically provide for, the first two alternations of *abab* are produced and that sequence is established as a patterned rule for the interaction that follows.

Insofar as the answerer of the summons does not use his right to talk again to introduce an extended utterance, the work of SA sequences may be seen to extend over a yet larger span of conversation. By "not introducing an extended utterance," I mean that he simply employs one of what might be called the "assent terms" of the society, such as "mmhmm" or "yes" or "yeah," or "uh huh." Under that circumstance the following may be the case: As the initial response to the summons establishes the answerer's availability and commits him to attend the next utterance of the summoner (that is, ensures his continued availability for the next remark), this obligation to listen and this ensurance that he will, may be renewable. Each subsequent "uh huh" or "yes" then indicates the continuing availability of its speaker and recommits him to hear the utterance that may follow. Availability may, in this way, be "chained," and, in fact, speakers with extended things to say may routinely leave slots open for the other to insert an "uh huh," thereby recalling them to and recommitting them to the continuing course of the activity.[12]

It was remarked earlier that conversation is a "minimally two-party" activity. That requirement is not satisfied by the mere copresence of two persons, one of whom is talking. It requires that there be both a "speaker" and a "hearer." (That "hearership" can be seen as a locus of rules, and a status whose incumbency is subject to demonstration, is suggested by some of Sacks' work.) To behave as a "speaker" or as a "hearer" when the other is not observably available is to subject oneself to a review of one's competence and "normality." Speakers without hearers can be seen to be "talking to themselves." Hearers without speakers "hear voices." (But cf. Hymes 1964e on cultural variations in the definition of participants in speech events.) SA sequences establish and align the roles of speaker and hearer, providing a summoner with evidence of the availability or unavailability of a hearer, and a prospective hearer with notice of a prospective speaker. The sequence constitutes a coordinated entry into the activity, allowing each party occasion to demonstrate his coordination

---

[12] It is as wry recognition of the operation and subversion of this mechanism that a standard joke of the society may be appreciated. In it, a tired husband returns from the office, sinks gratefully into his easy chair and opens the evening paper to the sports page. His nagging wife, however, wishes to unburden herself of the accumulated troubles of the day and begins an extended monologue. Routinely, she leaves a slot of silence and he dutifully inserts "Yes, dear," until, dimly aware that all is not as it appears to be, she says, "Are you ignoring me?" and he replies "Yes, dear."

with the other, a coordination that may then be sustained by the parties demonstrating continued speakership or hearership. It is by way of the status of items such as "uh huh" and "mmhmm" as demonstrations of continued, coordinated hearership that we may appreciate the fact that they are among the few items that can be spoken while another is speaking without being heard as "an interruption."

13

A Kinesic-Linguistic Exercise: The Cigarette Scene

RAY L. BIRDWHISTELL

Ray L. Birdwhistell is Professor of Communications, Annenberg School of Communications, at the University of Pennsylvania and Senior Research Scientist, Eastern Pennsylvania Psychiatric Institute. He received his doctorate from the University of Chicago and has taught at the University of Kentucky, the Foreign Service Institute, and the University of Buffalo. Inventor of the field of kinesics, for two decades he has been concerned with the analysis of communicative behavior as a complex whole.

In this sketch of the development of kinesic research and its current status, Birdwhistell brings out the bittersweet tension so far inherent in it. Body motion is undeniably essential to interpretation of communicative conduct, and, as Birdwhistell shows in his discussion of linguistic and kinesic interdependence, it sometimes substitutes for linguistic means. Sociolinguists concerned with the study of natural conversation are becoming increasingly aware of the need for both visual and audio records in the interpretation of interactional sequences. Some rules of alternation thus must hold across, or between, verbal and nonverbal modalities (and rules of co-occurrence, of course, involve them). "Movers" (like "speakers") presumably have a competence, a characterizable knowledge and ability, in terms of which they

From *Kinesics and Context: Essays on Body Motion Communication* by Ray L. Birdwhistell. Copyright © 1970 by the Trustees of the University of Pennsylvania. By permission of the author and The University of Pennsylvania Press.

interpret and accomplish body motion, both as an autonomous mode of communication and as a mode integrated with language in social interaction. Because its mechanisms and functions are so largely out of awareness, nonverbal behavior should illustrate, better than most forms of cultural behavior, the same kind of patterning as language (see Sapir 1949c:556–557). Yet units and patterns of nonverbal behavior prove difficult to determine with certainty; even short segments are found almost infinitely rich for continued analysis.

If definitive progress is slow, it may be because "nonverbal behavior" conflates several aspects of patterning that must be discretely analyzed, a problem Birdwhistell discusses in terms of the relation of kinesic to extra-kinesic (parakinesic) phenomena. It may be that differences between linguistic and nonlinguistic codes in means and functions override such common organization as the human brain might be expected to confer. It may be also that structure cannot be ascertained apart form semantic and "functional" analysis (see Ervin-Tripp, Chapter 7, for a discussion of function), and that observational identification, however necessary, must ultimately depend upon ethnographic consultation of native intuition (see Sapir 1949g, and also Hockett 1955, on the dashed hope that sound spectographs would solve problems of phonological identification).

It is certain that the progress of the field has been slow because the necessarily painstaking research has depended upon a very few men. The material discussed in this chapter was filmed in 1956 and is part of a larger body of data to be treated more extensively by a group of anthropologists, psychologists, and linguists in the forthcoming *The Natural History of an Interview* (McQuown, in preparation). The linguistic model that has helped shape kinesic research (that of Trager and Smith) has been supplanted within linguistics by transformational-generative grammar. This has meant a shift in emphasis from behaviorally oriented observation and analysis to a concern with the more abstract and not directly observable rules relating meaning to sound (Chomsky and Halle 1968). But linguists of the latter school have not concerned themselves with modalities of communication apart from language, or with the difference that their approach might make for kinesic analysis.

Interest in the formal analysis of nonverbal communication processes is rapidly increasing, however. A collection of Birdwhistell's essays has recently appeared in paperback (1970). Work along similar lines is now being carried on by several other groups of researchers concerned with diagnosis of behavior in psychiatric interviews (Mahl 1968; Scheflen 1964). Of interest to students of social interaction is the work of Condon and his collaborators (1969, 1970), who, turning away from the earlier atomistic emphasis on isolation of phoneme-like units of motion, have begun to focus on "self synchrony" (on changes in the flow of body motion in relation to speech) and "interactional synchrony" (body change patterns of listeners in relation to the speech and body motion change patterns of speakers). There are indications that this type of analysis may be particularly useful in the study of communication in ethnically diverse societies.

Paul Ekman and his associates (Ekman and Friesen 1969) at the University of California, San Francisco, are focusing on some of the broader gestural complexes analyzed in terms of their physiological properties and communicative function. They distinguished five major categories of nonverbal behavior: (1) emblems, nonverbal acts which have a direct verbal translation, i.e., greetings, gestures of assent, etc.; (2) illustrators, movements tied to speech which serve to illustrate the spoken word; (3) affective displays such as facial signs indicating happiness, surprise, fear, etc.; (4) regulators, acts which maintain and regulate the act of speaking; (5) adaptors, signs originally linked to bodily needs, such as brow wiping, lip biting, etc. Computer aided methods for the isolation of these categories in video tape or film records have been developed materially reducing the otherwise considerable time required for analysis (Ekman, Friesen, and Tausig 1971).

In yet another direction, Cicourel and Boese have begun a study of deaf and dumb sign language. Their preliminary results indicate that sign language can be described in terms of syntactic rules and rules of stylistic contraction and emphasis much like those of spoken language (Cicourel and Boese 1971).

Every issue of the theory and description of communicative conduct arises forcefully in the study of nonverbal modalities: the relation between universal and culturally specific features (see Ekman and Friesen 1968); the relation between linguistic and other methodological approaches (see Greimas 1968); the uncertainty as to adequate parameters of description and initial "etic" frameworks; and the paucity of adequate data and adequately trained investigators for integrating communicative form (or means) with communicative purpose. Renewed interest in primate behavior and comparative study of signaling across species make human nonverbal signaling all the greater a challenge. Additional related readings are provided by Crystal (1969), Crystal and Quirk (1964), Dance (1968), Cazden, Hymes, and John (1971), Goffman (1964), Key (in press), LaBarre (1964), Rensky (1966), and Sebeok, Hayes, and Bateson (1964).

Doris and Gregory, as the camera is reloaded and again begins to record the scene, are reseated upon the sofa. Each has a stein of the homemade beer supplied by Doris. Doris looks from Gregory to her beer stein and at the matches which Gregory is holding. Her left hand carries the cigarette to her mouth after her right leaves the stein on the coffee table before them. Gregory continues: "He's a very, very bright four-and-a-half-year-old. Why, that drawing that he brought in is very advanced for four-and-a-half." As he talks, he opens the match folder, extracts a match, strikes the match under the closed flap, moves the lighted match into position and makes contact with her cigarette as he terminates his vocalization. As he talks, Doris moves in concert with his match manipulations until her cigarette is lighted. She speaks: "I suppose all mothers think their kids are smart, but I have no worries about that child's intellectual ability." A ⅔ second lag between "child's" and "intellectual" was equaled by another between "intellectual" and "ability." Gregory speaks, his first words coterminous with the latter hesitation and "ability": "No, that's a very smart one." As Doris talks, her right hand drops to the table edge and then past it slightly to the left to adjust her shoe strap before she drops her hand backward to the couch. This movement, with its momentary shifts, are still in concert with Gregory's, who, after Doris' cigarette is lighted, forms a triangular movement in the air which terminates with the extinguishing of the match and its disposal in the ash tray. This scene begins at (plus or minus ten frames) #12529 and is concluded by (plus or minus 10 frames) #12784.

Introduction

"The Cigarette Scene," an interactional sequence of some 18 seconds in duration, has remained a type site for linguistic-kinesic analysis throughout the decade following the original work on the Doris-Gregory films.[1] Filming techniques have improved, budgets have become sufficiently large to permit extensive recording on sound film of half-hour and hour-long sequences of conversation, interview, and interaction, and, with Jacques Van Vlack's development of the frame count B Roll, the correlation of the vocalic and the movement stream has become more precise. Other films have attracted our research interest, but this scene, in which Gregory and Doris contemporaneously discuss the merits of Doris' four-year-old son, Bruce, and engage in a ritual dancelike lighting of Doris' cigarette, has remained a rich, only partially analyzed corpus. The special cadence of this piece of interaction, which Gregory (frames 12756-12786 and 12786-12826) terminates by a batonlike change of pace, marks the scene as critical and relevant to any final appraisal of the Gregory-Doris reciprocal. The seeming irrelevance of the body movement to the content exchanged by the participants and the glove-fit coherence of the rhythmic movements of the two participants to the instrumental act of cigarette lighting has made the scene useful for demonstration purposes. In our earlier assessments, the dramatic quality of the interchange masked out the significance of other behavior in the performance. The parakinesic category, "Rhythmic-Disrhythmic," in the first appraisals, subsumed data that, as our analyses became more refined, were to be analyzable as stress kinemes and suprasegmental kinemorphemes. This present exercise attempts to bring the earlier research in line with some more recently developed techniques.

Kine to Kineme

As reported elsewhere (Birdwhistell 1952, 1958, 1961), the theory and methodology of kinesics has been consistently influenced by that of descriptive and structural linguistics. From the initial morphological discoveries, it has been clear that visible communicative behavior exhibited formal properties at least analogic to those describable for audible behavior. I have been fortunate to be in constant consultative contact with linguistic researchers, and this contact shaped the research design and terminology constructed for kinesic research. At the same time, because of a deep appreciation of linguistic discipline and rigor, I

[1] From *The Natural History of an Interview*. Norman A. McQuown, ed., in preparation, 1956– . The research for this still unpublished report was initiated at the Center for the Behavioral Sciences, during the summer of 1956. Gregory Bateson, Henry Brosin, Charles Hockett, Norman A. McQuown, Frieda Fromm-Reichmann, and the author selected 10 minutes of sound-filmed interview taken earlier by Bateson for examination. Research of the scenes from this corpus given special attention has continued sporadically by McQuown and his students, Birdwhistell and his students, and by Henry Brosin until the time of this writing (June, 1967).

have reacted against the fashionable and often careless preemption of the "etic-emic" distinctions. Throughout kinesic research, every attempt has been made to be cautious about the abstraction of isolable elements of body motion (kines) into manipulable classes of allokines (kinemes). "Complementary distribution" is an idea of great methodological force for the linguist and has proved to be an efficient tool for phonologic analysis. Because of the multiple layering of body motion behavior, both in body part and temporal arrangement, the distributional qualities of units of kinemorphology are more difficult to assess in the empirical data.

At the present writing, a kineme is a class of allokines *which can be demonstrated in kinemorphs* to be substitutable.

Note: *If more than one allokine is discovered to be present in the same structural neighborhood,* the kine representing it may be either:

a. a member of more than one kinemic class or
b. an insufficiently refined kine; or
c. the morphology has been insufficiently analyzed and we are probably dealing with an intersection of levels in the behavioral stream

The distinctions between kine and kineme, kinemorph and kinemorpheme, remain useful and efficient. However, these terms are heuristic devices. Until we become much more secure as to the morphology and syntactics of kinesics (even for American English movers) our emic assignments must be registered as tentative. The history of phonological research is reassuring to the kinesicist timid about working models; tomorrow's research will validate the model or obliterate it.

Sight and Sound

The earliest work in kinesics attempted only the crudest correlation of body motion and speech behavior (Birdwhistell 1952). I had yet to comprehend either the feasibility or necessity of sound film recording and was, in fact, resistant to the idea early suggested by McQuown that the future of kinesic-linguistic research as related to social processes depended upon intensive and parallel phonetic and microkinesic recording and analysis. As an anthropologist, I was attracted by grosser elements which I felt could be abstracted and organized by the careful scansion of the complex message stream. The isolation of these, I believed, would lead to the understanding of communication—for me then, as now, the dynamic structure which sustains order and creativity in social interaction.

The complex data which began to emerge as body motion research became involved in cross-cultural comparisons of human body motion, and the encouragement of Henry Lee Smith, Jr., and George L. Trager to study body motion as a structure with its own rules of order combined to force me to concentrate upon the visible and silenced behavior of human beings. Small stretches of films and access to a slow-motion projector by 1956 laid the groundwork for the analysis of the American kinesic system. As research proceeded, the presence of vocalization or auditor behavior was not ignored. However, it was recorded at the articulatory level as body motion behavior—not as speech behavior. Even the preliminary attempts to abstract this data, however, made it clear that beyond the circumoral activity involved in speech production, behavior appeared which seemed related to or was at least usually modified by the presence of vocalization. It was not until the Palo Alto group[2] began its research conferences that the delineation of such behavior became relevant to kinesic research.

Out of these conferences, out of the co-research with Smith and Trager, and out of the subsequent ongoing research at Eastern Pennsylvania Psychiatric Institute and at Western Pennsylvania Psychiatric Institute and Clinic[3] came ideas which led to the isolation of a variety of circum-speech body behavioral abstractions. These abstractions cover behavior characteristic of conversation, but which seems to have differing structural properties than those which could be traced for the phenomena assigned to kinesics proper.

In the Cigarette Scene, the acts of lighting the cigarette, Gregory's manipulation of the match, and Doris' adjustment of her shoe strap may be termed *instrumental behavior.* Moreover, the fact that Doris and Gregory are seated for an extended conversation is, at one level, instrumental. To say that an act is instrumental, however, does not define it, in itself, as without signal or message value. The performance of any act in the presence of others must be comprehended as having the stamp of individual and social practice. Yet, at this writing, acts such as walking, smoking, eating, knitting, woodworking, still must be filed as "instrumental" and/or "task oriented" until we know more about their communicative structure.[4] However, as we can see from the analysis of the scene, the assignment of instrumentality to the larger frame of behavior must not preclude the examination of concurrent behavior, whether such behavior

[2] Gregory Bateson, Ray Birdwhistell, Henry Brosin, Frieda Fromm-Reichmann, and Charles Hockett.

[3] The work of Harvey Sarles, William Condon, Felix Loeb, and Joseph Charny at Western Pennsylvania Psychiatric Institute and Clinic has been invaluable both as a check upon and as a creative incentive to the work here at Eastern Pennsylvania Psychiatric Institute.

[4] The work of Marvin Harris is an approach to this problem. See *The Nature of Cultural Things* (New York: 1964). See also the review by Duane Metzger in the *American Anthropologist* 67, no. 5, pt. 1 (1965):1293.

is at first glance integral to or apparently trivial to the immediate task accomplishment. There is a temptation to see instrumental acts in a social situation as "carriers" of other messages. Yet there is an equal justification, from another point of view, of assigning priority to the communicational act. At the moment, I am using the concept of *alternating context.* Either can be the context for the other.

There is a second type of customary behavior which resists kinesic analysis while having patterned form and discernible message value. Included in this category, the *demonstratives,* would be such acts as gestural mapping, the illustrative movements customary as accompaniments to female discussions of dressmaking and design or of cosmetological arrangements of the hair. To the same category belong the illustrative movements which accompany male discussions of fishing or cabinet making and which often accompany male discussions of sporting events. From the limited cross-cultural data available it is clear that demonstratives are conventionalized forms, but they do not appear to follow kinesic rules, at least among American movers. No definitive demonstratives appear in this particular scene. However, the limited tridirectional sweep which is employed by Gregory as he extinguishes the match and which is followed by the larger cigarette movement to change the cadence of the scene may, as we get more comparative data, be both "instrumental" and "demonstrative." The act is clearly, at one level, instrumental. However, without supporting data, we cannot define the *act* itself as demonstrative —the change of cadence may very well be at times, in and of itself, demonstrative.

The durations of both instrumental behavior and demonstrative behavior are often longer than that of the accompanying syntactic sentences. This need not be so. For example, a speaker may circumscribe a shape in the air while describing an object and the air picture may be coextant with the nominal clause. Comparably, an instrumental act, whether referred to in the context of accompanying speech or not, may be completed within or beyond the stretches of the speech behavior.

There is a third type of body behavior which, while still only crudely understood, should be mentioned here. This behavior is characteristic of all conversational and nonconversational interactional situations. *Interactional behavior* includes a variety of behaviors of part or whole bodies as they move toward or away from, or maintain careful spacing among, participants of an interactional scene. Hall (1959, 1966) has done pioneering work in the isolation of certain aspects of these phenomena in his work upon proxemics. Scheflen's (1966) analysis of the movement patterns in the psychiatric interview provides still another dimension to the understanding of body shifts as messageful. His study, related to Bateson and Mead's (1942) earlier work of complementary, mirroring, and parallel movements of participants, indicates that there is a discoverable logic which marks segments of interaction. The work of Condon on "synchrony" and "dissynchrony" in interaction is further suggestive of overall interpersonal movement patterns which promise, as analysis proceeds, to supply us with measures of interactional communicative signals.[5] A number of behavioral categories are reported as relevant to the examination of the interaction. Often this behavior, which ranges from the presence of a rhythmic cadence to the interaction to a disassociation in the behavior of the actors to the extent that they appear to be in isolation from one another, seems almost to be a running comment to the participants about the interaction (see also Birdwhistell 1961). Bateson's concept of "metacommunicational" is of relevance here. Perhaps the term "metainteractional" would leave the function of such variations in behavior more open for further investigation. In the case of the Cigarette Scene, going beyond the data provided by our corpus, Doris' activity might be interpreted as a demand upon Gregory for a relationship more interpersonally involved than he has seemed to engage in before. As hostess, *she* has provided beer. Her nonlexical request for Gregory to light her cigarette *may* be no more than an act to elicit a formalizing etiquette. At some level of analysis his act can be seen as the reciprocal of hers. The cadence of which we spoke above, which distinguishes this part of the scene from the remaining 20 minutes, sustains itself until Gregory cuts the beat in half with the waved match and cigarette. This action is special and must ultimately be accounted for in any description of the interaction. However, the point being made here is that while Doris moves her hands and arms and shifts her body, and while Gregory moves his hands and body in a concert beat, other things are continuing to happen. The "dance" is no more exclusive than is her "shoe fixing"—interaction is multidimensional in time and structure.

To return to the data, Doris, while continuing to talk about her son, turns away from Gregory, "reaches" for a glass which she does not take, drops the heel of her shoe away from her foot and then adjusts the strap and lets her hand fall away from the shoe before it swings back to touch the table again. Meanwhile, she has "closed" her body, moving her torso closer to her legs as she talks about "all mothers think their kids are smart". . . . Her hand touches the table on "but." She then turns back to Gregory and focuses upon him as she says, "I have no worries about that child's intellectual ability" while shaking her head with animation. Here again is a "layer" of behavior which cannot be accounted for either in

---

[5] Personal communication with William Condon. His analysis of fine-grained movement reveals that there is very close coordination in the fine movement of interactants in conversation.

strictly kinesic structure or in either of the categories laid out above. The quality of the film makes it impossible for us to confirm the impression that as she talks the tonus of her face changes. Nor can we determine whether the tight mouth-limited smile with which the scene began, taken together with the tonus shift, forms a cross-referencing signal that calls attention to the signal value of the complexity of her utterance. These phenomena which are recorded as parakinesic are detectable when we contrast these scenes with others in the larger film. However, "interpretation" of these would require more data than are supplied by all of the film and tape at our disposal.

Since the stretch which we are examining contains no clear examples of *kinesic markers,* these movements, which seem to be tied to particular semologic forms, require no discussion here. These movements customarily but irregularly appear in utterance situations in conjunction with ambiguous pronominals, in situations where the lexeme is ambiguous about tense, position, possession, and plurality, and in situations where adverbial clauses appear to require reinforcement or modification. The fact that these are lacking or submerged within other phenomena in this stretch may or may not be of significance. The string upon which we will concentrate in this discussion is Doris' "I suppose all mothers think their kids are smart, but I have no worries about that child's intellectual ability." When compared to comparable strings within the larger corpus, there is a kind of stereotypy here to her speech behavior. It is impossible from the available data to determine whether this stereotypy arises from the fact that she has used this sentence before in her dealings with the outside world, whether her words are somehow fillers for a critical relationship shift, or, whether what we hear is not stereotypy at all but what Fromm-Reichmann once described in conference as the "voice of despair." At any rate, regardless of our rationalization, the absence of discernible markers is worthy of note and may become of significance as we come to know more about the codes of interaction.

In this exercise our focus is upon what Doris *says* in this situation. It is not our present problem to determine what she *means.* At the same time, operating upon the assumption that description approaches explanation as it deals with a greater proportion of the available data, it should be profitable to describe our corpus more adequately. Charles Hockett originally transcribed this string, and his transcription was modified only slightly by an independent analysis by Norman McQuown. Trager-Smith conventions are used here, although modified slightly for Hockett's purposes.

In an attempt to get some kind of perspective upon the lexical aspect of this piece, twelve women of comparable age and social class background to that of Doris were given a typescript in standard English orthography and asked to comment upon it. All except one commented that this was standard "woman talk," i.e., a preliminary apology followed by a proud statement about the child, unusual only in the presence of the "but" rather than the expected "and." The one exception to the "woman talk" generalization came from an informant who said, "It's a sentence to hide the 'but.' She is very concerned about her child." The general attitude of these informants about the "but" was consistent with the appraisal of the psychiatrists, Henry Brosin and Frieda Fromm-Reichmann, who saw the central lexical signal of the sentence in the conjunction. (It is worthy of note that four of a control group of six women, when showed this sentence among five other sentences and asked to recall them 5 minutes later, wrote this sentence as "I suppose [one case 'guess'] all women think their kids are smart [two cases, 'bright'] and I have no worries [one case, 'I'm not worried'] about that child's [three cases, 'my child's'] intellectual ability.")

Careful review of the linguistic evidence (see Charts 13.1a, 1b, 1c)

chart 13.1a

Linguistic Transcription: "I Suppose All Mothers Think Their Kids Are Smart But"

```
1c***                       ♀-                                    -♀
fn**<                                             ∩ —
VSg*ʔm                                                          ?
Int   3          2                          3   2   3   #        :
StrJ  ∧       ∧      ∧       ∧       ∧          ∧       /         :
Sgm ay + spoz + ɔhl + məðərz + θink + ðer + kidz ər + smart  ǀ  bət  :
     I   suppose  all  mothers  think  their kids are  smart      but
```

(673) (676) (683) (688) (694)   (705) (711) (716) (719) (724) (730) (732)

676 683 686 691   698 702 706 710 718   725

---

* ?,h,r,ə,m, Vocal Segregates (Trager).
** <, Crescend (Hockett); ∩ Drawling (Trager).
*** ♀, Rasp (Trager).

Phonetic transcription omitted. Circled numbers are numbers assigned 1956.
Open numbers are from edge reading of sound film 1967.

---

provides the following discussion. Doris' customary discourse pattern contains long strings of secondary stress. Moreover, the tertiary on "I" at the start of the string is not unusual. What is more unusual are the two double cross junctures within such a short string. Doris customarily has

chart 13.1b

Transcription: "I Have No Worries About"

```
*In
VSg     hr ?ə?m?—?
Int          |2        3       3    2|  2
StrJ         | /       ∧       ∧    / |
Sgm          |ay + haev + now + wəriyz |əbawt +
              I    have   no    worries  about
```

756 757   764 767 773 780 785

752 755   760 763   778

* Overloud (Trager).

chart 13.1c

Transcription: "That Child's Intellectual Ability"

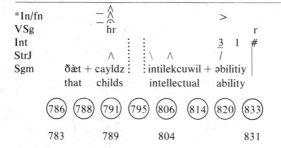

```
*In/fn     − ∧
           − ∧                    >
VSg          hr                        r
Int          : :            3   1   #
StrJ       ∧ : :\ ∧              /
Sgm     ðæt + cayldz : :intilekcuwil + əbilitiy |
        that   childs     intellectual   ability
```

786 788 791 795 806 814 820 833

783   789   804   831

* > Fading (Hockett).

very long strings without terminal junctures. This is a phenomenon common in psychiatric interviews (this is not ostensibly such an interview) and has been interpreted as a device to avoid interruption or interpretation. The segregates here again are not unusual in her speech patterning. The paralinguistic rasp over "think their kids are smart" is consistent with other portions of the larger protocol. The drawl over "are smart but I have no worries about that child's" is not, in the fact that it conveys portions of two syntactic sentences, a common device for her. *If we were trying to assess her meanings,* the use of drawl here would deserve further comparative attention. Studies of silence remain preliminary among linguists. "Hesitations" and "pauses" have been remarked upon by a number of students as worthy of study, but even when they are statistically appraised, we still know relatively little about the conventional use of the devices. However, in the case of Doris, the roughly ¼ second between "worries" and "about" and between "child's" and "intellectual" seem worthy of note, particularly if we are in pursuit (consciously or not) of some kind of evidence that the utterance implies that she does have worries and among those worries, some about her child. Even though we are not here preoccupied with meaning, it is always with us, and an increase in our data might amplify our understanding of the situation. Let us see how this sentence is marked kinesically.

Kinesic Junctures

From the beginning of the systematic investigation of American movement patterns it was evident that we were not dealing with a set of isolated and disconnected gestural forms. The discovery of kinesic junctures in the behavior of American (including American-English-speaking Canadians) movers laid the groundwork for structural kinesics. Not only were movement segments tied together morphologically, but longer segments and complex forms were joined or separated by junctural conventions. The fact that streams of body behavior were segmented and connected by demonstrable behavioral shifts analogic to double cross, double bar, and single bar junctures in the speech stream enhanced the research upon kinemorphology and freed kinesics from the atomistic amorphy of earlier studies dominated by "gestures" and "sign" language. Moreover, when we attempted to study interactional situations, by means of context analysis (Scheflen 1966), the need for rigor demanded markers to give us some way of explicitly breaking the behavioral stream, of segmenting out sections for special comparative attention. The fact that the kinesic markers, while at times coextant with the linguistic markers, often gave us a very different shape contributed to our assessment of data that did not seem to fit within linguistic terminal junctures. This became particularly evident when the major body shift which I termed the kinesic triple cross juncture served to relate and segment much longer stretches of conversational behavior. While not entirely accurate, we have come to see the behavioral stretch marked by kinesic triple cross junctures as comparable to paragraphing or stanzaing in writing. We have not attempted the systematic research necessary to relate this juncture to content but, as of this writing, the best statement possible is that it is often but not always related to shifts in content *or* to shifts in relationship patterning. Only further research will permit security as to whether such phenomena as these are separate, interdependent, or in free distribution.

During the past several years, research upon complex strings of speech taken from conversation and compared with the production of simple and complex statistical formulas (Birdwhistell 1968) has provided us with two other junctural forms. The first of these, the "tie" juncture, has been detected only in conjunction with spoken nominal constructions and will be demonstrated (p. 395). The second, the "hold" juncture, occurs regularly in conjunction with complex strings of discourse and apparently has a discretely semologic function. The hold juncture, involving a particular body part which holds a position while other parts continue to perform other functions, connects included and apparently intrusive variation in content, maintains the coherence of complex themes, and bridges apparently trivial diversionary or explanatory discourse excursions. These six kinesic junctures are working tools. The primitive state of kinesic research does not permit us at the moment to see them either as structurally equivalent or as of more than one level of activity. My *hunch* is that the single bar and the tie juncture will turn out to be at a different level than are the double cross, the double bar, the triple cross, and the hold. However, this may be a result of the types of data I have been analyzing rather than a matter of structure.

Tentative Kinemes of Juncture

Symbol	Term	Gross Behavioral Description
K#	Double cross	Inferior movement of body part followed by "pause." Terminates structural string.
K//	Double bar	Superior movement of body part followed by "pause." Terminates structural strings. Homomorph in initial and medial or parallel positions *may* be a kinemorpheme which permits K# in terminal position. We have no data which illustrate coexistence of a terminal K// in conjunction with a complex kinemorphemic construction containing "K//" in other positons.
K ##	Triple cross	Major shift in body activity (relative to customary performance). Normally terminates strings marked by two or more K#s or K//s. However, in certain instances K ## may mark termination of a single item kinic construction, e.g., in auditor response, may exclude further discussion or initiate subject or activity change.
K=	Hold	A portion of the body actively involved in construction performance projects an arrested position while other junctural activity continues in other body areas.
K/	Single bar	Projected held position, followed by "pause." Considerable idiosyncratic variation in performance; "pause" may be momentary lag in shift from body part to body part in kinemorphic presentation or may involve full stop and hold of entire body projection activity.
K.	Tie	A continuation of movement, thus far isolated only in displacement of primary stress, discussed below (p. 399 ff).

The Stress Kinemes

Three of the junctural kinemes were isolated prior to the initiation of serious research and analysis designed to *integrate* kinesic and linguistic data. K#, K//, and, although not given separate status, K# were easily detectable as operative forms in complex kinemorphic constructions. Only as linguistic-kinesic analysis proceeded, however, did K/, K=, and K. emerge in that order from the behavioral stream. From this time on, work proceeded, in a sense, in two directions. Microanalysis permitted the abstraction of the kinic stream from articulatory description to the point that complex kinemorphs could be abstracted. Fortunately, early hunches that shifts in body part, of intensity or breadth of movement, marked movement from kinemorph to kinemorph held up in a sufficiently large number of cases that, as the "terminal" junctures were isolated, their function in relation to strings of kinemorphs could be postulated and a primitive syntactics could be derived to permit the investigation of bounded sequence of behavior. This proved immediately productive.

The Cigarette Scene as a unit for study was originally chosen because of the unique interactional cigarette lighting. While the film was being changed, Doris reported to Gregory that a psychologist had examined her son and felt that he did not need any special attention. The sound made by the camera starting seemed to trigger Doris and she makes a major body shift which is recorded as a kinesic triple cross. The termination of the scene is marked by Gregory's body shift and match lid closing which follows directly upon his triangular cigarette wave. The cameraman shifts his focus and we are precluded from determining whether Doris acquiesces to his juncture. The fact that after a 34-frame duration of silence she places her hand firmly on the table as she shifts indicates that she has. It is worthy of comment that even after this major shift they continue to discuss the little boy's personality.

Doris' string, with which we are concerned here, is marked:

$$\text{K·} \quad \text{K/} \quad \text{K\# K\#} \quad \text{K=}$$
$$\text{K/(?)}$$

//I suppose all mothers think their kids are smart but I have no worries

$$\text{K/} \quad\quad\quad \text{K·} \quad\quad \text{K\#}$$

about that child's intellectual ability//.
(See Charts 3a, b, and c below for correlation with linguistic transcription.)

The kinesic single bar, noted in the phonational gap between "worries" and "about," is questioned because while her head activity is the only part in manifest movement, it, *in its activity,* meets the minimal articulatory requirement for held part. However, there is no manifest (in relationship to her ongoing movement pattern) stop in that activity. Analysis of the film does not lead me to see the presence of the morpheme of "dead pan," nor can I find any evidence of "destressed," discussed below under the stress kinemes. The "hesitation" in the head sweeps is assigned single bar status, but I hold little confidence in the assignment. It may be simply that kinesics, like linguistics, must learn how to deal with cessations of activity which are not codable by any prevalent classification system. The K= is manifest; her very active torso holds over the remaining stretch. I suspect that it is the K= which gives the impression of the presence of a K/.

McQuown and I had insisted that the analysis of human communicational behavior was in such a primitive state that, insofar as time permitted, we could not afford either in the linguistic or kinesic transcriptions to dispense with the most microscopic recording achievable within the state of the art. We felt that it would be more profitable in the long run to do shorter stretches in an intense fashion than to do longer stretches of macrorecording. In the annotated transcript which accompanies *The Natural History of an Interview,* the reader will find that the kinesic "macro" is often crude and arbitrary. Unlike linguistics with its background of research, kinesics had no canons which would regulate the size and relevance of shapes which we termed "macro." On the other hand, the past 10 years have given me little reason to vary my decision that microanalysis is, *for our purposes,* sufficiently fine-grained if every third frame of a movie taken at 24 frames a second is recorded.[6] As the years have passed, the micro line has continued to supply data to and confirm hypotheses made about conclusions derived at much higher levels of analysis.

Data have a way of hiding in a corpus and have in themselves little power of resistance to false, overfine, or overgross retrieval techniques. In the case of the behaviors that were to become the kinesic stress phonemes, two factors served to obscure them. The first of these factors came from an all-too-available classification called "speech effort" into which I placed the nonkinemorphic activity which occurred between the isolated junctures. Naively and innocently influenced by the fact that these activities were roughly correlatable with shifts in vocalic pitch and stress and reinforced in my conclusions by introspective support as I mimicked the speech patterns, I at first dismissed such evident variations in movement as artifacts of speech production. The difficulty of matching

---

[6] The elegant work of Condon, Sarles, Loeb, Charny, and their colleagues to my mind constitutes a partial affirmation of this position. Moreover, there seems every reason to believe from their reported data that an articulatory kinesics is developing which will ease the microrecording of exotic movement systems.

speech and movement because of the crudity of our correlational techniques contributed to the artifact theory. Only later, when Henry Lee
Smith, Jr., and George L. Trager worked to strengthen my knowledge of
descriptive linguistics and to sharpen my ear, did it become evident that,
while clearly production of speech strings requires effort or at least is not
laborless, the regularities I was becoming aware of could not (because of
their systematically variable appearance) be so dismissed.

Kinesic stresses are discussed at length elsewhere (Birdwhistell 1970:
128–147). It is enough to say here that four distinct variations in movement pattern, usually with the head, the hand, or the brows, serve to mark
the flow of speech. These have been termed "primary" /∨/, "secondary"
/∧/, "unstressed" /—/, and "destressed" /○/. At least one stress occurs
between all kinesic terminal junctures. By definition this is a primary
stress. The following example from a film may serve to illustrate the
stresses. In response to the question //What was John's last name?//,
//Doe// is marked by a single movement, //Doe//. If the emphasis is upon
John (not Harry), in the question, the question itself would be marked
with //John// under primary kinesic stress and //last name// either has a
secondary plus unstressed, two secondarys, or two unstressed.

Thus:

//Jo∨hn's la∧st na—me// or //Jo∨hn's la∧st na∧me// or //Jo∨hn's la‾st na‾me//.

The stressing is reversed if "name" not "John" is being emphasized.

Thus:

//Jo∧hn's la—st na∨me// or //Jo∧hn's la∧st na∨me// or //Jo‾hn's la—st na∨me//.

The third stress of "unstressed" was derived following the isolation of
"destressed," the fourth stress which is a reduction of stress below the
norm of the produced string. In the filmed corpus was discovered:

//Wha∧t i—s Johns yo○u kno○w Bi∧lls frie∨nds la∧st na∨me//.

The string takes on more form when the kinesic junctures are added:

K// ∧ — ∨ K=○ ○ K/∧ ∨ K# ∧ ∨ K#
//What is Johns you know Bills friends last name//.

Although several thousands of exercises have been run from sound
filmed data, it is still not possible to establish a rule which states an absolute relationship between these kinesic stresses and junctures and the
linguistic stress and intonation patterns (by the Smith-Trager conventions)
which accompany them. In general, a primary kinesic stress tends to
coincide with the primary linguistic stress. Yet, in more than 20 per cent

of the cases it does not. Perusal of the data indicates that the highest point of loudness and pitch, when these points coincide, is usually marked by a kinesic primary. However, this does not always occur. A long string of linguistic secondary stresses or a long string of phonation at a pitch 2 level is usually marked by destressed, but not always. In nominal phrases which are often marked by kinesic secondary-primary or kinesic primary-secondary or kinesic tertiary-primary, the kinesic stress may be consistent with or differ from the linguistic stresses. To summarize: while, statistically, kinesic stress patterning tends to be consistent with linguistic stress patterning, this is not invariable. I assume that further research at the semologic level and greater refinement of research with relationship to both linguistic and kinesic stress patterning will provide more perspective upon these phenomena. I am attracted by a conception of communicative structure which would include the possibility that, at least for American English, kinesic and linguistic suprasegmentals may be in free variation. However, I would hasten to say that the burden of proof for such a proposition would at the present state of knowledge rest upon me.

The concept "free variation," a useful one for structural analysis, may be misleading to the reader concerned with either psychological or sociological considerations of meaning. All that the term is intended to designate is the fact that forms of a given level are substitutable without special structural adaptation *at that level*. Throughout the structures of either linguistic or kinesic phenomena, "emic" forms are abstracted from class members, which are described as being in free variation with one another. However, there is no implication here that the choice of one of a series of alternatives (defined in structural terms) at any level of structure is not of consequence at the level of social interaction. The difference between /ðə/ and /ðiy/ (thuh and the) may at one level of analysis be seen as trivial but at another be of great consequence. These forms, under certain morphological or syntactical analyses, may be seen as identical, but, at the semological level, as well as at the phonological, as absolutely distinct. Comparably, the fact that in a stream of action the movement of the head may be seen to transport all kinesic stress signals, while in another stream a movement of the brows or, in another, the hand is utilized for this activity, is of little consequence in kinemorphological analysis. However, this may be of definitive significance for questions asked of this data at the level of social interaction.

When the tentative hypothesis is established that at certain levels of analysis we may discover, as research proceeds, structural forms from kinesics which are substitutable for structural forms from linguistics, there is no suggestion that the "choice" made by the conversant is not of consequence to the *interaction*. We are postulating an interdependence of linguistic and kinesic *structure,* not a final equivalence of semological or interactional function. In the discussion to follow, it will be seen that structural distinctions are made in the abstracted speech stream which do not appear in the abstracted movement stream and *vice versa*. At one level of analysis it is possible to say that the kinesic suprasegmental activity is functioning to make distinctions that *might* have been made by the linguistic suprasegmentals, and that we could not have been aware of these distinctions if we examined only the audible aspects of the activity stream. It is furthermore possible to say that these same (at this level of analysis) distinctions *could* have been made in the linguistic stream without an alteration in the structural activity in the kinesic stream. All that we are saying is that *unless we analyze both the linguistic and kinesic stream*, we have no way of knowing *what distinctions* have been made by the conversant.

There is a temptation to say that when one channel carries a distinction which is not made by the other, the fuller channel carries the "real" meaning. This implies that a given performance has *a* particular meaning. Under no circumstances must the reader be misled by the heuristically limited corpus which we are examining in this exercise. From the examination of extensive sound-filmed interactional sequences, I have every reason to posit the proposition that in human experience there are at all observational times many streams of meaning in process. The particular section of the stream we analyze is always a partial one, and only as we come to comprehend the larger rules of communicational structure will we be able to determine the relevant meanings in particular sequences. In short, it is my hope that as we gain more complete control of the varisized forms of both linguistics and kinesics, we shall be able to examine limited sequences with an increased control over the data we ignore when we limit our corpus. I think a great part of the arguments popular in linguistics today about "grammar," syntax, and meaning are viable only because of the limited universe which is under scrutiny.

The kinemes of stress combine to form a set of suprasegmental kinemorphemes which have been tested in studies of complex sentences and statistical formulas. These are:

Stress Kinemes		Suprasegmental Kinemorphemes
/∨/	=	/v/
/∧∨/or/-∨/or/-∧/	=	/ ⌣ /
/∨∧/or/∨-/or/∧-/	=	/ ⌣ /
/-V̆-/or/V̆/or/-V̆∧/	=	/ ⌣ /
/∨̆K|∨/or/∨K#∨/or/∨ ⌢ ∨/	=	/ ⌣⌣ /[7]
/◯◯K|/or/◯◯K#/or/◯◯|||/	=	/-◯-/
/◯◯∨/	=	/ *∨ /
/∨◯◯/	=	/ √ /

---

[7] / ⌣⌣ / and /-◯-/ may as research develops turn out to be at a higher level of structure. The fact that the form crosses terminal junctures may or may not require such placement.

Charts 13.2a, 2b, and 2c, below, will demonstrate the kinic, the kinemic, and the kinemorphemic levels of analysis of Doris' circumlexical stress behavior. The structural balance of this selected segment is immediately obvious. The /K=/ is the added factor in the latter section of the utterance. However, ignoring this, if the suspected /K// is added, our type becomes:

chart 13.2a

Kinemorphic, Kinemic, and Kinic Transcriptions

K_1	K·	⌒	⌐		#	∨ #
K_2	− − ∨ K|	− ∨ ∧	−	−K#	∨ K#
K_3	hn	hn hn			an

I suppose all mothers think their kids are smart but

K_1 KINEMORPHIC
K_2 KINEMIC
K_3 KINIC

chart 13.2b

K_1	⌒⌒⌒ ∨	K =	K/(?)
K_2	∧ − − ∨	K =	K/(?) −
K_3	hn	hn	(torsohold)

I   have   no   worries   about

chart 13.2c

K_1	⌒		K#
	K·		
K_2	− − ∨ ∧	−	K#
K_3	hn hn		−(torsohold)

that   child's   intellectual   ability

This balance could be related to the cadence in which Gregory and Doris are moving in their interactional dance. On the other hand, this may be a stylistic factor related to the production of a stereotypic utterance. At this stage of kinesic and communicational research, however, such statements remain little more than conjecture. (One of my assistants who was proofreading this chapter points out that the sentence above, when spoken aloud, has the same quality of balance in its accompanying suprasegmental structure.)

A final task remains for this exercise. In Charts 13.3a, 3b, and 3c, the linguistic and kinesic materials are assembled for comparison.

A linear examination of the charts points up a series of items for special examination:

1. The movement of the kinesic stress from its expectable position, either over /mothers/ or over /all/ as in //all mŏthers// or //ăll mothers//, gives us a form //all mŏthers// as in //hot dŏg// which contrasts with //hŏt dog// and //hŏt dŏg//.

2. The form //their kids// in the string is specially marked by the kinesic primary-secondary form.

3. Neither of these distinctions appear to be marked either in linguistic stress or intonation (verboid marker?).

chart 13.3a

Linguistic and Kinesic Transcriptions

K_1 　　　　 ⌒ 　|　　 ⌐ 　　　　# ∨#
　　　　　　 K

K_2 　— 　— 　∨ 　K| 　— 　∨ 　∧ 　— 　— 　K# 　∨K#
K_3 　　　　　 hn 　　　　 hn 　hn 　　　　　　　　　 an

I suppose all mothers think their kids are smart but

K_1 KINEMORPHIC
K_2 KINEMIC
K_3 KINIC

1c***			♀-					-♀
fn** <					⌒—			
VSg*ʔm								?
Int	3		2			3̲ 2 3	#	⋮
StrJ	∧	∧	∧	∧	∧	∧	/	⋮
Sgm	ay + spoz + ɔhl + mæð ərz + Өink + ðer + kidz ər + smart						bət	⋮

　I 　suppose 　all 　mothers 　think 　their 　kids are 　smart 　　but

(673) (676) (683) (688) (694) 　(705) (711) (716)(719) (724)(730) (732)

　676 　683 　686 　691 　　　698 　702 　706 710 　718 　　725

---

[1] Phonetic transcription omitted. Circled numbers are numbers assigned 1956. Open numbers are from edge reading of sound film 1967.
* ʔ, h, r, ə, m, Vocal Segregates (Trager).
** < , Crescend (Hockett); ⌒, Drawling (Trager).
*** ♀, Rasp (Trager).

chart 13.3b

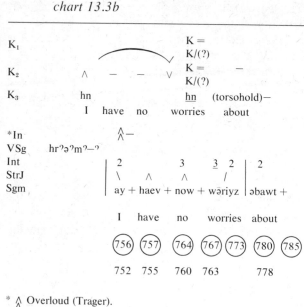

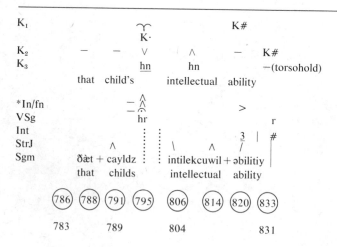

* ⋀ Overloud (Trager).

chart 13.3c

4. The kinesic single bar between /mothers/ and /think/ is unmarked in the linguistic stream.

5. The linguistic stress and intonation appearing over /smart/ is absent in the kinesic line but may be subsumed under the kinesic /#/.

6. The kinesic primary stress over /but/, bounded by kinesic double

cross junctures, in emphasis seems comparable to but not identical with the rather complicated linguistic situation in which /but/ is not specially denoted in either pitch or stress but is followed by a "pause" and glottal stop, and is the nexal point for the paralinguistics. /But/ is included within the rasp, which marks //think their kids are smart *but*// and is, at the same time, within the drawl which covers //*but* I have no worries about that childs//. It is furthermore excluded from the overloud which extends over //I have no worries about that childs//.

7. The initial /I/ is kinesically unmarked while being at pitch 3. This may be a function of the cigarette lighting which masks either a kinesic stress or a pronominal marker. The second /I/ is marked with a kinesic secondary (perhaps flavored by a pronominal marker) while she speaks with tertiary stress over /I/.

8. The intonation pattern of 3-3-2, as marked by Hockett, over /no worries/ has some parallel in the primary kinesic stress over /worries/. I think that the kinesic stress pattern of secondary-primary or primary-secondary that might have been expected in this construction may have been absorbed in the kinemorphic construction of "head-shaking" which extends over //I have no worries about that childs//.

9. The kinesic primary stress which is pulled to a point *between* /childs/ and /intellectual/ to give us a form parallel to /all mothers/ is of special interest. More statistically normal forms would have been either:

$$\overset{\wedge}{\text{//that}}\ \overset{\wedge}{\text{childs}}\ \overset{\wedge}{\text{intellectual}}\ \overset{\vee}{\text{ability//}}\ \text{or}$$

$$\overset{\vee}{\text{//that}}\ \overset{\wedge}{\text{childs}}\ \overset{\wedge}{\text{intellectual}}\ \overset{\wedge}{\text{ability//}}\ \text{or}$$

$$\overset{\wedge}{\text{//that}}\ \overset{\vee}{\text{childs}}\ \overset{\vee}{\text{intellectual}}\ \overset{\wedge}{\text{ability//}}.$$

The /‿/ recorded for the last form indicates a continuation of movement which seems to cross kinesic junctures, either of single bar or double cross. The linguistic pause, marked by Hockett, may be of consequence in the case. The segregates and the termination of the overloud and drawl are also to be noted here.

Summary

The nine points listed above are sufficient to illustrate some of the complexities which confront the linguist, the kinesicist, or the communication analyst who would attempt an assessment of the relationship between kinesic and linguistic phenomena at this level of analysis. This limited segment, containing two syntactic sentences, represents an abstracted corpus which is short enough to be subjected to intense analysis but does not seem to contain sufficient information to settle many of the questions which come to mind. One general point may be made from these data. Any discourse analysis, conversational analysis, communicational analysis, or interactional analysis which would attend to but one modality—lexical, linguistic, or kinesic—must suffer from (or, at least, be responsible for) the assumption that the other modalities maintain a steady or non-influential state.

part three

GENESIS, MAINTENANCE, AND CHANGE OF LINGUISTIC CODES

14

Social Meaning
in Linguistic Structure:
Code-Switching in Norway[1]

JAN-PETTER BLOM AND JOHN J. GUMPERZ

Jan-Petter Blom is a lecturer in social anthropology and member of the Research Institute for Social Anthropology at the University of Bergen. He has done fieldwork in rural Norway and, most recently, in the Bahamas, on folklore, social structure, and ethnomusicology.

John J. Gumperz is a professor of anthropology at the University of California, Berkeley. He received his doctorate in Germanic linguistics at the University of Michigan and has taught at Cornell University and Deccan College in Poona. He has done fieldwork in India, Norway, and among minority groups in the United States.

This study of the meaning of linguistic choice in a Norwegian community exemplifies what is meant by an integrated sociolinguistic approach. Ethnography and linguistics both are drawn upon, technically and conceptually; but more than that, the outcome is an understanding of social constraints and linguistic rules as parts of a single communicative system. The conceptual framework for the social analysis here leans on the work of Leach (1954) and Barth (1966) and Goffman (1964).

The stability of the valued local form of speech, as well as the potential for change in speech patterns within the

[1] Some of the data cited in this study were given in preliminary form in previous publications (Gumperz 1964b and Gumperz 1966). The authors are grateful to Einar Haugen, Aaron Cicourel, and Richard Howell for their comments. Field work for the study was sponsored by the Institute of Sociology, University of Oslo, Norway. We are grateful to Professor Sverre Holm of that institution for support and encouragement. Mr. Gumperz' stay in Norway was made possible through a senior postdoctoral fellowship from the National Science Foundation.

community, is discussed. To show the relationships between social and linguistic alternatives presupposes the technical analysis of specific features of speech, as well as also, of social relations (particularly of participation in closed and open networks) and of the diversity of local value systems. It requires an experimental approach such as the one employed. It also requires a unitary frame of reference; here the whole network is viewed from the standpoint of actors in particular social situations as they adopt strategies constrained by the existing communicative repertoire.

As in Part 1 of this volume, the present study concerns values expressed in certain genres of speech, particularly self-identity and pride in informal conversations. As in Part 2, this study deals with rules; here, rules of alternation that govern the linguistic repertoire of an entire community. The components of the repertoire themselves are defined by co-occurrence rules. One can also describe the study as making problematic a series of things sometimes taken for granted: (1) given that members of the community consider there to be two varieties of code, to what extent and in what way are the varieties actually linguistically distinct? Blom and Gumperz find a single linguistic system, differentiated by features similar to what Labov (Chapter 19) calls variables. Notice that definition of the two varieties, Ranamål and Bokmål, cuts across several formal sectors of language (phonology, lexis, morphology). (2) Given that elicitation brings out these differences, what is the case in everyday interaction? Some features found in elicitation sessions are never found in spontaneous speech. (3) Given the linguistic reality of the two varieties, why are both maintained? Unintelligibility can hardly be a factor since most speakers control the entire range of both. To speak of persistence of dialects in remote or less advanced areas is merely to name the phenomenon, not to explain it. Again, since the adult population has access to both varieties, the explanation must lie in the social meanings of the two. (4) If social symbolism is the basis, what is its nature? How is it actually expressed? Blom and Gumperz introduce the concepts of *setting, situation,* and *event,* taken as stages recognized in the enactment of personal strategies, to analyze the meaning of choice between the two varieties. An important distinction is made between *situational switching,* where alternation between varieties redefines a situation, being a change in governing norms, and *metaphorical switching,* where alternation enriches a situation, allowing for allusion to more than one social relationship within the situation. In Hemnes situational switching involves change in participants and/or strategies, metaphorical switching involves only a change in topical emphasis. (Cf. Albert's Burundi case of role switching initiated by an aristocrat talking to a peasant, described in terms of change of topic and purpose.)

Notice the experimental presentation of the unconscious status of metaphorical switching among the members of the open network (i.e., a network of relationships with reference points outside the local community); and criticism of it in terms of the folk concept of *knot* 'artifical speech.' Goffman (1961) provides an additional related reading. A collection of Gumperz' papers dealing with similar issues has recently appeared (Gumperz 1971).

In recent discussions of the problem of language and society, Bernstein (1961, 1964a) explores the hypothesis that social relationships act as intervening variables between linguistic structures and their realization in speech. His formulation suggests that the anthropologists' analysis of social constraints governing interpersonal relationships may be utilized in the interpretation of verbal performances. This chapter attempts to clarify the social and linguistic factors involved in the communication process and to test Bernstein's hypothesis by showing that speaker's selection among semantically, grammatically, and phonologically permissible alternates occuring in conversation sequences recorded in natural groups is both patterned and predictable on the basis of certain features of the local social system. In other words, given a particular aggregate of people engaged in regular face-to-face interaction, and given some knowledge of the speakers' linguistic repertoire (Gumperz 1964b), we wish to relate the structure of that repertoire to the verbal behavior of members of the community in particular situations.

Data on verbal interaction derives from approximately two months' field work in Hemnesberget, a small commercial and industrial town of about 1300 inhabitants in the center of the Rana Fjord, close to the Arctic circle in northern Norway. The settlement owes its existence to the growth of local trade and industry following the abolition of government-sanctioned trade monopolies covering most of northern Norway in 1858. Since the Middle Ages, these monopolies had kept the area's economy dependent upon a small elite of merchant and landholding families with connections to southern Norway, separated by great differences in wealth, culture, and education from the tenant farmers, fishermen, estate laborers, and servants who formed the bulk of the populace. Apart from a few shop owners and government officials, present-day Hemnesberget residents are mostly descendants of these latter groups. They have been attracted to the town from the surroundings by new economic opportunities there, while a hundred years of relatively free economic development have splintered the old ruling circles. Many of this former elite have moved away, and the remainder no longer form a visible social group in the region.

Present inhabitants of Hemnesberget earn their livelihood mainly as craftsmen in family workshops or in the somewhat larger boat-building and lumber-processing plants, all of which are locally owned. The area serves as a major source of wood products and fishing equipment for the northernmost part of Norway. A significant group of merchant middlemen deal in locally produced boats and other products, which they ship north for resale, and maintain sales agencies for motors and other appliances and manufactured goods from the south.

While at the beginning of the century Hemnesberget was the most important communications and commercial center in the area, it has been eclipsed in recent years by government-sponsored economic development which has turned the town of Mo i Rana, at the mouth of Rana Fjord, into Norway's major iron- and steel-producing center. The region of Mo has grown from about 1000 inhabitants in 1920 to almost 9000 in 1960, largely through immigration from the region of Trøndelag and southern Norway. It now boasts several modern department stores, hotels, restaurants, and cinemas. The railroad from Trondheim in the south through Mo and on north to Bodø was completed shortly after World War II, and the road system is steadily improving. All these new communication arteries, however, now bypass Hemnesberget, which has all but lost its importance as a communication link for both land and sea traffic.

Although the immediate ecological environment has changed greatly, Hemnesberget remains an island of tradition in a sea of change. There is a regular once-a-day boat service to Mo, buses leave for the railroad station twice a day, and a few people commute to Mo by private automobile or motorcycle. However, the bulk of the residents spend most of their working and leisure time in and around Hemnesberget. Those who can afford it build vacation cabins in the unsettled areas across the fjord a few miles away. Our interviews uniformly show that social events in Mo i Rana are only of marginal interest to local inhabitants.

The Community Linguistic Repertoire

Most residents of Hemnesberget are native speakers of Ranamål (R), one of a series of dialects which segment northern Norway into linguistic regions roughly corresponding to other cultural and ecological divisions (Christiansen 1962). As elsewhere in Norway, where local independence and distinctness of folk culture are highly valued, the dialect enjoys great prestige. A person's native speech is regarded as an integral part of his family background, a sign of his local identity. By identifying himself as a dialect speaker both at home and abroad, a member symbolizes pride in his community and in the distinctness of its contribution to society at large.

Formal education, however, is always carried on in the standard, the language of official transactions, religion, and the mass media. Norwegian law sanctions two standard languages: Bokmål (formally called Riksmål) and Nynorsk (formerly Landsmål), of which only Bokmål (B) is current in northern Norway.

Education is universal and, allowing for certain individual differences in fluency, all speakers of Ranamål also control the standard. Both Bokmål and Ranamål, therefore, form part of what we may call the community linguistic repertoire (Gumperz 1964b), the totality of linguistic resources which speakers may employ in significant social interaction. In their everyday interaction, they select among the two as the situation demands. Members view this alternation as a shift between two distinct entities, which are never mixed. A person speaks either one or the other.

The fact that the two varieties are perceived as distinct, however, does not necessarily mean that their separateness is marked by significant linguistic differences. Pairs such as Hindi and Urdu, Serbian and Croatian, Thai and Laotian, and many others which are regarded as separate languages by their speakers are known to be grammatically almost identical. The native's view of language distinctions must thus be validated by empirical linguistic investigation.

We began our analysis by employing standard linguistic elicitation procedures. A series of informants selected for their fluency in the dialect were interviewed in our office and were asked to produce single words, sentences, and short texts, first in the dialect and then in the standard, for taping or phonetic recording by the linguist. These elicitation sessions yielded a series of dialect features which are essentially identical to those described by Norwegian dialectologists (Christiansen 1962).

The vowel system distinguishes three tongue heights—high: front unrounded i, front rounded y, central rounded u, back rounded o; mid: front unrounded e, front rounded ö, back rounded å; low: front unrounded æ, front rounded ø, back a.

Consonants occur either singly or as geminates. Vowels are phonetically short before geminates, consonant clusters, and palatalized consonants. There are two series of consonants: unmarked and palatalized. Unmarked consonants include stops p, b, t, d, k, g; spirants f, v, s, š, j, ç; nasals m, n, ŋ; trill r, lateral l, and retroflex flap ḷ. The palatal series contains tj, dj, nj, and lj. On the phonetic level, a set of cacuminal or retroflex allophones occur for the sequences rs [š], rd [d], rt [t], and rn [ṇ].

The local pronunciation of the standard differs from the "pure" dialect as follows: Bokmål does not have the phonemic distinction between the palatalized and nonpalatalized series of consonants. Only nonpalatalized consonants occur. In addition, it does not distinguish between mid front rounded /ö/ and low front rounded /ø/; only the former occurs. On the purely phonetic level, dialect allophones of the phonemes /æ/ and /a/ are considerably lower and more retracted than their standard equivalents. The dialect furthermore has a dark allophone [ł] of /l/ where the standard has clear [l]. The cacuminal or retroflex allophones of /s/, /d/, /t/, and /n/, and the flap /ḷ/, however, which are commonly regarded as dialect features, are used in both varieties, although they tend to disappear in highly formal Bokmål.

Morphological peculiarities of the dialect include the masculine plural indefinite suffix *-æ* and the definite suffix *-an*, e.g., (R) *hæstæ* (horses), *hæstan* (the horses), contrasting with (B) *hester* and *hestene*. In verb inflection the dialect lacks the infinitive suffix *-e* and the present suffix *-er* of regular verbs. Further differences in past tense and past participle markers and in the assignment of individual words to strong or weak inflectional classes serve to set off almost every dialect verb from its standard Norwegian equivalent. Here are some examples of common regular and irregular verbs and their standard equivalents:

Infinitive		*Present*		*Past*		*Past Participle*		
(R)	(B)	(R)	(B)	(R)	(B)	(R)	(B)	
finj	*finne*	*finj*	*finner*	*fanj*	*fant*	*fønje*	*funnet*	(find)
vara								
or *va*	*være*	*e*	*ær*	*va*	*var*	*vøre*	*vært*	(be)
få	*få*	*får*	*får*	*fekk*	*fikk*	*fått*	*fått*	(get)
stanj	*stå*	*står*	*står*	*sto*	*sto*	*stie*	*stått*	(stand)
jær	*jøre*	*jær*	*jør*	*jol*	*jøre*	*jort*	*jort*	(do)
læs	*lese*	*læs*	*leser*	*læst*	*leste*	*læst*	*lest*	(read)
ta	*ta*	*tek*	*tar*	*tok*	*tokk*	*tatt*	*tatt*	(take)
						or *tiçe*		

Other important dialect features appear in pronouns, common adverbs of time, place, and manner, conjunctions, and other grammatically significant function words. Here is a list of some of the most common distinctive forms of personal pronouns and possessive pronouns:

(B)	(R)	
jæjj	*og*	(I)
mæjj	*meg*	(me)
dæjj	*deg*	(you)
hann	*hanj*	(he)

(B)	(R)	
hunn	*ho*	(she)
hanns	*hanjs*	(his)
hennes	*hinjers*	(hers)
dere	*dåkk*	(you)(plural)
di	*dæmm**	(theirs)

* Sometimes also *di* and *deres.*

Interrogatives, relatives, and indefinites:

(B)	(R)	
såmm	*så*	[who, which (relative)]
va	*ke*	[what (interrogative)]
vemm	*kem*	(who)
noe	*nåkka*	(something)
vorfårr	*kefør*	(what for)
vilket	*kefør nokka*	[which (thing)]
vilken	*kefør nann*	[which (person)]
vær	*kvar*	(every)
en	*ein*	(one)

Adverbs and conjunctions:

(B)	(R)	
till	*tell*	(to, toward)
menn	*mænn*	(but)
hær	*her*	(here)
fra	*ifra*	(from)
mellam	*imeljæ*	(in between)
vordan	*kelesn*	(how)
viss	*vess*	(if)

These data constitute empirical evidence to support the view of the dialect as a distinct linguistic entity. By comparing information collected in this manner with local speech forms elsewhere in northern Norway, dialectologists interested in historical reconstruction identify Ranamål as one of a series of northern Norwegian dialects set off from others by the fact that it shows influences of eastern Norwegian forms of speech (Christiansen 1962). In this discussion however, we are concerned with social interaction and not with history, and this leads us to raise somewhat different problems.

The elicitation sessions which provide the source data for dialect grammars are conducted in the linguist's, and not in the informant's, frame of reference. Although by asking speakers to speak in the dialect, the linguist may be interested in purely descriptive or historical information, the native speaker, mindful of the association between dialect, local culture, and local identity, is, of course, anxious to present his locality in the best possible light. Consistency of performance in linguistic interview sessions might well be the result of the interviewer's presence; it need not reflect everyday interaction. Furthermore, when comparisons with other forms of speech are made, it is the linguist's analysis which serves as the basis for these comparisons, not the speaker's performance.

Ranamål and Bokmål as Codes in a Repertoire

In order to understand how natives may perceive the dialect standard language differences, some further discussion of the way in which distinctions between what are ordinarily treated as separate linguistic systems may be manifested in everyday speech is necessary. Thus if we compare a bilingual's pronunciation of the Norwegian sentence *vill du ha egg og beiken till frokast?* with the same speaker's pronunciation of the English equivalent "Will you have bacon and eggs for breakfast?" the two utterances will show phonetic distinctions in every segment. The Norwegian voiced spirant [v] has much less spirantal noise than its English equivalent, the [i] is tense as compared to the lax English [i], the Norwegian [l] may be clear or dark but it is phonetically different from English [l]. The Norwegian central rounded [u] in *du* has no direct English equivalent. In *egg* the Norwegian has a tense [e] and the [g] has an aspirate release, whereas in English the vowel is lax and [g] has a voiced release. Similarly, the Norwegian has a stressed vowel in *beiken* [æi] whereas the English has [ey]. Bilinguals whose entire articulation shifts in this way can be said to have two distinct articulation ranges in addition to two sets of grammatical rules.

Analysis of recordings of Hemnesberget speakers' switching from the dialect to the standard reveals a different situation. In a sentence pair like *hanj bor på nilsen's paŋšonat* and its Bokmål equivalent *hann bor pa nilsen's paŋsonat* "He lives in Nilsen's pensionat," only the realizations of /a/, /ł/, and /nj/ which appear in our list of dialect characteristics differ. In other relevant respects the two utterances are identical. Furthermore, even in the case of these dialect characteristics, speakers do not alternate between two clearly distinguishable articulation points; rather, the shift takes the form of a displacement along a scale in which palatalized consonants show at least three degrees of palatalization, strong [nj], weak [nʲ], and zero [n] and /a/ and /æ/ each show three degrees of retraction and lowering.

While the switch from Norwegian to English implies a shift between two distinct structural wholes, the Bokmål-Ranamål alternation, in phonology at least, seems more similar to conditions described by Labov (1966b) for New York speech. A speaker's standard and dialect performance can be accounted for by a single phonetic system. The bulk of the constituent phones within this system are marked by relatively stable, easily identifiable points of articulation. The palatalized consonants and the vowels listed here differ in that they vary within a much greater articulation range. They are instances of what Labov has called variables (1964b). It is the position of such variables along the scale of possible articulations which, when evaluated along with morphological information, signals dialect vs. standard speech.

Not all items identified in our elicitation sessions as Ranamål features function as variables, however. The contrast between /ø/ and /ö/ was never produced spontaneously. In normal discourse only [ö] occurs. Furthermore, as stated previously, the flap allophone /l/ and the retroflex stop allophones which find a prominent place in dialect grammars are also used in local Bokmål as well as in eastern varieties of standard Norwegian; thus their status as dialect markers is doubtful.

Our texts also reveal some individual differences in the pronunciation of the palatalized consonant and vowel variables. While the normal dialect speech of most residents shows strong palatalization of these consonants and extreme vowel retraction, some of the more highly educated younger residents normally have medium palatalization and medium vowel retraction. Regardless, however, the direction of variation is the same for all individuals.

In the realm of morphology-syntax it is also possible to set up a single set of grammatical categories to account for what on the surface seem like striking differences between the two varieties. All nouns, e.g., appear in an indefinite form consisting of the noun stem and in an indefinite form made up of stem plus suffixed article, both of which are inflected for singular and plural. There are three subcategories of noun gender: masculine, feminine, and neuter, and the case categories are shared. Verbs appear in imperative, infinitive, present, past, and past participle forms. Basic function word categories, including pronouns, conjunctions, and adverbs, are shared, etc.

Ranamål shows a few peculiarities in the order of pronouns and verbs in sentences such as (R) *ke du e ifrå,* (B) *vor ær du fra* "Where are you from?" But even without detailed analysis, it is obvious that these differences correspond to relatively low-order syntactic rules. The majority of the distinctions between the dialect and the standard thus do not affect the basic grammar but only what we may call the morphophonemic realization of shared grammatical categories.

Even at the morphophonemic level, variation is not without pattern.

Examination of such alternates as (B) *till,* (R) *tell* "to"; (B) *fikk,* (R) *fekk* "received"; (B) *hest,* (R) *hæst* "horse"; and (B) *menn,* (R) *mænn* "but" suggests a general process of lowering of front vowels in the dialect. This lowering process is also found elsewhere in Norway, although it may occur in different linguistic forms. Similarly, other sets of alternates such as *icce/ikke* "not," *dæmm/di* "they," and *ifra/frå* "from" are common in other Norwegian regions.

Leaving aside historical considerations, it is almost as if all dialect variation within Norway were generated by selection of different forms from a common reservoir of alternates. Ranamål differs from other dialects not so much because it contains entirely different features but because of the way in which it combines features already found elsewhere. Furthermore, Hemnesberget pairs such as (B) *lærer,* (R) *lerar,* and (B) *hær,* (R) *her,* which conflict with the lowering process just mentioned, suggest that here as elsewhere selection may at times be motivated by social pressures favoring maintenance of distinctions (Ramanujan 1967). No matter what the actual historical facts are, however, the narrow range of variation we find lends support to our view of dialect features as variables within a single grammatical system.

The effect of structural similarities on speakers' perception of speech differences is somewhat counterbalanced by the fact that choice among these variables is always restricted by sociolinguistic selection constraints such that if, for instance, a person selects a standard morphological variant in one part of an utterance, this first choice also implies selection of pronunciation variables tending toward the standard end of the scale. A speaker wishing to ask for another's place of residence may, e.g., start his sentence either with (R) *ke* "where" or (B) *vor.* In the first case, the rest of the sentence will read *hanj e ifrå* "is he from?" In the second case, it will be *ær hann fra; vor* and *hanj* do not co-occur. Similarly, selection of *e* "is" requires dialect pronunciation; the form *ær* "is" would sound odd if it appeared in the same sentence with *hanj.*

It is the nature of these selection constraints and the manner in which they cut across the usual boundaries of phonology and morphology to generate co-occurrences among phonetic and allomorphic and lexical variables, which lends the Ranamål-Bokmål variation its peculiar stamp, and sets it off, e.g., from the phonologically similar situation in New York. Sociolinguistic selection rules also account to some extent for the speaker's view of the two varieties as separate entities.

Since the dialect and the standard are almost isomorphic in syntax and phonetics and vary chiefly in morphophonemics, and since most speakers control the entire range of variables, it would be unreasonable to assume, as is frequently done wherever two distinct dialects are spoken, that selection patterns affecting the just-mentioned selection rules are motivated by considerations of intelligibility. The most reasonable assumption is that the linguistic separateness between the dialect and the standard, i.e., the maintenance of distinct alternates for common inflectional morphemes and function, is conditioned by social factors.

Some idea of how this came about can be obtained by considering the conditions under which the two varieties are learned. The dialect is acquired in most homes and in the sphere of domestic and friendship relations. As a result, it has acquired the flavor of these locally based relationships. However, dialect speakers learn the standard in school and in church, at a time when they are also introduced to national Norwegian values. It has therefore become associated with such pan-Norwegian activity systems.

Since the adult population has equal access to both sets of variants, however, the developmental argument does not provide sufficient explanation for the maintenance of distinctness. Immigrants to urban centers around the world, e.g., frequently give up their languages after a generation if social conditions are favorable to language shift. The hypothesis suggests itself, therefore, that given the initial acquisition patterns, the dialect and the standard remain separate because of the cultural identities they communicate and the social values implied therein. It is this aspect of the problem that we intend to explore in the remaining sections of the chapter. Before we proceed, however, something more needs to be said about the process of social symbolization.

Students of communication usually distinguish between semantics proper, or reference, and pragmatics (Ervin-Tripp 1964). Reference indicates verbal categorization of objects' actions and experience in terms of their objective properties; pragmatics deals with the effect of symbols of various kinds on speakers and listeners, i.e., with the significance of what is communicated for the actors involved. Most discussions of pragmatics ordinarily do not distinguish between individual intent and interpersonal significance of usage patterns, although it is evident that without such a distinction it would be impossible to explain the fact that the same message may indicate praise in some instances and disapproval in others. Effective communication requires that speakers and audiences agree both on the meaning of words and on the social import or values attached to choice of expression. Our discussions will be confined to the latter. We will use the term *social significance,* or *social meaning,* to refer to the social value implied when an utterance is used in a certain context.

In general, the assignment of value to particular objects or acts is as arbitrary as the referential naming of objects. Just as a particular term may refer to a round object in one group and a square object in another, so also the value of actions or utterances may vary. Thus the same term may indicate geographical distinctions in one community and symbolize social stratification elsewhere. Social meanings differ from referential meanings in the way in which they are coded. Whereas reference is coded largely through words, social meaning can attach not only to acoustic signs but also to settings, to items of background knowledge, as well as to particular word sequences. In Hemnes, e.g., values attached to a person's family background or to his reputation as a fisherman are important in understanding what he says and influence the selection of responses to his actions.

It must also be pointed out that referential meanings are at least to some extent recoverable through the study of individual words, they are, to use Pike's (1967) term, segmental, while social meanings are not. A sentence like *ke du e ifrå* "Where are you from?" can be divided into units of reference like *ke* "where," *du* "you," *e* "are," and *ifrå* "from." Social significance attaches to the utterance as a whole; it is not segmentable into smaller component stretches. Sociolinguistic co-occurrence patterns along with intonation contours enable the speaker to group language into larger pragmatic wholes and to interpret them in relation to signs transmitted by other communicative media.

Local Organization and Values

Social life in Hemnesberget shows a fluidity of class structure quite similar to that described for southern Norway by Barnes (1954). Extremes of poverty and wealth are absent. Expressions of solidarity such as "'We all know each other here in Hemnes," and "We are all friends here" recur in our interviews. The majority of those who claim local descent show a strong sense of local identification. To be a *hæmnesværing* "Hemnes resident" in their view is like belonging to a team characterized by commonalty of descent. Members of this reference group act like kin, friends, and neighbors, cooperating in the pursuit of community ideals. In everyday behavior they symbolize this quality of their ties through greetings, exchanges of personal information, and general informality of posture toward fellow members. The dialect is an important marker of their common culture. Residents of neighboring settlements, of Mo i Rana, as well as other Norwegians, stand apart from this local community. They are potential competitors who must at least initially be treated with reserve. Their dialects are said to be different. The linguist interested in structural significance may wish to disregard such variation as minor. Nevertheless, they have important social meanings for intercommunity communication within the Rana region. They are constantly commented upon and joked about and seem to play an important role in the maintenance of local identity.

Despite the intense sense of local identification, perceptions of closeness within this local group are not everywhere the same among Hemnes residents. More detailed interviews and observations of visiting and recreational patterns and of the exchange of assistance suggest a clear distinction between personal relations and the more general local relations. The actual range of effective personal relations for any single individual tends to be fairly small and stable over time. For most people it includes only certain near kin, in-laws, neighbors, or fellow workers. The community can thus be described as segmented into small nuclei of personal interaction. Since these groups are not marked linguistically, however, the behavioral signs of friendliness and equality constitute a communicative idiom which applies to both these nuclei and to other relations or shared local identification.

The meaning attached to local descent and dialect use—to being part of the "local team"—is clearly seen when we consider those members of the community who dissociate themselves from this "team." Traditionally, in northern Norway the local community of equals was separated from the landowning commercial and administrative elite by a wide gulf of social and judicial inequality. Since the latter were the introducers and users of standard Norwegian, the standard form was—and to some extent still is—associated with this inequality of status. Many of the functions of the former elite have now been incorporated into the local social system. Individuals who fill these functions, however, continue to be largely of nonlocal descent. Although they may pay lip service to locally accepted rules of etiquette and use the dialect on occasion, their experience elsewhere in Norway, where differences in education, influence, and prestige are much more pronounced, leads them to associate the dialect with lack of education and sophistication. Therefore, they show a clear preference for the standard.

Such attitudes are unacceptable to locals, who view lack of respect for and refusal to speak the dialect as an expression of social distance and contempt for the "local team" and its community spirit. It is not surprising, therefore, that their loyalty to the dialect is thereby reaffirmed. For a local resident to employ (B) forms with other local residents is in their view to *snakk fint* or to *snakk jalat* "to put on airs."

Since the different social meanings which attach to the dialect are regular and persistent, they must in some way be reinforced by the pattern of social ties. This relationship can best be described if we consider the socioecological system which sustains the community. There is a correlation between a person's regional background, his reference group, and the niche he occupies in this system (Barth 1964). This information enables us to segment the local population into three distinct categories: (1) artisans, (2) wholesale-retail merchants and plant managers, and (3) service personnel. Members of the first two categories are the basic producers of wealth.

The more than 50 percent of the population which falls into the first category includes draftsmen who may or may not own their own shops, as well as workmen employed in the larger plants and their dependents. Most of them are locally born or have been drawn to Hemnes from the surrounding farms by the demand for their skills. Since they live and work among their relatives and among others of the same social background, they tend to choose their friends and spouses from within their own reference group and thus become strong supporters of local values.

Wholesale-retail merchants buy lumber products and finished boats from producers in the Rana area, furnishing them with supplies and gear and appliances in exchange. They sell boats, lumber products, and fishing supplies to customers all the way up to the northernmost tip of Norway. Relationships between merchants and their customers most commonly take the form of long-term credit arrangements based on personal trust in which credit is given to artisans against their future production. Also part of the second category are the managers of large local enterprises who achieve their position partly because of their special commercial and managerial skills and partly through their ability to get along with and keep the confidence of owners, workers, and foremen.

Like artisans, members of category 2 are largely of local descent. Although they tend to be in the higher income brackets, they maintain kin and conjugal relationships among craftsmen and fishermen-farmers. The fact that their livelihood depends to a great extent on their standing within the system of locally based relations leads them to associate more closely with the local values. The circumstances of their commercial enterprises, however, also take them outside this local network. They must be able to act within the urban commercial ethic, and they must also maintain personal ties with their customers in the north and elsewhere. The range of their social connections includes both local and supralocal ties, involving different and sometimes conflicting standards of behavior. The result is that while they maintain strong loyalty to general local values, they tend to avoid close personal ties with their kin in the first category and confine their friendships to others who are in similar circumstances.

The third category is a composite one, consisting of individuals whose position depends on the productivity of others. It includes persons engaged in purely local services—private and administrative—of all kinds such as salesmen, clerks, repairmen, shopkeepers, professionals, and those who are employed in repair shops and in transportation. The sociocultural background of these people varies. Those who perform manual labor tend to be of local descent and are culturally indistinguishable from members of the first category. The same is true for the lower echelons of employees in stores and in administrative offices. Among the owners of retail businesses, clothing, shoe, pastry, and stationary shops, many belong to families who have moved to Hemnesberget from other urban or semiurban centers in northern Norway. Their kin and friendship relations tend to be dispersed among these communities, and this leads them to identify with the differentiated nonlocal middle-class value system. Shopowners of local background also aspire to these standards, at the same time trying to maintain their position in the "local team" by showing loyalty to its values. Professionals are similarly drawn to Hemnes from the outside because of their technical expertise. The more stable core of this group, the schoolteachers, tend to be of north Norwegian background. Doctors, veterinarians, dentists, and priests frequently come from the south. Invariably their values are those of the pan-Norwegian elite.

Economic conditions in Hemnes leave little room for the academically trained and those with technical skills outside local niches. Consequently, young people from all categories who aspire to higher education must spend most of their student years away from Hemnes and will eventually have to seek employment somewhere else. While they remain students, however, they are partly dependent on their families. They tend to return home during the summer vacation and seek local employment.

Contextual Constraints

Previous sections have dealt with the linguistic repertoire, internal cultural differences, and relevant features of social organization. We have suggested that linguistic alternates within the repertoire serve to symbolize the differing social identities which members may assume. It is, however, evident from our discussion that there is by no means a simple one-to-one relationship between specific speech varieties and specific social identities. Apart from the fact that values attached to language usage vary with social background, the same individual need not be absolutely consistent in all his actions. He may wish to appear as a member of the local team on some occasions, while identifying with middle-class values on others. In order to determine the social significance of any one utterance, we need additional information about the contextual clues by which natives arrive at correct interpretations of social meaning.

Recent linguistic writings have devoted considerable attention to speech events as the starting point for the analysis of verbal communication. It has been shown that aside from purely linguistic and stylistic rules, the form of a verbal message in any speech event is directly affected by (a) the participants (i.e., speakers, addressees, and audiences); (b) the ecological surroundings; and (c) the topic or range of topics (Hymes 1964e; Ervin-Tripp 1964).

In visualizing the relationship between social and linguistic factors in speech events, it seems reasonable to assume that the former restrict the selection of linguistic variables in somewhat the same way that syntactic environments serve to narrow the broader dictionary meanings of words.

For the purpose of our analysis, we can thus visualize verbal communication as a two-step process. In step 1, speakers take in clues from the outside and translate them into appropriate behavioral strategies. This step parallels the perceptual process by which referential meanings are converted into sentences. In step 2, these behavioral strategies are in turn translated into appropriate verbal symbols. The determinants of this communicative process are the speaker's knowledge of the linguistic repertoire, culture, and social structure, and his ability to relate these kinds of knowledge to contextual constraints. For Hemnesberget, it seems useful to describe these constraints in terms of three concepts representing successively more complex levels of information processing.

We will use the term *setting* to indicate the way in which natives classify their ecological environment into distinct locales. This enables us to relate the opportunities for action to constraints upon action provided by the socially significant features of the environment. First, and most important among local settings in Hemnesberget, is the home. Homes form the center for all domestic activities and act as meeting places for children's peer groups. Houses are well built and provide ample space for all. Also, friends and kin prefer the privacy of meetings at home to restaurants or other more public places.

Workshops and plants where productive activity is carried on are separated for the most part from residential areas, although some families continue to live next to their workshops along the shore of the fjord. The work force normally consists of male members of the group of owners, whether managed by a single nuclear family or by a group of families connected by filial, sibling, or in-law ties. Employees in the larger plants frequently also include groups of kin who work together as work teams. In view of the homogeneity of workers, it is not surprising that the place of work frequently forms the center for informal gathering among males. In offices, shops, and merchant establishments, however, where the expertise requirements favor socially more differentiated personnel, work relations tend to be less colored by preexistent social ties.

A second group of settings lacks the specific restrictions on personnel which mark those just mentioned. These include the public dock, where visiting boats and the steamer are moored, as well as a few of the larger stores, e.g., the co-operative society store located near the central square, the square itself, and the community park. Here all local residents may meet somewhat more freely without commitments, subject, of course, to the constraints imposed by lack of privacy. The primary school, the junior high school, the church, and community meeting hall all form somewhat more restricted meeting grounds for more formal gatherings such as classroom sessions, religious services, political meetings, meetings of various voluntary associations, and occasional movies. The church is used only for church services.

The socioecological restrictions on personnel and activities still allow for a wide range of socially distinct happenings. The school, e.g., is used for class sessions during the day and for meetings of voluntary associations during the evening. Similarly, in the town square, men gather for discussions of public affairs, women shoppers stop to chat with acquaintances, adolescent peer groups play their various games, etc. A closer specification of social constraints is possible if we concentrate on activities carried on by particular constellations of personnel, gathered in particular settings during a particular span of time. We will use the term *social situation* to refer to these. Social situations form the background for the enactment of a limited range of social relationships within the framework of specific status sets, i.e., systems of complementary distributions of rights and duties (Barth 1966).

Thus alternative social definitions of the situation may occur within the same setting, depending on the opportunities and constraints on interaction offered by a shift in personnel and/or object of the interaction. Such definitions always manifest themselves in what we would prefer to call a *social event*. Events center around one or at the most a limited range of topics and are distinguishable because of their sequential structure. They are marked by stereotyped and thus recognizable opening and closing routines. The distinction between situation and event can be clarified if we consider the behavior of Hemnes residents who are sometimes seen in the community office, first transacting their business in an officially correct manner, and then turning to one of the clerks and asking him to step aside for a private chat. The norms which apply to the two kinds of interaction differ; the break between the two is clearly marked. Therefore, they constitute two distinct social events, although the personnel and the locale remain the same.

The terms setting, social situation, and social event as used here can be considered three successively more complex stages in the speaker's processing of contextual information. Each stage subsumes the previous one in such a way that the preceding one is part of the input affecting the selection rules of the next stage. Thus, a speaker cannot identify the social situation without first having made some decision as to the nature of the setting. To demonstrate how these factors influence language usage in Hemnesberget, we turn now to some examples drawn from participant observation.

The fact that the dialect reflects local values suggests that it symbolizes relationships based on shared identities with local culture. Casual observations and recording of free speech among locals in homes, workshops, and the various public meeting places where such relationships are assumed do indeed show that only the dialect is used there. However, statuses defined with respect to the superimposed national Norwegian system elicit the standard. Examples of these are church services, presentation of text material in school, reports, and announcements—but not necessarily informal public appeals or political speeches—at public meetings. Similarly, meetings with tourists or other strangers elicit the standard at least until the participants' identity becomes more clearly known.

Situational and Metaphorical Switching

When within the same setting the participants' definition of the social event changes, this change may be signaled among others by linguistic clues. On one occasion, when we, as outsiders, stepped up to a group of locals engaged in conversation, our arrival caused a significant alteration in the casual posture of the group. Hands were removed from pockets and looks changed. Predictably, our remarks elicited a code switch marked simultaneously by a change in channel cues (i.e., sentence speed, ryhthm, more hesitation pauses, etc.) and by a shift from (R) to (B) grammar. Similarly, teachers report that while formal lectures—where interruptions are not encouraged—are delivered in (B), the speakers will shift to (R) when they want to encourage open and free discussion among students. Each of these examples involves clear changes in the participants' definition of each other's rights and obligation. We will use the term *situational switching* to refer to this kind of a language shift.

The notion of situational switching assumes a direct relationship between language and the social situation. The linguistic forms employed are critical features of the event in the sense that any violation of selection rules changes members' perception of the event. A person who uses the standard where only the dialect is appropriate violates commonly accepted norms. His action may terminate the conversation or bring about other social sanctions. To be sure language choice is never completely determined; sociolinguistic variables must be investigated empirically. Furthermore, situations differ in the amount of freedom of choice allowed to speakers. Ritual events, like the well-known Vedic ceremonies of South Asia, constitute extreme examples of determination, where every care is taken to avoid even the slightest change in pronunciation or rhythm lest the effectiveness of the ceremony be destroyed. The greetings, petitions, and similar routines described by Albert (Chapter 2) similarly seem strictly determined.

In Hemnesberget, as our example will show later on, speakers are given relatively wide choice in vocabulary and some choice in syntax. Selection rules affect mainly the variables discussed previously. Values of these variables are sociolinguistically determined in the sense that when, on the one hand, we speak of someone giving a classroom lecture or performing a Lutheran church service or talking to a tourist, we can safely assume that he is using (B) grammatical forms. On the other hand, two locals having a heart-to-heart talk will presumably speak in (R). If instead they are found speaking in (B), we conclude either that they do not identify with the values of the local team or that they are not having a heart-to-heart talk.

In contrast with those instances where choice of variables is narrowly constrained by social norms, there are others in which participants are given considerably more latitude. Thus official community affairs are largely defined as nonlocal and hence the standard is appropriate. But since many individuals who carry out the relevant activities all know each other as fellow locals, they often interject casual statements in the dialect into their formal discussions. In the course of a morning spent at the community administration office, we noticed that clerks used both standard and dialect phrases, depending on whether they were talking about official affairs or not. Likewise, when residents step up to a clerk's desk, greeting and inquiries about family affairs tend to be exchanged in the dialect, while the business part of the transaction is carried on in the standard.

In neither of these cases is there any significant change in definition of participants' mutual rights and obligations. The posture of speakers and channel clues of their speech remain the same. The language switch here relates to particular kinds of topics or subject matters rather than to change in social situation. Characteristically, the situations in question allow for the enactment of two or more different relationships among the same set of individuals. The choice of either (R) or (B) alludes to these relationships and thus generates meanings which are quite similar to those conveyed by the alternation between *ty* or *vy* in the examples from Russian literature cited by Friedrich (Chapter 9). We will use the term *metaphorical switching* for this phenomenon.

The semantic effect of metaphorical switching depends on the existence of regular relationships between variables and social situations of the type just discussed. The context in which one of a set of alternates is regularly used becomes part of its meaning, so that when this form is then employed in a context where it is not normal, it brings in some of the flavor of this original setting. Thus a phrase like "April is the cruelest month" is regarded as poetic because of its association with T. S. Eliot's poetry. When used in natural conversation, it gives that conversation some of the flavor of this poetry. Similarly, when (R) phrases are inserted metaphorically into a (B) conversation, this may, depending on the circumstances, add a special social meaning of confidentiality or privateness to the conversation.

The case of the local who, after finishing his business in the community office, turns to a clerk and asks him to step aside for a private chat further illustrates the contrast between metaphorical and role switching. By their constant alternation between the standard and the dialect during their business transaction, they alluded to the dual relationship which exists between them. The event was terminated when the local asked the clerk in the dialect whether he had time to step aside to talk about private affairs, suggesting in effect that they shift to a purely personal, local relationship. The clerk looked around and said, "Yes, we are not too busy." The two then stepped aside, although remaining in the same room, and their subsequent private discussion was appropriately carried on entirely in the dialect.

The Experiment

Our discussion of verbal behavior so far has relied largely on deductive reasoning supported by unstructured ethnographic observation. Additional tests of our hypothesis are based on controlled text elicitation. We have stated that gatherings among friends and kin implying shared local identities must be carried on in the dialect. If we are correct in our hypothesis, then individuals involved in such friendly gatherings should not change speech variety regardless of whether they talk about local, national, or official matters.

In order to test this, we asked local acquaintances whom we knew to be part of the network of local relationships to arrange a friendly gathering at which refreshments were to be served and to allow us to record the proceedings as samples of dialect speech. Two such gatherings were recorded, one in the living room of our local hosts, and the other in the home of an acquaintance. The fact that arrangements for the meeting were made by local people means that the groups were self-recruited. Participants in the first group included two sisters and a brother and their respective spouses. One of the men was a shopkeeper, one of the few in this category who claims local descent; his brothers-in-law were employed as craftsmen. All three men are quite literate compared to workmen elsewhere in the world and well read in public affairs. They are active in local politics and experienced in formal committee work. The second group included three craftsmen, friends and neighbors who worked in the same plant, and their wives. One of these had served as a sailor on a Norwegian merchant vessel for several years and spoke English. Participants were all quite familiar with standard Norwegian, and our recorded conversations contain several passages where the standard was used in quoting nonlocal speech or in statements directed at us.

Methodologically, self-recruitment of groups is important for two reasons. It insures that groups are defined by locally recognized relationships and enables the investigator to predict the norms relevant to their interaction. Furthermore, the fact that participants have preexisting obligations toward each other means that, given the situation, they are likely to respond to such obligations in spite of the presence of strangers. Our tape recording and our visual observations give clear evidence that this in fact was what occurred.

Our strategy was to introduce discussion likely to mobilize obligations internal to the group, thus engaging members in discussion among themselves. This proved to be relatively easy to do. When a point had been discussed for some time, we would attempt to change the subject by injecting new questions or comments. In doing this, we did not, of course, expect that our own interjections would predictably affect the speakers' choice of codes. Participants were always free to reinterpret our comments in any way they wished. Nevertheless, the greater the range of topics covered, the greater was the likelihood of language shift.

As a rule, our comments were followed by a few introductory exchanges directed at us. These were marked by relatively slow sentence speeds, many hesitation pauses, and visual clues indicating that people were addressing us. Linguistically, we noted some switching to the standard in such exchanges. After a brief period of this, if the topic was interesting, internal discussion began and arguments that referred to persons, places, and events we could not possibly be expected to have any knowledge about developed. The transition to internal discussion was marked by an increase in sentence speed and lack of hesitation pauses and similar clues. The tape recorder was run continously during the gatherings, and after some time participants became quite oblivious to its presence.

Only those passages which were clearly recognizable as internal discussion were used in the analysis; all others were eliminated. The texts obtained in this way consist of stretches of free discussion on diverse topics. The following passages show that our hypothesis about the lack of connection between code switching and change in topic was confirmed.

Group I: Topic: Chitchat about Local Events

GUNNAR: *ja de va ein så kåmm idag—ein så kåmm me mælka—så så hanj de va så varmt inj på mo i går—ja, sa eg, de va no iççe vent anjæ dåkk må no ha meir enn di anjrann bestanjdi.*

Yes, there was one who came today—one who came with milk—so he said it was so warm in Mo yesterday. Yes, I said, there is nothing else to be expected, you people must always have more than anybody else.

Topic: Industrial Planning
ALF: *her kunj ha vǫre eit par sånn mellomstore bedreftæ på ein førti-fæmti manu so ha beșæftigæ denna fålke detta så ha gådd ledi amm vinjtærn.*

There might have been here some medium-size plants employing forty to fifty men which then could offer work to those who have nothing to do in winter.

. *Topic: Governmental Affairs*

OSCAR: *vi jekk inj før denn forste injstiljingæ ifrå šeikommitenn.*

'We supported the first proposal made by the Schei Committee.'

Item 1 deals with a local topic in a somewhat humorous way; items 2 and 3 concern planning and formal governmental affairs. All these passages are clearly in the dialect. Of the phonological variables, [nj] and [lj] show the highest degree of palatalization and [a] and [æ] the highest degree of retraction throughout. Morphophonemic dialect markers are (R) *ein* "one," *så* "who," *iççe* "not," *dåkk* "you," *meir* "more," *her* "here," *jekk* "went," *ifrå* "from." Even lexical borrowings from the standard such as *injstiljing* "proposal" and *bedreftæ* "plants" are clearly in dialect phonology and morphology. We find one single instance of what seems to be a standard form: (B) *mellom/* (R) *imelja* "middle." But this only occurs as part of the borrowed compound *mellomstore* "medium-size." In several hours of conversation with both groups, marked by many changes in topic, we have found a number of lexical borrowings but not a clear instance of phonological or grammatical switching, in spite of the fact that all informants clearly know standard grammar.

While our hypothesis suggests that switching is constrained in those situations which allow only local relationships to be enacted, it also leads us to predict that whenever local and nonlocal relationships are relevant to the same situation, topical variation may elicit code switching. To test this, we selected members of a formerly quite active local peer group. For the last few years these individuals had all been at universities in Oslo, Bergen, and Trondheim. They returned home in the summer either for vacation or to take up local employment. In conventional interview sessions, all participants claimed to be pure dialect speakers and professed local attitudes about dialect use. They thus regarded themselves as members of the local "team." As fellow students, however, they also shared statuses that are identified with pan-Norwegian values and associated with the standard. Our assumption then is that if topical stimuli are introduced which elicit these values, switching may result.

Three gatherings were arranged in the home of one of our informants. Refreshments were again served. Elicitation strategies were similar to those employed with the first two groups, and similar ranges of topics were covered. The examples cited here show that our hypothesis was again confirmed.

Group III: Topic: Chitchat about Drinking Habits

BERIT: *ja, ja, mæn vi bjynjt anjer veien du—vi bjynjt i barnelošen—så vi har de unjajort.*

Yes, yes, we started the other way, we started in the children's antialcoholic league. So we have finished all that.

Topic: Industrial Development

BERIT: *jo da viss di bare fikk de te lønn seg—så e i værtfall prisnivåe hær i Rana skrudd høger enn de e vanligvis anner stann i lanne.*

Yes, if they could only manage to make it profitable—so in any case the prices tend to be higher here in Rana than is common in other places in the country.

Topic: Informal Statement about University Regulations

OLA: *mænn no ha dæmm læmpæ pa de.*

But now they have relaxed that.

Topic: Authoritative Statement about University Regulations

OLA: *de voel du mellom en faemm saeks.*

You choose that from among five or six.

Comparison of Berit's and Ola's first statement with their second statements shows considerable shifting in each case. Thus Berit's second utterance has such unpalatalized forms as *anner* (vs. *anjer*), and raised and less retracted [a] in *da*. She also uses standard variables (B)*fikk*/(R)*fekk*, (B)*viss*/(R)*vess*, (B)*værtfall*/(R)*kvartfall*, (B)*hær*/(R)*her*, etc. Ola's second statement is characterized by (B)*mellon*/(R)*imelja* and (B)en/(R)ein. Similarly, his [æ] in *fæm* and *sæks* is raised and fronted. In neither case is the shift to the standard complete—after all the situation never lost its informality. Berit's statement still contains dialect words like (R)*lønn*/(B)*lønne* "to be profitable"; (R)*stan*/(B)*steder* "places"; and Ola has (R)*væl*/(B)*velger* "to choose." What we see then is a breakdown of co-occurrence rules, an erosion of the linguistic boundary between Ranamål and Bokmål. The tendency is to switch toward standard phonology while preserving some morphophonemic and lexical dialect features of (R). Features retained in this manner are largely those which also occur in other local dialects and to some extent also in Nynorsk. They have thus gained some acceptance as proper dialect forms. Those characteristics which locals refer to as broad speech, i.e., those that are known as local peculiarities, tend to be eliminated.

It must also be noted that Berit and Ola also differ in their pronunciation of the phonological variables. Ola's normal pronunciation shows the strong palatalization of consonant and extreme vowel retraction characteristic of most residents. Berit's normal pronunciation has medium palatalization and medium retraction. Both, however, switch in the same direction, in response to similar situational and topical clues, and this agreement on the rules of stylistic manipulation is clearly more important in this case than the mere articulatory difference in Berit's and Ola's speech.

The social character of the style switch was clearly revealed when the tape-recorded conversations were played back to other Hemnes residents. One person who had been working with us as a linguistic informant at first refused to believe that the conversations were recorded locally. When he recognized the voices of the participants, he showed clear signs of disapproval. Apparently, he viewed the violation of co-occurrence rules as a sign of what is derogatorily called *knot* "artificial speech" in colloquial Norwegian. Some of the participants showed similar reactions when they heard themselves on tape. They promised to refrain from switching during future discussion sessions. Our analysis of these later sessions, however, revealed that when an argument required that the speaker validate his status as an intellectual, he would again tend to use standard forms in the manner shown by Berit and Ola. Code selection rules thus seem to be akin to grammatical rules. Both operate below the level of consciousness and may be independent of the speaker's overt intentions.

Additional information about usage patterns in group III was provided through a fortunate accident. One of our sessions with this group was interrupted by a somewhat mentally retarded young person, who has the habit of appearing in peoples' homes to solicit assistance for his various schemes. Here are some examples of remarks addressed to him by Berit and Solveig, of all the members of the group, the most prone to use standard forms. Her normal pronunciation shows the least amount of consonant palatalization. She is socially more marginal to Hemnes than other members of the group.

Group III: Topic: Talking to a Retarded Local Youth

BERIT: *e de du så vikarier fφrr hanj no.*
                Are you a stand-in for him now?

SOLVEIG: *hanj kanj jo jett gåte, haj kanj no va me.*
                He is good at word games, he should participate.

Both Berit and Solveig's pronunication in these examples become identical with the ordinary speech of Ola and of the members of group I. The extreme palatalization of [nj] and the lowering of [a] is not normal for them; they clearly are talking down in this case. Their stylistic range, as well as their facility in switching, seem to be greater than those of the others.

In comparing the behavior of the first two groups with that of group III, we find two different kinds of language-usage patterns. All three groups speak both the dialect and the standard. Groups I and II, however, show only situational switching. When members talk to each other, differences of formality or informality to topic are reflected only in the lexicon. Pronunciation and morphology do not change. Those groups shift to (B) phonology and grammar only when remarks are addressed directly to us who count as outsiders or in indirect quotes of such matters as government rules, on officials' statements, etc. In such instances of situation switching, therefore, Ranamål and Bokmål are kept separate throughout by strict co-occurrence restrictions. In group III, however, deviation from the dialect results both from metaphorical and situation switching. Metaphorical switching, furthermore, involves a breakdown of the co-occurrence restrictions characteristic of situational shifts.

The dialect usage of locals, on the one hand, corresponds to their view that the two varieties are distinct, and to their insistence on maintaining the strict separation of local and nonlocal values. For the students, on the other hand, the distinction between dialect and standard is not so sharp. Although they display the same general attitudes about the dialect as the team of locals, their behavior shows a range of variation rather than an alternation between distinct systems. It reflects a de facto recognition of their own nonlocal identification.

A fourth conversational group further illustrates the internal speech diversity in the community. The principal speakers here are two men, A and B, and C, who is A's wife. All come from families who tend to dissociate themselves from the egalitarian value system of the local team. Their normal style of speech was Bokmål for remarks directed, at us as well as for in-group speech. Only in a few instances when A began telling local anecdotes did he lapse into Ranamål. (R) forms were introduced as metaphorical switches into what were basically (B) utterances to provide local color, indicate humor, etc., in somewhat the same way that speakers in group III had used (B) forms in (R) utterances.

In the course of the evening A and C's teen-age daughter joined the conversation. She expressed attitudes toward the dialect which are quite similar to those of the students in group III and thus are somewhat different from those of her parents. The few samples we have of her speech show (R) phonology similar to that of Berit and Solveig in group III.

Although the picture of language usage derived from the four groups seems at first highly complex, it becomes less so when viewed in relation to speakers' attitudes, interactional norms, and local values. All Hemnes residents have the same repertoire. Their linguistic competence includes control of both (R) and (B) rules. They vary in the way in which they use these rules. Expressed attitudes toward (R) and (B) do not provide an explanation for these differences in speech behavior. The most reasonable explanation of the ways in which these groups differ seems to be that the dual system of local values, differences in individual background, and the various social situations in which members find themselves operate to affect their interpretation of the social meaning of the variables they employ.

Conclusion

Our analysis in this chapter is based on the assumption that regularities in behavior can be analyzed as generated from a series of individual choices made under specifiable constraints and incentives (Barth 1966). This position implies an important break with previous approaches to social structure and to language and society. Behavioral regularities are no longer regarded as reflections of independently measurable social norms; on the contrary, these norms are themselves seen as communicative behavior. They are reflected in what Goffman (1959) calls the rules of impression management or, in our terms, in the social meanings which constrain the actor's adoption of behavioral strategies in particular situations.

In interactional sociolinguistics, therefore, we can no longer base our analyses on the assumption that language and society constitute different kinds of reality, subject to correlational studies. Social and linguistic information is comparable only when studied within the same general analytical frame work. Moving from statements of social constraints to grammatical rules thus represents a transformation from one level of abstraction to another within a single communicative system.

As Bernstein (1961) has pointed out, verbal communication is a process in which actors select from a limited range of alternates within a repertoire of speech forms determined by previous learning. Although ultimately this selection is a matter of individual choice, our chapter shows that the rules of codification by which the deep structure of interpersonal relations is transformed into speech performances are independent of expressed attitudes and similar in nature to the grammatical rules operating on the level of intelligibility. They form part of what Hymes (1972) has called the speaker's communicative competence. Sociolinguistic constraints on the selection of variables seem to be of central importance in this codification process. We argued that they determine the speaker's perception of the utterances as a unit of social meaning. By accepting the native's view of what is and what is not properly part of a dialect or language, linguists have tended to assume these co-occurrences rather than investigate them empirically. We have attempted to develop descriptive procedures suitable for the empirical investigation of these rules by combining various ethnographic field techniques with conventional linguistic elicitation methods.

In Hemnes, where Ranamål and Bokmål communicate the same objective information, we were led to ask how the apparent separateness of the dialect and the standard can exist and be maintained. Ethnographic investigation suggests the hypothesis that Ranamål has social value as a signal of distinctness and of a speaker's identification with others of local descent. This social significance of the dialect can only be understood by contrast with the meanings which locals assign to the standard, the language of nonlocal activities. The standard is associated with education and power on the national scene and carries connotations of differences in rank which are unacceptable in the realm of informal local relations. When used casually among Hemnes residents, therefore, it communicates dissociation from the "local team."

Since most Hemnes natives live, marry, and earn their livelihood among others of their own kind, their values are rarely challenged. Their personal relations have all the characteristics of network closure (Barnes 1954). On the other hand, those with nonlocal background and who maintain significant ties in other communities tend to seek their friends among those in similar circumstances, even though they may have resided in Hemnes for more than a generation. Their contacts with members of the "local team" remain largely nonpersonal, focusing around single tasks, and are thus similar in kind to nonlocal contacts. This lack of personal ties between individuals of dissimilar backgrounds and cultural identification reinforces the general social meanings ascribed to the dialect by those who share local background and identity, and thus contributes to maintaining the separateness of dialect and standard.

While this information provides the background for our study, it does not explain the fact that all residents frequently switch between the dialect and the standard. This can only be explained through the analysis of particular speech events. The concepts of setting, social situation, and social event represent an attempt to explain the natives' conception of their behavioral environment in terms of an ordered set of constraints which operate to transform alternative lines of behavior into particular social meanings. Our distinction between metaphoric and role switching shows how constraints at different levels of inclusiveness produce appropriate changes in the way speech performances are interpreted.

Although locals show an overt preference for the dialect, they tolerate and use the standard in situations where it conveys meanings of officiality, expertise, and politeness toward strangers who are clearly segregated from their personal life. In private gatherings where people meet as natives and equals, a speaker's use of standard variables suggests social dissociation, an attitude which is felt to be out of place. Although the students in our experimental sessions meet as locals and friends, they differ from other members of the local team because they share the additional status of intellectuals. This fact modifies the social meaning of standard forms when they are used among the students. To refrain from using standard forms for these topics which elicit participants' shared experience as intellectuals would constitute an unnatural limitation on their freedom of expression. Group IV demonstrates the effect of intracommunity differences in value systems on language-usage patterns. Because of this identification with the urban middle classes, the adult members of this group use (B) as their normal form of speech while employing (R) only for special effect. Such usage distinctions, however, are not necessarily very stable. The teen-age daughter of the adult members seems to follow local usage, thus symbolizing her identification with her peer group rather than with her family.

Our experiments, and the analysis presented in this chapter, demonstrate the importance of social or nonreferential meaning for the study of language in society. Mere naturalistic observation of speech behavior is not enough. In order to interpret what he hears, the investigator must have some background knowledge of the local culture and of the processes which generate social meaning. Without this it is impossible to generalize about the social implication of dialect differences. The processes studied here are specific to particular small communities. Predictions of language maintenance or language shift in larger societies will, of course, have to depend on statistical generalizations. More studies along the lines suggested here, however, should materially improve the validity of such generalizations. For Hemnesberget, the fate of the dialect seems assured as long as local identification maintains its importance, and the socioecological system continues to prevent any significant accumulation of individuals who, like the students, fail to maintain the situational barrier between the dialects and the standard.

15

Domains and the Relationship between Micro- and Macrosociolinguistics

JOSHUA A. FISHMAN

Joshua A. Fishman is a professor of sociology at Yeshiva University. He has been concerned with multilingualism and the social role of language for some years. Having completed studies of language loyalty in the United States, and Spanish-English bilingualism among Puerto Ricans in the New York area, he is now engaged in research on language policy and development. The theoretical framework, as well as part of the data presented in this chapter, are contained in an earlier article (Fishman 1965), of which the present essay is an extension and revision.

Fishman is here concerned with situations of language choice, as are Blom and Gumperz, but the focus and the methods employed are instructively different. Blom and Gumperz treat norms and other factors all as dimensions of one communicative system as input to a single set of rules. The potential for change in the situation is detected, but information as to the larger society and history is used as context to illuminate the set of rules itself. The emphasis is on the individual choosing among alternative modes of behavior in accordance with linguistic and social constraints. Fishman, however, is concerned with behavioral norms seen as jural rules (see Introduction) and defined in sociological terms as regularities which stand apart from individual behavior. He concentrates on stable systems of choice, or "proper" usage as he calls it, specifically excluding situations of change where these norms no longer hold. Fishman's key concept, *domain,* is intended to relate specific language choices, from which it is an abstraction, to general institutions and spheres of activity, both in one society and, comparatively, between societies. Concern with changing situations is not dealt with in terms of formulated rules and linguistic variation but at the level of changes in spheres of activity and institutions. Whereas Blom and Gumperz place participant observation and analysis of spontaneous speech at the center of their approach, Fishman employs techniques more characteristic of large-scale social investigations, including self-report instruments, census, word association, test together with factor analysis and analysis of variance. The approach taken here is akin to the correlational view of language described by William Bright (1966) and discussed in the Introduction.

Further difference lies in the materials studied and in the approach taken. Both chapters are concerned with successful prediction, but the Norwegian case of variables within one linguistic matrix clearly requires close phonetic and other linguistic specification, whereas the Puerto Rican case can be approached in terms of two grossly distinguishable wholes.

Notice in Fishman's discussion of *topic* that this salient dimension of rule-governed choices is shown to depend on more than one underlying process. The implicit danger to which Fishman calls attention is that success in stating rules and predicting use may remain at a "surface structure" level and may not reach the level at which the predictable regularities are generated. In both this and the preceding chapter there is the concern of relating individual choices to relatively stable patterns, but whereas Blom and Gumperz align themselves with the view that the latter are generated from the former, Fishman treats the individual choices as being derived from stable patterns. (It is worthwhile to compare the Blom-Gumperz schema of setting-situation-event with the scheme of relationships in Fig. 15.1 of the present chapter.)

Domain analysis is linked to the analysis of cultural scenes discussed by Frake (Chapter 3), although the definition of domain here differs from the ethnoscientific definition of the term. Fishman points out that a fixed set of domains cannot be prescribed in advance for all cases. He envisages different categories of participant (e.g.,

children), different types of social context (e.g., immigrant-host contexts), and different levels of focus (e.g.,
social-psychological vs. societal-institutional). While
concerned with the establishment of the validity of the
constructs for the particular Puerto Rican study,
Fishman locates the findings of appropriate domains first
of all in the integrative intuition of the investigator. He
implies that the heuristic value of the concept of domain
does not depend on any one method of data collection
and analysis. Additional related readings are provided
by: Ferguson (1966), Gumperz (1961), Rona (1966),
Rubin (1968), and Fishman (1970).

The Analysis of Multilingual Settings

Multilingual speech communities differ from each other in so
many ways that every student of societal multilingualism must grapple
with the problem of how best to systematize or organize the manifold differences that are readily recognizable between them. This chapter is
directed to a formal consideration of several descriptive and analytic variables which may contribute to an understanding of *who* speaks *what* language to *whom* and *when* in those speech communities that are characterized by widespread and relatively stable multilingualism. It deals
primarily with "within-group (or intragroup) multilingualism" rather than
with "between-group (or intergroup) multilingualism," i.e., it focuses upon
those multilingual settings in which a single population makes use of two
(or more) "languages" or varieties of the "same language" for internal
communicative purposes (Fishman 1967). As a result of this limitation,
mastery or control of *mother tongue* and *other tongue* [or, more generally,
of the various languages or varieties constituting the speech community's
linguistic repertoire (Gumperz 1962)] may be ruled out as a crucial variable since the members of many speech networks *could* communicate
with each other quite easily in any of their available codes or subcodes. It
seems clear, however, that habitual language choice in multilingual
speech communities or speech networks is far from being a random
matter of momentary inclination, even under those circumstances when it
could very well function as such from a purely probabilistic point of view
(Lieberson 1964). "Proper" usage dictates that only *one* of the theoretically coavailable languages or varieties *will* be chosen by particular
classes of *interlocutors* on particular kinds of *occasions* to discuss particular kinds of *topics*.

438   Genesis, Maintenance, and Change of Linguistic Codes

What are the most appropriate parameters in terms of which these choice patterns can be described in order to attain both factual accuracy and theoretical parsimony, and in order to facilitate the integration of small-group and large-group research rather than its further needless polarization? If we can solve the problem of how to describe language choice in stable, within-group bilingual settings (where the limits of language mastery do not intrude), we can then more profitably turn (or return) to the problem of choice determinants in less stable settings such as those characterizing immigrant-host relationships and between-group multilingual settings more generally (Fishman 1964).

A HYPOTHETICAL EXAMPLE

American students are so accustomed to bilingualism as a "vanishing phenomenon," as a temporary dislocation from a presumably more normal state of affairs characterized by "one man, one language," that an example of stable intragroup bilingualism may help to start off our discussion in a more naturalistic and less bookish vein.

A government functionary in Brussels arrives home after stopping off at his club for a drink. He *generally* speaks standard French in his office, standard Dutch at his club, and a distinctly local variant of Flemish at home.[1] In each instance he identifies himself with a different speech network to which he belongs, wants to belong, and from which he seeks acceptance. All of these networks—and more—are included in his overarching speech community, even though each is more commonly associated with one speech variety than with another. Nevertheless, it is not impossible to find occasions at the office in which he speaks or is spoken to in one or another variety of Flemish. There are also occasions at the club when he speaks or is addressed in French; finally, there are occasions at home when he communicates in standard Dutch or even French.

Our hypothetical government functionary is most likely to give and get Flemish at the office when he bumps into another functionary who hails from the very same Flemish-speaking town. The two of them grew up together and went to school together. Their respective sets of parents strike them as being similarly "kind- but- old- fashioned." In short, they share many common experiences and points of view (or think they do, or pretend they do), and, therefore, they tend to speak to each other in the

[1] This example may be replaced by any one of a number of others: standard German, Schwytzertütsch, and Romansch (in parts of Switzerland); Hebrew, English, and Yiddish in Israel; Riksmaal, Landsmaal, and more local dialectal variants of the latter in Norway; standard German, Plattdeutsch, and Danish in Schleswig; French, standard German, and German dialect in Luxembourg, etc.

language which represents for them the intimacy that they share. The two do not cease being government functionaries when they speak Flemish to each other; they simply prefer to treat each other as intimates rather than as functionaries. However, the careful observer will also note that the two do not speak Flemish to each other invariably. When they speak about world affairs, or the worlds of art and literature, not to mention the world of government, they tend to switch into French (or to reveal far more French lexical, phonological, or even grammatical influence in their Flemish), even though (for the sake of our didactic argument) the mood of intimacy and familiarity remains clearly evident throughout.

Thus our overall problem is twofold: (a) to recognize and describe whatever higher order regularities there may be in choosing among the several varieties that constitute the repertoire of a multilingual speech community (so that we need not always remain at an anecdotal and clinical level of analysis) and (b) nevertheless, to provide for and recognize the interpersonal fluctuation (= lower order societal patterning) that remains even when higher order societal patterning is established.

TOPIC

The fact that two individuals who usually speak to each other primarily in X nevertheless switch to Y (or vacillate more noticeably between X and Y) when discussing certain topics leads us to consider topic per se as a regulator of language use in multilingual settings.

The implication of topical regulation of language choice is that certain topics are somehow handled "better" or more appropriately in one language than in another in particular multilingual contexts. However, this greater appropriateness may reflect or may be brought about by several different but mutually reinforcing factors. Thus, some multilingual speakers may "acquire the habit" of speaking about topic *x* in language X partially because that is the language in which they are *trained* to deal with this topic (e.g., they received their university training in economics in French), partially because *they (and their interlocutors)* may *lack the specialized terms* for a satisfying discussion of *x* in language Y,[2] partially because *language Y itself may currently lack as exact or as many terms* for handling topic *x* as those currently possessed by language X, and par-

[2] This effect has been noted even in normally monolingual settings, such as those obtaining among American intellectuals, many of whom feel obliged to use French or German words in conjunction with particular professional topics. English lexical influence on the language of immigrants in the United States has also often been explained on topical grounds. The importance of topical determinants is discussed by Haugen (1953, 1956) and Weinreich (1953) and, more recently, by Gumperz (1962) and Susan Ervin-Tripp (1964). It is implied as a "pressure" exerted upon "contacts" in Mackey's descriptions of bilingualism (1962, 1965, 1966).

tially because *it is considered strange* or inappropriate to discuss *x* in language Y. The very multiplicity of sources of topical regulation suggests that *topic* may not in itself be a convenient analytic variable when language choice is considered from the point of view of the larger societal patterns and sociolinguistic norms of a multilingual setting, no matter how fruitful it may be at the level of face-to-face interaction per se. What *would* be helpful for larger societal investigations and for intersocietal comparisons is an understanding of how topics reflect or imply regularities which pertain to the major spheres of activity in any society under consideration. We may be able to discover the latter if we inquire *why* a significant number of people in a particular multilingual setting at a particular time have received certain kinds of training in one language rather than in another; or *what it reveals* about a particular multilingual setting if language X *is* currently actually less capable of coping with topic *x* than is language Y. Does it not reveal more than merely a topic-language relationship at the level of particular face-to-face encounters? Does it not reveal that certain socioculturally *recognized spheres of activity* are, at least temporarily, under the sway of one language or variety (and, therefore, perhaps, under the control of certain speech networks) rather than others? Thus, while topic is doubtlessly a crucial consideration in understanding language choice variance in our two hypothetical government functionaries, *we must seek a means of examining and relating their individual, momentary choices to relatively stable patterns of choice that exist in their multilingual speech community as a whole.*

Domains of Language Behavior

1. The concept of domains of language behavior seems to have received its first partial elaboration from students of language maintenance and language shift among *Auslandsdeutsche* in pre-World-War-II multilingual settings.[3] German settlers were in contact with many different non-German-speaking populations in various types of contact settings and were exposed to various kinds of sociocultural change processes. In attempting to chart and compare the fortunes of the German language under such varying circumstances Schmidt-Rohr (1963) seems to have been the first to suggest that *dominance configurations* needed to

---

[3] The study of language maintenance and language shift is concerned with the relationship between change or stability in habitual language use, on the one hand, and ongoing psychological, social, or cultural processes of change and stability, on the other hand (Fishman 1964, 1966; Nahirny and Fishman 1965).

be established to reveal the overall status of language choice in various domains of behavior. The domains recommended by Schmidt-Rohr were the following nine: the family, the playground and street, the school, the church, literature, the press, the military, the courts, and the governmental administration. Subsequently, other investigators either added additional domains [e.g., Mak (1935), who nevertheless followed Schmidt-Rohr in overlooking the work sphere as a domain], or found that fewer domains were sufficient in particular multilingual settings [e.g., Frey (1945), who required only home, school, and church in his analysis of Amish "triple talk"]. However, what is more interesting is that Schmidt-Rohr's domains bear a striking similarity to those "generally termed" spheres of activity which have more recently been independently advanced by others interested in the study of acculturation, intergroup relations, and bilingualism [e.g., Dohrenwend and Smith (1962)].

Domains are defined, regardless of their number,[4] in terms of *institutional contexts and their congruent behavioral co-occurrences. They attempt to summate the major clusters of interaction that occur in clusters of multilingual settings and involving clusters of interlocutors.* Domains enable us to understand that *language choice* and *topic,* appropriate though they may be for analyses of individual behavior at the level of face-to-face verbal encounters, are, as I suggested, related to widespread sociocultural norms and expectations. By recognizing the existence of domains it becomes possible to contrast the language of topics for individuals or particular subpopulations with the predominant language of domains for larger networks, if not the whole, of a speech community.

2. The appropriate designation and definition of domains of language behavior obviously calls for considerable insight into the sociocultural dynamics of particular multilingual speech communities at particular periods in their history. Schmidt-Rohr's domains reflect not only multilingual settings in which a large number of spheres of activity, even those that pertain to governmental functions, are theoretically open to both or all of the languages present but also those multilingual settings in which such permissiveness is at least sought by a sizable number of interested parties. Quite different domains might be appropriate if one were to study habitual language use among children in these very same settings. Certainly, immigrant-host contexts, in which only the language of the host society is recognized for governmental functions, would require other and perhaps fewer domains, particularly if younger generations constantly

---

[4] We can safely reject the implication encountered in certain discussions of domains that there must be an invariant set of domains applicable to all multilingual settings. If language behavior is reflective of sociocultural patterning, as is now widely accepted, then different kinds of multilingual speech communities should benefit from analyses in terms of different domains of language use, however defined and validated.

leave the immigrant society and enter the host society. Finally, the domains of language behavior may differ from setting to setting not only in terms of number and designation but also in terms of level. Thus in studying acculturating populations in Arizona, G. C. Barker [who studied bilingual Spanish Americans (1947)] and Barber [who studied trilingual Yaqui Indians (1952)] formulated *domains at the level of sociopsychological analysis:* intimate, informal, formal, and intergroup. Interestingly enough, the domains defined in this fashion were then identified with domains at the *societal-institutional level* mentioned previously. The "formal" domain, e.g., was found to coincide with religious-ceremonial activities; the intergroup" domain consisted of economic and recreational activities as well as of interactions with governmental-legal authority, etc. The interrelationship between domains of language behavior defined at a societal-institutional level and domains defined at a sociopsychological level (the latter being somewhat closer to the topical-situational analyses discussed earlier) may enable us to study language choice in multilingual settings in newer and more fruitful ways.

3. The "governmental administration" domain is a social nexus which normally brings certain kinds of people together *primarily* for a certain *cluster of purposes.* Furthermore, it brings them together *primarily* for a certain set of *role relations* (discussed later) and in a delimited *environment.* Thus, domain is a sociocultural construct abstracted from topics of communication, relationships between communicators, and locales of communication, in accord with the institutions of a society and the spheres of activity of a speech community, in such a way that *individual behavior and social patterns can be distinguished from each other and yet related to each other.*[5] The domain is a higher order summarization which is arrived at from a detailed study of the face-to-face interactions in which language choice is imbedded. Of the many factors contributing to and subsumed under the domain concept, some are more important and more accessible to careful measurement than others. One of these, topic, has already been discussed. Two others, role relation and locale, remain to be discussed. Role relations may be of value to us in accounting for the fact that our two hypothetical governmental functionaries, who usually speak an informal variant of Flemish to each other at the office, except when they talk about technical, professional, or sophisticated "cultural" matters, are themselves not entirely alike in this respect. One of the two tends to slip into French more frequently than the other. It would not be surprising to discover that he is the supervisor of the other.

---

[5] For a discussion of the differences and similarities between "functions of language behavior" and "domains of language behavior" see Fishman (1964). "Functions" stand closer to sociopsychological analysis, for they abstract their constituents in terms of individual motivation rather than in societal institutions.

DOMAINS AND ROLE RELATIONS

In many studies of multilingual behavior the family domain has proved to be a very crucial one. Multilingualism often begins in the family and depends upon it for encouragement if not for protection. In other cases, multilingualism withdraws into the family domain after it has been displaced from other domains in which it was previously encountered. Little wonder then that many investigators, beginning with Braunshausen several years ago (1928), have differentiated *within* the family domain in terms of "speakers." However, two different approaches have been followed in connection with such differentiation. Braunshausen [and, much more recently, Mackey (1962, 1965, 1966)] have merely specified family "members": father, mother, child, domestic, governess and tutor, etc. Gross (1951), however, has specified *dyads* within the family: grandfather to grandmother, grandmother to grandfather, grandfather to father, grandmother to father, grandfather to mother, grandmother to mother, grandfather to child, grandmother to child, father to mother, mother to father, etc. The difference between these two approaches is quite considerable. Not only does the second approach recognize that interacting members of a family (as well as the participants in most other domains of language behavior) are *hearers* as well as *speakers* (i.e., that there may be a distinction between multilingual *production*) but it also recognizes that their language behavior may be more than merely a matter of individual preference or facility but also a matter of *role relations*. In certain societies particular behaviors (including language behaviors) are *expected* (if not required) of *particular individuals vis-a-vis each other* (Goodenough 1965a).

The family domain is hardly unique with respect to its differentiability into role relations. *Each domain can be differentiated into role relations that are specifically crucial or typical of it* in particular societies at particular times. The religious domain (in those societies where religion can be differentiated from folkways more generally) may reveal such role relations as cleric-cleric, cleric-parishioner, parishioner-cleric, and parishioner-parishioner. Similarly, pupil-teacher, buyer-seller, employer-employee, judge-petitioner, all refer to specific role relations in other domains. It would certainly seem desirable to describe and analyze language use or language choice in a particular multilingual setting in terms of the crucial role relations within the specific domains considered to be most revealing for that setting.[6] The distinction between own-group-in-

---

[6] These remarks are not intended to imply that *all* role-relation differences are necessarily related to language-choice differences. This almost certainly is *not* the case. Just which role-relation differences *are* related to language-choice differences (and under what circumstances) is a matter for empirical determination within each multilingual setting as well as at different points in time within the same setting. In general the verification of significantly different clusters of *allo-roles* (as well as significantly different clusters of allo-topics and allo-cales) (see later discussion) is a prerequisite for the empirical formulation of domains.

terlocutor and other-group-interlocutor may also be provided for in this way when intergroup bilingualism becomes the focus of inquiry.

DOMAINS AND LOCALES

Bock (1964), Ervin-Tripp (1964), and Gumperz (1964b) have presented many examples of the importance of locale as a determining component of situational analysis. If one meets one's clergyman at the racetrack, the impact of the locale on the topics and role relationships that normally obtain is likely to be quite noticeable. However, we must also note that domains too are locale related in the sense that most major social institutions are associated with a very few primary locales. Just as topical appropriateness in face-to-face language choice is indicative of larger scale societal patterns, and just as role appropriateness in face-to-face language choice is similarly indicative, so the locale constraints and local appropriatenesses that obtain in face-to-face language choice have their large-scale implications and extrapolations.

THE CONSTRUCT VALIDITY OF DOMAINS

A research project dealing with Puerto Rican bilingualism in the Greater New York City area has yielded data which may help clarify the construct validity of domains as well as the procedure for their recognition. Since domains are a higher order generalization than *congruent situations* (i.e., from situations in which individuals interacting in appropriate role relationships with each other, in the appropriate locales for these role relationships, and discussing topics appropriate to their role relationships), it was first necessary to try out and revise intuitive and rather clinical estimates of the widespread congruences that were felt to obtain. After more than a year of participant observation and other data-gathering experiences, it seemed to Greenfield (1968) that five domains could be generalized from the innumerable situations that he had encountered in the Puerto Rican speech community. He tentatively labeled these "family," "friendship," "religion," "education," and "employment" and proceeded to determine whether a typical *situation* could be presented for each domain as a means of collecting valid self-report data on language choice. As indicated on p. 445 each domain was represented by a congruent person (interlocutor), place, and topic in the self-report instrument that Greenfield constructed for use with high school students.

Greenfield's hypothesis was that within the Puerto Rican speech community, among individuals who knew Spanish and English equally well, Spanish was primarily associated with family and secondarily with friendship (the two, family and friendship, constituting the intimacy value clus-

Domain	Interlocutor	Place	Topic
Family	Parent	Home	How to be a good son or daughter
Friendship	Friend	Beach	How to play a certain game
Religion	Priest	Church	How to be a good Christian
Education	Teacher	School	How to solve an algebra problem
Employment	Employer	Workplace	How to do your job more efficiently

ter), while English was primarily associated with religion, work, and education (the three constituting the status-stressing value cluster).[7] In order to test this hypothesis, he initially presented two seemingly congruent situational components and requested his subjects (a) to select a third component in order to complete the situation as well as (b) to indicate their likelihood of using Spanish or English if they were involved in such a situation (and if they and their Puerto Rican interlocutors knew Spanish and English equally well). Section I of Table 15.1 shows that Greenfield's predictions were uniformly confirmed among those subjects who selected congruent third components. The domains for which Spanish was reported were, from most often to least, family, friendship, religion, employment, and education, regardless of whether the third component selected was a person, place, or topic.

However, as Blom and Gumperz (Chapter 14), Fishman (1968b), and others have indicated, seemingly incongruent situations frequently occur and are rendered understandable and acceptable (just as are the seemingly ungrammatical sentences that we hear in most spontaneous speech). Interlocutors reinterpret incongruencies in order to salvage some semblance of the congruency in terms of which they understand and function within their social order (c.f. Garfinkel, Chapter 10). Were this not the case, then no seemingly congruent domains could arise and be maintained out of the incongruencies of daily life. In order to test this assumption, Greenfield subsequently proceeded to present his subjects with two incongruent components (e.g., with a person from one hypothetical domain and with a place from another hypothetical domain) and asked them (a) to select a third component in order to complete the situation, as well as (b) to indicate their likelihood of using Spanish or English in a situation so constituted. Greenfield found that the third component was overwhelmingly selected from one or the other of the two domains from which he had selected the first two components, not from some third domain. Furthermore, in their attempts to render a seemingly incongruous situation somewhat more congruent, his subjects' language preferences left *the normal relationship between domains and language choice substantially unal-*

---

[7] For a discussion of the significance of value clusters in the study of diglossic societies and the relationship between domain analysis and value analysis see Fishman (1968b).

tered (*directionally*), regardless of whether person, places, or topics were involved. Nevertheless, all domains became somewhat less different from each other than they had been in the fully congruent situations. Apparently, both individual indecisiveness and sociolinguistic norms governing domain regularity must be combined and compromised when incongruencies appear. Language choice is much more clear-cut and polarized in "usual" situations governed entirely by sociolinguistic norms of communicative appropriateness than they are in "unusual" situations which must be resolved by individual interpretation.

Greenfield's findings imply that the assumed relationship between face-to-face situations and larger scale societal domains obtains for self-report data. However, it remained necessary for other investigators to determine whether the domains adumbrated in this fashion have more general validity in the speech community under study.

On a reinterviewed sample of 124 cases the distributions obtained were practically identical to those shown here, indicating that the marginals reported here are quite stable.

The language replies to the census have been subjected to a factor analysis (verimax orthogonal rotation). The following five-factor solution appeared to be most revealing:

A language census conducted among all 431 souls in a two-block Puerto Rican neighborhood in Jersey City yielded the data shown in Table 15.2. Above and beyond examining the replies obtained to the individual census items, the reader should direct his attention to the results of the factor analysis. If domains are more than the investigator's etic reclassification of situations, then they should also become apparent from factor analysis, which in essence asks: Which items tend to be answered in a consistent fashion? Of the five domains extracted from this analysis, all four domains considered appropriate for census questioning (language in the context of family, education, work, and religion) appeared as separate factors, namely, I. Spanish: literacy (= education), II. Spanish: oral (= family), IV. Spanish: at work, and V. Spanish: in religion. In addition, an English factor also emerged, indicating that although English is not associated with specific domains for the population as a whole (it *is* so associated for children, as we will see), its relation to Spanish is not one of displacement or transition. An orthogonal English factor indicates that (as in other speech communities marked by relatively stable and widespread bilingualism) there is no need for one language to be learned or used at the *expense* of the other in the population under study. Other accounts of language censuses and the research problems which they pose are provided by Kloss (1929) and Lieberson (1966a).

A third (and, for this presentation, final) indication of the construct validity of domains as analytic parameters for the study of large-scale sociolinguistic patterns is yielded by Edelman's data (1968). Here we note that when the word-naming responses of bilingual Puerto Rican

table 15.1

Spanish- and English-Usage Self-Ratings in Various Situations for Components Selected by Bilingual Ss*

I. Congruent Situations: Two "congruent" components presented; S selects third congruent component and language appropriate to situation (1 = All in Spanish; 5 = all in English)

Congruent Persons Selected

	Parent	Friend	Total	Priest	Teacher	Employer	Total
Mean	2.75	3.38	3.08	4.67	4.92	4.77	4.77
s.d.	1.67	1.22	1.15	0.68	0.30	0.44	0.37
n	12	13	13	12	12	13	13

Congruent Places Selected

	Home	Beach	Total	Church	School	Work Place	Total
Mean	2.33	3.50	2.60	3.80	4.79	4.27	4.34
s.d.	1.11	1.37	1.14	1.57	0.58	1.39	0.99
n	15	6	15	15	14	15	15

Congruent Topics Selected

	Family	Friendship	Total	Religion	Education	Employment	Total
Mean	1.69	3.33	2.64	3.80	4.78	4.44	4.38
s.d.	0.95	1.24	0.98	1.52	0.55	1.15	0.75
n	16	18	18	15	18	18	18

II. Incongruent Situations: Two "incongruent" components presented; S selects any third component and language appropriate to situation (1 = All in Spanish; 5 = all in English)

All Persons Selected

	Parent	Friend	Total	Priest	Teacher	Employer	Total
Mean	2.89	3.48	3.50	4.65	4.73	4.38	4.66
s.d.	1.41	1.21	0.73	0.63	0.42	0.74	0.57
n	13	13	13	13	13	8	13

All Places Selected

	Home	Beach	Total	Church	School	Work Place	Total
Mean	2.63	3.86	2.77	3.71	4.39	4.42	4.10
s.d.	0.80	1.05	0.73	1.36	1.03	0.98	0.85
n	15	5	15	15	15	15	15

All Topics Selected

	Family	Friendship	Total	Religion	Education	Employment	Total
Mean	2.88	3.81	3.26	3.07	3.65	3.81	3.49
s.d.	1.07	1.16	1.05	1.03	1.59	1.06	0.79
n	18	16	18	18	17	18	18

* From Greenfield 1968.

table 15.2

Language Census

Item	Yes†	Little †	no*	np*
1. Can understand Spanish conversation?	779	135	019	067
2. Can speak Spanish (conversation)?	833	077	016	074
3. Can read newspapers/books in Spanish?	397	049	318	237
4. Can write letters in Spanish?	390	030	339	241
5. Can understand English conversation?	571	176	183	070
6. Can speak English (conversation)?	536	181	216	067
7. Can read newspapers/books in English?	455	130	206	209
8. Can write letters in English?	387	063	327	223

Item	Span†	Eng†	Both†	NP†
9. First language understood (conversation)?	886	002	039	072
10. First language spoken (conversation)?	884	—	0.23	093
11. First language read (newspapers/books)?	401	—	297	302
12. First language written (letters)?	383	002	276	339
13. Most frequently spoken at home?	657	088	183	072
14. Most frequently read at home?	267	051	357	325
15. Most frequently written at home?	339	014	255	392
16. Most frequently spoken with fellow workers?	137	049	137	677
17. Most frequently spoken with supervisor?	046	009	264	680
18. Most frequently spoken with clients/customers	032	014	035	919
19. Language of instruction in school?	339	237	167	257
20. Language liked most (conversation)?	362	285	186	167
21. Language of priest's/minister's sermon?	452	137	193	206
22. Language of silent prayer?	469	123	151	257
23. Language of church service?	427	160	193	220

On a reinterviewed sample of 124 cases the distributions obtained were practically identical to those shown here, indicating that the marginals reported here are quite stable.

The language replies to the census have been subjected to a factor analysis (verimax orthogonal rotation). The following five-factor solution appeared to be most revealing:

No.	Suggested Factor Name	Items (Loadings)
I	Spanish: literacy	4(93), 3(92), 15(89), 12(88), 11(87), 19(71), 14(70), 20(54)
II	English (oral and written)	7(89), 6(88), 5(84), 8(82)
III	Spanish: oral	9(78), 1(71), 2(66), 10(63), 13(38)
IV	Spanish: at work	18(79), 16(73), 17(55)
V	Spanish: in religion	21(93), 23(89), 22(40)

* Fishman 1968a.
† Percents carried to three places; decimals omitted.

table 15.3a

Mean Number of Words Named by Young Schoolchildren*

$(N = 34)$

Age	Language	Domain				
		Family	Education	Religion	Friendship	Total
6–8	English	6.2	8.2	6.6	8.3	7.3
	Spanish	7.6	6.2	5.8	6.4	6.5
	Total	6.9	7.2	6.2	7.4	6.9
9–11	English	11.7	12.8	8.7	10.9	11.0
	Spanish	10.5	9.4	7.2	9.7	9.2
	Total	11.1	11.1	7.9	10.3	10.1
Total	English	9.0	10.5	7.7	9.6	9.2
	Spanish	9.0	7.8	6.5	8.0	7.8
	Total	9.0	9.1	7.1	9.0	8.5

*Edelman 1968.

children in Jersey City were analyzed in accord with the domains derived from Greenfield's and Fishman's data reported here (Tables 15.1 and 15.2) significant and instructive findings were obtained. The most Spanish domain for all children was "family" (Table 15.3a). The most English domain for all children was "education." The analysis of variance (Table 15.3b) indicates that not only did the children's responses differ significantly by age (older children giving more responses in both languages than did younger children), by language (English yielding more responses than did Spanish), and by domain (church yielding fewer responses than did any other domain), but that these three variables *interact significantly* as well. This means that one language is much more associated with certain domains than is the other and that this is differentially so by age. This is exactly the kind of finding for which domain analysis is particularly suited. Its utility for inter-society comparisons and for gauging language shift would seem to be quite promising.

THE INTEGRATION OF MACRO- AND MICROPARAMETERS

The situational analysis of language and behavior represents the boundary area between micro- and macrosociolinguistics. The very fact that a baseball conversation "belongs" to one speech variety and an electrical

table 15.3b

Analysis of Variance of Young Schoolchildren's Word-Naming Scores

Source	df	Mean Square	F_{95}	F_{95}	F_{99}
Between subjects	33				
C (age)	1	689.30	19.67*	4.17	7.56
D (sex)	1	15.54	0.44	4.17	7.56
CD	1	87.87	2.51	4.17	7.56
Error (b)	30	35.05			
Within subjects	235				
A (domain)	1	123.13	11.11*	4.17	7.56
B (language)	3	64.18	9.30*	2.71	4.00
AB	3	21.71	6.66*	2.71	4.00
AC	3	20.51	2.97*	4.17	7.56
AD	3	0.96	0.14	4.17	7.56
BC	1	16.50	1.49	2.71	4.00
BD	1	42.08	3.80	2.71	4.00
ABC	3	8.00	2.45	2.71	4.00
ABD	3	2.23	0.68	2.71	4.00
ACD	3	4.51	0.65	4.17	7.56
BCD	1	14.62	1.32	2.71	4.00
ABCD	3	2.66	0.82	2.71	4.00
Error (w)	207				
Error$_1$ (w)	89	6.90			
Error$_2$ (w)	29	11.08			
Error$_3$ (w)	89	3.26			
Total	268				

* Significant at or above the 0.01 level.
† Significant at or above the 0.05 level.

engineering lecture "belongs" to another speech variety is a major key to an even more generalized description of sociolinguistic variation. The very fact that humor during a formal lecture is realized through a *meta-phorical switch* to another variety (Blom and Gumperz, Chapter 14) must be indicative of an underlying sociolinguistic *regularity,* which obtained before the switch occurred, perhaps of the view that lecture-like or formal situations are generally associated with one language or variety whereas levity or intimacy is tied to another. Without such a view, *without a more general norm assigning a particular topic or situation, as one of a class of such topics or situations, to one language rather than to another, meta-phorical purposes could neither be served nor recognized.*

As with all constructs (including situations, role relationships, and speech events), domains originate in the integrative intuition of the investigator. If the investigator notes that student-teacher interactions in classrooms, school corridors, school auditoriums, and school laboratories of elementary schools, high schools, colleges, and universities are all realized via the high variety (H), as long as these interactions are focused upon educational technicality and specialization, he may begin to suspect that these congruent situations all belong to a single (educational) *domain.* If he further finds that incongruent situations involving an educational and a noneducational ingredient are, by and large, predictably resolved in terms of H rather than the low variety (L) if the third ingredient is an educational time, place, or role relationship, he may feel further justified in positing an educational domain. If informants tell him that the predicted language or variety would be appropriate in most of the examples he can think of that derive from his notion of the educational domain, whereas they proclaim that it would not be appropriate for examples that he draws from a contrasted domain, and, finally, *if the construct helps clarify and organize his data, and, particularly, if it arises as a compositing feature of his data*—then the construct is as usefully validated as is that of situation or event—with one major difference.

Whereas particular speech acts can be apportioned to the speech events and social situations in which they transpire (Hymes, Chapter 1) the same cannot be done with respect to such acts in relation to societal domains. Domains are extrapolated from the *data* of "talk" rather than being an actual component of the *process* of talk. However, domains are as real as the very social institutions of a speech community and, indeed, they show a marked paralleling with such major social institutions (G. C. Barker 1947) and the somewhat varied situations that are congruent with them. There is an undeniable difference between the social institution, "the family," and any particular family, but there is no doubt that the societal regularities concerning the former must be derived from data on many instances of the latter. Once such societal regularities are formulated, they can be utilized to test predictions concerning the distributions of societally patterned variation in "talk."

Thus domains and social situations reveal the links that exist between micro- and macrosociolinguistics. The members of diglossic speech communities can come to have certain views concerning their varieties or languages because these varieties are associated (in behavior and in attitude) with particular domains. The H variety (or language) is considered to reflect certain values and relationships within the speech community, whereas the L variety is considered to reflect others. Certain individuals and groups may come to advocate the expansion of the functions of L into additional domains. Others may advocate the displacement of L entirely and the use of H solely. Neither of these revisionist views could be held or advocated without recognition of the reality of domains of language-and-behavior (in terms of *existing* norms of communicative appropriations) on the part of members of speech communities. The high culture values with which certain varieties are associated and the intimacy and folksiness with which others are congruent are both derivable from domain-appropriate norms governing characteristic verbal interaction.

There are several levels and approaches to sociolinguistic description and a host of linguistic, sociolinguistic, and societal constructs within each (Fig. 15.1). The choice among them depends on the particular

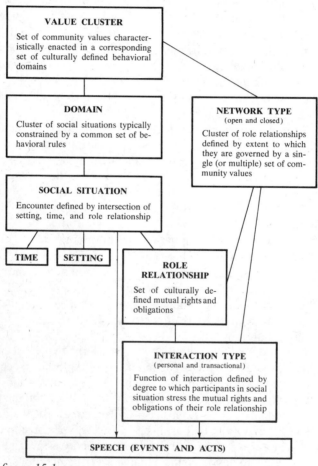

figure 15.1

Relationships among some constructs employed in sociolinguistic analysis (Cooper 1968).

problem at hand. This is necessarily so. Sociolinguistics is of interest to students of small societies as well as to students of national and international integration. It must help clarify the change from one face-to-face situation to another. It must also help clarify the different language-related beliefs and behaviors of entire social sectors and classes. It must be as useful and as informative to sociologists pursuing intersocietal and intrasocietal topics as it is to linguists pursuing more contextualized synchronic description.

It would be foolhardy to claim that one and the same method of data collection and data analysis be utilized for such a variety of problems and purposes. It is one of the hallmarks of scientific social inquiry that methods are selected as a *result* of problem specifications rather than independently of them. Sociolinguistics is neither methodologically nor theoretically uniform. Nevertheless, it is gratifying to note that for those who seek such ties the links between micro- and macroconstructs and methods exist (as do a number of constructs and methods that have wide applicability through the entire range of sociolinguistics). Just as there is no societally unencumbered verbal interaction so are there no large-scale relationships between language and society that do not depend on individual interaction for their realization. Although there is no mechanical part-whole relationship between them, micro- and macrosociolinguistics are both conceptually and methodologically complementary.

16

Ethnic Processes
on the Pathan-Baluch Boundary

FREDRIK BARTH

Fredrik Barth is a professor of social anthropology and director of the Research Institute for Social Anthropology at the University of Bergen, Norway. He has done fieldwork in Iran, Pakistan, Sudan, and most recently in New Guinea. One of his principal interests is a transactional model of social organization (Barth 1966). The present chapter was originally published as part of the Georg Morgenstierne Felicitation volume (Redard 1964).

The stability of language boundaries in multitribal areas is in large part determined by the structure of tribal systems. Taking a sociological insight of the linguist Georg Morgenstierne as his starting point, Barth explains the northward expansion of the Baluchi language in Pakistan in terms of capacity to assimilate and organize potential personnel, given a situation of fragmentation and social mobility. The considerations usually invoked by linguists would have predicted expansion not of the Baluch but of the Pathans. The Pathans are more numerous, of greater population density, more prosperous, probably have a higher rate of fertility, and are acknowledged to be more agressive militarily. Yet in spite of numerical superiority and greater prestige, Pashto, the Pathan langauge, is retreating before Baluchi.

In explaining this seemingly anomalous situation Barth, by implication, at least, suggests that the analysis

From *Indo-Iranica. Mélanges preséntés à Georg Morgenstierne a l'occasion de son soixante-dixieme anniversaire.* Edited by Georges Redard. 1964. Otto Harrassowitz, Wiesbaden.

of language maintenance and language shift (see Fishman 1965 for a discussion of this problem) requires considerably more information about intrasocietal social processes internal to the societies concerned than is usually adduced. Units such as "a tribe," "a culture," "a caste," or "a nation" cannot be taken for granted and member populations treated as culturally uniform (cf. Moerman 1965 and 1968a for a different approach to similar problems). Nor does the common assumption that societal or geographical isolation is crucial to maintenance of cultural diversity accord with the ethnographic facts. Barth's position is explained in detail in his introduction to a recent collection of ethnographic investigations of ethnic boundaries (Barth 1969). Here he demonstrates that ethnic boundaries frequently persist in spite of the regular movement of personnel across them and in spite of regular and institutionalized intergroup communication [just as language boundaries are often maintained in regions of almost total bilingualism (Gumperz 1969)]. There must therefore be, he argues, social processes of exclusion and incorporation which lead to the maintenance of such boundaries. Taking an interactional point of view of social structure similar to that developed by Goffman (1959), he views ethnic categories as categories of ascription by which actors identify themselves by expressing particular cultural values and speaking particular languages. The social necessity (or advantage) of maintaining such identifications is conditioned by a combination of underlying factors (cultural interactional norms, intrasocietal power relationships, ecology, or by factors of demography, etc.) which must be studied empirically for each case.

In the present situation, Barth begins by questioning the identification of Pathans and Baluch as two completely distinct social entities. He deals with them as component groups operating within the same ecological system—i.e., as members of a single linguistically diverse speech region. He then proceeds to examine in detail the social conditions which could lead an individual to identify himself as a member of one or the other subgroup. His analysis of the two groups as part of a single social whole is justified on grounds of both intergroup mobility and communication and common culture. Pathan and Baluch share the fundamental cultural principles of patrilineality, honor, and obligation. They differ in political organization. Pathan communities are based on councils of equals where a person's ability to survive economically is in part based on his ability to muster community support. Individuals who for reasons of war or personal misfortune, etc., no longer possess the resources for participation in the competition among equals must turn to others for protection. If they fail to find support among their former equals, their alternative is to attach themselves to a Baluch chief and enter into a hierarchically organized patron-client relationship with him.

Notice that the different systems of social organization also involve differences in norms of verbal interaction and lead to differential distribution of speech skills and verbal genres. Among the Pathan, on the one hand the right to speak in one's local councils requires skilled use of Pashto rhetoric in formal debate. Furthermore, the egalitarian ethic emphasizing communality of background apparently also operates to exclude bilingualism. Among the Baluch, on the other hand, political communication is between different levels of authority and may be carried by bilingual intermediaries. The use of Baluchi is required only in a type of formalized ritual exchange. Former Pathan groups may therefore retain informal colloquial Pashto for intragroup communication while using Baluchi on specialized occasions. (Cf. Bernstein, Chapter 17, on the relationship between social relations and speech skills.)

Although Barth deals with relatively remote tribal groups, his approach to social organization has important implications for the understanding of sociolinguistic phenomena in complex Western societies. In these societies, even more than in the case discussed by Barth, ethnically distinguishable groups are tightly enmeshed in a single social system. Yet, most of our models for the description of such groups, or subgroups, are models designed to describe primarily the aspects of mechanical, rather than organic, solidarity. Note that Barth has a way of isolating both similarities and differences in culture and that he is careful to point out the behavioral consequences of an individual's choice among alternate value systems. He also separates culture from ecology and shows the effect of common ecological systems on different value systems, and on speech behavior. A similar approach applied to Western society might provide some revealing insight into subtle behavioral variations in such societies. Additional related readings are provided by Gumperz (1962), Trevor Hill (1958), Hymes (1968b), Pride (in press), Salisbury (1962), and Brudner (1969).

Linguistic studies on the Indo-Iranian borderland throw light on the historical processes of ebb and flow of language areas and on the role of contagion, borrowing, and linguistic substrata, as well as genetic processes, in language development. In his many contributions to the subject, Georg Morgenstierne has referred to the importance of social structure in these processes. Thus in an early statement he comments on how "the tribal system of the Baloches and Brahuis, which in contrast to that of the Pathans favours the assimilation of racially foreign elements into the tribe, has no doubt led to frequent changes of language within many Baloch and Brahui clans" (1932:8–9). As a tribute to his insight, I should like to demonstrate the validity of this contrast, and show its relevance to trends along the Pathan-Baluch language boundary. Briefly, I wish to demonstrate that the recent northward spread of Baluchi at the expense of Pashto in the hill country west of the Suleiman range (Fig. 16.1) depends precisely on the structural differences in the tribal systems of these two peoples, to which Morgenstierne refers. The discussion is based mainly on material collected during social anthropological fieldwork among Pathans in 1954 (see Barth 1959a,b) and in 1960, and among the Marri by the late Robert N. Pehrson in 1955 (see Pehrson 1966).

The relationship between *tribal* and *ethnic identity* and language needs to be established. The often-cited Pashto proverb that "he is Pathan who *does* Pashto, not who *speaks* Pashto" can illustrate the absence of any necessary correlation. Yet, in the tribal areas, it is true to say that tribal membership presupposes linguistic fluency. In contrast to some other of the tribal systems of the Middle East [e.g., South Persia (cf. Barth 1961:130ff)], tribal political structures constitute linguistic communities and depend on constant internal cross-communication. In the case of Pathan tribes, these structures are essentially acephalous and are constituted by lineage councils (*jirgas*) arranged in a hierarchy of inclusiveness. Within councils of every level the interests—and in the longer run, survival—of individuals and segments can only be secured through debate, requiring the skilled use of the idiom.

Baluch tribes, however, are socially stratified and have a centralized form, and the structure is composed of channels of communication through echelons of leaders. In such a system foreign language bodies might be encapsulated and communicate upwards through a bilingual

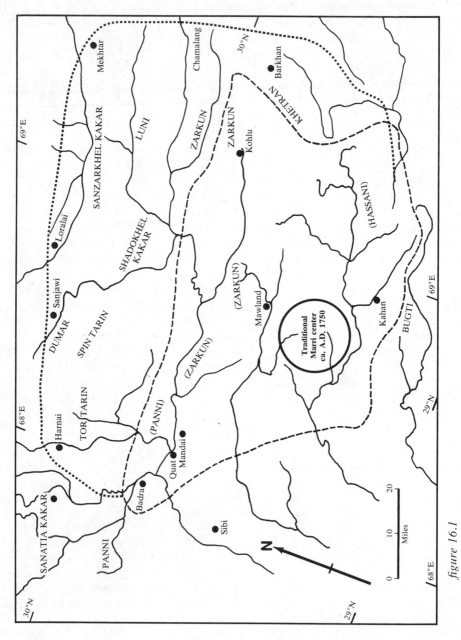

figure 16.1

Ethnic processes on the Pathan-Baluch boundary

leader, as do linguistic minorities in South-Persian tribes. However, in their precarious niche as nomadic mixed herders in a harsh environment, the widely dispersed Baluch camps and segments depend for survival also on another network of communication, mediating information on the availability of grazing, water, and the movements of other persons and camps rather than political decisions. This network is formalized in the Baluch institution of *hal*—exchanges of information given in a peculiar intonation and stereotyped phrases as formal greetings whenever tribesmen meet. In both cases, in other words, membership in a tribe implies membership in a linguistic community.

In seeking the causes for the growth and expansion of Baluch-speaking tribes at the expense of Pathans, it is convenient first to discuss some of the more self-evident possibilities. Indeed a number of factors of undeniable relevance in a situation of competition between tribes seem rather to favor the Pathans. With respect to aggregate numbers, Pathans greatly outnumber Baluchis; likewise in their over-all density in their respective territories. In the zone of contact that concerns us here (Marri/Bugti vs. Panni/Tarin/Kakar/Luni/Zarkun/Powindah), the same holds true, and Pathan villages and camps are consistently larger than those of the Baluchis. Relative prosperity is also on the side of the Pathans—there is a general ecological gradient of improvement from south to north, and this is mirrored in greater capital accumulation (in dwellings, irrigation developments, flocks, movable property, and weapons) among the Pathans. Relative rates of natural population growth are difficult to assess in the absence of detailed demographic information. Doubtless both populations produce a surplus, as evidenced by their history of invasions of the plains, and the wide dispersal of both groups through contemporary labor migration. But the small door-to-door censuses I have suggest a higher rate of fertility among Pathan than Baluch, as one would expect in their better environment. Finally, in military aggressiveness the reputation of Pathan tribes exceeds that of Baluchis, both in their mutual estimation and in the judgement of third parties, though perhaps more because of the Pathans' better weapons than any difference in the value placed in the two cultures on bravery and fighting.

A number of considerations would thus lead one to expect the pressure along the boundary to be primarily from Pathan to Baluch country. In the hill regions, until recently, for all practical purposes, uncontrolled by any external government, one would expect these pressures to express themselves in fighting, conquest, and over-all expansion. There can be no doubt about the anarchy that prevailed in the area (cf. Bruce 1900), which resulted in a complex history of conquest and local succession (Dames 1904). Yet this very anarchy created the situation where structural features of the tribal organizations of the competing peoples become overwhelmingly important. Frequently, wars and plundering forays inevitably tear numbers of people loose from their territorial and social contexts: splinter groups, fleeing survivors, and families and communities divested of their property, as well as nuclei of predators, are generated. From such processes of fragmentation and mobility, a vast pool of personnel results —persons and groups seeking social identity and membership in viable communities. The growth rates of such communities will then depend not so much on their natural fertility rates as on the capacity of their formal organization to assimilate and organize such potential personnel.

In this respect, there are striking contrasts between Pathan and Baluch tribal organization, though the difference in the cultural bases on which each is built is slight. Fundamentally, both tribal forms derive from the shared principles of *patrilineality, honor,* and *obligation.* Let me try to sketch these common bases, and then show how the two systems derive from them.

1. The *patrilineal* principles are followed in both tribes: Political rights in the tribe and rights in the tribal estate are vested in men and transmitted in male line only. Though persons may lose status and rights because of their mother's lower status, they can never gain rights through their mother, only through their father. A man's political position inside his lineage and tribe is thus fixed through agnatic descent.

2. A position in the tribe implies a patrimony of *honor* which must be defended against slights from persons with whom one claims to be equal. An unrequited grievance is a blemish on one's honor which only *talion* or blood revenge can eliminate. A failure to take revenge is an acceptance of inequality and brings about a loss of honor and position. From the time they are very small, Pathan boys learn to fight with their peers to defend their honor (*izzat*), just as the Baluch boy who fails to hit back when other boys beat him is scolded for being *beghairat*—'without honor.'

3. Finally, the honor of a tribesman involves an *obligation* toward those who depend on his position: his guests, his family who are his legal wards, and those who have sought his protection as clients (*hamsayah*). Thus hospitality, patronage, and physical dependence form a complex with clear political implications.

Pathan tribal organization is based on these principles, as realized for political and judicial purposes through the mechanism of the council (*jirga*). One might say that the model for the whole system is the group of brothers, independent men with separate interests who, by virtue of their common blood, keep peace and can unite as a corporate body through joint decision making on the basis of equality. Extending the notion of common blood (among patrilineal relatives only), ever-widening circles of "brotherhood" are defined by ever-deepening genealogies, producing a hierarchy of merging segments and lineages based on common descent. Each such segment becomes corporate in the form of a council of its living male members, who sit together as agnates with equal rights. It also follows that the right to speak in one small, local council implies the right to speak in every council of higher order within the merging series.

Another important feature of the Pathan tribal system is its territorial aspect. Groups and their segments hold rights to different types of joint estate. Persons thus obtain access to agricultural land and to grazing areas by virtue of agnatic status; as a result, units are also territorial units, and localities and districts tend to be named after the tribal segment inhabiting them—names which again usually derive from the common ancestor of that descent segment.

The aspect of equality between council members indicates the relevance of honor, point 2, to council procedure. This has tactical implications since acts which compromise the honor of fellow council members will lead to retaliation or blood revenge, even against superior force. For the person who is insulted cannot permit the blemish to remain—he can sit on the council and act as a tribesman only if he can defend his honor and assert his equality. It is therefore difficult for such councils to reach final decisions, and dangerous for the interested parties to use pressure on members to achieve compliance. Pathan tribes are well able to act strongly in defense of shared, short-term interests or basic values or in the pursuit of gain, but generally fail to pursue more long-term strategies, or to reach agreement on compromises requiring joint action.

Where a Pathan's honor is lost through a dishonorable act of failure to extract revenge, he loses his capacity to defend his life and interests in the council. He must then either flee the country or seek the protection of another man as noted under point 3. Seeking the protection of one man is, however, lowering yourself before *all* the tribesmen, and in most situations the unfortunate chooses emigration—so Pathans often say that "he who leaves his tribal land has either committed incest with his mother or failed to revenge his father." It also follows from the preceding that to accept *hamsayahs* is in most Pathan areas a commitment that men would prefer to avoid. In the egalitarian setting of the council, the value of clients as a fighting force is more than offset by the disputes they may cause—liabilities which fall squarely on the shoulders of their patron. Only in rich environments, where the control over a large labor force gives great economic returns, are such clients an advantage (as, e.g., in Bannu in preadministration times, and in Malakand Agency today).

It should be emphasized that this description holds even where, as in many of the southern Pathan tribes, sardars and maliks are found. An investigation of actual decision making shows that these leaders have little authority, and political processes take place within the framework of egalitarian lineage councils. The tribal growth pattern that follows from these features is characteristic: It might be called vegetative, based on natural increase (with a certain loss through individual emigration) and tending toward a ramifying, branching form where local growth is associated with rapid segmentation.

Baluch tribal organization, though derived from the same concepts, is not based on the particular mechanism of the egalitarian council. Though defense of honor among equals is important, it thus does not become built into the *political* system as a major tactical consideration. A model for the Baluch political system is the relationship between a father and his sons—one of authority stemming from status, and common submission to this authority as the basis for joint action. Instead of working in terms of rhetoric and rallying of equals, with the ultimate sanction of *talion*, the Baluch political and judicial mechanism is based on *vertical* communication between ordinary men and big leaders, with communal action as the ultimate sanction. Political activity thus mainly takes place between unequals, and the important principle that is brought into play is not honor but obligation, as sketched under point 3. Tribal status in such a system does not require an assertion of equality but is based on a chain of clientage and patronage between minor and major leaders in a hierarchy. A Baluch tribe as a whole becomes divided into segments in a formal pattern very much like a Pathan tribe, and membership and position in the system are ascribed on the basis of patrilineal descent; but the politically crucial aspect of the organization is the recognition of a political clientship tie to the leader of each group by its members. These leaders again work in the same "vertical" pattern—political maneuver does not involve appeal to equals in a council, but communication with and mobilization of more influential, higher echelon leaders.

At the top of this hierarchy sits the sardar, who has no equal, only even more influential connections: with the Khan of Kalat and the government of the plains. Sardars maintained their influence in the tribe by playing their inferiors (*waderas* and *mukadams*) off against each other, and by substantial bribes and personal favors—the patron's reciprocal to the client's request for protection.

The territorial estate of a Baluch tribe is also allocated differently from that of Pathans. Among the Marri, grazing rights to the whole tribal area are held by the sardar and accessible to any Marri by payment of a tax (*gahl*), which has now been dispensed with. Agricultural land is held individually (until recently by leaders only) or jointly by very large tribal sections in a system of periodic reallotment. Such systems have also been common among Pathans; but among them the allocation of fields to subsegments and families follows the schema of their genealogical relations, while among the Marri equal shares are given to all men within the section, regardless of genealogical pattern. There is thus no identity between tribal subunits and territorial units; as might be expected, place names in Marri area have no reference to social groups, though they sometimes derive from the personal names of prominent men, past or present.

When a man in this system is dishonored, the consequences are of a different order from what they are for Pathans. Conflicts of honor and revenge between equals lead to fission of their immediate group, but need not in fact be resolved between the parties since territorial separation can take place without consequences for the persons' positions in the political structure. A relationship of clientship to the same leader can thus be maintained by enemies, though the conflict may also be such as to involve the leader and thus force one faction to secede. But where a man or group does secede, this implies no important loss of rank, and a new clientship relation may be established to another leader. Again in contrast to the Pathans, such seceders are welcomed in their new status: The importance and influence of a Baluch leader is roughly commensurate with the number of his effective followers, and the decision to grant new followers protection and rights lies with him and need not be debated and accepted by a council of his equals.

The normal growth pattern that will result in such a system is in part different from that of the Pathan system. Further segmentation does not follow automatically with growth in every generation: Natural growth can take place within fixed political units, merely increasing their size. And where persons secede or are expelled from one segment, they can be accommodated in an equivalent position in another segment, without loss of tribal status.

The structural differences sketched here imply clear differences in assimilative capacities of the two forms of tribal organization. Disorganized personnel such as is generated at a high rate during relatively anarchic periods is readily incorporated in a Baluch tribe: Persons may seek the protection of, and swear fealty to, a recognized leader within that tribe. In the case of the Marri, their tribal organization was also clearly thought of as predatory organization, and for purposes of offense and increased loot, as well as defense, it was in everybody's interest to increase the personnel. Thus one Marri leader, himself of Pathan descent, explained to me: "In those days there was war [*jang*]—nobody asked who is your father, brother—you joined the force [*lashkar*], moved and conquered and moved again."

Though the same military consideration also held for Pathan tribes along the boundary, incorporation of personnel into their tribal system would either require that newcomers accept servile status or that a plenary meeting of the whole tribe agreed to accept them as equals, allotted them a compact block of land, and determined their position in the tribal schema of segmentation. Though both of these forms of incorporation have occurred, they are rare, and one would expect the growth rate by incorporation into Baluch tribes far to exceed that of Pathan tribes.

There can be little doubt that such is the case. None of the Pathan tribes along the boundary have sections or, to my knowledge, persons claiming Baluch descent, and the vast majority of tribesmen have recognized agnatic status, though some incorporation of other Pathan groups has taken place, e.g., among the Kakar and Luni (*Baluchistan District Gazetteer* II:76, 85). The tiny Zarkun tribe, partly encapsulated in Marri territory, is the only one that admits to a (rather fanciful) compound origin, explaining the name as meaning *zar koum*—"thousand nations"—and their origin as being a defensive confederation against the Marri to which each Pathan tribe contributed one family. The presence of so many small, genealogically distant tribes along the boundary (Panni stem: Isot/Barozai; Miani stem: Luni/Jafar/Lats; Zarkun; var. Tarins, etc.) is evidence of this general failure of assimilative growth.

In the Marri tribe, however, all sections have traditions of incorporation, and many sections and subsections trace Pathan descent, often to existing Pathan tribes. Of the three main branches of the Marri, the Ghazani contains subsections of various origins, the Loharanis are half-constituted by the Shiranis, tracing descent from the Pathan tribe of that name, and the Bijaranis are regarded as predominantly of Pathan origin. Among the Bijaranis the Powadhi section has had the most prolific recent growth. Mentioned in most texts (based on early and poor material) as a not particularly significant subsection, their leader is today virtually autonomous in his relation to the Bijarani leader; and the growth of the section has taken place so predominantly through incorporation of Pathans that it is referred to as "Pathan" by other Marris, though it is uniformly Baluchi speaking.

This rapid population growth of the Marri tribe, based in large part on assimilation, has expressed itself also in territorial expansion. Growth without political subdivision has progressively tipped the military scales in favor of the Marris; over the last hundred years parts of Panni, Luni, Zarkun, and Tarin land have been conquered, and the linguistic boundary moved accordingly. The broken fragments of Pathan tribes along the boundary, and the Wanechi language remnant among them, suggest that the northward trend has both considerable consistency and antiquity. Under present more peaceful conditions, increasing numbers of Marris also penetrate with their flocks into Pathan country as far north as Loralai and Mekhtar—an encroachment which the administrative authorities battle against but are unable to stop.

The northward expansion of the Baluchi language area in the hill country west of the Suleiman range is thus an aspect of rather complex processes of incorporation and exclusion along the ethnic boundary by which Pathans become assimilated into Baluch tribal organization rather than a simple case of Baluch population growth and expansion. An analysis of tribal organization illuminates some of the critical factors underlying the linguistic spread.

17

A Sociolinguistic Approach
to Socialization; with Some Reference
to Educability

BASIL BERNSTEIN

Basil Bernstein is Professor of Sociology and director of the Sociolinguistics Research Unit at the Institute of Education, London University. For some years his research has been concentrated on speech as a central process in social theory. He has conducted extensive investigations into the social implications of differences in speech in London.

In the present chapter Bernstein sets forth the theoretical perspective that forms the basis for his work. The distinction between elaborated and restricted codes, for which he is internationally noted, is developed as part of a general theory of the processes by which fundamental properties of social systems—division of labor, belief, type of solidarity, family roles, modes of social control—are linked and maintained (or changed). The present essay is a general introduction to the work which was written especially for this volume—the supporting data appear in a series of papers and monographs (e.g., Bernstein and Henderson 1969; Brandis and Henderson 1970; Cook, 1972; Hasan 1972; Turner and Mohan 1970; Robinson and Rackstraw 1972; Bernstein 1971).

The essential thing is that Bernstein identifies a set of significant dimensions and systematically relates them. The dimensions and relationships are richly productive, both of research and further thought, but most important is that Bernstein shows that sociolinguistics can and must come to grips with general social theory. There is so much to discover in the structure of speech that discovery may remain exciting for its own sake for some time to come. If, however, as Bernstein maintains, speech systems are generated, or controlled, by forms of social relations, then discoveries, however fascinating and well described, cannot be explained without a theory that embraces social relations. [Cf. the relationship between descriptive and explanatory adequacy in Chomsky's grammatical theory (1966).] If sociolinguistic research often begins as an extension of linguistics, it must end as an intension of the social sciences—but in the idiom of disciplines that is only to say that it changes from a way of studying language to a way of studying man as a social being.

Much of the initial effort of sociolingusitics is to show as problematic what is often taken for granted. Bernstein does this. His work makes it impossible ever again to pass over the problem of the functions of speech with the "truism" that language is very important because it serves to transmit culture. English, then, transmits English culture. As this essay shows, the primary questions are: How? Which parts of culture? For whom? [Cf. in this respect Bernstein and Henderson 1969.]

A dichotomy such as elaborated and restricted codes lends itself to dichotomous thinking. Bernstein warns against it, but the point needs to be emphasized. First of all, a given individual, family, or group may (and most certainly will) commonly make use of both kinds of codes (more exactly, of more than one of the varieties of coding indicated in the chapter). It is not a question of assigning persons, families, or classes to a single type of code but rather of ascertaining the scope of their repertoire of types of coding, and any hierarchy among them. Bernstein does focus on the dominant, or preferred, coding of a person or group, and hence his concepts are to be understood as ideal types. The present chapter, and the detailed research, show that the types are degrees of more and less, not of all or nothing (see Cook 1972).

Second, while the types themselves may be defined by a particular co-occurrence property (that of contrast in range, or predictability, or alternatives), their use is subject to rules of alternation. Bernstein observes that context is a major control upon syntactic and lexical selection. One would not be surprised to find the quantitative measure to vary by social position and situation, as do the phonological variables studies by Labov (Chapter 19).

Third, the distinctions are not evaluations, and certainly not pejorative evaluation. Each type of coding is seen as appropriate to the social matrix that gives rise to it; the rewards, costs, and possible failures of each are recognized. The differences do come under evaluation, and sanction, within a complex society, especially where individuals of different social background are brought into close contact. They do show sources of stress under conditions of social mobility, and Bernstein is concerned to point out such implications. Either type of coding may show warmth, respect for personal dignity, etc. ("Individual oriented" might be more helpful in connotation that "person oriented" in this regard.)

Restricted code use on the one hand, relies heavily on gestures, intonation, and verbal metaphor to express respect, familiarity, etc., toward addressees or to indicate attitude (certainty about, sureness of, etc.) toward a message. These nonverbal signs are fully intelligible only to audiences who share the speaker's cultural background (home, ethnic identity, intellectual interests, etc.). In elaborated codes, on the other hand, a much greater amount of such attitudinal information is expressed by verbal means. To the extent that these verbal devices are taught in public schools (accessible to all, regardless of home background), elaborated codes are more suitable for cross-cultural communication (Gumperz 1970a).

Children used to predominantly restricted coding, i.e., who have not had practice in much elaborated code use, tend to have difficulty in culturally diverse, big city school systems. As Bernstein points out elsewhere (1969), teachers in such schools tend to be unable to deal with the modes of communication of culturally different children, and this accounts for much of the children's lack of educational success (see also Gumperz 1970b). Given a communality of cultural background, however, those skilled in restricted code usage may have some advantage insofar as it is true that the paralinguistic signals carry the true import of speech wherever they conflict with the import of the words. (Cf. Bateson et al. 1956; Hymes 196lb:321). Note also, e.g., that dramatic performances as well as music and poetry tend to rely heavily on restricted code-like metaphoric devices, and that in many situations verbal explicitness of the sort typical of elaborated coding is inappropriate, even a sign of incompetence. It should also be stressed that these functional notions are entirely independent of "ungrammatical" or substandard features, and that it is orientation and use of communicative modes that is in question, not fundamental capacity for logical analysis and conceptual thought (see Labov 1969a).

Finally, the distinctions do not point to wholly fixed, received sets of linguistic habits. Bernstein points out that frequency and length of talk are not what is in question. In the first instance, size of vocabulary and scope of grammatical competence are not at issue either (although long-range consequences might be expected). Long stretches of complex syntax, if only taken over as language forms that cannot be used in creative, unpredicted, individuating ways, would count as a restricted, not an elaborating, use (Barnes et al. 1969:61). As the preceding phrase indicates, it would be more appropriate perhaps to speak of elaborat*ing* and restrict*ing* codes, or better yet, of elaborated and restricted cod*ing*. It is of the essence of Bernstein's approach that it is concerned with a mode of action (not a countersign of social class): Witness the term *communication codes,* and the stress on the statement *"A social role can then be considered as a complex coding activity. . . ."* (It is helpful to keep in mind the origin of this aspect of Bernstein's approach in the late Hughlings Jackson's distinction between "now-coding" and "then-coding," i.e., between ad hoc formulation of what one is saying (likely to be reflected in more and longer hesitation pauses, as well as less predictability of forms used), and use of preformulated expressions (greetings, sayings, and commonplaces provide obvious examples).

The key to the linkage between codes, role systems, families, communication systems, and modes of social control is the notion of range of alternatives. Codes are elaborated or restricted, according to whether it is difficult or easy to predict their linguistic alternatives; role systems are open or closed, according to whether they permit or reduce range of alternatives for realization of verbal meaning; families are person oriented or positional, according to whether decision making is based on the psychological (individual) qualities or formal (socially defined) status of persons, implying a greater or lesser range within which decisions are open to discussion; communication systems are open or closed, according to this last dimension (openness of decisions to discussion); family type and communication system jointly entail another important dimension, that of role discretion—in the person-oriented, open type there is greater role discretion, i.e., greater range of alternatives of the role in different social situations, while in the positional, more closed type, there is less role discretion. With modes of social control, matters are somewhat more complex; personal and positional modes are both subtypes of *appeal,* itself contrasted to the imperative mode; but the basis of all three distinctions is again role discretion (the range of alternatives accorded).

Two further dimensions multiply the range of alternatives within the theory itself. With regard to role systems, two orders, or areas, of meaning are noted, those of object and person, with respect to each of which a role system might be open (encouraging novel meanings, hence alternatives) or closed. There may thus be "object" or "person" oriented codes, either elaborated or restricted. Later, two variants for each such type of code are suggested, considering whether the code is used to explore (primarily?) means or ends. There are thus at least eight possible types of code, four of them person oriented and four object oriented, each four subdivided as to elaborated and restricted, and again, as to means and ends focus. Morever, the two orders of meaning, person and object orientation, are presented as *areas* with regard to which a role system may be open or closed. Both pertain to any given role system. In principle, then, a person, family, or group might be characterizable in any one of sixteen ways (assuming an exclusive or dominant mode). The table on page 470 shows the possibilities; each cell contains one of the possible combinations of person and object orientation. Possibly, the dominance of orientation toward one area, or order, of meaning is so great as to obviate any need to consider more than eight possibilities [El(e), El(m), R(e), R(m) for

			Object Orientation*			
			Elaborated		Restricted	
			Ends	Means	Ends	Means
Person Orientation	Elaborated	Ends {P	El(e),	E1(e),	El(e),	El(e),
		{O	El(e)	El(m)	R(e)	R(m)
		Means {P	El(m),	El(m),	El(m),	El(m),
		{O	El(e)	El(m)	R(e)	R(m)
	Restricted	Ends {P	R(e),	R(e),	R(e),	R(e),
		{O	El(e)	El(m)	R(e)	R(m)
		Means {P	R(m),	R(m),	R(m),	R(m),
		{O	El(e)	El(m)	R(e)	R(m)

* P, person orientation; O, object orientation; El, elaborated; R, restricted; (e) ends; (m) means.

both person orientation (any column in the table) and object orientation (any row)]. In any case, when one singles out, say, a person-oriented elaborated code (means variant) for discussion in relation to a type of social control, one must understand a preferred or dominant mode of coding (not an absence of coding with respect to the other order, in this case, object).

Notice that Bernstein's work could be developed to account for the origin and maintenance of particular genres of speech. In the context of family types and forms of social control he observes that "special forms of arbitration, reconciliation, and explanation will develop. It would be interesting if Bernstein's approach should yield predictions different in this regard from that of Roberts (see Roberts and Forman, Chapter 6). The two are, of course, distinct both in basis in the verbal genres to which they most readily apply, Roberts dealing with salient expressive models, games, and the like, whereas Bernstein's approach points to speech structures that have yet to be well described or even identified for many cultures, e.g., what counts as an apology, a request, an instruction. Sociolinguistic description here would enrich both approaches. Certainly, in extending Bernstein's theory to societies of which the investigator lacks a participant's knowledge, many difficult, yet rewarding, ethnographic problems arise—the distribution of restricted coding according to formality or politeness of situation, or type of political authority (one suspects that the

Pathans described by Barth favor elaborated coding in political communication, the Baluchi not). It is essential to bear in mind that restricted coding (e.g., a genre such as "small talk") is as much an accomplishment as elaborated coding; those who have the knowledge and skill to manage it in one set of circumstances may not in another, and some may be unsuccessful altogether. In any community to be able to identify "small talk," to recognize where it is and is not done, and to discover what comfort or success in it presuppose, might be especially revealing.

Bernstein places his work in relation to that of Whorf. Whorf, of course, did not consider the form of social relationships, or differences in function within a single language. He did, however, specify that it was not a language as such but rather a consistent active selection of its resources, a *fashion of speaking,* that was to be studied. Bernstein's delineation of communication codes can be seen as giving Whorf's insight new life and sociological substance. There is a further parallel between the two approaches. Whorf held that different languages entail different world views; that thesis itself implies a single universal relationship between languages and world views. Multilingualism and cross-cultural differences in the use of language in socialization make the functional implication something to be demonstrated, not taken for granted (Hymes 1966a). Bernstein's theory implies a single universal relationship between linguistic and paralinguistic channels, on the one hand, and social systems (including ingredients of world view), on the other. It assumes that personal (individualized) meanings and novel intent are always made explicit, and elaborated, through relatively novel, unpredictable words and syntax, never through selection and elaboration of conventionalized verbal means (e.g., proverbs) and/or paralanguage. The range of alternatives, or unpredictability within the one (words and syntax) matches the range of alternatives in the other. Bernstein's view gives added, realistic dimension to the notion of the "creative" use of language (Chomsky 1966); but its assumptions can and should be tested cross-culturally. Indeed, a great importance of Bernstein's work for the development of sociolinguistics is that it provides a theory that stimulates, gives immediate theoretical point to, ethnographic work.

The final section of the chapter indicates the range of suggestiveness of the theory. It is not without bearing on subjects as seemingly remote as interviewing (Strauss and Schatzmann 1955), liturgical reform, and structural analysis of myth. In societies where myths convey official cultural meaning through terse, traditional materials, personal meaning may find expression through imagery and tone in ways that very much suggest an institutionalized form of restricted coding (Hymes 1968a). Additional related readings are provided by Gardner (1966); Mead (1937, 1964a); Sapir (1949b, 1949c, 1949e).

If a social group, by virtue of its class relation, i.e., as a result of its common occupational function and social status, has developed strong communal bonds; if the work relations of this group offers little variety; little exercise in decision making; if assertion, if it is to be successful must be a collective rather than an individual act; if the work task requires physical manipulation and control rather than symbolic organization and control; if the diminished authority of the man at work is transformed into an authority of power at home; if the home is overcrowded and limits the variety of situations it can offer; if the children socialize each other in an environment offering little intellectual stimuli; if all these attributes are found in one setting, then it is plausible to assume that such a social setting will generate a particular form of communication which will shape the intellectual, social, and affective orientation of the children.

I am suggesting that if we look into the work relationships of this particular group, its community relationships, its family role systems, it is reasonable to argue that the genes of social class may well be carried not through a genetic code but through a communication code that social class itself promotes. Such a communication code will emphasize verbally the communal rather than the individual, the concrete rather than the abstract, substance rather than the elaboration of processes, the here and now rather than exploration of motives and intentions, and positional rather than personalized forms of social control. To say this about a communication system is not to disvalue it, for such a communication system has a vast potential, a considerable metaphoric range and a unique esthetic capacity. A whole range of diverse meanings can be generated by such a system of communication. It so happens, however, that this communication code directs the child to orders of learning and relevance that are not in harmony with those required by the school. Where the child is sensitive to the communication system of the school and thus to its orders of learning and relation, then the experience of school for this child is one of symbolic and social development; where the child is not sensitive to the communication system at school, then this child's experience at school becomes one of symbolic and social change. In the first case we have an elaboration of social identity; in the second case, a change of social identity. Thus between the school and community of the working class child there may exist a cultural discontinuity based upon two radically different systems of communication.

THE SOCIAL ORIGINS OF
COMMUNICATION CODES

I shall spend the rest of this section examining how different forms of communication arise. I shall argue that the particular form of a social relation acts selectively upon what is said, when it is said, and how it is said. The form of the social relation regulates the options that speakers take up at both syntactic and lexical levels. For example, an adult talking to a child will use a form of speech in which both the syntax and vocabulary are relatively simple. The speech used by members of an army combat unit on maneuvers will clearly be different from the same members' speech at a padre's evening. To put it another way, the consequences of the form the social relation takes, are transmitted in terms of certain syntactic and lexical selections. Thus different forms of social relation can generate very different speech systems or communication codes (Ervin-Tripp 1964, 1969; Gumperz 1964b; Hymes 1967; Blom and Gumperz, Chapter 14).

I shall argue that different speech systems or codes create for their speakers different orders of relevance and relation. The experience of the speakers may then be transformed by what is made significant or relevant by different speech systems. As the child learns his speech, or in the terms I shall use here, learns specific codes which regulate his verbal acts, he learns the requirements of his social structure. The experience of the child is transformed by the learning generated by his own apparently voluntary acts of speech. The social structure becomes, in this way, the substratum of the child's experience essentially through the manifold consequence of the linguistic process. From this point of view, every time the child speaks or listens, the social structure is reinforced in him and his social identity shaped. The social structure becomes the child's psychological reality through the shaping of his acts of speech.

The same argument can be stated rather more formally. Individuals come to learn their social roles through the process of communication. A social role from this point of view is a constellation of shared, learned meanings through which individuals are able to enter stable, consistent, and publically recognized forms of interaction with others. *A social role can then be considered as a complex coding activity controlling both the creation and organization of specific meanings and the conditions for their transmission and reception.* Now if the communication system which defines a given role is essentially that of speech, it should be possible to distinguish critical social roles in terms of the speech forms they regulate. By critical social roles I mean those through which the culture is transmitted. These roles are learned in the family, in the age or peer group, in the school, and at work. These are the four major sets of roles learned in the process of socialization. As a person learns to subordinate his behavior to the linguistic code through which the role is realized, then orders of meaning, of relation, of relevance are made available to him. The complex of meanings, e.g., generated within the role system of a family, reverberates developmentally in the child to inform his general conduct. Children who have access to different speech systems or codes, i.e., children who learn different roles by virtue of their family's class position in a society, may adopt quite different social and intellectual orientations and procedures despite a common potential.

The concept code, as I shall use it, refers to the principle which regulates the selection and organization of speech events. I shall briefly outline two fundamental types of communication codes and consider their regulative functions. These codes will be defined in terms of the relative ease or difficulty of predicting the syntactic alternatives which speakers take up to organize meanings. If it is difficult to predict across a representative range the syntactic options or alternatives taken up in the organization of speech, this form of speech will be called an elaborated code. In the case of an elaborated code, the speaker will select from a wide range of syntactic alternatives, and these will be flexibly organized. A restricted code is one where it is much less difficult to predict, across a representative range, the syntactic alternatives, as these will be drawn from a narrow range. Whereas there is flexibility in the use of alternatives in an elaborated code, in the case of a restricted code the syntactic organization is marked by rigidity. Notice that these codes are not defined in terms of vocabulary or lexes. Jargon does not constitute a restricted code. However, it is likely that the lexical differentiation of certain semantic fields will be greater in the case of an elaborated code.

It is clear that context is a major control upon syntactic and lexical selections, consequently, it is not easy to give general linguistic criteria for the isolation of the two codes. Derivations from the theory would be required in order to describe syntactic and lexical usage by any one speaker in a specific context.[1] The definitions given in the text would have increasing relevance to the extent that speakers could freely determine for themselves the nature of the constraints upon their syntax and lexes. In other words, the less rigid the external constraints upon the speech, the more appropriate the general definitions. The more rigid the external constraints, the more specific the criteria required. It is also important to point out that the codes refer to cultural *not* genetic controls upon the options speakers take up. The codes refer to *performance* not to competence in Chomsky's sense of these terms. There may be different *performances* for every degree of competence. It is certainly the case that these codes can be seen as different kinds of communicative competence as this concept is expounded by Dell Hymes (1970d).

If a speaker is oriented toward an elaborated code, then the code will facilitate the speaker in his attempts to make explicit (verbally) his intentions. If a speaker is oriented toward a restricted code, then this code will not facilitate the verbal expansion of the speaker's intent. In the case of an elaborated code the speech system requires more complex planning than in the case of a restricted code. For example, in the case of an elaborated code the time dimension of the verbal planning of the speech is likely to be longer (provided that the speaker is not quoting from himself) than in the case of a restricted code [Bernstein 1962, 1964b (especially the postscript)]. It will be argued that the events in the environment which take on significance when these codes are used are different, whether the events be social, intellectual, or affective. Those two codes, elaborated and restricted, are generated by a particular form of social relation. Indeed they are likely to be a realization of different social structures. They do not necessarily develop solely because of a speaker's innate ability.

We can now ask what is responsible for the simplification and rigidity of the syntax of a restricted code. Why should the vocabulary across certain semantic fields be drawn from a narrow range? Why are the speaker's intentions relatively unelaborated verbally? Why should the speech controlled by a restricted code tend to be fast, fluent, with reduced articulatory clues, the meanings often discontinuous, condensed, and local, involving a low level of syntactic and vocabulary selection where the "how" rather than the "what" of the communication is important; above all, why should the meaning of the person be implicit rather than verbally explicit? Why should the code orient its speakers to a low level of causality?

[1] Research carried out by the Sociological Research Unit shows that there are considerable differences between middle-class and working-class five-year-old children at five years and seven years of age in their ability to switch grammar and lexes in accordance with the nature of the context. [See Hawkins 1968; Henderson 1968; also Hakulinen, Lewis, and Taylor (in preparation).]

A restricted code will arise where the form of the social relation is based upon closely shared identifications, upon an extensive range of shared expectations, upon a range of common assumptions. Thus a restricted code emerges where the culture or subculture raises the "we" above "I."[2] Such codes will emerge as both controls and transmitters of the culture in such diverse groups as prisons, the age group of adolescents, army, friends of long standing, between husband and wife. The use of a restricted code creates social solidarity at the cost of the verbal elaboration of individual experience. The type of social solidarity realized through a restricted code points toward mechanical solidarity, whereas the type of solidarity realized through elaborated codes points toward organic solidarity (Durkheim 1933). The form of communication reinforces the *form* of the social relation rather than creating a need to create speech which uniquely fits the intentions of the speakers. Restricted codes do not give rise to verbally differentiated "I's." If we think of the communication pattern between married couples of long standing, then we see that meaning does not have to be fully explicit, a slight shift of pitch or stress, a small gesture, can carry a complex meaning. Communication goes forward against a backcloth of closely shared identifications and affective empathy which removes the need to elaborate verbal meanings and logical continuity in the organization of the speech. Indeed, orientation in these relationships is less toward *verbal* but more toward extraverbal means. For extraverbal means are likely to be used to transmit intentions, purposes, and qualifications. It follows from this that speakers limited to a restricted code may well have difficulty in switching from this form of communication to other forms of communication which presuppose different role relations and so different social orientations. Thus a restricted code may limit certain kinds of role switching. However, it must be pointed out that a restricted code may be entirely appropriate for certain contexts.

An elaborated code will arise wherever the culture or subculture emphasizes the "I" over the "we." It will arise wherever the intent of the other person cannot be taken for granted. Inasmuch as the intent of the other person cannot be taken for granted, then speakers are forced to elaborate their meanings and make them both explicit and specific. Meanings which are discrete and local to the speaker must be cut so that they are intelligible to the listener. And this pressure forces the speaker to select from among syntactic alternatives and encourages differentiation of vocabulary. In terms of what is transmitted verbally, an elaborated code

---

[2] In different ways Vygotsky, Sapir, and Malinowski have drawn attention to the simplification of grammar and the lack of specificity in lexes where social relationships are based upon closely shared assumptions and identifications.

encourages the speaker to focus upon the experience of others as different from his own. In the case of a restricted code, what is transmitted verbally usually refers to the other person in terms of a common group or status membership. What is said here epitomizes the social structure and its basis of shared assumptions. Thus restricted codes could be considered status or positional codes, whereas elaborated codes are oriented to persons. An elaborated code, in principle, presupposes a sharp boundary or gap between self and others which is crossed through the creation of speech which specifically fits a differentiated "other." In this sense, an elaborated code is oriented toward a person rather than a social category or status. In the case of a restricted code, the boundary or gap is between sharers and nonsharers of the code. In this sense a restricted code is positional or status *not* person oriented. It presupposes a generalized rather than a differentiated other.

In the case of an elaborated code, the orientation is toward the verbal channel, for this channel will carry the elaboration of the speaker's intentions. In the case of restricted codes, to varying degrees it is the extraverbal channels which become objects of special perceptual activity. It is important to point out that restricted code users are not nonverbal, only that the speech is of a different order from that controlled by an elaborated code. If an elaborated code creates the possibility for the transmission of individual symbols, then a restricted code creates the possibility for the transmission of communalized symbols. I now want to discuss differences in the type of social roles which are realized through these two codes.

OPEN AND CLOSED ROLE SYSTEMS

Let us first consider the range of alternatives that a role system (say that of the family) makes available to individuals for the verbal realization of meanings. Here we need to distinguish between two basic orders of meaning, one which refers to interpersonal and intrapersonal relationships and one which refers to relationships between objects—object meanings and person meanings. We could call a role system which reduced the range of alternatives for the realization of verbal meaning a closed type. It would follow that the greater the reduction in the range of alternatives, the more communal or collective the verbal meanings and the lower the order and more rigid the syntactic and vocabulary selections—thus the more restricted the code. However, we could call a role system which permitted a range of alternatives for the realization of verbal meanings an open type. It would follow that the greater the range of alternatives permitted by the role system, the more individualized the verbal meanings, the higher the order, and the more flexible the syntactic and vocabulary selection and so the more elaborated the code.[3]

We can now take this simple dichotomy a little further by picking up the distinction between object and person orders of meaning. A role system may be open or closed with respect to the alternatives it permits for the verbal realization of object or person meanings (Fig. 17.1).

Role Systems

	Elaborated code (person)	Open	Elaborated code (object)

Verbal MEANINGS   Person ———————————————————— Object

	Restricted code (person)	Closed	Restricted code (object)

Now in the area where the role system is open, novel meanings are likely to be encouraged and a complex conceptual order explored. In the area where the role system is closed, novel meanings are likely to be discouraged and the conceptual order limited. Where the role system is of the closed type, verbal meanings are likely to be assigned. The individual (or child) steps into the meaning system and leaves it relatively undisturbed. Where the role system is of the open type, the individual is more likely to achieve meaning on his own terms, and here there is the potential of disturbing or changing the pattern of received meanings. We can begin to see that in the area where the role system is open, there is an induced motivation to explore and actively seek out and extend meanings; where the role is closed, there is little induced motivation to explore and create novel meanings. Let us take this a little further. Where the role system is open, the individual or child learns to cope with ambiguity and isolation in

[3] Our research shows that the speech of middle-class children compared to working-class children at five years of age is more likely to show greater differentiation in the open set lexical choices within the nominal group, *and* that these children are more flexible in their use of the grammatical options they take up within the nominal group. The working-class children are more likely to select pronouns as heads (especially third person pronouns). Where pronouns are used as head, the possibility of both modification and qualification is considerably reduced. Further, our research shows [as does that of Loban (1966)] that middle-class children are more likely, in certain contexts, to use more frequently than working-class children modal verbs of uncertainty or possibility. A detailed discussion of this work will be found in a future Sociological Research Unit monograph (Hawkins and Turner, in preparation).

the creation of verbal meanings; where the role system is closed, the individual or child forgoes such learning. On the contrary, he learns to create verbal meanings in social contexts which are unambiguous and communalized. Such an individual or child may experience considerable tension and role conflict if he persistently attempts to individualize the basis of his syntactic and vocabulary selections, and thus attempts to create or point toward an open role system. Notice that what is a source of strain here is precisely that which an individual or child learns to do if he is socialized into an open role system. Thus a source of role strain in restricted codes is precisely the role relationship appropriate to an elaborated code.

We have now outlined a framework which shows a causal connection between role systems, communication codes, and the realization of different orders of meaning and relevance. Emphasis has been laid upon the relationship between roles and codes. It is possible for a person to be able to write in an elaborated code but not to be able to speak it, for he may not be able to manage the face-to-face requirements of the role (over and above the matter of dialect). This may apply, e.g., to a bright working-class boy whose early socialization has offered little training in the social role. In the same way, object and person forms of an elaborated code not only create different orders of meaning; they are realized through different role relations. It may well be that the cultural tension between the sciences, especially the applied sciences, and the arts reflects the different role relations which control object and person forms of the elaborated code.

The organization of education often produces cleavage and insulation between subjects and levels, and this serves to reduce role and code switching between person and object modes of the elaborated code and from restricted to elaborated codes.

If we ask what are the general social forces which influence the development of elaborated and restricted codes and their two modes, the answer is likely to be found in two sources. These shape the culture and role systems of the four major socializing agencies, the family, the age group (or peer group), the school, and work. One major source of the movement from restricted to elaborated codes lies in increases in the complexity of the division of labor. This changes both the nature of the occupational roles and their linguistic bases. The two modes of the elaborated code may well be affected by the movement of economics from goods to service types. The shift from a goods to a service economy may well promote the development of the person mode of an elaborated code. The second major source of code orientation is likely to be the character of the central value system. Pluralistic societies are likely to produce strong orientations toward the person mode of an elaborated code, whereas monolithic societies are likely to strengthen the orientation towards the object mode. It should be remembered that persons can be treated as objects.

COMMUNICATION CODES
AND EDUCABILITY

I have been trying to show how the nature of the division of labor and the character of the central value system affects communication codes through the way they affect the culture and role systems of the major socializing agencies, especially the family and school. Social class position regulates the occupational function, the intrafamilial and interfamilial relationships, and responsiveness to the school. Thus we can expect, broadly speaking, to find both modes of an elaborated code within the middle class together with restricted codes. In the lower working class we could expect to find a high proportion of families limited to a restricted code. We might further expect that upwardly mobile working-class children would move toward the object rather than the person mode of the elaborated code.

Where children are *limited* to a restricted code, primarily because of the subculture and role systems of the family, community, and work, we can expect a major problem of educability whose source lies not in the genetic code but in the culturally determined communication code.

Children limited to a restricted code learn a code where the extraverbal tends to become a major channel for the qualification and elaboration of individual experience. *This does not mean that such children's speech output is relatively reduced.* The verbal planning of the speech, relative to an elaborated code, involves a relatively low order and rigidity of syntactic organization. The interpersonal and intrapersonal, although clearly perceived and felt, are less verbally differentiated. The concept of self-development through a restricted code does not, itself, become an area of enquiry, as in the case of an elaborated code, particularly one whose orientation is toward persons. In the case of an elaborated code, such a code points to the possibilities which inhere in a complex conceptual hierarchy for the organization and expression of inner experience. This is much less the case where experience is regulated by a restricted code, for this code orients its speakers to a less complex conceptual hierarchy and so to a low order of causality. What is made available for learning through elaborated and restricted codes is radically different. Social and intellectual orientations, motivational imperative and forms of social control, rebellion, and innovation are different. Thus the relative backwardness of many working-class children who live in areas of high population density or in rural areas may well be a culturally induced backwardness transmitted by the linguistic process. Such children's low performance on verbal IQ tests, their difficulty with abstract concepts, and their failures within the language area, their general inability to profit from the school all may result from the limitations of a restricted code. For these children the school induces a change of code and with this a change in the way the children relate to their kin and community. At the same time we often offer these children grossly inadequate schools with less than able teachers. No wonder they often fail—for the "more" tend to receive more and become more, while the socially defined "less" receive less and become less.

I want to make one final point. A restricted code contains a vast potential of meanings. It is a form of speech which symbolizes a communally based culture. It carries its own esthetic. It should not be disvalued. We must ensure that the material conditions of the schools we offer, their values, social organization, forms of control and pedagogy, the skills and sensitivities of the teachers are refracted through an understanding of the culture these children bring to the school. After all, we do no less for the middle-class child. The problem does not stop there. Housing conditions must be improved, social services extended, and preschool education developed.

We cannot say what a child is capable of, as we do not have a theory of what an optimum learning environment looks like; and even if such a theory existed, we are unwilling to redirect national expenditure toward physically creating it for children, on the scale required.

FAMILY ROLE SYSTEMS, SOCIAL CONTROL, AND COMMUNICATION

I shall now look more closely at the relationships between role systems and communication codes, as the connection between social class and communication codes is too imprecise. Such a relationship omits the dynamics of the causal relationship. In order to examine these dynamics, it is necessary to look at the nature of the role system of a family and its procedures of social control. The basic requirement of such an analysis is that it is predictive and so gives rise to measurable criteria for evaluating the interrelationships between role systems, forms of social control, and linguistic orientations.

It is possible to evaluate family role systems by reference to the principles which for any one family control the allocation of decision making. Thus we could consider the effect of the allocation of decision making on the extent and kind of interactions between members of the family. Let us postulate two types of families—positional and person-oriented families.[4]

Positional Families. If the area of decision making is invested in the members' formal status (father, mother, grandfather, grandmother, age of child, or sex of child), this type of family will be called positional. (It is not necessarily authoritarian or "cold" rather than "warm.") In such a family there would be a clear separation of roles. There would be formally defined areas of decision making and judgments accorded to members of the family in terms of their formal status. In such a family type we could expect close relationships and interactions between the parents and grandparents. Further, we could expect that the parents would closely regulate the child's relationships with his age peers (if middle class) or the child's relationship with his peers would be relatively independent of the parents' regulation (if working class). Thus in certain positional families the socialization of the child might well be through his own age mates. Positional families, it is suggested, would give rise to a weak or *closed* communication system.

Person-Oriented Families. By contrast we could consider a family type where the range of decisions, modifications, and judgments were a function of the psychological qualities of the person rather than a function of the formal status. In such families there is clearly a limit to the interactions set by age development and status ascription. However, status ascription would be reduced (age, sex, age relations) compared to positional families. Unlike certain positional families the socialization of the children would never be left to the child's age group. The behavior of the child in his peer group would be subject to discussion with parents rather than to their legislation. Person-oriented families would give rise to a strong or "open" communication system.

DISCUSSION: POSITIONAL-PERSONAL FAMILY TYPES AND OPEN AND CLOSED COMMUNICATION SYSTEMS

Person-Oriented Families—Open Communication System. In these families the limits on the extent to which decisions may be open to discussion would be set by the psychological characteristics of the person rather than by his formal status. Simply, the ascribed status of the member, for

---

[4] This distinction between positional and personal forms of control was set out by the author in a paper in 1963. At that time the term *status* was used instead of positional. The terms *positional* and *personal* have also been used by Hanson (1965). However, Hanson's discussion is somewhat differently focused, for he sees positional relationships as contractual and personal relationships as noncontractual.

many activities, would be weakened by his *achieved* status. The children, e.g., would achieve a role within the communication system in terms of their unique social, affective, and cognitive characteristics. Clearly, if there is reduced segregation of role and less formal definition, then the parents *and* the children operate with a greater range of alternatives; i.e., with greater role discretion. In as much as the *role discretion* is wide (the range of alternatives of the role in different social situations), then individual choices can be made and offered. Verbal communication, of a particular kind, is generated. It is not just a question of more talk but talk of a particular kind. Judgments, their bases and consequences, would form a marked content of the communications. The role system would be continuously eliciting and reinforcing the verbal signaling and the making explicit of individual intentions, qualifications, and judgments. The role system would be continuously accommodating and assimilating the different intents of its members. Looked at from another point of view, the children would be socializing the parents as much as the parents were socializing the children; for the parents would be very sensitive toward the unique characteristics of the children. These would be verbally realized and so enter into the communication system. Thus there would develop an "open" communication system which would foster and provide the linguistic means and role learning for the verbal signaling and making explicit of individual differences, together with the explication of judgments and their bases and consequences. Of fundamental importance, the role system would promote communication and orientation toward the motives and dispositions of others. Note also that in such a family the child learns to *make* his role rather than having it formally assigned to him. Children socialized within such a role and communication system learn to cope with ambiguity and ambivalence, although clearly there may well be pathological consequences if insufficient sense of boundary is not provided.

Positional Families—Closed Communication Systems. In this type of family we said that judgments and the decision-making process would be a function of the *status* of the member rather than a quality of the person. There would be segregation of roles and a formal division of areas of responsibility according to age, sex, and age-relation status. Boundary areas, instead of generating discussion and accommodation, might well become border disputes settled by the relative power inhering in the respective statuses. The children's communication system might well be "open" only in relation to their age mates, who would then become a major source of learning and relevance. If socialization is reciprocal in person-oriented families, it tends to be unilateral in positional families. The role system here is less likely to facilitate the verbal elaboration of individual differences and is less likely to lead to the verbal elaboration of judgments and their bases and consequences; it does not encourage the verbal exploration of individual intentions and motive. In a person-oriented family the child's developing self is differentiated by the continuous adjustment to the verbally realized and elaborated intentions, qualifications, and motives of others. In positional families the child takes over and responds to status requirements. Here he learns what can be called a communalized role as distinct from the individualized role of person-oriented families. In positional families, the range of alternatives which inhere in the roles (the role discretion) is relatively limited; consequently, the communication system reduces the degree of individual selection from alternatives. Of course, within positional families there is sensitivity toward persons, but the point is that these sensitivities are less likely to be raised to a level of verbal elaboration so that they can become objects of special perceptual activity and control. Within positional families the child develops either within the unambiguous roles within his family *or* within the clearly structural roles of his age-mate society or both. Thus these children are less likely to learn to cope with problems of role ambiguity and ambivalence. They are more likely to avoid or foreclose upon activities or problems which carry this potential.

SOCIAL CONTROL AND FAMILY TYPES

It is clear that these two family types generate radically different communication systems which we have characterized as open and closed. It has been suggested that there are important socializing and linguistic consequences. I want now to outline differences in their forms of social control with again special reference to uses of spoken language.

We have said that inasmuch as a role system is person rather than position oriented, then it is a relatively more unstable system. It is continuously in the process of assimilating and accommodating the verbally realized but different intentions, qualifications, and motives of its members. Tensions will arise which are a function of the characteristics of the role system. Special forms of arbitration, reconciliation, and explanation will develop. These tensions only in the last resource will be managed in terms of relative power which inheres in the respective statuses. Social control will be based upon linguistically elaborated meanings rather than upon power. However, it is clearly the case that power in the end is still the ultimate basis of authority.

In positional families where the status arrangements reduce the instability which inheres in person-oriented families, social control will be affected either through power or through the referring of behavior to the universal or particular norms which regulate the status. Thus in person-oriented families social control is likely to be realized through verbally elaborated means oriented to the person, while in positional families social control is likely to be realized through less elaborated verbal means, less oriented to the person but more oriented toward the formal status of the regulated (child).

It is of crucial importance to analyze the procedures of social control, for I want to show, among other things, that person-oriented families, very early in the child's life, sensitize him toward and actively promote his language development in order that they can apply their favored modes of control. In positional families the modes of social control depend less upon individually created and elaborated verbal meanings, and so within these families there is less need to sensitize the child toward, and promote the early development of, verbally elaborated forms of speech.

MODES OF SOCIAL CONTROL[5]

I shall distinguish initially between imperative modes of control and control based upon appeals. Two forms of appeal will be further distinguished. Underlying these distinctions in modes of control is the role discretion (the range of alternatives) accorded.

Imperative Modes. This mode of control reduces the role discretion accorded to the regulated (child). It allows the child only the external possibilities of rebellion, withdrawal, or acceptance. The imperative mode is realized through a restricted code (lexicon prediction): "Shut up," "Leave it alone," "Get out," or extraverbally through physical coercion.

APPEALS

These are modes of control where the regulated is accorded varying degrees of discretion in the sense that a range of alternatives, essentially linguistic, are available to him. Thus social control which rests upon appeals does permit, to different degrees, reciprocity in communication and so linguistically regulated learning. These appeals may be broadly broken into two types and each type further classified into subtypes. The two broad types are positional and personal appeals.

Positional Appeals. Positional appeals refer the behavior of the regulated (child) to the norms which inhere in a particular or universal status.

---

[5] A coding manual for social control has been developed and applied to the speech of mothers and their children. This manual gives a range of delicate subdivisions within imperative, positional, and personal forms of control. The coding manual, constructed by B. Bernstein, and J. Cook, is available from the Sociological Research Unit, University of London Institute of Education.

Positional appeals do not work through the verbal realization of the personal attributes of the controllers (parents) or regulated (children).
Some examples now follow:
"You should be able to do that by now" (age status rule).
"Little boys don't cry" (sex status rule).
"People like us don't behave like that" (subcultural rule).
"Daddy doesn't expect to be spoken to like that" (age relation rule).
Positional appeals are not necessarily disguised forms of the imperative mode. Consider the following situation where a child is learning his sex role. A little boy is playing with a doll.

MOTHER: "Little boys don't play with dolls."
CHILD: "I want the dolly."
MOTHER: "Dolls are for your sister."
CHILD: "I want the doll" (or he still persists with the doll).
MOTHER: "Here, take the drum instead."

As compared with a situation where the mother says:

"Why do you want to play with the doll—they are so boring—why not play with the drum?"

The essence of positional appeals is that in the process of learning the rule, the child is explicitly linked to others who hold a similar universal or particular status. The rule is transmitted in such a way that the child is reminded of what he shares in common with others. Where control is positional, the rule is communalized. Where control is positional, the "I" is subordinate to the "we." Positional control is realized through a specific linguistic variant. As will be shown later, positional appeals can be given in restricted *or* elaborated codes. They can be complex linguistically and conceptually, as in the case of a West Point or public school boy who is reminded of his obligations and their origins. Where control is positional, the child (the regulated) learns the norms in a social context where the relative statuses are clear-cut and unambiguous. Positional appeals may lead to the formation of shame rather than guilt. In the case of positional appeals, however, certain areas of experience are less verbally differentiated than in the case of personal appeals. Positional appeals transmit the culture of subculture in such a way as to increase the similarity of the regulated with others of his social group. They create boundaries. If the child rebels, he very soon challenges the bases of the culture and its social organization, and this may force the controller (parent/teacher) into the imperative mode.

Personal Appeals. In these appeals the focus is upon the child as an individual rather than upon his formal status. Personal appeals take into account interpersonal or intrapersonal components of the social relationship. They work very much at the level of individual intention, motive, and disposition and consequently are realized through a distinctive linguistic variant. This again can be within restricted or elaborated codes. It will be the case that the areas of experience verbally differentiated through personal appeals are very different from the experiences controlled by positional appeals. The following example might help to bring out the distinctions.

Imagine a situation where a child has to visit his grandfather who is unwell and the child does not like to kiss him because the grandfather has not shaved for some time. One mother says to the child before they go:

MOTHER: "Children kiss their Grandpa" (positional).
CHILD: "I don't want to—why must I kiss him always?"
MOTHER: "He's not well—I don't want none of your nonsense" (positional reason) (imperative).

Another mother says in the same context:

MOTHER: "I know you don't like kissing Grandpa, but he is unwell and he is very fond of you."

The second example is perhaps blackmail, but note that the child's intent is recognized explicitly by the mother and linked to the wishes of another. Causal relations at the interpersonal level are made. Further, in the second example, there is the appearance of the child having a choice (discretion). If the child raises a question, more explanation is given. The mother, so to speak, lays out the situation for the child, and the rule is learned in an individualized interpersonal context. The rule is, so to speak, *achieved* by the child. The child, given the situation and the explanation, opts for the rule. In the first example, the rule is simply *assigned* in a social relationship which relies upon latent power for its effectiveness. Here we see another difference between positional and personal appeals in that rules are assigned in positional control and achieved in personal control.

Where control is personal, whole orders of learning are made available to the child which are not there if control is positional. Where control is personal, each child learns the rule in a context which, so to speak, uniquely fits him, and a language through which this is realized. Where control is positional, learning about objects, events, and persons is reduced and the child comes to learn that the power which inheres in authority may soon be revealed. Where control is personal, as distinct from where it is positional, the status differences are less clear-cut and ambiguities and ambivalences are verbally realized. I should point out, although I have no time to develop this, that there may well be patholog-ical consequences to extensive use of personal appeals.

Finally, if positional appeals do lead to the development of shame, per-sonal appeals may lead to the formation of guilt.

In the case of person-oriented appeals, the rights of the controller or parent which inhere in his formal status are less likely to come under at-tack than in the case of positional appeals. For in the case of personal ap-peals, what may be challenged are the reasons the controller gives or even a specific condition of the controller or parent (e.g., "Do you always have a headache when I want to play?"). Thus personal appeals may act to pro-tect the normative order from which the controller derives his rights. For here there is an attenuation of the relationship between power and the rule system. In the case of positional appeals which shift rapidly to the impera-tive mode of control, the formal rights of the controller or parent may well be challenged, and with this the whole normative order from which the controller derives his rights can come under attack. Imperative/positional forms of control under certain conditions may lead the socialized to turn to alternative value systems. Further, where control is personal, the basis of control lies in linguistically elaborated individualized meanings. This may lead to a situation where the child attains autonomy, although his sense of social identity may be weakened. Such ambiguity in the sense of social identity, the lack of boundary, may move such children toward a radical closed value system and its attendant social structure. However, where control is positional, and, even more, where it is imperative, the child has a strong sense of social identity, but the rules which he learns will be tied to specific contexts and his sense of autonomy may well be reduced. Finally, a child socialized by controllers who favor positional or imperative procedures becomes highly sensitive to specific role relations in the context of control. Such a child may be bewildered, initially, when placed in a context of control where personal procedures are used as he may lack the orientation and the facility to take up the different options or alternatives which this form of control makes available. Person-oriented forms of control may induce role strain where the child has been socia-lized through imperative or positional forms of control.

I have briefly outlined, with special reference to communication, imper-ative, positional and personal modes of social control. It is very clear that in any one family, or even in any one context of control, all three modes may be used. It is also likely to be the case within a family that parents may share control modes or each may use a different mode. We can, how-ever, distinguish between families or, at a greater level of delicacy, between parents, in terms of their preferred modes of control. It follows that we could also distinguish the modes of control which are used in any one context. We can summarize the consequences for learning which inhere thus:

Mode	Learning	Level of Learning
Imperative	Hierarchy	Restricted code
Positional	Role obligation and differentiation	Restricted code
		Elaborated code
Personal	Interpersonal	Restricted code
	Intrapersonal	Elaborated code

We can now link positional families with closed systems of communication with positional imperative modes of control. We could, in principle, distinguish between positional families whose preferred mode of control was imperative power (the lower working class?) from positional families where the preferred mode was positional appeals with relatively little physical coercion. We could distinguish between positional families according to whether the dominant code was elaborated or restricted. In the same way we could link person-oriented families with open communication systems operating with personal appeals. We could again distinguish between such families in terms of the dominant general code, elaborated or restricted. The latter tells us about the degree of openness of the communication system and its conceptual orientation. Thus the roles which children learn in those various families, their conceptual orientations, their perception of and use of language, should differ.[6]

Means and Ends Variants

It may be that we can now sepeculate about the dynamics of object and person modes of the two general codes as these were discussed in the early part of this chapter. You may remember that here we suggested that a communication system could be open or closed with reference to relationships between objects or relationships within or between persons. We should bear in mind that persons, if they are treated in their status capacity can be likened to objects.

We could in principle distinguish between two variants of "person" and "object" oriented elaborated or restricted codes (Fig. 17.2)

1. Object- or person-oriented codes can lead to the exploration of means or ends. Thus we might consider that an object code (means) is likely to be used by members of the applied sciences where indi-

---

[6] It should be clear that in this discussion I have drawn upon a range of work in the literature of sociology and social psychology (in particular, Bott 1957; Foote 1961, Chapter V; Nye and Berardo 1966; Bronfennbrenner 1958).

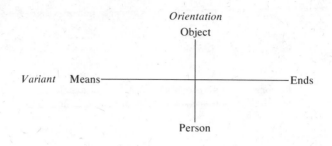

viduals tend to work *within* established principles and derive from them specific applications. In the case of an object code (ends) the individual is less concerned with the specific application of established principles but more concerned with the explorations, than we might expect its orientation to be, toward objects at the level of means.

2. If the form of control is personal appeal and the code restricted, we might expect that the children would move initially toward a person-oriented restricted code of either the means of ends type. The predominant characteristic of the individuals in the quadrant would be their potentiality for change.

3. Families which use predominantly positional forms of control and elaborated codes are likely to socialize their children into an object-oriented elaborated code (means) where the code referents may be either relationships between objects (future applied scientists?) *or* where the code referents are the status characteristics of persons (military, bureaucratic position?).

4. Families which use predominantly personal forms of control are likely to develop a person-oriented elaborated code (means) where the referents emphasized are likely to be inner states and processes of the person. We might expect that such sociolinguistic socialization is likely to orient the children initially toward social positions which involve control relationships over persons.

5. It is difficult to speculate about the social origins of elaborated codes (ends), for the social psychology of creativity is still in its infancy. We might say that such socialization would induce (a) marked egocentricity, (b) risk taking, and (c) flexibility of boundary. In terms of the model used, we might then expect that where positional and personal forms of control were very much parent specific then the child might be faced with a basic tension between inner and outer which he resolves by creative restructuring.

It is clearly the case that occupational functions of children are not simply given by primary socialization but are dominated by the nature of the educational and occupational systems. The point here is to emphasize the need for research to examine the linguistic consequences of role and control systems within families.

SOCIAL CLASS, POSITIONAL AND PERSONAL FAMILIES, AND SOCIAL CHANGE

On this analysis we might find positional families who were deeply im-bedded in their community operating essentially with imperative modes of control and where the children were socialized through unsupervised age peers or mates. Here we could expect the development of restricted codes (object) to be the hard core of the language/educability problem. It should also be possible to locate within the working class families who were moving toward personal forms of control within the general rubric of a restricted code. These families, we would expect, would be less tightly imbedded within their local community, perhaps through rehousing or where the parents were actively confronting the complex relationships between their local subculture and the cultures of the wider society. Here we might find an orientation toward a restricted code (person) or a move-ment toward an elaborated code (person).

A further point is worth making. Within working class positional large families we should expect a marked difference between boys and girls in their use of language. Girls, especially older girls in such families, tend to take on mothering roles. They also, of equal relevance, mediate between parents and sibs. Their role then is more complex as it combines a normal sib role with that of mediator, and with that of controller. Further, girls are less tied to the activity-oriented, group-dominated peer-group social structure such as that of boys. Thus girls, especially older girls in such families, are likely to be person-oriented and to have to rely upon forms of control based upon linguistically elaborated meanings rather than upon physical coercion. Finally, they are placed in a situation involving a vari-ety of role and code switching, e.g., girl-girl, girl-boy, girl controlling girls, girl controlling boys, girl mediating between parents and other sibs. These factors are likely to develop the girl's orientation toward a more differen-tiated, more individualized use of language.[7]

Within the middle class we should be able to isolate positional and person-oriented families who, on this argument, should orientate their

---

[7] Henderson's research (quoted previously), as other research, indicates a marked superi-ority in the form-class usage of working-class girls as compared to working-class boys. It is possible, however, that our very *eliciting techniques* may well create contexts for girls in which they can demonstrate a socially promoted superiority. We have reason to believe that such superiority in girls is not wholly the result of earlier biological development. The girls (five years of age) of middle-class mothers who score low on an index of reported com-munication offer speech where the lexes is less differentiated than the lexes of middle-class girls whose mothers score high on an index of reported communication. The findings of B. Bernstein and W. Brandis (1968) indicate that there is a subgroup of *middle-class* mothers (positional) who explain less and are more coercive in the socializing of the *girl* than in the socializing of the boy. Thus, different uses of language by boys and girls may partly derive from family and age-group role learning. They may also be a function of the eliciting con-texts constructed to obtain speech.

children *initially* (formal education could change this) to the two modes of object and person of an elaborated code. In the earlier section of this chapter suggestions were made as to the social origins of elaborated and restricted codes in terms of the increases in the complexity of the division of labor and the character of the central value system. We shall now turn our attention to the social conditions which may produce positional and person-oriented families within the middle-class and the working class.[8] The literature strongly suggests that the traditional working-class family is of the positional type. For here we find insulation between working-class and middle-class subcultures and social relationships (a product of the class system); high population density within limited territories; low rate of social mobility (through educational failure) producing intragroup marriage; social solidarity arising out of similarity of economic function and interests; unemployment; reciprocity of services and mutual help between families arising partly out of low income (in the United States a common ethnic origin and subculture) sustaining the transmission of this particular subculture. The weakening of the positional family type, closed systems of communication limited to a restricted code, would result from the play of forces which would differentiate the family from its community and so weaken the transmission of collective beliefs, values, and the subsequent detailed regulation of behavior.

In England since the war, this has begun to happen as a result of:

1. Greater affluence, greater geographical mobility, and, therefore, greater responsiveness to a wide range of influences which has been partly assisted by mass media.
2. Rehousing into areas of relatively low population density.
3. A change in the power position of the wife through her independent earning capacity.
4. A change in attitude both toward education and child development on the part of the working-class groups and, therefore, greater responsiveness to education and subsequent social mobility.
5. A change in the solidarity between workers arising out of, until recently, full employment and higher earnings.
6. A shift in the division of labor away from goods to that of a services economy. This is part of a long-term trend from a goods to a service economy, an economy which is now more person than object oriented.

These different forces are beginning to weaken the transmission of the

---

[8] D. Miller and Swanson (1968) provide a very interesting attempt to distinguish between entrepreneurial and bureaucratic families.

communally based, socially insulated working-class subculture and have created the conditions for more individualized family systems.[9]

This is not to say that the working-class subculture has been eroded and replaced by middle-class beliefs, values, and norms, but only that there now exists the *conditions* for more individualized and less communalized relationships.

In the United States (and I am really not entitled to discuss this) the situation is much more complex. Apart from attempts of the school which so far have not been outstandingly successful, the most important influence upon change of linguistic code is probably the Civil Rights movement. This movement and its various organizations is bringing about a change in the Negro's view of his own subculture, his relation to the white culture, and his attitude toward education. This movement has produced powerful charismatic leaders at both national and local levels, who are forcing Negroes to reassess, reexamine, their structural relationship to the society. This confrontation (despite the violence) is likely to make new demands upon linguistic resources and to challenge the passivity of the old subculture and its system of social relationships. The language of social protest, with its challenging of assumptions, its grasping toward new cultural forms, may play an important role in breaking down the limitations of subculturally bound restricted codes.

Middle-class changes in the orientations of family types, however, might well reflect changes in the character of middle-class occupations; in particular, the movement from entrepreneurial to managerial, professional and service type occupations. At the same time, the indeterminancy of the value system has individualized choice and changed the basis of authority relationships within the family. The "science" of child development and its popularization through books, papers, and journals has also had an important influence, given the just-stated conditions, in shaping role relationships and communication within middle-class families. It is likely that the personalizing of socialization agencies has gone further in the United States than in the United Kingdom. It is important to point out that family types may also be very influenced by the nature of religious and political beliefs. On the whole, pluralistic societies like those in the United States and the United Kingdom are likely to produce strong tendencies toward personalized socialization agencies, whereas societies with monolithic centrally planned and disseminated value systems are likely to develop highly positional socializing agencies, generating object-oriented communication codes.

---

[9] A good account of this movement is given by Goldthorpe and Lockwood (1963). For a general analysis of the effects of the interrelationships between the division of labor and the central value system upon the structure of socializing agencies, see Parsons (1964), Chapter 8.

REPRISE

Let me now retrace the argument. First, we started with the view that the social organization and subculture of the lower working class would be likely to generate a distinctive form of communication through which the genes of social class would be transmitted. Second, two general types of communication codes were postulated and their social origins and regulative consequences analyzed. Third, it was suggested that the subculture of the lower working class would be transmitted through a restricted code while that of the middle class would realize both elaborated and restricted codes. This causal link was considered to be very imprecise and omitted the dynamics of the process. The fourth step entailed the construction of two types of family role systems, positional and personal, their causally related "open" and "closed" communication systems, and their procedures of social control. The fifth step made the causal link between restricted and elaborated codes and their two modes with positional and person-oriented family role systems. Finally, factors affecting the development and change of family types were discussed.

SOME CONSEQUENCES OF CHANGE OF
HABITUAL LINGUISTIC CODE

I should like finally to consider some possible consequences of linguistic code switching. In contemporary societies, both in the West and in the newly developing societies, educational institutions are faced with the problem of encouraging children to change and extend the way they normally use language. In terms of this chapter, this becomes a switch from restricted to elaborated codes. A change in linguistic code implies more than a change in syntactic and lexical selection. The view taken here and in other publications is that linguistic codes are basic controls on the transmission of a culture or subculture and are the creators of social identity. Changes in such codes involve changes in the *means* whereby order and relevance are generated. Changes in codes involve changes in role relationships and in procedures of social control.

Elsewhere (Bernstein 1965) I have distinguished my position from that of Whorf, but I believe that there are distillations or precipitations from the general system of meanings which inhere in linguistic codes which exert a diffuse and generalized effect upon the behavior of speakers. What I am tentatively putting forward is that imbedded in a culture or subculture may be a basic organizing concept, concepts, or themes whose ramifications may be diffused throughout the culture or subculture. The speech forms through which the culture or subculture is realized transmits this organizing concept or concepts within their gestalt rather than through any one set of meanings.

The following diagram sets out the application of this essentially Whorfian thought to the linguistic codes and their social controls discussed in this chapter:

CODES
Restricted

OBJECT		PERSON
Authority		*Authority*
Piety		Identity

Positional ———————————————————————————————Personal
Controls

Rationality		Identity
OBJECT		PERSON

Elaborated

Positional restricted code (object). The basic organizing concept here would form around the concepts of authority or piety.

Personal restricted code (person). The basic organizing concepts here would be authority/identity in a state of unresolved tension. By "identity" I simply mean a preoccupation with the question: "Who am I?"

Positional elaborated code (object). The basic organizing concept here would center about the concept of rationality.

Personal elaborated code (person). The basic organizing concept would refer to the concept of identity.

On this view an educationally induced change of code from a restricted code (object) to an elaborated code (person) involves a shift in organizing concepts from authority/piety toward identity. From an organizing concept which makes irrelevant the question of personal identity to an organizing concept which places the notion of identity in the forefront of the personality. Individuals who are in the process of making such a switch of codes are involved in a basic cultural change at the level of meanings and at the sociological level of role. We need to know much more about the social and psychological consequences of radical shifts in linguistic codes.

It may be that the switch from a restricted code (object) is more likely to be toward an elaborated code (object) than toward the person mode of an elaborated code. In concrete terms we might expect working-class children to move toward the applied sciences than toward the verbal arts. This shift from authority to rationality for working-class children may involve a less traumatic change in their role relations, systems of meanings and control, than a shift from authority to identity. Authority and rationality are both positional in the sense that the individual works *within* a framework, within a system or structure, without a critical problem of ambiguity of ends. Where the organizing concept transmitted by the code is that of identity, the individual is faced with ambiguity at the level of ends and often moans. This speculation on no account should be taken to mean that it is more appropriate for individuals limited to a restricted code (object) to be guided toward the applied sciences or routine low-level supervisory functions, where persons are often treated as objects but only that it may be expected that they may well make these choices rather than choose the verbal arts. They are more likely to be concerned with object processes than interpersonal and intrapersonal processes.

One might further expect that the individuals starting from restricted codes (person) will move toward elaborated codes (person) rather than toward elaborated codes (objects). If they were to move toward the latter mode, it would be perhaps one where persons are treated as objects. Individuals in this quadrant, if they switch to elaborated codes, are likely to be restless in their search for belonging, or they might accept some belief system which creates it for them. It is thought that many may become teachers, writers, or community protest leaders, or perhaps become involved in dropout movements or deviant. This code switch involves major problems of culture conflict.

There are relatively few individuals who are capable of managing equally both modes of an elaborated code, although one suspects that the social sciences contain many of these. The meanings, roles, and controls entailed in these two modes are somewhat antithetical. At the basis of the meanings of an elaborated code (object) is the notion of one integrated system which can generate order. In an odd way it is objective idealist in character. At the basis of the meanings of an elaborated code (person) is a pluralism, a range of possibilities. It is subjective idealist or romantic in character. *Another way of seeing this might be to suggest that the major latent function of an elaborated code (object) is to remove ambiguity, while the major latent function of an elaborated code (person) is to create it.* In this brief discussion I have not referred to the means/ends variants of object- and person-oriented linguistic codes. They should be borne in mind.

These are poorly worked out thoughts. [They have been developed by

Mary Douglas (1967).] My excuse for including them is to point up the need for discussion of more general issues involved in the changing of forms of speech.

Conclusion

I have attempted within the confines of this chapter to work on a broad canvas in which particular problems of language and educability may be placed within a much broader setting. The chapter is really a plea for more extensive research into the social constraints upon the emergence of linguistic codes, the conditions for their maintenance and change, and above all their regulative functions.

18

The Stylistic Significance
of Consonantal Sandhi
in Trukese and Ponapean

JOHN L. FISCHER

John L. Fischer is a professor of anthropology at Tulane University. He received his doctorate from Harvard University, where he has also taught. The present chapter draws on several years of fieldwork on Truk and on Ponape; Dr. Fischer has done fieldwork in Acton, Massachusetts, and Japan. His major research interests include socialization, social structure, folklore, and language. This chapter is a slightly revised version of an original paper published in the *American Anthropologist* (Fischer 1965).

This short discussion points toward a number of important lines of research. The particular phenomenon, *sandhi* (or morphophonemic alternation) is common in languages. [An English analogue would be found in finance: financial, province: provincial, justice: justicial, where (despite the spelling) the final /s/ in the first of each pair alternates with an /s/ ('sh' sound) before the adjectival ending -ial in the second of each pair.] Fischer points out that the normal, or unmarked, consequence of consonantal sandhi *differs as between* these two historically related languages. He asks why. One course is to see whether there are differences between the two societies that might match the differences in normal linguistic form. Suggestive differences do exist, in the attitudes toward each language and toward speaking itself. Pon-

From "The Stylistic Significance of Consonantal Sandhi in Trukese and Ponapean." Reproduced by permission of the American Anthropological Association from the *American Anthropologist*, Vol. 67, pp. 1495–1502, December, 1965.

apeans value conciseness, emotional restraint, formal etiquette, while Trukese value loquacity and show greater freedom of expression. A second course is to consider the unusual, or marked, form. The evidence again suggests a contrast between the two societies, and a complementary one. In effect, there appears to be *sociolinguistic* alternation in each society such that on Ponape the marked form expresses abruptness, freedom of expression, aggression; on Truk the marked form expresses greater restraint, politeness, gentleness.

Notice that it is not just correlation between the normal aspects of language and of culture but the value of the corresponding marked forms in actual speech events, that is decisive, for both the existence of a relationship between linguistic form and social structure and its explanation. The contrast in unmarked forms suggests, and the social meaning of the marked forms would seem to prove, that the phonetic features involved have a common expressive value in both societies.

Interpretation of the marked forms depends on recognizing that they serve more than one function. In themselves, it would seem, the marked forms are conventional *stylistic* devices, defined by their relation to the normal phonological forms. In some uses they serve the metalinguistic function of clarity, in others, of expression and persuasion (and in some, both). [Mitchell-Kernan (Chapter 5) and Gumperz (1970b) provide similar analyses of marking.]

Fischer considers alternative historical explanations for the Trukese-Ponapean contrast but finds the best explanation to lie in a view of the relation of linguistic features to social life quite like that of Labov (Chapter 19) and Barth (Chapter 16). Where variation or alternation exists, it may be given meaning, and selective pressures over time will then operate in terms of such meaning. Fischer adds to this view the important point that expressive, as well as social, meaning must be considered; and he shows that expressive features must be taken into account in the study of universals of language and of language change. He indicates ways in which this line of research should be further pursued, with regard to sociolinguistic investigation in the field, and with regard to other linguistic features whose selection might also be found to have similar explanation. Additional related readings are provided by Guiraud (1967) and Stankiewicz (1964).

This chapter[1] examines a phonological process in Trukese and Ponapean and suggests possible differences in the significance of its use and omission as between these two related Micronesian languages. It also proposes a common, perhaps universal, expressive value for the types of sound sequence involved in the phonological process. Finally, the chapter considers the implications for linguistic change of such stylistic choices as conditioned by social structure and underlying cultural attitudes toward speech.

The Sandhi Rules

Trukese and Ponapean are mutually unintelligible but have rather similar structures. The degree of their relationship may be roughly gauged by the fact that they share about 40% of the Swadesh hundred-word basic vocabulary list (indicating perhaps some 3000 years of separation). The inventories of consonant phonemes are quite similar. For purposes of this chapter we may note that both languages have the same number of genetically equivalent and phonetically quite similar stops and nasals (the two types of consonant involved in the phonological process to be discussed).

In both Trukese and Ponapean there are various phonetic accommodations at the boundaries of words adjoining one another in the same construction in fluent casual speech. Some of these accommodations involve simply the substitution of one allophone for another of the same phoneme. Instead of the allophone that would occur finally if the word were uttered in isolation, there occurs an allophone characteristic of word-medial position. A particularly striking illustration of this for English speakers concerns the Trukese phoneme /n/. The [n] allophone usually found in word-

[1] This chapter is a revised and expanded version of a paper first read at the winter meeting of the Linguistic Society of America in New York, December 1964, and subsequently published in the *American Anthropologist* (Fischer 1965). I wish to express my thanks to Marshall Durbin, Dell Hymes, William Labov, and Ernst Pulgram for very helpful advice on a number of points. Hymes in particular has provided extensive comment. Data discussed cussed herein are derived principally from texts and daily experience in the use of languages obtained during residence in the Caroline Islands 1949–1953. I was greatly aided in my initial understanding of the two languages by the availability of the unpublished sketches of Trukese by Dyen (1965) and of Ponapean by Garvin (1949), although my chief informants spoke slightly different dialects. Responsibility for the full formation of this chapter remains my own.

final position is replaced by the flap allophone [r] (which is regularly found between vowels in words) when the next word of the construction begins with a vowel. Thus, the final /n/ of *nükiin* 'outside,' pronounced [n] when the word is used in isolation, is pronounced [r] in a phrase such as *nukun iimw* [nüküriimʷ] 'outside the house.'

Other phonetic accommodations may be interpreted as involving additions or substitutions of phonemes. Changes such as these are often referred to as *sandhi*, after the term employed by Sanskrit grammarians. (In modern linguistic theory, the changes treated here are technically morphophonemic since they are dependent on grammatical relationships; i.e., the changes cannot be explained in terms of the occurrence of the particular sounds as such but only in terms of their occurrence in relation to word boundaries and syntactic constructions.)

The relevant rules for consonantal sandhi in Trukese and Ponapean are as follows (we are now considering fluent speech without special expressive import):

1. If a final consonant of one word and the initial consonant of the following word are heterorganic (i.e., articulated at significantly different points in the vocal passage), an epenthetic vowel is introduced. This holds in either language. Thus Ponapean *emen* 'one (living thing)' and *kaeru* 'frog' (the latter a Japanese loan—the example is from a modern love song text) yield *emen-i kaeru* 'one frog' or 'a frog.' The vowel *i* is inserted between the heterorganic consonants /n/ and /k/ but bears no additional meaning. Similarly, Trukese *imwen* 'house of' and *ppw* 'dirt' yield *imwen-i-ppwun* 'house of dirt,' 'native-style house.' An *i* is inserted without change of meaning, and the dental /n/ and labial /ppw/ remain unchanged.

2. If the final consonant of one word and the initial consonant of the following word are homorganic (i.e., articulated at essentially the same point in the vocal passage), a vowel usually is not inserted and a consonant cluster results. Here we reach the phenomena that are the special concern of this chapter. Under similar general conditions in both languages, sandhi operates so as to eliminate or prevent one type of consonant cluster in both languages, but the type of cluster eliminated in one language is precisely the type retained in the other. In other words, the favored types of cluster are diametrically opposed.

The conditions for such sandhi are that the first of the two words juxtaposed in the construction end in a nasal or a stop, and that the second begin with a stop. (We speak here of the form of a word as pronounced in isolation; this form is taken as the base or underlying form.) As noted, the final consonant of the first word and the initial consonant of the second must also be homorganic. Sandhi affects the first of the two consonants, the second remaining unchanged.

In Trukese, sandhi operates to produce clusters of two identical stops (articulated as a single long stop), while in Ponapean sandhi operates to produce clusters of nasal plus stop. Thus in Trukese, if the juxtaposition of two words results in a cluster of two identical stops, no phonemic change occurs. Thus, Trukese *otoot* 'husk' (verb) plus *taka* 'ripe coconut' yield *otoot taka* 'husking coconuts.' The double *t* cluster remains phonemically unchanged. On the other hand, if a homorganic cluster of nasal plus stop occurs at adjoining word boundaries, the nasal is normally replaced by the corresponding stop, resulting in a double stop (technically, regressive assimilation). Thus, Trukese *aetin* 'youth of-' and *Toon* 'Tol Island' yield *aetit Toon* 'youth of Tol Island.' In this example, the final /n/ of the first word has been replaced by the homorganic stop /t/.

Conversely, in Ponapean, if the juxtaposition of two words results in a homorganic cluster of nasal plus stop at the adjoining boundaries, no phonemic change occurs, but if the sequence results in a double stop at the boundaries, the first stop is replaced by the homorganic nasal (technically, progressive assimilation. Thus, Ponapean *meen* 'person of' and *Tiati* (a place name) yield *meen Tiati* 'person of Tiati.' Unlike Trukese, the final /n/ does not change. But in *aak* 'mangrove' plus *kɔ* 'those, the,' yielding *aa kɔ* 'those mangroves,' the stop at the end of the first word (/k/) is replaced by the corresponding homorganic nasal (/ŋ/).

If we represent nasals by N, stops by S, and the particular point of articulation by subscript a, we may summarize the interlinguistic differences in which we are interested by the following formulae:

	Underlying Forms	Results of Sandhi
Truk	$\ldots N_a\,S_{a\cdot}\ldots$	$\ldots S_a\,S_{a\cdot}\ldots$
	$\ldots S_a\,S_{a\cdot}\ldots$	$\ldots S_a\,S_{a\cdot}\ldots$
Ponape	$\ldots N_a\,S_{a\cdot}\ldots$	$\ldots N_a\,S_a$
	$\ldots S_a\,S_{a\cdot}\ldots$	$\ldots N_a\,S_{a\cdot}\ldots$

I might add here that in both languages the most common cases in which the juxtaposition of words results in a cluster of nasal plus stop, the first ends in the construct suffix -*Vn* 'of,' while the second begins with a dental or alveolar stop. As we have seen, such clusters are modifiable by sandhi in Trukese but not in Ponapean. The most common cases in which the juxtaposition of words results in a double stop cluster probably involve nouns ending in -*k* (the most common stop in both languages), followed by one of several plural demonstratives, which always begin with *k*- in Ponapean and often do so in Trukese. As we have seen, these cases are modifiable by sandhi in Ponapean but not in Trukese.

In view of the above, we may speak of the clusters of two identical stops as a normally "preferred" type of consonant cluster in Trukese, and of the clusters of nasal plus homorganic stop as a normally "preferred" type in Ponapean.[2]

Cultural Significance of Sandhi

There are two lines along which the significance of these contrasting preferences for type of consonantal cluster can be explored. One is to relate the preferred type in each culture to other cultural characteristics on which Truk and Ponape contrast, and attempt to discern some sort of relationship between the linguistic and the other traits. Since the sandhi changes are the ordinary, but not the inevitable, result of the conditions described, one can also examine in each culture the contexts and circumstances of the *omission* of the preferred type and the selection of its alternate. Both lines of inquiry involve the expressive value of the two types of consonant cluster. We shall consider first cultural contrasts in characteristic attitudes toward speech as influenced by social structure, for this would seem to be a promising, even essential, area in which to begin a search for relationships between intra- and extra-linguistic factors.

CULTURAL ATTITUDES TOWARD
SPEECH AS INFLUENCED BY
SOCIAL STRUCTURE

In this section I wish to consider what Hymes has called the relativity of role or function of language in societies (1966a). Most of us are perhaps accustomed to thinking of the function of language as a universal and stable thing which should vary little or not at all from one society to the next. However, if we think about it a bit, we recognize that within our own society language can serve many distinguishable functions, and it becomes plausible that in some other society the balance among these functions, if not the total inventory of functions, might be considerably different.

Elsewhere I have discussed differences between Ponapean and Trukese a little more fully (1966), but would like to note a few points here which seem significant for apprehending the typical attitudes of members of the

---

[2] A complete description of Trukese and Ponapean sandhi would require various qualifications and additions that are not given in detail since they would be irrelevant to the problem of this chapter. Suffice it to note that there are some dialectal variations in sandhi in both languages; that epenthetic vowels can be introduced between certain homorganic consonants, especially between a stop and a *following* nasal; that at least in some dialects heterorganic consonant clusters without an intervening epenthetic vowel result at times from prosodic considerations, such as number and length of syllables in the two words.

two cultures toward their languages and toward speech in general:

1. *Fluency versus precision in speaking.* Ponapeans value concise, well-chosen speech. Trukese value loquacity and fluency, and are less concerned with careful choice of words. . . . In spite of a generally greater emphasis on personal achievement in Ponape, there is a greater emphasis on verbal productivity in Truk.

2. *Overt expression of emotion.* The control of emotion in public is greatly emphasized in Ponape (cf. Bascom 1965:16–17), while relatively free expression of at least some kinds of emotion is allowed in Truk.

3. *Joking, lying.* Ponapean joking is milder and more controlled, while Trukese joking is relatively more aggressive and freer. For instance, it is common to hear one Trukese tell another that he is lying and this is usually a joke. Ponapeans make this charge much less frequently and when they do it is more likely to be taken and intended as a serious insult.

4. *Etiquette.* Formal etiquette is highly developed on Ponape. This includes the use of two or more levels of respect vocabulary toward chiefs and other social superiors (cf. Garvin and Riesenberg 1952). In Truk respect vocabulary is weakly developed. Such respect behavior as exists is about as strong toward matrilineal of the opposite sex as toward the highest chiefs, perhaps stronger (cf. Goodenough 1951); in other words, even the existing respect behavior on Truk is not so deeply involved in social stratification in the usual sense of the term.

In brief, we may say in comparing the two cultures that the Ponapeans place greater value on precision and quality of speech, while the Trukese place greater value on fluency and quantity of speech. These preferences appear related to the greater emphasis on formal etiquette in Ponape, and beyond that, to differences in social structure. The differences in social structure have been discussed elsewhere and will not be repeated in detail here (for a short summary and further references, see Fischer 1957; for a recent summary of references on Ponape see Bascom 1965). Very briefly, on Ponape as compared with Truk, greater individual social mobility is possible and at the same time rank differences are much more elaborate and important, with the result that speech is pervaded by a striving to be courteous to near equals and superiors.

Of course, great variations in speech situations do exist within both cultures. The Trukese can be polite in their own language and the Ponapeans can be informal, but the predominance of politeness and informality varies by culture. To give a simple example, I have heard a young boy address the most respected Trukese chief by an abbreviated version of his personal name, whereas in Ponape even a close intimate of a high chief, such as his wife or younger brother, would normally address him by his title, even in rather informal situations. In other words, while formal and informal speech are found in both cultures, the formal forms are much more widely used in Ponapean, the informal in Trukese.

INTRACULTURAL VARIATION IN
USES OF CONSONANT CLUSTERS

By noting the association of type of preferred consonant cluster with the characteristic cultural attitudes toward speech described above we might be led to form the hypothesis that clusters of nasal plus stop, preferred in Ponapean, in some fashion express typical Ponapean attitudes toward speech, and that double stop clusters, preferred in Trukese, in some fashion express typical Trukese attitudes toward speech. This hypothesis would be strengthened if we could examine more closely situational variation in the use of consonantal sandhi in each language and find that where sandhi tends to be omitted (and thus the frequency of the preferred type of consonant cluster reduced) there is evidence of a special attitude toward speech contrasting with the culturally dominant attitude, or a marking of the message as of some special or specialized import. For, as noted, the sandhi changes are by no means completely automatic in either language, and the frequency of their use varies by speaker and situation.

To some extent the situations in which sandhi is omitted in either culture are parallel, and the import of the omission is much the same. Sandhi changes may be omitted in either language whenever it is desired to speak with special clarity, as in talking to a very small child or to a foreigner learning to speak the language, or when talking against a background of interfering noise. The changes are, of course, also omitted whenever there is hesitation between two words in a sequential construction.

Other data, however, suggest that the omission of consonantal sandhi may also have some special expressive significance, one which contrasts as between the two languages; further, that this differing expressive value for omission of sandhi is related to an expressive value shared by the two cultures with respect to each of the two types of consonant cluster in question. The observations supporting this view are not numerous but are, I believe, suggestive.

Regarding the expressive omission of consonantal sandhi in Ponapean (i.e., preserving double stops at word boundaries rather than changing the first stop to the corresponding nasal), the only time when I heard this done consistently between native speakers in a situation of ordinary audibility was during a rather outrageous speech in which a chief who had recently won out in a long dispute over rights to certain traditional titles was forcefully castigating his opponents and attempting to cow them into permanent submission. This is quite unusual behavior for modern Ponapean chiefs, who, like their subjects, generally try to give the impression that they are reasonable and gentle. Rather than directly express his anger a chief will usually try to manage an unruly subject through go-betweens if he suspects there is a chance of serious open resistance. This chief, on this one occasion only, regularly omitted consonantal sandhi at all word junctures, resulting in many double consonant clusters, especially double *k*'s in his speech. I spoke with him many times on other occasions and never noticed the slightest tendency in this direction, nor did I ever notice such a tendency in other speakers in speech to other native speakers in situations of ordinary audibility. It is true that in the situation described, the speaker was trying to state his position very clearly, and no doubt this is relevant to the omission of sandhi, but the point to note is that the clarity was for the purpose of expressing aggression, of telling certain members of his audience something which he knew they did not want to hear. The omission of sandhi in this situation therefore facilitated the expression of aggression. It is of special interest that the more formal form without sandhi should be used to express aggression since it would seem to be more common for informal, slurred forms characteristic of rapid speech to result from aggressive feelings.

For Trukese I can report no single dramatic incident such as this, but can give my general impression that some tendency toward the omission of sandhi in Trukese characterizes polite speech, as toward strangers of greater age, or in formal public gatherings. For what it is worth, I would note that consonantal sandhi does not occur as far as I know in the texts of love songs in Truk, although the epenthetic vowels, another sandhi feature, are especially common in songs in both languages. Admittedly, musical reasons could help to account for the epenthetic vowels and the retention of nasal stop clusters. But if double stops give an impression of greater force in both languages, it may also be significant that I have recorded them in consonantal sandhi in texts of Trukese spells, where the intent is presumably to compel some event by magical power.

Thus we find various bits of ethnographic evidence, as just reported, supporting the notion that there is a common expressive significance for each of the two types of consonant cluster in the two languages. Specifically, in both languages the double stops seem to have the values of abruptness and freedom of emotional expression, including the expression of aggression, while the clusters of nasal plus stop seem to have the values of restraint, politeness, and gentleness. To the extent that these expressive considerations influence the use of sandhi, we may say that the use and omission of sandhi have contrasting expressive value as between the two cultures.

POSSIBLE UNIVERSAL EXPRESSIVE
VALUE OF TYPES OF CONSONANT
CLUSTER

The apparent similarities between the two cultures in the expressive value of these two types of consonant cluster may lead us to consider further whether there may not be something appropriate in these cultural meanings from the point of view of a potentially universal phonetic symbolism. If found, this would give further support to the thesis. It would appear that in any language it would be natural for double stops to be articulated more forcefully than single stops or nasal stop clusters: in order to ensure most economically that a single stop is not held too long (and thus confused with a double stop), it helps to close it with less force, preparing for its prompt release. Increasing the number of double stops by whatever optional means would then be suitable for expressing aggression since it would result in a more forceful articulation, considered as a gesture of the speech organs. In Ponapean, of course, this effect is achieved by *elimination* of consonantal sandhi, as in the angry chief's speech, while in Trukese it is achieved through the *normal operation* of consonantal sandhi.

By analogy, the clusters of nasal plus stop may be regarded as a less forceful vocal gesture. Especially when they are substituted for double stop clusters, as in Ponapean sandhi, they may be interpreted gesturally as a dulling or blunting of the abruptness of the double stop cluster.

FUNCTIONAL LOAD

While I believe that the expressive value and stylistic role of consonant clusters discussed herein are probably in part dependent on universal phonetic symbolism, I do not believe that the "stylistic functional load" of these or similar consonant clusters is equal in all languages in which they can occur. The expressive value of the consonant clusters would be slight if there were no opportunity in actualizing particular constructions for choice between the two types of cluster—double consonants versus clusters of nasal plus other homorganic consonants. Since such a choice does exist frequently in both languages, it can actively serve an important expressive function. Of course, in any language in which the two types of cluster existed in different words or constructions, there is still a little opportunity for an expressive function to be served insofar as approximate synonyms might be selected at times on the basis of their phonetic shape, e.g., as an English speaking writer might select "large" in preference to "big" because he found the open (low) vowel of the first in some way more expressive than the closed (high) vowel of the second.

We may say, therefore, that the development of optional sandhi affecting these consonant clusters in the two languages has provided an opportunity for speakers to make especially great stylistic use of what may be a universal tendency or potential in phonetic symbolism. In the context of human culture as a whole, then, the occurrence of sandhi may be said to be marked (or potentially marked) in relation to its absence, and the normal speech of the two cultures in question can be seen as marked as aggressive, and restrained, respectively, just in virtue of normal phonological process, as against a hypothetical universal baseline. However, in the context of a single culture, it is the omission of the normal phonological process, sandhi, that is marked, as against the known cultural (and morphonemic) baseline. On this view, in Trukese it is restrained speech that is marked, in Ponapean aggressive.

Historical Considerations

Whatever the reasons for the expressive significance of these consonant clusters, whether universal or particular to these two cultures, there are grounds for suspecting that it is the contrasting attitudes toward language in the two cultures that have provided a selective pressure in favor of one type of consonantal sandhi in Trukese and another type in Ponapean.

PHONETIC ECONOMY

It is hard to interpret the difference in type of consonantal sandhi in terms of phonetic economy. While either type of sandhi results in a kind of economy by reducing the number of consonant clusters which the speaker must produce and the listener identify, the two languages considered in themselves appear to offer no evidence that either form of sandhi results in a cluster which is easier to pronounce than the original cluster since the Trukese form of sandhi (nasal plus homorganic stop changing to double stop) results in precisely the type of consonant cluster which Ponapean sandhi eliminates, and vice versa.

RECENT ACCULTURATION

The question was raised as to whether the learning of Japanese by the speakers of one or the other language during the period of Japanese administration between the two world wars could have altered the possible consonant clusters in very recent times. This possibility can be conclusively ruled out for several reasons:

1. A majority of the speakers of both languages remained monolingual during the Japanese period.
2. Nearly all Trukese or Ponapeans who learned some Japanese did so imperfectly and simply used the most appropriate phonemes and phoneme combinations of their mother tongue to approximate Japanese pronunciation.
3. The types of consonant clusters favored at word boundaries

by sandhi shifts are the only types found within indigenous morphemes; the consonant clusters within morphemes are generally subject to no variation at present and are presumably more stable historically.

4. Exposure to the Japanese language was roughly equal for speakers of the local Trukese and Ponapean dialects which I studied.

5. Both types of consonant cluster under consideration—double stops and nasal-stop clusters—occur frequently in Japanese.

The other major non-Micronesian languages with which there has been some contact are English, Spanish, and German. The first three reasons apply to these languages as well, the first two with even greater force.

We cannot at present rule out conclusively the possibility that after initial differentiation of the two languages prehistoric contact with one or more other Pacific languages influenced the divergent development of sandhi patterns, but I consider this explanation less probable than the one offered. I think there is some suggestion of greater Polynesian contact for Ponapean, but Polynesian languages generally lack all consonant clusters, and presumably have for some time.

WORLD VIEW, SOCIAL STRUCTURE, AND LINGUISTIC CHANGE

Consonant clusters occur within words and within morphemes in both languages. Here there is at present less room for stylistic choice: in Trukese one generally finds a double stop (or fricative) where in the cognate Ponapean word (if there is one) one finds a nasal-stop (or nasal-fricative) cluster. However, it seems to me plausible that we may infer a time in the past when "free variation," i.e., variation conditioned by expressive or social factors and not by linguistic factors, existed in both languages with respect to these *internal* consonant clusters. I think it is also reasonable to infer that the significance in the internal clusters was the same as that of the corresponding clusters at adjoining word boundaries. If this is granted, then we have an instance of an effect of stylistic preferences conditioned by social structure on phonological change. If more instances can be documented and studied in greater detail, we may ultimately be able to develop a general social-psychological theory for the interpretation of much phonological change.

The argument with respect to phonology (specifically, formation of consonant clusters) is similar to the argument of a paper of mine with respect to syntax—specifically, the construction of noun phrases. In both works I compare the genetically related languages and cultures of Truk and Ponape and infer that long-standing differences in world view have led to linguistic change along different lines. The basic theme of both papers is that:

World view can have influence on linguistic change . . . through its effect on attitudes toward speech and language. . . . Given a fairly consistent set of attitudes toward speech over a period of time, the linguistic alternatives of style which express the preferred attitudes at one period . . . will tend to increase in frequency and become obligatory. . . . At the same time . . . new alternatives must develop to express the same sort of attitudes (Fischer 1966:182).

World view is further relatable to social structure. As has been indicated, the basic difference between the two societies, one from which a number of others flow, is the greater emphasis on political and social hierarchy in Ponape. Ponapean hierarchy entails, for one thing, a much greater concern with politeness and control of emotions among the Ponapeans as compared with the Trukese. There is in Ponape less free play for verbal aggression, joking or serious. In the present work I have argued that this politeness and carefulness with speech extends to phonology, favoring less "forceful" consonant clusters in Ponapean, and have presented some evidence suggesting that the people of both cultures attribute similar expressive significance to the forcefulness of the different types of cluster.

In the paper on syntax I argue for another effect of social hierarchy on the two languages. In the more differentiated and more hierarchical society, Ponape, there is a stronger assumption that the listener has a different point of view from the speaker. Consequently there is a greater concern for speaking carefully and economically—to say what one has to say but to avoid saying anything extra which might be misinterpreted. At the same time there is less willingness to suffer interruption when one "has the floor." Ponapean noun phrase construction contributes to these values by its tightness: i.e., in the context of actual discourse it is usually easier to infer the end of a Trukese noun phrase than its Ponapean equivalent because of the differences in order of presentation of information. It is therefore easier to interrupt the Trukese noun phrase before its completion, once the end has been inferred, or to prepare to seize the floor as soon as it does end.

More recently, in an unpublished paper presented at the 1967 annual meeting of the American Anthropological Association in Washington, D.C., I have examined some regularities in combinations of syntactic rules noted by Joseph Greenberg (1963) in a diverse sample of world languages, and have attempted an interpretation of these along lines similar to those of my 1966 paper on Trukese and Ponapean noun phrase construction. Greenberg's sample contains a wide range of syntactic variables which show no difference between Trukese and Ponapean. A number of these variables show a tendency toward scaling, suggesting to me a single underlying rhetorical variable on the order of "looseness/tightness" or "suspense/directness," as I have discussed previously for the noun phrase in Trukese and Ponapean. As I interpret Greenberg's data, Japanese is at one end of the scale and four languages—Berber, Hebrew, Welsh, and Zapotec—are at the other end.

Unfortunately for my argument, Trukese noun phrase construction turns out to be more like Japanese than does Ponapean, although in terms of social structure and values about speech Japanese culture appears to me to be closer to Ponapean than it is to Trukese—and I have conducted fieldwork in all three cultures. As far as dominant subject-verb-object (SVO) order is concerned, Japanese has what I regard as the most "suspenseful" of the three common orders, SOV, while Ponapean and Trukese are both like English, SVO, which is an intermediate order. (The other extreme order is VSO.) Probably greater weight should be given to the subject-verb-object order than to internal order of noun phrases since either subject or object can itself be a complex noun phrase; SVO order therefore involves an ordering of greater chunks of the sentence. I have no simple explanation which satisfies me to explain these apparent inconsistencies. Possibly more focused fieldwork on the ethnography of speaking in these cultures would reveal that I have not chosen the correct rhetorical and social variables. There are a number of genres of language use (various kinds of narrative and songs, poetry, oratory, courting, gossip, age-graded discourse, etc.) in relation to which stylistic choices might be intensively investigated.

However, I am still inclined to think that the scaling of certain syntactic variables suggests the operation of some sort of universal rhetorical or expressive factor. Further work with a larger number of variables and a larger sample of world language may enable us ultimately to develop a general social psychological theory for the interpretation of much linguistic change.

19

On the Mechanism
of Linguistic Change

WILLIAM LABOV

William Labov is a professor of linguistics at the University of Pennsylvania. He received his doctorate from Columbia University where he also taught for a number of years. He is a member of the Committee on Sociolinguistics of the Social Science Research Council. His research has concentrated on the observation and explanation of linguistic change in English, analysis of conversation and narrative, and the development of more adequate linguistic analyses through the incorporation of quantitative patterning and social features. The present chapter is reprinted from a Georgetown University monograph edited by Charles Kreidler (1965). Part of the discussion of Labov's paper also reprinted there is reproduced in an appendix at the end of the chapter. A more detailed discussion of some of the notions in this chapter is provided by Weinreich, Herzog, and Labov (1968).

Some thirty years ago Edward Sapir objected that "In linguistics, abstracted speech sounds, words and the arrangement of words have come to have so authentic a vitality that one can speak of 'regular sound changes' and 'loss of genders' without knowing or caring who opened their mouths, at what time, to communicate what to whom" (1949d:579). Sapir criticized the arbitrary boundaries drawn by "the many kinds of segmental scientists of

From "On the Mechanism of Linguistic Change." Reprinted from Georgetown University Monograph Series on Languages and Linguistics, No. 18, edited by Charles W. Kreidler, pp. 91–114 and pp. 131–132.

man," arguing that "we need never fear to modify, prune, extend, redefine, rearrange, and reorient our sciences of man as social being, for these sciences cannot point to an order of nature that has meaning apart from the directly experienced perceptions and values of the individual" (1949d:578, 581). Much of the study of linguistic change has continued to deserve Sapir's stricture. Labov shows how research not afraid to "extend, redefine, rearrange, and reorient" current segmentations of the study of man can succeed in observing what has been pronounced unobservable, find regularity in what was thought to be confusion, and begin to answer some of the fundamental questions posed by the universal fact of linguistic change.

The present chapter begins and ends with reference to data from the speech community. The implication is that data on the internal structure of the language, i.e., linguistic forms collected by the traditional elicitation procedures, in which these forms are abstracted from ordinary verbal interaction, do not provide a proper basis for the explanation of linguistic change. One must have data on attitudes and use as well. Indeed the phrase means more than that. It is not enough simply to add (or correlate) information from the speech community to the linguistic analysis. The two kinds of data are interlocked and must be obtained and analyzed together. Note that the speech community is defined not by the presence or absence of a particular dialect or language but by the presence of a common set of normative values in regard to linguistic features. (One might speak of a criterion of social rather than merely "referential" intelligibility.)

This concept of the data and conception of the speech community has led to the development of new and highly ingenious elicitation techniques capable of simulating some of the significant variations in social context which characterize everyday verbal interaction. Labov discovered that although individual speech varies greatly, New Yorkers are alike in the way in which they adapt their pronunciation and grammar in differing social situations and in the way in which they judge or evaluate the social significance of the forms they hear. (See Labov 1966b for a full account of field techniques and results.) Previous investigators who had confined themselves simply to recording linguistic forms in formal interview sessions had been defeated by the heterogeneity of what they found and thought of New York only as a locale of great mixture of speech. Labov showed that underneath the heterogeneity of what people say is a considerable homogeneity of social meaning and of evaluation of what is said, New York City shows in perhaps extreme form what is true for any community (see e.g., that described by Blom and Gumperz, Chapter 14); a synchronic description cannot be static, but must take the perspective called by Jakobson (1962) "dynamic synchrony."

Labov's concern in this chapter is to develop a theory of some of the processes that contribute to the diversity within speech communities, while at the same time reflecting the common evaluations that unite them. He is concerned first to show that *sound change,* a classic locus of linguistic theory, can indeed be observed and be described (as against some neogrammarian views), and then to show that its occurrence can be explained (a possibility dismissed, or trivialized, by some generative grammarians (Postal 1968:283–284)). Central to the approach is recognition of a new concept, the *linguistic variable,* as the unit of change (see the Introduction and also Ervin-Tripp, Chapter 7). The linguistic variable is by definition a feature subject to social evaluation, hence requiring data from the speech community for its description, and at the same time making explanation possible (through concomitant variation between the linguistic and social data). At any one time some features of a language will be subject to social evaluation, moving through the statuses of *indicator, marker,* and perhaps *stereotype* indicated in the outline of states of change.

Linguistic change is seen as an adaptive process, as linguistic evolution. Its adequate study must deal with three problems, *transition, embedding,* and *evaluation*— finding the route, the sociolinguistic matrix, and the social meaning of a change. In both the studies reported here (Martha's Vineyard and New York City) self-identity is found to be at the root of linguistic change (see the Norwegian study by Blom and Gumperz, Chapter 14, and Bernstein, Chapter 16). In the first, native status as a Vineyarder is the key. In New York City socioeconomic class and, most of all, ethnic identity are most important. In both, of course, age enters (other work of Labov has formalized generation as one of the contextual features to which a linguistic rule is sensitive).

Notice the necessity of placing data in terms of the identity of the speaker and the context of speech. Only by treating data as situated in these two respects could the patterning be discerned. Survey techniques were used to place the New York City speakers in terms of socio-economic class. Diverse modes of elicitation were used to deal with contextual style. Recognizing self-consciousness as the crucial factor, whose effects could not be eliminated, Labov proceeded to control for it, and indeed, to turn it to advantage. Four contextual styles were differentiated, reading of isolated words from a list giving the most self-conscious speech, the telling of an incident in which one's life had been in danger giving the least self-conscious. Statistical techniques were, of course, required to show the stable patterns that emerged, for these were patterns not of presence and absence of features but of greater and lesser incidence. Notice that it is not the absolute values of the percentages of a feature, according to class and context but the reliable (and valid) pattern of relationship between values that counts. Another investigator or another day might show a different absolute but not a different relative incidence.

Like Blom and Gumperz, Labov found people unaware of their own usage of language and holding values about speech in terms of which their usage would be stigmatized by the larger community. Such research gives a dynamic dimension to the thesis of the unconscious patterning of linguistic and other behavior developed by Boas, Sapir, and Lévi-Strauss and indicates some specific explanations of that dimension, e.g., the relationship between hypercorrection and position just below the highest social level. The conflict between two sets of values (see Bernstein, Chapter 17) is significant. In his general monograph Labov (1966b) speaks of the great linguistic insecurity of the average New York speaker. Participation in a particular linguistic change may be a sensitive index of social mobility and struggle.

Labov's research disproves the recurrent view that linguistic change can be bifurcated between a purely internal process of the origin of changes and an external process of their spread, such that social factors enter only into the second (see, most recently, Postal 1968:284). The other view can be seen as an attempt to avoid recognition of linguistics as partly a social science, as a field whose problems require some use of social science methods for their solution. Such a view must ignore clear cases of social motivation of sound change (see Fischer 1958; Hymes 1964d:450; as well as the Martha's Vineyard case in this chapter), and retreat to a position from which the meaningfulness of linguistic change to "the directly experienced perceptions and values of the individual" is either invisible or explained away (cf. Postal 1968:283: "There is no more reason for languages to change than there is for automobiles to add fins one year and remove them the next").

If the description and explanation of linguistic change require data beyond that with which most linguists are used to dealing, it is not, Labov stresses, multiplication of data in itself that matters but theoretically motivated selection of data, and rigor in its analysis. Additional related readings are provided by Malkiel (1960) and Martinet (1952).

Introduction

This chapter outlines the approaches to the explanation of linguistic change which are being followed in our current research within the context of the speech community. It is now clear that many theoretical problems of linguistic structure cannot be resolved without data from the speech community. This point of view is developed in detail in Labov 1964a. Here I will focus on the converse proposition—that linguistic change cannot be explained by arguments drawn from purely internal relations within the system, even if external, sociolinguistic relations are recognized as additional conditioning factors. In the mechanism of linguistic changes which we have observed, the two sets of relations are interlocked in a systematic way.

The investigations which form the basis for the present discussion are studies of linguistic change on the island of Martha's Vineyard, and in New York City; the principal focus will be on the process of sound change. The chief techniques used in this research have been described in several previous papers and publications, along with a certain amount of the data and the findings (see Labov 1963, 1964a, 1964b, 1965, 1966a, 1966b, 1968). The data to be presented here may be considered representative of a much larger set of facts and correlations derived from these studies.

The problems of linguistic evolution. Despite the achievements of nineteenth century historical linguistics, many avenues to the study of linguistic change remain unexplored. In 1905, Meillet noted that all of the laws of linguistic history that had been discovered were merely possibilities (Meillet 1921:16): "It remains for us to discover the variables which permit or incite the possibilities thus recognized."

The problem as we face it today is precisely that which Meillet outlined sixty years ago, for little progress has been made in ascertaining the empirical factors which condition historical change. There has actually been a retrograde movement in this respect in the sense that treatments of linguistic change which are essentially ahistorical have become popular. Chronological detail is deliberately set aside in such articles as those by Pilch (1955) and Halle (1962).

The chief problems of linguistic evolution might be summarized as five questions:

1. What are the causes of the continual origination of new linguistic changes?
2. By what mechanism do changes proceed?
3. Is there an adaptive function to linguistic evolution?[1]
4. Is there an over-all direction of linguistic evolution?
5. What are the universal constraints upon linguistic change?

One approach to linguistic evolution is to study changes completed in the past. This has, of course, been the major strategy of historical linguistics, and it is the only possible approach to the last two questions—the direction of linguistic evolution, and the universal constraints upon change. On the other hand, the questions of the mechanism of change, the inciting causes of change, and the adaptive functions of change are best analyzed by studying in detail linguistic changes in progress. The mechanism of linguistic change will be the chief topic of the discussion to follow; however, many of the conclusions will plainly be relevant to the questions of inciting causes and adaptive functions of change, and it will be apparent that more complete answers to these three questions will require methods similar to those used here.

An essential presupposition of this line of research is the claim that the same mechanisms which operated to produce the large scale changes of the past may be observed operating in the current changes taking place around us.

---

[1] This question is all the more puzzling when we contrast linguistic with biological evolution. It is difficult to discuss the evolution of the plant and animal kingdoms without some reference to adaptation to various environments. But what conceivable adaptive function is served by the efflorescence of the Indo-European family? On this topic, see Labov (1964a) and Hymes (1961a).

A Strategy for the Study
of Linguistic Changes in Progress

Although answers to the first three questions given above are the ultimate goals of our current research, they do not represent the actual strategy used. For the empirical study of changes in progress, the task can be sub-divided into three separate problems which jointly serve to answer the questions raised above.

1. The *transition* problem is to find the route by which one stage of a linguistic change has evolved from an earlier stage. We wish to trace enough of the intervening stages so that we can eliminate all but one of the major alternatives. Thus questions of the regularity of sound change, of grammatical influence on sound change (Malkiel 1960), of "push chains" versus "pull chains" (Martinet 1952), of steady movement versus sudden and discontinuous shifts, are all aspects of the transition problem.

2. The *embedding* problem is to find the continuous matrix of social and linguistic behavior in which the linguistic change is carried. The principal route to the solution is through the discovery of correlations between elements of the linguistic system and between those elements and the non-linguistic system of social behavior. The correlations are established by strong proof of concomitant variation: that is, by showing that a small change in the independent variable is regularly accompanied by a change of the linguistic variable in a predictable direction.

The concept of the linguistic variable is that developed in Labov 1964c. The definition of such a variable amounts to an empirical assertion of co-variation, within or without the linguistic system. It appears that the fundamental difference between an explanation of a linguistic change and a description is that a description makes no such assertion. In terms of a description of change, such as that provided by Halle (1962), there is no greater probability of the change taking place in the observed direction as in the reverse direction. Note that the embedding problem is presented here as a single problem, despite the fact that there are two distinct aspects: correlations within the linguistic system and with elements outside the system. The main body of this chapter provides justification for this decision.

3. The *evaluation* problem is to find the subjective (or latent) correlates of the objective (or manifest) changes which have been observed. The indirect approach to this problem correlates the general attitudes and aspirations of the informants with their linguistic behavior. The more direct approach is to measure the unconscious subjective reactions of the informants to values of the linguistic variable itself.

With tentative solutions to these problems in hand, it would be possible to provide an explanation of a linguistic change which answers the three questions of inciting cause, mechanism, and adaptive function. As in any other investigation, the value of an explanation rises in relation to its generality, but only to the extent that it rests upon a foundation of reliable and reproducible evidence.

The Observation of Sound Change

The simplest data that will establish the existence of a linguistic change is a set of observations of two successive generations of speakers —generations of comparable social characteristics which represent stages in the evolution of the same speech community. Hermann (1929) obtained such data at Charmey in 1929 by developing the original observations of Gauchat (1905), obtained in 1899. We have such data for Martha's Vineyard, adding the 1961 observations to the 1933 data of the *Linguistic Atlas* (Kurath 1941). For New York City, we add the current data of 1963 to the *Linguistic Atlas* data of 1940; in addition, we have many other reports, including the excellent observations of Babbitt in 1896, to add further time depth to our analysis (Frank 1948; Kurath and McDavid, Jr. 1961; Hubbell 1949; Babbitt 1896).

Solutions to the transition problem proposed here will depend upon close analysis of the distribution of linguistic forms in *apparent time*—that is, along the dimension formed by the age groups of the present population. Such an analysis is possible only because the original simple description of change in *real time* enables us to distinguish age-grading in the present population from the effects of linguistic change (Hockett 1950).

The evidence obtained in the research reported here indicates that the regular process of sound change can be isolated and recorded by observations across two generations. This process is characterized by a rapid development of some units of a phonetic sub-system, while other units remain relatively constant. It affects word classes as a whole rather than individual words: yet these classes may be defined by a variety of conditions, morphophonemic and grammatical as well as phonetic. It is regular, but more in the outcome than in its inception or its development. Furthermore, it appears that the process of sound change is not an autonomous movement within the confines of a linguistic system but rather a complex response to many aspects of human behavior.

Some comment is required on the possibility of observing regular sound since arguments inherited from the neogrammarian controversy have impeded the progress of empirical research in this area. The inheritors of the neogrammarian tradition, who should be most interested in the empirical study of regular change in progress, have abandoned the arena of meaningful research in favor of abstract and speculative arguments. Indeed, Bloomfield (1933:347, 365) and Hockett (1958:439, 444) have maintained that phonetic change cannot in principle be observed by any of the techniques currently available. Hockett writes: "No one has yet observed sound change: we have only been able to detect it via its consequences. We shall see later that a more nearly direct observation would be theoretically possible, if impractical, but any ostensible report of such an observation so far must be discredited." His theoretical proposal is that "over a period of fifty years we made, each month, a thousand accurate acoustic records . . . all from the members of a tight-knit community." The suggestion to multiply the data in this way is not necessarily helpful, as the experience of sociological survey analysts has shown: for relatively small numbers are needed to measure change in a population if the bias of selection is eliminated or minimized. Otherwise, we merely multiply the errors of measurement.

Hockett proceeds to identify sound change with a level of random fluctuations in the action of the articulatory apparatus, without any inherent direction, a drift of the articulatory target which has no cognitive, expressive, or social significance. According to Hockett, the variables responsible for sound change include "the amount of moisture in the throat, nose and mouth of the speaker, random currents in his central nervous system, muscular tics . . . the condition of the hearer's outer ear [presence of wax or dirt]" (1958:443–444). All of the empirical observations of change in progress which have been reported are explained as the results of a complex process of borrowing, and are relegated to a type of linguistic behavior known as the fluctuation or conflict of forms. No claims are made for the regularity of this process, and so the basic tenet of the regularity of sound change has been deprived of all empirical significance. Furthermore, the changes which actually are observed are regarded as unsystematic phenomena, to be discussed with anecdotal evidence, subject to forces "quite outside the linguist's reach," factors which "elude our grasp," fluctuations "beyond our powers" to record (Bloomfield 1933:343–368).

The evidence of current research suggests that this retreat was premature, that the regular process of sound change can be observed by empirical methods. The refinements in methodology called for are not the mechanical elaborations suggested by the writers cited above; for the mere multiplication of data only confounds analysis and perpetuates the bias of selection. It is rigor in the analysis of a population and in the selection of informants which is required. Furthermore, we need ingenuity in the resolution of stylistic variation, to go beyond the sterile method of endless dissection into idiolects. With such techniques, we find that regularity emerges where only confusion was seen before. Random fluctuations in articulation can certainly be found: indeed, this is the level of "noise" which prevents us from predicting the form of every utterance which our informants will make. But it would be an error to ascribe a major role to such fluctuations in the economy of linguistic change. The forces which direct the observed changes appear to be of an entirely different order of magnitude, and the changes take place much more rapidly than any process of random drift could account for.

Thus the following table contrasts the two points of view:

Neogrammarian:	Sound change	Fluctuation of forms	Ultimate regularity
Present discussion:	Sublinguistic fluctuations	Sound change	Ultimate regularity

A single example of a sound change recently observed will be used to illustrate the general approach to solving the transition, embedding, and evaluation problems. This example is one of the simplest cases—that of the centralization of (aw) on Martha's Vineyard. In the development of this case, some new evidence will be presented on the mechanism of sound changes which has not been published before.

The Centralization of (aw) on Martha's Vineyard

We begin with a clear-cut case for the existence of a linguistic change from observations in real time. In 1933, Guy Lowman found no more than the barest trace of centralization of /aw/; the significant variation observed was the fronting of /aw/ from [aU] to [æU]. In 1961, a comparable set of older eighth generation descendants of Yankee settlers from the same villages showed a very pronounced centralization of /aw/— now clearly the variable (aw). (In the notation used here, parentheses indicate the linguistic variable, while slashes indicate bi-unique phonemes and brackets phonetic notation as usual. Thus (aw) represents the variable in general; (aw-2) is a particular value of the variable; (aw)-22 is an average index score for the variable.)

The *transition* problem is studied through a detailed examination of the distribution of forms through apparent time—that is, through the various age levels in the present population. In this case, as in many others, the original sample was too small to allow us to study differences in age levels; only four informants were chosen on Martha's Vineyard in 1933. The first step in the analysis is to construct a quantitative index for discrete values of the variable. The original impressionistic scale had six levels. Instrumental measurements of a sample of these ratings indicated that four levels could be distinguished with a high degree of conformity to formant positions (see Labov 1963:286–287).

aw-0	[aU]
aw-1	[a ⊥ U]
aw-2	[ɐU]
aw-3	[əU]

The index of centralization was constructed from this scale by averaging the numerical values assigned to each variant. Thus (aw)-00 would mean no centralization at all, while (aw)-3.00 would mean consistent centralization at the level of [əU]. This index was applied to interviews with 69 informants by rating each of the words in which (aw) occurred. The first approach to the transition problem can then be made by correlating average (aw) index scores for these interviews with the age level of the speakers. The first three columns of Table 19.1 show a regular correlation, in which the centralization index rises regularly for four successive age levels.

table 19.1

Centralization Indexes by Age Level

Generation	Age level	(aw)-	(ai)-
Ia	Over 75	0.22	0.25
Ib	61–75	0.37	0.35
IIa	46–60	0.44	0.62
IIb	31–45	0.88	0.81

The over-all tendency of Table 19.1 represents an amalgamation of many different types of speakers and many different trends in the use of (aw). Figure 19.1 presents a more detailed analysis of the transition problem for a critical sub-group. Here are displayed the percentage distribution of lexical items for eight individuals from 92 to 31 years of age. The horizontal axes show the four coded levels of the variable (aw). The vertical axes are the percentages of lexical items used with each variant. The vocabulary is broken into two sections that are tabulated separately: the solid line represents words in which (aw) is followed by a voiceless obstruent, as in *out, house, about, mouth;* the broken line represents all other words (and principally those ending in a nasal, as in *town, found,* or with no consonant final, as in *now, how,* etc.) [The phonetic conditioning was actually much more complex than this, and both following and preceding consonants are involved (Labov 1963:290).]

The first diagram, *a,* in Fig. 19.1 is not that of an individual but shows the composite results for the four *Linguistic Atlas* informants interviewed in 1933. They show only the barest trace of centralization. The second

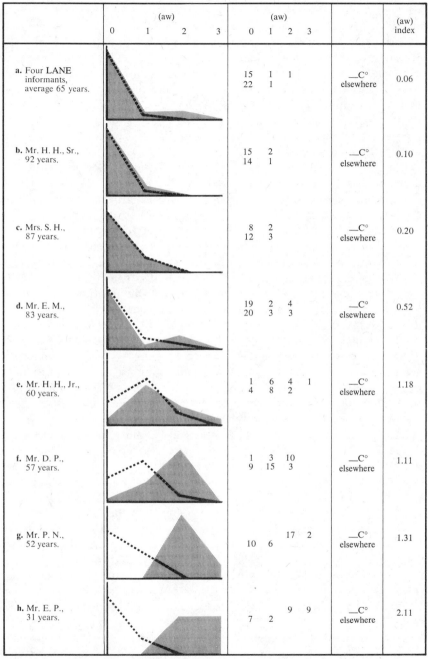

	(aw)				(aw)					(aw) index
	0	1	2	3	0	1	2	3		
a. Four LANE informants, average 65 years.					15 22	1 1	1		—C° elsewhere	0.06
b. Mr. H. H., Sr., 92 years.					15 14	2 1			—C° elsewhere	0.10
c. Mrs. S. H., 87 years.					8 12	2 3			—C° elsewhere	0.20
d. Mr. E. M., 83 years.					19 20	2 3	4 3		—C° elsewhere	0.52
e. Mr. H. H., Jr., 60 years.					1 4	6 8	4 2	1	—C° elsewhere	1.18
f. Mr. D. P., 57 years.					1 9	3 15	10 3		—C° elsewhere	1.11
g. Mr. P. N., 52 years.					10	6	17	2	—C° elsewhere	1.31
h. Mr. E. P., 31 years.					7	2	9	9	—C° elsewhere	2.11

figure 19.1

Stages in the centralization of (aw) on Martha's Vineyard, Massachusetts

diagram, *b*, is that of the oldest informant of 1961, a man 92 years old. The average age of the *Atlas* informants was 65 years; Mr. H. H., Sr., would have been 64 years old in 1933, and so he is of the same age group. His centralization profile is quite similar to that of the *Atlas* informants in *a*. In *c*, we have an 87-year-old woman who shows only a slight increase in centralization. Diagram *d*, Mr. E. M., 83 years old, indicates a small but distinct increase in the occurrence of variant (aw-2). Mr. H. H., Jr., in *e*, is considerably younger; he is 61 years old, the first representative of the next generation since he is the son of Mr. H. H., Sr. Here we have a marked increase in centralization, with both classes of words centered about a norm of (aw-1). In *f*, Mr. D. P., 57 years old, shows a distinct difference between words ending in voiceless obstruents and all others; the first are now centered about a norm of (aw-2), while the second group is concentrated at (aw-1). This process is carried further in *g*, the speech of Mr. P. N., 52 years old, who shows perfect complementary distribution. Before voiceless obstruents, /aw/ has an allophone which is almost always (aw-2), while before other terminals it is usually uncentralized. And at this point, there is no overlap in the distribution. Finally, in *h*, the most extreme case of centralization, we see an even sharper separation: this is Mr. E. P., 31 years old, the son of Mr. D. P. in *f*.

On the right hand side of Fig. 19.1 are the figures for the actual numbers of lexical items observed, and the composite index scores for each of the eight cases. It may be noted that (aw) is only one-third as frequent as (ay); the regularity which appears here does not require a vast corpus of observations. The regularity emerges through the controlled selection of informants, methods of elicitation, and of recording the data.

The eight diagrams of Fig. 19.1 represent the most homogeneous type of population. All of the speakers are Yankee descendants of the original settlers of the island, all are interrelated, many from the same families, with similar attitudes towards the island. All had rural upbringing, and worked as carpenters or fisherman, with one exception. Thus the continuous development of centralization represents the very model of a neogrammarian sound change, accomplished within two generations.

The *embedding* problem was first approached by correlating the centralization of the obviously related variables (ay) and (aw)—that is, the change of (aw) was embedded in the system of upgliding diphthongs. The *Atlas* records indicate a moderate degree of centralization in the 1930s, so that we know that the centralized forms of (ay) preceded the rise of (aw). The fourth column of Table 19.1 shows a close correlation of the two variables, with (ay) slightly in the lead at first, but (aw) becoming more dominant at the end. This pattern was repeated when the variables were correlated with a number of independent extra-linguistic factors: the occupation, education, and geographic location of the speaker, and most importantly, the ethnic group to which he belonged. The significant differences in the transition rates of these various sub-groups allowed the following statement of a solution to the embedding problem:

The centralization of (aw) was part of a more general change which began with the centralization of (ay). This initial change proceeded from a moderate level of (ay) centralization which was probably a regional recessive trait inherited from the original settlers of the island. The increase of centralization of (ay) began in a rural community of Yankee fisherman descended directly from these original settlers. From there, it spread outward to speakers of the same ethnic group in other occupations and in other communities. The structurally symmetrical variable (aw) began to show similar tendencies early in this process. The change was also adopted by the neighboring Indian group at Gay Head, and a generation later, spread to the large Portuguese group in the more settled sections of the island. In these two ethnic groups, centralization of (aw) overtook and surpassed centralization of (ay).

Figure 19.1 would lead us to believe that the phonetic environment of (aw) was a powerful factor in the initiation of the sound change. Moreover, we can observe that the centralization of (ay) also showed a strong tendency towards phonetic conditioning in Generation Ib, similar to that displayed for (aw) in Generation IIb.[2] However, phonetic restriction on (ay) was overridden in the following generation, so that Generation II shows a uniform norm for (ay) in all phonetic environments. This development would support the view that phonetic conditioning does not play a significant role as an inciting cause of the centralization of (aw), but acts rather as a conditioning factor which may be eliminated by further change.

On Martha's Vineyard, the *evaluation problem* was approached by analyzing a number of clues to the subjective attitudes towards island life which appeared in the course of the interviews. Attitudes toward summer tourists, toward unemployment insurance, toward work on the mainland, toward other occupational and ethnic groups, were correlated with data obtained from community leaders and historical records, and then with the linguistic variables. It appeared that the rise of (aw) was correlated with the successive entry into the main stream of island life of groups that had previously been partially excluded. It was concluded that a social value had been (more or less arbitrarily) associated with the centralization of (ay) and (aw), and that social value could best be expressed as "native status as a Vineyarder." Thus to the extent that an individual felt able to claim and maintain status as a native Vineyarder, he adopted increasing centralization of (ay) and (aw). Sons who had tried to earn a living on the mainland, and afterwards returned to the island

---

[2] This phonetic conditioning is more in the nature of a continuum than that for (aw). The complete data for a speaker of the same age and background as Mr. H. H., Jr. of Fig. 19.1 are given in Labov (1963:289).

developed an even higher degree of centralization than their fathers had used. But to the extent that a Vineyarder abandoned his claim to stay on the island and earn his living there, he also abandoned centralization and returned to the standard uncentralized forms.

The solution to the evaluation problem is a statement of the social significance of the changed form—that is, the function which is the direct equivalent of the meaning of the form in its grammatical function. In the developments described here, the grammatical function of /ay/ and /aw/ has remained constant. It is plain that the non-grammatical (or non-referential) functions which are carried by these phonological elements are the essential factors in the mechanism of the change. This conclusion can be generalized to many other instances of more complex changes in which the net result is a radical change of grammatical function. The sound change observed on Martha's Vineyard did not produce phonemic change, in which units defined by grammatical function were merged or split. But many of the changes in progress that have been observed in New York City did produce such mergers and splits on the level of the bi-unique phoneme.[3] One such change is the raising of (oh), the vowel of *law, talk, off, more,* etc., which will serve to illustrate many aspects of the mechanism of linguistic change not relevant to the simpler example on Martha's Vineyard.

The Raising of (oh) in New York City

It was not possible to make a direct attack upon the transition problem in New York City. Although the records of the *Linguistic Atlas* showed sporadic raising of (oh) at a fairly low level, the *Atlas* informants in New York City were not selected systematically enough so that we could construct a comparable sample in 1963.

Convenience was apparently a greater factor in the selection of *Atlas* informants in New York than on Martha's Vineyard. The great bulk of the New York population was poorly represented in the sample, including the working class and lower middle class. The old-family stock used for *Atlas* interviews represents only a very small fraction of the ethnic composition of the city, at most 1 or 2 percent. Furthermore, an over-all comparison of the usage of this variable by older and younger speakers did not show the clear-cut and regular progression which we saw for (aw) on Martha's Vineyard. It was suspected that the reason for this difficulty was

---

[3] The far-reaching shifts and mergers observed in the long and ingliding vowel system of New York City, to be discussed here, do not affect the morphophonemic system. The detailed distribution of the variables in the process of change appear to provide evidence for the systematic status of the bi-unique phoneme. See Labov (1964a) for discussion.

the greater tendency towards stylistic variation among New Yorkers, and the heterogeneity of the population in terms of socio-economic class and ethnic membership. Therefore it was necessary to attack the embedding problem first, before the transition problem.

The variable (oh) is a part of the system of long and ingliding vowels in the vernacular pattern of New York City speech which is essentially *r*-less: that is, where final and pre-consonantal /r/ does not occur as a consonantal glide. Thus (oh) occurs in the word class of *law, talk, broad, caught, off,* and *more, four, board,* etc. To establish a quantifiable index, five variants were coded as follows:

$$
\begin{array}{ll}
(\text{oh-1}) & [\text{U:}^{\text{a}}] \\
(\text{oh-2}) & [\text{O:}^{\perp}\text{ɔ}^{\text{-ɪə}}] \\
(\text{oh-3}) & [\text{ɔ:}^{\perp\text{ə}}] \\
(\text{oh-4}) & [\text{ɔ:}] \\
(\text{oh-5}) & [\text{ɒ:}]
\end{array}
$$

The codification of these variants can be assisted by the use of some modal reference points. (oh-1) is at the level of the vowel of (r-less) *sure;* (oh-3) is the level of the most common Northern vowel in (r-pronouncing) *or, nor;* (oh-4) at cardinal I.P.A. [ɔ]; (oh-5) at the level of eastern New England *cot.* The (oh) index score was established by taking the numerical average of the variants recorded in any given portion of speech, and multiplying by ten. Thus the consistent use of (oh-2) would give a score of (oh)-20, and a consistent use of (oh-4), a score of (oh)-40.

A method was developed in the New York City study for isolating a range of well-defined contextual styles in the speech of individual informants, and average index scores were determined for each style. A systematic approach to the sampling of a large urban population was utilized, embodying the techniques of survey methodology, and average index scores for various sub-groups of the sample population were determined for each style. The embedding problem was then attacked by correlating the five chief linguistic variables each with each other, and with other elements of the linguistic system, with the level of stylistic variation in which they were recorded, and with the independent variables of socio-economic class (occupation, education and income), sex, ethnic group, and age level. (The embedding problem is treated here as one problem, not two, in accordance with the general logic of this chapter.)

Correlations of (oh) with socio-economic class revealed that the irregular distribution of (oh) in the population as a whole was partly due to the fact that the change had not yet affected all social classes. Figure 19.2 is a style stratification diagram for (oh) in which the transition state of this variable can be seen in synchronic section. The horizontal axis represents the ten socio-economic levels used for this analysis, grouped informally into lower class, working class, lower middle class, and upper

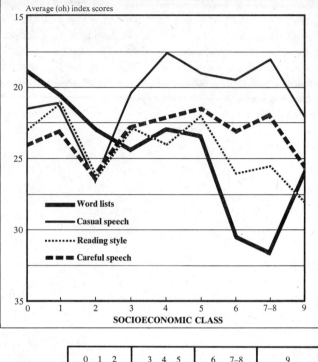

figure 19.2

Style stratification of (oh) for nine socio-economic sub-classes

	0 1 2	3 4 5	6 7–8	9
Socioeconomic class	Lower class	Working class	Lower middle class	Upper middle class
Stylistic stratification	None	Slight	Extreme	Moderate
(oh) in casual speech	Low	High	High	Low

middle class. The vertical axis represents the average (oh) index scores: the lower values of (oh) are at the top, representing the higher, closer vowels, and the higher values of (oh) are at the bottom, indicating more open vowels. The index scores for each socio-economic group are entered on the diagram for each stylistic context, and values for the same style are connected along straight lines.

Figure 19.2 indicates that (oh) is not a significant variable for lower class speakers, who do not use particularly high values of this vowel and show no stylistic stratification at all. Working class speakers show a recent stage in the raising of (oh): very high vowels in casual speech, but otherwise very little stratification in the more formal styles, and little tendency towards the extreme, hypercorrect (oh-4) and (oh-5). But lower middle class speakers show the most developed state of the sound change, with high values in casual speech, and extreme stylistic stratification. Finally, the upper middle class group is more moderate in all respects than the lower middle class, still retaining the pattern of stylistic stratification.

The ethnic group membership of New York City speakers is even more relevant to their use of (oh) than socio-economic class. Figure 19.3 shows the differences between speakers of Jewish and Italian background in the

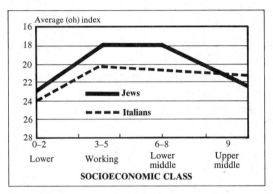

figure 19.3

Class stratification diagram for (oh) by ethnic group in causal speech

treatment of (oh) in casual speech. For all but the upper middle class, the Jewish group uses higher levels of (oh). The Negro group does not show any significant response to the variable (oh), and shows a constant index of performance at a low level. As noted above, the lower class in general is similarly indifferent to (oh). Table 19.2 shows Jewish and Italian ethnic groups only, with the lower class excluded. Table 19.2 shows that both Jewish and Italian speakers have participated in the raising of (oh), but the increase seems to have reached its maximum early for the Jewish group, and later for the Italian group. A separate solution for the transition problem is therefore required for each ethnic group.

The *transition problem* for the Italian group can be seen analyzed in Figure 19.4. The procession of values is not absolutely regular since socio-economic membership, sex, and other factors affect the values; nevertheless, there is a steady upward movement from the oldest speakers on the right to the youngest speakers on the left. Within the present sample of New York City speakers, this is the finest resolution of the transition problem which can be obtained.[4]

---

[4] Figure 19.4 includes Italian informants who refused the original interview, and whose speech patterns were sampled by the television interview, as described in Appendix D of Labov (1966b).

table 19.2

Average (oh) Indexes by Age Level and Ethnic Group in Casual Speech

Age	Jews	Italians
8–19	17	18
20–35	18	18
36–49	17	20
50–59	15	20
60–	25	30

The *embedding problem* for (oh) requires an intricate set of correlations with other elements in the linguistic system, in addition to the extralinguistic correlations exemplified above. We find that (oh) is firmly embedded within the sub-system of long and ingliding vowels, and also related structurally to other vowel sub-systems. Quantitative studies of these relations fall into five sets:

1. There is a strong correlation between the height of (oh) and the height of the corresponding front ingliding vowel (eh) in the word class of *bad, ask, dance,* etc. This variable originated as a raising of /æh/, but

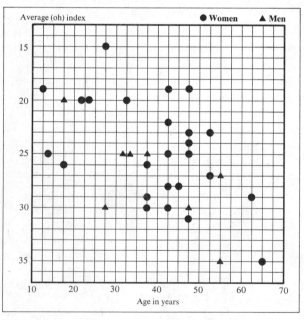

figure 19.4

Distribution of (oh) index scores for Italian subjects by age

early in the evolution of New York City speech it merged with /eh/, the word class of *bare, bared, where,* etc. The relation between (eh) and (oh) is strikingly parallel to that of (ay) and (aw) on Martha's Vineyard, the variable (oh) became specialized in the usage of a particular ethnic group: to the extent that the Italian group shows higher use of (eh) in casual speech, the Jewish group shows higher values of (oh), until the difference is largely resolved in the youngest age level by merger of (eh) and /ih/, (oh) and /uh/.

2. The variable (oh) also has close relations with the higher ingliding vowel /uh/. As we observe higher and higher variants of (oh) in the casual speech of the younger informants, it becomes apparent that a merger of (oh) and /uh/ is imminent. This merger has undoubtedly occurred in the youngest speakers in our sample from the working class and lower middle class. In fact, we have many informants who show the merger even in the most formal styles, in the reading of isolated word lists, and we can conclude *a fortiori* that the merger exists in casual speech. Close study of the variants of their casual speech shows the merger as an accomplished fact: though most listeners who are not conscious of the overlap will hear *beer* as higher than *bear,* it is in fact indistinguishable out of context.

3. There is also a close correlation between (oh) and /ah/, the long tense vowel heard in *guard, father, car,* etc. The variable (ah) represents the choice of back or center options for the subclasses of *hot, heart, hod,* and *hard* (with the last two generally homonymous); lower values of (oh) are correlated with low center positions of the vowels in these word classes. This correlation is independent of socio-economic class or ethnic group. Whereas (oh) is firmly embedded in the socio-linguistic structure of the speech community, /ah/ is not. As a linguistic variable, (ah) seems to be a function only of the height of (oh): a purely internal variable. [The quantitative correlations are given in Chapter 12 of Labov 1966b. The relationship of (oh) and (ah) held even within a single ethnic group.]

4. (oh) is also related to the variable height of the vowel in *boy, coil,* etc., (oy) in the front upgliding system. The height of the vowels in *coil* and *call* seem to vary directly together in casual speech, but only (oh) is corrected to lower values in more formal styles. (oh) carries the major burden of social significance, and is the focus of non-systematic pressure from above.

5. Finally, we find that (oh) and (oy) are jointly correlated with the variable (ay), which represents the backing or fronting of the first element of the diphthong in *my, why, side,* etc. High values of (oh) and (oy) are correlated with back values of (ay), and low values of (oh) and (oy) with low center values of (ay).

Beyond these immediate correlations, there are more indirect, diffuse relations with such variables as (aw) and /ih/, through which (oh) is connected with all of the other vowels in the vernacular system of New York

City speech. This is not the place to pursue the full details of this intricate set of structural correlations within the linguistic system; however, it should be apparent that a full solution to the embedding problem will reveal the ways in which the internal relations of linguistic elements determine the direction of sound change, in a manner which provides empirical confirmation for the view of linguistic structure expressed by Martinet (1955). (See the Appendix.) We can summarize the most important relations that center about (oh) in the following notation, which defines the structural units on the left hand side of the equations as linguistic variables:

$$(oh) = f_1(St, C, E, A, Sx, (eh)) \qquad St = Style$$
$$(ah) = f_2((oh)) \qquad\qquad\qquad\quad C = \text{Socio-economic class}$$
$$(oy) = f_3((oh)) \qquad\qquad\qquad\quad E = \text{Ethnic group}$$
$$(ay) = f_1((ah)) = f_4(f_2((oh))) \qquad A = \text{Age level}$$
$$(ay) = f_5((oy)) = f_5(f_3((oh))) \qquad Sx = Sex$$

In New York City, the *evaluation problem* was approached more directly than on Martha's Vineyard. The unconscious subjective reactions of the informants to each of the variables were determined. The details of this method have been presented elsewhere.[5] In general, we can say that the reliability of the tests can be measured by the high degree of uniformity showed by New Yorkers in contrast to the scattered results from those raised outside of New York City.

The subjective reaction responses to (oh) give us a clear view of the social significance of the variable, as shown in Table 19.3. The majority of informants responded to the test in a way consistent with the stigmatized status of high (oh).[6] Just as the solution to the embedding problem showed no significant stylistic response to (oh) for lower class speakers, here we find that lower class speakers showed no significant (oh)-negative response. The other groups showed (oh)-negative response in proportion to the average height of (oh) used in their own casual speech, and to the degree of stylistic stratification in their speech patterns. This result illustrates a principle which holds quite generally in New York City: that those who used the highest percentage of a stigmatized form in casual speech were the most sensitive in stigmatizing it in the speech of others. Thus the lower middle class speakers between the ages of 20 and 39, who use the highest values of (oh) in their own casual speech, show 100%

[5] In addition to Chapter XI of Labov (1966b), the most detailed presentation of this method is in "Subjective Dimensions of a Linguistic Change in Progress," a paper given before the Linguistic Society of America in Chicago, December, 1963.

[6] The (oh)-negative response shown here consisted of rating three speakers lower on a scale of job suitability when they pronounced sentences with high, close (oh) vowels, as compared to sentences with no significant variables. Those making the ratings were unaware that they were rating the same speakers.

table 19.3

Percentage of (oh)-Negative Response by Socio-economic Class and Age Level

Age Level	Lower Class [SEC 0-2]	Working Class [SEC 3-4]	Lower Middle Class [SEC 5-8]	Upper Middle Class [SEC 9]
20–39	25	80	100	60
40–59	18	60	62	57
60–	33	[00]	—	—

		N		
4	10	11	5	
11	15	13	7	
6	1	—	—	

(oh)-negative response. Similarly, we find that the percentages of (oh)-negative response among Jewish and Italian speakers is proportionate to the height of (oh) in casual speech.

This solution to the evaluation problem can hardly be called satisfactory. It is not clear why a group of speakers should adopt more and more extreme forms of a speech sound which they themselves stigmatize as bad speech. (Many subjects reacted to the test with violent and unrealistic ratings; as, for example, marking a person who used high vowels for *coffee* and *chocolate* as not even speaking well enough to hold a factory job.) Some further explanation must be given.

First of all, it has become clear that very few speakers realize that they use the stigmatized form themselves. They hear themselves as using the prestige forms which occur sporadically in their careful speech and in their reading of isolated word lists. Secondly, the subjective responses tapped by our test are only the overt values—those which conform to the value systems of the dominant middle class group. There are surely other values, at a deeper level of consciousness, which reinforce the vernacular speech forms of New York City. We have not yet measured these more obscure forms systematically, but through anecdotal evidence we can be sure of their existence—values which cluster about the themes of group identification, masculinity, friendship ties, and so on.

In the case of the alternate preference of Jewish and Italian ethnic groups for (oh) and (eh), we can put forward a reasonable suggestion based upon the mechanism of hypercorrection. *Hypercorrection* is used here not to indicate the sporadic and irregular treatment of a word class but the movement of an entire word class beyond the target point set by the prestige model. This mechanism is evident on Martha's Vineyard, as well as in New York. The influence of the Yiddish sub-stratum leads to a loss of the distinction between low back rounded and unrounded vowels in first-generation Jewish speakers of English, so that *cup* and *coffee* have the same vowel. In second-generation speakers of Jewish descent, the reaction against this tendency leads to a hypercorrect exaggeration of the distinction, so that (oh) becomes raised, tense, and over-rounded. A parallel argument applies to Italian speakers. This suggestion is all the more plausible since hypercorrection has been demonstrated to be an important mechanism of linguistic change in a variety of circumstances. (I am indebted to Marvin Herzog for this suggestion.)

The Mechanism of Sound Change

Solutions to the transition, embedding, and evaluation problems have been illustrated by two examples, drawn from Martha's Vineyard and New York City. It is possible to apply the results of our work with these and other variables to a provisional answer to the question: what is the mechanism by which sound change proceeds? The following outline is based upon analysis of twelve sound changes: three on rural Martha's Vineyard, and nine in urban New York City. The stages suggested here are necessarily ordered in approximately the manner listed, but there are some re-arrangements and permutations in the data observed.

1. The sound changes usually originated with a restricted sub-group of the speech community, at a time when the separate identity of this group had been weakened by internal or external pressures. The linguistic form which began to shift was often a marker of regional status with an irregular distribution within the community. At this stage, the form is an undefined linguistic variable.

2. The changes began as generalizations of the linguistic form to all members of the sub-group; we may refer to this stage as *change from below*, that is, below the level of social awareness. The variable shows no pattern of stylistic variation in the speech of those who use it, affecting all items in a given word class. The linguistic variable is an *indicator*, defined as a function of group membership.

3. Succeeding generations of speakers within the same subgroup, responding to the same social pressures, carried the linguistic variable further along the process of change, beyond the model set by their parents. We may refer to this stage as *hypercorrection from below*. The variable is now defined as a function of group membership and age level.

4. To the extent that the values of the original sub-group were adopted by other groups in the speech community, the sound change with its associated value of group membership spread to these adopting groups. The function of group membership is now re-defined in successive stages.

5. The limits of the spread of the sound change were the limits of the

speech community, defined as a group with a common set of normative values in regard to language.

6. As the sound change with its associated values reached the limits of its expansion, the linguistic variable became one of the norms which defined the speech community, and all members of the speech community reacted in a uniform manner to its use (without necessarily being aware of it). The variable is now a *marker,* and begins to show stylistic variation.

7. The movement of the linguistic variable within the linguistic system always led to readjustments in the distribution of other elements within phonological space.

8. The structural readjustments led to further sound changes which were associated with the original change. However, other subgroups which entered the speech community in the interim adopted the older sound change as stage 1. This *re-cycling* stage appears to be the primary source for the continual origination of new changes. In the following development, the second sound change may be carried by the new group beyond the level of the first change.

(Stages 1–8 dealt with *change from below;* stages 9–13 concern *change from above.*)

9. If the group in which the change originated was not the highest status group in the speech community, members of the highest status group eventually stigmatized the changed form through their control of various institutions of the communication network.

10. This stigmatization initiated *change from above,* a sporadic and irregular correction of the changed forms towards the model of the highest status group—that is, the *prestige model.* This prestige model is now the pattern which speakers hear themselves using: it governs the audio-monitoring of the speech signal. The linguistic variable now shows regular stylistic stratification as well as social stratification, as the motor-controlled model of casual speech competes with the audio-monitored model of more careful styles.

11. If the prestige model of the highest status group does not correspond to a form used by the other groups in some word class, the other groups will show a second type of *hypercorrection:* shifting their careful speech to a form further from the changed form than the target set by the prestige group. We may call this state *hypercorrection from above.*

12. Under extreme stigmatization, a form may become the overt topic of social comment, and may eventually disappear. It is thus a *stereotype,* which may become increasingly divorced from the forms which are actually used in speech.

13. If the change originated in the highest status group of the community, it became a prestige model for all members of the speech community. The changed form was then adopted in more careful forms of

speech by all other groups in proportion to their contact with users of the prestige model, and to a lesser extent, in casual speech.[7]

Many of the stages in the mechanism of sound change outlined here are exemplified in the two detailed examples given above. The centralization of (aw) on Martha's Vineyard did not provide the evidence to decide this question. There is no doubt, however, that the centralization of (aw) is a secondary change, produced by the re-cycling process when the centralization of (ay) reached stage 8.

To place the raising of (oh) in this outline, it is necessary to consider briefly the evolution of the New York City vowel system as a whole. The first step in the historical record is the raising of (eh). We have reason to believe that the merger of /æh/ with /eh/ began in the last quarter of the nineteenth century (see Babbitt 1896). The upward movement of the linguistic variable (eh) continued beyond this merger, leading to the current cumulative merger of /eh/ with /ih/ among most younger New Yorkers. For the entire community, (eh) is subject to the full force of correction from above: the change has reached stage 11, so that the linguistic variable is defined by co-variation with social class, ethnic membership, age level, and contextual style. The raising of (oh) was the first re-cycling process which began when (eh) reached stage 8. The major burden of the raising of (oh) has been carried by the Jewish ethnic group; the extreme upward social mobility of this group has led to a special sensitivity to (oh) in the lower middle class. Thus the merger of /oh/ and /uh/ has gone quite quickly, and (oh) has reached stage 11 for the lower middle class; yet it has hardly touched stage 1 for the lower class.

The third stage in the re-cycling process occurred when (oh) reached stage 8. The structural re-adjustments which took place were complex: (oy) and (ah) were closely associated with (oh), and were defined as linguistic variables only by their co-variation with (oh). Thus the raising of (oy) and the backing of (ah) were determined by internal, structural factors. Change from above is exerted upon (oh), but not upon (oy). In careful speech, a New Yorker might say [Its ɒːl tɪn fUːɫl], *It's all tin foil*. But the shift of (ah) and (oy) have in turn led to a shift of (ay), and this process has apparently begun a third re-cycling. Indeed, the backing of (ay) has reached stage 8 itself, and produced an associated fourth recycling, the fronting of (aw). There are indications that (ay) has evolved to stage 9, with the beginning of overt correction from above, although (aw) has reached only stage 4 or 5 (for details, see Labov 1966b, Chapter 12).

It is evident that the type of structural re-adjustments that have been considered here require a linguistic theory which preserves the geometry

---

[7] We find some support in these observations for the idea that people do not borrow much from broadcast media or from other remote sources, but rather from those who are at the most one or two removes from them in age or social distance.

of phonological space. The structural relations found here are strikingly parallel to those established by Moulton (1962) in his study of co-variation of mid and low vowels in Swiss German dialects. The techniques, the area, the societies studied are quite different, and the coincidence of results provides strong empirical evidence for the view of phonological structure advanced by Martinet. Both studies show strong evidence for co-variation of low vowels along the front-to-back dimension with back vowels along the dimension of height. Distinctive feature theory, in the form utilized by Halle (1962), dissolves the geometry of phonological space into a set of independent dimensions. Even if a phonetic form of distinctive features is provided with scalar values, distinctive feature theory has no rationale for co-variation of grave and acute with compact and diffuse. Nevertheless, the purely internal equilibria projected by Martinet do not provide a coherent theory of the mechanism of sound change. In the scheme that has been outlined here, they are only part of a more comprehensive process, embedded in the sociolinguistic structure of the community.

Conclusion

This discussion has focused on the theme that internal, structural pressures and sociolinguistic pressure act in systematic alternation in the mechanism of linguistic change. It can no longer be seriously argued that the linguist must limit his explanations of change to the mutual influences of linguistic elements defined by cognitive function. Nor can it be argued that a changing linguistic system is autonomous in any serious sense. Here I have attempted to carry the argument beyond the mere cataloguing of possibilities by introducing a large body of evidence on sound changes observed in progress. On the basis of this evidence, we can make the stronger claim that it is not possible to complete an analysis of structural relations within a linguistic system, and then turn to external relations. The re-cycling process outlined here suggests the kind of answer we can make to the basic questions of the inciting causes of linguistic change, and the adaptive functions of change, as well as the mechanism by which change proceeds. We can expect that further investigations will modify the outline given here, but that data from the speech community will continue to form an essential part in the analysis of linguistic change.

Discussion

The following excerpt from the discussion of Mr. Labov's paper reprinted in Kreidler (1965) may clarify the problem of linguistic determinants of sound change:

MR. GUMPERZ: I have another question for Professor Labov. You say that your studies show a connection between the movement of /ay/ and /oy/. Is there any reason why you could predict that /ey/ will not be affected?

MR. LABOV: In terms of the concept of phonological space I have developed here, nothing could be more clear than that /ey/ would not rise. First, there is a system of long vowels and/or centering diphthongs, which originally were related like this:

$$ \begin{array}{cc} \text{ih} & \text{uh} \\ \text{eh} & \text{oh} \\ & \text{ah} \end{array} $$

In the community investigated, the high-front and mid-front have merged, and the high-back and mid-back have merged, forming a triangular system:

$$ \begin{array}{cc} [\text{I:}^{\text{ə}}]\text{eh} & \text{oh}[\text{U:}^{\text{ə}}] \\ & \text{ah} \end{array} $$

Then, there is a system of forward-upgliding diphthongs, originally like this:

$$ \begin{array}{cc} \text{iy} & \\ \text{ey} & \text{oy} \\ & \text{ay} \end{array} $$

There is a hole in the high-back position since there is no /uy/ (very few New Yorkers say *buoy* or [*chop*] *suey* as one syllable). As /oy/ moves upward to fill the hole, /ay/ moves to the back. The result is that a skewed system becomes perfectly symmetrical:

$$ \begin{array}{cc} \text{iy} & \text{oy}[\text{U}^{\text{I}}] \\ \text{ey} & \text{ay}[\alpha^{\text{I}}] \end{array} $$

The pronunciation [mɔ′ bu′] 'my boy' is the most extreme form, but it shows the direction in which the change is headed. This is repeated in the system of backward-upgliding diphthongs, in which we have:

$$ \begin{array}{cc} \text{iw} & \text{uw} \\ & \text{ow} \\ & \text{aw} \end{array} $$

Our theory of phonological space would predict that /aw/ would move forward to [æ^{U}] paralleling the movement of /ay/ to [α^{I}]. And this, in fact, is what happens — there is detailed quantitative evidence to show that to the extent that /ay/ moves to the back, /aw/ moves to the front, yielding:

$$ \begin{array}{cc} \text{iw} & \text{uw} \\ \text{aw} & \text{ow} \end{array} $$

There is no reason for /ey/ to rise, because it is now structurally parallel to /ay/, not /oy/. I think we have here a remarkable demonstration of the internal structural pressures that Martinet has discussed in his *Economie*.[8]

[8] Andre Martinet, *Économie des changements phonétiques* (1955).

appendix 1
Background Reading

1. Predecessors in general linguistics
2. General linguistics: current trends
3. Historical linguistics
4. Dialectology and social dialectology
5. Methods of fieldwork and description
6. Sociological perspective
7. A short list of principal collections, monographs and journals

1. Predecessors in General Linguistics

Modern sociolinguistics is in many ways a renewal of long-standing interests. The three great American contributors to general linguistics in the first half of the century are also the three men of most importance in shaping interests relevant to the study of language as an aspect of social life: Franz Boas, Edward Sapir, and Leonard Bloomfield. The major statement by Boas is his "Introduction" to the *Handbook of American Indian Languages* (Bulletin of the Bureau of American Ethnology 40, Part 1) (Washington, D.C.: 1911). Sapir's *Language* (New York: Harcourt, Brace, 1921) is still read for its insights as to the relation of language to culture, as are his seminal essays, collected in D. G. Mandelbaum (ed.), *Selected writings of Edward Sapir* (Berkeley: University of California Press, 1949). Bloomfield's *Language* (New York: Holt, Rinehart and Winston, Inc., 1933) was the standard text for a generation, establishing orientations to the speech community and its description, and is still read for its masterful presentation of historical linguistics. On these pioneers, see discussion and bibliography in Hymes (ed.), *Language in culture and society* (New York: Harper & Row, 1964); a more detailed analysis of the development of American work with regard to a linguistic approach to social life is given in Hymes, "Linguistic method of ethnography," in P. L. Garvin (ed.), *Method and theory in linguistics* (The Hague: Mouton, 1970). On the Sapir tradition, see Hymes, "Morris Swadesh and the first Yale School" in Swadesh, *Origin and diversification of languages* (Chicago: Aldine, 1971).

An early classic by a Danish scholar is Otto Jespersen, *Mankind, nation and the individual from a linguistic point of view* (Oslo, 1925; now reprinted, Bloomington: Indiana University Press, 1964). In England the central earlier figures were Bronislaw Malinowski, especially his *Coral gardens and their magic; Part 2: The language of gardening* (London: Allen Unwin, 1935; reprinted, Bloomington: Indiana University Press, 1968), and J. R. Firth. For Firth's views, see his *Papers in linguistics 1934-1951* (London: Oxford University Press, 1957) and F. R. Palmer (ed.) *Selected papers 1952-1959* (Bloomington: Indiana University Press, 1969). In France, Antoine Meillet took a social point of view in major writings, such as the famous essay, "Comme les mots changent leur sens," *L'année sociologique* (1905-1906). Meillet and Ferdinand de Saussure (*Cours de linguis-*

tique generale (Paris: Payot, 1916), were influenced by the sociological perspective of Émile Durkheim, whose own classic work, *Elementary forms of religious life* (Paris: 1912; English translation, London: G. Allen, 1915; New York: The Free Press, 1947), has much about the social role of language.

A major force for a social point of view in linguistics has been the Prague School; see selections in P. Garvin (ed.), *A Prague school reader in aesthetics, literary structure and style* (Washington, D.C.: Georgetown University Press, 1969), and Josef Vachek (ed.), *A Prague school reader in linguistics* (Bloomington: Indiana University Press, 1964). See also a special number of the current *Travaux Linguistique de Prague* 3 (1971), devoted to an assessment of the prewar school.

2. General Linguistics: Current Trends

H. A. Gleason, Jr., *An introduction to descriptive linguistics* (New York: Holt, Rinehart and Winston, Inc., 1961) gives a still useful introduction to American descriptive practice in the recent period. J. Greenberg, *Anthropological Linguistics* (New York: Random House, 1968) provides a nonpartisan account of descriptive and historical linguistics from a structural standpoint. The dominant trend in linguistic analysis today of course is tranformational generative grammar in the form given it by Noam Chomsky. Chomsky's first monograph, *Syntactic structures* (The Hague: Mouton, 1957) remains essential reading; his more recent views stem from the revised model presented in *Aspects of the theory of syntax* (Cambridge, Mass.: MIT Press, 1965). A general introduction to Chomsky's development of syntactic theory and to its larger implications is found in J. Lyons, *Noam Chomsky* (New York: Viking, 1970). Lyons' *Introduction to theoretical linguistics* (Cambridge: Cambridge University Press, 1968) is probably the best general introduction to contemporary grammatical theory. As a practical introduction to technical transformational generative grammar, note R. A. Jacobs and P. S. Rosenbaum, *English transformational grammer* (Waltham, Mass.: Blaisdell, 1968).

A younger group of linguists have developed an alternative perspective within the Chomskyan framework. This approach, commonly called "generative semantics," is well illustrated in E. Bach and R. Hamms (eds.), *Universals in linguistic theory* (New York: Holt, Rinehart and Winston, Inc., 1968). An excellent study, presenting Chomsky's *Aspects* model more clearly than Chomsky, and then showing cogently the lines of criticism that lead to development of a semantic approach, is P. Seuren, *Operators and nuclei* (Cambridge: Cambridge University Press, 1969).

Notice that the scope of the term "linguistic theory" has come to be narrowed in practice to "theory of grammar"; works concerned with linguistic theory in this sense have by no means the scope and relevance of the books on language by Sapir and Bloomfield.

A critical analysis, uniting a social standpoint with transformational generative grammar, has been developed by W. Labov. See especially two major articles, "The study of language in its social context," *Studium Generale* 23:30–87 (1970), and "The notion of 'system' in creole studies," in D. Hymes (ed.), *Pidginization and creolization of languages* (Cambridge: Cambridge University Press, 1971).

An approach generically influenced by the Firthian concern with social meaning is being developed in England by M. A. K. Halliday. His work has also been influenced by the continuing concern of Prague School linguistics with functional perspective on syntax. See Halliday's "Language structure and language function," in J. Lyons (ed.), *New horizons in linguistics* (Baltimore: Penguin Books, 1970), a collection with a number of other useful articles on many aspects of the study of language.

The school of linguistic analysis developed by Kenneth L. Pike, known as tagmemics, has an essentially sociolinguistic foundation; see Pike, *Language in relation to a unified theory of the structure of human behavior* (The Hague: Mouton, 1967). (The concern of tagmemics with functional aspects of syntactic units is taken up into the formalization developed by Seuren (see above).)

The lines of work inspired by Halliday and Pike both are being developed in the analysis of texts and discourse in such a way as to make these larger contexts of linguistic units relevant to their grammatical analysis. In general, models of grammar which start from semantic rather than syntactic function are the more realistic and relevant to sociolinguistics; and models whose semantics include social as well as referential meaning are *a fortiori* most realistic and relevant.

The approach being developed by Sydney Lamb takes as its premise that language in the mind is in the form of a network rather than a set of rules (as modelled in transformational grammar); Lamb applies the approach of his stratificational analysis to all aspects of meaning and culture. See his *Outline of stratificational grammar* (Washington, D.C.: Georgetown University Press, 1966).

A broad perspective on linguistics in relation to social and humanistic concerns continues to be maintained by an eminent leader of the prewar Prague School, Roman Jakobson, who has had a special impact on American linguistics through residence in the United States since early in the Second World War. Jakobson's development of a functional perspective can be seen in a major essay, "Linguistics and poetics," in T. A. Sebeok (ed.), *Style in language* (Cambridge, Mass.: MIT Press, 1960). Jakobson's comprehensive view of linguistic theory is set forth in "Linguistics in its relation to other sciences," *Actes du Xe Congres International des Linguistes* (Bucharest: 1969). A cognate view of the scope of general linguistics is presented in Hymes, "Linguistics—the field," *International Encyclopedia of Social Sciences* (New York: Macmillan, 1968).

3. Historical Linguistics

Two standard works are W. P. Lehmann, *Historical linguistics; an introduction* (New York: Holt, Rinehart and Winston, Inc., 1962) and H. M. Hoenigswald, *Language change and linguistic reconstruction* (Chicago: University of Chicago Press, 1960), an advanced and in some respects definitive work. The second part of Bloomfield's *Language* is still useful as an introduction and has been reissued separately for this purpose as *Language history* (New York: Holt, Rinehart and Winston, Inc., 1966).

The development of a sociolinguistic perspective may have the effect of restoring the study of language change to the central place in linguistic theory which it once enjoyed. Such possibilities are broached in the efforts toward a reconstruction of the explanation of change in language by U. Weinreich, W. Labov, and M. Herzog, "Empirical foundations for a theory of language change," in W. P. Lehmann and Y. Malkiel (eds.), *Directions for historical linguistics: a symposium* (Austin: University of Texas Press, 1968), and in the character and scope of the study of the processes of standardization, pidginization and creolization. For these last see P. S. Ray, *Language standardization* (The Hague: Mouton, 1963); J. Fishman, C. Ferguson and J. Das Gupta (eds.), *Language problems of developing nations* (New York: Wiley, 1968) and D. Hymes (ed.), *Pidginization and creolization of languages* (Cambridge: Cambridge University Press, 1971).

A unified approach to language change will of necessity integrate historical linguistics (conceived as study of change as internal to a language) with what is often segregated as language history (conceived as factors external to a language). A major question in language history is maintenance and loss of language; see J. Fishman, "Language maintenance and language shift as a field of inquiry," *Linguistics* 9:32–70 (1964) and his monograph, *Language loyalty in the United States* (The Hague: Mouton, 1966). On the related problems of language planning and language politics, see two important recent volumes, E. Haugen, *Language conflict and language planning* (Cambridge, Mass.: Harvard University Press, 1966), which gives a detailed analysis of the Norwegian case, and J. Das Gupta, *Language politics and language planning in modern India* (Berkeley: University of California Press, 1970), in which the pressure-group theory of political science is applied.

For the recent revival of a long-term evolutionary perspective on language change, see B. Berlin and P. Kay, *Basic color terms* (Berkeley: University of California Press, 1970), and M. Swadesh, *Origin and diversification of languages* (ed. J. Sherzer) (Chicago: Aldine, 1971).

4. Dialectology and Social Dialectology

S. Pop, *La dialectologie. Apercu historique et methodes d'enquetes linguistiques* (Louvain, 1950) is the standard reference for earlier work. H. Kurath, *Handbook of the linguistic geography of New England* (Washington, D.C.: American Council of Learned Societies, 1939) provides an excellent concise introduction to the development and practice of standard European dialectology with reference to its application in the United States. A. MacIntosh, *Introduction to a survey of Scottish dialects* (Edinburgh: Thomas Nelson, 1952) provides a more modern, structurally-oriented introduction, including attention to stylistic alternation between dialects and standard languages. The major study in modern urban dialectology, essentially redefining the entire subject, is W. Labov, *The social stratification of English in New York City* (Washington, D.C.: Center for Applied Linguistics, 1966). Whereas earlier dialectology had focussed on differentiation of dialects, Labov develops a methodology for comprehending the dominant phenomenon of modern life, reintegration of diverse dialects within a complex speech community.

The sociolinguistic character of intimate contact and diffusion among language varieties is given fundamental treatment in U. Weinreich's *Languages in contact* (New York: Linguistic Circle of New York, 1953; reprinted, The Hague: Mouton).

5. Methods of Fieldwork and Description.

Earlier works in descriptive linguistics retain their usefulness for sociolinguistics, because of their attention to the actual problems of observation, recording and description of speech. See K. L. Pike, *Phonemics* (Ann Arbor: University of Michigan Press, 1947) and E. A. Nida, *Morphology* (Ann Arbor: University of Michigan Press, 1949). W. Samarin, *Field linguistics: a guide to linguistic field work* (New York: Holt, Rinehart and Winston, Inc., 1967) is the basic introduction to elicitation and analytic procedure. W. Smalley, *Manual of articulatory phonetics,* rev. ed. (Tarrytown, N.Y.: Practical Anthropology, 1968) provides the best introduction to the mastery and use of phonetic transcription.

Sociolinguistic description must extend to whatever features of verbal communication have conventional social meaning. The problems of description of paralinguistic aspects of speech, including intonation, are dealt with by D. Crystal, *Prosodic systems and intonation in English* (Cambridge: Cambridge University Press, 1968) and "Prosodic and paralinguistic correlates of social categories," in E. Ardener (ed.), *Social anthropology and language* (ASA Monographs 10) (London: Tavistock, 1971). The related problems of description of gesture and body motion are treated from an anthropological perspective by R. Birdwhistell, *Kinesics and context* (Philadelphia: University of Pennsylvania Press, 1970); a different system of analysis is developed by P. Ekman and W. Friesen, "The repertoire of non-verbal behavior: categories, origins, usage and coding," *Semiotica* 1:49–98 (1969).

Paralinguistics and kinesics have together played an important part in the development of the general study of communicative codes; see T. Sebeok, A. Hayes and M. C. Bateson (eds.), *Approaches to semiotics* (The Hague: Mouton, 1964). E. T. Hall, *The silent language* (New York: Doubleday, 1959) is a challenging introduction to the significance of nonverbal phenomena. For a generalized structuralist approach to semiotic phenomena, see R. Barthes, *Elements of semiology* (London: Jonathan Cape, 1969). Since 1968, see the journal *Semiotica* and its associated series of monographs.

Many aspects of sociolinguistic description intersect problems of stylistics. See the historical introduction by P. Guiraud, *La stylistique* (Que Sais-je, 646) (Paris: Presses Universitaires de France, 1961); the report of a conference in T. A. Sebeok (ed.), *Style in language* (Cambridge, Mass.: MIT Press, 1960); the recent collection by S. Chatman and S. Levin (eds.), *Essays on the language of literature* (Boston: Houghton Mifflin, 1967); and since 1967, the journal *Language and Style*. A close relation also exists between sociolinguistics and work under the heading of rhetoric; *cf.* M. Steinmann, Jr. (ed.), *New rhetorics* (New York: Scribners, 1967). Not to be neglected here is the seminal influence of Kenneth Burke, whose *Philosophy of literary form* (Baton Rouge: Louisiana State University Press, 1941) *Grammar of motives* (Englewood Cliffs, N.J.: Prentice-Hall, 1945) and *Rhetoric of motives* (Englewood Cliffs, N.J.: Prentice-Hall, 1950) have been variously reprinted and have influenced many students of the workings of language. For an overview, see Burke's article "Dramatism," in the *International Encyclopedia of the Social Sciences* (New York: Macmillan, 1968).

Philosophical interest in the analysis of speech acts intersects sociolinguistic problems also. The seminal work is J. L. Austin, *How to do things with words* (Cambridge, Mass.: Harvard University Press, 1962). The philosophical significance of speech acts is treated in an important book, *Speech acts* (Cambridge: Cambridge University Press, 1969), by John Searle, who is currently developing a new general classification; *cf.* also Q. Skinner, "On performing and explaining linguistic actions," *The Philosophical Quarterly 21(82):1–21 (1971)* for an analysis of philosophical issues that affect sociolinguistic explanation.

Two special publications of the American Anthropological Association present a broad picture of anthropological interests and contributions to the ethnographic analysis of meaning: A. K. Romney and R. G. D'Andrade (eds.), *Transcultural studies in cognition* (Washington, D.C., 1964) and E. A. Hammel (ed.), *Formal semantic analysis* (Washington, D.C., 1965). Representative basic papers are collected in S. Tyler (ed.), *Cognitive anthropology* (New York: Holt, Rinehart and Winston, Inc., 1969). R. Burling, *Man's many voices* (New York: Holt, Rinehart and Winston, Inc., 1970) is an introduction to this field as well as to several other areas of sociolinguistics. A sociolinguistic perspective on ethnographic semantics and cognitive anthropology is sketched in Hymes, "A perspective for linguistic anthropology," in S. Tax (ed.), *Horizons in anthropology* (Chicago: Aldine, 1964) and "Two types of linguistic relativity," in W. Bright (ed.) *Sociolinguistics* (The Hague: Mouton, 1966).

The contributions of folkloristic materials to the analysis of meaning in texts and events have experienced a renascence in the work of C. Lévi-Strauss on myth and of Victor Turner and Mary Douglas on ritual. E. Leach, *Lévi-Strauss* (New York: Viking Press, 1970) is a critical introduction to Lévi-Strauss' approach; for Lévi-Strauss' own work, see the series *Mythologiques,* beginning with *The raw and the cooked* (New York: Harper & Row, 1968). On ritual, see V. Turner, *The ritual process* (Ithaca, N.Y.: Cornell University Press, 1967) and Mary Douglas, *Purity and danger* (London: Penguin Press, 1968) and *Natural symbols* (New York: Pantheon, 1970), in the latter of which use is made of Bernstein's sociolinguistic categories. A general series in anthropological analysis of symbolism has been launched through Cornell University Press under Turner's editorship. On the analysis of a specific genre of event, *cf.* J. Peacock, *Rites of modernization* (Chicago: University of Chicago Press, 1968). For developments within folklore proper, *cf.* Americo Paredes and Richard Bauman (eds.), *Towards new perspectives in folklore* (Austin: University of Texas Press, 1971; also, *Journal of American Folklore* 84(1) (1971), and K. Goldstein, special editor, "Folklore and communication," in *Semiotica* 5 (1972, in press). See also the major study by A. Lomax, *Folk song style and culture* (Washington, D.C.: American Association for the Advancement of Science, 1968), which unites textual detail and event structure, and T. Kochman, *Language and expressive role behavior in the black inner city* (in preparation), showing application of a folkloristic perspective to sociolinguistic material.

Guides to ethnographic research oriented toward speech include, first of all, D. Slobin (ed.), *A field manual for cross-cultural study of the acquisition of communicative competence* (Berkeley: ASUC Bookstore, 1967), comprising elicitation procedures for a number of aspects of language acquisition. See also D. Hymes, R. Darnell, and J. Sherzer, *A guide to the field study of speech use* (New York: Holt, Rinehart and Winston, Inc., in preparation). J. Flavell *et al., The development of communication and role-taking skills in children* (New York: Wiley, 1968) provides many useful examples of situations for eliciting role-taking and role-switching behavior. R. G. Barker and H. F. Wright, *Midwest and its children* (New York: Harper & Row, 1954) remains an unrivalled source of insight into the observation of behavior in relation to community settings. Aspects of ethnographic method are discussed by Frake, Metzer, Conklin, and others in Tyler, *Cognitive anthropology* (cited above). See also M. Freilich, (ed.), *Marginal natives* (New York: Harper & Row, 1970) and A. Epstein (ed.), *The craft of social anthropology* (London: Tavistock, 1967). A book in an ethnographic spirit is E. J. Webb, D. T. Campbell, R. D. Schwartz, and L. Sechrest, *Unobtrusive measures* (Chicago: Rand McNally, 1966).

C. A. Ferguson, *Language structure and language use* (Palo Alto, Calif.: Stanford University Press, 1971) contains articles on problems of sociolinguistic description and measurement by a pioneer in the field. J. Rubin, *National bilingualism in Paraguay* (The Hague: Mouton, 1968) shows the use of a survey and questionnaire method in a community and at a national level. Major aspects of survey and related methods of description are treated in papers in J. Fishman (ed.), *Advances in the sociology of language* (The Hague: Mouton, 1971). W. Labov, *The social stratification of English in New York City* offers many insights into the process of obtaining socially relevant and valid speech; see also the methodological observations in his "The study of language in its social context," *Studium Generale* 23: 30–87 (1970) and "Some principles of linguistic methodology," *Language in society* 1 (1972, in press). Problems of fieldwork are also discussed in R. Shuy, W. Wolfram and W. K. Riley, *Field techniques in an urban language study* (Washington, D.C.: Center for Applied Linguistics, 1968).

6. Sociological Perspective

A useful general introduction to social anthropology is R. Firth, *Elements of social organization* (Boston: Beacon Press, 1961 (2d ed.)). The social theory relevant to sociolinguistics depends heavily on notions of diversity developed in the work of E. R. Leach, *Political systems of highland Burma* (Cambridge, Mass.: Harvard University Press, 1954) and A. F. C. Wallace, *Culture and personality* (New York: Random House, 1961; 2d ed., 1970). A pungent review of present social theory is provided by P. S. Cohen, *Modern social theory* (London: Heinemann, 1968). Two contrastive perspectives in cultural anthropology are developed cogently by M. Harris, *The rise of anthropological theory* (New York: Crowell, 1968) and W. H. Goodenough, *Method in cultural anthropology* (Chicago: Aldine, 1970). Basic to the analysis of linguistic interaction is the perspective developed in the writings of E. Goffman, such as *Presentation of self in everyday life* (New York: Doubleday, 1959) and *Behavior in public places* (New York: Free Press, 1963), as to the underlying structure of social gatherings; so also the perspective developed by F. Barth in *Models of social organization* (London: Royal Anthropological Institute, Occasional Paper 23, 1966), and in Barth (ed.), *Ethnic groups and boundaries: the social organization of culture difference* (London: Allen & Unwin, 1969), as to the larger social processes the condition and arise from interaction. A recent collection concerned with sociological approaches to interaction is H. P. Blumer (ed.), *Symbolic interaction* (Englewood Cliffs, N.J.: Prentice-Hall, 1969). G. Bateson deals with some of the basic concepts of communication relevant to sociolinguistics in his contribution in D. D. Jackson (ed.), *Communication, family and marriage* (Palo Alto, Calif.: Science and Behavior Books, 1968); *cf.* also J. Ruesch and G. Bateson, *Communication: the social matrix of psychiatry* (New York: Norton, 1951).

A major sociological trend interacting with sociolinguistics is ethnomethodology. See H. Garfinkel, *Studies in ethnomethodology* (Englewood Cliffs, N.J.: Prentice-Hall, 1967); J. Douglas (ed.), *Understanding everyday life* (Chicago: Aldine, 1971); H. P. Dreitzel (ed.), *Recent sociology no. 2: patterns of communicative behavior* (New York: Macmillan, 1970), M. Speier and R. Turner (eds.), *Studies in socialization* (New York: Basic Books, 1971), and H. Garfinkel and H. Sacks (eds.), *Contributions to ethnomethodology* (Bloomington: Indiana University Press, forthcoming). See also A. Cicourel, *Method and measurement in sociology* (New York: Free Press, 1966) for a critique of sociological research from ethnomethodological perspective. H. Sacks, *Social aspects of language: the organization of sequencing in language* (Englewood Cliffs, N.J.: Prentice-Hall, in press) gives a more complete exposition of the principles presented in Chapter 11 of this volume.

Some of the impetus to sociolinguistics has come from work by social psychologists. Notable among these is R. W. Brown, whose *Words and things* (New York: Free Press, 1958) remains a valuable discussion of many topics. Brown's *Social psychology* (New York: Free Press, 1970) is a textbook that contains extensive discussion of issues pertinent to sociolinguistics. A. Diebold's survey of psycholinguistic work in the second edition of C. Osgood and T. A. Sebeok (eds.), *Psycholinguistics* (Bloomington: Indiana University Press, 1966), takes up a number of sociolinguistic topics. An excellent introduction to the field of sociolinguistics by a scholar versed in sociolinguistics is D. Slobin, *Psycholinguistics* (Glenview, Ill.: Scott, Foresman, 1971). The papers in J. Macnamara (ed.), *Problems of bilingualism* (*Journal of Social Issues* 23(2) (1967)) offer sociological perspective on what is often conceived as a purely psychological problem; *cf.* especially W. E. Lambert, "A social psychology of bilingualism," pp. 91–109. Lambert's work generally is an outstanding contribution from social psychology to sociolinguistics.

7. *A Short List of Principal Collections, Monographs, and Journals in the Development of Sociolinguistics in the United States,* 1953–1972 (chronologically arranged)

U. Weinreich, *Languages in contact.* New York: Linguistic Circle of New York, 1953.

E. Haugen, *The Norwegian language in America: a study in bilingual behavior.* 2 vols. Philadelphia: University of Pennsylvania Press, 1953; 2d ed., Bloomington: Indiana University Press, 1969.

H. Hoijer (ed.), *Language in culture.* Chicago: University of Chicago Press, 1954.

K. L. Pike, *Language in relation to a unified theory of the structure of human behavior.* Part 1, Preliminary edition. Santa Ana, Calif.: Summer Institute of Linguistics,1954.

E. Haugen, *Bilingualism in the Americas: a bibliography and research guide.* (American Dialect Society, 26). Montgomery, Alabama: University of Alabama Press, 1956.

C. A. Ferguson and J. J. Gumperz (eds.), *Linguistic diversity in South Asia: studies in regional, social, and functional variation.* (Research Center in Anthropology, Folklore, and Linguistics, Publication 13; *International Journal of American Linguistics* 26 (3), Part 3). Bloomington, 1960.

F. A. Rice (ed.), *Study of the role of second languages in Asia, Africa and Latin America.* Washington, D.C.: Center for Applied Linguistics, 1962.

D. Hymes (ed.), *Language in culture and society.* New York: Harper Row, 1964.

A. K. Romney and R. G. D'Andrade (eds.), *Transcultural studies of cognition.* Washington, D.C.: American Anthropological Association, 1964.

J. J. Gumperz and D. Hymes (eds.), *The ethnography of communication.* Washington, D.C.: American Anthropological Association, 1964.

R. Shuy (ed.), *Social dialects and language learning.* Champaign, Ill.: National Council of Teachers of English, 1965.

W. Bright (ed.), *Sociolinguistics.* The Hague: Mouton, 1966.

J. A. Fishman, *Language loyalty in the United States.* The Hague: Mouton, 1966.

W. Labov, *Social stratification of English in New York City.* Washington, D.C.: Center for Applied Linguistics, 1966.

S. Lieberson (ed.), *Explorations in sociolinguistics. Sociological Inquiry* 36 (2) (1966); also, Research Center in Anthropology, Folklore and Linguistics, Publication 44, *International Journal of American Linguistics* 33 (2), Part 2, Bloomington, Indiana, 1967.

J. Macnamara (ed.), *Problems of bilingualism. Journal of Social Issues* 33 (2) (1967).

J. Fishman (ed.), *Readings in the sociology of language.* The Hague: Mouton, 1968.

J. A. Fishman, C. A. Ferguson, R. Das Gupta (eds.), *Language problems in developing nations.* New York: Wiley, 1968.

J. Fishman, *Sociolinguistics*. Rowley, Mass: Newberry House, 1970.
E. Ardener (ed.), *Social anthropology and language*. (Association of Social Anthropologists Monographs 10). London: Tavistock Press, 1971.
J. A. Fishman (ed.), *Advances in the sociology of language*. The Hague: Mouton, 1971.
D. Hymes (ed.), *Pidginization and creolization of languages*. Cambridge: Cambridge University Press, 1971.
T. A. Sebeok (ed.), *Current Trends in linguistics 12: Linguistics and adjacent arts and sciences*. The Hague: Mouton, 1972. (Section on sociology and anthropology.)

A variety of journals publish articles in sociolinguistics. The principal English language journals are:

African Language Review. London: School of Oriental and African Studies.
American Anthropologist. Washington, D.C.: American Anthropological Association.
Anthropological Linguistics. Bloomington: Department of Anthropology, Indiana University.
Journal of Linguistics. Cambridge: Cambridge University Press.
Language. Washington, D.C.: Linguistic Society of America.
Language in Society. Cambridge: Cambridge University Press.
Le Mondo Lingvo-Problemo. The Hague: Mouton.
Linguistics. The Hague: Mouton.
Man. London: Royal Anthropological Institute of Great Britain and Ireland.
Southwestern Journal of Anthropology. Albuquerque: Department of Anthropology, University of New Mexico.

appendix 2

Outline Guide for the Ethnographic Study of Speech Use

JOEL SHERZER AND REGNA DARNELL

This guide stems from a search of ethnographic literature to obtain information documenting the range of cross-cultural variability in the use of speech.[1] Ethnographies seldom explicitly describe speech use, but information was obtained from some seventy-five societies (in different degrees of detail). On the basis of those examples, the questions presented here have been devised. The questions are intended to serve as a stimulus for much-needed fieldwork focused on speech, and to indicate lines along which such work might proceed. The questions are *not* a check list to be followed mechanically. The ways in which individual questions must be phrased will vary from society to society. Moreover, not every possible question about the use of speech has been included. Within the general range indicated by the questions in the guide, an investigator in a given society may well focus on certain areas of particular significance.

To avoid awkward phrasing, many questions appear in a "yes" or "no" form. All such questions should be understood to be asking not only for a report of presence or absence but also for details: under what circumstances or conditions, for what group, for what purpose, etc.? Thus, when it is asked, "Is speaking regarded as a satisfying activity?" the intended answer is not simply "yes" or "no". Probably, the answer is "yes" under some conditions for some persons in every society. A full answer might include "more so for older people than for younger," "for men but not for women," "during the winter ceremonial season," etc.

The questions are accompanied by paragraphs labeled "Discussion." These paragraphs indicate some of the motivation for the questions, and ways in which they might be interpreted.

---

[1] The original version of the full guide was prepared under an Office of Education Grant during 1966–1967 with Dell Hymes as the principle investigator. Research assistants were Regna Darnell, Helen Hogan, Virginia Hymes, Sheila Seitel, Joel Sherzer, and K. M. Tiwary. A full version of the guide (the questions presented here together with the ethnographic examples on which they are based) with more detailed theoretical discussion, is currently being prepared for publication. The authors alone are responsible for any shortcomings in the present version of the guide.

The guide is subdivided into five sections:

1. Analysis of the use of speech
2. Attitudes toward the use of speech
3. Acquisition of speaking competence
4. The use of speech in education and social control
5. Typological generalizations

1. Analysis of the Use of Speech

Discussion: Much of linguistic theory has been concerned with study of language in abstraction from its use in speech. Here we are concerned with the kinds of questions one would ask if language is not abstracted in such a way. We do not think that we are merely adding a level to the traditional linguistic description. Rather, we are looking at linguistic data from a different perspective, one which integrates language with the *other* components involved in its use: features of *setting, participant,* etc. Instead of postulating "an ideal speaker-listener, in a completely homogeneous speech-community" (Chomsky 1965), and describing what is in effect the code of a single, limited form of speech, we assume a diversified speech community and take our goal to be a description of the many different *ways of speaking* which exist in the community. These *ways of speaking* and the relations among them are structured, or "rule-governed," just as is language. The usual description of a language, from this point of view, deals with only a portion, sometimes a somewhat arbitrary portion, of the structure of speaking in a community.

The questions that follow are intended to suggest the analytical steps an ethnographer might take in attempting to characterize the use of speech among a particular group of people. (1) He or she must first discover the *components* (or dimensions) that are relevant to speech use, and what in the particular group count as instances of these. (2) He or she must describe the relationships or rules among the various relevant components.[2]

I. What are the *components* involved in the use of speech?

Discussion: The potential components of speech use listed later have proven useful (necessary?) to analysis of the material on which the present guide is based. They are not to be used as a check list but rather as a guide to the kinds of factors which enter into the relationships or rules governing the use of speech. They stand to a complete analysis as does a phonetic grid to a phonological description; but at the present preliminary stage of work in this field the list cannot be either exhaustively specific or discrete. The items of the present list are clearly interdependent and possibly overlapping. They have been identified at a level sufficiently general to be maximally useful now.

In different cases, different components and different numbers of components will prove to be relevant. It is the task of the ethnographer to show which are relevant, and in what relationships, in the society under consideration. These various relationships among components are the ways of speaking for that society. The

[2] See Hymes, Chapter 1, for a more complete discussion of the problems involved in a description of speech usage.

present terminology is necessarily provisional. Work is still at a stage in which choice among existing terms, and creation of needed new terms, is problematic. One of the urgent tasks is development of an adequate terminology.

A. Linguistic varieties: What are the linguistic varieties in use in the community?

Discussion: The community, and its members, are conceived as having *linguistic repertoires,* composed of *linguistic varieties.* Varieties are defined in terms of their functional roles, independently of historical provenience (same or related languages, dialects) and of structural connection (Pig Latin, Mazateco whistle speech). Research has shown that the same contrast in function may be served, and the same underlying other relations entailed, by what in one case are wholly unrelated languages, in another related dialects, in another shift in phonological styles or in just certain elements (e.g., pronouns) within a single dialect and style. What is asked for here, then, are the linguistic varieties which function in the community, placed first of all in terms of such dimensions as formal/informal, public/private, out-group/in-group, etc.

1. To what extent are the identities and relationships of the linguistic varieties known or conscious?
2. What language-derived verbal or nonverbal codes are in use (i.e., Pig Latin, thieves' cant, whistle speech, sign language, drum signaling, etc.)?

B. Linguistic units of description: What are the local categories of speech acts, speech events, speech situations, and genres?

Discussion: Neither linguists nor anthropologists have as yet developed adequate units of description for speech use. The sentence, as ordinarily treated by linguists, is valid only for a narrowly referential function of language. It is abstracted from social meaning and relationships of use of concern to us here. And it is increasingly clear that limitation to the sentence misses generalizations, even of the narrowly syntactic sort. The text, or discourse, is more promising, but probably too gross. The various purposes accomplished in language—how people insult, show deference, command, request information, curse, greet, take leave, etc.—do not come in sentences or whole texts. We are not sure what they do come in, but would suggest the *speech act* as the minimal structural unity in a description of speech use.[3] In terms of conventional linguistic units (phonological, grammatical) it may range greatly in locus and size. *Speech acts* may be embedded in larger units such as genres, on the one hand, and discourse structures, speech events, and speech situations, on the other. It is clearly a task of the linguistic ethnographer and also, we believe, of the linguist, to describe the structure of such units. Note that the *unit of description* (the speech act) is included among the components; this is because we believe that speech acts and speech events can be adequately described only in relation to the other components of speech use with which they interact.

C. Topic: What is the *topic* (or *topics*) of the message, act, or event?
D. Channel: Through what *channels* may a message be transmitted (i.e., spoken, written, sung, whistled, drummed, etc.)?

---

[3] See Hymes, Chapter 1, for a discussion of this and other terms needed for a description of speech usage.

E. Key: What are the various *keys, tones,* or *manners* in which a message may be delivered?

F. Participants: What are the possible categories of *participants* in the uses of speech?

Discussion: *Audience* and *spokesman* must be considered as well as the more traditional *sender* and *receiver, addressor,* and *addressee.*

G. Setting: What are the times and places which serve as bounds or contexts of speech usages?

H. Ends: What are the *ends, goals,* or *purposes* of the speech usage under consideration?

I. Norms of interaction: What are the specific behaviors and proprieties that accompany speech usages?

II. Rules for the use of speech: What *relationships* exist among the components just described?

2. Attitudes Toward the Use of Speech

Discussion: It must be stressed that the answers to questions in this or any other section are often relevant to other sections as well. Thus a particular fact about the use of speech (e.g., that children may not speak on certain occasions) can be seen as

1. A *rule* for the use of speech which can be expressed in terms of relationships among components
2. An attitude about the place of certain members of the community vis-à-vis communication or
3. Part of the process of the learning of the use of speech

I. General attitudes toward speaking
A. What aspects of speaking (if any) are related to conceptions of the ideal or typical individual, man, woman, or child? Ideal exemplars of particular roles (i.e., chief, warrior, spokesman, herald, father, etc.)?

1. Is the use of speech important in the definition of roles, i.e., is the use of speech part of the qualification for membership?
2. Is the use of speech instrumental in the social marking of roles?

B. What are the characteristics of *speaking well?*
Discussion: At least two foci seem possible here:

1. Focus on the performance or message, i.e., what is it about the performance or message that makes it good or effective?
2. Focus on participant, i.e., what personal characteristics of participants make them good or effective speakers?
These two foci are not intended to represent two different questions; rather they are put forth as two aspects of a single one.

C. What is the permissible range of speech behavior? Are there conceptions of idiosyncracies, exceptions, speech defects? What are the individual and/or societal consequences of aberrant behavior with regard to speaking?

D. Is speaking regarded as a satisfying activity? Easy or difficult? Rewarding or not? What aspects of speaking are considered satisfying? Is speaking considered more satisfying under certain circumstances or for certain groups of people? Do people seek or are they given opportunities to display competence in speaking?

E. When are people *taciturn* or *voluble?*

    Discussion: Actually, we are asking here two different questions: (1) Are there cross-cultural differences regarding when people are *voluble* and when they are *taciturn?* and (2) is the dimension *taciturnity-volubility* relevant to the society under investigation, i.e., do such concepts exist?

    1. What personality traits or personal characteristics are associated with differences on this dimension?

    2. Are there differences associated with different roles, social categories, or different stages in the life cycle?

II. Attitudes toward languages, dialects, varieties, etc.

A. Are there beliefs concerning the nature and origin of language and speech? What are they?

B. What are the attitudes taken toward each of the linguistic varieties used in the community? How are these attitudes expressed? Are there concepts of correctness (or other normative notions) with regard to the varieties in use? Is one variety considered *correct* or *standard?* What are the criteria of correctness? Who may judge correctness? Do hypercorrect forms arise?

C. What are the attitudes taken toward neighboring languages or languages known to exist?

    Discussion: The boundary between this question and the previous one is not always clear. If community A uses the language of its neighbor, community B, for certain functions (even if not all members of A speak B), we often would want to consider B one of the varieties in use in A.[4]

Final discussion for section 2: A full description of attitudes toward language and speech would include the relative importance of speech among other means of communication as well as of the place of speaking within social interaction as a whole. The question of over-all communication is considered here only when it clarifies the use of speech in a given society or when one culture does with speech what another does with facial gesture, another through body movements, etc.

3. Acquisition of Speaking Competence

    Discussion: The use of the terms *infant* and *child* in italics in this section is intended to indicate that they are ethnocentric. Our own society expects a child to respond to training only when he can walk and talk; an infant is not expected to meet such demands. Other societies do not make this distinction in the same way. (See section 4, part I.) The terms thus are understood to refer to whatever categories the society recognizes, whether or not they are named.

I. Is the notion *infant* (distinct from *child*) relevant to the society's conception of the life cycle with reference to the acquisition of speaking competence?

[4] For a fuller treatment of this problem, see Hymes 1968b:23–48.

II. Is there an explicit native theory (or theories) with regard to the acquisition of speaking competence?

A. How are an *infant's* first cries or words interpreted?

1. Is it believed that the *infant* will always utter certain words first? What are these words?
2. What interpretation (if any) is given to an *infant's* crying?
3. What interpretation (if any) is given to a *child's* first (or early) utterance (or utterances)?

B. Are there ways of explaining or contributing to [apart from explicit teaching (see part III)] the distribution or acquisition of speaking competence?

1. Are any characteristics (physical, social, etc.) of the *infant* (*child*) or of its circumstances of birth, etc., thought to predispose or predetermine its later communicative behavior, especially its verbal ability? What and how?
2. Are there practices [apart from explicit teaching (see part III)] thought to encourage or discourage, ensure or prevent particular kinds of communicative behavior? Particular speaking skills?

III. How are speaking skills transmitted?

A. How are skills in language (abstracted from use) transmitted? In other words, how are grammar and vocabulary acquired?
B. Are the various linguistic varieties used in the community learned in different ways, in a particular order?
C. How are skills in the use of language transmitted? In other words, how do people learn to greet, converse, curse, gossip, etc.?
D. Is the learning of speaking skills a source of pride, a focus of concern?

IV. What is the general place of *children* in communication?

A. Are there special varieties or uses of speech restricted to use among *infants* (*children*)? restricted to use between *children* and adults? Is there a special *baby talk?* Is it intentionally taught? Is it approved or disapproved?
B. Can *children* participate in all uses of speech? If only some, which ones? Are there some speech situations at which *children* may be present but not participate?

4. The Use of Speech in Education and Social Control

Discussion: Much of the ethnographic literature dealing with children or acquisition of culture in general has been done from the point of view of culture and personality studies in anthropology. This section attempts to show how speech might be relevant to the description of socialization as well as how socialization might be relevant to the study of speech use.

I. Life cycle

A. What is the relation of speech to the definition of stages, periods, or transitions in life? Are the stages named?

1. Is the use of speech important in the definition of stages, i.e., is the use of speech part of the qualification for membership in a class of persons at a given stage of the life cycle?
2. Is the use of speech instrumental to the social marking of stages in the life cycle?

II. Learning and teaching
   A. Does the society have an explicitly formulated philosophy of education? For what purposes is it formulated (i.e., for use in child training or only in response to inquiry by the ethnographer)? What is the place of language and speech in the *native theory* of learning and teaching?
   B. What is the role of language (explicit verbalization) and speech in the actual transmission of knowledge or skills?
      Discussion: The distinction between learning by *participation and observation* and learning by *explicit verbalization* is not always clear-cut. Rather, we envisage here a continuum with societies tending toward one end or the other.
   C. Do methods of teaching vary with recognized stages in the life cycle? Setting? According to what is being taught?

III. Social control
   A. Does the society have an explicitly formulated philosophy of social control?
   B. What is the role of language and speech in social control?
   C. Do means of social control vary with recognized stages in the life cycle, membership in various social categories, setting, etc.? Do they vary according to the offense?

5. *Typological Generalizations*

I. What broad patterns in the use of speech emerge from analysis of a particular culture? Note especially attitudes toward speaking common throughout a given society, ritual idioms cross-cutting many speech events, certain social dimensions which are always relevant.
II. Are there patterns of speech use characteristic of culture areas? Culture area is understood here to mean such broad areas as North America, South America, Africa, and Oceania.
III. Are there patterns of speech use characteristic of particular kinds of speech community, e.g., societies with a particular level of sociocultural complexity or particular types of social organization?

Bibliography

Abasolo-Domingo, Maria, 1961, Child-rearing practices in barrio Cruz Na Ligas. Master's thesis, University of the Philippines, Quezon City.

Abrahams, Roger D., 1962, Playing the dozens. *Journal of American Folklore* 75:209–220.

———, 1964, *Deep down in the jungle. Negro narrative folklore from the streets of Philadelphia.* Hatboro, Pa: Folklore Associates.

———, 1968, Introductory remarks to a rhetorical theory of folklore. *Journal of American Folklore* 81:143–158.

Abrahams, Roger, and Richard Bauman, 1971, Sense and nonsense in St. Vincent: speech behavior and decorum in a Caribbean community. *American Anthropologist* 73:762–772.

Albert, Ethel, 1964, "Rhetoric," "logic," and "poetics" in Burundi: culture patterning of speech behavior. In John J. Gumperz and Dell Hymes (eds.), The ethnography of communication. *American Anthropologist.* 66, pt. 2 (6):35–54.

Arewa, E. Ojo, and Alan Dundes, 1964, Proverbs and the ethnography of speaking folklore. In John J. Gumperz and Dell Hymes (eds.), The ethnography of communication. *American Anthropologist* 66, 6:70–85.

Ausubel, Nathan (ed.), 1948, *A treasury of Jewish folklore.* New York: Crown.

Ayoub, Milla, 1962, Bi-polarity in Arabic kinship terms. *Proceedings of the Ninth International Congress of Linguistics* (edited by H. G. Lunt), The Hague: Mouton.

Babbitt, E. H., 1896, The English of the lower classes in New York City and vicinity. *Dialect Notes,* 1:457–464.

Bach, Adolf, 1960, Deutsche Dialectgeographie. Heidelberg: Carl Winter.

Bach, Emmon, and Robert T. Harms (eds.), 1968, *Universals in linguistic theory.* New York: Holt, Rinehart and Winston, Inc.

Bales, R. F., 1951, *Interaction process analysis.* Cambridge, Mass.: Addison-Wesley.

Bales, R. F., F. Strodtbeck, T. Mills, and Mary E. Roseborough, 1951, Channels of communication in small groups. *American Sociological Review* 16:461–468.

Baluchistan Gazeteer, 1907, Baluchistan District Gazeteer Series II. Allahabad: The Pioneer Press.

Baratz, Joan C., and Roger W. Shuy (eds.), 1969, *Teaching Black children to read.* Washington, D.C.: Center for Applied Linguistics.

Barber, Carrol, 1952, Trilingualism in Pascua; social functions of language in an Arizona Yaqui village. M.A. thesis, University of Arizona, Tucson.

Barker, G. C., 1947, Social functions of language in a Mexican American community. *Acta Americana* 5:185–202.

Barnard, F. M., 1965, *Herders' social and political thought: from enlightenment to nationalism.* London: Clarendon Press.

Barnes, Douglas, James Britton, and Harold Rosen, 1969, *Language, the learner, and the school.* London: Penguin.

Barnes, John A., 1954, Class and committees in a Norwegian island parish. *Human Relations* 8:39–58.

Barry III, Herbert, Margaret K. Bacon, and Irvin L. Child, 1967, Definitions, ratings, and bibliographic sources for child-training practices of 110 cultures. In Clellan S. Ford (ed.), *Cross-cultural approaches: readings in comparative research.* New Haven, Conn: HRAF Press.

Barth, Fredrik, 1959a, *Political leadership among Swat Pathans.* London: London School of Economics and Political Science.

———, 1959b, Segmentary opposition and the theory of games. *Journals of the Royal Anthropological Institute* 89:5–21.

———, 1961, *Nomads of South Persia.* London: G. Allen.

———, (ed.), 1963, *The role of the entrepeneur in social change in northern Norway.* Bergen: Norweigna Universities Press.

———, 1964, Ethnic processes in the Pathan-Baluchi boundary. In *Indo-Iranica: mélanges présentes a Georg Morgenstierne a l'occasion de son soixante-dixième anniversaire.* Wiesbaden: Otto Harrassowitz.

———, 1966, *Models of social organization.* Royal Anthropological Institute of Great Britain and Ireland, Occasional Papers, London.

———, (ed.), 1969, *Ethnic groups and boundaries. The social organization of culture difference.* London: Allen & Unwin.

Barthes, Roland, 1966, Introduction a l'analyse structurale des recits. *Communications,* Centre D'Etudes Des Communications de Masse, Paris.

Bascom, William R., 1965, *Ponape: A Pacific economy in transition.* University of California Publications, Anthropological Records, 22. Berkeley: University of California Press.

Basso, Keith, 1970, To give up on words: silence in the Western Apache culture. *Southwestern Journal of Anthropology* 26 (3):213–230.

Bateson, Gregory, and Margaret Mead, 1942, *Balinese character.* Special Publication of the New York Academy of Sciences 2, New York.

Bateson, Gregory, D. D. Jackson, J. Haley, and J. Weakland, 1968, Toward a theory of schizophrenia. In Don D. Jackson (ed.), *Communication, family and marriage.* (Human Communication, Vol. 1). Palo Alto, Calif. Science and Behavior Books, pp. 31–54. [1956, *Behavioral Science* 1:251–264.]

Beardsley, Monroe, 1962, The metaphorical twist. *Philosophy and Phenomenological Research* 22 (3):293.

Bellugi, Ursula, 1967, The acquisition of negation. Ph.D dissertation, Harvard Graduate School of Education, Cambridge, Mass.

Ben-Amos, Dan, 1969, Analytical categories and ethnic genres. *Genre* 2:275–301.

Berger, Peter, 1967, *The sacred canopy.* New York: Doubleday.

Bergler, L., 1938, On the resistance situation: the patient is silent. *Psychoanalytic Review* 25:170–186.

Berlyne, D. E., 1960, *Conflict, arousal, and curiosity.* New York: McGraw-Hill.
Bernstein, Basil, 1961, Social structure, language, and learning. *Educational Research* 3:163–176.
———, 1962, Linguistic codes, hesitation phenomena, and intelligence. *Language and Speech* 5:31–46.
———, 1963, Family role systems, socialization, and communication. *Paper presented at Conference on Cross-Cultural Research into Childhood and Adolescence, University of Chicago, Chicago.
———, 1964a, Elaborated and restricted codes: their social origins and some consequences. In John J. Gumperz and Dell Hymes (eds.), The ethnography of communication. *American Anthropologist* 66, 6, 2: 55–69.
———, 1964b, Aspects of language in the genesis of the social process. In Dell Hymes (ed.), *Language in culture and society,* pp. 251–263. New York: Harper & Row.
———, 1965, A socio-linguistic approach to social learning. In J. Gould (ed.), *Penguin Survey of the Social Sciences.* Harmondsworth: London: Penguin.
———, 1968, *Language, primary socialization, and education.* University of London Institute of Education, Sociological Research Unit Monographs. London: Routledge.
———, 1969, A critique of the concept of compensatory education. Mimeographed.
———, (ed.), 1971, *Class codes and control,* vols. 1 and 2. London: Routledge.
Bernstein, Basil, and W. Brandis, 1968, *Social class, communication, and control.* In *Social class, language, and communication.* University of London, Institute of Education, Sociological Research Unit Monographs. London: Routledge.
Bernstein, Basil, and Dorothy Henderson, 1969, Social class differences in the relevance of language to socialization. *Sociology* 3:1–20.
Bettelheim, Bruno, 1962, *Symbolic wounds: Puberty rites and the envious male.* New York: Collier.
Birdwhistell, Ray L., 1952, *Introduction to kinesics* (photo-offset). Foreign Service Institute. Louisville: University of Louisville Press. (Available in microfilm only from University Microfilms, Inc., 313 North First Street, Ann Arbor, Michigan.)
———, 1958, Implications of recent developments in communication research for evolutionary theory. *Report on the ninth annual round table meeting on linguistics and language studies* (edited by W. M. Austin). Washington, D.C: Georgetown University Press.
———, 1961, Paralanguage: 25 years after Sapir. In Henry Brosin (ed.), *Lectures in experimental psychiatry.* Pittsburgh, Pa: University of Pittsburgh Press.
———, 1968, Communication: a continuous multi-channel process. In *Conceptual bases and applications of the communicational sciences.* New York: Wiley.
———, 1970, *Kinesics and context: Essays on body motion communication.* Philadelphia: University of Pennsylvania Press.
Bloomfield, Leonard, 1933, *Language.* New York: Holt, Rinehart and Winston, Inc.
Bock, Philip K., 1964, Social structure and language structure. *Southwestern Journal of Anthropology* 20 (4):393–403.
Bolinger, Dwight, 1958, *Interrogative structures of American English.* Montgomery: University of Alabama Press.

Bott, E., 1957, *Family and social network*. London: Tavistock Press.
Bradburn, Norman M., 1963, Achievment and father dominance in Turkey. *Journal of Abnormal and Social Psychology* 67:464–468.
Brandis, W., and Dorothy Henderson (eds.), 1968, *Social class, language, and communication*. University of London, Institute of Education, Sociological Research Unit Monographs. London: Routledge.
Braunshausen, Nicolas, 1928, Le bilinguisme et le famille. In *Le bilinguisme et l'education*. Geneva-Luxembourg: Bureau International d'Education.
Brent, S. B., and Evelyn W. Katz, 1967, A study of language deviations and cognitive processes. OEO-Job Corps Project 1209, Progress Report No. 3., Wayne State University, Detroit, Michigan.
Bright, William (ed.), 1966, *Sociolinguistics*. The Hague: Mouton.
Bright, J. O, and William Bright, 1965, Semantic structures in Northwestern California and the Sapir-Whorf Hypothesis. *American Anthropologist* 67, 5 (2):249–258.
Bronfenbrenner, U., 1958, Socialization and social class in time and space. In E. Maccoby et al. (eds.), *Readings in social psychology*. New York: Holt, Rinehart and Winston, Inc.
Brown, Roger W., 1958, *Words and things*. New York.: Free Press.
——, 1965, *Social psychology*. New York: Free Press.
Brown, Roger W., and Marguerite Ford, 1961, Address in American English. *Journal of Abnormal and Social Psychology* 62:375–385. [Reprinted in Dell Hymes (ed.), *Language in culture and society*, pp. 234–244. New York: Harper & Row.]
Brown, Roger W., and A. Gilman, 1960, The pronouns of power and solidarity. In T. Sebeok (ed.), *Style in language*, pp. 253–276. Cambridge, Mass.: M.I.T. Press.
Bruce, R. I., 1900, *The forward policy and its results*. London: Longmans.
Brudner, Lilyan, 1969, The ethnic component of social transactions. Ph. D. dissertation, Department of Anthropology, University of California, Berkeley.
Bruner, Edward M., 1955, Two processes of change in Mandan-Hidatsa kinship terminology. *American Anthropologist* 57:840–850.
Buchler, Ira R., and R. Freeze, 1966, The distinctive features of pronominal systems. *Anthropological Linguistics* 8, 8:78–105.
Bulatao, Jaime, 1962, Philippine values: the Manileno's mainsprings. In Frank Lynch (ed.), *Four readings on Philippine values*. Institute of Philippine Culture Papers 2. Quezon City: Ateneo de Manila University Press.
Burke, Kenneth, 1941, *Philosophy of literary form*. Baton Rouge: Louisiana State University Press.
——, 1945, *A grammar of motives*. Englewood Cliffs, N.J.: Prentice-Hall. (Republished by University of California Press, Berkeley, 1969.)
——, 1950, A rhetoric of motives. Englewood Cliffs, N.J.: Prentice-Hall. (Republished by University of California Press, Berkeley, 1969.)
Burton, Roger V., and John W. M. Whiting, 1961, The absent father and cross-sex identity. *Merrill-Palmer Quarterly* 7:85–95.
Calame-Griaule, Geneviève, 1965, *Ethnologie et langage. La parole chez les Dogon*. Bibliotheque des sciences humaines. Paris: Gallimard.
Cambridge University Reporter, January 15, 1969, p. 890.
Cansever, Gocke, 1965, Psychological effects of circumcision. *British Journal of Medical Psychology* 38:321–331.
Capell, A., 1966, *Studies in socio-linguistics*. The Hague: Mouton.

Cassirer, Ernst, 1961, *The logic of the humanities.* New Haven, Conn.: Yale University Press. (Translated from Zur Logik des Kulturwissenschaften Goteborg, 1942.)

Cazden, Courtney, Vera John, and Dell Hymes (eds.), 1971, *The functions of language in the classroom.* New York: Teachers College Press.

Chatman, Seymour, and Samuel E. Levin (eds.), 1967, *Essays on the language of literature.* Boston: Houghton Mifflin.

Chomsky, Noam, 1965, *Aspects of the theory of syntax.* Cambridge, Mass.: M.I.T. Press.

———, 1966, *Cartesian linguistics.* New York: Harper & Row.

———, 1968, *Language and mind.* New York: Harcourt.

Chomsky, Noam, and M. Halle, 1968, *The sounds of American English.* New York: Harper & Row.

Christiansen, Hallfried, 1962, *Målet i Rana.* Oslo: Institut for Sociologi, Universitetet i Oslo.

Cicourel, Aaron, 1970, The acquisition of social structure: towards a developmental sociology of language and meaning. In Jack Douglas (ed.), *Existential Society.* New York: Appleton.

Cicourel, Aaron, and Robert Boese, 1971, Sign language acquisition and the teaching of deaf children. In C. Cazden, V. John, and Dell Hymes (eds.), *The functions of language: an anthropological and psychological approach.* New York: Teachers College Press.

Cohen, Percy S., 1968, *Modern social theory.* London: Heinemann.

Colby, Benjamin N., 1966, Ethnographic semantics: a preliminary survey. *Current Anthropology* 7 (1):3-32.

Coldevin, Axel, 1958, *Et bidrag til Rana-bygdens Socialhistorie.* Oslo: Institutt for Sociologi, Universitetet i Oslo.

Conklin, Harold C., 1962, Lexicographical treatment of folk taxonomies. In F. W. Householder, Jr., and Sal Saporta (eds.), *Problems in lexicography. International Journal of American Linguistics* 18, 2, pt. IV:119-141.

———, 1964, Ethnogenealogical method. In Ward Goodenough (ed.), *Explorations in cultural anthropology.* New York: McGraw-Hill.

Cook, Jenny, 1972, *Social Control and Socialization.* London: Routledge.

Cooper, Robert L., 1968, How can we measure the roles which a bilingual's languages play in his everyday behavior? In William Mackey (ed.), *Proceedings of the International Seminar on the Measurement and Description of Bilingualism.* Ottawa: Canadian Commission for UNESCO, 1968.

Corpuz, Onofre D., 1965, *The Philippines.* Englewood Cliffs, N.J.: Prentice-Hall.

Crystal, David, 1969, *Prosodic systems and intonation in English.* London: Cambridge University Press.

Crystal, David, and Randolph Quirk, 1964, *Systems of prosodic and paralinguistic features in English.* The Hague: Mouton.

Dalby, David, 1970, *Black through white.* Bloomington: Indiana University African Studies Program.

Dalby, David, in preparation, Americanisms that may once have been Africanisms. In Thomas Kochman (ed.), Language and expressive role behavior in the black inner city.

Dames, M. L., 1904, *The Baloch race.* Asiatic Society Monographs, 4. London: Royal Asiatic Society.

Dance, Frank X. W. (ed.), 1968, *Human communication theory.* New York: Holt, Rinehart and Winston, Inc.

Das Gupta, Jyotirindra, 1970, Language conflict and national development: group politics and national language policy in India. Berkeley, Calif.: University of California Press.

Das Gupta, Jyotirindra, and John J. Gumperz, 1969, "Language communication and control in North India." In J. A. Fishman, C. A. Ferguson, and J. Das Gupta (eds.), *Language problems in developing nations*. New York: Wiley.

Dennis, Wayne, 1940, *The Hopi child*. Charlotteville, Va: University of Virginia Press.

De Saussure, Ferdinand, 1916, *Cours de linguistique generale*. Paris: Payot. [*Course in general linguistics* (translated by Wade Baskin). New York: Philosophical Library, 1958.]

Diebold, A. R., 1963, *Code-switching in Greek-English bilingual speech*. Reports of the thirteenth annual round table meetings on linguistics and language study. Georgetown University Monograph 15. Washington, D.C.: Georgetown University Press.

Dikeman, Bessie, and Patricia Parker, 1964, Request forms. Term paper for Speech 160B. University of California, Berkeley.

Dohrenwend, Bruce P., and Robert J. Smith, 1962, Toward a theory of acculturation. *Southwest Journal of Anthropology* 18:30–39.

Dollard, J., and F. Auld, Jr., 1959, *Scoring human motives: a manual*. New Haven, Conn.: Yale University Press.

Douglas, Jack, 1971, *Understanding social life*. Chicago: Aldine.

Douglas, Mary, 1967, *The contempt of ritual*. Aquinas lecture. Oxford: Black Friars.

Drach, K., B. Kobashigawa, C. Pfuderer, and D. Slobin, 1969, The structure of linguistic input to children. Language Behavior Research Laboratory working paper no. 14, University of California, Berkeley.

Duncan, Hugh Dalziel, 1968, *Symbols in society*. New York: Oxford.

Dundes, Alan, 1966a, Here I sit: a study of American latrinalia. Papers of the Kroeber Anthropological Society 34:91–105.

———, 1966b, Metafolklore and oral literary criticism. *The Monist* 60:505–516.

Durkheim, E., 1933, *On the division of labour in society*. London: Macmillan.

———, 1950, *The rules of sociological method* (translated from the French by Sarah A. Solovay and John H. Mueller and edited by George E. G. Catlin). New York: Free Press.

Du Toit, Brian M., 1966, Riddling traditions in an isolated South African community. *Journal of American Folklore* 79:471–475.

Dyen, Isidore, 1965, Sketch of Trukese grammar. American Oriental Society, Essay 4. From typed version, Washington, D.C.: Pacific Science Board, 1948.

Ebeling, Gerhard, 1966, *Theology and proclamation*. Philadelphia: Fortress Press. (Translated from *Theologie und Verkündigung*. Tübingen: 1962).

Edelman, Martin, 1968, The contextualization of children's bilingualism. In Joshua Fishman, R. L. Cooper, Roxana Ma, et al. (eds.), *Bilingualism in the barrio*. Final report to DHEW under contract no. OEC-1-7-062817-0297. New York: Yeshiva University.

Eggan, Dorothy, 1948, The general problem of Hopi adjustment. *American Anthropologist* 45:357–373. [Cited from Clyde Kluckhohn and Henry Murray (eds.), *Personality in nature, society, and culture*, pp. 220–235. New York: Knopf, 1943.]

Ekman, Paul, and Wallace Friesen, 1968, Nonverbal behavior in psychotherapy research. In J. Shlien (ed.), *Research in psychotherapy*, vol. III, pp. 179–216. American Psychological Association.

————, ————, 1969, The repertoire of non-verbal behavior: Categories, origins, usage and coding. *Semiotica* 1 (1):49–98.

Ekman, Paul, Wallace Friesen, and T. Tausig, 1969, VID-R and SCAN: Tools and methods for the automated analysis of visual records. In G. Gerbner, O. Holsti, K. Krippendorf, W. Paisley, and P. Stone (eds.), *The analysis of communication content*, pp. 297–312. New York: Wiley.

Ervin, Susan M., 1964, Language and TAT content in bilinguals. *Journal of Abnormal Social Psychology* 68:500–507.

Ervin-Tripp, Susan M., 1964, An analysis of the interaction of language, topic, and listener. In John J. Gumperz and Dell Hymes (eds.), The ethnography of communication. *American Anthropologist* 66, 6, pt. II:86–102.

————, 1967, As Issie learns English. In John Macnamara (ed.), Problems of bilingualism, *Journal of Social Issues* 23 (2):78–90.

————, 1968, Becoming a bilingual. Working paper no. 9, Language Behavior Research Laboratory, University of California, Berkeley.

————, 1968, Proceedings of the 1967 UNESCO conference on the description and measurement of bilingualism.

————, 1969, Sociolinguistics. In L. Berkowitz (ed.), *Advances in experimental social psychology*. vol. 4, pp. 91–165. New York: Academic Press, Inc.

————, 1970a, Social dialects in developmental sociolinguistics. In Roger W. Shuy, Irwin Feigenbaum, and Allene Grognet (Investigators), *Sociolinguistic Theory, Materials, and Training Programs: Three related studies.* [Final Report, OEC-3-9-180357-0400 (010), U.S. Department of Health, Education and Welfare.] Center for Applied Linguistics, Washington, D.C.

————, 1970b, Structure and process in language acquisition. Twenty-first Annual Round Table Meeting on Linguistics and Language Studies. School of Languages and Linguistics. Georgetown University. Washington, D.C.

Eslao, Nena B., 1962, Child-rearing among the Samal of Manubul, Siasi, Sulu. *Philippine Sociological Review* 10:80–91.

Evans, I. H. N., 1951, Fifty Dusun riddles. *Sarawak Museum Journal* 5:553–561.

————, 1954, More Dusun riddles. *Sarawak Museum Journal* 6:20–35.

————, 1955, Some Dusun proverbs and proverbial sayings. *Sarawak Museum Journal* 6:233–244.

Faris, James, 1966, The dynamics of verbal exchange: a Newfoundland example. *Anthropologica* 8:235–248.

————, 1968, Validation in ethnographical description: the lexicon of "occasions" in Cat Harbour. *Man* (new series) 3:112–124.

Fay, Percival 1918–1920, The use of *tu* and *vous* in Moliere. Berkeley University of California Publications in Modern Philology, 7, pp. 227–286.

Ferguson, Charles A., 1964a, Diglossia. In Dell Hymes (ed.), *Language in culture and society*, pp. 429–437. New York: Harper & Row.

————, 1964b, Baby talk in six languages. In John J. Gumperz and Dell Hymes (eds.), The ethnography of communication. *American Anthropologist* 66, 6, pt. II:103–114.

————, 1966, National sociolinguistic profile formulas. In William Bright (ed.), *Sociolinguistics*, pp. 309–314. The Hague: Mouton.

————, 1971, *Language structure and language use*. Stanford, Calif.: Stanford University Press.

Ferguson, Charles A., and John J. Gumperz, 1959, Linguistic diversity in south Asia: Studies in Regional, and Functional Variation. [RCAFL-P 13; *International Journal of American Linguistics* 26 (3), pt. III].

Fischer, J. L., 1957, The eastern Carolines. New Haven, Conn: Human Relations Area Files.

———, 1958, Social influence in the choice of a linguistic variant. *Word* 14:47–56. [Reprinted in Dell Hymes (ed.), 1964, *Language in culture and society,* pp. 483–488. New York: Harper & Row.]

———, 1964, Words for self and others in some Japanese families. In John J. Gumperz and Dell Hymes (eds.). *American Anthropologist* 66, 6, pt. II:115–132.

———, 1965, The stylistic significance of consonantal Sandhi in Trukese and Ponapean. *American Anthropologist* 67:1495–1502.

———, 1966, Syntax and social structure: Truk and Ponape. In William Bright (ed.), *Sociolinguistics,* pp. 168–182. The Hague: Mouton. (Proceedings of the UCLA Sociolinguistics Conference, 1964.)

Fishman, Joshua A., 1964, Language maintenance and language shift as fields of inquiry. *Linguistics* 9:32–70.

———, 1965, Who speaks what language to whom and when. *La Linguistique* 2:67–88.

———, 1966, Language loyalty in the United States. The Hague: Mouton.

———, 1967, Bilingualism with and without diglossia; diglossia with and without bilingualism. In J. Macnamara (ed.), Problems of bilingualism. *Journal of Social Issues* 23, 2:29–38.

———, 1968a, A sociolinguistic census of a bilingual neighborhood. In J. A. Fishman, R. L. Cooper, Roxana Ma, et al. (eds.), *Bilingualism in the barrio.* Final report to DHEW under contract no. OEC-1-7-062817-0297. New York: Yeshiva University.

———, 1968b, Sociolinguistic perspective on the study of bilingualism. *Linguistics* 39:21–49.

Fishman, Joshua, Charles A. Ferguson, and Jyotirindra Das Gupta, 1968, *Language problems of developing nations.* New York: Wiley.

Fock, Niels, 1965, Cultural aspects of the "oho" institution among the Waiwai. Proceedings of the International Congress of Americanists, pp. 136–140.

Foote, N. N. (ed.), 1961, *Household decision-making: consumer behavior.* vol. 4. New York: New York University Press.

Ford, Clellan S. (ed.), 1967, *Cross-cultural approaches: readings in comparative research.* New Haven, Conn.: HRAF Press.

Frake, Charles O., 1960, The eastern Subanun of Mindanao. In G. P. Murdock (ed.), *Social structure in Southeast Asia.* Chicago: Quadrangle Books.

———, 1962, The ethnographic study of cognitive systems. In T. Gladwin and W. C. Sturtevant (eds.), *Anthropology and human behavior.* Washington, D.C.: Anthropological Society.

———, 1963, Litigation in Lipay: A study in Subanun law. The proceedings of the Ninth Pacific Science Congress, 1957, vol. 3, Bangkok.

———, 1964a, How to ask for a drink in Subanun. In John J. Gumperz and Dell Hymes (eds.), The ethnography of communication. *American Anthropologist* 66, 6, pt. II:127–132.

———, 1964b, A structural description of Subanun "religious behavior." In Ward H. Goodenough (ed.), *Explorations in cultural anthropology: essays in honor of George Peter Murdock.* New York: McGraw-Hill.

———, 1964c, Notes on queries in ethnography. In A. Kimball Romney and R. G. D'Andrade (eds.), Transcultural studies in cognition. *American Anthropologist* (special publication), 66, 3, pt. II.

———, 1964d, The diagnosis of disease among the Subanun of Mindanao. In Dell

Hymes (ed.), *Language in culture and society,* pp. 193–211. New York: Harper & Row.

————, 1966, Review of riddles in Filipino folklore. *American Anthropologist* 68:245–246.

Frank, Y. A., 1948, The speech of New York City. University of Michigan Ph.D. dissertation, Ann Arbor, Michigan.

Frey, J. William, 1945, Amish triple talk. *American Speech* 20:85–98.

Friedrich, Paul, 1964, Semantic structure and social structure: an instance from Russian. In Ward H. Goodenough (ed.), *Explorations in cultural anthropology.* New York: McGraw-Hill.

————, 1966, Structural implications of Russian pronominal usage. In William Bright (ed.), *Sociolinguistics,* pp. 214–253. The Hague: Mouton.

Fries, Charles C., 1952, *The structure of English.* New York: Harcourt.

Gardner, Peter M., 1966, Symmetric respect and memorate knowledge: the structure and ecology of individualistic culture. *Southwestern Journal of Anthropology* 22:389–415.

Garfinkel, Harold, 1966, Comments. In William Bright (ed.), *Sociolinguistics,* pp. 322–333. The Hague: Mouton.

————, 1967, *Studies in ethnomethodology.* Englewood Cliffs, N.J.: Prentice-Hall.

Garfinkel, Harold, and Harvey Sacks, 1969, On formal structures of practical actions. In John C. McKinney and Edward Tiryakian (eds.), *Theoretical sociology: perspectives and developments.* New York: Appleton.

Garvin, Paul L., 1949, Linguistic study of Ponape. Washington, D.C.: Pacific Science Board. Typed.

————, (ed.), 1969. *A Prague school reader.* Washington, D.C.: Georgetown University Press.

————, 1952, Respect behavior on Ponape. *American Anthropologist* 54:201–220.

Gauchat, L., 1905, *L'unite phonetique dans le patois d'une commune.* Halle.

Gayton, Ann H., and Stanley Newman, 1940, Yokuts and western Mono myths. University of California Publications, Anthropological Records, 5, Berkeley.

Geertz, C., 1960, *The religion of Java.* New York: The Free Press.

Geoghegan, William, 1970, Balangingi' Samal address terminology. Ph.D. dissertation, University of California, Berkeley.

————, 1971a, Information processing systems in culture. In Paul Kay (ed.), *Explorations in mathematical anthropology.* Cambridge, Mass.: M.I.T. Press.

————, 1971b, Natural information processing rules: Formal theory in applications to ethnography. Monograph III. Language Behavior Research Laboratory. University of California, Berkeley.

Georges, Robert A., and Alan Dundes, 1963, Toward a structural definition of the riddle. *Journal of American Folklore* 76:111–118.

Goffman, Erving, 1953. Communication conduct in an island community. Ph.D. dissertation, Department of Sociology, University of Chicago.

————, 1959, The presentation of self in everyday life. New York: Doubleday.

————, 1961, *Encounters:* Two Studies in the Sociology of interaction. Indianapolis: Bobbs-Merrill.

————, 1963, *Behavior in public places.* New York: Free Press.

————, 1964, The neglected situation. In John J. Gumperz and Dell Hymes (eds.), The ethnography of communication. *American Anthropologist* 66, 6, pt. II: 133–137.

————, (ed.), 1967, Alienation from interaction. In *Interaction ritual: essays in face to face behavior,* pp. 113–136. Chicago: Aldine. [1957, *Human Relations* 10:47–59.]

Goldthorpe, J., and D. Lockwood, 1963, Affluence and the class structure. *Sociological Review* 11:133–163.

Goodenough, Ward H., 1951, Property, kin, and community of Truk. Yale University Publications in Anthropology, 46. New Haven, Conn.: Yale University Press.

————, 1964, Cultural anthropology and linguistics. In Dell Hymes (ed.), *Language in culture and society,* pp. 36–39. New York: Harper & Row. [Reprinted from Report of the *Seventh Annual Round Table Meeting on Linguistics and Language Study,* Monograph Series on Languages and Linguistics, 9 (edited by Paul L. Garvin), pp. 109–173. Washington, D.C.: Georgetown University Press, 1957.]

————, 1965a, Rethinking "status" and "role": toward a general model of the cultural organization of social relationships. In M. Banton (ed.), *The relevance of models of anthropology.* London: Tavistock.

————, 1965b, Personal names and modes of address in two Oceanic societies. In Melford Spiro (ed.), *Context and meaning in cultural anthropology.* New York: Free Press.

Greenberg, J. H., 1963, Some universals of grammar with particular reference to the order of meaningful elements. In Joseph Greenberg (ed.), *Universals of language.* Cambridge, Mass.: M.I.T. Press.

————, 1966, Language universals. In T. Sebeok (ed.), *Current trends in linguistics, vol. 3,* pp. 61–112. The Hague: Mouton.

————, 1968, *Anthropological linguistics.* New York: Random House, Inc.

Greenfield, Lawrence, 1968, Spanish and English usage self-ratings in various situational contexts. In J. A. Fishman, R. L. Cooper, Roxana Ma, et al. (eds.), *Bilingualism in the barrio.* Final report to DHEW under contract no. OEC-1-7-062817-0297. New York: Yeshiva University.

Greimas, A. G., 1968, Gesture. *Communications.* Paris.

Grimshaw, Allen, 1968, Sociolinguistics. In Wilber Schramm, et al. (eds.), *Handbook of communication.* New York: Rand McNally & Co.

————, 1969, Language as obstacle and as data in sociological research. *Items* 23, 2.

Gross, Feliks 1951, Language and value changes among the Arapho. *International Journal of American Linguistics* 17:10–17.

Guiraud, Pierre, 1961, *Lastylistic.* 3d ed. Paris: Presses Universitaire de France.

————, 1967, *Structures etymologiques du lexique français.* Paris: Librairie Larousse.

Gumperz, John J., 1961, Speech variation and the study of Indian civilization. *American Anthropologist* 63:976–988. [Reprinted in Dell Hymes (ed.), 1964, *Language in culture and society,* pp. 416–428. New York: Harper & Row.

————, 1962, Types of linguistic communities. *Anthropological linguistics* 4, 1:28–40.

————, 1964a, Hindi-Punjabi code-switching in Delhi. In H. G. Lunt (ed.), *Proceedings of the ninth international congress of linguists,* pp. 1115–1124. The Hague: Mouton.

————, 1964b, Linguistic and social interaction in two communities. In John J. Gumperz and Dell Hymes (eds.), The ethnography of communication. *American Anthropologist* 66, 6, pt. II:137–154.

————, 1966, On the ethnology of linguistic change. In William Bright (ed.), *Sociolinguistics,* pp. 27–49. The Hague: Mouton.

————, 1967, On the linguistic markers of bilingual communication. In J. Macnamara (ed.), Problems of bilingualism. *Journal of Social Issues* 23, 2:48–57.

————, 1969, Communication in multilingual societies. In Stephen Tyler (ed.), *Cognitive anthropology.* Holt, Rinehart and Winston, Inc.

————, 1970a, Sociolinguistics and communication in small groups. Working paper no. 33, Language Behavior Research Laboratory, University of California, Berkeley.

————, 1970b, Verbal strategies in multilingual communication. Working paper no. 36, Language Behavior Research Laboratory, University of California, Berkeley. [Report of the Twenty-First Annual Round Table Meeting on Linguistics and Language Studies (Monograph Series on Languages and Linguistics, Number 23), James Alatis (ed.). Georgetown University, Washington, D.C., 1970.]
[In Roger Abrahams and Rudy Troike (eds.), *Language, culture, and education.* Prentice-Hall. In preparation.]

————, 1971, *Language in social groups: Essays by John J. Gumperz.* Language Science and National Development Series, Anwar S. Dil, General Editor. Palo Alto, Calif.: Stanford University Press.

Gumperz, John J., and Eduardo Hernandez, 1971, Bilingualism, bidialectalism, and classroom interaction. In Courtney, Cazden, Dell Hymes, and Vera John (eds.), *The function of language in the classroom.* New York: Teachers College Press.

Gumperz, John J., and Dell Hymes (eds.), 1964, The ethnography of communication. *American Anthropologist* 66, 6, pt. II.

Gumperz, John J., and C. M. Naim, 1960, Formal and informal standards in Hindi regional language area. In Charles A. Ferguson and John J. Gumperz (eds.), Linguistic diversity in South Asia. RCAFL-P 13 *International Journal of American Linguistics* 26 (3), pt. III:92–118.

Gunter, R., 1966, On the placement of accent in dialogue: a feature of context grammar. *Journal of Linguistics* 2:159–179.

Guthrie, George, and Peptia Jiminez Jacobs, 1966, Child-rearing and personality development in the Philippines. University Park: Pennsylvania State University Press.

Haas, Mary R., 1964, Men's and women's speech in Koasati. In Dell Hymes (ed.), *Language in culture and society,* pp. 228–232. New York: Harper & Row.

Hakulinen, A., B. Lewis, and S. Taylor, in preparation, Seven-year-old children and the contextual use of language. University of London, Institute of Education, Sociological Research Unit Monographs. London: Routledge, 1968.

Hall, Edward T., 1959, *The silent language.* New York: Doubleday.

————, 1963, A system for the notation of proxemic behavior. *American Anthropologist* 65:1003–1026.

————, 1964, Adumbration as a feature of intercultural communication. In John J. Gumperz and Dell Hymes (eds.), The ethnography of communication. *American Anthropologist* 66, 6, pt. II:154–163.

————, 1966, *The hidden dimension.* New York: Doubleday.

————, 1968, Proxemics. *Current Anthropology* 9:83–108.

Halle, Morris, 1962, Phonology in a generative grammar. *Word* 18:54–72.

Halliday, Michael A., 1967–1968, Notes on transitivity and the theme in English. *Journal of Linguistics* 3:37–81, 199–245; 4:179–215.

————, 1972, *An outlook on modern English*. London: Oxford.

Halliday, Michael A., Angus McIntosh, and Peter Strevens, 1964, *The linguistic sciences and language teaching*. London: Longmans.

Hammel, Eugene A. (ed.), 1965, Formal semantic analysis. *American Anthropologist* 67, 5, Part II.

Hampshire, Stuart, 1967, *Thought and action*. New York: Viking.

Hanson, D., 1965, Personal and positional influences in informal groups. *Social Forces* 44:246–258.

————, 1963, *Freedom and reason*. Oxford: Clarendon Press.

Harrah, David, 1961, A logic of questions and answers. *Philosophy and Science* 28:40–46.

Harris, Marvin, 1964, *The nature of cultural things*. New York: Random House, Inc.

Hart, Donn V., 1956, Halfway to uncertainty: a short autobiography of a Cebuano Filipino. *Journal of East Asiatic Studies* 5:255–277.

————, 1964, Riddles in Filipino folklore: an anthropological analysis. Syracuse, N.Y.: Syracuse University Press.

Hassan, Ruquaiya, 1968, *Grammatical cohesion in spoken and written English*. pt. I. (Programme in Linguistics and English teaching, Paper 7.) London: University College and Longmans.

————, 1972, *Language in the imaginative context: A sociolinguistic study of stories told by seven year old children*. London: Routledge.

Haugen, Einar, 1953, *The Norwegian language in America: a study in bilingual behavior*. 2 vols. Philadelphia: University of Pennsylvania Press.

————, 1956, Bilingualism in the Americas: a bibliography and research guide. *American Dialect Society* 26.

————, 1957, The semantics of Icelandic orientation. *Word* 13:447–459.

————, 1966, *Language conflict and language planning; the case of modern Norwegian*. Cambridge, Mass.: Harvard University Press.

Hawkins, P., 1968, Social class the nominal group and reference. Language and speech.

Hawkins, P., and G. Turner, in preparation, Aspects of the nominal, verbal, and adverbial group. Sociological Research Unit Monograph. University of London, Institute of Education, Sociological Research Unit Monographs. London: Routledge.

Haxthausen, August F. von, 1956, *The Russian Empire* (translated by R. Farrie). 2 vols. London: Chapman and Hall.

Henderson, D., 1968, Social class differences in form-class usage. In W. Brandis and Dorothy Henderson (eds.), *Social Class, Language and Communication*. University of London, Institute of Education, Sociological Research Unit Monographs. London: Routledge.

————, in press, Parental definitions of the relevance of speech in socialization. *Sociology*.

Henrie, Samuel N., 1969, A study of verb phrases used by five year old non standard Negro English speaking children. Ph.D. dissertation, University of California, Berkeley.

Hermann, M. E., 1929, Lautveränderungen in der Individualsprache einer Mundart. Nachrichten der Gesellschaft der Wissenshcaften zu Göttigen, *Philosophisch-historische Klasse* 11:195–214.

Hilger, Sister Inez, 1957, Araucanian child life and its cultural background. Smithsonian Miscellaneous Collections, 135, Publ. 4297, Washington, D.C.

Hill, Richard, and Kathleen S. Crittenden, 1968, Proceedings of the Purdue symposium on ethnomethodology. Institute for the Study of Social Change, Monograph 1. West Lafayette, Ind.: Purdue University.

Hill, Trevor, 1958, Institutional linguistics. *Orbis* 7:444–455.

Hockett, C. F., 1950, Age grading and linguistic continuity. *Language* 26, 4:449–457.

———, 1955, *A manual of phonology*. Indiana University Publications in Anthropology and Linguistics, II, Bloomington, Ind.

———, 1958, *A course in modern linguistics*. New York: Macmillan.

Hogan, Sister Helen Marie, 1967, An ethnography of communication among the Ashanti, M.A. dissertation, Department of Anthropology, University of Pennsylvania, Philadelphia.

Hoijer, Harry (ed.), 1954, Language in culture. Comparative Studies of Cultures and Civilizations, no. 3, Memoirs of the American Anthropological Association, no. 79. Chicago: University of Chicago Press.

Hollensteiner, Mary R., 1962, Reciprocity in the lowland Philippines. In Frank Lynch (ed.), *Four readings on Philippine values*. Institute of Philippine Culture Papers 2. Quezon City: Ateneo de Manila University Press.

Homans, G. C., 1958, Social behavior as exchange. *American Journal of Sociology* 62:597–606.

Howell, Richard, 1967, Linguistic choice as an index to social change. Ph.D. dissertation, University of California, Berkeley.

———, 1968, Linguistic choice and levels of social change. *American Anthropologist* 70:553–559.

Hubbell, A. F., 1950, *The pronunciation of English in New York City*. New York: King's Crown Press.

Human Relations Area Files (HRAF), New Haven, Conn.

Hyman, Herbert H., et al., 1954, *Interviewing in social research*. Chicago: University of Chicago Press.

Hymes, Dell, 1961a, Functions of speech: an evolutionary approach. In F. C. Gruber (ed.), *Anthropology and education*, pp. 55–83. Philadelphia: University of Pennsylvania Press.

———, 1961b, Linguistic aspects of cross-cultural personality study. In Bert Kaplan (ed.), *Studying personality cross-culturally*, pp. 313–359. New York: Harper & Row.

———, 1962, The ethnography of speaking. In T. Gladwin and W. C. Sturtevant (eds.), *Anthropology and human behavior*, pp. 13–53. Anthropological Society of Washington. Washington, D.C. (Reprinted in J. A. Fishman, *Readings in the sociology of language*, pp. 99–138. The Hague: Mouton, 1968.)

———, 1964a, A perspective for linguistic anthropology. In Sol Tax (ed.), *Horizons of anthropology*, pp. 92–107. London: Aldine.

———, 1964b, Directions in (ethno-) linguistic theory. In A. K. Romney and R. G. D'Andrade (eds.), Transcultural studies in cognition. *American Anthropologist* 66, 3, pt. II:6–56.

——— (ed.), 1964c, Modes of address (reference note). *Language in culture and society*, pp. 225–227. New York: Harper & Row.

———, (ed.), 1964d, *Language in culture and society*. New York: Harper & Row.

———, 1964e, Introduction: toward ethnographies of communication. In John J. Gumperz and Dell Hymes (eds.), The ethnography of communication. *American Anthropologist* 66, 6, pt. II:1–34.

———, 1966a, Two types of linguistic relativity. In William Bright (ed.), *Sociolinguistics*, pp. 114–165. The Hague: Mouton.

————, 1966b, On "anthropological linguistics" and congeners. *American Anthropologist* 68:143–153.

————, 1967, Models of the interaction of language and social setting. *Journal of Social Issues* 23 (2):8–28.

————, 1968a, The "wife" who "goes out" like a man: reinterpretation of a Clackamas Chinook myth. *Studies in Semiotics* 7 (3):173–199.

————, 1968b, Linguistic problems in defining the concept of "tribe." In June Helm (ed.), *Essays on the problem of tribe*. Seattle: University of Washington Press.

————, 1968c, Linguistics—the field. *International Encyclopedia of the Social Sciences* 9:351–371.

————, 1969, Linguistic aspects of comparative political research. In Robert T. Holt and John Turner (eds.), *Methodology of comparative research*. New York: Free Press.

————, 1970, Linguistic theory and the functions of speech. *Proceedings of international days of sociolinguistics,* Rome: Instituto Luigi Sturzo.

————, 1971a, The contribution of folklore to sociolinguistics. *Journal of American Folklore* 84 (1):42–50.

————, 1971b, Sociolinguistics and the ethnography of speaking. In Edwin Ardener (ed.), *Social anthropology and linguistics*, pp. 47–93. Association of Social Anthropologists Monograph 10. London: Tavistock.

————, 1972, *Towards communicative competence*. Philadelphia: University of Pennsylvania Press.

————, typescript, On personal pronouns; formal and phonesthematic aspects.

————, (ed.), 1971, *Creolization and pidginization of language*. London: Cambridge University Press.

Ingham, John Michael, 1968, Culture and personality in a Mexican village. Unpublished Ph.D dissertation, University of California, Berkeley.

Irvine, Judith Temkin, 1968, Speech and music in two cultures. Unpublished manuscript.

Jaberg, Karl, 1936, *Aspects geographique du langage*. Paris: Droz.

Jain, Dhanesh, 1969, Verbalization of respect in Hindi. *Anthropological linguistics* 11, 3:79–97.

Jakobson, Roman, *Kindersprache, Aphasie und allgemeine Laugesetze,* Uppsala Universitets Aarsskrift.

————, 1957, Shifters, verbal categories, and the Russian verb. Russian Language Project. Harvard University, Cambridge.

————, 1959, Boas' view of grammatical meaning. The anthropology of Franz Boas, essays on the centennial of his birth (edited by Walter Goldschmidt). American Anthropological Association memoir 89.

————, 1960, Linguistics and poetics. In T. Sebeok (ed.), *Style in language,* pp. 350–377. Cambridge: M.I.T. Press.

————, 1962, *Retrospect. Selected writings I: Phonology.* The Hague: Mouton.

Jakobson, Roman, and Morris Halle, 1956, *Fundamentals of language.* (*Janua Linguarum,* 1.) The Hague: Mouton.

————, [1962] *In retrospect. Selected writings I: Phonology.* The Hague: Mouton.

Jesperson, Otto, 1924, *The philosophy of grammar.* New York: Holt, Rinehart and Winston, Inc.

Joos, M., 1962, The five clocks. *International Journal of American Linguistics* 28, pt V.

Joseph, Sister Miriam, 1962, *Rhetoric in Shakespeare's time. Literary theory in Renaissance Europe.* New York: Harcourt.

Kantorovich, V., 1966, *ty i vy: Ametki pisatelya* ('*Ty* and *vy:* a writer's notes'). Moscow: Izd-vo pol. lit.

Kaspar, Walter, 1969, *The methods of dogmatic theology.* Shannon: Ecclesia Press. (Translated from *Die Methoden der Dogmatik—Einheit-und-Vielheit.* Munich: Kosel Verlag, 1967.)

Katz, Evelyn, 1966, A content-analytic method for studying themes of interpersonal behavior. *Psychological Bulletin* 66:419–422.

Keesing, F. M., and M. M. Keesing, 1956, *Elite communication in Samoa: a study in leadership.* Stanford, Calif.: Stanford University Press.

Key, Mary (ed.), in press, *Nonverbal communication: a reader in paralanguage and kinesics.*

Kiparsky, Paul, 1968, Tense and aspect in Indo-European syntax. *Foundations of Language* 4:30–57.

Kjolseth, J. R., 1967, Structure and process in conversation. Paper presented at the American Sociological Society meetings, San Francisco.

Klima, E. S., 1964, Relatedness between grammatical systems. *Language* 40:1–29.

Kloss, Heinz, 1929, Sprachtabellen als Grundlage fur Sprachstatistik, Sprachenkarten and fur eine allgemeine Sociologie der Sprachgemeinschaften. *Vieteljahrschrift fur Politik unde Geschichte* 1, 7:103–117.

Kochman, Thomas, 1969, "Rapping" in the black ghetto. *Trans-Action,* February 1969:26–34.

——— (ed.), in preparation, *Language and expressive role behavior in the black inner city.*

Kohl, Herbert, 1967, *Thirty-six children.* New York: New American Library.

Kohn, M. L., 1959a, Social class and parental values. *American Journal of Sociology* 64:337–351.

———, 1959b, Social class and the exercise of parental authority. *American Sociological Review* 24:352–366.

Kostomarov, V. G., 1967, Russkiy rechevoy stiket ('Russian speech etiquette'). *Russkiy yazyk za rubezhom* 1:56–62.

Kramer, M., H. Goldstein, R. H. Israel, and N. A. Johnson, 1956, Applications of life table methodology to the study of mental hospital populations. Psychiatric research reports of the American Psychiatric Association, June. 46–76.

Kreider, Charles W. (ed.), 1965, Report of the Sixteenth Annual Round Table Meeting on Linguistics and Language Studies. Washington, D.C.: Georgetown University Press.

Kroeber, Alfred L., 1909, Classificatory systems of relationship. *Journal of the Royal Anthropological Institute* 3 :77–85.

———, 1960, Evolution, history and culture. In Sol Tax (ed.), *Evolution after Darwin,* pp. 1–16. Chicago: University of Chicago Press.

Kurath, Hans, et al., 1941, *Linguistic atlas of New England.* Providence, R. I.: Brown University Press.

Kurath, Hans, and R. A. McDavid, Jr., 1961, *The pronunciation of English in the Atlantic States.* Ann Arbor, Mich.: University of Michigan Press.

La Barre, Weston, 1964, Paralinguistics, kinesics, and cultural anthropology. In T. A. Sebeok, A. S. Hayes, and Mary C. Bateson (eds.), *Approaches to semiotics,* pp. 191–220. The Hague: Mouton.

Labov, William, 1963, The social motivation of a sound change. *Word* 19:273-309.

————, 1964a, The aims of sociolinguistic research. Paper prepared for the Sociolinguistics Seminar held at Bloomington, Ind., in the summer of 1964 under the auspices of the Social Science Research Council.

————, 1964b, Phonological correlates of social stratification. In John J. Gumperz and Dell Hymes (eds.), The ethnography of communication. *American Anthropologist* 66, 6, pt. II:164-176.

————, 1964c, The linguistic variable as a structural unit. Paper given before the Washington, D.C., Linguistics Club, October.

————, 1965, Stages in the acquisition of standard English. In Roger Shuy (ed.), *Social dialects and language learning,* pp. 77-103. Champaign, Ill.: National Council of Teachers of English.

————, 1966a, Hypercorrection by the lower middle class as a factor in linguistic change. In William Bright (ed.), *Sociolinguistics*. The Hague: Mouton.

————, 1966b, The social stratification of English in New York City. Center for Applied Linguistics, Washington, D.C.

————, 1968, The reflections of social processes in linguistic structures. In Joshua Fishman (ed.), *A reader in the sociology of language.* The Hague: Mouton.

————, 1969a, The logic of non-standard English. Report on the Twentieth Annual Round Table Meeting on Linguistics and Language Studies, James Alatis (ed.), School of Language and Linguistics, Georgetown University. Washington, D.C.

————, 1969b, Contraction, deletion, and inherent variability of the copula. *Language* 45 (4):715-762.

————, in preparation, Rules for ritual insults. In Thomas Kochman (ed.), *Language and expressive role behavior in the black inner city.*

Labov, William, and Joshua Waletsky, 1967, Narrative analysis: oral versions of personal experience. In *Essays on the verbal and visual arts.* (Proceedings of 1966 spring meeting, American Ethnological Society.) Seattle: University of Washington Press.

Labov, William, Paul Cohen, Clarence Robins, and John Lewis, 1968, A study of the non-standard English of Negro and Puerto Rican speakers in New York City. vol. II. pp. 76-152. Department of Linguistics, Columbia University, New York.

Lamb, S., 1966, *Outline of stratificational grammar.* Washington, D.C.: Georgetown University Press.

Lambert, W., 1963, Psychological approaches to the study of language, pt. II, On second-language learning and bilingualism. *Modern Language Journal* 47:114-121.

————, 1967a, A psychology of bilingualism. In John Macnamara (ed.), Problems of bilingualism. *Journal of Social Issues* 23, 2:91-109.

————, 1967b, The use of *tu* and *vous* as forms of address in French Canada: a pilot study. *Journal of Verbal Learning and Verbal Behavior* 6:614-617.

Lambert, W., and G. R. Tucker, in press, *A social-psychological study of interpersonal modes of address. A French-Canadian illustration.*

Lambert, W. E., M. Anisfeld, and G. Yeni-Komshian, 1965, Evaluational reactions of Jewish and Arab adolescents to dialect and language variations. *Journal of Personality and Social Psychology* 2.

Landis, M. H., and H. E. Burtt, 1924, A study of conversations. *Journal of Comparative Psychology* 4:81-89.

Lanham, Richard A., 1968, *A handlist of rhetorical terms.* Berkeley: University of California Press.
Leach, Edmund, 1954, *Political systems of highland Burma.* Cambridge, Mass.: Harvard University Press.
————, 1960, The Sinhalese of the dry zone of northern Ceylon. In George Murdock (ed.), *Social structure in Southeast Asia.* Chicago: Quadrangle Books.
Leary, T., 1957, *Interpersonal diagnosis of personality.* New York: Ronald.
————, 1966, *Le langage et la société.* Paris: Gallimard.
Lefebvre, Henri, 1968, *The sociology of Marx.* London: Allen Lane, The Penguin Press.
Leroy-Bequlieu, Anatole, 1881, *L'empire des tsars et les Russes,* vol. 1. Paris: Hachette.
Lieberson, Stanley, 1964, An extension of Greenberg's measures of linguistic diversity. *Language* 40:526–531.
————, 1966a, Language questions in census. *Sociological Inquiry* 36:262–279.
————, (ed.), 1966b, Explorations in sociolinguistics. *Sociological Inquiry* 36, 2.
Loban, W., 1966, *Language ability.* Washington, D.C.: U.S. Department of Health, Education and Welfare.
Lounsbury, F. G., 1964, The formal analysis of Crow- and Omaha-type kinship terminologies. In G. P. Murdock (ed.), *Explorations in cultural anthropology.* New York: McGraw-Hill.
Lowie, R. H., 1917, Notes on the social organization of the Mandan, Hidatsa, and Crow Indians. American Museum of Natural History, Anthropological Papers, 21 (1).
————, 1937, *A history of ethnological theory.* New York: Holt, Rinehart and Winston, Inc.
Lynch, Frank, 1962a, Lowland Philippine values: social acceptance. In Frank Lynch (ed.), *Four readings on Philippine values.* Institute of Philippine Culture Papers 2. Quezon City: Ateneo de Manila University Press.
————(ed.), 1962b, *Four readings in Philippine values.* Institute of Philippine Culture Papers 2. Quezon City: Ateneo de Manila University Press.
McCawley, James, 1968, The role of semantics in grammar. In Emmon Bach and Robert Harms (eds.), *Universals in linguistic theory,* pp. 125–170. New York: Holt, Rinehart and Winston, Inc.
McIlwraith, T. F., 1948, *The Bella Coola Indians.* Toronto: University of Toronto Press.
Mack, John E., 1969, T. E. Lawrence: A study of heroism and conflict. *American Journal of Psychiatry* 125:1083–1092.
Mackey, William F., 1962, The description of bilingualism. *Canadian Journal of Linguistics* 7:58–85.
————, 1965, Bilingual interference: its analysis and measurement. *Journal of Communication* 15:239–249.
————, 1966, The measurement of bilingual behavior. *The Canadian Psychologist* 7:75–90.
Maclay, H., and S. Newman, 1960, Two variables affecting the message in communication. In Dorothy K. Wilner (ed.), *Decisions, values, and groups.* New York: Pergamon.
Macnamara, John (ed.), 1967, Problems of bilingualism. *Journal of Social Issues* 23:2.
McNeill, D., 1963, The psychology of *you* and *I;* a case history of small language system. American Psychological Association meeting.

McQuown, Norman (ed.), in preparation, The natural history of an interview. (1956–   ).

Mahl, G. F., 1968, Gestures and body movements in interviews. Paper presented at the Third Research in Psychotherapy Conference. (Chicago, June 1966; in Vol. III, American Psychological Association.)

Mak, Wilhelm, 1935, Zweisprachigkeit und Mischmundart in Oberschlesien, *Schlesisches Jahrbuch fur deutsche Kulturarbeit* 7:41–52.

Malay, Paula Carolina, 1957, Some Tagalog folkways. *Journal of East Asiatic Studies* 6:69–88.

Malinowski, Bronislaw, 1935, *Coral gardens and their magic,* vol. II. London: Allen and Unwin.

——, 1964, The dilemma of contemporary linguistics. In Dell Hymes (ed.), *Language in culture and society,* pp. 63–64. New York: Harper & Row. (Reprinted from *Nature* 140:172–173, 1937.)

Malkiel, Yakov, 1960, Paradigmatic resistance to sound change. *Language* 36:281–346.

Mandelbaum, David G. (ed.), 1949, *Selected writings of Edward Sapir in language, culture and personality.* Berkeley: University of California Press.

Manuel, E. Arsenio, 1955, Notes on Philippine folk literature. *Journal of East Asiatic Studies* 4:137–153.

Marsden, G., 1965, Content-analysis studies of therapeutic interviews: 1954–1964. *Psychological Bulletin* 63:298–321.

Martin, Samuel E., 1964, Speech levels in Japan and Korea. In Dell Hymes (ed.), *Language in culture and society,* pp. 407–415. New York: Harper & Row.

——, 1958, Speech level and social structure in Japan and Korea. Paper read at annual meeting, Asian Studies Association, New York.

Martinet, Andre, 1952, Function, structure, and sound change. *Word* 8:1–32.

——, 1955, Economie des changements phonetiques. Bibliotheca Romanica. Ser. Prima, Manualia et Commentationes, Vol X. Bern: Francke.

Mascall, E. L., 1968, *Words and images.* London: Darton, Longman, and Todd, Ltd. [1957, New York: Ronald Press Co.]

Mayer, Philip, 1951, The joking of "pals" in Gusii age-sets. *African Studies* 10:27–41.

Mead, Margaret, 1937, Public opinion mechanisms among primitive peoples. *Public Opinion Quarterly* 1:5–16.

——, 1942, *And keep your powder dry.* New York: Morrow.

——, 1948, Some cultural approaches to communications problems. In Lyman Bryson (ed.), *The communication of ideas,* pp. 9–26. New York: Harper & Row.

——, 1964a, Vicissitudes of the study of the total communication process. In T. A. Sebeok, A. S. Hayes, and M. C. Bateson (eds.), *Approaches to semiotics,* pp. 277–287. The Hague: Mouton.

——, 1964b, *Continuities in cultural evolution.* New Haven, Conn.: Yale University Press.

Meillet, Antoine, 1921, Linguistique historique et linguistique générale. *Revista di Scienzia* 4 (8).

Merleau-Ponty, M., 1967, Introduction to the prose of the world. *La Revue de Métaphysique et de Morale* 2:139–153, Paris. [Reprinted in *La prose du monde* (Paris: Gallimard) and in English as *Prose of the world* (Evanston, Ill.: Northwestern University Press, 1970.]

Messenger, John C., Jr., 1960, Anang proverb riddles. *Journal of American Folklore* 73:225–235.

Metcalf, George J., 1938, Forms of address in German (1500–1800). Washington University Studies, n.s., *Language and Literature* 7, St. Louis, Mo.

Metzger, Duane, 1965, Review of Harris 1964. *American Anthropologist* 67:1293–1296.

Metzger Duane, and Gerald Williams, 1963, Tenejapa medicine: the curer. *Southwestern Journal of Anthropology* 19:216–234.

Meyers, George C., and John M. Roberts, 1968, A technique for measuring preferential family size and composition. *Eugenics Quarterly* 15:164–172.

Miller, D., and G. E. Swanson, 1958, *The changing American parent.* New York: Wiley.

Miller, G. A., 1956, The magical number seven, plus or minus two: some limits on our capacity for processing information. *The Psychological Review* 63:81–97.

Miller, G. A., E. Calanter, and R. Pribham, 1960, *Plans and structure of behavior.* New York: Holt, Rinehart and Winston, Inc.

Miner, Horace M., and George de Vos, 1960, Oasis and casbah: Algerian culture and personality in change. Anthropological papers, no. 15, Museum of Anthropology, University of Michigan, Ann Arbor, Mich.

Moerman, Michael, 1965, Ethnic identification in a complex civilization: who are the Lue? *American Anthropologist* 6:1215–1230. (Reprint no. 214, Institute of International Studies. University of California, Berkeley.)

———, 1968a, Being Lue: uses and abuses of ethnic identification. American Ethnological Society, Proceedings of 1967 spring meeting, pp. 153–169. (Reprint no. 275, Southeast Asia Series, Institute of International Studies, University of California, Berkeley.)

———, 1968b, Analysis of Lue conversation: Providing accounts, finding breaches, and taking sides. Working Paper no. 12. Language-Behavior Research Laboratory. University of California, Berkeley.

———, 1969, Analysis of Thai conversation. In D. Sudnow (ed.), *Studies in interaction.* New York: Free Press.

Morgenstierne, G., 1932, *Report on a linguistic mission to Northwestern India.* Oslo: H. Ascheoug and Co., Cambridge, Mass.: Harvard University Press.

Moulton, William A., 1962, Dialect geography and the concept of phonological space. *Word* 18:23–33.

Murdock, George P., 1967, Ethnographic atlas: a summary. *Ethnology* 6:2.

Nader, Laura (ed.), 1969, *Law in culture and society.* London: Aldine.

Nahirny, Vladimir C., and Joshua A. Fishman, 1965, American immigrant groups: ethnic identification and the problem of generations. *Sociological Review* 13:311–326.

Neustupny, Jiri, 1968, Politeness patterns in the system of communication. Proceedings of the Eighth International Congress of Anthropological and Ethnological Sciences, Tokyo and Kyoto.

Newman, Stanley S., 1964, Vocabulary levels: Zuni sacred and slang usage. In Dell Hymes (ed.), *Language in culture and society.* New York: Harper & Row. [1954, Reprinted from *Southwestern Journal of Anthropology*, 11:345–354.]

Nurge, Ethel, 1965, Life in a Leyte village. Monograph 40, American Ethnological Society. Seattle: University of Washington Press.

Nydegger, William F., and Corinne Nydegger, 1966, *Tarong: an Ilokos barrio in the Philippines.* Six Cultures Series, vol. VI. New York: Wiley.

Nye, F. I., and F. M. Berardo, 1966, *Emerging conceptual frameworks in family analysis.* New York: Macmillan.

Oakshott, M., 1959, *The voice of poetry in the conversation of mankind.* London: Bowes and Bowes.

Öztürk, Orhan M., 1964, Folk treatment of mental illness in Turkey. In Ari Kiev (ed.), *Magic, faith, and healing: studies in primitive psychiatry today*, pp. 343–363. New York: Free Press.

Parain, Brice, 1969, *Petite metaphysique de la parole*. Paris: Gallimard. (Reviewed in *Times Literary Supplement*, Sept. 25, 1969:1084.)

Parsons, Talcott, 1964, *Personality and social structure*. New York: Free Press.

Passin, Herbert, 1966, Intra-familial linguistic usage in Japan. Monumenta Nipponica Monographs. *Studies in Japanese Culture*, 21:97–113, Tokyo: Sophia University.

Paulhan, Jean, 1913, *Les Hain-teny*. Paris: Gallimard.

Pehrson, R. N., 1966, The social organization of Marri Baluch (compiled by Fredrik Barth). Viking Fund Publications in Anthropology 43. New York: Wenner-Gren Foundation for Anthropological Research.

Perelman, Charles, 1963, The idea of justice and the problem of argument. London: Routledge.

Petrovitch, Gajo, 1967, *Marx in the mid-twentieth century*. New York: Anchor Books.

Pfuderer, Carol, 1968, A scale of politeness forms in English. Term paper for Speech 164A. University of California, Berkeley.

Phelan, John L., 1959, *The Hispanization of the Philippines: Spanish aims and Filipino responses, 1565–1700*. Madison: University of Wisconsin Press.

Philips, Susan U., 1970, Acquisition of rules for appropriate speech usage. Report on Round Table Meeting on Linguistics and Language Studies, George Alatis (ed.), School of Languages and Linguistics. Georgetown University. Washington, D.C.

Pierce, Joe E., 1964, *Life in a Turkish village*. New York: Holt, Rinehart and Winston, Inc.

Pike, Kenneth L., 1945, *The intonation of American English*. Ann Arbor, Mich: University of Michigan Press.

————, 1964, Towards a theory of the structure of human behavior. In Dell Hymes (ed.), *Language in culture and society*. New York: Harper & Row.

————, 1967, *Language in relation to the unified theory of the structure of human behavior*. (2nd rev. ed.). The Hague: Mouton.

Pike, Kenneth L., and C. C. Fries, 1949, Coexistent phonemic systems. *Language* 26:29–50.

Pilch, Herbert, 1955, The rise of the American English vowel pattern. *Word* 11:57–93.

Pitcher, E. G., and E. Prelinger, 1963, *Children tell stories: An analysis of fantasy*. New York: International Universities Press.

Polgar, Steven A., 1960, Biculturation of Mesquakie teenage boys. *American Anthropologist* 62:217–235.

Pool, I, 1959, *Trends in content analysis*. Urbana, Ill.: University of Illinois Press.

Pop, Sever, 1950, La dialectologie. Aperçu historique et methodes d'enquêtes linguistiques. pt. I, Dialectologie Romane; pt. II: Dialectologie non-Romane. Louvain: Chez l'auteur.

Post, Emily, 1922, *Etiquette*. New York: Funk & Wagnalls.

Postal, Paul, 1968, *Aspects of phonological theory*. New York: Harper & Row.

Potter, Charles F., 1950, Riddles. In Maria Leach and Jerome Fried (eds.), *Standard dictionary of folklore, mythology, and legend, vol. 2*. New York: Funk & Wagnalls.

Poussaint, A. F., 1967, A Negro psychiatrist explains the Negro psyche. *New York Times* magazine, August 20, p. 52ff.

Prator, Clifford H., 1970, The survey of language use and language teaching in East Africa. *Journal of the Language Association of Eastern Africa* 1(2):1–7.

Pride, J. B., 1971, Customs and cases of verbal behavior. In Edwin Ardener (ed.), *Social anthropology and linguistics,* pp. 95–117. Association of Social Anthropologists Monograph 10. London: Tavistock.

Priestly, J. B., 1926, *Talking.* New York: Harper & Row.

Ramanujan, A. K., 1967, The structure of variation: a study in caste dialects. In B. Cohn and M. Singer (eds.), *Social structure and social change in India.* London: Aldine.

Redard, G. (ed.), 1964, *Indo-Iranica. Mélange présentés a Georg Morgenstierne a l'occasion de son soixante-diexieme anniversaire.* Wiesbaden: Otto Harraesowitz.

Reichel-Dolmatoff, Gerardo, and Alicia Reichel-Dolmatoff, 1961, *The people of Aritama.* Chicago: University of Chicago Press.

Rensky, Miroslav, 1966, The systematics of paralanguage. *Travaux Linguistique de Prague* 2:97–102.

Revill, P. M., 1966, Preliminary report on paralinguistics in Mbembe (Eastern Nigeria). Tagmemic and matrix linguistics applied to selected African languages, by K. L. Pike, 245–254, appendix VIII. Final report, contract no. OE-5-14-065. Washington, D.C., U.S. Deptartment of Health, Education and Welfare, Office of Education, Bureau of Research.

Richards, I. A., 1955, *Speculative instruments.* Chicago: University of Chicago Press.

Richardson, Alan, 1964, *The Bible in the age of science.* London: SCM Press.

Roberts, John M., 1964, The self-management of cultures. In Ward H. Goodenough (ed.), *Explorations in cultural anthropology.* New York: McGraw-Hill.

———, 1965, Oaths, autonomic ordeals, and power. In Laura Nader (ed.), *American Anthropologist* 67, pt. 2, 6.

Roberts, John M., and Malcolm J. Arth, 1966, Dyadic elicitation in Zuni. *El Palacio* 73 (2):27–41.

Roberts, John M., and Fredrick Koenig, 1968, Focused and distributed status affinity. *Sociological Quarterly* 9:150–157.

Roberts, John M., and Brian Sutton-Smith, 1962, Child training and game involvement. *Ethnology* 1:166–185.

———, 1966, Cross-cultural correlates of games of chance. *Behavior Science Notes* 3:131–144.

Roberts, John M., Malcolm J. Arth, and Robert R. Bush, 1959, Games in culture. *American Anthropologist* 61:597–605.

Roberts, John M., Hans Hoffman, and Brian Sutton-Smith, 1965, Pattern and competence: a consideration of tick tack toe. *El Palacio* 72, 3:17–30.

Roberts, John M., Fredrick Koenig, and Richard B. Stark, n.d., Judged display: a consideration of a craft show. Manuscript.

Roberts, John M., Richard F. Strand, and Edwin Burmeister, 1971, Preferential pattern analysis. In Paul Kay (ed.), *Explorations in mathematical anthropology,* pp. 242–268. Cambridge: M.I.T. Press.

Roberts, John M., Brian Sutton-Smith, and Adam Kendon, 1963, Strategy in games and folktales. *Journal of Social Psychology* 61:185–199.

Roberts, John M., Wayne Thompson, and Brian Sutton-Smith, 1966, Expressive self-testing in driving. *Human Organization* 25:54–63.

Robinson, P., and S. Rackstraw, 1972, *A question of answers*. London: Routledge.

Romney, A. K., and Roy G. D'Andrade, 1964, Cognitive aspects of English kin terms. In A. K. Romney and Roy G. D'Andrade (eds.), Transcultural studies in cognition. *American Anthropologist* 66 (3) pt. 2:146–170.

Rona, Jose Pedro, 1966, The social and cultural status of Guarani in Paraguay. In William Bright (ed.), *Sociolinguistics*. The Hague: Mouton.

Royal Anthropological Institute, 1951, *Notes and queries of anthropology*. 6th ed. London: Routledge.

Rubin, Joan, 1962, Bilingualism in Paraguay. *Anthropological Linguistics* 4 (1):52–58.

———, 1968, *National bilingualism in Paraguay*. The Hague: Mouton.

Sachs, Jacqueline, 1967, Recognition memory for syntactic and semantic aspects of connected discourse. *Perception and Psychophysics* 2:437–442.

Sacks, Harvey, n.d., The diagnosis of depression. Manuscript.

———, in press, Social aspects of language; the organization of sequencing in conversation. Englewood Cliffs, N.J.: Prentice-Hall.

———, 1969, An initial investigation of the usability of conversational data for doing sociology. In D. Sudnow (ed.), *Studies in interaction*. New York: Free Press.

Salisbury, R. F., 1962, Notes on bilingualism and linguistic change in New Guinea. *Anthropological Linguistics* 4 (7):1–13.

Samarin, William, 1965, The language of silence. *Practical Anthropology* 12:115–119.

———, 1967, *Field linguistics: a guide to linguistic field work*. New York: Holt, Rinehart and Winston, Inc.

———, 1969, The art of Gbeya insults. *International Journal of American Linguistics* 35:323–329.

Sandys, Sir John Edwyn, 1920, *A history of classical scholarship*, vol. 1. 3d ed. New York: Cambridge University Press.

Sankoff, Gillian, 1968, Social aspects of multilingualism in New Guinea. Ph.D. thesis, McGill University, Montreal.

Santos, Angeles S., 1958, *Tsang libo at isang butong* ('One thousand and one riddles'). Malabon, Rizal, epifanio de los Santos College Kapariz Publication 2.

Sapir, Edward, 1949a, The emergence of the concept of personality in a study of cultures. In David G. Mandelbaum (ed.), *Selected writings of Edward Sapir*, pp. 590–597. Berkeley: University of California Press. (Reprinted from *Journal of Social Psychology* 5:408–415, 1934.)

———, 1949b, Culture, genuine and spurious. In David G. Mandelbaum (ed.), *Selected writings of Edward Sapir*, pp. 308–331. Berkeley: University of California Press. (Reprinted from *American Journal of Sociology* 29:491–492, 1924.)

———, 1949c, The unconscious patterning of behavior in society. In David G. Mandelbaum (ed.), *Selected writings of Edward Sapir*, pp. 544–559. Berkeley: University of California Press. (Reprinted from E. S. Dummer (ed.), *The unconscious*, pp. 114–142. New York: Knopf, 1927.)

————, 1949d, Psychiatric and cultural pitfalls in the business of getting a living. In David Mandelbaum (ed.), *Selected writings of Edward Sapir*, pp. 578–589. Berkeley: University of California Press. (Reprinted from Mental Health, Publication no. 9, pp. 237–244. American Association for the Advancement of Science, 1939.)

————, 1949e, Communication. In David Mandelbaum (ed.), *Selected writings of Edward Sapir*, pp. 104–109. Berkeley: University of California Press. (Reprinted from *Encyclopedia of the Social Sciences*, vol. 4, pp. 78–81. New York: Macmillan, 1933.)

————, 1949f, Why cultural anthropology needs the psychiatrist. In David Mandelbaum (ed.), *Selected writings of Edward Sapir*, pp. 590–597. Berkeley: University of California Press. (Reprinted from *Psychiatry* 1 (1938):7–12.)

————, 1949g, Sound patterns in language. In David Mandelbaum (ed.), *Selected Writings of Edward Sapir*, pp. 33–45. Berkeley: University of California Press. (Reprinted from *Language* 1 (1925):37–51.)

————, 1949h, Speech as a personality trait. In David Mandelbaum (ed.), *Selected writings of Edward Sapir*, pp. 533–543. Berkeley: University of California Press. (Reprinted from *American Journal of Sociology* 32 (1927):892–905.)

————, 1949i, Language. In David Mandelbaum (ed.), *Selected writings of Edward Sapir*, pp. 7–32. Berkeley: University of California Press. (Reprinted from *Encyclopedia of the Social Sciences*, vol. 9, pp. 155–169. New York: Macmillan, 1933.)

————, 1957, *Language, culture, and personality*. Berkeley: University of California Press. [Selections from the larger *Selected Writings of Edward Sapir* (edited by David B. Mandelbaum).]

————, 1964, Conceptual categories in primitive languages. In Dell Hymes (ed.), *Language in culture and society*. New York: Harper & Row. [1931, reprinted from *Science* 74:578.]

Sartre, Jean-Paul, 1963, *Search for a method*. New York: Knopf. (Translated from *Question de méthode*. Paris: Gallimard, 1960.)

Scheflen, Albert E., 1964, Communication and regulation in psychotherapy. *Psychiatry* 27:126–136.

————, 1965, *Stream and structure of communicational behavior: context analysis of a psychotherapy session*. Behavioral Studies Monograph 1. Philadelphia: Eastern Pennsylvania Psychiatric Institute.

————, 1966, Natural history method in psychotherapy: communicational research. In Louis A. Gottschalk and A. H. Auerbach (eds.), *Methods of research in psychotherapy*. New York: Appleton.

Schegloff, Emmanuel A., 1967, The first five seconds: the order of conversational openings. Unpublished Ph.D. dissertation, Department of Sociology, University of California, Berkeley.

Schmidt-Rohr, George, 1963, *Mutter Sprache*. Jena: Eugen Diederichs Verlag. (Title of first edition: *Die Sprache als Bildnerin der Völker*. Munich, 1932.)

Schneider, D. M., 1953, Yap kinship terminology and kin groups. *American Anthropologist* 55:215–236.

————, 1955, Kinship terminology and the American kinship system. *American Anthropologist* 57:1194–1208.

————, 1968, *American kinship*. Englewood Cliffs, N.J.: Prentice-Hall.

————, 1969, Componential analysis—a state-of-the-art review. Prepared for Wenner-Gren Symposium on "Cognitive studies and artificial intelligence research," Chicago.

Schneider, D. M., and J. M. Roberts, 1956, Zuni kin terms. Monograph 1, Notebook No. 3, Laboratory of Anthropology, University of Nebraska, Lincoln, Neb.

Schutz, Alfred, 1962. In Maurice Nateson (ed.), *Collected papers I: the problem of social reality*, p. 76. The Hague: Martinus Nijhoff.

———, 1964, Making music together. In Arvid Broderson (ed.), *Collected papers II: studies in social theory*. The Hague: Martinus Nijhoff.

———, 1966, Studies in phenomenological philosophy. In Ilse Schutz (ed.), *Collected papers III: studies in phenomenological philosophy*. The Hague: Martinus Nijhoff.

———, 1967, *The phenomenology of the social world*. Chicago: Northwestern University Press.

Scott, Charles T., 1965, Persian and Arabic riddles: a language-centered approach to genre definition. The Hague: Mouton. [Bloomington, Ind.: Indiana University Research Center in Anthropology, Folklore and Linguistics Publication 39], [*International Journal of American Linguisitcs* 31:4.]

Searle, John R., 1969, *Speech acts: an essay in the philosophy of language*. New York: Cambridge University Press.

Sebeok, Thomas A. (ed.), 1960, *Style in language*. Cambridge, Mass.: M.I.T. Press.

Sebeok, Thomas A.; Alfred S. Hayes; and Mary Catherine Bateson (eds.), 1964, *Approaches to semiotics*. The Hague: Mouton.

Seitel, Peter, 1971, An ethnographic report of one aspect of proverb usage among the Haya of Tanzania. Manuscript.

Seitel, Sheila, 1969, Ethnography of communication in four African societies. In Working Paper no. 16, Studies of Interaction. Language Behavior Research Laboratory, University of California, Berkeley.

Sherzer, Joel, 1967, An ethnography of communication of the Abipon. M.A. thesis, Philadelphia: University of Pennsylvania (published in French as *La parole chez les Abipone. L'Homme* 10 (1970):42–76).

Shuy, R., W. A. Wolfram, W. K. Riley, 1969, *Methods for the analysis of social dialect*. Washington, D.C.: Center for Applied Linguistics.

Silverberg, William, 1940, On the psychological significance of *Du* and *Sie. The Psychoanalytic Quarterly* 9:509–525.

Simmons, Donald C., 1958, Cultural functions of the Efik tone riddle. *Journal of American Folklore* 71:133–138.

Sinclair, Angus, 1951, *The conditions of knowing*. London: Routledge.

Skinner, B. F., 1957, *Verbal behavior*. New York: Appleton.

Skinner, Quentin, 1970, Conventions and the understanding of speech acts. *Philosophical Quarterly* 20 (79):118–138.

Slobin, D. I., 1963, Some aspects of the use of pronouns of address in Yiddish. *Word* 19:193–202.

———, A field manual for cross-cultural study of the acquisition of communicative competence. University of California, Berkeley. (A.S.U.C. Bookstore.)

Smith, Frank, and George A. Miller, 1966, *The genesis of language*. Cambridge, Mass.: M.I.T. Press.

Snyder, Gary, 1969, *Earth household: technical notes and queries to fellow Dharma revolutionaries*. New York: New Directions.

Sonnino, Lee A., 1968, *A handbook to sixteenth century rhetoric*. London: Routledge.

Soskin, W. F., and Vera John, 1963, The study of spontaneous talk. In R. G. Barker (ed.), *The stream of behavior*. New York: Appleton.

Spoehr, A., 1947, Changing kinship systems. Anthropological Series, Chicago Natural History Museum, vol. 33, no. 4.

Stankiewicz, Edward, 1964, Problems of emotive language. In Thomas A. Sebeok, Alfred S. Hayes, and Mary Catherine Bateson (eds.), *Approaches to semiotics*, pp. 239–264. The Hague: Mouton.

Steinmann, Martin, Jr. (ed.), 1967, *New rhetorics*. New York: Scribner.

Steinzor, B., 1949, The development and evaluation of a measure of social interaction. *Human relations* 2:103–122, 319–347.

Stephan, F. F., and E. G. Mischler, 1952, The distribution of participation in small groups: an exponential approximation. *American Sociological Review* 17:598–608.

Stewart, W. A. 1964, Urban Negro speech: sociolinguistic factors affecting English teaching. In R. Shuy (ed.), *Social dialects and language learning*. Champaign, Ill.: National Council of Teachers of English.

———, 1967, Sociolinguistic factors in the history of American Negro dialects. The *Florida FL Reporter* 5, 2:1–4.

Stirling, Paul, 1953, Social ranking in a Turkish village. *British Journal of Sociology* 4:31–44.

Strauss, Anselm, and Leonard Schatzmann, 1955, Cross-cultural interviewing: an analysis of interaction and communicative styles. *Human Organization* 14, 2:28–31.

Stross, Brian, 1964, Waiter-to-cook speech in restaurants. Term paper, Speech 160B, University of California, Berkeley.

Sturtevant, Wm., 1964, Studies in ethnoscience. *American Anthropologist* 66, 3, pt. 2.

Sutton-Smith, Brian, and John M. Roberts, 1964, Rubrics of competitive behavior. *Journal of Genetic Psychology* 105:13–37.

Sutton-Smith, Brian, John M. Roberts, and Robert M. Kozelka, 1963, Game involvement in adults. *Journal of Social Psychology* 60:15–30.

Sutton-Smith, Brian, and John M. Roberts, 1967, Studies of an elementary game of strategy. *Genetic Psychology Monographs* 75:3–42.

Sutton-Smith, Brian, John M. Roberts, and B. G. Rosenberg, 1964, Sibling association and role involvement. *Merrill-Palmer Quarterly of Behavior and Development* 1:25–38.

Swartz, Marc J., 1960, Situational determinants of kinship terminology. *Southwestern Journal of Anthropology* 16:393–397.

Tanner, Nancy, 1967, Speech and society among the Indonesian elite: a case study of a multilingual community. *Anthropological linguistics* 9, pt. III:15–40.

Trager, George L., 1958, Paralanguage: a first approximation. *Studies in Linguistics* 13:1–12. [Reprinted in Dell Hymes (ed.), *Language in culture and society*, 274–279, with bibliography. New York: Harper & Row, 1964.]

Trager, George L., and Henry Lee Smith, Jr., 1951, An outline of English structure. Studies in Linguistics, Occasional Papers, 3. Norman, Okla.: Battenburg Press. [Reprinted by the American Council of Learned Societies, Washington, D.C., 1956–1957.]

Tulisano, R., and J. T. Cole, 1965, Is terminology enough? *American Anthropologist* 67:747–748.

Turner, G., and B. Mohan, 1971, *A linguistic description and computer program for children's speech*. London: Routledge.

Tylor, Edward B., 1871, *Primitive culture*. London: John Murray.
Tyler, Stephen A., 1964, Koya kinship: the relation between roles and behavior. Unpublished Ph.D. dissertation, Stanford University, Stanford, Calif.
———, 1965, Koya language morphology and patterns of kinship behavior. *American Anthropologist* 67:1428–1440.
———, 1966, Context and variation in Koya kinship terminology. *American Anthropologist* 68:693–707.
———, 1967, *Formal analysis of Koya kinship terminology*. Emeneau Felicitation Volume (Edited by B. H. Krishnamurty). Poona, India: Linguistic Society of India.
———, 1969, *Cognitive anthropology*. New York: Holt, Rinehart and Winston, Inc.
Urban, Wilbur M., 1939, *Language and reality*. New York: Macmillan.
Veron, E., C. E. Sluzki, F. Korn, A. Kornblit, and R. Malfe, 1965, *Communications and neurosis*. Buenos Aires: University of Buenos Aires Institute Sociologia.
Wallace, Anthony F. C., 1961, The psychic unity of human groups. In Bert Kaplan (ed.), *Studying personality cross-culturally*, pp. 129–164. New York: Harper & Row.
Wallace, A. F. C., and John Atkins, 1960, The meaning of kinship terms. *American Anthropologist* 62:58–80.
Wallace, David, 1905, *The Russian empire*. 2 vols. New York: Henry Holt.
Watson, Jeanne, and R. J. Potter, 1962, An analytic unit for the study of interaction. *Human Relations* 15:245–263.
Watson, O. Michael, and T. D. Graves, 1966, Quantitative research in proxemic behavior. *American Anthropologist* 68:971–985.
Webster's third new international dictionary, 1967. Springfield, Mass.: G. & C. Merriam Company.
Weinreich, Uriel, 1953, Languages in contact. Linguistic Circle of New York.
———, 1963, On the semantic structure of language. In Joseph H. Greenberg (ed.), *Universals of language*, pp. 114–171. Cambridge, Mass.: M.I.T. Press.
———, 1968, Semantics and semiotics. *International encyclopedia of the social sciences* 14:164–169. New York: Macmillan.
Weinreich, Uriel, William Labov, and Marvin Herzog, 1968, Empirical foundations for a theory of language change. In W. Lehmann (ed.), *Proceedings of the Texas Conference on Historical Linguistics*, pp. 97–195. Austin: University of Texas Press.
Wheeler, Alva, 1967, Grammatical structure in Siona discourse. *Lingua* 19:60–77.
Whitely, W. H., 1966, Social anthropology, meaning, and linguistics. *MAN* 1:139–157.
——— (ed.), 1971, *Language use and social change*. London: Oxford.
Whiting, Beatrice Blyth (ed.), 1963, *Six cultures: studies in child rearing*. New York: Wiley.
Whiting, John W. M., and Irving L. Child, 1953, *Child training and personality: a cross-cultural study*. New Haven, Conn.: Yale University Press.
Whorf, Benjamin, 1957, Language, thought, and reality: selected writings of Benjamin Lee Whorf (edited by John B. Carroll). Cambridge, Mass.: M.I.T. Press.
Wilkinson, R. J., 1932, *A Malay-English dictionary* (Romanized). Mytilene, Greece.
Williams, Frederick, 1969, Psychological correlates of speech characteristics: on

sounding "disadvantaged." Institute for Research on poverty, University of Wisconsin, Madison, Wis. Typescript.

Williams, Thomas R., 1963, The form and function of Tambunan Dusun riddles. *Journal of American Folklore* 76:95–110.

Withers, Carl, and Sula Benet, 1954, *The American riddle book.* New York: Abelard-Schuman.

Wittgenstein, Ludwig, 1953, *Philosophical investigations.* Oxford: Blackwell.

Wolfram, Walter A., 1969, *A sociolinguistic description of Detroit Negro speech.* Washington, D.C.: Center for Applied Linguistics.

————, 1970, *The Detroit dialect survey.* Washington, D.C.: Center for Applied Linguistics.

Name Index

Subject Index